INDEX
TO
BOOK REVIEWS
IN
ENGLAND
1749–1774

Antonia Forster

Southern Illinois University Press

Carbondale and Edwardsville

*Copyright © 1990 by the Board of Trustees,
    Southern Illinois University*
All rights reserved
Printed in the United States of America
Designed by Robyn M. Laur
Production supervised by Natalia Nadraga

Library of Congress Cataloging-in-Publication Data

Forster, Antonia, 1951–
    Index to book reviews in England, 1749–1774 / Antonia Forster.
        p.   cm.
    *1. Books—Reviews—England—Indexes.   2. Literature, Modern—18th
century—Book reviews—Indexes.   3. English literature—18th
century—Book reviews—Indexes.   I. Title.*
Z1035.A1F67   1990
028.1'0942—dc19   88-18424
    ISBN 0-8093-1406-1   CIP

*The paper used in this publication meets the minimum requirements of
American National Standard for Information Sciences—Permanence
of Paper for Printed Library Materials, ANSI Z39.48-1984.* ∞

FOR

William, Clarissa, and Ralph

Contents

Preface ix

Acknowledgments xi

PART ONE

Introduction 3

PART TWO

Explanatory Note 21

Review Index 25

Preface

Book reviewing in the eighteenth century bore little resemblance to the operations of the great nineteenth-century journals; similarly, it bore little resemblance to the completely unimportant hackwork it has so often been said to be. Such inadequate efforts as the thirteen-word review of Gray's *Elegy*—"The excellence of this little piece amply compensates for its want of quantity"[1]—are fairly well known, but much less well-known are the reviewers' many early efforts to deal with new directions in poetry or, especially in the *Critical Review*, the increasing interest in fiction.

Reviewing in the nineteenth century, particularly during the Romantic period, has been reprinted and studied thoroughly by a number of scholars during recent decades, and its importance and influence have been demonstrated conclusively.[2] But reviewing, in anything approaching the modern sense of the term, began in the eighteenth century, with the *Monthly Review* in 1749, and there is much to be learned about its place in and impact on eighteenth-century literature. It is, for example, a depressing fact that the editor of a recent University Press of Virginia collection of essays on modern scholarly reviewing can summarize eighteenth-century reviewing in these inadequate and grossly inaccurate terms:

> In 1749 the *Monthly Review* began to publish analyses of recently published works of fiction, and the rival *Critical Review* followed suit soon after. But it was not until the nineteenth century that works of scholarship received notices of any sort in journals or the popular press, and even as late as the beginning of this century more often than not to "review" a written work meant to assess a new novel, drama, or volume of verse.[3]

Reviewing of scholarly books was well established in the seventeenth century, and even a glance at the table of contents of one volume of the *Monthly Review* or *Critical Review* would show the range of works reviewed and the fact that fiction, poetry, and drama take up a small percentage of the review journals' pages.

Studies of some aspects of eighteenth-century reviewing have been made, particularly by Smollett scholars interested in the *Critical Review*,[4] and Derek Roper's full-length 1978 study, *Reviewing before the Edinburgh: 1788–1802* (London: Methuen) examines the period at the end of the century. But, apart from W. Denham Sutcliffe's unpublished 1942 Oxford D. Phil. thesis, which attempts to cover all the journals for a period of fifty years, there have been no detailed studies of reviewing in a range of periodicals during its first quarter-century, either of the reviewers' practice or of the impact on authors of the beginnings of reviewing.

This book, it should be said quite unambiguously, will not fill that gap and does not attempt to do so. The Review Index, however, aims to provide ready access to the great majority of reviews of poetry, fiction, and drama during the period covered, and the Introduction aims to provide literally an introduction to the scope and methods of reviewing and to its place in literary life. The period covered extends from the formal beginnings of the new reviewing in 1749 when, aiming their labors only at the public, reviewers saw their task simply as that of being "tasters to the public," to the end of the first twenty-five years when reviewers had long since expanded their duties to include those of the "beadles of Parnassus" and "officers of the literary police," taking upon themselves the task and mission of ordering the literary world. The Introduction, by surveying some of the available material concerning the reviewers' public attitude to their self-appointed task, provides not a critical study of reviewing during this period but a background against which the reviewers' literary judgments can be examined.

The Review Index and Introduction stop short of the last quarter of the eighteenth century. This later period, the beginning of which is marked by the start of Kenrick's *London Review* in 1775, is the period of great expansion in review journals and other periodicals, as well as books in general, and is a new phase in the history of reviewing. Preparation of a much larger review index to cover the period from 1775 is well underway and will extend coverage to 1800.

Notes

1. *Monthly Review* 4 (1750–51): 309.
2. See, for example, John Wain, ed. *Contemporary Reviewers of Romantic Poetry* (London: Harrap, 1953); John O. Hayden, *The Romantic Reviewers 1802–1824* (London: Routledge & Kegan Paul, 1971); Donald H. Reiman, ed. *The Romantics Reviewed* 7 vols. in 9 parts (New York: Garland, 1972); and Theodore Redpath, ed. *The Young Romantics and Critical Opinion 1807–1824* (London: Harrap, 1973).
3. James O. Hoge, ed. *Literary Reviewing* (Charlottesville: University Press of Virginia, 1987), p. vii.
4. Most important are five articles by Claude E. Jones in the 1940s and 1950s: "Contributors to *The Critical Review* 1756–1785," *Modern Language Notes* 61 (1946): 433–441; "Dramatic Criticism in the *Critical Review*, 1756–1785," *Modern Language Quarterly* 20 (1959): 18–26; "The English Novel: A *Critical* View, 1756–1785," *Modern Language Quarterly* 19 (1958): 147–159 and 213–224; "Poetry and the *Critical Review*, 1756–1785," *Modern Language Quarterly* 9 (1948): 17–36; and "Smollett and the *Critical Review*," *Smollett Studies* (Berkeley and Los Angeles: University of California Press, 1942). Equally significant are five articles and a book written by Robert Donald Spector in the 1950s and 1960s: "Attacks on the *Critical Review*," *Periodical Post Boy* (1955): 6–7; "Additional Attacks on the 'Critical Review,'" *Notes and Queries* 201 (1956): 425; "Attacks on the 'Critical Review' in the 'Court Magazine,'" *Notes and Queries* 203 (1958): 308; "Further Attacks on the 'Critical Review'", *Notes and Queries* 200 (1955): 535; "The *Monthly* and its Rival," *Bulletin of the New York Public Library* 64 (1960): 159–161; and *English Literary Periodicals and the Climate of Opinion During the Seven Years' War* (The Hague: Mouton, 1966). A recent illuminating study is James G. Basker's *Tobias Smollett: Critic and Journalist* (Newark: University of Delaware Press, 1988).

Acknowledgments

A project of this kind could not have been carried out without the help of many people, amongst whom the chief are staffs of libraries on three continents. I am very grateful for the help of the staff of the British Library (especially that of David Paisey and of the E.S.T.C. staff), the Bodleian Library, the Cambridge University Library, the Beinecke and Sterling Libraries at Yale, the Folger Shakespeare Library, the Houghton, Sterling, and Pusey Libraries at Harvard, the Johns Hopkins University Library, the Library of Congress, the Lilly Library, the Newberry Library, the New York Public Library, the University of Pennsylvania Library, the University of Chicago Library, and the Library of the University of Illinois at Champaign-Urbana. The interlibrary loan staff (especially Linda Santos) of the Baillieu Library of the University of Melbourne were of very great help to me, and I have also appreciated the help of the Founders Memorial Library of Northern Illinois University and the Bierce Library of the University of Akron. In addition, I want to thank the Faculty of Arts of the University of Melbourne for the travel grants that allowed me to carry out the bulk of my research in England.

Many individuals have also given me help, advice, and encouragement. First among these is my husband, William Proctor Williams, but I also owe a debt of gratitude to my supervisor at the University of Melbourne, Dr. Peter Steele, and to Professor Edward A. Bloom, Chantal Brotherton-Ratcliffe, Professor Jan Fergus, Professor Rosalie Hewitt, Mrs. Felicity Hughes, Professor Robert D. Hume, Professor Paul J. Korshin, George and Jeannine Lockett, Professor Thomas Lockwood, Dr. Roger Lonsdale, Dr. Harold Love, Trevor Mills, James Mungal, Clarissa and Ralph Palmer, Dr. Susan Porterfield, Dr. Philip R. Rider, Mr. Derek Roper, Margaret Russell and the Malory Institute, Professor Sean Shesgreen, Professor James E. Tierney, Mrs. Kathleen Tillotson, and Maggie and Jock Tomlinson. And finally, I want to thank my parents.

PART ONE

Introduction

Reviewing in its first (and literal) sense, abstract and/or summary without evaluative comment, has been dated back as far as 140 B.C. but formal review journals date from the *Journal des Sçavans*, published in Paris and Amsterdam from 1665 to 1753. This and several later seventeenth-century journals, most notably the several journals headed by Michel de la Roche (including the *Memoirs of Literature* and the *Literary Journal*) and others such as the *History of the Works of the Learned*, led the way toward the *Monthly Review*.[1] But none of these was intended for readers other than "the Learned"; the increasing market of general readers in Great Britain, the readers who did much to make the *Gentleman's Magazine* and the *London Magazine* successful, was, until the middle of the eighteenth century, still generally left to find out about most publications from the bare bones of advertisements or from word of mouth.

The revolution that was to change the literary marketplace forever began quietly when the first number of "a new Periodical Work, entitled, THE MONTHLY REVIEW" was advertised on 20 May 1749. This new work was the first review journal in anything approaching the modern sense of the term, and it led eventually to a host of imitators, while remaining the leader in the field for fifty years. Its early success soon brought others attempting to join the bandwagon in the rapidly expanding periodicals market, but they were short-lived and the *Monthly* had no serious rivals until Smollett started the *Critical Review* seven years later. The surprising speed with which the reviewers in these two journals established a place for themselves in the literary world soon had the general magazines undertaking more-or-less systematic reviewing. But it remained true throughout the twenty-five-year period under consideration here that the reviews that really counted were those in the *Monthly* and the *Critical*. For the majority of authors and booksellers they were simply "the two Reviews" and the judgments delivered elsewhere, although they became a necessary part of most general publications and might stir up an occasional fuss, were not important. Indeed, one could read thirty attacks on reviewers from this period and not even discover the existence of reviewing in any other journals than the two leading ones. However, the fact remains that other journals were doing some reviewing and it is necessary to consider them as a part of the total picture.

On its initial appearance the *Monthly Review*'s announced efforts are modest. It is described in an early advertisement simply as "Giving an Account, with proper Abstracts, of the new Books, Pamphlets, &c. as they come out."[2] This advertisement lists the six books of which the first number "contains a View," and the fact that two of the six are works of poetry and a third a play is a clear pointer to one of the two most important ways in which this new journal was revolutionary.

When Ralph Griffiths, a London bookseller and former watchmaker who had been employed by Jacob Robinson, the publisher of *The History of the Works of the Learned*, started the *Monthly Review*, he did so from within the tradition of the earlier French and English journals, which saw reviewing as, to quote again his advertisement mentioned above, "Giving an Account, with proper Abstracts." That reviewing in this new journal came soon, in many instances, to mean more than summary and abstract, is apparent from its early volumes, and even the earliest reviews in the *Monthly* contain material of interest. In addition, as I have mentioned above, the *Monthly Review* dealt from its first number with imaginative literature instead of restricting itself, as had been the usual practice of its predecessors, to "works of the learned," and from the third number it promised to "register all the new Things in general, without exception to any, on account of their lowness of rank, or price."[3] During the first few years of its long life (it lasted until 1845, outliving the *Critical* by nearly thirty years), the *Monthly Review* can be seen to outgrow its long-established literary origins very quickly and to mark a new direction in literary

3

periodicals. A continuing journal paying regular attention to imaginative literature and containing an increasing amount of evaluative comment on the works reviewed was indeed something new.

The twentieth-century scholar is more likely to see individual reviews as isolated pieces than as the parts of large enterprises that they were to their editors and most readers in the eighteenth century. The account that follows attempts to provide a context to show something of the light in which the first practitioners of the new reviewing saw what they were doing; the self-consciousness of an essentially new enterprise means that the reviewers first in the *Monthly* and then in the *Critical* give a great deal of information to build up this context, and their rivals and imitators in other journals contribute as well.

The "Advertisement" added to the first number of the *Monthly Review* sets out briefly the aims and rationale of the new journal:

> When the abuse of title-pages is obviously come to such a pass, that few readers care to take in a book, any more than a servant, without a recommendation; to acquaint the public that a summary review of the productions of the press, as they occur to notice, was perhaps never more necessary than now, would be superfluous and vain. The cure then for this general complaint is evidently, and only, to be found in a periodical work, whose sole object should be to give a compendious account of those productions of the press, as they come out, that are worth notice; an account, in short, which should, in virtue of its candour, and justness of distinction, obtain authority enough for its representations to be serviceable to such as would choose to have some idea of a book before they lay out their money or time on it. This is the view and aim of the present undertaking; and as it must necessarily stand or fall by the merit of the execution, on that we rest the issue, without offering to prepossess the public in its favour.[4]

With these essentially modest aims the *Monthly Review* began the process of experimentation with form and content characteristic of so many modern periodicals.

The Review[5] took some years to settle into its final format, but the first basic pattern, that of two volumes a year each made up of six monthly numbers, was established by the beginning of 1752 with the sixth volume. The major portion of each number was then taken up with an average of ten main articles, with the rest of the items reviewed appearing in the monthly catalogue section, either as short articles, usually ranging from a few words to about a page in length, or, increasingly rarely, simply as listed items with title and publishing details but no comment. Some numbers concluded with a list of single published sermons, some with comment and some without. The eighth volume (January to June 1753) was the first to include an appendix as a seventh number, published halfway through the following month and made up of further review material together with an index to the whole volume. This format, two volumes a year each made up of six monthly numbers and an appendix, remained until 1790 and was followed by later review journals established in opposition to the *Monthly* (though the *Critical* was to mention often and ostentatiously that *it* avoided the "unnecessary incumbrance" that a supplement or an appendix would be to its readers). The only change to this format during the first twenty-five years of the *Monthly* was the later use of the appendix for reviews only of items in foreign languages. (The *Monthly Review*'s coverage of some foreign literature began early—an advertisement in January 1750 promises to "introduce an Account of the Works of the Learned and Ingenious in foreign Parts"[6]—but there is not very much of this until the *Critical Review*'s efforts spur the *Monthly* into renewed action.)

The initial decision to cover only "those productions of the press . . . that are worth notice" lasted for only two numbers, and the third followed its six main articles with a brief list of nineteen other items, some without comment, headed "Books published in July 1749" and carrying the prefatory announcement:

> We propose, for the future, to register all the new Things in general, without exception to any, on account of their lowness of rank, or price. But as it would exceed the limits of our plan, as well as prove disagreeable to many of our readers to give a large detail of some of our new productions, we shall content ourselves with giving a very brief account of them, in the manner following. (M.R.1, 1749: 238)

This precedent, once established, led to an ever-increasing stream of complaints in print from reviewers about the rubbish they were obliged to read, and in early numbers it was thought necessary to apologize for the inclusion of some items by repeating policy statements. Thus Griffiths'[7] brief review of a "miserable" collection entitled *D—n Sw—t's Medley*, which rouses him to anger because of "the prostitution of the name of the inimitable SWIFT, on such dirty occasions," begins: "We should have stood in need of an apology for mentioning this article, had not our plan obliged us to allow it some place in the Review" (M.R.2, 1749–50: 88).

The other side of such apologies were the explicit reminders of the service being done to the public by the reviewers, reminders thought necessary particularly during the early years when the reviewers were still establishing themselves:

> The public are, really, more obliged to us *Reviewers* than they imagine. We are necessitated to read every thing that comes out, and must, consequently, submit to the vile drudgery of going through those loads of trash, which are thrown in upon us under the denomination of *Lives, Adventures, Memoirs, Histories*, &c. (M.R.11, 1754: 470)

Even a glance at the Review Index will show the large numbers of works published "under the denomination of *Lives, Adventures, Memoirs, Histories,* &c."; a more careful examination will show that during the twenty-five-year period covered there were more than five hundred works beginning with or featuring these popular words in their titles.

Whatever their sufferings, as the reviewers point out, they are obliged, as "tasters to the public," to let the public know what is fit for consumption by readers (M.R.13, 1755: 399). In the very early years "tasters to the public" is a more effective term than "critic" for describing the reviewers' function, because, to start with, the reviewers do not call themselves critics. Just what they *were* doing it is necessary to establish before giving much attention to the reviews; far too often these early reviews have been judged according to standards their writers would not have recognized or valued. In the post-Pope era (phrases and lines from the *Essay on Criticism* were to be quoted with monotonous regularity by authors throughout the century as ammunition in their battles with reviewers; reviewers liked to use it, too),[8] the term "critic" was of doubtful and varying standing, reflected in passing remarks made in the reviews of this early period. The confusion is summed up by the author of a collection of poems entitled *Escapes of a Poetical Genius* when he or she comments in a footnote: "The name of a Critic is become odious; yet a Critic is one who judges of Literary Productions according to the Rules of Art, and a Reader to be coveted by all good Writers."[9]

The term "critic," as used in authors' prefaces during this period, had three main applications, sometimes separately identifiable and sometimes confusingly mixed. (Here I leave aside the separate application of the term to, as Johnson's *Dictionary* defines it, "A censurer; a man apt to find fault.") Nathaniel Weekes, an undistinguished poet whose works fared badly at the hands of the reviewers, discussed critics and criticism frequently in his prefaces and in the text of one of his poems. One of these references provides an example of two of the applications of the term. "There are at this Time," he says, "two different Societies of Critics; your Idlers at Coffee-Houses, and your Writers of Magazines."[10] In the first group one may include the theatre-going "critics" referred to or addressed so often in prologues and epilogues to plays, and in the second group the reviewers. The third application is, of course, still current today, although less strictly applied, and its meaning may be covered by the definition I have quoted in the paragraph above, as "one who judges of Literary Productions according to the Rules of Art." This last but earliest application, respectable because of its ancient origins but battered in the public literary arena by the attacks of Pope and others, had an uneasy alliance with its fellows.

From the beginning the Review's intention was to approach the business of reviewing with what Griffiths describes as the "agreeable and useful method" of quotation of extracts (M.R.1, 1749: 67), supported by summaries. This method continued to be used throughout the century in some articles, even while others (particularly the shorter monthly-catalogue articles that were obviously less suitable for the use of the abstract/extract method) soon came to contain expressions of critical opinion more in keeping with the modern ideas of reviewing that have developed since the great nineteenth-century journals. Comments on and explanations of the extract method of reviewing are frequent in the early volumes of the Review, indicating that, despite the well-established tradition, this new journal was conscious of a need to justify its approach and to establish itself with a new audience, a significant part of which would not have been in the market for the earlier learned journals. It might be argued that the abstract/extract method of reviewing is taking the easy way out, which is often true (although when the time and patience necessary to produce, for example, the exhaustive plot summaries of many novels, including Mrs. Radcliffe's long and complicated ones in the 1790s, are taken into account it can be seen that straight comment on the novels would have been easier). But it is necessary to keep in mind the Review's aims and its editor's conception of its function in relation to its audience.

Sometimes the *Monthly*'s reviewers, as "tasters" rather than critics, maintain that they are not there to give opinions, that their "business is to enter no farther into the province of criticism, than just so far as may be indispensibly necessary to give some idea of such books as come under [their] consideration" (M.R.2, 1749–50: 260). At other times, however, they defend the necessity of their offering their opinions because "it is expected of [them] to have a voice" (M.R.2, 1749–50: 219) and their "real judgment . . . the public have a right to" (M.R.13, 1755: 458). In fact, there are few reviews, long or short, in which opinions of some sort are not given; the traditional idea of simply presenting neutral information and leaving judgment up to readers is given lip service but seldom followed.

Exactly whose "real judgment" the public was getting in the pages of the *Monthly Review* at this time was known to almost no one, and reviewing remained anonymous throughout the twenty-five-year period and in all the journals covered by the Review Index. An advertisement in the *London Advertiser, and Literary Gazette* for 12 March 1751, describes the "Authors" of the *Monthly Review* as "Six Gentlemen of different Qualifications" (the title page of the journal at this time simply said it was "by Several Hands") and points out that this is "an Advantage which perhaps no Work of this Nature, in any Part of Europe, ever had before." As Griffiths' marked set of the journal and Nangle's *Index* show,[11] these six certainly included Griffiths himself (he did a great deal of reviewing at the beginning and remained a contributor to some extent throughout his life) and his close friend William Rose, who wrote the first review in the *Monthly*'s opening number and wrote a large number of reviews in the early years; John Cleland and John Hill were also contributors at this time.

When the *Monthly Review* was in its seventh year, and its staff of regular or occasional contributors had included such well-known figures as Theophilus Cibber, who did some drama reviewing, and Smollett, who reviewed two medical works and a novel, and lesser lights such as James Kirkpatrick and James Grainger (both poets and doctors), the *Critical* was preparing to launch itself into the literary scene with an arrogant fanfare in noticeable contrast to its predecessor's quiet beginnings. The public had been, as the *Gentleman's Magazine* pointed out rather sourly, "prepared to receive this elaborate work with proper respect, by a long ostentatious advertisement, that, like another Goliah, . . . [came] forth 'morning and evening, and presented itself more than forty days,' with insult and defiance."[12] Insult and defiance were certainly prominent among the hallmarks of the *Critical*'s early years, and in this the "long ostentatious advertisement" gave accurate promise of what was to come.

"This Work will not be patched up by obscure Hackney Writers, accidentally enlisted in the Service of an undistinguishing Bookseller," declared the December 1755 advertisement for the forthcoming journal, then intended for publication on 1 February 1756 under the title *The Progress or Annals of Literature and the Liberal Arts*.[13] Where the *Monthly Review* had needed to establish a general demand for an essentially new enterprise, the *Critical*'s task was different and Smollett, at this time the editor, went about his preparatory work with a vigor little hampered by considerations of truth or accuracy. Comprehensive and ill-natured attack on the unnamed existing journal was the chosen approach—and the groundwork was laid for a great deal of future sniping in the early volumes of the new Review.

The advertisement promises that the new journal will cover "all the Performances on the Subjects of Theology, Metaphysics, Physics, Medicine, Mathematics, History, and the Belles Lettres" and will describe, in addition, painting, sculpture, and architecture; it also promises grandly to revive "the true Spirit of Criticism" and vindicate "the cause of Literature" from the "venal and corrupted Jurisdiction" of the other journal. For the most part, despite its claims of gentlemanliness, impartiality, and goodwill, the advertisement makes savage attacks on its rival's staff of "obscure Hackney writers" and "sordid views of Avarice" (the *Critical*'s reviewers were also anonymous and it cost the same amount—one shilling—as the *Monthly* and had an editor rather more in need of money than Griffiths) and swears, while demonstrating most of these, to avoid "Interest, Faction, Envy or Malevolence."

The advertisement appeared a number of times, both in its original form and later with slight alterations, including that of the journal's title to *The Critical Review; or, Annals of Literature*. The version in the *Public Advertiser* for 2 February 1756 for the not-yet-published *Critical Review* has appended a concluding explanation for the non-appearance of the promised journal, "postponed till March, in Expectation of some Foreign Articles." This time the projected publication date was kept and the *Critical Review*, having expended considerable energy in preparatory blowing of its own trumpet, finally made its appearance.

For all its grandiose promises to reform the state of periodical criticism and Smollett's description of the enterprise, in a private letter, as "a small Branch of an extensive Plan which [he had] projected for a sort of Academy of the belles Lettres,"[14] the *Critical Review* follows, for the most part, the successful format and approach to criticism established by the *Monthly Review*. There are clear political and religious differences between the two journals, although the long-held belief that "the *Critical* was established under Tory and Church patronage to maintain principles in opposition to those of the *Monthly*"[15] is an oversimplification, but their methods and general literary principles do not differ greatly. The regular items of foreign literary intelligence and the attention paid at first to paintings, sculpture, and engravings "now in hand, or lately finished" are innovations (the *Monthly* had paid some attention to foreign literature before 1756, as I have mentioned, but not with any regularity), but the ordinary method of reviewing follows that developed by the *Monthly Review*, with extracts and summary making up much of the substance of each review.

The *Monthly Review* had succeeded in establishing a place in the literary market for the judgment of reviewers, and several short-lived imitators had attempted to jump onto the bandwagon. Now, in early 1756, the task before Smollett was that of surpassing or at worst equaling the sales of the *Monthly Review*, and such success, if it were to outlast the initial flurry of interest stirred up by the "long ostentatious advertisement," required the maintenance of an attractive or interesting image. The *Monthly Review* could lament in pained tones the debasing of literature by "indecent contests" between "mean, envious, and illiberal Competitors" (M.R.17, 1757: 373), but there is little doubt that disputes between authors and reviewers or reviewers and reviewers attracted public interest in the Reviews and led to increased sales. As the *Critical* says on one occasion, the attacks of furious writers served "no other purposes, but those of propagating their own want of talent and temper, and of increasing the demand for the Critical Review" (C.R.7, 1759: 167).

The *Critical*'s expressed willingness to receive contributions from its readers is an innovation and is clearly part of the desired image for the new journal as one in which criticism is properly the province of gentlemanly amateurs. Supporting this, a concluding note to the first number solicits "hints or assistance . . . from the learned and ingenious of every denomination" and addresses itself in particular to "the GENTLEMEN OF THE TWO UNIVERSITIES" for whom the *Critical*'s reviewers "profess the most profound veneration" (C.R.1, 1756: 96). (That the profundity of this veneration, if sincere, might tend rather to cast some doubt on the standing of the reviewers than to confirm their position as highly educated gentlemen does not seem to have occurred to the author—probably Smollett[16]—of the note.) Griffiths was generally opposed on principle to the use of contributions by outsiders and used them only occasionally, although it would seem that such contributions might save time and money, but the *Critical*'s attitude was different. The first number's request for "hints or assistance" and the declaration, in the preface to the first volume, of willingness to "thankfully receive all kinds of assistance" (C.R.1, 1756: sig.A2v) are made still more explicit in the second volume. In accordance with this aspect of the reviewers' plan, a number of reviews appear with headnotes such as "The following article was sent to our publisher, and as it seems to be written with spirit and candour, we shall insert it verbatim" (C.R.7, 1759: 89).

Readers' contributions are few, however; most of the reviewing is done by the *Critical*'s "Set of Gentlemen" whose identity during the early period covered by the Review Index, apart from the five in the Review's first two volumes (Smollett,

Francklin, Armstrong, Derrick, and Murdoch) is only occasionally able to be established.[17] Reviews by some major writers, such as Johnson and Goldsmith (both of whom, like a number of others during this period, reviewed for more than one journal—Johnson reviewed for the *Literary Magazine* too, Goldsmith for both Reviews, and John Hawkesworth and Owen Ruffhead reviewed for both the *Gentleman's Magazine* and the *Monthly Review*) have long been attributed to their authors but in general the identities of the reviewers in the *Critical* in its early years remain a mystery, as do most of those in the magazines.

The *Critical*'s reviewing methods are like the *Monthly*'s; the *Monthly Review*'s methods had proved successful and seemed to indicate the path to follow. Indeed, there seemed to be no other path, as one of the *Critical*'s reviewers explains: "We were always of opinion that appealing to an author's works, and supporting our judgment by quotations from them was the fairest method of determining their intrinsic merit that could possibly be made use of" (C.R.1, 1756: 484).

Here, as is so often the case, the *Critical Review* writes as if the other journal did not exist. But there are, particularly during the early years, a number of direct attacks on the "old woman" (the *Monthly Review*, by extension from the proprietor's wife, popularly supposed to play a part in the writing and editing of the journal, a legend for which there is no reliable evidence)[18] and the "illiterate bookseller," its proprietor, much of their contents couched in intemperate language; and some occasional carefully phrased sniping comes the other way from the *Monthly*. Griffiths appears a clear winner on points because the *Monthly*, the established journal, is generally able to maintain a tone of dignified but pained forbearance toward the newcomer yapping at its heels, whereas Smollett and the *Critical Review* tend to rise furiously to every real and imagined slight.

The *Critical*'s chief role, as it is presented to the public, is, as the preliminary advertisement promised it would be, that of reforming the state of criticism. Like the *Monthly*, the *Critical* complains a great deal about the "severe task of reading every new production" (C.R. 3, 1757: 384), but it shows little doubt concerning what is described as its "delicate task of directing the public taste with regard to criticism" (C.R.8, 1759: 271) and it lays down the law in all directions. Modest claims that the *Critical* is there to "exhibit" works, leaving final opinion up to the public, occur as they do in the *Monthly*, but in reality the *Critical*'s view is that, as Smollett puts it, "Every author who writes without talents is a grievance, if not an impostor, who defrauds the public; and every critic has a right to detect the imposition" (C.R.1, 1756: 287). The *Critical* appears to see itself as having not only a right but a positive moral duty to censure and repress authors, and determine which works may be fit or permitted to be successful with the public.

By this time the *Monthly* has long since abandoned any idea that it is not in the business of criticism and often discusses the role of the critic and defends its own critical practice, although its self-righteousness is generally less than that exhibited in the *Critical*'s early years. Both journals set out to do more than informing and entertaining the public; they also see themselves, at least in theory, as having a critical role to play in advising authors. The *Critical*'s forte is destructive criticism, although the *Monthly* enjoys this too, and the *Monthly* does rather more than its rival to at least purport to fulfill the role of the critic as the constructive helper and advisor of writers. In 1759 James Kirkpatrick refers to the *Monthly* reviewers' design "to act with constant equity between the Writers [they] review, and the Readers [they] intend to inform or entertain" (M.R.21, 1759: 467), and by 1767 it has become a struggle, a reviewer says, to "do *justice* to the Public, and at the same time answer the *expectations* of Authors" (M.R.36, 1767: 176). The struggle is, of course, more fancied than real; although such ungentlemanly and indelicate ideas are not mentioned, the review journals are in business to make money by pleasing the public.

There are in reality many more similarities than differences between the two journals, but they often disagree. It seems likely that the rivalry between the two journals provided an entertainment for readers which must, on occasion, have surpassed that provided by the journals' primary functions as "tasters to the public" or reformers of public taste. "Every Art is improved by the Emulation of Competitors," writes the *London Chronicle* in its first number;[19] be that as it may, by 1760 a correspondent to the *London Chronicle* writes that he takes both Reviews "for the same reason, and with the same success too, that Mr. Alworthy put his nephew under the tuition of *Thwackum* and *Square*."[20]

One sure guide to the success of the enterprise of general reviewing is the rapidly increasing number of journals attempting to join the new market. Between 1749 and 1760 at least nine new review journals started, most of them short-lived (the *Impartial Review*, for example, seems to have lasted for only one number in 1759), and many more general journals started review sections as regular features.

Thus the idea that a review journal was something "which no one, conversant in the Literary World, ought, in justice to themselves, to be without"[21] seems to have taken hold quite early. Whether or not the reading public was actually influenced in its book-buying habits and circulating-library use by reviewers' verdicts is very difficult to determine. Research by Jan Fergus and Ruth Portner into the bookselling records of the Clays in the Midlands suggests that the reviewers did not in fact have much influence,[22] but it is apparent from the early days of reviewing that authors and booksellers believed—or feared—that they did. Perhaps the most important indicator of the book trade's having accepted reviewers' verdicts as an integral part of their business is the early use of review material in advertisements for books. The earliest such advertisement I have found appears in *The General Advertiser* for Friday, 14 December 1750. The advertisement, for the then forthcoming *The Revolutions of Genoa*, quotes from the *Monthly Review*'s review of the original French edition of the work in March 1750, taking remarks from three places in the review but presenting them as a single, connected paragraph, with what was to become a typical footnote: "Vide the Character of the Original, in the Monthly Review, for March 1750." Although it must be pointed out that *The Revolutions of Genoa* was published by Ralph Griffiths, this use of review material in advertisements was soon to become established among booksellers in general and to appear both in any newspapers carrying book-advertisements and in the booksellers' advertisements printed at the end (or occasionally at the beginning) of published books. The most common way of using review material in these advertisements is for a brief quotation to be tacked on to the end of the usual book-advertisement and identified or authenticated by a note such as "The Monthly Review for March 1759, p.276, gives the following Character of this Work,"[23] "N.B. The Authors of the Critical Review, speaking of this Performance, say . . . ,"[24] or, in a rare reference to a journal other than the *Monthly* and *Critical* Reviews, "The WRITERS of the GENTLEMAN'S MAGAZINE give the following Account of this WORK."[25] At other times the bookseller will refer the reader directly to the review itself, without quoting from it (and with a clear assumption that the public in general would consult the Reviews regularly), with a note such as "See the Character of this Ode in the last Monthly Review"[26] or "For the Character of this Book, see the Critical Review for last Month."[27]

As eighteenth-century review journals normally purchased or borrowed the works for review *after* they had been advertised at publication and a high proportion of works were not readvertised for more than a few days after publication, it is more surprising that there are so many advertisements using review material than that most advertisements do not. The practice of readvertising books as "This day . . . published" often weeks and sometimes months or even years after the initial publication date is the most obvious and frequent factor enabling the use of review material, but there are others. Advertisements (for earlier books) appended to published books are, of course, not subject to the timing problems associated with the advertising of recently published works in newspapers, and some of these show a long lapse of time. For example, William Collins' anonymous *Oriental Eclogues*, published in 1757, carries on its last page a list of six other books published by Payne and the first of these, *The Matrimonial Preceptor*, is supported by quotations from reviews in the *Gentleman's Magazine* for March 1755 and the *Monthly Review* for May 1755.[28] Second or subsequent editions of works also provide opportunities for use of review material, sometimes after several years have elapsed, as when the fourth edition of *Youth's Friendly Monitor* is advertised in June 1756 with a quotation from the *Monthly Review* of October 1752.[29] Other circumstances of which occasional use is made include the English translation of a foreign work already reviewed as a foreign publication[30] and the publication of a subsequent volume or volumes of a work of which the first volume has already been reviewed.[31] One way or another, it is clear, many booksellers are ready to make use of review material as ammunition in advertising, in the expectation that quoting or mentioning one or more of the review journals will have a positive value in the eyes of the book-buying public.

In the early days of reviewing the modern

system of sending out free copies of books for review, before or after publication, did not exist, although an occasional author would send or request that his or her bookseller send a copy of a book to the *Monthly* and *Critical* Reviews. Thanks to some of Griffiths' surviving correspondence, most of it in the Bodleian Library, and to some public pronouncements in both the Reviews, we do know a fair amount about this aspect of the reviewing business (as we do, principally from Griffiths' correspondence, about the rates of pay for reviewers—between £2 and 4 guineas per octavo sheet of 16 pages).[32] Donald D. Eddy wrote as recently as 1979 that "presumably publishers sent free copies of books to periodicals for review" and that "it is also reasonable to assume that reviewers—then as now—were allowed to keep the books they reviewed,"[33] but the review journals and Griffiths' correspondence make it clear that such assumptions are incorrect.

The booksellers Edward and Charles Dilly are said to have sent out review copies[34] and Griffiths' correspondence shows that some authors sent copies of their works to the review journals,[35] but for the most part it appears that the Reviews had to obtain the publications for themselves. The *Critical* refers in a review to the fact that the "sons of Grub-street" should be grateful to the reviewers instead of resentful of them because "let them be never so dull, [the reviewers] are obliged to buy their performances" (C.R.8, 1759: 412). A letter from Griffiths to Messrs. Boydell in 1801 suggests that it has been normal for the Review to buy or borrow books for review; this letter apologizes for having kept (and accidentally damaged) a book returned therewith, and explains that he had thought that "the work was intended as a Present to the Reviewers" because it had been sent without a request.[36] Sometimes reviewers already have a copy of a book to be reviewed or say that they can get access to it;[37] generally, however, it is the Reviews' responsibility to obtain copies of all published works and distribute them to individual reviewers.

The usual procedure for obtaining copies for the *Monthly* and *Critical* Reviews appears to have been the same for both and to have been fairly simple: on the basis of booksellers' advertisements the editor or his representative sent a book collector to buy or borrow the publications (the *Monthly Review* makes a number of references to the "person who collects the new publications for us" [M.R.42, 1770: 416] and the "person who statedly collects the Publications necessary for the Review" [M.R.36, 1767: 496]). This procedure is by no means foolproof, of course, and often the reviewers are informed by readers of publications they have missed (although readers do not always give enough information; the reviewers are sometimes found replying to correspondents at the end of a monthly number with a request for more details "that [they] may know what to enquire for at the publishers" [M.R.42, 1770: 496]). Even after they have been informed about a work, perhaps one "printed in the country and never, that [they] have heard of, being advertised in the London papers" (M.R.47, 1772: 412), the reviewers sometimes confess defeat, as the *Critical* does to a correspondent from Brecon who has asked them to review a work: "they cannot find it, either at the places described, or any where else in London" (C.R.7, 1759: 88).

It is clear that the *Monthly*'s reviewers, at least, are not allowed to keep the review copies sent to them by Griffiths, and it appears that the copies were returned or sold back to booksellers. The *Monthly* sometimes refers to the fact that an earlier reviewed work mentioned by a correspondent is no longer to hand (see, for example, M.R.51, 1774: 80 and 248) and Griffiths' correspondence has several references by reviewers to formerly reviewed works now no longer in their possession.[38]

As many of the *Monthly*'s reviewers were living at some distance from London, there are frequent references in their letters to the difficulties of getting books and reviews back and forth by means of coaches, "by waggon," "by Union Shipping Company of Berwick," and by any other means available (Samuel Goodenough excuses himself on one occasion because "owing to a lame horse" he has been unable to dispatch his completed reviews).[39] It seems likely that the *Critical* shared these problems; there is a reference in the early years of the Review to the fact that the "gentlemen chiefly concerned in the Critical Review, live at a considerable distance from the press; and sometimes the printer has been so hurried at the latter end of the month, by their sending in the copy so late that he could not possibly furnish them with proof sheets for their correction" (C.R.4, 1757: 472). (The *Monthly* says on one occasion that periodical publications "rarely allow the Writers any opportunity of persuing the proof sheets" [M.R.

48, 1773: 248], but Griffiths' correspondence suggests that at least some of the reviewers saw proofs.)[40]

The many acccusations by disgruntled authors who liked to maintain that reviewing was done by incompetent, malicious hacks who reviewed because they could not write cannot stand for long in the face of all the information now available, but the myth still occasionally revives. The accusations of puffing, made at the time and regularly since, are more difficult to combat because there is some truth to them. The *Critical* and the *Monthly* could make grand declarations about the reviewers' duty to "guard the most scrupulously against the partialities of friendship, the prejudices of resentment, the suggestions of calumny, and the soothing incense of adulation" (C.R.8, 1759: 271), but we still see Griffiths commenting disingenuously on the publication (by himself) of the bowdlerized *Fanny Hill*, the *Critical* relentlessly puffing Smollett's works, the *Monthly* regularly publishing reviews by friends of the author and even, on rare occasions, by the author or translator himself (the *Critical* is just as likely as the *Monthly* to have done this too, and the manipulations of both Reviews by Charles Burney documented by Roger Lonsdale support this, but the surviving marked set of the *Monthly* provides proof generally lacking in the case of the other journal).[41] Such examples do not undermine eighteenth-century reviewing as a whole, however; the majority of reviews appear to have been writen conscientiously and with no more than the usual kinds of prejudices and quirks possessed by reviewers in all periods.

Authors' accusations and ill-wishing notwithstanding, their belief (often strenuously denied) in the power of the review journals is made abundantly clear in the innumerable attacks on reviews and reviewers in letters to magazines and newspapers; in poems, plays, novels, and pamphlets; and, increasingly often, in appeals to reviewers in prefaces. By 1759 many authors believe that "there are many Readers who seldom venture to judge for themselves, or, even, to peruse a Work until they are informed of its Character."[42] The *Monthly Review*'s timely recognition of the potential for creating a market for book reviews has led to remarkable success; the *Critical* has taken it as a matter of course that book reviewing is necessary and accepted that its initial task is to convince the public not that reviewing is necessary but that the *Critical*'s approach to reviewing will revive "the true Spirit of Criticism." And by January 1757, when the *London Chronicle* begins publication, the new journal refers lightly to the fact that there are "now, amongst other Disturbers of human Quiet, a numerous Body of *Reviewers* and *Remarkers*"[43] but goes on, as the *Critical* had done (but calmly and without any of the furious insults offered by the *Critical*), to try to show why its reviewing methods will be preferable to those already on offer in other journals.

A year earlier *The Repository, or General Review* had informed the public that its anthologizing work was "highly needful" because of the "great multitude of periodical pieces that now contend with each other, in exhibiting a variety of literary matter for public instruction and amusement."[44] Few of the new journals lasted long, apart from the *Critical Review*, the *Annual Register*, and the already successful *Gentleman's* and *London* magazines, but time after time they testify to the essential place carved out for themselves by the reviewers. The *Annual Register*, for example, in its preface to its first volume (covering 1758), announces its aim as being the "extensively useful" one of "uniting the plan of the Magazines with that of the Reviews"[45] and other magazines make it clear in their advertisements that their proprietors naturally include among "every . . . necessary Article either for Instruction or Amusement" a section devoted to "critical Remarks and Extracts from the latest Publications."[46] It is an accepted fact in 1761 that a new magazine is well advised to announce that it will offer "an impartial and critical Account of all the New Books, with Abstracts from the most valuable,"[47] and by 1769 an article in *Critical Memoirs of the Times* refers to the "necessity, which the editors of almost all our periodical publications have found themselves under, of giving some account of the productions of the press."[48]

This necessity, according to the writer in *Critical Memoirs of the Times*, "fully proves the utility of a design, which but few of [the periodicals] have been able to execute with tolerable propriety,"[49] and this, not surprisingly, is the line taken by many of the new journals or journals new to reviewing. Echoing the *Monthly Review*'s original statement of its role, journal after journal acknowledges the needs of "those who are not disposed to read every new work, or who really cannot afford to purchase them"[50] or those of their readers who "would wish to be acquainted with the literature of the times, without submitting to the disagreeable task of perusing *every new* book that may issue from the press."[51] New review journals, or review sections in journals, are necessary because of "the manner in which the duty of a critic is performed by the Monthly and Critical Reviewer"[52] who performs his task in "so imperfect a Manner";[53] like the *Critical Review* in 1756, a new journal such as the *Candid Review* is likely to inform the public that its "Design . . . is very different from that hath already appeared under a like Character."[54]

A review journal, were it "never so justly conducted," would nonetheless be sure to offend "a numberless tribe" of authors,[55] and some of the new journals see a good opportunity in this. With all of the multiplying attacks on reviewers, the author/editor of *Literary Annals: or, The Reviewers Reviewed* obviously thinks it a sound move to offer space in his journal "if any persons aggrieved think proper to reply" to the criticisms of "doughty Critics" in other journals,[56] and the *London Magazine* publishes so many attacks on the *Monthly Review* from 1769 onwards that they become one of its regular sections. Other journals offer a right of reply to their own criticisms if "any misunderstanding should arise, or personal offence be taken"[57] and if, in the case of *The Universal Catalogue*, "such Reply be a decent one, and with the Limits of [their] present Plan, and sent to the Publisher before the fifteenth Day of every Month."[58]

Attacks on the existing reviewers are, of course, a feature of the new journals, and many enjoy the "generous task of unmasking a set of modern pretenders to criticism, who under the immodest and specious title of Reviewers . . . have for near twenty years, exercised with impunity, a despotic, tyrannic sway, throughout the regions of genius."[59] In this arena too, like that of the disgruntled authors, references abound to "those two presumptuous and self-erected tribunals,"[60] "a set of *self-erected* critics, who have usurped a power more cruel than that of Procrustes, the tyrant of Attica,"[61] and to "these performances [which assume] the separate jurisdiction, as viceregents of the public, of sitting formally upon a trial for the life and death of all literary productions."[62] The reviewers' faults, particularly their "practice of censure and cavil, totally deviating from the purpose of their intention,"[63] serve as a basis for contrast when new journals promise that they "will not stoop to indulge in ill-nature, or in satire"[64] and that the "person of the author shall be deemed *sacred and inviolable*."[65] All of these attacks and promises have something to tell us both about the image of the reviewers and about their place in the literary world.

Journals, or sections of journals, comparing the two Reviews or, by reprinting different criticisms, giving the public a chance to do so, start early, and expressed motives for the practice vary. The *Universal Catalogue*, for example, considers that it will enable the public "from many Opinions to form a better judgment of each particular Work,"[66] whereas *The Repository*, sixteen years earlier, thinks it only just that the reviewers be "called to account" by the same means they use for authors.[67] As a correspondent to the *London Magazine* points out in October 1771, "a scheme of contrasting the opinion of the two Reviews . . . would certainly form a very agreeable article to many . . . readers, and shew the *candour* of our literary inquisitors in the clearest point of view to the public" (L.M.40, 1771: 504); certainly such schemes (of which the *London Magazine*'s effort in 1771 and 1772 is a good example) appear to have been popular with unhappy authors and with general readers.

Indeed, all kinds of battles in print appear to have been becoming steadily more popular. "The present taste for reading seems to have unhappily degenerated into the mere love of abuse," writes the *Gentleman's Magazine* sadly in a 1772 review, "and people buy pamphlets from the same motives which would carry them to a bear-garden" (G.M.42, 1772: 30). In fact the *Gentleman's Magazine* is better entitled to lament this development than the other three journals most involved in reviewing during this third quarter of the eighteenth century (the *Monthly* and *Critical* Reviews and the *London Magazine*) because it avoids becoming entangled in undignified brawls with authors, although it does make some sharp comments in reviews. For the *Gentleman's Magazine*, of course, book reviewing is, even after 1765, only one minor section of its contents. Even before the birth of the *Monthly Review* the *Gentleman's* makes the occasional very brief comment on a new publication, and this continues until December 1750 when its booklist, a regular feature since the magazine's beginning in 1731, is for the first time described in the table of contents as "Books and pamphlets with remarks." Only a few items in the booklist do have "remarks," and these are rarely more than a few words; this area of literary endeavor remains of very minor interest until 1765, with, sometimes, a whole year passing without any comments at all. Then in April 1765, when the importance of reviewing can no longer be questioned, the *Gentleman's* begins an expanded review section, "List of Books published; with Extracts," with a few books dealt with in some detail, some with up to half a page of comment. Reviewing methods are much the same as those employed in the full-scale Reviews, except that the *Gentleman's* reviews only a selection of the works published each month and does so on a much smaller scale, without the huge amounts of quotation regularly accompanying or making up many of the main-article reviews in the *Critical* or *Monthly*. (The *Gentleman's Magazine* has the distinction of having published the shortest review of all time—it consists simply of an exclamation point added to the title of the work—in volume 41, 1771; the review, on page 133, is of William Hodson's *The Dedication of the Temple of Solomon*.) The *London Magazine*'s later interest in reviewing I have already mentioned, but it too is slow in making any real feature of reviews. There is the occasional comment on a book before 1749 and its monthly booklists start including brief comments in August 1759 but, like its rival, the *Gentleman's*, the *London* has comments on only a few items in the lists. In October 1759 the lists begin to be described in the table of contents (but not at the head of the lists) as "Catalogue of Books, with Remarks," although this, like the comments, stops and starts during the next few years. Then it is in June 1767 that the *London Magazine*, once again behind the *Gentleman's*, makes a formal beginning of larger scale reviewing, with its "An Impartial Review of New Publications" containing eight items.

After formally joining the ranks of the reviewers, the *London Magazine* devotes, from the end of 1769, a significant portion of its attention to attacking the other reviewers, almost always those in the *Monthly Review*. Most of these attacks are in the form of letters from correspondents, month after month, but it is impossible to know how genuine these are. (The *Gentleman's Magazine* has some such letters, but comparatively few.) One after another these correspondents, with such names as "Crito" and "Aristarchus," criticize a particular review and say firmly that "so evasive, uncandid, and illiberal a criticism cannot be too much exposed" (L.M.39, 1770: 195) or that it will be a public service "to vindicate the valuable works of those learned and ingenious writers such *pseudo-critics* condemn, and to expose to just censure the *inane* productions of those *half-thinking* authors they commend" (L.M.39, 1770: 292). By the end of 1770 a correspondent, "X.Y.Z.," begins his letter, "finding you appropriate a part of your publication to criticisms on the Monthly Review, I take the liberty to send you my thoughts concerning it" (L.M.39, 1770: 608), and letters like this continue to be published over the next few years, together with regular items headed "The Reviewers reviewed" and other occasional ones concerning reviewing.

"The present age is an age of scriblers," a correspondent to the *London Magazine* writes in 1771 (L.M.40, 1771: 268), and naturally there are many to complain about the reviewers' ever-more-secure position in the literary world. There is, as before, agreement between authors and reviewers that the "reviewing of books is a business of much consequence"[68] and that "a literary Journal, conducted upon liberal principles, would be of equal service to the gentleman and the scholar" (L.M.40, 1771: 270), but there the agreement ends. Laments by authors (and perhaps their literary public) that existing journals merely disgrace the ideals of criticism recur regularly and this one, from "Anti-Zoilus" writing to the *London Magazine*, is typical:

A Journal of the productions of literature, conducted with fidelity, decency, and candour, would be a continual source of national respect and honour abroad, and of entertainment and instruction at home. But, to answer this great purpose, it is indispensibly necessary, that the conductors should be men of known honour and ability; who would not less disdain an ostentatious parade of the talents they have, than bold pretensions to those they have not; who, of the pieces they examine, would be less sollicitous to impose their own opinion as a standard for the opinion of their readers, than by a clear and just representation to enable every reader to form an opinion for himself. . . . (L.M.42, 1773: 184)

Such a "great purpose" can hardly be expected to be fulfilled by the *Monthly* and *Critical* Reviews, so often described as "these Pretenders to Criticism"[69] whose "judgment, as criticks, [is] shallow and despicable" (L.M.39, 1770: 86). Even a dictionary entry in 1772, in Joseph Nicoll Scott's new edition of Bailey's *New Universal Etymological English Dictionary*, remarks under the heading of "criticism" that there are "critics of every *size* and *complexion*" to be found at the time, "from an Addison or Sheffield, on the *one* hand; *down as low* as your *Monthly Reviews* and *Gentleman's Magazines* on the other."[70] The fact that the reviewers have "*set themselves up* as Judges of the Labours of the Learned, and Censors in the Republic of Letters"[71] and that "an office, to which only liberal learning and sound judgment, and ingenuous candour have an inalienable right, [has been] usurped by two setts of Pseudo-critics" (L.M.42, 1773: 184) continues to be commented on by disgruntled authors; what is really galling, of course, is the success crowning the usurpation.

The end of the third quarter of the eighteenth century is also the end of the first quarter-century of reviewing and the beginning of a new phase. In 1775 William Kenrick, reviewer, pamphleteer, dramatist, translator, and literary troublemaker, described by the *London Magazine* as "a haberdasher in the small wares of literature" (L.M.37, 1768: 445), began a new enterprise, *The London Review of English and Foreign Literature*. Like many of its predecessors, including the *Critical Review*, it promised various improvements "which the Proprietors of former Reviews [had] hitherto neglected";[72] in fact, during its short five-and-a-half-year life (it survived for only a year after Kennrick's death in June 1779), it did not make significant changes to the well-established successful formula of its predecessors. With the impact of reviewing still increasing—the poems, the prefaces, the advertisements and the pamphlets continued to multiply to attack or to plead with the reviewers—the eighties and nineties saw the establishment of several successful new review journals, beginning with the *English Review, or an Abstract of English and Foreign Literature* in 1783 and the *Analytical Review, or History of Literature, Domestic and Foreign, on an Enlarged plan* in 1788. As the *English Review*'s preface began:

> The wide diffusion of Science and Literature among all classes of society, gives birth to an endless multiplicity of performances, which engage the curiosity, and illustrate the efforts of men in their advances to refinement and perfection. To exhibit a faithful report of every new Publication, is an undertaking of very extensive utility. It affords the means of instruction to the studious, and it amuses the idle. It blends knowledge and relaxation; and ought to hold out and ascertain the progressive improvements, as well as the reigning follies of mankind. It is therefore, a matter of suprize, that two publications only of the critical kind should have been able to establish themselves in England.[73]

In the development of these "two publications . . . of the critical kind," their progress and steadily increasing importance in literary life, and, above all, in the growth of and changes to the relationship formed between authors, reviewers, and the reading public, it can be seen that a period not normally considered to be of great literary-historical interest is, on the contrary, of considerable consequence to the history of criticism and the history of literature.

The fact that this period with its newly wide and ever-increasing audience for literature should (not coincidentally) have produced a phenomenon that "inclosed what was once a common field" (C.R.30, 1770: 467) aroused a sense of grievance in authors which would far outlast the end of the period covered by this brief introduction. The hopeless fight to undermine and put an end to the reviewers, who were attaining positions of growing power and influence, and to forestall or bypass reviewers to speak directly to the public, makes this a lively and extremely interesting period.

The review journal, according to Walter Graham, "must be regarded by far the most important agent for the development of literary criticism in English before 1800";[74] the Reviews' regular attention to prose fiction, Robert D. Mayo argues convincingly, "helped beyond any other single agency (outside the obvious merits of the better novels themselves) to ensure for prose fiction a recognized place in the total eighteenth-century consciousness."[75] All this is a far cry from the long-held image of eighteenth-century reviewing, and study of reviews and of the relationship between reviewers, authors, and the reading public is clearly essential to understanding the literary life and criticism of the eighteenth century. It is hoped that the Review Index will facilitate this.

Notes

1. For information concerning these early developments see Roger Philip McCutcheon, "The Beginnings of Book-Reviewing in English Periodicals," *PMLA* 37 (1922): 691–706; Walter Graham, *English Literary Periodicals* (New York: Nelson, 1930), chapter 7; Edward A. Bloom, "'Labors of the Learned': Neoclassic Book Reviewing Aims and Techniques," *Studies in Philology* 54 (1957): 537–563; and Derek Roper, *Reviewing before the Edinburgh 1788–1802* (London: Methuen, 1978), chapter 1.
2. *The London Evening Post* 17–20 June 1749.
3. *Monthly Review* 1 (1749): 238. Subsequent references to the *Monthly Review*, taking this one as an example, will be abbreviated as M.R.1, 1749: 238, and will so appear in the text and notes. Similarly, the titles of the *Critical Review*, *Gentleman's Magazine*, and *London Magazine* will be abbreviated as C.R., G.M., and L.M., respectively.
4. This "Advertisement" is bound following the table of contents at the beginning of volume 1 of the *Monthly Review* in the Bodleian Library's copy (Griffiths' own annotated set) but is bound at the end of the first number, i.e., between pages 80 and 81, in the British Library's copy and the copy in the State Library of Victoria.
5. I have adopted the convention used by Walter Graham and Derek Roper (see note 1, above) and others, by which "Review" with an initial capital refers to a review journal and is thus clearly distinguishable from the individual "review" items.
6. *The General Advertiser* Tuesday, 16 January 1749–50.
7. All reviews in the *Monthly Review* were anonymous throughout its history, a practice followed by later journals, and preservation of the anonymity of his reviewers was important to Griffiths. However, his own cryptically annotated set of the Review survives in the Bodleian and enabled the identification of most of the reviewers by Benjamin Christie Nangle. Nangle published in 1934 and 1955 indexes to the contributors to the first and second series of the *Monthly Review* (1749 to 1789 and 1790 to 1815, respectively) and thereby put an end to any excuse for the surprisingly long-lived notion that the reviewing was done by Grub Street hacks. See *The Monthly Review, First Series, 1749–1789: Indexes of Contributors and Articles* (Oxford: Clarendon, 1934) and *The Monthly Review, Second Series, 1790–1815: Indexes of Contributors and Articles* (Oxford: Clarendon, 1955).
8. See my "Mr. Pope's Maxims," *The Age of Johnson* 2 (1987) 67-91.
9. *Escapes of a Poetical Genius* (London, 1752), p. 1. For the review see M.R.6, 1752: 155–156.
10. Nathaniel Weekes, *On the Abuse of Poetry. A Satire* (London, 1754), preface to second edition, p. iv.
11. See note 7, above.
12. *Gentleman's Magazine* 26 (1756): 141.
13. *Public Advertiser* Friday, 9 December 1755.
14. Letter to John Moore, 3 August 1756, in *The Letters of Tobias Smollett*, ed. Lewis M. Knapp (Oxford: Clarendon, 1970), p. 46.
15. Walter Graham, *English Literary Periodicals* (New York: Nelson, 1930), p. 213. See also Derek Roper's examination of this received "truth," "The Politics of the 'Critical Review', 1756–1817," *Durham University Journal* 22 (1961): 117–122, and Robert D. Spector, *English Literary Periodicals and the Climate of Opinion During the Seven Years' War* (The Hague: Mouton, 1966).
16. No equivalent of Nangle's *Index* to the contributors to the *Monthly Review* (see note 6, above) exists for the *Critical*. Derek Roper has identified the four contributors to the first two volumes of the *Critical Review* as Thomas Francklin, Samuel Derrick, John Armstrong, and Patrick Murdoch, in addition to Smollett himself (see Derek Roper, "Smollett's 'Four Gentlemen': The First Contributors to the *Critical Review*," *Review of English Studies* n.s. 10 [1955]: 38–44), and James G. Basker (see p. x, note 4) has identified many Smollett articles from 1756 to 1763, but little identification is possible for the rest of the journal's run.
17. See note 16, above.
18. Betty Rizzo's article on Isabella Griffiths in *A Dictionary of British and American Women Writers 1660–1800*, ed. Janet Todd (London: Methuen, 1984), pp. 142–143, decides to accept the story, chiefly on the grounds of Goldsmith's (not very reliable) word and a disinclination to believe Ralph Griffiths (whom she describes, with echoes of the

nineteenth-century Goldsmith-directed views of Griffiths, as "a man who lied for professional advantage whenever he thought it necessary" [p. 143]).
19. *The London Chronicle: or, Universal Evening Post* no. 1, Saturday, 1 January 1757, p. 1.
20. Letter signed "Tim Buck" and dated from Lincoln's Inn, 10 July 1760, in *London Chronicle* 8 (1760): 85.
21. Advertisement for the October 1749 number of the *Monthly Review*, *The General Advertiser* Thursday, 2 November 1749.
22. Jan Fergus and Ruth Portner, "Reviews and Readers: Provincial Subscribers to the *Monthly* and *Critical Reviews* and the Books They Read, 1758–80," paper delivered at the annual meeting of the Modern Language Association of America, 27 December 1985. For further information about the Clays' records and their contributions to literary history, see Jan Fergus, "Eighteenth-Century Readers in Provincial England: The Customers of Samuel Clay's Circulating Library and Bookshop in Warwick, 1770–72," *Papers of the Bibliographical Society of America* 78 (1984): 155–213 and "Women, Class, and the Growth of Magazine Readership in the Provinces, 1746–1780" in *Studies in Eighteenth-Century Culture* 16 (1986): 41–56, and Jan Fergus and Ruth Portner, "Provincial Bookselling in Eighteenth-Century England: The Case of John Clay Reconsidered," *Studies in Bibliography* 40 (1987): 147–163.
23. Advertisement for *The History of Portia*, *London Chronicle* 5 (1759): 341.
24. Advertisement for *Agenor and Ismena*, *London Chronicle* vol. 6 (1759): 602. This advertisement also appears appended to *Memoirs of the Chevalier de ***** (London, 1760), sig. (1+A3)v.
25. Advertisement for *The History of Margaret of Anjou Queen of England*, *The Evening Advertiser* no. 483, 9–12 April 1757.
26. Advertisement for *An Ode as presented to the Right Hon. William Pitt*, *Public Advertiser* Thursday, 2 June 1757.
27. Advertisement for *A Compendious History of the Popes*, *London Chronicle* 5 (1759): 592.
28. [William Collins], *Oriental Eclogues. Written originally for the Entertainment of the Ladies of Tauris. And now translated* (London, 1757), p. [24].
29. *Public Advertiser* Saturday, 5 June 1756.
30. See, for example, the advertisement for *Magazin des Enfans*, *London Chronicle* 2 (1757): 344. (And, of course, the advertisement for *The Revolutions of Genoa* I have mentioned above.)
31. See, for example, the advertisement for volume II of Madame de Maintenon's *Letters*, *London Chronicle* 5 (1759): 165.
32. There are many available references to the reviewers' rates of pay; most are later than the period covered here, but see the last of them below which establishes that the rates did not change much. See, for example, Bodl. Add. Mss. C89, fol. 197v, where Griffiths notes (in 1794) that he has agreed to pay John Leslie £4 per sheet, or fol. 369r, where J. Workman mentions (in an undated letter c. 1797) that Griffiths' terms are 3 guineas per sheet. See also Andrew Becket's complaint that for 280 articles in the *Monthly Review* he has been paid only £45 (letter to Griffiths 1790, quoted in *Dramatic and Prose Miscellanies. By Andrew Becket. . . . Edited By William Beattie, M.D.* 2 vols. [London: Virtue, 1838] vol. 1, p. xvii; for the response of Griffiths' friend and one-time partner, Thomas Becket, to his son's complaint, see Bodl. Add. Mss. C89, fol. 12); Samuel Badcock's statement to Griffiths in 1782 that the *Critical*'s reviewers are paid £2 "for all common articles" (Bodl. Add. Mss. C90, fol. 92); Percival Stockdale's mention of the *Critical*'s rate of pay in 1770 as being "poor; viz. two guineas a sheet" while the *Monthly Review* was paying 4 guineas a sheet (*The Memoirs of the Life, and Writings of Percival Stockdale; containing Many Interesting Anecdotes of the Illustrious Men With Whom He Was Connected. Written by Himself. In Two Volumes* vol. 2, [London: 1809] pp. 57–58); and an undated letter (c. 1795) from Griffiths to William Taylor in which he discusses the fact that the ordinary rate of pay "with *allowed exceptions* in favour of the more difficult branches of the business" has remained substantially unchanged in the fifty years of the Review's life and says that Taylor's rate of pay, now that he has "gone through [his] probation" and proved that his "abilities and

exertions were above the ordinary level and consequence," will be 3 guineas (J. W. Robberds, *A Memoir of The Life And Writings of the late William Taylor of Norwich* 2 vols. [London: Murray, 1843] vol. 1, pp. 130–132.
33. Donald D. Eddy, *Samuel Johnson Book Reviewer in the Literary Magazine: or, Universal Review 1756–1758* (New York and London: Garland, 1979), pp. 79–80.
34. Sylvester H. Bingham, "Publishing in the Eighteenth Century, with special reference to the firm of Edward and Charles Dilly" (Ph.D. dissertation, Yale University, 1937). Quoted in W. Denham Sutcliffe, "English Book-Reviewing 1749–1800" (D.Phil. thesis, Oxford University, 1942), p. 135.
35. See, for example, Bodl. Add. Mss. C89, fols. 163 and 326. See also Bodl. Mss. Montagu d.6, fol. 111, and d.10, fol. 51.
36. Bodl. Ms. Montagu d.7, fol. 336.
37. See, for example, Bodl. Add. Mss. C89, fols. 194v, 202r, and 277r.
38. See, for example, Bodl. Add. Mss. C89, fols. 48, 49, 198r, and 223.
39. For Goodenough's letter see Bodl. Add. Mss. C89, fol. 122; for some of the many other references to means of conveyance see fols. 61, 204, and 266.
40. See, for example, Bodl. Add. Mss. C89, fols. 225 and 297, the former requesting and the latter declining to see proofs.
41. See Roger Lonsdale, "Dr. Burney and the *Monthly Review*," *R. E. S.* n.s. 14 (1963): 346–358 and n.s. 15 (1964): 27–37, and *Dr. Charles Burney: A Literary Biography* (Oxford: Clarendon, 1965).
42. [James] Grainger, *A Letter to Tobias Smollett, M.D. Occasioned By his Criticism Upon a late Translation of Tibullus* (London, 1759), p. 1.
43. *London Chronicle* no. 1, Saturday, 1 January 1757, p. 1. In fact the *London Chronicle* did not engage in any regular original reviewing.
44. *The Repository, or General Review: consisting Chiefly of a Select Collection of Literary Compositions, extracted From all the celebrated Periodical Productions now Publishing: with Occasional Remarks.* [1] (1756) sig. A2r.
45. *The Annual Register, or a View of the History, Politicks, and Literature, Of the Year* [1758] 1 (1759): v.
46. Advertisement for *The Imperial Magazine; or, Complete Monthly Intelligencer*, *Public Advertiser* Tuesday, 10 February 1761.
47. Advertisement for *The Court Magazine; or, Royal Chronicle of News, Politics, and Literature, for Town and Country*, *Public Advertiser* 25 September 1761.
48. *Critical Memoirs of the Times: containing A Summary View of the Popular Pursuits, Political Debates, and Literary Productions of the Present Age* [1] (1769): 33.
49. *Critical Memoirs*: 33.
50. *Critical Memoirs*: 163.
51. *The Political Register; and Impartial Review of New Books* 1 (1767): 33.
52. *The Political Register*: 121–122.
53. Advertisement for *The Universal Catalogue*, *Public Advertiser* Friday, 31 January 1772.
54. Advertisement for *The Candid Review, and Literary Repository*, *Public Advertiser* Wednesday, 30 January 1765.
55. *The Repository*, sig. B1r.
56. *Literary Annals: or, The Reviewers Reviewed* no. 1 (1765): 30.
57. *Critical Memoirs of the Times* [1] (1769): vii.
58. Advertisement for *Universal Catalogue*, *Public Advertiser* Friday, 31 January 1772.
59. Letter signed "J.W.," *Critical Memoirs of the Times* [1] (1769): 163.
60. Letter signed "X.Z.," *Political Register* 1 (1767): 122.
61. Letter signed "Misocriticos," *Political Register* 1 (1767): 181.
62. *The Repository*, sig. B1v.
63. *Critical Memoirs of the Times* [1] (1769): 33.
64. *The Edinburgh Magazine and Review. By A Society of Gentlemen* 1 (1773–74): 4.
65. *Political Register* 1 (1767): 33.
66. Advertisement for *The Universal Catalogue*, *Public Advertiser* Friday, 31 January 1772.
67. J. M. S. Tompkins, *The Popular Novel in England 1770–1800* [1932] (London: Methuen, 1969): 14.
68. Ms. draft of letter to Ralph Griffiths (undated but contents date it to 1772), Folger Ms. Y.c.1133(1), fol. (1a)r.
69. R. Lovett, *The Electrical Philosopher* (Worcester, 1774), p. 259.
70. *A New Universal Etymological English Dictionary: . . . Originally compiled by N. Bailey . . . Revised and Corrected by Joseph Nicoll Scott, M.D. A New Edition* (London, 1772).

71. Lovett, *Electrical Philosopher*, p. 247.
72. *London Review of English and Foreign Literature* 1 (1775): iv.
73. *English Review, or an Abstract of English and Foreign Literature* 1 (1783): 3.
74. Walter Graham, *English Literary Periodicals* (New York: Nelson, 1930), p. 226.
75. Robert D. Mayo, *The English Novel in the Magazines 1740–1815* (Evanston: Northwestern University Press, 1962), p. 201.

PART TWO

Explanatory Note

It is the fate of those who toil at the lower employments of life to be rather driven by the fear of evil than attracted by the prospect of good; to be exposed to censure, without hope of praise; to be disgraced by miscarriage, or punished for neglect, where success would have been without applause, and diligence without reward.

Samuel Johnson

The Review Index is based primarily on the British Library's collections, both of the journals included and of the works reviewed. In an ideal world the Index would cover *all* the periodicals, including newspapers, that ever reviewed a book during this period and would include all works reviewed, whatever their subject or form; it would also then have taken perhaps twenty-seven years instead of the seven it did take, and have required research support on the scale of the ESTC's on both sides of the Atlantic. The Index *does* include all the principal journals doing reviewing and a significant representation of the minor ones available and appropriate.

As the Index could not cover all works reviewed, the decision was made to include works in English only in the categories of poetry, fiction, and drama. These categories are somewhat artificial; inevitably there will be items—particularly concerning fiction, where the lines between "history" of a sort and prose fiction are often hopelessly blurred—over the inclusion of which there may be disagreement. Artificial though the categories of poetry, fiction, and drama may be, the notion of such categories interested the reviewers, particularly those in the *Monthly Review*. In the pages of the *Monthly*, for example, fiction was, in the early years, variously included under the Monthly Catalogue headings of "History" or "Miscellaneous"; later, such headings as "Novels and Romances" began to be used. By the 1760s the *Monthly*'s Monthly Catalogue was using many new headings in addition to the old. Basic headings like "Poetry" and "Political" (a political poem might turn up in either) were supplemented by new ones such as "Heraldry," "Gardening," "Trade," "East Indies," and "Conjuration." The heading may even be used to insult, as when it is "Doggrel" (M.R.30, 1764: 489) or "Quackery" (M.R.53, 1775: 275), or when a poem is deliberately not placed in the poetical section because "so far from coming under that denomination, it is hardly measured rhyme" (M.R.55, 1776: 480).

What the Review Index can do is provide a list of most of the reviews of the 3,023 works it includes, as well as details of the works themselves, both from the review journals and, where I have been able to examine a copy of the work (as I have for all but 499 of them), from the works. Where there appears to be no surviving copy of a work, as is true for several hundred here (of course, many that I have not seen do survive in libraries I have not been able to visit or were inaccessible in libraries I did visit), the Index can provide some readily available details. Reference to the review journals also provides an important source of assistance with or confirmation of the publication dates of the many undated or misdated works of the period; when newspaper advertisements go on saying "This Day is Published" months and sometimes even years after the initial publication of a work, reference to the reviews can provide a necessary *terminus a quo*. (A survey of the *Critical* and the *Monthly*'s reviewing of 425 works of poetry, fiction, and drama published and advertised in 1756–57, 1761, 1765, and 1772 shows that both journals reviewed them on average in less than two months, with the *Critical Review* having a much better record for promptness in reviewing, as it did for the amount of space and prominence given to works of imaginative literature.) Many library catalogues have incorrect suggested publication dates for eighteenth-century works; the Index, in many cases, provides grounds for reconsideration.

Format

— The library name given is the one in which I examined a copy of the work; for many works there are also copies in other libraries.

— The information concerning format, price, and bookseller's name, given in parentheses for each item, comes from the review journals. If I have seen the work, title details come from the title page; if I have not, these details come from the review journals.

— The Index does *not* include reviews in newspapers.

— Translated, "altered," and adapted works have their main entry under the name of the translator, alterer, etc., if known, with a cross-reference under the original author's name. (In this period the line between translation/imitation/adaptation and original creation is too often blurred, and individual decisions on hundreds of items could not have been possible.)

— Where the author's "name" is only initials, the entry is under the title.

— Women writers are listed under the surname by which they are generally known, and not automatically under maiden names as in the British Library Catalogue. (Exceptions are Anna Laetitia Aikin, who was not yet Mrs. Barbauld at the time of publication of the work included here, and Catharine Trotter, whose *Works* included here were published under her maiden name of Cockburn.)

— The entries in the index are for books *reviewed*, which explains such apparent oddities as an entry for only volume 3 of Sarah Fielding's *David Simple* (the first two volumes were published in 1744) or an entry for only the bowdlerized version of *Fanny Hill* (the original edition predates the *Monthly Review*).

— From the magazines I include reviews only from the sections of reviews of published works and not reviews of drama as performance. This means, in many cases, that I have no magazine reviews for plays, as they were often not reviewed again as publications.

— A few items are noted as "listed" rather than reviewed. This is noted only for items listed (i.e., title and publication details are given but no comment is made) in the *Critical* or *Monthly* Reviews, where it is something out of the ordinary; the innumerable items merely listed in the magazines' book lists are not entered here.

Journals Included

Numbers in parentheses are the item numbers in R. S. Crane and F. B. Kaye, *A Census of British Newspapers and Periodicals 1620–1800* [1927] (London, 1979).

The Annual Register, or a View of the History, Politicks, and Literature, Of the Year [year] (C&K 16).

The British Magazine; or Monthly Repository for Gentlemen and Ladies (C&K 69).

The British Magazine and General Review of the Literature, Employment and Amusements of the Times (C&K 67).

The Candid Review and Literary Repository (C&K 90).

Critical Memoirs of the Times: containing A Summary View of the Popular Pursuits, Political Debates, and Literary Productions of the Present Age (C&K 1176).

The Critical Review; or, Annals of Literature (C&K 156).

The Gentleman's Magazine and Historical Chronicle (C&K 277).

The General Magazine of Arts and Sciences, Philosophical, Philological, Mathematical, Mechanical, &c. (C&K 266).

The London Magazine and Monthly Chronologer (C&K 398).

The London Review of English and Foreign Litera-

ture (C&K 410). [Only a few items were included from this journal, as it started in 1775. In its first few numbers this journal reviewed some works reviewed in the 1774 volumes of the *Monthly* and *Critical*, so these works have been included.]

The Literary Magazine; or, Universal Review (C&K 381).

The Monthly Review (C&K 580). [This journal had several minor title changes and settled on *The Monthly Review: or, Literary Journal. By Several Hands.*]

The Political Register; and Impartial Review of New Books (C&K 730).

The Town and Country Magazine; or, Universal Repository of Knowledge, Instruction and Entertainment (C&K 874).

The Universal Catalogue (C&K 901).

The Universal Museum and Complete Magazine of Knowledge and Pleasure (C&K 907).

Libraries Cited

British Library

Bodleian Library

Cambridge University Library

Folger Shakespeare Library

Houghton Library, Harvard

Widener Library, Harvard

Pusey Library, Harvard

Indiana University Library

Library of Johns Hopkins University

Library of Congress

Lilly Library, Indiana University

Newberry Library

New York Public Library

University of Pennsylvania Library

University of Chicago Library

Library of the University of Illinois at Champaign-Urbana

Beinecke Library, Yale

Sterling Library, Yale

Abbreviations

CAT. = the catalogue of the library concerned

ESTC = the British Library's published *Eighteenth-Century Short Title Catalogue*

N.C.B.E.L. = *The New Cambridge Bibliography of English Literature*

Review Index

Abbassai. An Eastern Novel
See: FALQUES, Marianne Agnès

The Absent Man: a Farce
See: BICKERSTAFFE, Isaac

The Abuse of Poetry
See: WEEKES, Nathaniel. *On the Abuse of Poetry*

The Accomplish'd Maid: A Comic Opera
See: GOLDONI, Charles

The Accomplish'd Rake
See: DAVYS, Mary

Achilles in Petticoats
See: COLMAN, George (the elder)

The Actor, a Poetical Epistle
See: LLOYD, Robert

1 ADAIR, James Makitrick. *The Methodist and Mimick. A Tale, In Hudibrastick Verse. By Peter Paragraph. Inscribed to Samuel Foot, Esq;* London, 1766 (4to. 1s.6d. Moran) CAMBRIDGE

Reviewed: *Monthly Review* 34 (1766): 395
Critical Review 24 (1767): 317–318
Gentleman's Magazine 37 (1767): 553–554
Universal Museum 3 (1767): 541

2 *Adam's Tail; or, the First Metamorphosis.* London, 1774 (4to. 1s.6d. Bell) NEWBERRY

Reviewed: *Monthly Review* 52 (1775): 355
Critical Review 38 (1774): 473

ADDISON, Joseph (adaptation)
See: *Rosamond, an Opera*

3 *An additional Scene to the Comedy of the Minor.* London, 1761 (8vo. 6d. Williams) BRITISH LIBRARY

Reviewed: *Monthly Review* 24 (1761): 158
Critical Review 11 (1761): 247

4 *The Address: a Fable*
NOT SEEN (4to. 6d. Nicoll)

Reviewed: *Monthly Review* 33 (1765): 324–325
Critical Review 20 (1765): 315
Gentleman's Magazine 35 (1765): 482

5 ADKINS, W. *The Hortonian Miscellany: Being a Collection of Original Poems, Tales, &c.* London, 1767 (8vo. 1s.6d. Bingley) BODLEIAN

Reviewed: *Monthly Review* 39 (1768): 165
Critical Review 24 (1767): 468
Gentleman's Magazine 37 (1767): 601–602
Universal Museum 4 (1768): 36

6 *Admiral Byng in the Elysian Shades, a Poem*
NOT SEEN (Fol. 6d. Withy)

Reviewed: *Monthly Review* 16 (1757): 287

7 *Admiral Vernon's Ghost; Being a full true and particular Account as how A Warlike Apparition appeared last Week to the Author, Clad all in Scarlet, and discoursed to him concerning the Present State of Affairs.* London, n.d. [ESTC-1758] (8vo. 6d. Burnet) BRITISH LIBRARY

Reviewed: *Monthly Review* 18 (1758): 185–186
Critical Review 5 (1758): 163–164

8 *The Adopted Daughter; or the History of Miss Clarissa B——.* 2 vols. London, 1767 (12mo. 6s. Noble) BRITISH LIBRARY

Reviewed: *Monthly Review* 35 (1766): 485
Critical Review 22 (1766): 469
London Magazine 36 (1767): 48

9 *The Adulterer. A Poem.* London, 1769 (4to. 1s. Bingley) BRITISH LIBRARY

Reviewed: *Monthly Review* 42 (1770): 76–77
Critical Review 28 (1769): 465–466

10 *The Adulteress.* London, 1773 (4to. 1s.6d. Bladon. 1773) BRITISH LIBRARY

Reviewed: *Monthly Review* 48 (1773): 318
Critical Review 35 (1773): 316
London Magazine 42 (1773): 196
Universal Catalogue [2] (1773) art. 380

11 *The Advantage of Misfortune: a Poem.* London, 1773 (4to. 1s. Ridley, &c. 1774) BRITISH LIBRARY

Reviewed: *Monthly Review* 50 (1774): 483
Critical Review 37 (1774): 315
London Magazine 43 (1774): 450–451
Universal Catalogue 3 (1774) art. 493

12 *The Advantages of Deliberation; or, the Folly of Indiscretion.* 2 vols. London, 1772 (12mo. 5s.sewed. Robinson and Roberts. 1772) UNIVERSITY OF PENNSYLVANIA

Reviewed: *Monthly Review* 46 (1772): 79
Critical Review 33 (1772): 83
Gentleman's Magazine 42 (1772): 85

13 *The Advantages of Repentance. A Moral Tale, Attempted in Blank Verse; and founded on the Anecdotes of a Private Family in *********shire.* London, n.d. [ESTC-1765] (8vo. 1s.6d. Tonson) BRITISH LIBRARY

Reviewed: *Monthly Review* 32 (1765): 152
Critical Review 19 (1765): 152
Candid Review 1 (1765): 137–139

The Adventures of a Bank Note
See: BRIDGES, Thomas

14 *The Adventures of a Black Coat. Containing a Series of Remarkable Occurrences and entertaining Incidents, That it was Witness to in its Peregrinations through the Cities of London and Westminster, in Company with Variety of Characters. As related by Itself.* London ed. reviewed; copy seen: Dublin, 1762 (12mo. 3s. Williams) BRITISH LIBRARY

Reviewed: *Monthly Review* 22 (1760): 548
Critical Review 9 (1760): 499

15 *The Adventures of a Jesuit: interspersed with Several Remarkable Characters, and Scenes in Real Life.* 2 vols. London, 1771 (12mo. 5s.sewed. Cook. 1771) BRITISH LIBRARY

Reviewed: *Monthly Review* 44 (1771): 92
Critical Review 30 (1770): 481
London Magazine 39 (1770): 631
Town & Country Magazine 3 (1771): 102

16 *The Adventures of a Kidnapped Orphan.* London, 1747 [1767–introduction refers to past event in 1758] (12mo. 2s.6d.sewed. Thrush) BRITISH LIBRARY

Reviewed: *Monthly Review* 37 (1767): 470
Critical Review 24 (1767): 345–349
Universal Museum 3 (1767): 595

17 *The Adventures of a Turk. Translated from the French.* 2 vols.
NOT SEEN (12mo. 6s. Coote)

Reviewed: *Monthly Review* 19 (1758): 580
Critical Review 7 (1759): 287

18 *The Adventures of a Valet. Written by Himself.* 2 vols. London, 1752 (12mo. 6s.bound. Robinson) BRITISH LIBRARY

Reviewed: *Monthly Review* 6 (1752): 110–123
London Magazine 21 (1752): 25–29

19 *The Adventures of an Author. Written by himself and a Friend.* 2 vols. London, 1767 (12mo. 6s. Robinson) BRITISH LIBRARY

Reviewed: *Monthly Review* 36 (1767): 238–239
Critical Review 23 (1767): 216–217
Gentleman's Magazine 37 (1767): 258–261

The Adventures of Captain Greenland
See: GOODALL, William

20 *The Adventures of Charles Villiers, an unfortunate Court Dependant.* 2 vols.
NOT SEEN (12mo. 5s. Bladon) [*Critical Review* gives name as Villers.]

Reviewed: *Monthly Review* 36 (1767): 173
Critical Review 22 (1766): 379

The Adventures of David Simple
See: FIELDING, Sarah

21 *The Adventures of Dick Hazard.* London, 1755 (12mo. 3s. Reeves) BRITISH LIBRARY

Reviewed: *Monthly Review* 11 (1754): 470

The Adventures of Emmera
See: YOUNG, Arthur

The Adventures of Ferdinand Count Fathom
See: SMOLLETT, Tobias

The Adventures of Harriet Sprightly
See: *The Adventures of Miss Harriet Sprightly*

22 *The adventures of Jack Smart*
NOT SEEN (12mo. 3s. Crowder)

Reviewed: *Monthly Review* 14 (1756): 360–361
Critical Review 1 (1756): 125–129

23 *The Adventures of Jack Wander. Written by Himself. Interspers'd with some Humorous Anecdotes, and Original Memoirs.* London, n.d. [ESTC-1766?] (12mo. 2s.6d. Jones) BRITISH LIBRARY

Reviewed: *Monthly Review* 34 (1766): 407
Critical Review 21 (1766): 470–471

The Adventures of Joe Thompson
See: KIMBER, Edward. *The Life and Adventures of Joe Thompson*

24 *The Adventures of Mark the Rambler. Written by himself*
NOT SEEN (8vo. 3s.6d. Williams)

Reviewed: *Monthly Review* 28 (1763): 404
Critical Review 15 (1763): 322

25 *The Adventures of Miss Beverly. Interspersed with Genuine Memoirs of a Northern Lady of Quality.* 2 vols. London, 1768 (12mo. 6s. Bladon) BRITISH LIBRARY

Reviewed: *Monthly Review* 38 (1768): 411–412
Critical Review 26 (1768): 209–212
London Magazine 37 (1768): 163
Universal Museum 4 (1768): 316

26 *The Adventures of Miss Harriet Sprightly, a Lady of Pleasure. Interspersed with the Histories and Characters, the Amours and Intrigues of several Personages well known in the polite World.* 2 vols.
NOT SEEN (12mo. 5s.sewed. Serjeant)

Reviewed: *Monthly Review* 34 (1766): 241
Critical Review 21 (1766): 237

27 *The Adventures of Miss Lucy Watson. A Novel.* London, 1768 (12mo. 2s.6d. Nicoll) BRITISH LIBRARY

Reviewed: *Monthly Review* 38 (1768): 72
Critical Review 25 (1768): 209–211
London Magazine 37 (1768): 276
Universal Museum 4 (1768): 93

28 *The adventures of miss Polly B–ch–rd and Samuel Tyrrel, Esq; Written by the lady herself. Wherein are introduced, the amours of Los Cardos and Zaphsharrak*
NOT SEEN (12mo. 3s. Woodyer)

Reviewed: *Monthly Review* 10 (1754): 147–148

The Adventures of Mr. George Edwards
See: HILL, John

29 *The Adventures of Mr. Loveill, Interspers'd with many Real Amours of the Modern Polite World.* London, 1750 (6s.) BRITISH LIBRARY

Reviewed: *Monthly Review* 3 (1750): 58

30 *The Adventures of Oxymel Classic, Esq; Once an Oxford Scholar.* 2 vols. London, 1768 (12mo. 6s. Flexney) HARVARD (HOUGHTON)

Reviewed: *Monthly Review* 38 (1768): 249
Critical Review 25 (1768): 464
London Magazine 37 (1768): 113
Universal Museum 4 (1768): 204

31 *The Adventures of Patrick O'Donnel, in his Travels through England and Ireland. Written by himself*
NOT SEEN (12mo. 2s.6d. Williams)

Reviewed: *Monthly Review* 29 (1763): 236
Critical Review 16 (1763): 138–142

The Adventures of Peregrine Pickle
See: SMOLLETT, Tobias

32 *The adventures of Shelim O Blunder, Esq; the Irish Beau.* London, n.d. [ESTC-1750?] (8vo. 1s. Carpenter) BRITISH LIBRARY

Reviewed: *Monthly Review* 5 (1751): 158

The Adventures of Sir Launcelot Greaves
See: SMOLLETT, Tobias

33 *The Adventures of Sylvia Hughes. Written by Herself.* London, 1761 (12mo. 3s. Williams) BRITISH LIBRARY

Reviewed: *Monthly Review* 23 (1760): 523
Critical Review 10 (1760): 486
London Magazine 29 (1760): 672
British Magazine 2 (1761): 46

The Adventures of Telemachus
See: SALIGNAC DE LA MOTHE FÉNÉLON, François

34 *The adventures of the Rd. Mr. Judas Hawke, the Rd. Mr. Nathan Briggs, Miss Lucretia Briggs, &c. Late Inhabitants of the Island Querumania. After the Manner of Joseph Andrews.* London, 1751 (12mo. 1s.6d. Waller) BRITISH LIBRARY

Reviewed: *Monthly Review* 5 (1751): 73–74

35 *The Adventures of William B–ds–w, commonly stiled Devil Dick, the son and brother to two pious ministers: Containing instructive accounts of his wicked exploits, during a course of several years, in company with Ann S–z–d, whom he afterwards married; the penitent reformation of both these profligates; their coming to a great estate of her father's; and their religious as well as generous behaviour to Will. Edgcomb, one of their iniquitous associates, who by their endeavours was happily reformed, and became a worthy gentleman farmer. Drawn up for the benefit of mankind, by Mr. B–ds–w's own hand, and published from his papers.* 2 vols.
NOT SEEN (12mo. 6s. Robinson, &c.)

Reviewed: *Monthly Review* 11 (1754): 470

Advice to new-married persons
See: QUILLET, Claude

AESOP. *Fables*
See: DRAPER, Charles

36 AESOP. *Select Fables of Aesop And Other Fabulists. In Three Books.* [Ed. and partly written by Robert DODSLEY.] Birmingham, 1761 (8vo. 3s. Dodsley) BRITISH LIBRARY

Reviewed: *Monthly Review* 24 (1761): 150–156
Critical Review 11 (1761): 122–127
British Magazine 2 (1761): 161
Annual Register 3 (1760): 265–271

37 *The affected Indifference, a Novel.* 2 vols. London, 1771 (12mo. 5s.sewed. Noble. 1771) BRITISH LIBRARY

Reviewed: *Monthly Review* 45 (1771): 503
Critical Review 32 (1771): 312

38 *The affecting Story of Lionel and Arabella, who, By a most unhappy Accident, first discover'd the Island of Madeira, and perish'd there.* London, 1756 (1s.6d. Griffiths) BRITISH LIBRARY

Reviewed: *Monthly Review* 14 (1756): 453
Critical Review 1 (1756): 253–255

The African Prince
See: DODD, William

39 *Age. An Essay. Addressed to Richard Tyrrell, Esq;*
NOT SEEN (4to. 1s. Burnet)

Reviewed: *Monthly Review* 21 (1759): 180–181
Critical Review 7 (1759): 558

40 *The Age of Dullness. A Satire. By a Natural Son of the late Mr. Pope. With a Preface giving some Account of his Mother, and how he came to the Knowledge of his Birth.* London, 1757 (4to. 1s. Brotherton) BODLEIAN

Reviewed: *Monthly Review* 16 (1757): 183
Critical Review 3 (1757): 87–88

41 *Agenor and Ismena; or, the War of the Tender Passions. A Novel. In Two Volumes. Translated from the French.* London, 1759 (12mo. 6s. Cooke) BRITISH LIBRARY

Reviewed: *Monthly Review* 21 (1759): 451
Critical Review 8 (1759): 408

London Magazine 28 (1759): 632
Critical Memoirs 1 (1769): 525

Agis: A Tragedy
See: HOME, John

42 *An Agreeable Companion For A Few Hours, either on the Road or at Home. In Several Fugitive Pieces. By a Gentleman of the University of Oxford.* London, 1773 (4to. 2s. Newbery. 1773) UNIVERSITY OF CHICAGO

Reviewed: *Monthly Review* 48 (1773): 159
Critical Review 34 (1772): 470
Gentleman's Magazine 43 (1773): 136–137
London Magazine 41 (1772): 598
Universal Catalogue [1] (1772) art. 1458

Agreeable Ugliness
See: SCOTT, Sarah

43 *Agriculture and Commerce, a Dialogue. Written in Autumn 1764.* London, 1765 (4to. 1s. Becket) BRITISH LIBRARY

Reviewed: *Monthly Review* 33 (1765): 85
Critical Review 19 (1765): 399–400
Gentleman's Magazine 35 (1765): 234
Candid Review 1 (1765): 326–328

44 AIKIN, Anna Laetitia (later Barbauld). *Poems.* London, 1773 (4to. 6s.sewed. Johnson. 1773) BRITISH LIBRARY

Reviewed: *Monthly Review* 48 (1773): 54–59 and 133–137
Critical Review 35 (1773): 192–195
London Magazine 42 (1773): 40
Town & Country Magazine 5 (1773): 267

45 AIKIN, John. *Essays on Song-Writing: With a Collection of such English Songs as are most eminent for Poetical Merit. To which are added, Some Original Pieces.* London, n.d. [ESTC-1772?] (8vo. 3s.6d.sewed. Johnson. 1772) BRITISH LIBRARY

Reviewed: *Monthly Review* 46 (1772): 538–539
Critical Review 33 (1772): 182–183
London Magazine 41 (1772): 188
Universal Catalogue [1] (1772) art. 278

46 *Airs and Chorusses in the Entertainment of the Sylphs, As performed at the Theatre-Royal, Covent-Garden. The Music entirely new, composed by Mr. Fisher.* [British Library copy lacks publishing details.] [ESTC-London, 1774] (8vo. 6d. Becket) BRITISH LIBRARY

Reviewed: *Monthly Review* 50 (1774): 157
Critical Review 37 (1774): 76

47 *Airs, Duets, Chorusses, &c. in the New Masque called the Druids. As performed at the Theatre-Royal, Covent-Garden. The words chiefly taken from Ben Jonson; the music composed by Mr. Fisher.* London, 1774 (8vo. 6d. Evans. 1774) BRITISH LIBRARY

Reviewed: *Monthly Review* 51 (1774): 484

48 AKENSIDE, [Mark]. *An Ode to the Country Gentlemen of England.* 1st ed. reviewed; copy seen 2d ed.: London, 1758 (4to. 6d. Dodsley) BRITISH LIBRARY

Reviewed: *Monthly Review* 18 (1758): 335–338

49 AKENSIDE, [Mark]. *An Ode to the late Thomas Edwards, Esq; Written in the Year M.DCC.LI.* London, 1766 (Fol. 6d. Dodsley) BRITISH LIBRARY

Reviewed: *Monthly Review* 34 (1766): 403
Critical Review 21 (1766): 389–391

50 AKENSIDE, Mark. *The Poems of Mark Akenside, M.D.* London, 1772 (4to. 1l.1s. Dodsley. 1772) BRITISH LIBRARY

Reviewed: *Monthly Review* 47 (1772): 428–437
Universal Catalogue [1] (1772) art. 419

Albion Restored
See: STEVENS, George Alexander

Albumazar. A Comedy
See: GARRICK, David

51 *Alcastor to Sophron. An Epistle.* London, 1755 (4to. 6d. Cooper) BODLEIAN

Reviewed: *Monthly Review* 12 (1755): 511–512

52 ALDINGTON, John. *A Poem On the Cruelty of Shooting: with Some tender Remarks on the 10th Day of May 1768, particularly on young Mr. Allen. Humbly dedicated to the Sons of*

Liberty. London, 1769 (8vo. Pyne) BRITISH LIBRARY

Reviewed: *London Magazine* 38 (1769): 439

53 ALDINGTON, John. *A Poem on the Various Scenes of Shooting. On a New Plan. By John Aldington, of Evesham, in Worcestershire, an experienced Fowler. Humbly recommended to the Gentlemen of the Gun.* London, 1767 (4to. 1s. Pridden) BRITISH LIBRARY

Reviewed: *Monthly Review* 37 (1767): 315
Critical Review 24 (1767): 225
Universal Museum 3 (1767): 484

54 D'ALENZON. *The Bonze, or Chinese Anchorite, an Oriental Epic Novel Translated from the Mandarine Language of Hoamchi-vam, a Tartarian Proselite, By Monsr. D'Alenzon.* 2 vols. London, 1769 (12mo. 6s.sewed. Dodsley, &c. 1768) BRITISH LIBRARY

Reviewed: *Monthly Review* 40 (1769): 370–373
Critical Review 27 (1769): 178–181
Gentleman's Magazine 39 (1769): 158
Critical Memoirs 1 (1769): 524
Town & Country Magazine [1] (1769): 213
Political Register 4 (1769): 388

Alfred, a Masque
See: GARRICK, David

55 *Alfred the Great; Deliverer of his Country. A Tragedy. By the author of the Friendly Rivals.* London, 1753 (8vo. 1s. Mechel) BRITISH LIBRARY

Reviewed: *Monthly Review* 8 (1753): 391–392

56 *All for Love; or, the World Well Lost. A new Romance, Founded entirely on Fiction.* London, 1762 (12mo. 2s. Freeman) BRITISH LIBRARY

Reviewed: *Monthly Review* 26 (1762): 319

57 *All in the Right: or, The Cuckold in Good Earnest. A Farce, in Two Acts. As it was agreed to be acted at A Certain Theatre.* London, 1761 (8vo. 1s. Nicoll) BRITISH LIBRARY

Reviewed: *Monthly Review* 26 (1762): 75
Critical Review 12 (1761): 481
British Magazine 2 (1761): 662

58 [ALLEN, Bennet]. *Modern Chastity: or, the Agreeable Rape. A Poem. By a Young Gentleman of Sixteen. In vindication of The Right Hon. Lord B--e.* London, 1768 (4to. 1s.6d. Bingley) BRITISH LIBRARY

Reviewed: *Monthly Review* 38 (1768): 248
Critical Review 25 (1768): 228
Gentleman's Magazine 38 (1768): 118
London Magazine 37 (1768): 160

59 ALLEN, Bennet. *A Poem inscribed to His Majesty.* London, 1761 (4to. 1s. Dodsley) BODLEIAN

Reviewed: *Monthly Review* 25 (1761): 398
Critical Review 12 (1761): 398

60 [ALLEN, Bennet]. *A Poem on the Peace.* London, 1764 (4to. 1s. Fletcher) BODLEIAN

Reviewed: *Monthly Review* 30 (1764): 238–239
Critical Review 17 (1764): 237

61 [ALLEN, Bennet]. *Satirical Trifles: consisting of An Ode, written on the first Attack of the Gout. To Mankind, an Ode. The Farewell, written at Woodcote, near Epsom. Epigrams. By B.A..* London, 1764 (4to. 1s. Fletcher) BRITISH LIBRARY

Reviewed: *Monthly Review* 31 (1764): 232
Critical Review 18 (1764): 158
General Magazine 1 (1764): 349–350

All's Right at Last: or, the History of Miss West
See: BROOKE, Frances

62 *An Allusion to the Tenth Ode of the Second Book of Horace; On a Report of the Right Honble. H—— F——, Esq; quitting all Public Employments, and, in a Religious Fit, retiring to H---d H——e: In the ever memorable Year M.DCC.LVII.* London, 1757 (Fol. 6d. J. Scott) CAMBRIDGE

Reviewed: *Monthly Review* 16 (1757): 603–604 [3d ed.]
Critical Review 4 (1757): 93

Almida, a Tragedy
See: CELESIA, Dorothea

63 *Almira. Being the History of a Young Lady Of good Birth and Fortune, but more distinguish'd Merit.* 2 vols. London, 1762 (12mo. 6s. Owen) LIBRARY OF CONGRESS

Reviewed: *Monthly Review* 25 (1761): 503
Critical Review 12 (1761): 480
British Magazine 3 (1762): 44

64 *Almira: or, the History of a French Lady of Distinction.* London, 1758 (12mo. 3s. Corbet) BRITISH LIBRARY

Reviewed: *Monthly Review* 18 (1758): 492
Gentleman's Magazine 28 (1758): 132–133

Almoran and Hamet
See: HAWKESWORTH, John

Alonzo. A Tragedy
See: HOME, John

Alonzo; or, the youthful Solitaire
See: NOTT, John

65 *Alphonso: or, the Hermit.* Cambridge, 1773 (4to. 1s. Cambridge printed; sold by Brown in London) BRITISH LIBRARY

Reviewed: *Monthly Review* 48 (1773): 159
London Magazine 41 (1772): 598
British Magazine & General Review 2 (1772): 631
Universal Catalogue [1] (1772) art. 1379

Alzuma, a Tragedy
See: MURPHY, Arthur

Amabella, A Poem
See: JERNINGHAM, Edward

Amana. A Dramatic Poem
See: GRIFFITH, Elizabeth

The Amaranth
See: HARTE, Walter

66 *The Ambassadors of Christ Delineated; in Divine Sketches taken from Real Life. Being A Characteristic Dialogue, copied from An Original Plan in the School of Evangelical Experience. Most humbly design'd to remove Prejudice, and promote the Gospel. Earnestly recommended to all Religious Sects, and Parties, who desire to hear the Word savingly. By a Lover of Truth.* London, 1762 (8vo. 6d. Keith) BRITISH LIBRARY

Reviewed: *Monthly Review* 26 (1762): 78–79

Amelia. A Musical Entertainment
See: CUMBERLAND, Richard

Amelia: or, The Distress'd Wife
See: JUSTICE, Elizabeth

Amilec; or the Seeds of Mankind
See: TIPHAIGNE DE LA ROCHE, Charles François

Amintas, an English Opera
See: TENDUCCI, Giusto Fernando

67 *The Amorous Friars: or, the Intrigues of a Convent.* London, 1759 (12mo. 3s. Fleming) BRITISH LIBRARY

Reviewed: *Monthly Review* 19 (1758): 581
Critical Review 7 (1759): 288

68 [AMORY, Thomas]. *The Life of John Buncle, Esq; Containing Various Observations and Reflections, Made in several Parts of the World; and Many extraordinary Relations.* London, 1756 (8vo. 6s. Noon) BRITISH LIBRARY

Reviewed: *Monthly Review* 15 (1756): 497–512 and 585–604
Critical Review 2 (1756): 219–227

69 [AMORY, Thomas]. *The Life of John Buncle, Esq; Containing Various Observations and Reflections in several Parts of the World, and Many Extraordinary Relations. Vol. II.* London, 1766 (8vo. 10s. Johnson) BRITISH LIBRARY

Reviewed: *Monthly Review* 35 (1766): 33–43 and 100–123
Critical Review 21 (1766): 470

70 [AMORY, Thomas]. *Memoirs of Several Ladies of Great Britain. Interspersed with Literary Reflexions, and Accounts of Antiquities and Curious Things. In Several Letters.* London, 1755 (8vo. 6s. Noon) BRITISH LIBRARY

Reviewed: *Monthly Review* 13 (1755): 128–138 and 202–225

L'Amour A-la-Mode
See: KELLY, Hugh

71 *The Amours and Adventures of Charles Careless, Esq.*
NOT SEEN (12mo. 6s. Fletcher)

Reviewed: *Monthly Review* 30 (1764): 328–329
Critical Review 17 (1764): 479–480
British Magazine 5 (1764): 377

72 *The Amours of Lais: or The Misfortunes of Love.* London, 1766 (12mo. 3s. Polingsby) BRITISH LIBRARY

Reviewed: *Monthly Review* 34 (1766): 241
Critical Review 21 (1766): 157

73 *The Amours of Zeokinizul, King of the Kofirans. Translated from the Arabic of the famous Traveller Krinelbol. With a Key.* London, 1749 (8vo. 1s.6d. Owen) BODLEIAN

Reviewed: *Monthly Review* 1 (1749): 412–423

The Amusing Instructor
See: HUMPHREYS, R.

74 ANACREON. *Odes of Anacreon*
NOT SEEN (4to. 1s. Russel)

Reviewed: *Monthly Review* 19 (1758): 94

ANACREON and others. *The Works of Anacreon and Sappho, with Pieces from ancient Authors*
See: GREENE, Edward Burnaby

ANACREON and others. *The works of Anacreon, Sappho, Bion, Moschus and Musaeus. Translated into English, by a Gentleman of Cambridge*
See: FAWKES, Francis

Analects in Verse and Prose
See: CAREY, George Saville

75 *The Anchoret. A Moral Tale. In a Series of Letters.* 3 vols. London, 1773 (12mo. 7s.6d. sewed. Newbery. 1773) BRITISH LIBRARY

Reviewed: *Monthly Review* 48 (1773): 71
Critical Review 34 (1772): 471–472
London Magazine 42 (1773): 39
Universal Catalogue [2] (1773) art. 68

Ancient and modern Rome, a Poem
See: KEATE, George

Ancient Scottish Poems
See: BANNATYNE, George

76 ANDREWS, Joseph. *Love and Chastity: A Poetical Essay. Occasioned by the melancholy catastrophe of Miss Bell. Humbly inscribed to the Ladies of Great Britain*
NOT SEEN (Fol. 1s. Williams)

Reviewed: *Monthly Review* 24 (1761): 278
Critical Review 11 (1761): 79

77 [ANDREWS, Miles Peter].*A new Musical Interlude called the Election. As it is performed at the Theatre Royal in Drury-Lane.* London, 1774 (8vo. 6d. Griffin) BRITISH LIBRARY

Reviewed: *Monthly Review* 51 (1774): 484–485
Critical Review 38 (1774): 319

78 ANDREWS, Robert. *Odes, Dedicated to the Honourable Charles Yorke, Esq. By Robert Andrewes, Author of the English Virgil. Dedicated to the Honourable Booth Grey, Esq;* Birmingham, 1766 (4to. 1s.6d. Johnson) BRITISH LIBRARY

Reviewed: *Monthly Review* 35 (1766): 407
Critical Review 22 (1766): 233–234
Gentleman's Magazine 36 (1766): 430

79 ANDREWS, Robert. *The Works of Virgil, Englished By Robert Andrews.* Birmingham, 1766 (8vo. 7s.6d. Printed by Baskerville, and sold at Mr. Sheinton's, a Grocer, in Great Russel-Street) BRITISH LIBRARY

Reviewed: *Monthly Review* 34 (1766): 405
Critical Review 22 (1766): 77

Andromache to Pyrrhus. An Heroick Epistle
See: JERNINGHAM, Edward

80 *Anecdotes of a Convent. By the Author of Memoirs of Mrs Williams.* 3 vols. London, 1771

(12mo. 7s.6d. Becket and De Hondt) BRITISH LIBRARY

Reviewed: *Monthly Review* 45 (1771): 144–148
Critical Review 31 (1771): 483–484

81 *Angelica; or Quixote in Petticoats. A Comedy, in Two Acts.* London, 1758 (8vo. 1s. Printed for the Author) LIBRARY OF CONGRESS

Reviewed: *Monthly Review* 19 (1758): 581–582
Critical Review 6 (1758): 525

82 *Angelicus and Fergusia, a Tale.* London, 1761 (8vo. 1s. Johnson) BRITISH LIBRARY

Reviewed: *Monthly Review* 25 (1761): 501
Critical Review 13 (1762): 78

83 *Angelina. Interspersed with the Histories of Dona Vittorina, Dom. Matheo, and the Chevalier de Riva Franca. Translated from the French.* London, 1753 (12mo. 3s. Hinton) BRITISH LIBRARY

Reviewed: *Monthly Review* 8 (1753): 394

The Anglers. Eight Dialogues in Verse
See: SCOTT, Thomas

Anningait and Ajutt
See: PENNY, Anne

D'ANOIS, Countess de
See: LA MOTHE, Marie Catherine, Comtesse D'Aulnoy

84 [ANSTEY, Christopher]. *Appendix to the Patriot: containing The Author's Conversations with his Bookseller, &c. &c.* Cambridge, 1768 (4to. 1s. Dodsley) BRITISH LIBRARY

Reviewed: *Monthly Review* 38 (1768): 408

85 [ANSTEY, Christopher]. *Memoirs of the Noted Buckhorse. In which, Besides a Minute Account of his past Memorable Exploits, That celebrated Hero is carried into higher Life; Containing some very Extraordinary Events. Interspersed with Remarkable Anecdotes of some Bloods of Fortune and Eminence, Companions of Mr. Buckhorse.* 2 vols. London, 1756 (12mo. 6s. Crowder) BRITISH LIBRARY

Reviewed: *Monthly Review* 15 (1756): 534–535
Critical Review 2 (1756): 275–276

86 [ANSTEY, Christopher]. *The New Bath Guide: Or, Memoirs of the B–r–d Family. In a Series of Poetical Epistles.* London, 1766 (4to. 5s. Dodsley) BRITISH LIBRARY

Reviewed: *Monthly Review* 34 (1766): 467–472
Critical Review 21 (1766): 369–373
Gentleman's Magazine 36 (1766): 241

87 [ANSTEY, Christopher]. *The New Bath Guide: Or, Memoirs of the B–r–d Family. In a Series of Poetical Epistles. The Third Edition.* London, 1766 (8vo. 5s. Dodsley) BRITISH LIBRARY

Reviewed: *Monthly Review* 35 (1766): 233–235
Critical Review 22 (1766): 156
Gentleman's Magazine 36 (1766): 241

88 [ANSTEY, Christopher]. *On the much lamented Death of the Marquis of Tavistock. The Second Edition.* London, 1767 (4to. 6d. Dodsley) HARVARD (HOUGHTON)

Reviewed: *Monthly Review* 36 (1767): 330–331

89 [ANSTEY, Christopher]. *The Patriot, a Pindaric Address to Lord Buckhorse.* Cambridge, 1767 (4to. 2s.6d. Dodsley) BRITISH LIBRARY

Reviewed: *Critical Review* 24 (1767): 469–470
Universal Museum 3 (1767): 36

90 [ANSTEY, Christopher]. *The Patriot: a Pindaric Address to Lord Buckhorse. The Second Edition. With an Appendix.* Cambridge, 1768 (4to. 3s. 6d. Dodsley) BRITISH LIBRARY

Reviewed: *Monthly Review* 38 (1768): 150
Critical Review 25 (1768): 151
Political Register 2 (1768): 62

91 [ANSTEY, Christopher]. *The Priest Dissected: a Poem, Addressed to the Rev. Mr. ––. Author of Regulus, Toby, Caesar, And other Satirical Pieces in the public Papers.* Bath, n.d. [ESTC-1774] (4to. 2s.6d. Dodsley. 1774) BRITISH LIBRARY

Reviewed: *Monthly Review* 51 (1774): 166–167
Critical Review 38 (1774): 71–73

Town & Country Magazine 6 (1774): 437
Universal Catalogue 3 (1774) art. 783

The Anti-Gallican
See: LONG, Edward

92 Anti-Midas: a Jubilee Preservative from Unclassical, Ignorant, False, and Invidious Criticism. London, 1769 (4to. 1s.6d. Payne) BRITISH LIBRARY

Reviewed: *Monthly Review* 41 (1769): 487
Critical Review 28 (1769): 466
Gentleman's Magazine 39 (1769): 600
London Magazine 38 (1769): 642

93 *Anti-Pantheon; or, Verses occasioned on reading a late Publication called, The Pantheon*
NOT SEEN (4to. 1s. Snagg. 1773)

Reviewed: *Monthly Review* 49 (1773): 318
Critical Review 36 (1773): 315
Universal Catalogue [2] (1773) art. 1116

94 *The Anti-Rosciad. By the Author.* London, 1761 (4to. 6d. Kearsly) BRITISH LIBRARY

Reviewed: *Monthly Review* 24 (1761): 354
Critical Review 11 (1761): 340
British Magazine 2 (1761): 326

95 *Anti-Thespis: or, a Vindication of the Principal Performers at Drury-Lane Theatre from the False Criticisms, Illiberal Abuse, and Gross Misrepresentations of the Author of a Poem lately published, entitled Thespis.* London, 1767 (4to. 1s.6d. Bladon) CAMBRIDGE

Reviewed: *Monthly Review* 36 (1767): 79
Critical Review 23 (1767): 60
Gentleman's Magazine 37 (1767): 34

96 *The Anti-Times: addressed to Mr. C——Ch–ch–ll; In Two Parts. By the Author.* London, 1764 (4to. 1s.6d. Hooper) HARVARD (HOUGHTON)

Reviewed: *Monthly Review* 31 (1764): 318
Critical Review 18 (1764): 317–318

97 *The Ants: a Rhapsody.* 2 vols. London, 1767 (12mo. 4s. Davis and Reymers) BRITISH LIBRARY

Reviewed: *Monthly Review* 37 (1767): 147
Critical Review 24 (1767): 32–34
Gentleman's Magazine 37 (1767): 410–411
London Magazine 36 (1767): 424
Universal Museum 3 (1767): 372
Political Register 1 (1767): 249

APOLLONIUS RHODIUS (translation)
See: EKINS, Jeffery. *The Loves of Medea and Jason*

98 *The Apostate Ecclesiastic, A Poem: Being Candid Animadversions on that Rev. Mock-Patriot Parson H**ne.* London, 1774 (4to. 1s. Bew. 1774) BRITISH LIBRARY

Reviewed: *Monthly Review* 51 (1774): 68
Critical Review 37 (1774): 315
London Magazine 43 (1774): 244
Universal Catalogue 3 (1774) art. 602

99 *The Apparition to a great Man; or Admiral Byng's Outcry for Justice. A Poem*
NOT SEEN (4to. 6d. Pyle)

Reviewed: *Monthly Review* 22 (1760): 515
Critical Review 9 (1760): 322

Appendix to the Patriot
See: ANSTEY, Christopher

Appius: a Tragedy
See: MONCREIFF, John

The Arbour: or the Rural Philosopher
See: COLE, Thomas

L'Arcadia in Brenta. A new opera
See: SAGREDO, Giovanni

Arcadia: or, the Shepherd's Wedding
See: LLOYD, Robert

Ariadne Forsaken. A Poem
See: CATULLUS, Caius Valerius

100 ARIEL (pseud.). *The Kenrickad: a Poem.* London, 1772 (4to. 1s. Griffin) BRITISH LIBRARY

Reviewed: *Monthly Review* 47 (1772): 411
Critical Review 34 (1772): 397

British Magazine & General Review 2 (1772): 629–630

Arimant and Tamira
See: ROBERTS, William Hayward

ARIOSTO, Ludovico (translations)
See: CROKER, Temple Henry. *The Satires*
HOOLE, John. *Orlando Furioso*
HOOLE, John. *A Translation of Part of the Twenty-third Canto*
HUGGINS, William. *Orlando Furioso*

ARISTAENETUS. *Love Epistles*
See: SHERIDAN, Richard Brinsley

ARISTOPHANES. *The Clouds*
See: WHITE, James

Armine and Elvira
See: CARTWRIGHT, Edmund

101 [ARMSTRONG, John]. *A Day: An Epistle to John Wilkes, of Aylesbury, Esq.* London, 1761 (4to. 1s. Millar) BRITISH LIBRARY

Reviewed: *Monthly Review* 24 (1761): 76–79
Critical Review 11 (1761): 73–75
British Magazine 2 (1761): 46

102 ARMSTRONG, John. *Miscellanies.* 2 vols. London, 1770 (12mo. 7s. Cadell) BRITISH LIBRARY

Reviewed: *Monthly Review* 42 (1770): 210–213
Critical Review 29 (1770): 340–348
London Magazine 39 (1770): 42–43
Town & Country Magazine 2 (1770): 72

103 [ARMSTRONG, John]. *Of Benevolence: an Epistle to Eumenes.* London, 1751 (Fol. 1s. Millar) BRITISH LIBRARY

Reviewed: *Monthly Review* 4 (1750–51): 480

104 [ARMSTRONG, John]. *Sketches: or Essays on Various Subjects. By Launcelot Temple, Esq;* London, 1758 (8vo. 1s.6d. Millar) BRITISH LIBRARY

Reviewed: *Monthly Review* 18 (1758): 580–588
Critical Review 5 (1758): 380–386
Gentleman's Magazine 28 (1758): 284
Literary Magazine 3 (1758): 227–228

105 [ARMSTRONG, John]. *Taste: An Epistle to a Young Critic.* London, 1753 (4to. 1s. Griffin) BRITISH LIBRARY

Reviewed: *Monthly Review* 8 (1753): 472

D'ARNAUD
See: BACULARD D'ARNAUD, François Thomas Marie de

106 [ARNE, Thomas Augustine]. *The Guardian Out-witted. A Comic Opera. As it is Performed At the Theatre Royal in Covent-Garden. The Musick composed by Tho. Aug. Arne, Doctor in Music.* [Libretto also by Arne.] London, 1764 (8vo. 1s. Lownds) BRITISH LIBRARY

Reviewed: *Monthly Review* 31 (1764): 474–475
Critical Review 18 (1764): 476

107 ARNOLD, Cornelius. *Commerce. A Poem. By Mr. Corns. Arnold.* London, 1751 (4to. 1s. Dodsley and Swan) NEWBERRY

Reviewed: *Monthly Review* 4 (1750–51): 476

108 ARNOLD, Cornelius. *Distress. A Poetical Essay. Humbly Inscribed to the Right Honourable John Earl of Radnor. The second Edition corrected and enlarged.* 1st ed. reviewed; copy seen 2d ed.: London, n.d. [ESTC-1750] (4to. 1s. Swan) BRITISH LIBRARY

Reviewed: *Monthly Review* 6 (1752): 156

109 ARNOLD, Cornelius. *The Mirror. A poetical Essay. In the Manner of Spenser.* n.p., 1755 [ESTC-London] (4to. 1s. Swan) BRITISH LIBRARY

Reviewed: *Monthly Review* 13 (1755): 454–456

110 *Art in Woman superior to Reason in Man. A Poem. Humbly inscribed to the Batchelors. By W--- G-----.* London, 1751 (Fol. 8pp. Bizet) HARVARD (HOUGHTON)

Reviewed: *Monthly Review* 5 (1751): 76

The Art of dressing the Hair. A Poem
See: PRATT, Ellis

The Art of Joking; or, an Essay on Witticism
See: SMILEWELL, Samuel (pseud.)

The Art of Living in London
See: SMITH, James

111 *The Art of Preserving. A Poem. Humbly inscribed to the Confectioner in Chief of the B–t–sh C–v–l–y.* London, 1759 (Fol. 1s. Burd) BRITISH LIBRARY

Reviewed: *Monthly Review* 21 (1759): 181
Critical Review 8 (1759): 163
Gentleman's Magazine 29 (1759): 385

Artaxerxes. An English Opera
See: METASTASIO, Pietro Antonio Domenico Bonaventura

The artful Priest; or the Virgin Sacrifice
See: HEIDEGGER, John James

112 *The Artless Lovers. A Novel. In a Series of Letters from Miss Lucy Wheatly in Town, to Miss Annabell Grierson in the Country.* 2 vols. London, 1768 (12mo. 6s. Wilkie) BRITISH LIBRARY

Reviewed: *Monthly Review* 40 (1769): 258–259
Critical Review 28 (1769): 372–373
Critical Memoirs 1 (1769): 525

113 *The A******'s Letter to the L***d M****r, Relative to His Polite Treatment of Mr. Wilkes. Versified by another A******n.* London, 1768 (4to. 1s. Hooper) BRITISH LIBRARY

Reviewed: *Monthly Review* 38 (1768): 406
Critical Review 25 (1768): 391
Universal Museum 4 (1768): 317

114 [ASPINWALL, Stanhope]. *Rodogune: or The Rival Brothers. A Tragedy. Done from the French of Mons. Corneille.* London, 1765 (8vo. 1s.6d. Dodsley) BRITISH LIBRARY

Reviewed: *Monthly Review* 33 (1765): 85
Critical Review 19 (1765): 393
Candid Review 1 (1765): 368–375

115 *The Assignation. A Sentimental Novel. In a Series of Letters.* 2 vols. London, 1774 (12mo. 6s. Noble) BRITISH LIBRARY

Reviewed: *Monthly Review* 50 (1774): 234
Critical Review 36 (1773): 477

Town & Country Magazine 6 (1774): 45
Universal Catalogue [2] (1773) art. 1332

116 *The Asylum; a Poem. By a Gentleman.* London, 1773 (4to. 2s. Davies. 1773) BRITISH LIBRARY

Reviewed: *Monthly Review* 49 (1773): 413
Critical Review 36 (1773): 475
London Magazine 42 (1773): 559
Town & Country Magazine 6 (1774): 45
Universal Catalogue [2] (1773) art. 1191

Athelstan. A Tragedy
See: BROWN, John

117 ATKINSON, Christopher. *A Poetical Sermon on the Benefit of Affliction, and the Reasonableness of an Entire Resignation to the Will of the Supreme Being. In Two Parts.* London, n.d. [ESTC-1765?] (4to. 1s.6d. Payne) BRITISH LIBRARY

Reviewed: *Monthly Review* 34 (1766): 165
Critical Review 21 (1766): 234

118 [ATKYNS, Lady]. *The Hermit. A Novel. By A Lady.* 2 vols. London, 1769 (12mo. 6s. Gardner) UNIVERSITY OF PENNSYLVANIA

Reviewed: *Monthly Review* 40 (1769): 520
Critical Review 28 (1769): 217–225

The Auction: A Modern Novel
See: WOODFIN, Mrs. A.

The Auction; a Poem
See: CHATTERTON, Thomas

The Auction, as it has been acted
See: CIBBER, Theophilus

D'AULNOY, Countess
See: LA MOTHE, Marie Catherine, Comtesse d'Aulnoy

119 AUSTIN, Mrs. *The Noble Family. In a Series of Letters.* 3 vols.
NOT SEEN (12mo. 9s. Pearch. 1771)

Reviewed: *Monthly Review* 45 (1771): 74

120 *Authentic Memoirs of the Countess de Barre, the French King's Mistress. Carefully collated*

from a Manuscript in the Possession of the Duchess of Villeroy, By Sir Francis N——. 1st ed. reviewed; copy seen 2d ed.: London, 1771 (12mo. 3s.bound. Roson. 1771) BRITISH LIBRARY

Reviewed: *Monthly Review* 44 (1771): 92
Critical Review 30 (1770): 488
London Magazine 39 (1770): 677–678
Town & Country Magazine 3 (1771): 44

121 AUTHER, John. *Divine poems on various subjects. By John Auther. The second edition, with additions*
NOT SEEN (8vo. Ward)

Reviewed: *Monthly Review* 9 (1753): 236

122 AVERAY, Robert. *Britannia and the Gods in Council; A Dramatic Poem: Wherein Felicity is predicted to Britain, the Causes of the present Disputes in Europe and America are debated, and their Issue prophetically determined*. London, n.d. [ESTC-1756] (4to. 1s. Kinnersley) BRITISH LIBRARY

Reviewed: *Monthly Review* 15 (1756): 84–85
Gentleman's Magazine 26 (1756): 308

Avon a Poem in three parts
See: HUCKILL, John

123 AYRE, [William]. *Four Ethic Epistles Opposing Some of Mr. Pope's Opinions of Man, as set forth in his Essay. I. With respect to the Universe. II. As an Individual. III. With respect to Society. IV. With respect to Happiness*. London, 1753 (8vo. 6d. Paterson) BRITISH LIBRARY

Reviewed: *Monthly Review* 7 (1752): 399

124 [BACON, Phanuel]. *Humorous Ethics: Or, an Attempt to Cure the Vices and Follies of the Age By a Method entirely New. In Five Plays, As they are now acting to the Life at the Great Theatre by His Majesty's Company of Comedians*. [Contains five plays—the three listed below plus *The Moral Quack* and *The Insignificants*.] London, 1757 (8vo. 6s.bound. Owen) CAMBRIDGE

Reviewed: *Monthly Review* 19 (1758): 406–407

125 [BACON, Phanuel]. *The Oculist. A Dramatic Entertainment of Two Acts*. London, 1757 (8vo. 1s. Owen) BRITISH LIBRARY

Reviewed: *Monthly Review* 17 (1757): 88
Critical Review 3 (1757): 554

126 [BACON, Phanuel]. *The Taxes, a Dramatick Entertainment*. London, 1757 (8vo. 1s. Owen) BRITISH LIBRARY

Reviewed: *Monthly Review* 16 (1757): 84
Critical Review 3 (1757): 86–87

127 [BACON, Phanuel]. *The Tryal of the Time-Killers. A Comedy of Five Acts*. London, 1757 (8vo. 1s.6d. Owen) BRITISH LIBRARY

Reviewed: *Monthly Review* 17 (1757): 605
Critical Review 4 (1757): 549

128 BACULARD D'ARNAUD, [François Thomas Marie de]. *Fanny: or, the Happy Repentance. From the French of M. D'Arnaud*. London ed. reviewed; copy seen: Dublin, 1767 (8vo. 2s. Becket) BODLEIAN

Reviewed: *Monthly Review* 35 (1766): 97–100
Critical Review 22 (1766): 80

BACULARD D'ARNAUD, [François Thomas Marie de]. *The Tears of Sensibility*
See: MURDOCH, John (trans.)

Bagatelles
See: MILLS, Andrew Hervey

129 BAGNALL, Gibbons. *Education: An Essay*. London, 1765 (4to. 1s. Baldwin) BRITISH LIBRARY

Reviewed: *Monthly Review* 32 (1765): 234–235
Critical Review 19 (1765): 150–151
Candid Review 1 (1765): 190–191

130 BAGNALL, Gibbons. *A New Translation of Telemachus* [*Critical Review* title: *The first Book of Telemachus in English Verse*]
NOT SEEN (12mo. 6d. Owen)

Reviewed: *Monthly Review* 15 (1756): 82–84
Gentleman's Magazine 26 (1756): 197
Listed: *Critical Review* 1 (1756): 291

131 BAKER, David Erskine. *The Muse of Ossian: A Dramatic Poem, Of Three Acts. Selected from the several poems of Ossian the Son of Fingal. As it is performed at the Theatre in Edinburgh.* Edinburgh, 1763 (12mo. 6d. Edinburgh) BRITISH LIBRARY

Reviewed: *Monthly Review* 29 (1763): 226

132 [BAKER, Henry]. *Essays Pastoral and Elegiac; containing, Morning; or, The Complaint. Noon; or, The Contest. Evening; or, The Exclamation. Night; or, The Wanderer. Addressed to the Right Hon. the Earl of Chesterfield. By A Gentleman, late of the Inner Temple.* London, 1756 (1s. Cooper) UNIVERSITY OF ILLINOIS

Reviewed: *Monthly Review* 15 (1756): 202–203
Critical Review 1 (1756): 482–483

133 BAKER, Thomas. *A Poem on the Winter Season: or, Mr. Hervey's Winter-Piece paraphrased*
NOT SEEN (4to. 6d. Ipswich, printed by William Creighton)

Reviewed: *Monthly Review* 20 (1759): 476

134 BAKER, T[homas]. *A Poem on Winter being a Versification of Mr. Hervey's Winter-Piece: With Part of his Contemplations on the Night. To which is added, A Poem addressed to Mr. Sutton, on Inoculation. By T. Baker. The second Edition, with large Additions and Alterations.* Ipswich, n.d. [ESTC-1760?] (4to. 1s. Hawkes) BRITISH LIBRARY

Reviewed: *Critical Review* 23 (1767): 141–142

135 *Balaam: or, the Antiquity of Scandal.* London, 1757 (4to. 6d. Cooper) BRITISH LIBRARY

Reviewed: *Monthly Review* 17 (1757): 280–281
Critical Review 4 (1757): 280

136 *A Ballad. To the Tune of Chevy Chase.* London, 1749 (Fol. 6 pp. 6d. Carpenter in Fleet-Street) BRITISH LIBRARY

Reviewed: *Monthly Review* 2 (1749–50): 58–59

137 BALLY, [George]. *The Day of Judgment. A Poem. Written for Mr. Seaton's Prize, but Rejected.* London, 1757 (4to. 1s. M. Cooper) BRITISH LIBRARY

Reviewed: *Monthly Review* 17 (1757): 400–402
Critical Review 4 (1757): 546–549

138 BALLY, George. *The Justice of the Supreme Being, a Poem.* Cambridge, 1755 (4to. 1s. B. Dod, &c.) BRITISH LIBRARY

Reviewed: *Monthly Review* 12 (1755): 159
Gentleman's Magazine 25 (1755): 93

139 BALLY, George. *The Providence of the Supreme Being. A Poem.* Cambridge, 1758 (4to. 1s. Cambridge printed, and sold by Merril there, and by Whiston &c. London) BRITISH LIBRARY

Reviewed: *Monthly Review* 19 (1758): 588
Gentleman's Magazine 28 (1758): 598–599

140 BALLY, George. *The Wisdom of the Supreme Being. A Poem.* Cambridge, 1756 (4to. 1s. B. Dod, &c.) BRITISH LIBRARY

Reviewed: *Monthly Review* 15 (1756): 678–681

141 [BANCROFT, Edward]. *The History of Charles Wentworth, Esq; in a Series of Letters. Interspersed With a Variety of Important Reflections, Calculated To improve Morality, and promote the Oeconomy of Human Life.* 3 vols. London, 1770 (12mo. 7s.6d.bound. Becket) NEWBERRY

Reviewed: *Monthly Review* 43 (1770): 67
Critical Review 29 (1770): 358–364
London Magazine 39 (1770): 267

The Banished Patriot
See: DELAMAYNE, Thomas Hallie

142 *The Banishment of Cupid, with the Birth of Hymen, And a Demon unknown to Antiquity. An Allegorical Poem, in the ancient Taste.* London, 1756 (4to. 1s. Crowder and Woodgate) BODLEIAN

Reviewed: *Monthly Review* 15 (1756): 185–189
Critical Review 1 (1756): 345–347

143 BANNATYNE, George. *Ancient Scottish Poems. Published from the MS. of George Bannatyne, MDLXVIII.* [Ed. Sir David Dalrymple,

Lord Hailes.] Edinburgh, 1770 (12mo. 4s. Cadell) BRITISH LIBRARY

Reviewed: *Monthly Review* 44 (1771): 42–48
Critical Review 30 (1770): 481
London Magazine 39 (1770): 632
Town & Country Magazine 2 (1770): 662

144 [BANNOC, Adolphus]. *The Apparition; or, Female Cavalier. A Story founded on Facts.* 3 vols.
NOT SEEN (12mo. 9s.bound. Noble)

Reviewed: *Monthly Review* 15 (1756): 536
Critical Review 3 (1757): 31–34

145 [BANNOC, Adolphus]. *The History of My Own Life. Being an Account Of many of the Severest Trials Imposed by an Implacable Father, upon the most Affectionate Pair That ever entered the Marriage State.* 2 vols. London, 1756 (12mo. 6s. Noble) BRITISH LIBRARY

Reviewed: *Monthly Review* 13 (1755): 398–399

Barbarossa. A Tragedy
See: BROWN, John

BARCLAY, John. *The Phoenix*
See: REEVE, Clara (trans.)

BAREBONES, Caustic (pseud.)
See: BRIDGES, Thomas

Barford Abbey
See: MINIFIE, Susannah

146 [BARNARD, Edward]. *Virtue the source of Pleasure.* London, 1757 (8vo. 3s.6d. J. Buckland) BRITISH LIBRARY

Reviewed: *Monthly Review* 17 (1757): 603
Critical Review 4 (1757): 277–278

147 BARNETT, [Richard]. *Odes*
NOT SEEN (4to. 1s. Hooper)

Reviewed: *Monthly Review* 25 (1761): 499–500

148 BARRETT, St[ephen]. *Ovid's Epistles, Translated into English Verse; With Critical Essays and Notes. Being part of a Poetical and Oratorical Lecture, read in the Grammar-School of Ashford, in the County of Kent; and calculated to initiate Youth in the first Rudiments of Taste.* London, 1759 (8vo. 3s.6d. Richardson) BRITISH LIBRARY

Reviewed: *Monthly Review* 20 (1759): 278–279
Critical Review 7 (1759): 31–39

149 BARTHOLOMEW, Ch. *Mead. A Poem To the Memory of Richard Mead, Late Physician to His Majesty, and Fellow of the Royal Society, &c. Wrote Originally in Latin, And Translated by the Rev. Mr. Ch. Bartholomew, A.B. Rector of West-Clandon in Surry.* London, 1756 (4to. 1s. Cooper) BODLEIAN

Reviewed: *Monthly Review* 14 (1756): 576–577

150 *The Basiliade: Or the Book of Truth and Nature; An Epic Poem. In fourteen Cantos in Prose. Translated from an Original Manuscript, of the Celebrated Indian Bramin and Philosopher Pilpay. Found among the Treasures of Mohammed Shah, Emperor of the Mogul Tartars, At the plunder of the city of Delhi, the Capital of Hindostan, By Thomas Khuli Khan.* 2 vols. London, 1761 (12mo. 6s. Hooper) LIBRARY OF CONGRESS [Library of Congress copy has vol. 1 only.]

Reviewed: *Monthly Review* 24 (1761): 352
Critical Review 11 (1761): 294–297
British Magazine 2 (1761): 265

The Battiad
See: MENDEZ, Moses

151 *The Battle of Epsom. A new Ballad.* London, 1763 (Fol. 1s. Williams) BRITISH LIBRARY

Reviewed: *Monthly Review* 29 (1763): 154
Critical Review 16 (1763): 72–73

The Battle of the Bonnets
See: BRIDGES, Thomas

152 *The Battle of the Briefs.* London, 1752 (4to. 1s. Webb) BRITISH LIBRARY

Reviewed: *Monthly Review* 5 (1751): 523

The Battle of the Genii
See: BRIDGES, Thomas

A Bavin of Bays
See: PERFECT, W.

153 BEACH, William Wither. *Abradates and Panthea. A Tale, extracted from Xenophon*. Salisbury, 1765 (4to. 1s. Fletcher) BRITISH LIBRARY

Reviewed: *Monthly Review* 32 (1765): 393
Critical Review 19 (1765): 394
Candid Review 1 (1765): 279

154 BEATTIE, James. *The Judgment of Paris. A Poem*. London, 1765 (4to. 1s.6d. Becket) BRITISH LIBRARY

Reviewed: *Monthly Review* 33 (1765): 23–27
Critical Review 19 (1765): 378–379
Gentleman's Magazine 35 (1765): 234
Candid Review 1 (1765): 360–365

155 [BEATTIE, James]. *The Minstrel; or, The Progress Of Genius. A Poem*. London, 1771 (4to. 1s.6d. Dilly. 1771) BRITISH LIBRARY

Reviewed: *Monthly Review* 44 (1771): 265–271
Critical Review 31 (1771): 143–144
Gentleman's Magazine 41 (1771): 221–222
London Magazine 40 (1771): 101–102

156 BEATTIE, James. *The Minstrel; or, The Progress of Genius. A Poem. The Second Book*. London, 1774 (4to. 1s.6d. Dilly. 1774) BRITISH LIBRARY

Reviewed: *Monthly Review* 51 (1774): 189–193
Critical Review 38 (1774): 351–354
Gentleman's Magazine 44 (1774): 531–532
London Magazine 43 (1774): 243–244
Town & Country Magazine 6 (1774): 660
Universal Catalogue 3 (1774) art. 636

157 BEATTIE, James. *Original Poems and Translations*. London, 1760 (8vo. 3s. Millar) BRITISH LIBRARY

Reviewed: *Monthly Review* 24 (1761): 393–395
Critical Review 11 (1761): 301–304
British Magazine 2 (1761): 265

158 BEATTIE, James. *Poems on several Subjects. A New Edition, Corrected*. London, 1766 (2s.6d. Johnston) BRITISH LIBRARY

Reviewed: *Critical Review* 21 (1766): 473–474

The Beau-Philosopher
See: MAINVILLERS, Genu Soalhat de

BEAUMONT, Madame
See: ÉLIE DE BEAUMONT, Anne Louise, or LE PRINCE DE BEAUMONT, Jeanne Marie

BEAUMONT, Francis, and John FLETCHER (adaptations)
See: COLMAN, George (the elder). *Philaster*
GARRICK, David. *The Chances*
HULL, Thomas. *The Royal Merchant*

159 *The Beauties of Poetry Display'd. Containing Observations on the different Species of Poetry, and the Rules of English Versification. Exemplified by A large Collection of beautiful Passages, Similies, and Descriptions, From the Writings of Addison, Akinside, Blacklock, Dryden, Gay, Garth, Grey, Milton, Pope, Prior, Rowe, Shakespeare, Smart, Swift, Thomson, Waller, West, Young, And other celebrated Poets*. 2 vols. London, 1757 (12mo. 6s. Hinton) BRITISH LIBRARY

Reviewed: *Monthly Review* 16 (1757): 581

Beauty, A Poetical Essay
See: PYE, Henry James

160 *The Beavers: A Fable*. London, 1760 (4to. 1s. Hooper) BRITISH LIBRARY

Reviewed: *Monthly Review* 23 (1760): 168–169
Critical Review 9 (1760): 494

The Bee
See: GOLDSMITH, Oliver

161 *The Beldames. A Poem*. London, 1759 (4to. 1s. Dodsley) BRITISH LIBRARY

Reviewed: *Monthly Review* 20 (1759): 215–216
Critical Review 7 (1759): 173
Gentleman's Magazine 29 (1759): 86–87

162 *Belle Grove; or, The Fatal Seduction*. 2 vols. NOT SEEN (12mo. 5s.sewed. Noble)

Reviewed: *Monthly Review* 44 (1771): 262
Critical Review 31 (1771): 232–233
London Magazine 40 (1771): 164
Town & Country Magazine 3 (1771): 213

163 *La Belle Philosophe, or the Fair Philosopher.* 2 vols.
NOT SEEN (12mo. 6s. Lowndes. 1774)

Reviewed: *Monthly Review* 50 (1774): 234
Critical Review 37 (1774): 76
London Magazine 43 (1774): 39
Town & Country Magazine 6 (1774): 155

DE BELLOY. *The Siege of Calais*
See: DENIS, Charles (trans.)

Beneficence. A Poetical Essay
See: *On Beneficence. A Poetical Essay*

164 BENNET, John. *Poems on several Occasions. By John Bennet, a Journeyman Shoemaker.* London, 1774 (8vo. 2s.6d. Evans. 1774) BRITISH LIBRARY

Reviewed: *Monthly Review* 51 (1774): 483
Critical Review 37 (1744): 473

165 [BENTLEY, Richard (the younger)]. *Patriotism, a Mock-Heroic. In Five Cantos.* London, 1763 (2s.6d. Hinxman) BODLEIAN

Reviewed: *Monthly Review* 29 (1763): 409–411
Critical Review 16 (1763): 390
Candid Review 1 (1765): 269–270

166 [BENTLEY, Richard (the younger)]. *Philodamus. A Tragedy.* London, 1767 (4to. 2s.6d. Dodsley) BRITISH LIBRARY

Reviewed: *Monthly Review* 36 (1767): 410
Critical Review 23 (1767): 399

167 BENTLEY, Samuel. *The River Dove: a Lyric Pastoral.* London, 1768 (4to. 1s. Stevens) BRITISH LIBRARY

Reviewed: *Monthly Review* 39 (1768): 317
Critical Review 26 (1768): 393
Universal Museum 4 (1768): 316

168 [BERKENHOUT, John]. *Three Original Poems; being the Posthumous Works of Pendavid Bitterzwigg, Esq; To which is added, The very remarkable Last Will and Testament of that well-known Author.* Oxford, n.d. [ESTC-1750?] (8vo. 54pp. 1s. Printed for T. Carnan, and sold by the booksellers at York, Leeds and Wakefield) BRITISH LIBRARY

Reviewed: *Monthly Review* 4 (1750–51): 377

169 *The Bertoldi at the court of King Alboino. A new comic opera, as it is acted at the Theatre-royal, in Covent-Garden*
NOT SEEN (8vo. 1s. Woodfall)

Listed: *Monthly Review* 11 (1754): 467

170 *Betsy: or, the Caprices of Fortune.* 3 vols.
NOT SEEN (12mo. 7s.6d. Baldwin)

Reviewed: *Monthly Review* 44 (1771): 333
Critical Review 31 (1771): 484

171 [BICKERSTAFFE, Isaac]. *The Absent Man: a Farce. As it is acted by His Majesty's Servants, at the Theatre-Royal, in Drury-Lane.* London, 1768 (8vo. 1s. Griffin) BRITISH LIBRARY

Reviewed: *Monthly Review* 38 (1768): 335
Critical Review 25 (1768): 315

172 [BICKERSTAFFE, Isaac]. *The Captive, A Comic Opera; As it is Perform'd at the Theatre-Royal in the Hay-Market.* London, 1769 (8vo. 1s.6d. Griffin. 1769) BRITISH LIBRARY

Reviewed: *Monthly Review* 41 (1769): 80
Critical Review 28 (1769): 75

173 [BICKERSTAFFE, Isaac]. *Daphne and Amintor. A Comic Opera, in One Act, As it is Performed at the Theatre Royal in Drury-Lane.* [Adapted from *L'Oracle* by Germain François Poullain de Saint Foix.] London, 1765 (8vo. 1s. Newbery) BRITISH LIBRARY

Reviewed: *Monthly Review* 33 (1765): 326–327
Critical Review 20 (1765): 316
Gentleman's Magazine 35 (1765): 483–484

174 [BICKERSTAFFE, Isaac]. *Doctor Last in his Chariot: A Comedy: As it is performed at the Theatre-Royal in the Hay-Market.* [Adaptation of Molière's *Le malade imaginaire*.] London, 1769 (8vo. 1s.6d. Griffin. 1769) BRITISH LIBRARY

Reviewed: *Monthly Review* 41 (1769): 80
Critical Review 28 (1769): 74–75
London Magazine 38 (1769): 377–379

175 [BICKERSTAFFE, Isaac]. *The Ephesian Matron. A Comic Serenata, After the Manner of the Italian. As it is performed at Ranelagh House. The Music by Mr. Dibdin.* London, 1769 (8vo. 1s. Griffin) BRITISH LIBRARY

Reviewed: *Monthly Review* 40 (1769): 512
Critical Memoirs [2] (1769): 198–200

176 [BICKERSTAFFE, Isaac]. *He Wou'd if he Cou'd; or, An Old Fool worse than Any: a Burletta. As it is performed at the Theatre Royal in Drury-Lane. The Music by Mr. Dibdin.* London, 1771 (8vo. 1s. Griffin. 1771) BRITISH LIBRARY

Reviewed: *Monthly Review* 44 (1771): 416
Critical Review 31 (1771): 314
Town & Country Magazine 3 (1771): 213

177 [BICKERSTAFFE, Isaac]. *The Hypocrite: a Comedy. As it is performed at the Theatre Royal in Drury-Lane. Taken from Moliere and Cibber, By the Author of the Alterations of the Plain-Dealer.* London, 1769 (8vo. 1s.6d. Griffin) BRITISH LIBRARY

Reviewed: *Monthly Review* 39 (1768): 491–492
Critical Review 26 (1768): 480
Gentleman's Magazine 38 (1768): 619–620

178 [BICKERSTAFFE, Isaac]. *Leucothoe. A Dramatic Poem.* London, 1756 (8vo. 1s.6d. Cooper) BRITISH LIBRARY

Reviewed: *Monthly Review* 15 (1756): 153–162

179 [BICKERSTAFFE, Isaac]. *Lionel and Clarissa. A Comic Opera. As it is Performed at the Theatre-Royal in Covent-Garden.* London, 1748 [1768] (8vo. 1s.6d. Griffin) BRITISH LIBRARY

Reviewed: *Monthly Review* 38 (1768): 245
Critical Review 25 (1768): 314
Political Register 2 (1768): 318–319

180 [BICKERSTAFFE, Isaac]. *Lionel and Clarissa: or, a School for Fathers. A Comic Opera. As it is Performed at the Theatre-Royal in Drury-Lane.* London, 1770 (8vo. 1s.6d. Griffin. 1770) BRITISH LIBRARY

Reviewed: *Monthly Review* 42 (1770): 145
Critical Review 29 (1770): 236–237

181 [BICKERSTAFFE, Isaac]. *Love in a Village; a Comic Opera. As it is performed at the Theatre Royal in Covent-Garden.* London, 1763 (8vo. 1s.6d. Newbery) LIBRARY OF CONGRESS

Reviewed: *Monthly Review* 27 (1762): 458
Critical Review 15 (1763): 40–42
British Magazine 4 (1763): 98

182 [BICKERSTAFFE, Isaac]. *Love in the City; a Comic Opera. As it is performed at the Theatre Royal in Covent-Garden. The Words Written and the Music Compiled By The Author of Love in a Village.* London, 1767 (8vo. 1s.6d. Griffin) BRITISH LIBRARY

Reviewed: *Monthly Review* 36 (1767): 164
Critical Review 23 (1767): 139
Gentleman's Magazine 37 (1767): 135

183 [BICKERSTAFFE, Isaac]. *The Maid of the Mill. A Comic Opera. As it is Performed at the Theatre Royal in Covent Garden. The Music Compiled, and the Words written By the Author of Love in a Village.* London, 1765 (8vo. 1s.6d. Newbery) BRITISH LIBRARY

Reviewed: *Monthly Review* 32 (1765): 155–156
Critical Review 19 (1765): 153–154
Candid Review 1 (1765): 120–125

184 [BICKERSTAFFE, Isaac]. *The Padlock: a Comic Opera: As it is perform'd by His Majesty's Servants at the Theatre-Royal in Drury-Lane.* 1st ed. reviewed; copy seen 2d. ed.: London, 1768 (8vo. 1s. Griffin) BRITISH LIBRARY

Reviewed: *Monthly Review* 39 (1768): 327
Critical Review 26 (1768): 388
Universal Museum 4 (1768): 541
Political Register 3 (1768): 383

185 [BICKERSTAFFE, Isaac]. *The Plain Dealer: a Comedy. As it is Performed at the Theatre Royal in Drury-Lane. With Alterations from Wycherley.* London, 1766 (8vo. 1s.6d. Lowndes) BRITISH LIBRARY

Reviewed: *Monthly Review* 34 (1766): 77–78
Critical Review 21 (1766): 61–62

186 [BICKERSTAFFE, Isaac]. *The Recruiting Serjeant. A Musical Entertainment As it is Perform'd at the Theatre-Royal in Drury-Lane.* London, 1770 (8vo. 1s. Griffin) BRITISH LIBRARY

Reviewed: *Monthly Review* 43 (1770): 498–499
Critical Review 30 (1770): 467–468
London Magazine 39 (1770): 677

187 [BICKERSTAFFE, Isaac]. *The Royal Garland, a new Occasional Interlude, in Honour of His Danish Majesty. Set to Music by Mr. Arnold, and performed at the Theatre Royal, Covent-Garden.* London, 1768 (8vo. 6d. Becket) BRITISH LIBRARY

Reviewed: *Monthly Review* 39 (1768): 327
Critical Review 26 (1768): 388
London Magazine 37 (1768): 556
Universal Museum 4 (1768): 541
Political Register 3 (1768): 383

188 [BICKERSTAFFE, Isaac]. *Thomas and Sally: or, The Sailor's Return. A Musical Entertainment. As it is performed at the Theatre-Royal in Covent-Garden. The Music composed by Doctor Arne.* London, 1761 (8vo. 1s. Kearsley) BRITISH LIBRARY

Reviewed: *Monthly Review* 23 (1760): 527
Critical Review 10 (1760): 483
London Magazine 29 (1760): 672

189 [BICKERSTAFFE, Isaac]. *'Tis Well it's no Worse: a Comedy. As it is Performed at the Theatre Royal in Drury-Lane.* London, 1770 (8vo. 1s.6d. Griffin. 1770) BRITISH LIBRARY

Reviewed: *Monthly Review* 43 (1770): 497–498
Critical Review 30 (1770): 440–445
Gentleman's Magazine 40 (1770): 578–582

190 [BICKNELL, John]. *Musical Travels through England. By Joel Collier, Organist.* London, 1774 (8vo. 1s. Kearsley. 1774) BRITISH LIBRARY

Reviewed: *Monthly Review* 51 (1774): 242
London Magazine 43 (1774): 499–500
Universal Catalogue 3 (1774): art. 1069

191 [BILLARDON DE SAUVIGNY, Louis Edmé]. *Oriental Apologues; or Instructive Fables. Translated from the French.* London, 1765 (4to. 2s. Davies) BRITISH LIBRARY

Reviewed: *Monthly Review* 32 (1765): 95–97
Critical Review 19 (1765): 47–50
Candid Review 1 (1765): 93–94

BION (translation)
See: LANGHORNE, John. *The Death of Adonis*

192 *The Birmingham Counterfeit; or, Invisible Spectator. A Sentimental Romance.* 2 vols. London, 1772 (12mo. 6s. Bladon) BRITISH LIBRARY

Reviewed: *Monthly Review* 46 (1772): 540
Critical Review 33 (1772): 325–327
Town & Country Magazine 4 (1772): 266

The Birth-Day of Folly
See: STEVENS, George Alexander

A Birth Day Offering to a young Lady
See: CANNING, George

193 [BISHOP, Samuel]. *An Ode To the Right Honourable the Earl of Lincoln, on the Duke of Newcastle's Retirement.* London, 1762 (4to. 6d. Kent) UNIVERSITY OF CHICAGO

Reviewed: *Monthly Review* 27 (1762): 75
Critical Review 13 (1762): 521–522
British Magazine 3 (1762): 324

BITTERZWIGG, Pendavid. *Three Original Poems*
See: BERKENHOUT, John

194 BLACKLOCK, [Thomas,] and others. *A Collection of Original Poems. By the Rev. Mr Blacklock, and other Scotch Gentlemen.* [For 2-vol. issue, see under *A Collection of Original Poems*.] Edinburgh, 1760 (12mo. 2s.sewed. Edinburgh, Donaldson. Sold also by Richardson &c. in London) BRITISH LIBRARY

Reviewed: *Monthly Review* 25 (1761): 507–508

195 BLACKLOCK, Thomas. *The Graham; an Heroic Ballad: in Four Cantos.* London, 1774 (4to. 2s.6d. Davies) BRITISH LIBRARY

Reviewed: *Monthly Review* 51 (1774): 316
Critical Review 38 (1774): 74–75
Gentleman's Magazine 44 (1774): 324
London Magazine 43 (1774): 399
Town & Country Magazine 6 (1774): 437
Universal Catalogue 3 (1774) art. 934

196 BLAKE, Robert. *The Triumph of Scipio, an Historical Poem On the late Rebellion*. London, 1758 (4to. 1s. Cooper) BODLEIAN

Reviewed: *Monthly Review* 18 (1758): 491

197 BLAND, John. *Genuine Happiness: a Poetical Essay. Address'd to the Young Club at Arthur's*. London, 1759 (4to. 1s. Townshend) BODLEIAN

Reviewed: *Monthly Review* 20 (1759): 575
Critical Review 7 (1759): 460–462
Gentleman's Magazine 29 (1759): 338

198 *The Blessings of Liberty Displayed. To which is added, the Fall of Corsica; a Poem. Third Edition, with Alterations and Additions*
NOT SEEN (8vo. 1s. Bladon)

Reviewed: *Critical Review* 30 (1770): 72

199 *The Blessings of Liberty displayed; with the Fall of Corsica: a Poem*
NOT SEEN (4to. 1s.6d. Bladon)

Reviewed: *Monthly Review* 41 (1769): 394
Critical Review 28 (1769): 379

200 *The Blessings of P****, and a Scotch Excise: or the Humbug Resignation. A Farce, in Two Acts. As it was lately Performed at the New Theatre in S--- A---y Street, by his M-----'s Company of Comedians*. London, 1763 (8vo. 1s. Abrahams) BRITISH LIBRARY

Reviewed: *Monthly Review* 28 (1763): 397
Critical Review 15 (1763): 393

201 *The Blood-Hounds, a Political Tale. Inscribed to the Earl of Bute*. London, 1763 (4to. 1s.6d. Griffin) BRITISH LIBRARY

Reviewed: *Monthly Review* 29 (1763): 472
Critical Review 16 (1763): 478

BODMER, Johann Jakob. *Noah* (translation)
See: COLLYER, Joseph

202 BOISSY, [Louis de]. *The Frenchman in London. A Comedy. From the French of Monsieur de Boissy*. London, 1755 (8vo. 1s. Crowder) BRITISH LIBRARY

Reviewed: *Monthly Review* 12 (1755): 384
Gentleman's Magazine 25 (1755): 142–143

203 BOLUS, Whirligig (pseud.). *The Quackade. A Mock Heroic Poem, in Five Cantos*. London, 1752 (4to. 2s.6d. Cooper) BRITISH LIBRARY

Reviewed: *Monthly Review* 6 (1752): 157

204 BOND, R[ichard]. *Poems, Divine and Moral. By R. Bond, Bookseller in Glocester*. Glocester, n.d. [ESTC-1769?] (4to. 2s.6d. Gloucester, printed for the Author, and sold by Caston, &c. in London) BRITISH LIBRARY

Reviewed: *Monthly Review* 40 (1769): 337–339
Critical Review 27 (1769): 236
Town & Country Magazine 1 (1769): 213

A Bone for the Chroniclers to pick
See: SHIRLEY, William

205 [BONHOTE, Elizabeth]. *The Fashionable Friend. A Novel*. 2 vols. London ed. reviewed; copy seen: Dublin, 1774 (12mo. 5s.sewed. Becket) BRITISH LIBRARY

Reviewed: *Monthly Review* 49 (1773): 69
Critical Review 36 (1773): 235–236
London Magazine 42 (1773): 302
Universal Catalogue [2] (1773) art. 732

206 [BONHOTE, Elizabeth]. *The Rambles of Mr. Frankly. Published By His Sister*. 2 vols. London, 1772 (12mo. 5s.sewed. Becket. 1772) UNIVERSITY OF PENNSYLVANIA

Reviewed: *Monthly Review* 48 (1773): 71–72
Critical Review 34 (1772): 472
London Magazine 41 (1772): 598–599
Universal Catalogue [1] (1772) art. 1471

207 *The Book of Lamentations for the Loss of his Royal Highness the Duke of Cumberland*
NOT SEEN (Fol. 6d. Cooke)

Reviewed: *Critical Review* 20 (1765): 394

208 *The Book of Nature. A Poem*. London, 1771 (4to. 1s. Carnan) BRITISH LIBRARY

Reviewed: *Monthly Review* 44 (1771): 343
Critical Review 31 (1771): 157
Gentleman's Magazine 41 (1771): 132
London Magazine 40 (1771): 104

209 *A book to help the young and gay / To pass the tedious hours away, &c.*
NOT SEEN (1s. 6d. Stamper)

Reviewed: *Monthly Review* 4 (1750–51): 479

The Booksellers. A Poem
See: DELL, Henry

210 [BOSWELL, James]. *The Cub; at New-Market: A Tale.* London, 1762 (4to. 1s. Dodsley) BRITISH LIBRARY

Reviewed: *Monthly Review* 26 (1762): 233
Critical Review 13 (1762): 273

211 BOURNE, Vincent. *Miscellaneous Poems: Consisting of Originals and Translations.* London, 1772 (4to. 11s.boards. Dodsley) BRITISH LIBRARY [ESTC: "This edition contains many poems which are falsely attributed to Bourne."]

Reviewed: *Monthly Review* 47 (1772): 150
Critical Review 33 (1772): 318–322

212 *The Bow-Street Opera, in Three Acts. Written on the Plan of the Beggar's Opera; all the most celebrated Songs of which are parodied, and the whole Piece adapted to modern Times, Manners, and Characters.* London, n.d. [ESTC-1773] (8vo. 1s.6d. Mariner, &c.) BRITISH LIBRARY

Reviewed: *Monthly Review* 49 (1773): 396
Critical Review 36 (1773): 476
London Magazine 42 (1773): 599
Universal Catalogue [2] (1773) art. 1189

213 [BOWDEN, John]. *The Explosion: or, an Alarming Providential Check to Immorality. A Poem. Occasioned by the late dreadful Explosion of Gunpowder, on the Fifth Day of November, 1772, in the City of Chester; whereby a Company assembled at a Puppet-Show, performed by George Williams, were blown up, and many killed and wounded. Wherein is given a lively, striking and particular Description of that most deplorably dreadful and alarming Catastrophe. Interspersed with serious and moral Reflections, Expostulations and Exhortations, to Readers in General; but particularly Magistrates and Clergy. To which is added, Notes; Theatrical Entertainments; and likewise other Notes, pertinent to the Subject of this Poem. The whole designed as a Terror to evil-doers, and an Alarm to those that are asleep. By a Citizen of Chester.* n.p., 1773 [ESTC-London] (8vo. 4to. 9d. Longman) BRITISH LIBRARY

Reviewed: *Critical Review* 35 (1773): 317

214 *The Box Return'd; or the City Satisfied. A Familiar Epistle from a Certain Great Man.* London, 1761 (4to. 1s. Moran) UNIVERSITY OF PENNSYLVANIA

Reviewed: *Monthly Review* 25 (1761): 398–399
Critical Review 12 (1761): 397–398
British Magazine 2 (1761): 622

215 BOYCE, Samuel. *An Ode, to the Right Honourable The Marquis of Hartington, Lord-Lieutenant of the Kingdom of Ireland.* London, 1755 (4to. 1s. Reeve) BRITISH LIBRARY

Reviewed: *Monthly Review* 13 (1755): 457–458

216 BOYCE, Samuel. *Paris; or, The Force of Beauty: a Poem. In Two Cantos.* London, 1755 (4to. 1s. Reeve) BRITISH LIBRARY

Reviewed: *Monthly Review* 12 (1755): 351–352

217 BOYCE, Samuel. *Poems on Several Occasions.* London, 1757 (8vo. 5s. Dodsley) BRITISH LIBRARY

Reviewed: *Monthly Review* 17 (1757): 185
Critical Review 4 (1757): 193–195

218 [BOYCE, Samuel]. *The Rover; or, Happiness at Last: A Pastoral Drama, As it was intended for the Theatre.* London, 1752 (4to. 1s. Cooper) BRITISH LIBRARY

Reviewed: *Monthly Review* 6 (1752): 316

219 BOYCE, Samuel. *The Thanksgiving Hymn of Adam, on his Recovery from Sickness. A Version from Gessner. By Samuel Boyce. To which is annexed, An Ode in Honour of His Majesty's Birth-Day, As it was performed at the Turk's-Head, in Gerrard-Street, Soho, Before the Soci-*

ety of Artists. London, 1762 (4to. 1s. Williams) LIBRARY OF CONGRESS

Reviewed: *Critical Review* 13 (1762): 524
British Magazine 3 (1762): 382

220 BOYCE, Tho. *A Specimen of Elegiac Poetry*. London, 1773 (4to. 1s. Becket. 1773) BRITISH LIBRARY

Reviewed: *Monthly Review* 48 (1773): 318–319
Critical Review 35 (1773): 315
London Magazine 42 (1773): 196
Universal Catalogue [2] (1773) art. 465

221 [BOYER, Jean Baptiste de, Marquis d'Argens]. *The Life and Amours of Count de Turenne, Originally wrote in French. By the Author of the Jews Letters*. 1st ed. reviewed; copy seen 2d ed.: London, 1762 (12mo. 2s. Williams) BRITISH LIBRARY

Reviewed: *Critical Review* 13 (1762): 270
British Magazine 3 (1762): 213

The Bracelet: or, the Fortunate Discovery
See: GUICHARD, Éléonore

222 BRAND, [Fitz]J[ohn]. *Conscience: an Ethical Essay*. London, 1773 (4to. 2s. Becket, &c. 1772) BRITISH LIBRARY

Reviewed: *Monthly Review* 48 (1773): 67–68
Critical Review 34 (1772): 470
London Magazine 42 (1773): 41
Universal Catalogue [1] (1772) art. 1506

223 BRECKNOCK, Timoleon. *An Epithalamion on the Nuptials of Lord Warkworth and Lady Anne [Susan?] Stuart. Inscribed to the Right Honourable the Countess of Northumberland* [*Monthly Review* gives name as Susan; *Critical Review* and *British Magazine* give it as Anne.] NOT SEEN (Fol. 6d. Marsh)

Reviewed: *Monthly Review* 31 (1764): 151–153
Critical Review 18 (1764): 79
British Magazine 5 (1764): 377

224 BRECKNOCK, Timoleon. *An Ode on His Majesty's Return*. London, 1755 (Fol. 6d. Swan) BRITISH LIBRARY

Reviewed: *Monthly Review* 13 (1755): 297
Gentleman's Magazine 25 (1755): 431

225 BRECKNOCK, T[imoleon]. *An Ode on His Most Sacred Majesty's Return*. London, 1752 (Fol. 6d. Purser) BRITISH LIBRARY

Reviewed: *Monthly Review* 7 (1752): 398–399

226 BRECKNOCK, [Timoleon]. *An ode to the right hon. sir Crisp Gascoigne, protector of the innocent, and late lord mayor of the city of London*
NOT SEEN (Fol. 6d. Corbett)

Reviewed: *Monthly Review* 10 (1754): 388
Gentleman's Magazine 24 (1754): 245

227 BRECKNOCK, T[imoleon]. *Prejudice Detected: an Ethic Epistle*. London, 1752 (4to. 1s. Owen) BRITISH LIBRARY

Reviewed: *Monthly Review* 6 (1752): 238–239

228 BREREWOOD, Thomas. *Galfred and Juetta; or, the Road of Nature. A Tale, In Three Cantos*. London, 1772 (4to. 2s.6d. Bladon. 1771) BRITISH LIBRARY

Reviewed: *Monthly Review* 45 (1771): 510
London Magazine 41 (1772): 31
Town & Country Magazine 4 (1772): 99

229 [BRET, Antoine]. *Lycoris: or, the Grecian Courtesan. Translated from the French, by a Gentleman*
NOT SEEN (12mo. 2s. Brotherton)

Reviewed: *Monthly Review* 24 (1761): 351
Critical Review 11 (1761): 338
British Magazine 2 (1761): 326

230 *Bribery and Corruption: or, the Journey to London: alias, the O****** in Town, at Windmill-College assembled*. London, n.d. [BLC-1765] (4to. 1s. Williams) BRITISH LIBRARY

Reviewed: *Monthly Review* 38 (1768): 149
Critical Review 25 (1768): 154

231 BRICE, Andrew. *The Mobiad: or, Battle of the Voice. An Heroi-Comic Poem, sportively satirical: Being a briefly historical, natural and lively, free and humorous, Description of an Exeter Election. In Six Canto's. Illustrated with such Notes as for some Readers may be supposed useful. By Democritus Juvenal, Moral Professor of Ridicule, and plaguy-pleasant Fel-*

low of Stingtickle College; Vulgarly Andrew Brice, Exon*. London, 1770 (8vo. 3s. Davies) BRITISH LIBRARY

Reviewed: *Critical Review* 30 (1770): 312–314

232 [BRIDGES, Thomas]. *The Adventures of a Bank Note*. 2 vols. London, 1770 (12mo. 5s.sewed. Davies) BRITISH LIBRARY [4 vols.]

Reviewed: *Monthly Review* 43 (1770): 152
Critical Review 30 (1770): 395
London Magazine 39 (1770): 482
Town & Country Magazine 2 (1770): 435

233 [BRIDGES, Thomas]. *The Adventures of a Bank Note. In Four Volumes. Vols. III and IV*. London, 1771 (12mo. 5s.sewed. Davies) BRITISH LIBRARY

Reviewed: *Monthly Review* 45 (1771): 333
Critical Review 31 (1771): 475

234 [BRIDGES, Thomas]. *The Battle of the Bonnets, a Political Poem. From the Erse*. London, n.d. [ESTC-1766?] (4to. 2s.6d. Bingley) BRITISH LIBRARY

Reviewed: *Monthly Review* 39 (1768): 80
London Magazine 37 (1768): 334
Political Register 3 (1768): 125

235 [BRIDGES, Thomas]. *The Battle of the Genii. A Fragment. In three Canto's. Taken from an ancient Erse Manuscript, supposed to be written by Caithsat, the Grandfather of Cuchullin. From the Plan of this Poem it is highly probable our great Milton took the Hint of his Battle of the Fallen Angels. Done into English by the Author of Homer Travestie*. London, 1765 (4to. 2s.6d. Hooper) BRITISH LIBRARY

Reviewed: *Monthly Review* 32 (1765): 276–279
Critical Review 19 (1765): 151
Candid Review 1 (1765): 222–223

236 [BRIDGES, Thomas]. *A Burlesque Translation of Homer. In Two Volumes. The Third Edition, Greatly Enlarged and Improved*. 2 vols. London, 1770 (12mo. 6s. Hooper) HARVARD (WIDENER)

Reviewed: *Critical Review* 30 (1770): 484

237 [BRIDGES, Thomas]. *Dido; a Comic Opera. As it is performed at the Theatre-Royal in the Hay-Market*. London, 1771 (8vo. 1s. Davies) BRITISH LIBRARY

Reviewed: *Monthly Review* 45 (1771): 152
Critical Review 32 (1771): 153
Gentleman's Magazine 41 (1771): 417
London Magazine 40 (1771): 370

238 [BRIDGES, Thomas]. *The first Volume of a new Translation of Homer's Iliad, adapted to the Capacity of honest English Roast Beef and Pudding Eaters. By Caustic Barebones, a broken Apothecary. To which is prefixed, some small Account of the abovesaid Mr. Barebones himself*
NOT SEEN (12mo. 2s.6d. Marriner)

Reviewed: *Monthly Review* 26 (1762): 454–458

239 [BRIDGES, Thomas]. *Homer Travestie: being a new Burlesque Translation of the Ten First Books of the Iliad. By the Translator. The Second Volume*. London, 1764 (Small 8vo. 2s.6d. Hooper) NEWBERRY

Reviewed: *Monthly Review* 30 (1764): 489
Critical Review 18 (1764): 239

240 [BRIDGES, Thomas]. *Homer Travestie: Being a new Translation of the Four First Books of the Iliad. By Cotton, Junior. To which is prefix'd, Some small Account of the Author*. London, 1762 (8vo. 2s.6d. Marriner) BRITISH LIBRARY

Reviewed: *Critical Review* 13 (1762): 519
British Magazine 3 (1762): 382

241 BRIMBLE, William. *Poems, attempted On various Occasions, by William Brimble, Of Twerton, near Bath, Carpenter. Written occasionally for Amusement, And now Publish'd At the Request of several of his Acquaintance*. Bath, 1765 (8vo. 2s.6d. Wilkie) BRITISH LIBRARY

Reviewed: *Monthly Review* 36 (1767): 241
Critical Review 24 (1767): 317

242 [BRISCOE, Sophia]. *The Fine Lady a Novel. By the Author of Miss Melmoth*. 2 vols. London, 1772 (12mo. 5s.sewed. Lowndes. 1772) BRITISH LIBRARY

Reviewed: *Monthly Review* 46 (1772): 457
Critical Review 33 (1772): 181–182
Universal Catalogue [1] (1772) art. 262

243 [BRISCOE, Sophia]. *Miss Melmoth: or, the New Clarissa. In Three Volumes.* London, 1771 (12mo. 9s. Lowndes. 1771) UNIVERSITY OF ILLINOIS

Reviewed: *Monthly Review* 45 (1771): 74
Critical Review 31 (1771): 479

244 *Britain, a Poem; in Three Books.* Edinburgh, 1757 (12mo. 1s.6d. Edinburgh. Sold by Millar &c. in London) BRITISH LIBRARY

Reviewed: *Monthly Review* 16 (1757): 462
Critical Review 4 (1757): 279–280

245 *Britain, Strike Home. A Poem. Humbly Inscribed to every Briton. By a true Antigallican.* London, 1756 (Fol. 6d. Legg) BRITISH LIBRARY

Reviewed: *Monthly Review* 14 (1756): 63

Britannia: A Masque
See: MALLET, David

246 *Britannia, a Poem. By a young Gentleman*
NOT SEEN (Fol. 1s. Gretton)

Reviewed: *Monthly Review* 26 (1762): 151
Critical Review 13 (1762): 166

247 *Britannia. A Poem. In Two Parts. By An Eton Scholar.* London, 1774 (4to. 1s. Harris) BODLEIAN

Reviewed: *Critical Review* 38 (1774): 392

Britannia: A Poem: With Historical Notes
See: GOUGH, James

248 *Britannia in Tears: an Elegy occasioned By the Dismission of the Right Honble. W. P---t, and H. L--ge, Esqrs; from the Service of their King and Country. Humbly Dedicated to the Right Honble. the Lord-Mayor, and the whole Court of Aldermen, except One; and to the Worthy Common-Council Men of this City.* London, 1767 (4to. 6d. Scott) UNIVERSITY OF PENNSYLVANIA

Reviewed: *Monthly Review* 16 (1757): 462–463

249 *Britannia's Precaution To Her Sons The Gentlemen, Clergy, and Freeholders of England, Against the approaching General Election. Most humbly inscribed to the Honourable Edward Vernon, Esq; late Vice-Admiral of the Blue. By the Author of Seventeen Hundred and Thirty nine: And the Hibernian Politicians.* London, n.d. [BLC-1754? / ESTC-1741] (Fol. 1s. Owen) BRITISH LIBRARY

Reviewed: *Monthly Review* 9 (1753): 155

250 *The British Coffee-house. A Poem.* London, 1764 (4to. 1s.6d. Nicoll) BRITISH LIBRARY

Reviewed: *Monthly Review* 30 (1764): 157
Critical Review 16 (1763): 479

251 *The British Hero, and ignoble Poltroon contrasted: or, the Principal Actors in the Siege and Defence of Fort St. Philip, and the Mediterranean Expedition, characterised. With some strictures on the French proceedings in America. An Ode*
NOT SEEN (4to. 1s. Robinson)

Reviewed: *Monthly Review* 15 (1756): 319

252 *The British Moralist; or, Young Gentleman and Lady's Polite Preceptor: Being a new Collection of Novels, Tales, Fables, Visions, Dreams, Allegories; Selected from those Writings of Brooke, Goldsmith, Johnson, Hume, Hawkesworth, Langhorne, Smollet, Sterne, Mulso, Murphy, Shenstone, Miss Carter, And other Celebrated Moderns, That have been published during the Last Ten Years. To which are added, I. An Introduction, containing rules for Acquiring True Politeness. II. Parallels between Ancient and Modern Characters. III. A Concise View of the Beauties of the British Constitution. In Two Volumes.* London, 1771 (12mo. 6s. Robinson and Roberts. 1771) UNIVERSITY OF ILLINOIS

Reviewed: *Monthly Review* 44 (1771): 499
Critical Review 32 (1771): 78
London Magazine 40 (1771): 226
Town & Country Magazine 3 (1771): 379

A British Philippic
See: REED, Joseph

253 *The British Spouter; or, Stage Assistant: Containing the most celebrated Prologues and Epilogues, That have been lately spoken, In the different Theatres, At the acting of the most eminent Plays.* London, 1773 (12mo. 1s.6d. Roson, &c. 1773) BRITISH LIBRARY

Reviewed: *Monthly Review* 49 (1773): 413
Critical Review 36 (1773): 476
Universal Catalogue [2] (1773) art. 1125

254 [BROMEHEAD, Joseph]. *The Melancholy Student. An Elegiac Poem. Written at Q-----'s College, Oxford, in the Year 1765.* Oxford, 1769 (4to. 6d. Rivington) BRITISH LIBRARY

Reviewed: *Monthly Review* 41 (1769): 477–478
Gentleman's Magazine 39 (1769): 357
London Magazine 38 (1769): 379

255 [BROOKE, Frances]. *All's Right at Last: or, the History of Miss West.* 2 vols. London, 1773 (12mo. 6s. Noble) BRITISH LIBRARY

Reviewed: *Monthly Review* 49 (1773): 409
Critical Review 36 (1773): 397
Town & Country Magazine 5 (1773): 669

256 [BROOKE, Frances]. *The History of Emily Montague. By the Author of Lady Julia Mandeville.* 4 vols. London, 1769 (12mo. 10s.sewed. Dodsley. 1769) BRITISH LIBRARY

Reviewed: *Monthly Review* 41 (1769): 231–232
Critical Review 27 (1769): 300–302
Gentleman's Magazine 39 (1769): 206
London Magazine 38 (1769): 213

257 [BROOKE, Frances]. *The History of Lady Julia Mandeville. In Two Volumes. By the Translator of Lady Catesby's Letters.* 2 vols. London, 1763 (12mo. 6s. Dodsley) BRITISH LIBRARY

Reviewed: *Monthly Review* 29 (1763): 159–160
Critical Review 16 (1763): 41–45

258 BROOKE, Frances (trans.). *Letters from Juliet Lady Catesby, To Her Friend Lady Henrietta Campley. Translated from the French.* [From the French of Marie Jeanne Riccoboni.] 1st ed. reviewed; copy seen 2d ed.: London, 1760 (12mo. 3s. Dodsley) BRITISH LIBRARY

Reviewed: *Monthly Review* 22 (1760): 521
Critical Review 9 (1760): 420
London Magazine 29 (1760): 224

259 BROOKE, [Frances]. *Memoirs of the Marquis de St. Forlaix. Translated from the French of Mons. Framery. By Mrs. Brooke.* 2 vols. London, 1770 (12mo. 5s. Dodsley. 1770) BRITISH LIBRARY

Reviewed: *Monthly Review* 43 (1770): 362–365
Critical Review 30 (1770): 417–420 [4 vols.]
Gentleman's Magazine 40 (1770): 621
London Magazine 39 (1770): 530
Town & Country Magazine 2 (1770): 547

260 BROOKE, [Frances]. *Memoirs of the Marquis de St. Forlaix. Translated from the French of Mons. Framery. By Mrs. Brooke. Vols. III and IV.* London, 1770 (12mo. 5s. sewed. Dodsley. 1770) BRITISH LIBRARY

Reviewed: *Monthly Review* 44 (1771): 48–51
Critical Review 30 (1770): 417–420 [4 vols.]

261 BROOKE, [Frances]. *Virginia a Tragedy, with Odes, Pastorals, and Translations.* London, 1756 (8vo. 2s.6d. Millar) BRITISH LIBRARY

Reviewed: *Monthly Review* 14 (1756): 560
Critical Review 1 (1756): 276–279

262 BROOKE, Henry. *The Earl of Essex. A Tragedy. As it is now Acting at the Theatre-Royal in Drury-Lane.* London, 1761 (8vo. 1s.6d. Davies) BRITISH LIBRARY

Reviewed: *Monthly Review* 24 (1761): 73–75
Critical Review 11 (1761): 29–36
Gentleman's Magazine 31 (1761): 45–46
London Magazine 30 (1761): 56
British Magazine 2 (1761): 46

263 BROOKE, [Henry]. *The Fool of Quality, or, the History of Henry Earl of Moreland. In Four Volumes. By Mr. Brooke. Vols. I and II.* London, 1765 (12mo. 3s.each. Johnston) UNIVERSITY OF PENNSYLVANIA [Vol. 1 of University of Pennsylvania copy is of 2d edition, 1767.]

Reviewed: *Monthly Review* 35 (1766): 145–146, 286–297 and 346–356
Critical Review 22 (1766): 197–204

264 BROOKE, [Henry]. *The Fool of Quality, or, the History of Henry Earl of Moreland. In Four Volumes. Vol. III. By Mr. Brooke.* London, 1768 (12mo. 3s. Johnston. 1768) UNIVERSITY OF PENNSYLVANIA

Reviewed: *Monthly Review* 39 (1768): 410–411
Critical Review 30 (1770): 459–460 [vols. 3, 4, & 5]
London Magazine 37 (1768): 275–276
Town & Country Magazine 3 (1771): 155 [vols. 3, 4, & 5]

265 BROOKE, [Henry]. *The Fool of Quality, or, the History of Henry Earl of Moreland. Vol. IV. By Mr. Brooke.* London, 1769 (12mo. 3s. Johnston. 1769) UNIVERSITY OF PENNSYLVANIA

Reviewed: *Monthly Review* 41 (1769): 318
Critical Review 30 (1770): 459–460 [vols. 3, 4, & 5]
London Magazine 38 (1769): 438–439
Town & Country Magazine 3 (1771): 155 [vols. 3, 4, & 5]

266 BROOKE, [Henry]. *The Fool of Quality, or, the History of Henry Earl of Moreland. Vol. V. By Mr. Brooke.* London, 1770 (12mo. 3s. Johnston) UNIVERSITY OF PENNSYLVANIA

Reviewed: *Monthly Review* 42 (1770): 330
Critical Review 30 (1770): 459–460 [vols. 3, 4, & 5]
London Magazine 39 (1770): 211
Town & Country Magazine 3 (1771): 155 [vols. 3, 4, & 5]

267 BROOKE, [Henry]. *Juliet Grenville: or, the History of the Human Heart. In Three Volumes. By Mr. Brooke.* 3 vols. London, 1774 (12mo. 7s.6d.sewed. Robinson. 1774) NEWBERRY

Reviewed: *Monthly Review* 50 (1774): 15–20
Critical Review 36 (1773): 443–453
Gentleman's Magazine 43 (1773): 607–610
London Magazine 42 (1773): 612
Town & Country Magazine 6 (1774): 45
Universal Catalogue 3 (1774) art. 53

268 [BROOKE, Henry]. *A New Collection of Fairy Tales. None of which were ever before printed. Containing Many Useful Lessons, Moral Sentiments, Surprising Incidents, and Amusing Adventures. In Two Volumes.* London, 1750 (12mo. 5s.bound. Davis, Hitch, Dodsley and Woodfall) HARVARD (HOUGHTON)

Reviewed: *Monthly Review* 3 (1750): 111

269 BROOKE, Henry. *Redemption: A Poem.* London, 1772 (4to. 1s.6d. White. 1772) BRITISH LIBRARY

Reviewed: *Monthly Review* 48 (1773): 68
Critical Review 35 (1773): 69–70
London Magazine 42 (1773): 91–92
Universal Catalogue [1] (1772) art. 1497

270 *The Brother. A Novel. By a Lady.* 2 vols. London, 1771 (12mo. 5s.sewed. Lowndes) BRITISH LIBRARY

Reviewed: *Monthly Review* 44 (1771): 262
Critical Review 31 (1771): 315
Gentleman's Magazine 41 (1771): 229

The Brothers, a Comedy
See: CUMBERLAND, Richard

The Brothers. A Tragedy
See: YOUNG, Edward

The Brothers. In Two Volumes
See: SMYTHIES, Miss

271 [BROWN, John]. *Athelstan. A Tragedy. As it is Acted at the Theatre Royal in Drury-Lane.* London, 1756 (8vo. 1s.6d. Davis) BRITISH LIBRARY

Reviewed: *Monthly Review* 14 (1756): 366
Critical Review 1 (1756): 148–162

272 [BROWN, John]. *Barbarossa. A Tragedy. As it is Perform'd at the Theatre-Royal in Drury-Lane.* London, 1755 (8vo. 1s.6d. Tonson) BRITISH LIBRARY

Reviewed: *Monthly Review* 12 (1755): 42–54

273 BROWN, [John]. *The Cure of Saul, A Sacred Ode.* London, 1763 (4to. 1s. Davis and Reymers) BRITISH LIBRARY

Reviewed: *Monthly Review* 28 (1763): 200–203

274 BROWN, Joseph. *A Poem on Joseph and his Brethren, from Joseph's Birth to the Reconciliation between them after the Funeral of Jacob their Father*
NOT SEEN (8vo. 1s.6d. Williams)

Reviewed: *Monthly Review* 37 (1767): 153
Critical Review 24 (1767): 74–75
Universal Museum 3 (1767): 372

BROWNE, Isaac Hawkins. *De Animi Immortalitate* (translations)
See: CRANWELL, John
GREY, Richard
HAY, William

275 [BROWNE, Isaac Hawkins]. *The Immortality of the Soul. A Poem. Book the First. Translated from the Latin.* London, 1754 (4to. 1s. Owen) BRITISH LIBRARY

Reviewed: *Monthly Review* 11 (1754): 77–78

276 BROWNE, Isaac Hawkins. *Poems upon Various Subjects, Latin and English. By the late Isaac Hawkins Browne, Esq; Published by his Son.* London, 1768 (8vo. 4s. Marsh) BRITISH LIBRARY

Reviewed: *Monthly Review* 38 (1768): 358–363
Critical Review 25 (1768): 126–131

277 BROWNE, Moses. *Percy-Lodge, A Seat of the Duke and Duchess of Somerset, a Poem; Written by Command of their late Graces, (In the Year 1749.) And Inscribed to the Right Honourable The (present) Countess of Northumberland.* London, 1755 (4to. 1s. Owen) BRITISH LIBRARY

Reviewed: *Monthly Review* 14 (1756): 60–61
Critical Review 1 (1756): 167–168

278 BROWNE, William. *The Works of William Browne. Containing Britannia's Pastorals: With Notes and Observations By The Rev. W. Thompson, late of Queen's-College, Oxford. The Shepherd's Pipe: consisting of Pastorals. The Inner-Temple Masque, never published before; and other Poems. With the Life of the Author.* 3 vols. London, 1772 (12mo. 7s.6d. sewed. Davies. 1772) BRITISH LIBRARY

Reviewed: *Monthly Review* 46 (1772): 526–530
Critical Review 33 (1772): 111–118
London Magazine 40 (1771): 570
Town & Country Magazine 3 (1771): 656–657

279 BROWNE, Sir William. *Appendix ad Opuscula, Odes, in imitation of Horace*
NOT SEEN (4to. 1s. Owen)

Reviewed: *Monthly Review* 38 (1768): 246
Critical Review 25 (1768): 151–152
Universal Museum 4 (1768): 93

280 BROWNE, Sir William. *Appendix II. to Opuscula. A Farewell-Oration, to the Chair of the College of Physicians, London. Spoken in the Comitia the Day after Saint Michael, MDDCCLXVII, appointed for renewing the college-administration; and fortified by a fire-engine, against the incendiary licentiates. Translated from the Latin.* London, 1768 (4to. 1s. Owen) BODLEIAN

Reviewed: *Monthly Review* 42 (1770): 143–144
Critical Review 29 (1770): 394–396
London Magazine 39 (1770): 318

281 BROWNE, Sir William. *Corrections In Verse, From The Father Of The College, On Son Cadogan's Gout-Dissertation: containing False Physic, False Logic, False Philosophy.* London, 1772 (4to. 6d. Dodsley) BRITISH LIBRARY

Reviewed: *Monthly Review* 47 (1772): 146
Critical Review 34 (1772): 239
Town & Country Magazine 4 (1772): 602
Universal Catalogue [1] (1772): art. 564

282 BROWNE, Sir William. *Ode, in Imitation of Horace, ode I. ad Maecenatem. Addressed to his Grace, John Duke of Montagu: The Most Beneficent of Mankind. Jan. XXX. MDCCXLVIII. To which Is Subjoined The Original Ode of Horace, Illustrated By a New Interpretation.* London, 1763 (4to. 1s.6d. Owen) BRITISH LIBRARY

Reviewed: *Monthly Review* 28 (1763): 400–401
Critical Review 15 (1763): 228–229

283 BROWNE, Sir William. *Ode. In Imitation of Horace, Ode III. L.III. Ivstvm Ac Tenacem Propositi Virum. Addressed To The Right Honourable Sir Robert Walpole: On Ceasing to Be Minister. February VI. MDCCXLI. Designed A Just Panegyric, On a Great Minister, The Glorious Revolution, Protestant Succession, And Principles of Liberty. To Which Is Added The Original Ode, Defended, In Commentariolo.* London, 1765 (4to. 1s. Owen) BRITISH LIBRARY

Reviewed: *Monthly Review* 32 (1765): 154–155
Critical Review 19 (1765): 152

284 BROWNSMITH, John. *The Rescue: or, Thespian Scourge. Being a Critical Enquiry Into the Merit of a Poem, Intituled, Thespis. With some Candid Remarks on the Modesty, Good-Nature, and Impartiality of that Piece. Written in Hudibrastic Verse. By John Brownsmith.* London, 1767 (4to. 1s.6d. Williams) FOLGER

Reviewed: *Monthly Review* 36 (1767): 162
Critical Review 23 (1767): 145

The Bruciad, an Epic Poem
See: HARVEY, John

285 *Brutus. A Monody to the Memory of Mr. Bruce.* Dublin, 1756 (4to. 16 pp. Dublin, printed for J. Smith) YALE (BEINECKE)

Reviewed: *Monthly Review* 14 (1756): 351–356

286 *The Bubbled Knights; or, Successful Contrivances. Plainly evincing, in two familiar instances lately transacted in this Metropolis, the Folly and Unreasonableness of Parents laying a Restraint upon their Childrens Inclinations, in the Affairs of Love and Marriage. In Two Volumes.* 2 vols. London, n.d. [1757] [BEINECKE CAT.–c. 1775] (12mo. 6s. Noble) YALE (BEINECKE) [Publication date of 1757 confirmed by ad in back of book for *The Muse in a moral Humour* also published 1757.]

Reviewed: *Monthly Review* 16 (1757): 178
Critical Review 3 (1757): 187

The Buck. A Poem
See: COATES, Charles

The Buds of Parnassus
See: NICHOLS, John

BUIRETTE DE BELLOY, Pierre Laurent. *The Siege of Calais*
See: DENIS, Charles

287 *Bum-Fodder for the Ladies. A Poem, upon Soft Paper.* London, 1753 (Fol. 6d. Lewis) BRITISH LIBRARY

Reviewed: *Monthly Review* 8 (1753): 392

288 [BURGOYNE, John]. *The Maid of the Oaks: a New Dramatic Entertainment. As it is performed at the Theatre-Royal, in Drury-Lane.* London, 1774 (8vo. 1s.6d. Becket. 1774) BRITISH LIBRARY

Reviewed: *Monthly Review* 51 (1774): 465–470
Critical Review 38 (1774): 392

289 [BURGOYNE, John]. *Songs, Chorusses, &c. in the Pastoral Entertainment of the Maid of the Oaks. As performed at the Theatre-Royal in Drury-Lane.* London, 1774 (8vo. 6d. Becket) BRITISH LIBRARY

Reviewed: *Monthly Review* 51 (1774): 394

290 BURNBY, John. *The Kentish Cricketers: a Poem. Being A Reply to a late Publication of a Parody on the Ballad of Chevy Chace; intituled, Surry Triumphant: or, the Kentish Men's Defeat.* Canterbury, 1773 (4to. 1s. Law, &c. 1773) BRITISH LIBRARY

Reviewed: *Monthly Review* 49 (1773): 317
Critical Review 36 (1773): 395
Gentleman's Magazine 43 (1773): 567–568
London Magazine 42 (1773): 509
Town & Country Magazine 5 (1773): 669

291 BURNE, James (trans.). *The Man of Nature. Translated from the French by James Burne.* [Translation of *L'élève de la nature* by Gaspard GUILLARD DE BEAURIEU.] 2 vols. [Vol. 1: *Solitude;* Vol. 2: *Society.*] London, 1773 (12mo. 6s. Cadell) BRITISH LIBRARY

Reviewed: *Critical Review* 35 (1773): 188–191
London Magazine 42 (1773): 91

Town & Country Magazine 5 (1773): 266
Universal Catalogue [2] (1773) art. 116

292 BURNEY, Charles (the elder). *The Cunning Man, a Musical Entertainment, in two Acts. As it is performed at the Theatre Royal in Drury-Lane. Originally written and composed by M. J. J. Rousseau. Imitated, and adapted to his original Music, By Charles Burney.* London, 1766 (8vo. 1s. Becket) BRITISH LIBRARY

Reviewed: *Monthly Review* 35 (1766): 406
Critical Review 22 (1766): 379
Gentleman's Magazine 36 (1766): 543

293 [BURTON, Philippina]. *Miscellaneous Poems, written By a Lady, Being her first Attempt.* 3 vols. London, 1768 (Small 8vo. 9s. sewed. Printed for the Author, and sold by Dodsley, &c.) BRITISH LIBRARY [vol. 1 only]

Reviewed: *Monthly Review* 38 (1768): 147
Critical Review 26 (1768): 314
London Magazine 37 (1768): 105–106

294 BURTON, Philippina. *A Rhapsody.* London, 1769 (4to. 2s.6d. Wilkie, &c.) BODLEIAN

Reviewed: *Monthly Review* 41 (1769): 156
London Magazine 38 (1769): 537

295 BUSHE, Amyas. *Socrates, a Dramatic Poem.* London, 1758 (4to. 3s. Dodsley) BRITISH LIBRARY

Reviewed: *Monthly Review* 19 (1758): 537–541
Critical Review 6 (1758): 89–95

296 *Bussy and Satan, a Fragment*
NOT SEEN (4to. 1s. Scott)

Reviewed: *Monthly Review* 26 (1762): 154
Critical Review 13 (1762): 165–166

297 BUTLER, Hillary. *The Mayor of Wigan, A Tale. To which is added, The Invasion, A Fable.* London, 1760 (8vo. 1s. Owen, &c.) BRITISH LIBRARY

Reviewed: *Monthly Review* 22 (1760): 342

298 BUTLER, Samuel. *The Genuine Remains in Verse and Prose of Mr Samuel Butler, Author of Hudibras. Published from the Original Manuscripts, formerly in the Possession of W. Longueville, Esq; With Notes By R. Thyer, Keeper of the Public Library at Manchester.* 2 vols. London, 1759 (8vo. 10s. Tonson) BODLEIAN

Reviewed: *Monthly Review* 21 (1759): 171–172
Critical Review 8 (1759): 1–10 and 208–212
Gentleman's Magazine 29 (1759): 336–337
Annual Register 2 (1759): 468–472

299 BUTTON, Edward. *A New Translation of The Persian Tales; From an Original Version of the Indian Comedies of Mocles; Wherein Care has been taken to expunge all those useless Repetitions, and trifling Circumstances, with which the Oriental Writings are encumbered: So that The Stories are rendered less tedious, and more instructive, the Whole being reduced into one small Volume. Designed For the Service and Amusement of the British Ladies. By Edward Button, Gent.* London, 1754 (12mo. 3s. Owen) BODLEIAN

Reviewed: *Monthly Review* 11 (1754): 395

The Button-Maker's Jests
See: KING, George

300 [BYROM, John]. *Enthusiasm; a Poetical Essay. In a Letter to a Friend in Town.* London, 1752 (Fol. 1s. Owen) HARVARD (HOUGHTON)

Reviewed: *Monthly Review* 5 (1751): 462

301 [BYROM, John]. *An Epistle to a Gentleman of the Temple. Occasioned by Two Treatises just published, wherein The Fall of Man Is differently Represented; viz. I. Mr. Law's Spirit of Prayer, II. The Bishop of London's Appendix. Shewing, That according to the plainest Sense of Scripture, the Nature of the Fall is greatly mistaken in the latter.* London, 1749 (Fol. 19pp. 1s. Printed for R. Spavan in Ivy Lane, Pater-noster-row) BRITISH LIBRARY

Reviewed: *Monthly Review* 1 (1749): 316

302 BYROM, John. *Miscellaneous Poems.* 2 vols. Manchester, 1773 (8vo. 10s. boards. Manchester printed; and sold by Rivington in London. 1773) BRITISH LIBRARY

Reviewed: *Monthly Review* 49 (1773): 241–246
Critical Review 36 (1773): 69

303 *Calista; or, the Injured Beauty: a Poem, founded on fact. Written by a Clergyman.* London, 1759 (4to. 1s. Griffin in Fetter-lane) NEW YORK PUBLIC LIBRARY

Reviewed: *Monthly Review* 21 (1759): 85
Critical Review 8 (1759): 86

The Call of Aristippus. Epistle IV
See: COOPER, John Gilbert

304 [CALLANDER, John]. *Hymn to the Power of Harmony. Humbly inscribed to the Right Honourable The Earl of Bute.* Edinburgh, 1763 (4to. 1s. Donaldson) BRITISH LIBRARY

Reviewed: *Monthly Review* 31 (1764): 397–398
Critical Review 18 (1764): 320

Cam. An Elegy
See: GREENE, Edward Burnaby

305 CAMBRIDGE, Richard Owen. *A Dialogue between a Member of Parliament and His Servant. In Imitation of the Seventh Satire of the Second Book of Horace.* London, 1752 (4to. 1s. Dodsley) BRITISH LIBRARY

Reviewed: *Monthly Review* 6 (1752): 237
Gentleman's Magazine 22 (1752): 147

306 [CAMBRIDGE, Richard Owen]. *An Elegy written in An Empty Assembly-Room.* London, 1756 (4to. 6d. Dodsley) BRITISH LIBRARY

Reviewed: *Monthly Review* 14 (1756): 454
Critical Review 1 (1756): 266
Gentleman's Magazine 26 (1756): 453

307 [CAMBRIDGE, Richard Owen]. *The Fable of Jotham: to the Borough-Hunters.* London, 1754 (Fol. 6d. Dodsley) BRITISH LIBRARY

Reviewed: *Monthly Review* 10 (1754): 78
Gentleman's Magazine 24 (1754): 51

308 [CAMBRIDGE, Richard Owen]. *The Fakeer: A Tale.* London, 1756 (4to. 6d. Dodsley) BRITISH LIBRARY

Reviewed: *Monthly Review* 14 (1756): 557–558
Critical Review 1 (1756): 318

309 [CAMBRIDGE, Richard Owen]. *The Genius of Britain. An Iambic Ode. Addressed to the Right Hon. William Pitt, Esq.* London, 1756 (4to. 6d. Cooper) BRITISH LIBRARY

Reviewed: *Monthly Review* 15 (1756): 652–653
Critical Review 2 (1756): 470–471

310 CAMBRIDGE, Richard Owen. *The Intruder, In Imitation of Horace, Book I. Satire IX.* London, 1754 (4to. 1s. Dodsley) BRITISH LIBRARY

Reviewed: *Monthly Review* 10 (1754): 156–157
Gentleman's Magazine 24 (1754): 97

311 [CAMBRIDGE, Richard Owen]. *The Scribleriad: an Heroic Poem. Book I The Scribleriad: an Heroic Poem. Book II.* [Books I and II have separate title pages; both dated London, 1751.] London, 1751 (4to. 1s.each. Dodsley) BRITISH LIBRARY

Reviewed: *Monthly Review* 4 (1750–51): 310
Gentleman's Magazine 21 (1751): 31–32 and 95

312 CAMBRIDGE, Richard Owen. *The Scribleriad. An Heroic Poem. In Six Books.* London, 1751 (4to. 6s.sheets. Dodsley) BRITISH LIBRARY

Reviewed: *Monthly Review* 5 (1751): 116–129

Cambridge. A Poem
See: CHRISTIAN, Ann

313 CAMERON, John. *The Messiah. In Nine Books.* Belfast, 1768 (8vo. 4s. Robinson & Roberts) BRITISH LIBRARY

Reviewed: *Monthly Review* 42 (1770): 161–167
Critical Review 29 (1770): 400
London Magazine 39 (1770): 319

CAMÕES, Luiz de (translation)
See: MICKLE, William Julius. *The First Book of the Lusiad*

314 *The Campaign; A True Story.* 2 vols. London, 1759 (12mo. 6s. Harrison) BRITISH LIBRARY

Reviewed: *Monthly Review* 20 (1759): 189–190
Critical Review 7 (1759): 78–79

Campanologia
See: WOTY, William

315 CAMPBELL, Duncan. *The Earth's Groans, and her Complaints against Man; enumerating The Iniquities she labours under; and an Exhortation to Repentance, in Heroick Verse. To which is added, the Faithful Soldier, and Fifty New Hymns and Spiritual Songs; seriously addressed to the Children of Adam the First*. London, 1756 (8vo. 1s. Buckland) BRITISH LIBRARY

Reviewed: *Monthly Review* 14 (1756): 573–574
Critical Review 1 (1756): 570–571

316 *A candid Appeal From the late Dean Swift to the Right Hon. the Earl of O-----y*. London, 1752 (4to. 6d. Owen) BRITISH LIBRARY

Reviewed: *Monthly Review* 6 (1752): 238

317 *Candid: or, All for the Best. Translated from the French of M. de Voltaire. Part II.* [Spurious continuation of *Candide*.] London, 1761 (12mo. 2s. Becket) BRITISH LIBRARY

Reviewed: *Monthly Review* 25 (1761): 155
Critical Review 12 (1761): 131–138
British Magazine 2 (1761): 495

318 *Candour: An Enquiry into the real Merits of the Salisbury Comedians*. London, 1768 (4to. 1s. Horsfield) BRITISH LIBRARY

Reviewed: *Monthly Review* 38 (1768): 71
Critical Review 24 (1767): 470

319 [CANNING, George]. *A Birth Day Offering to a young Lady from her Lover*. London, 1770 (4to. 6d. Dodsley) BODLEIAN

Reviewed: *Monthly Review* 42 (1770): 406
Critical Review 29 (1770): 148
London Magazine 39 (1770): 105
Town & Country Magazine 2 (1770): 72

320 [CANNING, George]. *An Epistle from William Lord Russell, to William Lord Cavendish*. 1st ed. reviewed; copy seen 2d ed.: London, 1763 (4to. 1s.6d. Becket, &c.) BRITISH LIBRARY

Reviewed: *Monthly Review* 29 (1763): 401–405
Critical Review 16 (1763): 391–392

321 [CANNING, George]. *Horace's First Satire Modernized, and Addressed to Jacob Henriques*. London, 1762 (4to. 1s. Cooke) BRITISH LIBRARY

Reviewed: *Monthly Review* 26 (1762): 232–233
Critical Review 13 (1762): 271
British Magazine 3 (1762): 158

322 CANNING, George. *Poems*. London, 1767 (4to. 10s.6d. Dodsley) BRITISH LIBRARY

Reviewed: *Monthly Review* 36 (1767): 447–449
Critical Review 23 (1767): 296

323 CANNING, George. *A Translation of Anti-Lucretius*. London, 1766 (4to. 10s.6d. Dodsley) BRITISH LIBRARY

Reviewed: *Monthly Review* 36 (1767): 190–194
Critical Review 22 (1766): 401–410

324 *The Canniniad; or, Betty's soliloquy in Newgate, on the night destined for her departure to her American settlement. A song, to the tune of, A lass that was laden with care*
NOT SEEN (Fol. 6d. C. Sympson)

Reviewed: *Monthly Review* 11 (1754): 234

The Canto added by Maphaeus
See: ELLIS, John

325 *The Cap and Staff, or the Recantation of the Rev. Captain Charles C------ll, addressed to John W-----s, Esq;* London, 1764 (4to. 2s.6d. Gibson) BRITISH LIBRARY

Reviewed: *Monthly Review* 30 (1764): 487
Critical Review 18 (1764): 62–63
British Magazine 5 (1764): 377

326 CAPELL, Edward (ed.). *Prolusions; or, select Pieces of antient Poetry—compil'd with great Care from their several Originals, and offer'd to the Publick as Specimens of the Integrity that should be found in the Editions of worthy Authors,—in three Parts; containing, I. The notbrowne Mayde; Master Sackvile's Introduction; and Overbury's Wife: II. Edward the third, a Play, thought to be writ by Shakespeare: III. Those excellent didactic Poems, intitl'd—Nosce teipsum, written by Sir John Davis: with a Pref-*

ace. London, 1760 (8vo. 3s.6d. Tonson) BRITISH LIBRARY

Reviewed: *Monthly Review* 22 (1760): 218–219
Critical Review 9 (1760): 127–130
British Magazine 1 (1760): 156

327 *The Capital. A satirical admonition. Addressed to every true lover of his country; but more particularly to the British clergy*
NOT SEEN (8vo. 1s. Staples)

Reviewed: *Monthly Review* 19 (1758): 587–588
Critical Review 6 (1758): 438
Gentleman's Magazine 28 (1758): 492

328 *The Captain in Love. A Tragi-Comical Novel.* 2 vols. London ed. reviewed; copy seen: Dublin, 1768 (12mo. 5s. Lownds) BRITISH LIBRARY

Reviewed: *Monthly Review* 38 (1768): 151
Critical Review 26 (1768): 360–363
Universal Museum 4 (1768): 148

The Captive, A Comic Opera
See: BICKERSTAFFE, Isaac

329 *The Captive; or, the History of Mr. Clifford. Translated from the French.* 2 vols. London, 1771 (12mo. 5s.sewed. Roson) BRITISH LIBRARY

Reviewed: *Monthly Review* 43 (1770): 400
Critical Review 30 (1770): 397–398
London Magazine 39 (1770): 529
Town & Country Magazine 2 (1770): 598

330 *The Captives: or, the History of Charles Arlington, Esq; and Miss Louisa Somerville.* 3 vols. London, 1771 (12mo. 7s.6d.sewed. Vernor. 1771) BRITISH LIBRARY

Reviewed: *Monthly Review* 45 (1771): 152
Critical Review 31 (1771): 483
Gentleman's Magazine 41 (1771): 417

331 [CARACCIOLI, Charles]. *Chiron: or, the Mental Optician.* 2 vols. London, 1758 (12mo. 6s. Robinson) BRITISH LIBRARY

Reviewed: *Monthly Review* 18 (1758): 276
Critical Review 5 (1758): 244–248
Gentleman's Magazine 28 (1758): 133–134

Caractacus
See: MASON, William

The Card
See: KIDGELL, John

332 CAREW, Thomas. *Poems, Songs, and Sonnets: together with a Masque. By Thomas Carew, Esq; One of the Gentlemen of the Privy-Chamber, and Sewer in Ordinary to King Charles I. A New Edition.* London, 1772 (12mo. 3s. Davies) BRITISH LIBRARY

Reviewed: *Monthly Review* 47 (1772): 70

333 [CAREY, George Saville]. *Analects in Verse and Prose, chiefly Dramatical, Satirical, and Pastoral.* 2 vols. London, 1770 (12mo. 5s.sewed. Shatwell) BRITISH LIBRARY

Reviewed: *Monthly Review* 44 (1771): 78
Critical Review 30 (1770): 466–467
Gentleman's Magazine 41 (1771): 85
London Magazine 40 (1771): 104

334 [CAREY, George Saville]. *The Magic Girdle: a Burletta. Taken from the French of Monsieur Rousseau. Set to Music by Mr. Barthelemon, and performed at Marybone Gardens.* [Adaptation from the French original of Jean Baptiste Rousseau.] London, 1770 (4to. 1s. Becket) BRITISH LIBRARY

Reviewed: *Monthly Review* 43 (1770): 151
Critical Review 30 (1770): 75

335 [CAREY, George Saville]. *Momus, a Poem; or a Critical Examination into the Merits of the Performers, and Comic Pieces, at the Theatre Royal in the Hay-Market.* London, n.d. [ESTC-1767] (4to. 1s. Almon) BRITISH LIBRARY

Reviewed: *Monthly Review* 37 (1767): 75
Critical Review 24 (1767): 74
London Magazine 36 (1767): 366
Universal Museum 3 (1767): 372

336 [CAREY, George Saville]. *The Noble Pedlar: a Burletta. As performed at Marybone-Gardens. Set to Music by Mr. Barthelemon.* London, 1770 (4to. 1s. Nicoll) HARVARD (HOUGHTON)

Reviewed: *Monthly Review* 43 (1770): 244
Critical Review 30 (1770): 151
Gentleman's Magazine 40 (1770): 383
Town & Country Magazine 2 (1770): 436

337 [CAREY, George Saville]. *The Old Women Weatherwise, an Interlude; As performed at the Theatre Royal in Drury-Lane*. London, 1770 (8vo. 6d. Bladon) BRITISH LIBRARY

Reviewed: *Monthly Review* 42 (1770): 495
Critical Review 29 (1770): 393

338 CAREY, George Saville. *Shakespeare's Jubilee, a Masque*. London, 1769 (8vo. 6d. Becket) BRITISH LIBRARY

Reviewed: *Monthly Review* 41 (1769): 238
Critical Review 28 (1769): 236–237
Gentleman's Magazine 39 (1769): 454

339 [CAREY, Henry]. *Cupid and Hymen; A Voyage to the Isles of Love and Matrimony. Containing A most Diverting Account of the Inhabitants of those Two Vast and Populous Countries, their Laws, Customs, and Government. Interspersed With many useful Directions and Cautions how to avoid the dangerous Precipices and Quicksands that these Islands abound with, and wherein so many Thousands, who have undertaken the Voyage, have miserably perished. By the Facetious H. C. and T. B. To which are added, A Map of the Island of Marriage; The Batchelor's Estimate of Expences attending a Married Life. The Married Man's Answer to it; None but Fools Marry, a Vindication of the Estimate; and a Boulster Lecture, &c. By Simon Single, Esq;* 4th ed. London, 1772 [Two of the earlier editions were in 1742 and 1746.] (12mo. 3s. Bladon) BRITISH LIBRARY

Reviewed: *London Magazine* 42 (1773): 92

340 [CAREY, Henry]. *True-Blue; or, the Press-Gang, a Musical Interlude: As revived at the Theatre-Royal In Covent-Garden*. London, 1770 (6d. Bell) CAMBRIDGE

Reviewed: *London Magazine* 39 (1770): 580

341 [CAREY, Patrick]. *Poems, From a Manuscript, written in the time of Oliver Cromwell.* London, 1771 (4to. 1s.6d. Murray. 1771) BRITISH LIBRARY

Reviewed: *Monthly Review* 44 (1771): 491
Critical Review 31 (1771): 314
London Magazine 40 (1771): 275

CARLET DE CHAMBLAIN DE MARIVAUX, Pierre. *Pharsamond*
See: LOCKMAN, John

CARLISLE, Earl of
See: HOWARD, Frederick, 5th Earl of Carlisle

CARON DE BEAUMARCHAIS, Pierre Augustin (adaptation)
See: GRIFFITH, Elizabeth. *The School for Rakes*

342 [CARR, John]. *Epponina: a Dramatic Essay. Addressed to the Ladies*. London, 1765 (8vo. 2s.6d. Beecroft) BRITISH LIBRARY

Reviewed: *Monthly Review* 32 (1765): 393
Critical Review 19 (1765): 393
Candid Review 1 (1765): 265–267

343 CARR, J[ohn]. *Extract of a Private Letter to a Critic*
NOT SEEN (Fol. 6d. Flexney)

Reviewed: *Monthly Review* 30 (1764): 323
Critical Review 17 (1764): 320

344 [CARR, John]. *Filial Piety: a Poem*. London, 1764 (4to. 6d. Flexney) BRITISH LIBRARY

Reviewed: *Monthly Review* 30 (1764): 69
Critical Review 17 (1764): 74

345 [CARR, John]. *The Life and Opinions of Tristram Shandy, Gentleman.* [Spurious vol. 3, published as if a continuation of Sterne's first 2 vols.] London, 1760 (12mo. 2s.6d. Scott) BRITISH LIBRARY

Reviewed: *Monthly Review* 23 (1760): 327
Critical Review 10 (1760): 237–238
London Magazine 29 (1760): 496
British Magazine 1 (1760): 602

346 [CARTER, Elizabeth]. *Poems on Several Occasions*. London, 1762 (8vo. 2s. Rivington) BRITISH LIBRARY

Reviewed: *Monthly Review* 26 (1762): 103–109
Critical Review 13 (1762): 180–[185]
British Magazine 3 (1762): 213

347 [CARTER, John]. *The Scotch Parents: or, the Remarkable Case of John Ramble, written by himself, (in the month of February, 1773)*. London, 1773 (12mo. 3s.6d. Bladon. 1773) BRITISH LIBRARY

Reviewed: *Monthly Review* 49 (1773): 69
London Magazine 42 (1773): 302
Universal Catalogue [2] (1773) art. 731

348 [CARTWRIGHT, Edmund]. *Armine and Elvira, a Legendary Tale. In Two Parts*. London, 1771 (4to. 2s. Murray) BRITISH LIBRARY

Reviewed: *Monthly Review* 45 (1771): 103–110
Critical Review 31 (1771): 396

349 [CARTWRIGHT, Edmund]. *Constantia, an Elegy, To the Memory of a Lady, lately deceased*. London, 1768 (4to. 1s. Becket) BODLEIAN

Reviewed: *Monthly Review* 39 (1768): 242–245
Critical Review 26 (1768): 229
London Magazine 37 (1768): 610
Universal Museum 4 (1768): 484

The Castle-Builders
See: STEVENS, Thomas

The Castle of Otranto
See: WALPOLE, Horace

350 CASWALL, George. *The Trifler. A Satire, inscribed to Lord ----- .* London, 1767 (4to. 1s.6d. Flexney) BRITISH LIBRARY

Reviewed: *Monthly Review* 36 (1767): 78
Critical Review 22 (1766): 470–471

Catharine and Petruchio
See: GARRICK, David

351 CATO REDIVIVUS. *Patriotism: a Political Satire*. London, 1767 (4to. 2s. Williams) BODLEIAN

Reviewed: *Monthly Review* 38 (1768): 71
Critical Review 24 (1767): 381–382

Gentleman's Magazine 37 (1767): 600–601
Universal Museum 3 (1767): 596

352 [CATULLUS, Caius Valerius]. *Ariadne Forsaken. A Poem.* [Translation of *Nuptiae Pelei*.] London, 1772 (4to. 1s.6d. Griffin) BRITISH LIBRARY

Reviewed: *Monthly Review* 47 (1772): 149–150
Critical Review 33 (1772): 490–491
London Magazine 41 (1772): 387
British Magazine & General Review 2 (1772): 65
Universal Catalogue [1] (1772) art. 871

Cautions to a Lady
See: CAYLEY, John

353 *The Cautious Lover; or, the History of Lord Woburn. By a Young Gentleman of Oxford. In Two Volumes*. London ed. reviewed; copy seen: Dublin, 1773 (12mo. 5s.sewed. Cadell. 1772) UNIVERSITY OF PENNSYLVANIA

Reviewed: *Monthly Review* 46 (1772): 265
Critical Review 33 (1772): 180–181
Town & Country Magazine 4 (1772): 100
Universal Catalogue [1] (1772) art. 112

The Cave of Morar
See: TAIT, John

354 *A Caveat to the Will of a Certain Northern Vicar. Addressed to the Reverend W. C********* Rector of K**** W****.* London, 1766 (4to. 2s. Flexney) BRITISH LIBRARY

Reviewed: *Monthly Review* 34 (1766): 324
Critical Review 21 (1766): 233–234

355 CAWTHORN, James. *Poems*. London, 1771 (4to. 6s.sewed. Bladon, &c. 1771) BRITISH LIBRARY

Reviewed: *Monthly Review* 45 (1771): 1–6
Critical Review 31 (1771): 213–216
London Magazine 40 (1771): 225
Town & Country Magazine 3 (1771): 213

356 [CAYLEY, John]. *Cautions to a Lady. A Poem. By the Author of Scarbrough*. York, 1771

(4to. 1s. Dodsley. 1771) NEW YORK PUBLIC LIBRARY

Reviewed: *Monthly Review* 44 (1771): 490

357 *Cecilia; or, the Eastern Lovers. A Novel. Translated from the French.* London, 1773 (12mo. 3s.bound. Bladon. 1773) BRITISH LIBRARY

Reviewed: *Monthly Review* 49 (1773): 150
Critical Review 36 (1773): 397
Town & Country Magazine 5 (1773): 669
Universal Catalogue [2] (1773) art. 632

358 [CELESIA, Dorothea]. *Almida, a Tragedy, As it is performed at The Theatre Royal in Drury-Lane. By a Lady.* [Altered from Voltaire's *Tancrède*.] London, 1771 (8vo. 1s.6d. Becket. 1771) BRITISH LIBRARY

Reviewed: *Monthly Review* 44 (1771): 150–155
Critical Review 31 (1771): 71
Gentleman's Magazine 41 (1771): 127–128
London Magazine 40 (1771): 46–47

359 [CELESIA, Dorothea]. *Indolence: a Poem. By The Author of Almida.* London, 1772 (4to. 1s. Becket. 1772) BRITISH LIBRARY

Reviewed: *Monthly Review* 46 (1772): 454
Critical Review 33 (1772): 254–255
Town & Country Magazine 4 (1772): 266
Universal Catalogue [1] (1772) art. 391

Cenia; or the supposed daughter
See: GRAFFIGNY, Françoise d'Issembourg d'Happoncourt

360 CENTLIVRE, [Susanna]. *The Works of the celebrated Mrs. Centlivre. In Three Volumes. Containing, Perjur'd Husband. Beaux's Duel. Gamester. Basset Table. Love at a Venture. Love's Contrivance. Busy Boy. Marplot in Lisbon. Platonic Lady. Perplex'd Lovers, Cruel Gift. Wonder, A Woman Keeps a Secret. Man's Bewitch'd. Gotham Election. Wife well Managed. A Bickerstaff's Burying. Bold Stroke for a Wife. Artifice. Stolen Heiress. With a New Account of her Life.* London, 1761 (12mo. 9s.boards or 10s.bound. Knapton, &c.) BRITISH LIBRARY

Reviewed: *Monthly Review* 23 (1760): 523–524
Critical Review 10 (1760): 486

CERVANTES SAAVEDRA, Miguel de. *Don Quixote* (translation)
See: SMOLLETT, Tobias. *The History and Adventures of the renowned Don Quixote*

361 *The Cestus of Venus; or, The Art of Charming. A Poem*
NOT SEEN (4to. 1s. Cabe)

Reviewed: *Monthly Review* 30 (1764): 68–69
Critical Review 17 (1764): 76–77

362 [CHAIGNEAU, William]. *The History of Jack Connor.* 2 vols. London, 1752 (12mo. 6s. Johnston) BRITISH LIBRARY

Reviewed: *Monthly Review* 6 (1752): 447–449

The Chances. A Comedy
See: GARRICK, David

The Chaplain. A Poem
See: GREENE, Edward Burnaby

363 CHAPPELOW, Leonard. *The Traveller: an Arabic Poem, intitled Tograi, Written by Abu-Ismael; Translated into Latin and publish'd with Notes in 1661, By Edward Pocock, D.D. Professor of Hebrew and Arabic in the University of Oxford, and Canon of Christ-Church. Now Render'd into English in the same Iambic Measure as the Original; with some additional Notes to illustrate the Poem, By Leonard Chappelow, B.D. Arabic Professor, and formerly Fellow of St. John's College, in the University of Cambridge.* [Translation of poem by ḤUSAIN IBN 'ALĪ.] Cambridge, 1758 (4to. 1s.6d. Thurlbourn, &c.) BRITISH LIBRARY

Reviewed: *Monthly Review* 20 (1759): 113–114

364 *Characters of the Age. A Panegyrico-Satirical Poem. (Wrote in the Year M, DCC, LVII.). With Notes Variorum. To which is prefixed, An Address to the Shade of the late Lord Bolingbroke.* London, 1758 (4to. 1s. No publisher's name) YALE (BEINECKE)

Reviewed: *Monthly Review* 19 (1758): 503–505

365 CHARITON. *The Loves of Chaereas and Callirrhoe. Written originally in Greek By Chariton of Aphrodisios. Now first translated into English.* 2 vols. London, 1764 (12mo. 6s. Becket and DeHondt) BRITISH LIBRARY

Reviewed: *Monthly Review* 30 (1764): 61–63
Critical Review 17 (1764): 37–39

366 *Charity: a Poetical Essay.* London, 1774 (4to. 1s. Horsfield) HARVARD (HOUGHTON) [Harvard has this cataloged under Peter Layard, but this is not Layard's Seaton Prize poem of the same title; it is an unsuccessful competitor.]

Reviewed: *Critical Review* 37 (1774): 156–157
London Magazine 42 (1773): 612

367 CHARKE, [Charlotte]. *The History of Henry Dumont, Esq; and Miss Charlotte Evelyn. Consisting of Variety of Entertaining Characters, and very Interesting Subjects; With some Critical Remarks on Comick Actors.* London, 1756 (12mo. 3s. Slater) UNIVERSITY OF PENNSYLVANIA

Reviewed: *Monthly Review* 14 (1756): 444–445
Critical Review 1 (1756): 136–138

368 [CHATER, John]. *The History of Tom Rigby.* 3 vols. London, 1773 [Vol. 1 misdated; ESTC-1733 {1773}] (12mo. 7s.6d.sewed. Vernon. 1773) BRITISH LIBRARY

Reviewed: *Monthly Review* 48 (1773): 154
Critical Review 34 (1772): 472
London Magazine 41 (1772): 598
Universal Catalogue [1] (1772) art. 1511

369 [CHATTERTON, Thomas]. *The Auction; a Poem: A Familiar Epistle to a Friend, With the head of Harpocrates, the God of Silence amongst the Egyptians, in a Ring.* London, 1770 (4to. 2s. Kearsly. 1770) BRITISH LIBRARY

Reviewed: *Monthly Review* 42 (1770): 98–100
Critical Review 29 (1770): 73
London Magazine 39 (1770): 43

370 [CHATTERTON, Thomas]. *An Elegy on the Much Lamented Death of William Beckford, Esq. Late Lord–Mayor of, and Representative in Parliament for, the City of London.* London, 1770 (4to. 1s. Kearsley) BRITISH LIBRARY

Reviewed: *Monthly Review* 43 (1770): 67
Critical Review 30 (1770): 72–73
London Magazine 39 (1770): 378

371 [CHATTERTON, Thomas]. *The Execution of Sir Charles Bawdin. Dedicated to Her Grace the Dutchess of Northumberland.* London, 1772 (4to. 2s.6d. Goldsmith) BRITISH LIBRARY

Reviewed: *Monthly Review* 47 (1772): 150
Critical Review 34 (1772): 234–236
British Magazine & General Review 1 (1772): 532
Universal Catalogue [1] (1772) art. 735

372 CHIARI, Pietro. *The Generous Lover: or the Adventures of the Marchioness De Brianville. In Three Volumes. Translated from the Original Italian of the Abbe Pietro Chiari.* London, 1771 (12mo. 7s.6d.sewed. Steel) YALE (STERLING)

Reviewed: *Critical Review* 32 (1771): 229–230

373 CHIARI, Pietro. *Rosara; or, the Adventures of an Actress: a Story from Real Life. Translated from the Italian of Pietro Chiari.* 3 vols. London, 1771 (12mo. 7s.6d.sewed. Baldwin) BRITISH LIBRARY

Reviewed: *Monthly Review* 44 (1771): 498
Critical Review 32 (1771): 231–232

374 *The Chimney-Sweepers, a Town Eclogue.* London, 1773 (4to. 1s. Ridley. 1773) BRITISH LIBRARY

Reviewed: *Monthly Review* 49 (1773): 65
Critical Review 36 (1773): 155

Chiron: or, the Mental Optician
See: CARACCIOLI, Charles

Chit-chat, or, natural characters
See: COLLET, John

Choheleth, or The Royal Preacher
See: FURLEY, J. Dennis

Chorus of the Dramatic Poem of Elfrida
See: MASON, William

375 CHRISTIAN, Ann. *Cambridge. A Poem.* London, 1756 (Fol. 6d. Reeve) BRITISH LIBRARY

Reviewed: *Monthly Review* 16 (1757): 461

376 *The Christian's Heart's Ease; or, Balm for Hurt Minds, a Sermon, In Verse.* London, n.d. [ESTC-1765?] (4to. 6d. Bladon) BRITISH LIBRARY

Reviewed: *Critical Review* 29 (1770): 239
London Magazine 39 (1770): 45

Chrysal: or, the Adventures of a Guinea
See: JOHNSTONE, Charles

377 CHURCHILL, C[harles]. *The Apology. Addressed to the Critical Reviewers.* London, 1761 (4to. 1s. Flexney) BRITISH LIBRARY

Reviewed: *Monthly Review* 24 (1761): 340–342
Critical Review 11 (1761): 409–411
British Magazine 2 (1761): 265

378 CHURCHILL, C[harles]. *The Author.* London, 1764 (4to. 2s.6d. Flexney, &c.) BRITISH LIBRARY

Reviewed: *Monthly Review* 30 (1764): 26–30
Critical Review 16 (1763): 446–448

379 CHURCHILL, C[harles]. *The Candidate. A Poem.* London, 1764 (4to. 2s.6d. Flexney) BRITISH LIBRARY

Reviewed: *Monthly Review* 30 (1764): 415
Critical Review 17 (1764): 365–370
General Magazine 1 (1764): 240–242

380 CHURCHILL, C[harles]. *The Conference. A Poem.* London, 1763 (4to. 2s.6d. Kearsley, &c.) BRITISH LIBRARY

Reviewed: *Monthly Review* 29 (1763): 385–389
Critical Review 16 (1763): 443–446

381 CHURCHILL, C[harles]. *The Duellist. A Poem. In Three Books.* London, 1764 (4to. 2s.6d. Kearsly, &c.) BRITISH LIBRARY

Reviewed: *Monthly Review* 29 (1763): 531–538
Critical Review 17 (1764): 39–43
General Magazine 1 (1764): 44–45

382 CHURCHILL, C[harles]. *An Epistle to William Hogarth. By C. Churchill.* London, 1763 (4to. 2s.6d. Coote) HARVARD (HOUGHTON)

Reviewed: *Monthly Review* 29 (1763): 134–138
Critical Review 16 (1763): 63–67

383 CHURCHILL, C[harles]. *The Farewell. A Poem.* London, 1764 (4to. 2s.6d. Flexney) BRITISH LIBRARY

Reviewed: *Monthly Review* 30 (1764): 487
Critical Review 18 (1764): 57–62
British Magazine 5 (1764): 377
General Magazine 1 (1764): 299–300

384 [CHURCHILL, Charles]. *The Ghost. By the Author.* London, 1762 (4to. 4s. Flexney) BRITISH LIBRARY

Reviewed: *Monthly Review* 26 (1762): 313–315 and 27 (1762): 316
Critical Review 14 (1762): 301–309
British Magazine 3 (1762): 606

385 CHURCHILL, C[harles]. *The Ghost. Book IV.* London, 1763 (4to. 2s.6d. Flexney) BRITISH LIBRARY

Reviewed: *Monthly Review* 29 (1763): 397
Critical Review 16 (1763): 335–338

386 CHURCHILL, C[harles]. *Gotham. A Poem. Book I.* London, 1764 (4to. 2s.6d. Flexney, &c.) BRITISH LIBRARY

Reviewed: *Monthly Review* 30 (1764): 151–154
Critical Review 17 (1764): 144–146
General Magazine 1 (1764): 94–95

387 CHURCHILL, C[harles]. *Gotham. A Poem. Book II.* London, 1764 (4to. 2s.6d. Kearsly, &c.) BRITISH LIBRARY

Reviewed: *Monthly Review* 30 (1764): 291–296
Critical Review 17 (1764): 288–292
General Magazine 1 (1764): 150–151

388 CHURCHILL, C[harles]. *Gotham. A Poem. Book III.* London, 1764 (4to. 2s.6d. Flexney) BRITISH LIBRARY

Reviewed: *Monthly Review* 31 (1764): 101–105
Critical Review 18 (1764): 107–111
British Magazine 5 (1764): 433

389 CHURCHILL, C[harles]. *Independence. A Poem. Addressed to the Minority.* London, 1764 (4to. 2s.6d. Almon, &c.) BRITISH LIBRARY

Reviewed: *Monthly Review* 31 (1764): 271–275
Critical Review 18 (1764): [265]-[270]
General Magazine 1 (1764): 500–503

390 [CHURCHILL, Charles]. *Night: An Epistle to Robert Lloyd. By the Author.* London, 1761 (4to. 1s. Flexney) BRITISH LIBRARY

Reviewed: *Monthly Review* 25 (1761): 451–454
Critical Review 12 (1761): 370–372
British Magazine 2 (1761): 622

391 CHURCHILL, C[harles]. *Poems by C. Churchill. Containing The Conference. The Author. The Duellist. Gotham, in Three Books. The Candidate. The Farewell. The Times. Independence. And Fragment of Journey. Volume II.* London, 1765 (4to. 10s.6d. Flexney) BRITISH LIBRARY

Reviewed: *Monthly Review* 32 (1765): 315
Critical Review 19 (1765): 311–313

392 CHURCHILL, C[harles]. *Poems. Containing. The Rosciad. The Apology. Night. The Prophecy of Famine. An Epistle to William Hogarth. And The Ghost, in Four Books.* London, 1763 (4to. 13s.sewed. Flexney, &c.) BRITISH LIBRARY

Reviewed: *Monthly Review* 29 (1763): 397–398
Critical Review 16 (1763): 338

393 CHURCHILL, C[harles]. *The Prophecy of Famine. A Scots Pastoral. By C. Churchill. Inscribed to John Wilkes, Esq;* London, 1763 (4to. 2s.6d. Kearsley) UNIVERSITY OF PENNSYLVANIA

Reviewed: *Monthly Review* 28 (1763): 56–61
Critical Review 15 (1763): 60–62
British Magazine 4 (1763): 98

394 [CHURCHILL, Charles]. *The Rosciad. By the Author.* London, 1761 (4to. 1s. Flexney) BRITISH LIBRARY

Reviewed: *Critical Review* 11 (1761): 209–212
British Magazine 2 (1761): 161

395 CHURCHILL, C[harles]. *The Rosciad. The Third Edition, Revised and Corrected.* London, 1761 (4to. 1s.6d. Flexney) BRITISH LIBRARY

Reviewed: *Monthly Review* 24 (1761): 278
Critical Review 11 (1761): 339–340

396 CHURCHILL, C[harles]. *The Times. A Poem.* London, 1764 (4to. 2s.6d. Flexney, &c.) BRITISH LIBRARY

Reviewed: *Monthly Review* 31 (1764): 201–205
Critical Review 18 (1764): 198–203
General Magazine 1 (1764): 454–456

397 CHURCHILL, W. *The Temple of Corruption. A Poem.* London, 1770 (4to. 2s.6d. Flexney. 1770) BODLEIAN

Reviewed: *Monthly Review* 42 (1770): 144
Critical Review 29 (1770): 145–146

398 *Churchill: an Elegy.* Bristol, 1765 (4to. 6d. Baldwin) BRITISH LIBRARY

Reviewed: *Monthly Review* 33 (1765): 165
Critical Review 20 (1765): 164

Churchill Defended, a Poem
See: STOCKDALE, Percival

399 *Churchill dissected. A Poem.* London, 1764 (4to. 1s.6d. Nicoll) BRITISH LIBRARY

Reviewed: *Monthly Review* 31 (1764): 276–277
Critical Review 18 (1764): 318–319

400 *Churchill's Epistle to William Hogarth, Esq. Re-Versified. With Notes.* London, 1763 (4to. 2s.6d. Burd) HARVARD (HOUGHTON)

Reviewed: *Monthly Review* 29 (1763): 471–472
Critical Review 17 (1764): 75

401 CIBBER, Colley. *A Rhapsody upon the Marvellous: Arising from the First Odes of Horace and Pindar. Being a Scrutiny into Ancient Poetical Fame, Demanded by Modern Common Sense.* London, 1751 (4to. 1s. Printed for W. Lewis near Covent-Garden) BRITISH LIBRARY

Reviewed: *Monthly Review* 4 (1750–51): 221–226

402 CIBBER, Colley. *Verses to the Memory of Mr. Pelham, Addressed to His Grace the Duke of Newcastle.* London, n.d. [ESTC-1754] (Fol. 6d. Joliffe) BRITISH LIBRARY

Listed: *Monthly Review* 10 (1754): 305
Reviewed: *Gentleman's Magazine* 24 (1754): 193

CIBBER, Colley (adaptation)
See: DIBDIN, Charles. *Damon and Phillida*

403 CIBBER, Susanna Maria (trans.). *The Oracle. A Comedy of One Act. As it is acted at the Theatre-Royal in Covent-Garden.* [Translated from the French of Germain François POUILLAIN DE SAINT FOIX.] London, 1752 (8vo. 1s. Dodsley) BRITISH LIBRARY

Reviewed: *Monthly Review* 6 (1752): 239–240
Gentleman's Magazine 22 (1752): 146–147

404 [CIBBER, Theophilus]. *The Auction, as it has been acted several nights with great applause, at the Theatre-Royal in the Hay-market, Mr. Cibber Auctioneer*
NOT SEEN (8vo. 6d. Baily)

Reviewed: *Monthly Review* 17 (1757): 183
Literary Magazine 2 (1757): 393–394

The Citizen of the World
See: GOLDSMITH, Oliver

405 *The City Patricians. A Poem.* London, 1773 (4to. 2s.6d. Allen. 1773) BRITISH LIBRARY

Reviewed: *Monthly Review* 49 (1773): 230
Critical Review 36 (1773): 234–235
London Magazine 42 (1773): 509
Universal Catalogue [2] (1773) art. 1048

406 *City Patriotism displayed; a Poem. Addressed to Frederick Lord North*
NOT SEEN (4to. 1s. Dixwell)

Reviewed: *Monthly Review* 49 (1773): 231
Critical Review 36 (1773): 315
London Magazine 42 (1773): 456
Town & Country Magazine 5 (1773): 603

407 CLANCY, Michael (trans.). *Memoirs of M. de Meilcour, translated from the French of the younger Crebillon. By Michael Clancy*
NOT SEEN (12mo. 2s.6d. Nourse)

Reviewed: *Monthly Review* 4 (1750–51): 158

408 [CLARKE, Edward]. *A Letter to a Friend in Italy. And Verses occasioned on Reading Montfaucon.* London, 1755 (4to. 6d. Baldwin) BRITISH LIBRARY

Reviewed: *Monthly Review* 13 (1755): 456–457

409 CLARKE, John. *The Adventures of Telemachus, The Son of Ulysses. Book the First. Translated into Blank Verse. By Mr. John Clarke.* London, 1773 (4to. 1s.6d. Allen. 1773) LIBRARY OF CONGRESS

Reviewed: *Monthly Review* 49 (1773): 316

410 [CLARKE, Richard]. *The Nabob: or, Asiatic Plunderers. A Satyrical Poem. In a Dialogue between a Friend and the Author To which are annexed, A few fugitive Pieces of Poetry.* London, 1773 (4to. 2s.6d. Townsend) BRITISH LIBRARY

Reviewed: *Monthly Review* 49 (1773): 229
Gentleman's Magazine 43 (1773): 392–393
Universal Catalogue [2] (1773) art. 941

411 *Cleanthes and Semanthe. A Dramatic History. By the Author of Leonora. In Two Volumes.* London, 1764 (12mo. 6s. Davies) HARVARD (HOUGHTON)

Reviewed: *Monthly Review* 31 (1764): 159–160
Critical Review 18 (1764): 75–76
British Magazine 5 (1764): 377

412 [CLEAVER, William]. *Elegies of Tyrtaeus, translated into English Verse; with Notes, and the Original Text.* London, 1761 (8vo. 1s.6d. Payne) BRITISH LIBRARY

Reviewed: *Monthly Review* 26 (1762): 57–58
Critical Review 13 (1762): 167–168
British Magazine 3 (1762): 158

413 [CLEAVER, William]. *Two Elegies. I. The Bee. II. The Bulfinch.* London, 1763 (4to. 6d. Dodsley) BRITISH LIBRARY

Reviewed: *Monthly Review* 28 (1763): 185–187
Critical Review 15 (1763): 153–154

414 [CLELAND, John]. *Memoirs of a Coxcomb.* London, 1751 (12mo. 3s.sewed. Griffiths) BRITISH LIBRARY

Reviewed: *Monthly Review* 5 (1751): 385–387

415 [CLELAND, John]. *Memoirs of Fanny Hill.* [Bowdlerised version, published by Griffiths, of *Memoirs of a Woman of Pleasure.*] London, n.d. [ESTC-1750] (12mo. 3s. bound in calf) BRITISH LIBRARY

Reviewed: *Monthly Review* 2 (1749–50): 431–432

416 [CLELAND, John]. *The Surprises of Love, exemplified in the Romance of a Day, or An Adventure in Greenwich-Park, last Easter; The Romance of a Night, or A Covent-Garden-Adventure; The Second Edition; With the Addition of Two Stories, never before in Print, entitled, The Romance of a Morning, or The Chance of a Sport; The Romance of an Evening, or Who would have thought it?* London, 1765 (12mo. 2s.6d.sewed. Lownds) BRITISH LIBRARY

Reviewed: *Monthly Review* 32 (1765): 156–157
Critical Review 18 (1764): 480

417 [CLELAND, John]. *The Times. A Second Epistle to Flavian*
NOT SEEN (4to. 1s. Burd)

Reviewed: *Monthly Review* 22 (1760): 515–516
Critical Review 9 (1760): 417–419

418 [CLELAND, John]. *The Times! An Epistle to Flavian.* London, 1759 (4to. 1s. Pottinger) BRITISH LIBRARY

Reviewed: *Monthly Review* 21 (1759): 354–356
Critical Review 8 (1759): 325

419 [CLELAND, John]. *Titus Vespasian: a Tragedy. By the Author of Memoirs of a Coxcomb.* London, 1760 (8vo. 1s.6d. Griffiths) LILLY

Reviewed: *Monthly Review* 22 (1760): 168
London Magazine 29 (1760): 56

420 [CLELAND, John (trans.)]. *Tombo-Chiqui: or, the American Savage. A Dramatic Entertainment. In Three Acts.* London, 1758 (8vo. 1s. Hooper & Morley) BRITISH LIBRARY

Reviewed: *Monthly Review* 18 (1758): 648
Critical Review 5 (1758): 199–206

421 [CLELAND, John]. *The Woman of Honor.* London, 1768 (12mo. 9s. Lowndes) BRITISH LIBRARY

Reviewed: *Monthly Review* 39 (1768): 83–84
Critical Review 25 (1768): 284–294
Universal Museum 4 (1768): 204

Clementina, a Tragedy
See: KELLY, Hugh

Clementina; or, the History of an Italian Lady
See: HAYWOOD, Eliza

422 *Cleora: or, The Fair Inconstant. A Recent and Authentic History of the Life and Adventures of a celebrated Lady of Distinction, lately very eminent in High Life. Compiled from Genuine Materials; interspersed with Variety of Real and Entertaining Incidents; and executed by an Impartial Hand.* London, 1752 (12mo. 3s. Cooper) BRITISH LIBRARY

Reviewed: *Monthly Review* 6 (1752): 311

423 CLINCH, William. *Poems on Several Occasions. Consisting of Odes, Epigrams, Pastorals, &c. Together with Remarks on The Memoirs of the young Prince of Anamboe, in a Poetical Epistle to the Author. To which is prefix'd, A Dedication to His Royal Highness Prince Present. By the Rev. Mr. William Clinch, B.A. Late of Magdalen-College, Oxon.* London, n.d. [FOLGER CAT.-1749] (8vo. pamphlet. 1s. Printed for G. Jones in Ludgate-street) FOLGER

Reviewed: *Monthly Review* 2 (1749–50): 176

424 *Clio; or, a Secret History of the Life and Amours Of the late Celebrated Mrs. S——N——M. Written by Herself, in a Letter to Hillarius.* London, 1752 (12mo. 2s.6d. Cooper) UNIVERSITY OF PENNSYLVANIA

Reviewed: *Monthly Review* 6 (1752): 148–149

425 CLIVE, [Catherine]. *The Rehearsal: or, Bays in Petticoats. A Comedy In Two Acts. As it is performed at the Theatre Royal in Drury-lane.* London, 1753 (8vo. 1s. Dodsley) BRITISH LIBRARY

Reviewed: *Monthly Review* 8 (1753): 392
Gentleman's Magazine 23 (1753): 150

426 *La Cloche De L'Ame: or Conscience the loudest Knell. A Satyr. Occasioned by several late Complaints from Places of Public Resort, of the too long and frequent tolling of the Bells at Deaths and Funerals. To which is added, Vigiliana Novissima: or the reformed Watchman. The second Edition, with several considerable Alterations and Additions* NOT SEEN (8vo. 6d. Towers, 1774)

Reviewed: *Monthly Review* 50 (1774): 316–317
Universal Catalogue 3 (1774) art. 321

427 *Clodius, a Poem. Addressed to C. Churchill, and the Writers in the Opposition. By G. T.* London, 1764 (4to. 1s.6d. Nicoll) HARVARD (HOUGHTON)

Reviewed: *Monthly Review* 30 (1764): 415
Critical Review 17 (1764): 320

428 *The Cloister: or, the Amours of Sanfroid, a Jesuit, and Eulalia, a Nun. Translated from the French.* London, 1758 (12mo. 3s. Fleming) UNIVERSITY OF PENNSYLVANIA

Reviewed: *Monthly Review* 19 (1758): 581
Critical Review 7 (1759): 288
General Magazine 1 (1764): 98

429 *The Coach-Drivers, a Political Comic Opera. Adapted to The Music of several eminent Composers.* London, 1766 (8vo. 1s. Flexney) BRITISH LIBRARY

Reviewed: *Critical Review* 22 (1766): 228–232
Gentleman's Magazine 36 (1766): 430–432

430 *The Coach-Drivers, a political Comic Opera. Adapted to The Music of several eminent Composers. To which is subjoined, a Letter of Thanks to the Compilers of the Critical Review, for the Encomiums which they have Let Slip, on that Performance. The Second Edition.* London, 1766 (8vo. 1s.6d. Flexney) BRITISH LIBRARY

Reviewed: *Critical Review* 22 (1766): 382

431 *The Coal-Heavers. A Mock-Heroic Poem, in Two Cantos: Humbly Inscribed to the Inhabitants of Lynn Regis, in Norfolk.* Lynn, 1774 (Fol. 1s. Newbery. 1774) BRITISH LIBRARY

Reviewed: *Monthly Review* 51 (1774): 69
London Magazine 43 (1774): 399
Universal Catalogue 3 (1774) art. 892

432 [COATES, Charles]. *The Buck. A Poem.* London, 1767 (4to. 1s. Smith) BRITISH LIBRARY

Reviewed: *Monthly Review* 36 (1767): 239
Critical Review 23 (1767): 226
Gentleman's Magazine 37 (1767): 262

433 COBDEN, Edward. *A Poem, Sacred to the Memory of Queen Anne, for Her Bounty to the Clergy.* London, 1756 (4to. 6d. Baldwin) BRITISH LIBRARY

Reviewed: *Monthly Review* 14 (1756): 580–581
Critical Review 1 (1756): 570

The Cobler: or, A Wife of Ten Thousand
See: DIBDIN, Charles

434 *Cobleriana; or, The Cobler's Medley. Being a choice Collection of the Miscellaneous Pieces, In Prose and Verse, Serious and Comic, of Jobson the Cobler, of Drury-Lane.* London, 1768 (12mo. 5s. Wilkie) CAMBRIDGE

Reviewed: *Monthly Review* 40 (1769): 79
Critical Review 26 (1768): 479
Gentleman's Magazine 38 (1768): 620–621
Universal Museum 4 (1768): 652

435 COCKBURN, Catharine. *The Works of Mrs. Catharine Cockburn, Theological, Moral, Dramatic, and Poetical. Several of them now first printed. Revised and published, With an Account of the Life of the Author, by Thomas Birch, M.A. F.R.S.* [Cockburn is more commonly known by her married name of Trotter.] 2 vols. London, 1751 (8vo. 2 vols. Sold at the Subscription price, which was half a Guinea. Knapton) BRITISH LIBRARY

Reviewed: *Monthly Review* 5 (1751): 102–116, 184–194, 241–256 and 353–357
Gentleman's Magazine 21 (1751): 190

436 COCKINGS, George. *Arts, Manufactures, and Commerce: a Poem*. London, n.d. [ESTC-1769] (8vo. 1s.6d. Cooke, &c.) BRITISH LIBRARY

Reviewed: *Monthly Review* 39 (1768): 485
Critical Review 26 (1768): 379–380
London Magazine 37 (1768): 667
Universal Museum 4 (1768): 596

437 COCKINGS, George. *Benevolence and Gratitude: a Poem*. London, 1772 (8vo. 40 pp. 2s.) BRITISH LIBRARY

Reviewed: *British Magazine & General Review* 2 (1772): 554
Universal Catalogue [1] (1772) art. 1298

438 COCKINGS, George. *The Conquest of Canada; or the Siege of Quebec. An Historical Tragedy. Of Five Acts*. London, 1766 (8vo. 6d. Cooke) BRITISH LIBRARY

Reviewed: *Monthly Review* 35 (1766): 76–78
Critical Review 21 (1766): 471–473

439 COCKINGS, George. *War: a Heroic Poem. From the Taking of Minorca by the French, to the Raising of the Siege of Quebec, by General Murray. By George Cockings*. London, 1760 (8vo. 3s. Cook) NEW YORK PUBLIC LIBRARY

Reviewed: *Monthly Review* 23 (1760): 412
Critical Review 10 (1760): 322

Codrus: A Tragedy
See: RASBOTHAM, Dorning

440 COFFEY, Charles. *The Beggar's Wedding. An Opera. As it is Acting with great Applause at the Theatre-Royal in Drury-Lane. With the Prologue and Epilogue*. London, 1763 (8vo. 1s. Horsfield) BRITISH LIBRARY

Reviewed: *Monthly Review* 28 (1763): 248

441 [COLE, Thomas]. *The Arbour: or the Rural Philosopher. A Poem*. London, 1756 (4to. 6d. Dodsley) BRITISH LIBRARY

Reviewed: *Monthly Review* 14 (1756): 260
Critical Review 1 (1756): 163

Colin and Lucy. A Fragment
See: MILLS, Andrew Hervey

442 *A Collection of Hymns adapted to Public Worship. The Second Edition, corrected*. 1st ed. reviewed; copy seen 2d ed.: Bristol, n.d. [ESTC-1770?] (12mo. 3s. Bristol, printed by Pine, and sold in London by Buckland, &c.) BRITISH LIBRARY

Reviewed: *Monthly Review* 43 (1770): 67
Critical Review 29 (1770): 477

443 *A Collection of Novels, never before printed, founded on facts, serious and whimsical. Containing I. Fatal charity. II. The unfortunate little French pastrycook. III. The comical doctor. IV. The professor: an oriental tale. (Addressed in particular to the citizens of Bristol.) V. Sophia: or the double escape*
NOT SEEN (12mo. 3s. Trye)

Reviewed: *Monthly Review* 18 (1758): 498
Critical Review 5 (1758): 349

444 *A Collection of Original Poems. By Scotch Gentlemen*. [Vol. 1 is reissue of volume listed under BLACKLOCK.] 2 vols. Vol. 1: Edinburgh, 1760; vol. 2: Edinburgh, 1762 (12mo. 5s. Dodsley) BRITISH LIBRARY

Reviewed: *Monthly Review* 27 (1762): 226–227 [vol. 2 only]
Critical Review 13 (1762): 495–499
British Magazine 3 (1762): 269

A Collection of Poems in Four Volumes (1755)
See: DODSLEY, Robert

A Collection of Poems in Six Volumes (1758)
See: DODSLEY, Robert

445 *A Collection of Poems. In four Volumes. By several Hands. Vols. III and IV*. [See next item for vols. I and II.] London, 1770 (8vo. 6s. sewed Pearch) BRITISH LIBRARY

Reviewed: *Monthly Review* 39 (1768): 242
Critical Review 26 (1768): 229

446 *A Collection of Poems in Two Volumes. By several Hands.* 1st ed. reviewed; copy seen 2d ed.: London, 1770) (8vo. 6s.sewed. Pearch) BRITISH LIBRARY

Reviewed: *Monthly Review* 39 (1768): 242
Critical Review 26 (1768): 229

A Collection of Poems, The Productions of the Kingdom of Ireland
See: WHYTE, Samuel

447 *A Collection of pretty Poems, for the Amusement of Children six foot high. Interspersed with a series of Letters, from Cousin Sam to Cousin Sue, On the Subject of Criticism, Poetry, and Politics.* London, n.d. [ESTC-1770?] (1s. Printed for the Booksellers of Europe, Asia, Africa, and America; and sold at the Bible and Sun in St. Paul's Church-yard) BRITISH LIBRARY

Reviewed: *Monthly Review* 16 (1757): 463

448 *A Collection of ridiculous Stories*
NOT SEEN (12mo. 1s.6d. Hinxman)

Reviewed: *Monthly Review* 26 (1762): 318
Critical Review 13 (1762): 523
British Magazine 3 (1762): 382

A Collection of the Moral and Instructive Sentiments . . .Contained in the Histories of Pamela, Clarissa, and Sir Charles Grandison
See: RICHARDSON, Samuel

A Collection of the Most esteemed Pieces of Poetry
See: MENDEZ, Moses

449 [COLLET, John]. *Chit-chat, or, natural characters, and the manners of real life, represented in a series of interesting adventures.* 2 vols. London, 1755 (12mo. 5s. Dodsley) BRITISH LIBRARY

Reviewed: *Monthly Review* 12 (1755): 388

COLLIER, Jane. *The Cry* (with Sarah FIELDING)
See: FIELDING, Sarah

COLLIER, Joel (pseud.)
See: BICKNELL, John

450 [COLLIGNON, Charles]. *Happiness, an Epistle to a Friend*
NOT SEEN (4to. 6d. Dodsley)

Reviewed: *Monthly Review* 30 (1764): 324

451 [COLLINS, William]. *Oriental Eclogues. Written originally for the Entertainment of the Ladies of Tauris. And now translated.* London, 1757 (4to. 6d. Payne) BRITISH LIBRARY

Reviewed: *Monthly Review* 16 (1757): 486–489

452 COLLINS, William. *The Poetical Works of Mr. William Collins. With Memoirs of the Author; and Observations on his Genius and Writings. By J. Langhorne.* London, 1765 (Small 8vo. 3s.bound. Becket) BRITISH LIBRARY

Reviewed: *Monthly Review* 32 (1765): 293–298
Critical Review 19 (1765): 214–215
Candid Review 1 (1765): 302–307

453 [COLLYER, Joseph]. *The Messiah. Attempted from the German of Mr. Klopstock. To which is prefix'd his Introduction on Divine Poetry.* [From the German original of Friedrich Gottlieb KLOPSTOCK.] 2 vols. London, 1763 (Small 8vo. 6s. Dodsley) BRITISH LIBRARY

Reviewed: *Monthly Review* 30 (1764): 69–70
Critical Review 16 (1763): 417–429

454 COLLYER, Joseph. *Noah. Attempted from the German of Mr. Bodmer. In Twelve Books.* [From the German original of Johann Jakob BODMER.] 2 vols. London, 1767 (6s. Dodsley) BRITISH LIBRARY

Reviewed: *Monthly Review* 36 (1767): 235–236
Critical Review 23 (1767): 280–281

455 COLLYER, Mary. *The Death of Abel. In Five Books. Attempted from the German of Mr. Gessner.* [From *Der Tod Abels* by Salomon GESSNER.] London, 1761 (12mo. 3s. Dodsley) BRITISH LIBRARY

Reviewed: *Monthly Review* 26 (1762): 109–112
Critical Review 13 (1762): 76
Gentleman's Magazine 32 (1762): 25–27
British Magazine 3 (1762): 102
Annual Register 4 (1761): 286–291

456 [COLLYER, Mary]. *Felicia to Charlotte: being Letters from a Young Lady in the Country, to Her Friend in Town. Containing a Series of the most interesting Events, interspersed with Moral Reflections; chiefly tending to prove, that the Seeds of Virtue are implanted in the Mind of Every Reasonable Being.* 2 vols. London, 1749 (12mo. 3s.bound. Printed for Mess. Payne and Bouquet in Pater-noster-row.) BRITISH LIBRARY

Reviewed: *Monthly Review* 2 (1749–50): 229 (vol. 2)

457 [COLMAN, George (the elder)]. *Achilles in Petticoats. An Opera. As it is performed at the Theatre-Royal in Covent-Garden. Written by Mr. Gay, With Alterations. The Music entirely new, by Dr. Arne.* London, 1774 (8vo. 1s. Lowndes) BRITISH LIBRARY

Reviewed: *Monthly Review* 50 (1774): 74
Critical Review 36 (1773): 476
Gentleman's Magazine 43 (1773): 611–612
Universal Catalogue [2] (1773) art. 1319

458 COLMAN, George (the elder), with David GARRICK. *The Clandestine Marriage, a Comedy. As it is Acted at the Theatre-Royal in Drury-Lane.* London, 1766 (8vo. 1s.6d. Becket and Co.) BRITISH LIBRARY

Reviewed: *Monthly Review* 34 (1766): 215–219
Critical Review 21 (1766): 221–225

459 COLMAN, George (the elder). *The Comedies of Terence, Translated into Familiar Blank Verse.* London, 1765 (4to. 1l.1s.boards. Becket, &c.) BRITISH LIBRARY

Reviewed: *Monthly Review* 32 (1765): 360–370
Critical Review 19 (1765): 321–331

460 COLMAN, George (the elder). *The Comedies of Terence, Translated into Familiar Blank Verse. The Second Edition, revised and corrected.* 2 vols. 2d ed. London, 1768 (8vo. 12s. Becket) BRITISH LIBRARY

Reviewed: *Monthly Review* 38 (1768): 402–403
Critical Review 26 (1768): 375

461 [COLMAN, George (the elder)]. *Comus: a Masque. Altered from Milton. As performed at the Theatre-Royal in Covent-Garden. The Musick Composed by Dr. Arne.* London, 1772 (8vo. 1s. Lowndes, &c.) BRITISH LIBRARY

Reviewed: *Monthly Review* 47 (1772): 407–408
London Magazine 41 (1772): 491
British Magazine & General Review 2 (1772): 553
Universal Catalogue [1] (1772) art. 1290

462 [COLMAN, George (the elder)]. *The Deuce is in Him. A Farce of Two Acts. As it is performed at the Theatre Royal in Drury Lane.* London, 1763 (8vo. 1s. Becket, &c.) BRITISH LIBRARY

Reviewed: *Monthly Review* 29 (1763): 464
Critical Review 16 (1763): 383–385

463 [COLMAN, George (the elder)]. *The English Merchant, a Comedy. As it is acted at the Theatre-Royal in Drury-Lane.* [Imitated from Voltaire's *Le café ou L'Écossaise*.] London, 1767 (8vo. 1s.6d. Becket) BRITISH LIBRARY

Reviewed: *Monthly Review* 36 (1767): 224–229
Critical Review 23 (1767): 214–216
Gentleman's Magazine 37 (1767): 126–130

464 [COLMAN, George (the elder)]. *The Fairy Prince: A Masque: As it is performed at the Theatre-Royal in Covent-Garden.* [From Ben Jonson's *Masque of Oberon*.] London, 1771 (8vo. 1s. Becket) BRITISH LIBRARY

Reviewed: *Monthly Review* 45 (1771): 411
Critical Review 32 (1771): 392

465 [COLMAN, George (the elder)]. *A Fairy Tale. In Two Acts. Taken from Shakespeare. As it is Performed at the Theatre-Royal In Drury-Lane.* [*N.C.B.E.L* describes it: "From A Midsummer's Dream via Garrick's The Fairies, 1755."] London, 1763 (8vo. 6d. Tonson) BRITISH LIBRARY

Reviewed: *Monthly Review* 30 (1764): 245
Critical Review 17 (1764): 238

466 [COLMAN, George (the elder)]. *The History of King Lear. As it is performed at the Theatre Royal in Covent Garden.* London, 1768 (8vo. 1s. Becket) BRITISH LIBRARY

Reviewed: *Monthly Review* 38 (1768): 245
Critical Review 25 (1768): 148–149

467 COLMAN, George (the elder). *The Jealous Wife: a Comedy. As it is Acted at the Theatre-Royal in Drury-Lane*. London, 1761 (8vo. 1s.6d. Newbery, &c.) BRITISH LIBRARY

Reviewed: *Monthly Review* 24 (1761): 180–192
Critical Review 11 (1761): 131–141
British Magazine 2 (1761): 98

468 [COLMAN, George (the elder)]. *Man and Wife; or, the Shakespeare Jubilee. A Comedy, of Three Acts. As it is performed at the Theatre Royal in Covent-Garden*. London, 1770 (8vo. 1s.6d. Baldwin, &c.) BRITISH LIBRARY

Reviewed: *Monthly Review* 41 (1769): 394–395
Critical Review 28 (1769): 377–378

469 COLMAN, George (the elder). *The Man of Business, a Comedy. As it is Acted at the Theatre-Royal in Covent-Garden*. London, 1774 (8vo. 1s.6d. Becket) BRITISH LIBRARY

Reviewed: *Monthly Review* 50 (1774): 205–207
Critical Review 37 (1774): 135–140
Universal Catalogue 3 (1774) art. 226

470 [COLMAN, George (the elder)]. *The Musical Lady. A Farce. As it is Acted at the Theatre-Royal in Drury-Lane*. London, 1762 (8vo. 1s. Becket and Co.) BRITISH LIBRARY

Reviewed: *Monthly Review* 26 (1762): 238
Critical Review 13 (1762): 266–267
British Magazine 3 (1762): 158

471 [COLMAN, George (the elder)]. *The Oxonian in Town. A Comedy, in Two Acts, As it is Performed at the Theatre Royal in Covent Garden*. London, 1770 (8vo. 1s. Becket &c.) BRITISH LIBRARY

Reviewed: *Monthly Review* 41 (1769): 395
Critical Review 28 (1769): 376–377

472 [COLMAN, George (the elder)]. *Philaster, a Tragedy. Written by Beaumont and Fletcher. With Alterations. As it is acted at the Theatre-Royal in Drury-Lane*. London, 1763 (8vo. 1s. Tonson) BRITISH LIBRARY

Reviewed: *Monthly Review* 29 (1763): 320
Critical Review 16 (1763): 303–304

473 [COLMAN, George (the elder), and Bonnell THORNTON (eds.)]. *Poems by eminent Ladies. Particularly Mrs. Barber, Mrs. Behn, Miss Carter, Lady Chudleigh, Mrs. Cockburn, Mrs. Grierson, Mrs. Jones, Mrs. Killigrew, Mrs. Leapor, Mrs. Madan, Mrs. Masters, Lady M.W. Montague, Mrs. Monk, Dutchess of Newcastle, Mrs. K. Philips, Mrs. Pilkington, Mrs. Rowe, Lady Winchelsea*. 2 vols. London, 1755 (12mo. 6s. Baldwin) BRITISH LIBRARY

Reviewed: *Monthly Review* 12 (1755): 512

474 [COLMAN, George (the elder)]. *Polly Honeycombe, a Dramatic Novel of One Act. As it is now Acted at the Theatre-Royal in Drury-Lane*. London, 1760 (8vo. 1s. Becket) BRITISH LIBRARY

Reviewed: *Monthly Review* 23 (1760): 524
Critical Review 10 (1760): 486
London Magazine 29 (1760): 672
British Magazine 2 (1761): 46

475 [COLMAN, George (the elder)]. *The Portrait; a Burletta. As it is performed at the Theatre-Royal, in Covent-Garden. The Music by Mr. Arnold*. London, 1770 (8vo. 1s. Becket) BRITISH LIBRARY

Reviewed: *Monthly Review* 43 (1770): 498
Critical Review 30 (1770): 468
London Magazine 39 (1770): 677

476 [COLMAN, George (the elder), and Robert LLOYD]. *Two Odes*. London, 1760 (4to. 1s. H. Payne) BRITISH LIBRARY

Reviewed: *Monthly Review* 23 (1760): 57–63
Critical Review 9 (1760): 496–499
London Magazine 29 (1760): 328

477 [COLTON, Henry]. *The Elopement; or Perfidy Punished*. 3 vols.
NOT SEEN (12mo. 7s.6d.sewed. Noble. 1772)

Reviewed: *Monthly Review* 45 (1771): 503
Critical Review 32 (1771): 392

478 [COLVILL, Robert]. *Eidyllia: or Miscellaneous Poems, On Losing Milton: an Ode. To Isa-*

bella: an Ode. The Fair Matron: an Ode. Virtue's Expostulation: an Ode. To Adversity: an Ode. Philocles: a Monody. The Muses triumphant over Venus: a Tale. With a Hint to the British Poets. By the Author of Animadversions upon the Reverend Doctor Brown's three essays on the Charactericks; and of a Criticism on the late Reverend Mr. Holland's Sermons. Edinburgh, 1757 (4to. 1s.6d. Edinburgh: Hamilton and Co.—London: Noon, Payne &c.) BRITISH LIBRARY

Reviewed: *Monthly Review* 18 (1758): 277–278

479 [COMBE, William]. *Sanitas, Daughter of Aesculapius, to David Garrick, Esq; a Poem.* London, 1772 (4to. 2s. Kearsly, &c. 1772) BRITISH LIBRARY

Reviewed: *Monthly Review* 46 (1772): 168
Critical Review 33 (1772): 84
Gentleman's Magazine 42 (1772): 84
London Magazine 41 (1772): 88
Town & Country Magazine 4 (1772): 100
Universal Catalogue [1] (1772) art. 127

480 COMBERBACH, Roger. *The Contest; In which is exhibited a Preface In Favour of Blank Verse; With an Experiment of it, in An Ode, Upon the British Country Life, By Roger Comberbach, Esq; An Epistle from Dr. Byrom to Mr. Comberbach, In Defence of Rhyme; And An Eclogue by Mr. Comberbach, In Reply to Dr. Byrom.* London and Chester, n.d. [ESTC-1755?] (8vo. 6d. Longman in London, and J. Lawston in Chester) BRITISH LIBRARY

Reviewed: *Monthly Review* 13 (1755): 95–99
Gentleman's Magazine 25 (1755): 287

481 COMMON, Doll (pseud.). *The Pittiad: A Satire.* London, 1759 (4to. 6d. Mariner) BRITISH LIBRARY

Reviewed: *Critical Review* 8 (1759): 176
Gentleman's Magazine 29 (1759): 184

482 *The Companion for the Fire-side; or Winter-evening's Amusement. Being a curious Collection of instructive Stories, Tales, Fables, Allegories, Historical Facts, &c. selected from the best Writers in several Languages*
NOT SEEN (12mo. 3s. Cooke)

Reviewed: *Monthly Review* 39 (1768): 83
London Magazine 37 (1768): 163

483 *A Companion in a Post-Chaise; or, an Amusement for a Leisure Hour at Home: containing A careful Selection from the Most approved and entertaining Pieces, in Verse and Prose, That have appeared for many Years past.* Salisbury, 1773 (8vo. 3s. Salisbury printed, and sold by Crowden in London. 1773) BRITISH LIBRARY

Reviewed: *Monthly Review* 50 (1774): 69
Universal Catalogue [2] (1773) art. 1294

484 *The Complaint. And Appeal of Authors to the Court of Apollo. In Two Epistles to Fidelio.* London, 1763 (4to. 1s. Wilson and Fell) FOLGER

Reviewed: *Monthly Review* 30 (1764): 68
Critical Review 17 (1764): 79–80

485 *The Complaint of Liberty.* London, 1767 (4to. 1s. Cadell) BODLEIAN

Reviewed: *Monthly Review* 40 (1769): 88
Critical Review 26 (1768): 472–473
Gentleman's Magazine 38 (1768): 581
London Magazine 37 (1768): 666
Universal Museum 4 (1768): 652

The Compleat Marksman
See: COOTE, Robert

Comus: a Masque
See: COLMAN, George (the elder)

486 *The Conaught Wife. A Comedy of Two Acts. As it is performed At the Theatre in Smock-Alley, Dublin.* London, 1767 (8vo. 1s. Williams) BRITISH LIBRARY

Reviewed: *Monthly Review* 36 (1767): 163–164
Critical Review 23 (1767): 139–140

487 *The Conciliator*
NOT SEEN (4to. 1s.6d. Kearsly)

Reviewed: *Critical Review* 17 (1764): 397

The Concubine: a Poem
See: MICKLE, William Julius

488 *The Conflict: or, the History of Miss Sophia Fanbrook.* 3 vols. London, 1767 (12mo. 9s. Noble) BRITISH LIBRARY

Reviewed: *Monthly Review* 36 (1767): 173
Critical Review 22 (1766): 380

489 *Conjugal Love: An Elegy*
NOT SEEN (4to. 6d. Cambridge printed, and sold by Davies, &c. in London. 1772)

Reviewed: *Monthly Review* 46 (1772): 538
Critical Review 34 (1772): 70
British Magazine & General Review 1 (1772): 532
Universal Catalogue [1] (1772) art. 734

490 *The Conquest of Corsica by the French. A Tragedy. By a Lady.* London, 1771 (12mo. 6d. Printed for the Author. Sold by Carter) BRITISH LIBRARY

Reviewed: *Monthly Review* 46 (1772): 168
Critical Review 33 (1772): 255

491 *The Conspirators. A Tragi-Comic Opera. As it was Acted in England and Ireland, Without Applause.* Carrickfergus, 1749 (8vo. 1s.) BRITISH LIBRARY

Reviewed: *Monthly Review* 1 (1749): 397–398

Constantia, an Elegy
See: CARTWRIGHT, Edmund

492 *Constantia and her Daughter Julia, an Italian History; with A Discourse on Romances.* 2 vols. London ed. reviewed; copy seen: Dublin, 1769 (12mo. 2 pamphlets. 4s.stitched. Robinson and Co.) NEWBERRY

Reviewed: *Monthly Review* 40 (1769): 344–345
Critical Review 27 (1769): 311
London Magazine 38 (1769): 267–268
Critical Memoirs 1 (1769): 525

493 *Constantia; or, A True Picture of Human Life, represented in fifteen Evening Conversations, after the manner of Boccace. To which is prefixed, A short Discourse on Novel Writing.* 2 vols. London ed. reviewed; copy seen: Dublin, 1751 (12mo. 6s.bound. Millar) BRITISH LIBRARY

Reviewed: *Monthly Review* 5 (1751): 8–23

494 *Constantia; or, the Distressed Friend. A Novel.* London, 1770 (12mo. 3s. Johnston. 1770) BRITISH LIBRARY

Reviewed: *Monthly Review* 43 (1770): 152
Critical Review 29 (1770): 364–366
London Magazine 39 (1770): 267

Constantine: a Tragedy
See: FRANCIS, Philip

495 *Contemplation.* London, 1753 (4to. 1s. Dodsley) BODLEIAN

Reviewed: *Monthly Review* 8 (1753): 393
Gentleman's Magazine 23 (1753): 202

The Contemplative Man
See: LAWRENCE, Herbert

496 *The Contest. A Poem.* London, 1764 (4to. 1s.6d. Almon) BRITISH LIBRARY

Reviewed: *Monthly Review* 30 (1764): 323
Critical Review 17 (1764): 320
General Magazine 1 (1764): 195

The Contrast. A Familiar Epistle
See: MORELL, Charles

497 *The Contrast: or, History of Miss Weldon and Miss Mosely.* 2 vols.
NOT SEEN (12mo. 5s.sewed. Noble)

Reviewed: *Monthly Review* 44 (1771): 173
Critical Review 31 (1771): 232

498 *The Convent: or, the History of Julia.* 2 vols. London, 1767 (12mo. 6s. Lowndes) BRITISH LIBRARY

Reviewed: *Monthly Review* 36 (1767): 172
Critical Review 23 (1767): 145–146

499 *The Converts: a Familiar Ode. Addressed to Sir G----- L--------, Chan-----r of the E-----r.* London, 1756 (Fol. 6d. Morgan) BRITISH LIBRARY

Reviewed: *Monthly Review* 14 (1756): 454
Critical Review 1 (1756): 317–318

500 CONWAY, Mr. *The Depopulated Vale: a Poem. By Mr. Conway.* London, 1774 (4to. 2s. Swift. 1774) YALE (BEINECKE)

Reviewed: *Monthly Review* 50 (1774): 484
Universal Catalogue 3 (1774) art. 757

501 [COOKE, Thomas]. *A Hymn to May*. London, 1754 (Fol. 1s. Dodsley) BRITISH LIBRARY

Reviewed: *Monthly Review* 10 (1754): 385

502 [COOKE, Thomas]. *An Ode on Beauty, To which are prefixed Some Observations on Taste, And on the Present State of Poetry in England*. London, 1749 (Fol. 11pp. 6d. Printed for Mrs. Cooper and Mr. Dodsley) BRITISH LIBRARY

Reviewed: *Monthly Review* 2 (1749–50): 87–88

503 [COOKE, Thomas]. *An Ode on Benevolence: To which are prefixed Observations on Education, Taste, and Poetry*. London, 1753 (Fol. 1s. Cooper) BRITISH LIBRARY

Reviewed: *Monthly Review* 8 (1753): 391

504 [COOKE, Thomas]. *An Ode on Pleasure*. London, 1754 (Fol. 6d. Cooper) BRITISH LIBRARY

Reviewed: *Monthly Review* 10 (1754): 304–305
Gentleman's Magazine 24 (1754): 145–146

505 [COOKE, Thomas]. *An Ode on Poetry, Painting, and Sculpture*. London, 1754 (Fol. 1s. Dodsley) BRITISH LIBRARY

Reviewed: *Monthly Review* 10 (1754): 156

506 [COOKE, Thomas]. *An Ode on the Powers of Poetry: To which are prefixed Observations on Taste, And on the Present State of Poetry and Criticism in England*. London, 1751 (Fol. 6d. Cooper) BRITISH LIBRARY

Reviewed: *Monthly Review* 4 (1750–51): 373

507 [COOKE, Thomas]. *A Prologue on Comic Poetry, and an Epilogue on the Comic Characters of Women, As spoke at the Theatre Royal in Covent-Garden, with a Pastoral Dialogue As performed at the same Theatre: to which is prefixed an Ode to John Rich, Esq*; London, 1753 (Fol. 1s. Purser) BRITISH LIBRARY

Reviewed: *Monthly Review* 7 (1752): 475

508 [COOKE, Thomas]. *Pythagoras an Ode. To which are Prefixed Observations on Taste, and on Education*. London, 1752 (Fol. 1s. Franklin) BRITISH LIBRARY

Reviewed: *Monthly Review* 6 (1752): 317

509 [COOKE, Thomas]. *The Tryal of Hercules, an Ode on Glory, Virtue and Pleasure*. London, 1752 (Fol. 1s. Cooper) BRITISH LIBRARY

Reviewed: *Monthly Review* 5 (1751): 464

510 COOKE, William. *The Conquest of Quebec: a Poem. Occasioned by the Premium offered by the Right Honourable the Earl of Litchfield, Chancellor of the University of Oxford*. London, 1769 (4to. 1s.6d. Davis and Reymers. 1769) BRITISH LIBRARY

Reviewed: *Monthly Review* 40 (1769): 515–517
Critical Review 27 (1769): 467–469
Town & Country Magazine 1 (1769): 381

511 COOPER, E[dward]. *A Collection of Elegiac Poesy. All Originals: To which is added Bewdley; A descriptive Poem in Blank Verse: and A Poem on Malvern Spaw*. London, n.d. (8vo. 1s.6d. Printed for the Author) BODLEIAN

Reviewed: *Monthly Review* 23 (1760): 410

512 COOPER, E[dward]. *The Elbow-Chair: a Rhapsody*. London, 1765 (4to. 1s.6d. Newbery) BRITISH LIBRARY

Reviewed: *Monthly Review* 33 (1765): 325–326
Critical Review 20 (1765): 314–315
Gentleman's Magazine 35 (1765): 482

513 [COOPER, John Gilbert]. *The Call of Aristippus. Epistle IV. To Mark Akenside, M.D. By the Author of the three former Epistles of Aristippus*. London, 1758 (4to. 1s. Dodsley) BRITISH LIBRARY

Reviewed: *Monthly Review* 18 (1758): 74–79
Critical Review 5 (1758): 196–198

514 [COOPER, John Gilbert]. *Epistles to the Great, from Aristippus in Retirement*. London, 1757 (4to. 1s.6d. Dodsley) BRITISH LIBRARY

Reviewed: *Monthly Review* 18 (1758): 74–79
Critical Review 4 (1757): 498–504

515 [COOPER, John Gilbert]. *A Father's Advice to his Son: an Elegy. Written a hundred and fifty years ago, and now first published from a manuscript found among the papers of a late Noble Lord.* London, 1759 (4to. 6d. Cooper) BRITISH LIBRARY

Reviewed: *Monthly Review* 20 (1759): 475
Critical Review 7 (1759): 462
Gentleman's Magazine 29 (1759): 339

516 [COOPER, John Gilbert]. *Poems on several Subjects. By the Author of the Life of Socrates.* London, 1764 (12mo. 2s. Dodsley) BRITISH LIBRARY

Reviewed: *Monthly Review* 30 (1764): 486–487
Critical Review 18 (1764): 158–159
General Magazine 1 (1764): 195

517 COOPER, John Gilbert. *The Tomb of Shakespear. A Poetical Vision.* London, 1755 (4to. 6d. Dodsley) BRITISH LIBRARY

Reviewed: *Monthly Review* 12 (1755): 353–355
Gentleman's Magazine 25 (1755): 143

518 [COOPER, John Gilbert (trans.)]. *Ver-Vert: or, the Nunnery Parrot. An Heroic Poem In Four Cantos. Inscribed to the Abbess of D****. Translated from the French of Monsieur Gresset.* [From the French original by Jean Baptiste Louis GRESSET.] London, 1759 (4to. 1s.6d. Dodsley) BRITISH LIBRARY

Reviewed: *Monthly Review* 20 (1759): 225–229
Critical Review 7 (1759): 175–178
Gentleman's Magazine 29 (1759): 87–88

519 [COOPER, Maria Susanna]. *The Exemplary Mother: or, Letters between Mrs. Villars and her Family. Published by a Lady, From the Originals in her Possession.* 2 vols. London, 1769 (12mo. 5s.sewed. Becket. 1769) BRITISH LIBRARY

Reviewed: *Monthly Review* 40 (1769): 476–480
Critical Review 27 (1769): 297–299
London Magazine 38 (1769): 213

520 [COOPER, Maria Susanna]. *Letters between Emilia and Harriet.* London, 1762 (8vo. 3s. Dodsley) BRITISH LIBRARY

Reviewed: *Monthly Review* 26 (1762): 154–155
Critical Review 13 (1762): 159
London Magazine 31 (1762): 112

521 [COOPER, William]. *The Will of a certain Northern Vicar: carefully copied from The Original, Deposited in his own Cabinet, at N-------- upon T---.* London, 1765 (4to. 6d. Bunce) BRITISH LIBRARY

Reviewed: *Monthly Review* 33 (1765): 164–165
Critical Review 20 (1765): 159

522 *The Cooper. A Musical Entertainment. In Two Acts. As it is performed at the Theatre Royal in the Haymarket. The Music composed By Dr. Arne.* London, 1772 (8vo. 1s. Cox. 1772) BRITISH LIBRARY

Reviewed: *Monthly Review* 47 (1772): 72
Critical Review 34 (1772): 155
British Magazine & General Review 2 (1772): 77
Universal Catalogue [1] (1772) art. 878

523 *Cooper's Hill. A Poem. Addressed to Sir Watkin Williams Wynne, Bart.* London, n.d. [ESTC-1766] (4to. 2s.6d. Wood) BRITISH LIBRARY

Reviewed: *Monthly Review* 36 (1767): 162
Critical Review 22 (1766): 380–381

524 *Cooper's Well. A Fragment, Written by the honourable Sir John Denham, Knight of the Bath, and Author of the Celebrated Poem of Cooper's Hill, found amongst the Papers of a late Noble Lord. Dated in the year 1667.* London, 1767 (4to. 2s. Moran) BRITISH LIBRARY

Reviewed: *Monthly Review* 38 (1768): 70–71
Critical Review 24 (1767): 469
Gentleman's Magazine 37 (1767): 640
Universal Museum 4 (1768): 36
Political Register 2 (1768): 64

525 COOTE, Robert. *The Compleat Marksman: or, The True Art of Shooting-Flying: A Poem.*

London, n.d. (8vo. 1s. Henderson) BODLEIAN

Reviewed: *Monthly Review* 14 (1756): 453
Gentleman's Magazine 26 (1756): 197–198

526 [COOTE, Robert]. *The Compleat Marksman: Or, The True Art of Shooting Flying. A Poem*
NOT SEEN (8vo. 1s. Cooke)

Reviewed: *Monthly Review* 37 (1767): 315
Critical Review 24 (1767): 223–224
Universal Museum 3 (1767): 484

COPYWELL, J. (pseud.)
See: WOTY, William

527 *Coquetilla; or, Envy its own Scourge: Containing the Adventures of several great Personages. From a Manuscript late in the Possession of a Gentleman famous for his acquaintance with the great World*
NOT SEEN (12mo. 2s.6d. Leacroft. 1771)

Reviewed: *Monthly Review* 45 (1771): 152
Critical Review 31 (1771): 482

528 *Corinna Vindicated*. London, 1759 (Fol. 6d. Cooper) CAMBRIDGE

Reviewed: *Monthly Review* 20 (1759): 279

Coriolanus: or the Roman Matron
See: SHERIDAN, Thomas

CORNEILLE, Pierre (translations/adaptations)
See: ASPINWALL, S. *Rodogune*
    WHITEHEAD, William. *The Roman Father*

529 *The Coronation: a Poem. Humbly addressed to Nobody who was there. By a Spectator*. London, 1761 (4to. 1s. Dodsley) BODLEIAN

Reviewed: *Monthly Review* 25 (1761): 398
Critical Review 12 (1761): 403
British Magazine 2 (1761): 622

The Coronation of David
See: WISE, Joseph

The Correspondence of Theodosius and Constantia
See: LANGHORNE, John

Corruption. A Satire
See: SHAW, Cuthbert

530 *Corsica, an Ode*. London, 1768 (4to. 6d. Ridley) HARVARD (HOUGHTON)

Reviewed: *Monthly Review* 39 (1768): 401
Critical Review 26 (1768): 378–379
Gentleman's Magazine 38 (1768): 533
Universal Museum 4 (1768): 597
Political Register 3 (1768): 384

531 [COSENS]. *The Oeconomy of Beauty; in a series of Fables: Addressed to The Ladies*. London, 1772 (4to. 5s.3d.sewed. Wilkie, &c. 1772) BRITISH LIBRARY

Reviewed: *Monthly Review* 47 (1772): 282–286
Critical Review 34 (1772): 372–374
Gentleman's Magazine 42 (1772): 328–329
London Magazine 41 (1772): 337
Town & Country Magazine 4 (1772): 660
British Magazine & General Review 1 (1772): 534–536
Universal Catalogue [1] (1772) art. 979

532 COSTIN, John. *A song of praise to the almighty*
NOT SEEN (8vo. 6d. Cooper)

Reviewed: *Monthly Review* 5 (1751): 77

COTTON, Junior (pseud.)
See: BRIDGES, Thomas

COTTON, John Daniel. *Lachrymae elegiacae* (translation)
See: ITCHENER, George

533 [COTTON, Nathaniel]. *Visions in Verse, for the Entertainment and Instruction of Younger Minds*. London, 1751 (8vo. 104pp. 1s.6d. Dodsley) BRITISH LIBRARY

Reviewed: *Monthly Review* 4 (1750–51): 310

534 *The Country Coquet; or, Miss in Her Breeches. A Ballad Opera. As it May be Acted at the Theatre-Royal in Drury-Lane. By a young Lady*. London, 1755 (1s. Reeve, &c.) BRITISH LIBRARY

Reviewed: *Monthly Review* 13 (1755): 467–46

535 *The Country Cousins: or, a Journey to London. A Novel. In Two Volumes.* 2 vols. London, 1767 (12mo. 6s. Noble) YALE (STERLING)

Reviewed: *Monthly Review* 36 (1767): 173
London Magazine 36 (1767): 206

536 *The Country Election; A Farce: In Two Acts.* London, 1768 (8vo. 1s. Hooper) BRITISH LIBRARY

Reviewed: *Monthly Review* 38 (1768): 144
Critical Review 25 (1768): 59–60
Universal Museum 4 (1768): 93

The Country Justice. A Poem
See: LANGHORNE, John

537 *The Country Seat; or Summer Evenings Entertainments. Translated from the French.* 2 vols. London, 1762 (12mo. 5s. Lownds) BRITISH LIBRARY

Reviewed: *Monthly Review* 27 (1762): 71–72
Critical Review 14 (1762): 156

The Country Wife, a Comedy
See: LEE, John

Court and Country
See: JOHNSON, Samuel (dancing master)

538 *Court-Intrigues. Or the Secret History of Ardelisa, A Story founded on Facts, and illustrated with Anecdotes of Persons in real Life.* London, 1759 (12mo. 3s. Cabe) BRITISH LIBRARY

Reviewed: *Monthly Review* 20 (1759): 565

The Court of Alexander. An Opera
See: STEVENS, George Alexander

The Court of Cupid
See: THOMPSON, Edward

539 *The Court of Thespis; being a Collection Of the most admired Prologues and Epilogues That have appeared for many Years; Written by some of the most approved Wits of the Age, viz.* Garrick, Colman, Foote, Murphy, Lloyd, &c. London, 1769 (12mo. 1s.6d.sewed. Richardson and Urquhart) BRITISH LIBRARY

Reviewed: *Monthly Review* 41 (1769): 478
Critical Review 28 (1769): 302–303
London Magazine 38 (1769): 586

540 [COURTENAY, John]. *An Epistle (moral and philosophical) from an Officer At Otaheite. To Lady Gr*s**n*r. With Notes, Critical and Historical. By the Author of The Rape of Pomona.* London, 1774 (4to. 1s.6d. Evans. 1774) BRITISH LIBRARY

Reviewed: *Monthly Review* 52 (1775): 188
London Magazine 43 (1774): 608
London Review 1 (1775): 66–67

541 [COURTENAY, John]. *The Rape of Pomona. An Elegiac Epistle, from the Waiter at Hockrel, to the Honourable Mr. L--tt--n.* 1st ed. reviewed; copy seen 2d ed.: London, 1773 (4to. 1s. Bladon. 1773) BRITISH LIBRARY

Reviewed: *Monthly Review* 48 (1773): 509
Critical Review 35 (1773): 393
Gentleman's Magazine 43 (1773): 291
London Magazine 42 (1773): 249
Universal Catalogue [2] (1773) art. 605

The Courtesan
See: THOMPSON, Edward

The Courtezans: a Comedy Of Two Acts
See: TOWNLY, Charles

542 *Covent-Garden, a Satire.* London, 1756 (4to. 1s. Legg) BRITISH LIBRARY

Reviewed: *Monthly Review* 14 (1756): 64
Critical Review 1 (1756): 164–166

543 [COVENTRY, Francis]. *The History of Pompey the little: or, the Life and Adventures of a Lap-Dog.* London, 1751 (272pp. 3s.bound. Cooper) BRITISH LIBRARY

Reviewed: *Monthly Review* 4 (1750–51): 316–317, 329–337 and 457–465

544 [COVENTRY, Francis]. *Penshurst. Inscribed to William Perry, Esq; and the Honble. Mrs. Elizabeth Perry.* London, 1750 (4to. 1s. Dodsley) BRITISH LIBRARY

Reviewed: *Monthly Review* 2 (1749–50): 331–335

545 COWLEY, A[braham]. *Select Works of Mr. A. Cowley; with a Preface and Notes by the Editor.* [Ed. Richard HURD.] 2 vols. London, 1772 (Small 8vo. 6s.sewed. Cadell. 1772) BRITISH LIBRARY

Reviewed: *Monthly Review* 48 (1773): 10–18
London Magazine 41 (1772): 288
British Magazine & General Review 1 (1772): 547
Universal Catalogue [1] (1772) art. 774

546 [COWPER, Ashley]. *Poems and Translations. By the Author of the Progress of Physic.* London, 1769 (8vo. 1s. Sanby) BRITISH LIBRARY

Reviewed: *Monthly Review* 36 (1767): 408
Critical Review 23 (1767): 293–295
Political Register 1 (1767): 486

547 [COWPER, William]. *Il Penseroso. An Evening's Contemplation in St. John's Church-Yard, Chester. A Rhapsody, Written more than Twenty Years ago, and Now (First) published. Illustrated With Notes Historical and Explanatory.* London, 1767 (4to. 1s. Longman) HARVARD (HOUGHTON)

Reviewed: *Monthly Review* 36 (1767): 409
Critical Review 23 (1767): 296
Political Register 1 (1767): 56

548 COYER, [Gabriel François]. *A Supplement to Lord Anson's Voyage round the World. Containing A Discovery and Description of the Island of Frivola. To which is prefix'd An Introductory Preface by the Translator.* London, 1752 (8vo. 1s. Millar and Whiston) BRITISH LIBRARY

Reviewed: *Monthly Review* 6 (1752): 233

549 [CRADOCK, Joseph]. *Village Memoirs: In a Series of Letters between A Clergyman and his Family in the Country, and his Son in Town.* 2d ed. London, 1775 [1st ed. published 1765] (8vo. 2s.6d.sewed. Davies) BRITISH LIBRARY

Reviewed: *Monthly Review* 52 (1775): 139–143
Critical Review 38 (1774): 449–455
London Magazine 44 (1775): 201

550 CRADOCK, J[oseph]. *Zobeide. A Tragedy. As it is Acted at the Theatre-Royal in Covent-Garden.* [Adaptation from Voltaire.] London, 1771 (8vo. 1s.6d. Cadell. 1771) BRITISH LIBRARY

Reviewed: *Monthly Review* 45 (1771): 491–493
Critical Review 32 (1771): 459–464
Gentleman's Magazine 42 (1772): 81–83
London Magazine 40 (1771): 611

551 CRADOCK, Thomas. *A Poetical Translation of the Psalms of David. From Buchanan's Latin into English Verse.* London, 1754 (8vo. 2s.6d.sewed) BRITISH LIBRARY

Reviewed: *Monthly Review* 10 (1754): 385

552 CRANCOCC, Vortigern (pseud.). *Trifles: By Vortigern Crancocc, Esq. A.B.C.D. and E.F.G.H.I. and K.L.M.N. and O.P.Q.R.S. and T.U.V.W.X.Y.Z.* London, 1772 (12mo. 2s.6d. sewed. Bladon. 1772) BRITISH LIBRARY

Reviewed: *Monthly Review* 47 (1772): 73
Critical Review 33 (1772): 501
London Magazine 41 (1772): 336
British Magazine & General Review 2 (1772): 61–64
Universal Catalogue [1] (1772) art. 875

553 [CRANE, Edward]. *The Fair Parricide. A Tragedy of Three Acts. Founded On a late melancholy Event.* London, 1752 (8vo. 1s. Waller) BRITISH LIBRARY

Reviewed: *Monthly Review* 6 (1752): 396

554 CRANWELL, J[ohn]. *The Christiad, a Poem In Six Books; translated from the Latin of Marcus Hieronymus Vida.* Cambridge, 1768 (8vo. 5s. Dodsley) BRITISH LIBRARY

Reviewed: *Monthly Review* 38 (1768): 409
Critical Review 25 (1768): 311
Universal Museum 4 (1768): 205

555 CRANWELL, J[ohn]. *A Poem on the Immortality of the Soul. Translated from the Latin of Isaac Hawkins Brown Esq;* Cambridge, 1765 (4to. 1s.6d. Rivington) BRITISH LIBRARY

Reviewed: *Critical Review* 18 (1764): 475

556 CRAWFORD, Charles. *Sophronia and Hilario: An Elegy. By Charles Crawford, Esq. Author of the Dissertation on the Phaedon of Plato.* London, 1774 (4to. 1s.6d. Becket. 1774) FOLGER

Reviewed: *Monthly Review* 50 (1774): 407–408
Critical Review 37 (1774): 315
London Magazine 43 (1774): 244
Town & Country Magazine 6 (1774): 268
Universal Catalogue 3 (1774) art. 512

Crazy Tales
See: STEVENSON, John Hall

CRÉBILLON père et fils
See: JOLYOT DE CRÉBILLON

557 *The Crisis. An Ode, to John Wilkes, Esq;* London, 1763 (4to. 6d. Williams) BRITISH LIBRARY

Reviewed: *Monthly Review* 29 (1763): 398
Critical Review 16 (1763): 389–390

558 *The Crisis: Being Three State Poems On the following Subjects; I. The Northern Dictator. A Dialogue between a Highland Peer, and his Vassals. II. On the Reduction and Surrender of the Havannah, and Conclusion of the late Peace. III. Caledonia. A Description of that fertile and beautiful Kingdom. Written on the Dismission of the present glorious Minority. And humbly addressed to The Honourable Assembly in Albemarle-Street.* London, 1764 (8vo. 6d. Williams) BRITISH LIBRARY

Reviewed: *Monthly Review* 30 (1764): 487
Critical Review 17 (1764): 471
General Magazine 1 (1764): 243–244

559 [CRISP, Samuel]. *Virginia. A Tragedy. As it is acted in the Theatre-Royal in Drury-Lane, by His Majesty's Servants.* London, 1754 (8vo. 1s. Tonson) BRITISH LIBRARY

Reviewed: *Monthly Review* 10 (1754): 221–231

560 CROKER, Temple Henry (ed.). *The Satires of Ludovico Ariosto.* London, 1759 (8vo. 3s. Millar) BRITISH LIBRARY

Reviewed: *Monthly Review* 20 (1759): 572–575
Critical Review 7 (1759): 180

CRONZECK, Baron
See: SCHOENAICH, Christoph Otto von, Baron

Cross Purposes: a Farce
See: O'BRIEN, William

561 CROWLEY, Thomas. *The Life and Adventures of Mad. de la Sarre*
NOT SEEN (8vo. 2s.6d.sewed. Johnson)

Reviewed: *Monthly Review* 43 (1770): 155–156
Critical Review 30 (1770): 317
London Magazine 39 (1770): 482

The Crucifixion. A Poem
See: WEEKES, Nathaniel. *The Messiah. A Sacred Poem* [Book 2]

562 *The Cruel Disappointment; or, the History of Miss Emmeline Merrick: a Novel (founded on Fact.).* 2 vols.
NOT SEEN (12mo. 6s. Bladon)

Reviewed: *Monthly Review* 36 (1767): 410
Critical Review 23 (1767): 464

A Crust for the Critics
See: NELTHORPE, George

The Cry. A new Dramatic Fable
See: FIELDING, Sarah, and Jane COLLIER

563 *The Cub. A Satire. Dedicated to Lord Holland.* London, n.d. [ESTC-1774] (4to. 1s.6d. Allen) BRITISH LIBRARY

Reviewed: *Monthly Review* 51 (1774): 65–67
Critical Review 38 (1774): 152
Town & Country Magazine 6 (1774): 464
Universal Catalogue 3 (1774) art. 480

The Cub; at New-Market
See: BOSWELL, James

564 *Cuckoldom Triumphant or, Matrimonial Incontinence Vindicated. Illustrated with Intrigues Public and Private, Ancient and Modern. By a Gentleman of Doctors Commons. To which is added, A Looking Glass for Each Sex.* 2 vols. London, n.d. [ESTC-1775?] (12mo. 5s.sewed. Thorn) BRITISH LIBRARY

Reviewed: *Monthly Review* 45 (1771): 153
Critical Review 32 (1771): 154

Gentleman's Magazine 41 (1771): 417
London Magazine 40 (1771): 463
Town & Country Magazine 3 (1771): 480

565 [CUMBERLAND, Richard]. *Amelia. A Musical Entertainment of Two Acts. As it is performed at the Theatre-Royal in Covent-Garden.* London, 1768 (8vo. 1s. Griffin) BRITISH LIBRARY

Reviewed: *Monthly Review* 38 (1768): 335

566 [CUMBERLAND, Richard]. *Amelia. A Musical Entertainment Of Two Acts.* London, 1771 (8vo. 1s. Becket) BRITISH LIBRARY

Reviewed: *Monthly Review* 45 (1771): 507
Critical Review 32 (1771): 470
London Magazine 40 (1771): 611

567 [CUMBERLAND, Richard]. *The Banishment of Cicero. A Tragedy.* London, 1761 (4to. 2s.6d. Walter) BRITISH LIBRARY

Reviewed: *Monthly Review* 24 (1761): 395–400
Critical Review 11 (1761): 332–333

568 [CUMBERLAND, Richard]. *The Brothers, a Comedy. As it is performed at the Theatre-Royal in Covent-Garden.* London, 1770 (8vo. 1s.6d. Griffin) BRITISH LIBRARY

Reviewed: *Monthly Review* 41 (1769): 478–479
Critical Review 28 (1769): 443–447
Gentleman's Magazine 39 (1769): 594–596
London Magazine 38 (1769): 640–641

569 [CUMBERLAND, Richard]. *An Elegy, written on Saint Mark's Eve.* London, 1754 (4to. 6d. Cooper) HARVARD (HOUGHTON)

Reviewed: *Monthly Review* 10 (1754): 305
Gentleman's Magazine 24 (1754): 146

570 [CUMBERLAND, Richard]. *The Fashionable Lover; A Comedy: As it is acted at the Theatre-Royal in Drury-Lane.* London, 1772 (8vo. 1s.6d. Griffin. 1772) BRITISH LIBRARY

Reviewed: *Monthly Review* 46 (1772): 167–168
Critical Review 33 (1772): 85
Gentleman's Magazine 42 (1772): 80–81
British Magazine & General Review 1 (1772): 263–267

571 [CUMBERLAND, Richard]. *The Note of Hand; or, Trip to Newmarket. As it is acted at the Theatre-Royal in Drury-Lane.* London, 1774 (8vo. 1s. Becket. 1774) BRITISH LIBRARY

Reviewed: *Monthly Review* 50 (1774): 156–157
Critical Review 37 (1774): 158
Universal Catalogue 3 (1774) art. 225

572 [CUMBERLAND, Richard]. *The Summer's Tale: a musical Comedy of three Acts. As it is performed at the Theatre Royal in Covent-Garden.* London, 1765 (8vo. 1s.6d. Dodsley) BRITISH LIBRARY

Reviewed: *Monthly Review* 33 (1765): 489–490
Critical Review 20 (1765): 460–465

573 [CUMBERLAND, Richard]. *Timon of Athens, Altered from Shakespear. A Tragedy. As it is acted at the Theatre-Royal in Drury-Lane.* London, 1771 (8vo. 1s.6d. Becket. 1771) BRITISH LIBRARY

Reviewed: *Monthly Review* 45 (1771): 507–508
Critical Review 32 (1771): 470

574 [CUMBERLAND, Richard]. *The West Indian: a Comedy. As it is performed at the Theatre Royal in Drury-Lane. By the Author of the Brothers.* London, 1771 (8vo. 1s.6d. Griffin. 1771) BRITISH LIBRARY

Reviewed: *Monthly Review* 44 (1771): 142–150
Critical Review 31 (1771): 112–116
Gentleman's Magazine 41 (1771): 124–127
London Magazine 40 (1771): 102–103

575 CUNNINGHAM, J[ohn]. *The Contemplatist: A Night Piece.* London, 1762 (4to. 6d. Payne) BRITISH LIBRARY

Reviewed: *Monthly Review* 27 (1762): 333–337
Critical Review 14 (1762): 318–319

576 CUNNINGHAM, J[ohn]. *An Elegy on a Pile of Ruins.* London, 1761 (4to. 6d. Payne) BODLEIAN

Reviewed: *Monthly Review* 25 (1761): 328–330
Critical Review 12 (1761): 319–320
British Magazine 2 (1761): 550

577 CUNNINGHAM, J[ohn]. *Fortune, an Apologue*. London, 1765 (4to. 6d. Dodsley) BODLEIAN

Reviewed: *Monthly Review* 32 (1765): 185–188
Critical Review 19 (1765): 152

578 CUNNINGHAM, John. *Poems, chiefly Pastoral*. Newcastle, 1766 (8vo. 4s. Dodsley) BRITISH LIBRARY

Reviewed: *Monthly Review* 34 (1766): 351–355
Critical Review 21 (1766): 226–229
Gentleman's Magazine 36 (1766): 193

579 CUNNINGHAM, Josias. *No. 1. Of a Collection of select, original, miscellaneous Poems* NOT SEEN (Fol. 1s.6d. Jones)

Reviewed: *Monthly Review* 32 (1765): 75

Cupid and Hymen; A Voyage to the Isles of Love and Matrimony
See: CAREY, Henry

580 *Cupid turned Spy upon Hymen; or, Matrimonial Intrigues in polite Life*. 2 vols.
NOT SEEN (12mo. 5s.boards. Roson)

Reviewed: *Monthly Review* 45 (1771): 153
Critical Review 32 (1771): 230

Cupid's Revenge: an Arcadian Pastoral
See: GENTLEMAN, Francis

581 *Curtain Lectures; or, Matrimonial Misery Displayed. In a Series of interesting Dialogues, between Married Men and their Wives. In every Station and Condition of Life*. London, 1770 (12mo. 2s.6d. Cooke) NEWBERRY

Reviewed: *Monthly Review* 39 (1768): 485
Critical Review 26 (1768): 376–378
Universal Museum 4 (1768): 596

Cymon. A Dramatic Romance
See: GARRICK, David

Cynthia and Daphne. Translated from the Italian of Il Cavalier Marino
See: MARINI, Giovanni Battista

CYRANO DE BERGERAC, Hercule Savinien de (translation)
See: DERRICK, Samuel

Dalinda: or, The Double Marriage
See: HAYWOOD, Eliza

582 [DALRYMPLE, Hugh]. *Rodondo; or, the State Jugglers. Cantos I. and II*. London, 1763 (8vo. 1s.each. Nicoll) BRITISH LIBRARY

Reviewed: *Monthly Review* 28 (1763): 73 [Canto 1] and 161 [Canto 2]
Critical Review 15 (1763): 126–130
British Magazine 4 (1763): 98

583 [DALRYMPLE, Hugh]. *Rodondo; or, the State Jugglers. Canto III*. London, 1770 (8vo. 1s. W. Nicoll. 1770) BRITISH LIBRARY

Reviewed: *Monthly Review* 42 (1770): 250
Critical Review 29 (1770): 144–145
London Magazine 39 (1770): 104
Town & Country Magazine 2 (1770): 72

584 [DALRYMPLE, Hugh]. *Woodstock: an Elegy*. London, 1761 (4to. 1s. Wilson) NEWBERRY

Reviewed: *Monthly Review* 25 (1761): 62–64
Critical Review 12 (1761): 76–77
British Magazine 2 (1761): 437

585 DALTON, John. *A Descriptive Poem, addressed to Two Ladies, At their Return from Viewing The Mines near Whitehaven. To which are added, Some Thoughts On Building and Planting, to Sir James Lowther, of Lowther-Hall, Bart*. London, 1755 (4to. 1s. Rivington) BRITISH LIBRARY

Reviewed: *Monthly Review* 11 (1754): 487–489
Gentleman's Magazine 24 (1754): 581

Damon and Phillida
See: DIBDIN, Charles

The Danger of the Passions
See: ERBIGNY, Henri Lambert d', Marquis de Thibouville

Daphne and Amintor
See: BICKERSTAFFE, Isaac

586 *Daphnis and Menalcas: A Pastoral. Sacred to the Memory of the Late General Wolfe. And humbly inscribed to the Right Honourable Wil-*

liam Pitt, Esquire. London, 1759 (4to. 1s. Dodsley) BRITISH LIBRARY

Reviewed: *Monthly Review* 21 (1759): 454–455
Critical Review 8 (1759): 413–414
Gentleman's Magazine 29 (1759): 544
London Magazine 28 (1759): 631

587 DAVIES, John. *The Original, Nature, and Immortality of the Soul, a Poem. With an Introduction concerning Human Knowledge. Written by Sir John Davis, Attorney-General in Ireland to King James the First. The Fourth Edition, Corrected. With An Account of the Author's Life and Writings.* London, 1759 [previous editions 1697, 1714, 1715, 1749] (12mo. 2s.6d.sewed. Browne) BRITISH LIBRARY

Reviewed: *Monthly Review* 21 (1759): 556–559

588 DAVIES, John. *The Poetical Works of Sir John Davies, Consisting of his Poem on the Immortality of the Soul: The Hymns of Astraea; and Orchestra a Poem on Dancing, in A Dialogue between Penelope and one of her Wooers. All published from a corrected Copy, Formerly in the Possession of W. Thompson of Queen's Coll. Oxon.* London, 1773 (12mo. 3s. Davies. 1773) BRITISH LIBRARY

Reviewed: *Monthly Review* 48 (1773): 510
Critical Review 35 (1773): 313–314

589 [DAVYS, Mary]. *The Accomplish'd Rake; or, The Modern fine Gentleman. Being the Genuine Memoirs of a certain Person of Distinction.* London, 1756 (12mo. 3s. Noble) BRITISH LIBRARY

Reviewed: *Monthly Review* 13 (1755): 510

590 [DAWE, Anne]. *The Younger Sister.* 2 vols. London, 1770 (12mo. 5s.sewed. Lowndes) BRITISH LIBRARY

Reviewed: *Monthly Review* 42 (1770): 487–488
Critical Review 30 (1770): 143–146
London Magazine 39 (1770): 531
Town & Country Magazine 2 (1770): 547

591 [DAWES, Richard]. *The Origin of the Newcastle Burr. A Tale, In Hudibrastic Verse.* London, 1767 (8vo. 6d. Nicoll) BODLEIAN

Reviewed: *Monthly Review* 37 (1767): 75
Critical Review 23 (1767): 462

592 [DAY, Thomas, and John BICKNELL]. *The Dying Negro, a Poetical Epistle, supposed to be written by A Black, (Who lately shot himself on board a Vessel in the River Thames;) to his intended Wife.* London, 1773 (4to. 1s. Flexney) BRITISH LIBRARY

Reviewed: *Monthly Review* 49 (1773): 63
Critical Review 36 (1773): 70–71
Gentleman's Magazine 43 (1773): 503–505
Town & Country Magazine 5 (1773): 434
Universal Catalogue [2] (1773) art. 753

A Day: An Epistle to John Wilkes
See: ARMSTRONG, John

A Day in Vacation at College
See: DODD, William

593 *The Day of Doom: a Poem. In two Books.* London, 1754 (4to. 1s. Owen) UNIVERSITY OF ILLINOIS

Reviewed: *Monthly Review* 10 (1754): 511–512
Gentleman's Magazine 24 (1754): 295

594 *The day of judgment; a poem, in two books*
NOT SEEN (1s. Keith)

Reviewed: *Gentleman's Magazine* 24 (1754): 390

The Day of Judgment: a Poetical Essay
See: GLYNN, Robert

595 *Dean Swift for ever: or, Mary the cook-maid to the earl of Orrery*
NOT SEEN (Fol. 1s. Robinson)

Reviewed: *Monthly Review* 7 (1752): 79

596 *The Death of a Friend. A Poem, in blank Verse*
NOT SEEN (4to. 6d. Walter)

Reviewed: *Monthly Review* 33 (1765): 85
Critical Review 19 (1765): 316
Candid Review 1 (1765): 298

The Death of Bucephalus
See: SCHOMBERG, Ralph

597 *A Declaration. By an Old Plebeian.* London, 1762 (4to. 3d. Kent) YALE (BEINECKE)

Reviewed: *Monthly Review* 28 (1763): 72–73
Critical Review 14 (1762): 477

598 [DELAMAYNE, Thomas Hallie]. *The Banished Patriot, or, the Exile Returned. An Heroic Fragment.* London, 1768 (4to. 1s.6d. Williams) BODLEIAN

Reviewed: *Monthly Review* 38 (1768): 406
Critical Review 25 (1768): 390
Universal Museum 4 (1768): 317

599 DELAMAYNE, Thomas Hallie. *The Oliviad. By Thomas Hallie De-la–Mayne, Esq;* London, 1762 (4to. 1s.6d. Scott) UNIVERSITY OF ILLINOIS

Reviewed: *Monthly Review* 28 (1763): 162

600 [DELAMAYNE, Thomas Hallie]. *The Patricians: or, A Candid Examination into the Merits of the Principal Speakers of the House of Lords. By the Author of the Senators.* London, 1773 (4to. 2s.6d. Kearsly. 1774) BRITISH LIBRARY

Reviewed: *Monthly Review* 48 (1773): 160
Critical Review 35 (1773): 159
London Magazine 42 (1773): 92
Town & Country Magazine 5 (1773): 134
Universal Catalogue [2] (1773) art. 243

601 [DELAMAYNE, Thomas Hallie]. *A Review of the Poem entitled "The Patricians:" or, a Re-examination into the Merits of the principal Speakers of the House of Lords. By the Author of a Review of the Poem of "The Senators"* NOT SEEN (4to. 1s.6d. Wilkie. 1773)

Reviewed: *Monthly Review* 49 (1773): 65
Critical Review 35 (1773): 474
Universal Catalogue [2] (1773) art. 633

602 [DELAMAYNE, Thomas Hallie]. *A Review of the Poem, intitled, The Senators; or, A Re-Examination into the Merits of the principal Performers of St. Stephen's Chapel. Part I* NOT SEEN (4to. 1s.6d. Wilkie)

Reviewed: *Monthly Review* 47 (1772): 151
Critical Review 34 (1772): 70
London Magazine 41 (1772): 388
Universal Catalogue [1] (1772) art. 1011

603 [DELAMAYNE, Thomas Hallie]. *A Review of the Poem intitled "The Senators:" or, A Re-Examination into the Merits of the principal Performers of St. Stephen's Chapel. Part II.* London, 1772 (4to. 1s.6d. Wilkie) NEWBERRY

Reviewed: *Monthly Review* 47 (1772): 240
London Magazine 41 (1772): 440

604 [DELAMAYNE, Thomas Hallie]. *The Senators: or, A Candid Examination into the Merits Of The Principal Performers of St. Stephen's Chapel.* London, 1772 (4to. 2s.6d. Kearsly. 1772) BRITISH LIBRARY

Reviewed: *Monthly Review* 46 (1772): 538
Critical Review 33 (1772): 410
Gentleman's Magazine 42 (1772): 284–285
London Magazine 41 (1772): 287
Town & Country Magazine 4 (1772): 266
British Magazine & General Review 1 (1772): 533
Universal Catalogue [1] (1772) art. 737

605 DELAP, [John]. *Elegies.* London, 1760 (4to. 6d. Dodsley) BRITISH LIBRARY

Reviewed: *Monthly Review* 22 (1760): 518–520
Critical Review 9 (1760): 320–321
British Magazine 1 (1760): 140 [324]

606 [DELAP, John]. *Hecuba, a Tragedy. As it is Acted at the Theatre Royal in Drury-Lane.* London, 1762 (8vo. 1s.6d. Dodsley) BRITISH LIBRARY

Reviewed: *Monthly Review* 25 (1761): 506–507
Critical Review 13 (1762): 53–58
British Magazine 3 (1762): 101

607 *The Delicate Embarrassments. A Novel.* 2 vols. London, 1769 (Small 8vo. 6s. Robinson and Roberts) BRITISH LIBRARY

Reviewed: *Monthly Review* 40 (1769): 259
Critical Review 27 (1769): 310
London Magazine 38 (1769): 213
Critical Memoirs 1 (1769): 525

608 [DELL, Henry]. *The Booksellers. A Poem.* London, 1766 (4to. 1s.6d. Dell) CAMBRIDGE

Reviewed: *Monthly Review* 34 (1766): 481
Critical Review 21 (1766): 394
Gentleman's Magazine 36 (1766): 241

609 [DELL, Henry]. *The Frenchified Lady Never in Paris, Taken from Dryden and Colley Cibber, Poets Laureat, Acted at the Theatre-Royal in Covent-Garden, With Universal Applause.* London, 1757 (8vo. 1s. Crowder) BRITISH LIBRARY

Reviewed: *Monthly Review* 16 (1757): 453

610 [DELL, Henry]. *Minorca. A Tragedy. In Three Acts.* London, 1756 (8vo. 1s. Scott) UNIVERSITY OF PENNSYLVANIA

Reviewed: *Monthly Review* 15 (1756): 532–533
Critical Review 2 (1756): 284–285

611 [DELL, Henry]. *The Mirrour. A Comedy. In Three Acts. With the Author's Life, and an account of the Alterations.* [From Thomas Randolph's *The Muses looking-glasse*.] London, 1756 (8vo. 1s.6d. Scott) BRITISH LIBRARY

Reviewed: *Monthly Review* 15 (1756): 681–682
Critical Review 2 (1756): 284–285

612 [DELL, Henry]. *The Spouter, or the Double Revenge. A Comic Farce, In Three Acts. As it was intended to be Acted.* London, 1756 (8vo. 1s. Crowder) BRITISH LIBRARY

Reviewed: *Monthly Review* 14 (1756): 67
Critical Review 1 (1756): 146

The Demi-Rep
See: THOMPSON, Edward

613 DENIS, C[harles], and R[obert] LLOYD (trans.). *The Moral Tales of M. Marmontel. Translated from the French by C. Denis and R. Lloyd.* [From the French original of Jean François MARMONTEL.] 2 vols. London, 1764 (5s. Kearsly) BODLEIAN

Reviewed: *Monthly Review* 30 (1764): 59–61

614 DENIS, Charles. *Select Fables.* London, 1754 (8vo. 6s. Tonson) BRITISH LIBRARY

Reviewed: *Monthly Review* 10 (1754): 305

615 [DENIS, Charles (trans.)]. *The Siege of Calais. A Tragedy. From the French of Mr. De Belloy. With Historical Notes.* [From the French original of Pierre Laurent BUIRETTE DE BELLOY.] London, 1765 (8vo. 1s.6d. Fletcher) BRITISH LIBRARY

Reviewed: *Monthly Review* 33 (1765): 83–84
Critical Review 19 (1765): 479
Candid Review 1 (1765): 307–310

616 DENTON, [Thomas]. *The House of Superstition. A Poem.* London, 1762 (4to. 6d. Hinxman) BRITISH LIBRARY

Reviewed: *Monthly Review* 26 (1762): 458–462
Critical Review 13 (1762): 439
British Magazine 3 (1762): 269

617 [DENTON, Thomas]. *Immortality: or, the Consolation of Human Life. A Monody.* London, 1754 (4to. 1s. Dodsley) BRITISH LIBRARY

Reviewed: *Monthly Review* 12 (1755): 54–57

618 DERRICK, [Samuel]. *The Battle of Lora. A Poem. With some Fragments* NOT SEEN (8vo. 6d. Dodsley)

Reviewed: *Monthly Review* 27 (1762): 157–158
Critical Review 13 (1762): 364

619 [DERRICK, Samuel]. *Fortune, a Rhapsody. Inscribed to Mr. Garrick.* London, 1751 (4to. 24pp. 1s. Manby and Cox) BRITISH LIBRARY

Reviewed: *Monthly Review* 5 (1751): 462–463

620 [DERRICK, Samuel]. *A Poetical Dictionary; or, the Beauties of the English Poets, alphabetically displayed. Containing The Most Celebrated Passages in the following Authors, viz. Shakespear, Johnson, Dryden, Lee, Otway, Beaumont, Fletcher, Lansdowne, Butler, Southerne, Addison, Pope, Gay, Garth, Rowe, Young, Thompson, Mallet, Armstrong, Francis, Warton, Whitehead, Mason, Gray, Akenside, Smart, &c.* 4 vols. London, 1761 (12mo. 12s. Newbery) BRITISH LIBRARY

Reviewed: *Monthly Review* 25 (1761): 231
Critical Review 11 (1761): 163

621 DERRICK, Samuel. *Sylla. A Dramatic Entertainment, Presented at the King's Theatre in Berlin. On the 27th Day of March, 1753. Being the Birth-Day of the Queen-Mother. Translated from the French of the King of Prussia.* London, 1753 (8vo. 1s. Vaillant) BRITISH LIBRARY

Reviewed: *Monthly Review* 9 (1753): 154–155
Gentleman's Magazine 23 (1753): 346

622 DERRICK, Samuel. *The Third Satire of Juvenal, translated into English Verse*
NOT SEEN (4to. 1s. Dodsley)

Reviewed: *Monthly Review* 12 (1755): 229–230

623 DERRICK, Samuel (trans.). *A Voyage to the Moon: with Some Acount of the Solar World. A Comical Romance. Done from the French of M. Cyrano de Bergerac.* London, 1754 (12mo. 1s.6d. Vaillant) BRITISH LIBRARY

Reviewed: *Monthly Review* 9 (1753): 314–315

624 *The Descent of Caesar on Britain. A poetical Essay*
NOT SEEN (4to. 6d. Davey and Law)

Reviewed: *Monthly Review* 21 (1759): 455
London Magazine 28 (1759): 631

A Description of Millenium Hall
See: SCOTT, Sarah

The Desert Island, a Dramatic Poem
See: MURPHY, Arthur

The Deserter; a New Musical Drama
See: DIBDIN, Charles

The Deserter: A Poem
See: JERNINGHAM, Edward

The Deuce is in Him
See: COLMAN, George (the elder)

625 DE VERE, Marquis (pseud.). *The Life and Adventures of the Prince of Salermo: Containing An Account of his Adventures at Venice, and in Hungary; his captivity at Damas, and amour with an Ottoman Princess, together with his return to Italy: with many entertaining descriptions of the Laws, Customs and Manners of the several Countries, through which he travelled. By the Marquis de Vere, a Venetian Nobleman.* London, 1770 (12mo. 2s.6d.sewed. Roson) BRITISH LIBRARY

Reviewed: *Monthly Review* 42 (1770): 251

626 *The Dialogue. Addressed to John Wilkes, Esq.* London, 1770 (4to. 1s.6d. Wilkie. 1770) BRITISH LIBRARY

Reviewed: *Monthly Review* 42 (1770): 145
Critical Review 29 (1770): 147

627 *A Dialogue between Mars and Britannia, on the present Peace. —With Observations and Reflections*
NOT SEEN (4to. 6d. Parker)

Reviewed: *Monthly Review* 29 (1763): 312
Critical Review 16 (1763): 232

628 *A Dialogue in Hudibrastick Verse. Occasioned by the Publication of a Volume of Poems by T----- U-----d*
NOT SEEN (4to. 6d. Hawes)

Reviewed: *Monthly Review* 39 (1768): 80
Critical Review 25 (1768): 392
Universal Museum 4 (1768): 260

629 [DIBDIN, Charles]. *The Cobler: or, A Wife of Ten Thousand. A Ballad Opera. In Two Acts. As it is performed at the Theatre-Royal, Drury-Lane.* London, 1774 (8vo. 1s. Becket. 1774) BRITISH LIBRARY

Reviewed: *Monthly Review* 51 (1774): 485
Critical Review 38 (1774): 480

630 [DIBDIN, Charles]. *Damon and Phillida. Altered from Cibber into a Comic Opera. With the Addition of New Songs and Chorusses. As it is performed at the Theatre Royal in Drury-Lane. The Music entirely new, composed by Mr. Dibdin.* [ESTC: "An adaptation by Charles Dibdin of Colley Cibber's abridgment of his own 'Love in a Riddle.'"] London, 1768 (8vo. 1s. Griffin) BRITISH LIBRARY

Reviewed: *Monthly Review* 39 (1768): 492

631 [DIBDIN, Charles]. *The Deserter; a New Musical Drama, as it is performed at the Theatre-Royal in Drury-Lane.* [From the French original of Michel Jean SEDAINE.] London, 1773 (8vo. 1s. Becket. 1773) BRITISH LIBRARY

Reviewed: *Monthly Review* 49 (1773): 395–396
Critical Review 36 (1773): 396
Universal Catalogue [2] (1773) art. 1205

632 DIBDIN, [Charles]. *The Shepherd's Artifice, a Dramatic Pastoral. As it is perform'd at the Theatre Royal in Covent Garden. The Words written and the Music compos'd by Mr. Dibdin*. London, 1765 (8vo. 1s. Becket) BRITISH LIBRARY

Reviewed: *Monthly Review* 32 (1765): 315
Critical Review 19 (1765): 393–394
Gentleman's Magazine 35 (1765): 234
Candid Review 1 (1765): 279

633 [DIBDIN, Charles]. *The Waterman; or, The First of August: a Ballad Opera, In Two Acts. As it is performed at the Theatre-Royal, Hay-Market*. London, 1774 (8vo. 1s. Becket) BRITISH LIBRARY

Reviewed: *Monthly Review* 51 (1774): 246
Critical Review 38 (1774): 154
Universal Catalogue 3 (1774) art. 1049

634 [DIBDIN, Charles]. *The Wedding Ring, a Comic Opera. In Two Acts. As it is performed at the Theatre Royal in Drury Lane*. London, 1773 (8vo. 1s. Becket. 1773) BRITISH LIBRARY

Reviewed: *Monthly Review* 48 (1773): 153
Critical Review 35 (1773): 160
Universal Catalogue [2] (1773) art. 224

635 *Did you ever see such Damned Stuff? Or, So-Much-The-Better. A Story Without Head or Tail, Wit or Humor*. London, 1760 (12mo. 2s. Seyffert) BRITISH LIBRARY

Reviewed: *Monthly Review* 23 (1760): 84
Critical Review 10 (1760): 157
British Magazine 1 (1760): 434

636 DIDEROT, [Denis]. *Dorval; or, the Test of Virtue. A Comedy. Translated from the French of Monsieur Diderot.* [Translation of *Le fils naturel*.] London, 1767 (8vo. 1s.6d. Dodsley) BRITISH LIBRARY

Reviewed: *Monthly Review* 36 (1767): 410
Critical Review 23 (1767): 463
London Magazine 36 (1767): 206

637 DIDEROT, [Denis]. *The Father, a Comedy. Translated from the French of Monsieur Diderot, By the Translator of Dorval, &c. (Amsterdam Edition, 1758)*. Lynn, 1770 (4to. 3s. Baldwin. 1770) LIBRARY OF CONGRESS

Reviewed: *Monthly Review* 44 (1771): 175
Critical Review 31 (1771): 71
Gentleman's Magazine 41 (1771): 86
Town & Country Magazine 3 (1771): 44

Dido, a Comic Opera
See: BRIDGES, Thomas

638 [DIGARD DE KERGUETTE, Jean]. *True Merit, true Happiness; Exemplified in the Entertaining and Instructive Memoirs of Mr. S———.* [Translation of *Memoires et aventures d'un bourgeois*.] 2 vols. London, n.d. [ESTC-1757?] (12mo. 6s. Noble) BRITISH LIBRARY

Reviewed: *Monthly Review* 16 (1757): 453
Critical Review 3 (1757): 467–469

639 DINE, William. *Poems on Several Occasions*. Lewes, 1771 (8vo. 1s. Robinson and Roberts. 1771) BODLEIAN

Reviewed: *Monthly Review* 45 (1771): 511
Critical Review 32 (1771): 469–470

Discord: a Satire
See: HURD, Richard

The Discovery. A Comedy
See: SHERIDAN, Frances

640 *The Discovery. An ode to mr. P****m*. London, 1752 (4to. 6d. Vaillant) BRITISH LIBRARY

Reviewed: *Monthly Review* 6 (1752): 317

641 *The Disguise, A Dramatic Novel*. 2 vols. London, 1771 (12mo. 5s.sewed. Dodsley. 1771) BRITISH LIBRARY

Reviewed: *Monthly Review* 44 (1771): 334
Critical Review 31 (1771): 315
Town & Country Magazine 3 (1771): 261

642 *The Disinterested Marriage: or, the History of Mr. Frankland.* 2 vols. London, 1774 (12mo. 6s. Noble) BODLEIAN

Reviewed: *Monthly Review* 49 (1773): 409–410
Critical Review 36 (1773): 398
Universal Catalogue [2] (1773) art. 1129

643 *The Distressed Lovers: or, the History of Edward and Eliza. In a Series of Letters.* 2 vols. London, 1768 (12mo. 5s. Robinson and Roberts) BRITISH LIBRARY

Reviewed: *Critical Review* 25 (1768): 54–57
Universal Museum 4 (1768): 36

644 *The Distrest Wife, or the History of Eliza Wyndham; related In a Journey from Salisbury. In Two Volumes.* London, 1768 (8vo. 5s. Wilkie) HARVARD (HOUGHTON)

Reviewed: *Monthly Review* 39 (1768): 83
Critical Review 25 (1768): 294–295
London Magazine 37 (1768): 163
Universal Museum 4 (1768): 204

The Divorce. A Musical Entertainment
See: DUBOIS, Lady Dorothea

645 *The Divorce. In a Series of Letters to and from Persons of high rank.* 2 vols.
NOT SEEN (12mo. 5s.sewed. Baldwin)

Reviewed: *Monthly Review* 44 (1771): 497–498
Critical Review 31 (1771): 315

646 *D---n Sw----t's Medley. Containing, I. His Scheme for making Religion and the Clergy useful; with his Observations on the Cause and Cure of the Piles, and some useful Directions about wiping the Posteriors. II. Reasons against Coition, a Discourse delivered to a private Congregation, on the following Text. I Cor.vii.I,27. It were good for a man not to touch a woman—Art thou loosed from a wife; seek not a wife. Ex infinito ne causam causa sequatur. Lucret. Vera redit facies, dissimulata perit. Pet. Arb. III. The Natural History of the Arbor Vitae, of the Tree of Life. Nec minus Arboribus succi genitabilis humor Sufficitur. Buchan. Psal. civ. Together With several other curious and entertaining Things, not mentioned in the Title.* Dublin printed, London reprinted; n.d. [ESTC-1749?] (12mo. 1s. No publisher) BRITISH LIBRARY

Reviewed: *Monthly Review* 2 (1749–50): 88–89

647 [DOBBS, Francis]. *Modern Matrimony. A Poem. To which is added, The Disappointment. An Elegy. By the Author of the Irish Chief: or, The Patriot King.* Dublin, 1773 (23pp. 1s.6d. Griffin) BRITISH LIBRARY

Reviewed: *Universal Catalogue* [2] (1773) art. 92

648 DOBBS, Francis. *The Patriot King; or, Irish Chief. A Tragedy. Performed at the Theatre in Smock-Alley, Dublin.* London, 1774 (8vo. 1s.6d. Bew. 1774) BRITISH LIBRARY

Reviewed: *Monthly Review* 51 (1774): 484

649 DOBSON, William. *Anti-Lucretius of God and nature, a Poem, Written in Latin By the Cardinal De Polignac: Rendered into English By the Translator of Paradise Lost.* London, 1757 (4to. 1s.6d. Manley) BRITISH LIBRARY

Reviewed: *Monthly Review* 17 (1757): 44–47
Critical Review 4 (1757): 90

650 DOBSON, William. *The Prussian Campaign. A Poem: Celebrating The Atchievements of Frederick the Great, In the Years 1756–57.* London, n.d. [ESTC-1760?] (4to. 1s. Manby) BRITISH LIBRARY

Reviewed: *Monthly Review* 18 (1758): 624
Critical Review 6 (1758): 81–83

DOBSON, William. *The Prussian Campaign.* See also: JONES, Henry. *The Patriot Enterprize*

The Doctor Dissected
See: IRELAND, Stella

Doctor Last in his Chariot
See: BICKERSTAFFE, Isaac

651 [DODD, William]. *The African Prince, When in England, to Zara, at his Father's Court.*
NOT SEEN (4to. 15pp. 6d. Printed for Payne and Bouquet)

Reviewed: *Monthly Review* 1 (1749): 240

652 [DODD, William]. *A Day in Vacation at College. A Burlesque Poem*. London, 1751 (4to. 1s. Owen) BRITISH LIBRARY

Reviewed: *Monthly Review* 5 (1751): 160
Gentleman's Magazine 21 (1751): 335

653 [DODD, William]. *An Epistle to a Lady, Concerning some important and necessary Truths in Religion*. London, 1753 (4to. 1s. Dodsley, &c.) BRITISH LIBRARY

Reviewed: *Monthly Review* 9 (1753): 478

654 [DODD, William]. *A New Book of the Dunciad: Occasion'd By Mr. Warburton's New Edition of The Dunciad Complete. By a Gentleman of one of the Inns of Court. With several of Mr Warburton's own Notes, and likewise Notes Variorum*. London, 1750 (1s. Payne and Bouquet) BRITISH LIBRARY

Reviewed: *Monthly Review* 3 (1750): 369–375

655 DODD, [William]. *Poems*. London, 1767 (8vo. 5s. Printed for the Author) BRITISH LIBRARY

Reviewed: *Monthly Review* 37 (1767): 395
Critical Review 24 (1767): 198–203
Gentleman's Magazine 37 (1767): 553
Universal Museum 3 (1767): 484
Political Register 1 (1767): 388–389

656 [DODD, William]. *The Sisters; or the History of Lucy and Caroline Sanson, Entrusted to a false Friend*. 2 vols. London, 1754 (12mo. 6s. Walker) BRITISH LIBRARY

Reviewed: *Monthly Review* 10 (1754): 308

657 DODD, William. *Thoughts on the Glorious Epiphany of the Lord Jesus Christ. A Poetical Essay written At Southampton in the year MDCCLVII. Sacred to Friendship*. London, 1758 (8vo. 1s.6d. Dilly) BRITISH LIBRARY

Reviewed: *Monthly Review* 18 (1758): 185

658 DODSLEY, R[obert]. *Cleone. A Tragedy. As it is Acted at the Theatre Royal in Covent-Garden*. London, 1758 (8vo. 1s.6d. Dodsley) BRITISH LIBRARY

Reviewed: *Monthly Review* 19 (1758): 582–583
Critical Review 6 (1758): 463–475

659 [DODSLEY, Robert (ed.)]. *A Collection of Poems In Four Volumes. By Several Hands. Vol. IV*. London, 1755 (12mo. 3s. Dodsley) BRITISH LIBRARY

Reviewed: *Monthly Review* 12 (1755): 382

660 [DODSLEY, Robert (ed.)]. *A Collection of Poems in Six Volumes. By Several Hands. Vols. V and VI*. London, 1758 (12mo. 6s. Dodsley) BRITISH LIBRARY

Reviewed: *Monthly Review* 18 (1758): 533–538

661 [DODSLEY, Robert (ed.)]. *Fugitive Pieces, on Various Subjects. By Several Authors*. 2 vols. London, 1761 (8vo. 6s. Dodsley) BRITISH LIBRARY

Reviewed: *Monthly Review* 26 (1762): 77
Critical Review 12 (1761): 398–399

662 [DODSLEY, Robert]. *Melpomene: or The Regions of Terror and Pity. An Ode*. London, 1757 (4to. 6d. Cooper) BRITISH LIBRARY

Reviewed: *Monthly Review* 17 (1757): 377–378
Critical Review 4 (1757): 465–467

663 DODSLEY, R[obert]. *Miscellanies. By the late R. Dodsley*. [Vol. 2 of *Trifles*, published in 1745; British Library copy has only half-title.] n.p., n.d. (8vo. 5s.bound. Dodsley. 1772) BRITISH LIBRARY

Reviewed: *Monthly Review* 47 (1772): 489
Critical Review 35 (1773): 70
Universal Catalogue [1] (1772) art. 1382

664 DODSLEY, R[obert]. *Public Virtue, A Poem. In three Books. I. Agriculture. II. Commerce. III. Arts*. London, 1753 (4to. 2s.6d.sewed. Dodsley) BRITISH LIBRARY

Reviewed: *Monthly Review* 10 (1754): 30–36
Gentleman's Magazine 23 (1753): 543

665 *Don Coblero: or, The Mock Baron. A Burlesque Poem*. London, 1763 (8vo. 1s. Hinxman) BRITISH LIBRARY

Reviewed: *Monthly Review* 29 (1763): 311
Critical Review 15 (1763): 324

666 [DONALDSON, William]. *The Life and Adventures of Sir Bartholomew Sapskull, Baronet. Nearly allied to most of the Great Men in the three Kingdoms. By Somebody.* 2 vols. London, 1768 (12mo. 6s. Williams) BRITISH LIBRARY

Reviewed: *Monthly Review* 39 (1768): 83
Critical Review 26 (1768): 312

667 DONALDSON, William. *North America, a Descriptive Poem. Representing The Voyage to America, a Sketch of that Beautiful Country; with Remarks upon the Political Humour and singular Conduct of its Inhabitants. To which are subjoined, Notes, Critical and Explanatory.* London, 1757 (8vo. 1s. Shepheard) BRITISH LIBRARY

Reviewed: *Monthly Review* 16 (1757): 460–461

668 [DORAT, Claude Joseph]. *The Fatal effects of Inconstancy; or, Letters of the Marchioness de Syrcé, The Count de Mirbelle, and others. Translated from the French.* [Name "Mirbelle" is misspelled "Mirbeele" on title page to vol. 1.] 2 vols. London, 1774 (12mo. 5s.sewed. Bew. 1774) BRITISH LIBRARY

Reviewed: *Monthly Review* 51 (1774): 238
Critical Review 38 (1774): 393
Universal Catalogue 3 (1774) art. 1161

669 [DOSSIE, Robert]. *The Statesman Foil'd. A Musical Comedy of Two Acts. Performed at the Theatre Royal in the Hay-Market. The Musick composed by Mr. Rush.* London, 1768 (8vo. 1s. Becket) BRITISH LIBRARY

Reviewed: *Monthly Review* 39 (1768): 163
Universal Museum 4 (1768): 372
Political Register 3 (1768): 126

670 *The Double Disappointment; or, the History of Charles Marlow. In a Series of Letters. In Two Volumes.* London, 1774 (12mo. 439pp. 6s.bound. Hookman) UNIVERSITY OF PENNSYLVANIA [University of Pennsylvania has vol. 1 only.]

Reviewed: *Universal Catalogue* 3 (1774) art. 518

671 *The Double Intrigue; or, the Adventures of Ismael and Selima. A Novel.* London, n.d. [BLC–c. 1755] (8vo. 1s. Corbet) BRITISH LIBRARY

Reviewed: *Monthly Review* 5 (1751): 75

The Double Mistake
See: GRIFFITH, Elizabeth

Douglas: a Tragedy
See: HOME, John

672 [DOW, Alexander]. *Sethona; a Tragedy. As it is performed at the Theatre-Royal in Drury-Lane.* London, 1774 (8vo. 1s. Becket. 1774) BRITISH LIBRARY

Reviewed: *Monthly Review* 50 (1774): 202–205
Critical Review 37 (1774): 209–212
Universal Catalogue 3 (1774) art. 326

673 [DOW, Alexander]. *Tales, Translated from the Persian of Inatulla of Delhi.* 2 vols. London, 1768 (12mo. 6s. Becket. 1768) BRITISH LIBRARY [British Library has vol. 1 only.]

Reviewed: *Monthly Review* 40 (1769): 221–232
Critical Review 27 (1769): 136–140
Gentleman's Magazine 39 (1769): 158
London Magazine 38 (1769): 103–104
Critical Memoirs [1] (1769): 142–149
Town & Country Magazine [1] (1769): 101
Political Register 4 (1769): 392

674 DOW, Alexander. *Zingis. A Tragedy. As it is performed at the Theatre-Royal in Drury-Lane.* London, 1769 (8vo. 1s.6d. Becket and Co.) BRITISH LIBRARY

Reviewed: *Monthly Review* 40 (1769): 50–54
Critical Review 27 (1769): 80
Gentleman's Magazine 39 (1769): 40–44
London Magazine 38 (1769): 42

675 *The Downfal of the Association. A Comic Tragedy. In Five Acts.* Winchester, 1771 (8vo. 1s.6d. Winchester, printed for the Author; and sold by Crowder, &c. in London. 1771) BRITISH LIBRARY

Reviewed: *Monthly Review* 45 (1771): 152
Critical Review 31 (1771): 475
Gentleman's Magazine 41 (1771): 325

676 DOWNING, G[eorge]. *The Parthian Exile, a Tragedy. As performed several Times at Coventry and Worcester. By G. Downing, Comedian.* Coventry, 1774 (8vo. 1s.6d. Robinson. 1774) NEW YORK PUBLIC LIBRARY

Reviewed: *Monthly Review* 51 (1774): 245–246
Critical Review 37 (1774): 396

677 [DOWNMAN, Hugh]. *An Elegy Wrote under a Gallows. With a Preface concerning the Nature of Elegy.* London, n.d. [ESTC-1770?] (4to. 6d. Richardson and Urquhart) BRITISH LIBRARY

Reviewed: *Monthly Review* 39 (1768): 163–165
Critical Review 25 (1768): 465
Universal Museum 4 (1768): 317

678 DOWNMAN, Hugh. *Infancy. A Poem. Book the First.* London, 1774 (1s. Kearsly. 1774) BRITISH LIBRARY

Reviewed: *Monthly Review* 50 (1774): 482–483
Critical Review 38 (1774): 71
London Magazine 43 (1774): 450
Town & Country Magazine 6 (1774): 437
Universal Catalogue 3 (1774) art. 616

679 DOWNMAN, Hugh. *The Land of the Muses: a Poem in the Manner of Spenser. With Poems on several Occasions.* Edinburgh, 1768 (4to. 2s.6d. Baldwin) BRITISH LIBRARY

Reviewed: *Monthly Review* 39 (1768): 242
Critical Review 26 (1768): 191–198
Universal Museum 4 (1768): 484

680 [DOWNMAN, Hugh]. *The Soliloquy, a Poem, Occasioned by a late Decision.* Edinburgh, n.d. [ESTC-1770?] (4to. 6d. Richardson and Urquhart) BRITISH LIBRARY

Reviewed: *Monthly Review* 38 (1768): 498
Critical Review 25 (1768): 465
Universal Museum 4 (1768): 317

The Dramatic History of Master Edward, Miss Ann . . .
See: STEVENS, George Alexander

681 DRAPER, Charles. *Fables Translated from Aesop, and Other Authors. To which are subjoined, A Moral in Verse, And an Application in Prose, Adapted to each Fable. Embellished with Cuts from the best Designs.* London, 1760 (12mo. 3s. Bristow) BRITISH LIBRARY

Reviewed: *Monthly Review* 23 (1760): 162–163
Critical Review 10 (1760): 240

682 DRAPER, W. H.. *The Morning Walk; or, City Encompass'd. A Poem in Blank Verse. With a Prologue and Appendix, from the best Poets on similar Subjects. Dedicated to the Right Honourable the Earl of Bath.* London, 1751 (8vo. 1s.6d. Cooper) BRITISH LIBRARY

Reviewed: *Monthly Review* 5 (1751): 77

683 DRAYTON, Michael. *The History of Queen Mab; or, the Court of Fairy. Being The Story upon which the Entertainment of Queen Mab, now exhibiting at Drury-lane, is founded.* London, 1751 (8vo. 6d. Cooper) BRITISH LIBRARY

Listed: *Monthly Review* 4 (1750–51): 303

684 DRAYTON, Michael. *The Works of Michael Drayton, Esq; A Celebrated Poet in the Reigns of Queen Elizabeth, King James I, and Charles I. Containing, I. The Battle of Agincourt. II. The Baron's Wars. III. England's Heroical Epistles. IV. The Miseries of Queen Margaret, the Unfortunate Wife of the most Unfortunate King Henry VI. V. Nymphydia: the Court of Fairy. VI. The Moon Calf. VII. The Legends of Robert Duke of Normandy, Matilda the Fair, Pierce Gaveston, and Tho. Cromwell Earl of Essex. VIII. The Quest of Cynthia. IX. The Shepherd's Sirena. X. Poly-Olbion, with the Annotations of the learned Selden. XI. Elegies on several Occasions. XII. Ideas. XIII. The Owl. XIV. The Man in the Moon. XV. Odes and other Lyrick Poesies. XVI. Pastorals. XVII. The Muses Elysium. XVIII. Noah's flood. XIX. Moses his Birth and Miracles. XX. David and Goliah.* 4 vols. London, 1753 (8vo. 1l. Reeve) BRITISH LIBRARY

Reviewed: *Monthly Review* 9 (1753): 187

685 *The Dream; or, England invaded. A Poem. By a young gentleman of sixteen*
NOT SEEN (4to. 6d. Lever)

Reviewed: *Monthly Review* 14 (1756): 366

686 *Dress. A Satire. Inscrib'd To the Ladies, On some recent Irregularities. To which is added, Philander and Aspasia.* London, 1754 (8vo. 6d. Reeve) BRITISH LIBRARY

Reviewed: *Monthly Review* 10 (1754): 510
Gentleman's Magazine 24 (1754): 294

687 *The Drivers: a Dialogue.* Cambridge, 1770 (4to. 1s. Cambridge printed, and sold by Dodsley &c. in London) BRITISH LIBRARY

Reviewed: *Monthly Review* 42 (1770): 75–76
Critical Review 28 (1769): 460
Gentleman's Magazine 39 (1769): 600
London Magazine 38 (1769): 641

The Druid's Monument
See: TAIT, John

688 DRUMMOND, Thomas. *Poems sacred to Religion and Virtue.* London, 1756 (8vo. 2s.6d. Wilson and Durham) BRITISH LIBRARY

Reviewed: *Monthly Review* 15 (1756): 128–135

689 *The Drunken News-Writer: a Comic Interlude. As it is performed at the Theatre-Royal in the Haymarket. With a new Song, Set to Music, and Sung in Character.* London, 1771 (8vo. 6d. Smith, in Greek-street) BRITISH LIBRARY

Reviewed: *Monthly Review* 44 (1771): 261
Critical Review 31 (1771): 231
Gentleman's Magazine 41 (1771): 238

DRYDEN, John (adaptation)
See: GARRICK, David. *King Arthur*

690 DRYDEN, John. *The Miscellaneous Works of John Dryden, Esq; containing all his Original Poems, Tales, and Translations. Now first Collected and Published together In Four Volumes With Explanatory Notes and Observations. Also an Account of His Life and Writings.* [Ed. Samuel Derrick.] 4 vols. London, 1760 (8vo. 1l.4s. Tonson) BRITISH LIBRARY

Reviewed: *Monthly Review* 23 (1760): 239

691 [DUBOIS, Lady Dorothea]. *The Divorce. A Musical Entertainment. As sung at Marybone Gardens. The Music composed by Mr. Hook.* London, 1771 (4to. 14pp. 1s. Wheble) LIBRARY OF CONGRESS

Reviewed: *Universal Catalogue* [1] (1772) art. 1097
British Magazine & General Review 2 (1772): 260

692 DUBOIS, Lady Dorothea. *Theodora, a Novel.* 2 vols. London, 1770 (12mo. 6s. Printed for the Author, and sold by Nicoll, &c.) BRITISH LIBRARY

Reviewed: *Monthly Review* 43 (1770): 65–66
Critical Review 29 (1770): 474
Gentleman's Magazine 40 (1770): 625
London Magazine 39 (1770): 378
Town & Country Magazine 2 (1770): 378

693 DUCK, [Stephen]. *Caesar's Camp: or, St. George's Hill. A Poem.* London, 1755 (4to. 1s. Dodsley) BRITISH LIBRARY

Reviewed: *Monthly Review* 12 (1755): 158–159

694 [DUDLEY, Sir Henry Bate]. *Henry and Emma, a new poetical Interlude, altered from Prior's Nut Brown Maid, with additions and a new Air and Chorus, (the Music by Dr. Arne.) As Performed on Wednesday, April 13, 1774, at the Theatre-Royal in Covent-Garden for the Benefit of Mrs. Hartley.* London, 1774 (8vo. 6d. Davies) BRITISH LIBRARY

Reviewed: *Monthly Review* 50 (1774): 409
Critical Review 37 (1774): 474
Universal Catalogue 3 (1774) art. 500

The Duel. A Play
See: O'BRIEN, William

695 [DUFF, William]. *The History of Rhedi, The Hermit of Mount Ararat. An Oriental Tale.* London, 1773 (12mo. 3s. Cadell. 1773) BRITISH LIBRARY

Reviewed: *Monthly Review* 49 (1773): 410
Critical Review 36 (1773): 283–286
London Magazine 42 (1773): 351
Universal Catalogue [2] (1773) art. 939

696 *Dumont, or The Hermitage. A British Story*
NOT SEEN

Reviewed: *London Magazine* 42 (1773): 149

697 [DUNCAN, John]. *An Essay on Happiness. In Four Books*. London, 1762 (4to. 2s.6d. Dodsley) BRITISH LIBRARY

Reviewed: *Monthly Review* 27 (1762): 228
Critical Review 14 (1762): 156–157

698 DUNCAN, John. *An Essay on Happiness, In Four Books. The Second Edition, Revised and much Enlarged*. London, 1772 (8vo. 5s.bound. Cadell. 1773) BRITISH LIBRARY

Reviewed: *Monthly Review* 48 (1773): 439–443
Critical Review 35 (1773): 400
Universal Catalogue [2] (1773) art. 131

699 [DUNCOMBE, John]. *An Evening Contemplation in a College. Being a Parody on the Elegy in A Country Church-Yard. By another Gentleman of Cambridge*. London, 1753 (4to. 6d. Dodsley) BRITISH LIBRARY

Reviewed: *Monthly Review* 9 (1753): 478–479
Gentleman's Magazine 23 (1753): 592

700 DUNCOMBE, John. *The Feminiad. A Poem. By John Duncombe, M.A. Fellow of Corpus Christi College, Cambridge*. London, 1754 (4to. 1s. Cooper) BRITISH LIBRARY

Reviewed: *Monthly Review* 10 (1754): 371–374
Gentleman's Magazine 24 (1754): 146

701 [DUNCOMBE, John]. *Horace, Book II. Satire VII. Imitated: or, a Dialogue between A Man of Fashion and His Valet. Inscribed to Richard Owen Cambridge, Esq; By Sir Nicholas Nemo, Knt*. London, 1752 (4to. 6d. Bathurst) BRITISH LIBRARY

Reviewed: *Monthly Review* 6 (1752): 311–312

702 DUNCOMBE, John. *Poems. I. The Prophecy of Neptune. II. On the Death of the Prince of Wales. III. Ode presented to the Duke of Newcastle at Cambridge. IV. Ode to the Hon. J. Y.* London, 1756 (4to. 1s. Dodsley) BRITISH LIBRARY

Reviewed: *Monthly Review* 14 (1756): 61–63
Critical Review 1 (1756): 262–263

703 [DUNCOMBE, John]. *Surry Triumphant: or the Kentish-Mens Defeat. A New Ballad; being A Parody on Chevy-Chace*. London, 1773 (4to. 1s. Johnson, 1773) BRITISH LIBRARY

Reviewed: *Monthly Review* 49 (1773): 231
Critical Review 36 (1773): 235
Gentleman's Magazine 43 (1773): 450–452
London Magazine 42 (1773): 509
Universal Catalogue [2] (1773) art. 1034

704 DUNCOMBE, [William] (ed.). *The Works of Horace In English Verse. By Several Hands. Collected and Published by Mr. Duncombe. With Notes Historical and Critical. Volume the First*. London, 1757 (8vo. 5s. Dodsley) BRITISH LIBRARY

Reviewed: *Monthly Review* 18 (1758): 45–52

705 DUNCOMBE, William and J[ohn], and others. *The Works of Horace. In English Verse. By Several Hands. Illustrated with Notes Historical and Critical. Volume the Second and Last*. 2 vols. London, 1759 (8vo. 5s. Dodsley) BRITISH LIBRARY

Reviewed: *Monthly Review* 21 (1759): 197–201
Gentleman's Magazine 29 (1759): 287

706 DUNCOMBE, W[illiam] and J[ohn] (eds.). *The Works of Horace, In English Verse, by Mr. Duncombe, Sen. J. Duncombe, M.A, and Other Hands. With Notes Historical and Critical. The Second Edition. To which are added, Many Imitations, now first published*. 4 vols. London, 1767 (12mo. 12s. White) BRITISH LIBRARY

Reviewed: *Monthly Review* 37 (1767): 1–8
Critical Review 24 (1767): 266–275
Political Register 1 (1767): 484

707 DUNKIN, [William]. *The Bramin: an Eclogue. To Edmund Nugent, Esq;* London, 1751 (4to. 6d. Baldwin) BRITISH LIBRARY

Reviewed: *Monthly Review* 4 (1750–51): 480

708 DUNKIN, William. *An Epistle To the Right Honourable Philip Earl of Chesterfield. To which is added, an Eclogue. By William Dunkin, D.D*. Dublin printed, London reprinted; 1760 (8vo. 1s. Griffiths) FOLGER

Reviewed: *Monthly Review* 22 (1760): 175–176
Critical Review 9 (1760): 232–235

709 DUNKIN, William. *The Poetical Works of the late William Dunkin, D.D. To which are added, His Epistles, etc. To The Late Earl of Chesterfield.* 2 vols. London, 1774 (4to. 1l.1s. Nicol, &c. 1774) BRITISH LIBRARY

Reviewed: *Monthly Review* 50 (1774): 355–359
Critical Review 37 (1774): 106–112
London Magazine 43 (1774): 240

The Dupe, a Comedy
See: SHERIDAN, Frances

710 *Du Plessis's Memoirs: Or, Variety of Adventures. Interspersed with Characters and Reflections moral, satirical, instructive and humorous.* 2 vols. London ed. reviewed; copy seen: Dublin, 1757 (12mo. 6s. Reeve) BRITISH LIBRARY

Reviewed: *Monthly Review* 16 (1757): 179
Critical Review 3 (1757): 113–118

D'URFEY, Young (pseud.)
See: FORREST, Frederick

711 DYER, John. *The Fleece: a Poem. In Four Books.* London, 1757 (4to. 5s. Dodsley) BRITISH LIBRARY

Reviewed: *Monthly Review* 16 (1757): 328–340
Critical Review 3 (1757): 402–415
Literary Magazine 2 (1757): 134–136

712 DYER, R. *The Carnation; To the Honourable Miss Grace Pelham. A Poem upon Her Marriage to the Honourable Lewis Watson, Esq;* London, 1753 (4to. 1s. Dodsley) BRITISH LIBRARY

Reviewed: *Monthly Review* 8 (1753): 392
Gentleman's Magazine 23 (1753): 150

The Dying Negro, a Poetical Epistle
See: DAY, Thomas, and John BICKNELL

713 *Each Sex in their Humour: Or, the Histories of the Families of Brightley, Finch, Fortescue, Shelburne, and Stevens. Written by a Lady of Quality, Whilst she was abroad on her Travels, and found among her Papers, since her Decease.* 2 vols. London, 1764 (12mo. 6s. Noble) BRITISH LIBRARY

Reviewed: *Monthly Review* 30 (1764): 75
Critical Review 16 (1763): 449–452

The Earl of Douglas: a Dramatick Essay
See: WILSON, John

The Earl of Warwick, a Tragedy (1766)
See: FRANCKLIN, Thomas

The Earl of Warwick; or, the King and Subject (1764)
See: HIFFERNAN, Paul

714 *The East India Culprits. A Poem. In Imitation of Swift's "Legion Club." (By an Officer, who was present at the Battle of Plassey.).* London, 1773 (4to. 1s.6d. Kearsly. 1773) BRITISH LIBRARY

Reviewed: *Monthly Review* 48 (1773): 413
Critical Review 35 (1773): 474
Town & Country Magazine 5 (1773): 378
Universal Catalogue [2] (1773) art. 606

Edgar and Emmeline
See: HAWKESWORTH, John

715 [EDGCUMBE, Richard]. *An Epistle from the Hon. R--- E---- to his Dear Nanny. To which is Added, A Satire on L--d O-----y's Remarks on the Life and Writings of Dean S--ft.* London, 1752 (Fol. 6d. Sold by R. Lion; a fictitious name) BRITISH LIBRARY

Reviewed: *Monthly Review* 7 (1752): 319

716 *Edward. A Novel. Dedicated (by Permission) to Her Majesty.* 2 vols. London, 1774 (12mo. 6s. Davies. 1774) BRITISH LIBRARY

Reviewed: *Monthly Review* 51 (1774): 72
Critical Review 37 (1774): 475
London Magazine 43 (1774): 448–449
Universal Catalogue 3 (1774) art. 884

Edwin and Emma
See: MALLET, David

The Effusions of Friendship and Fancy
See: LANGHORNE, John

717 *The Egg, Or the Memoirs of Gregory Giddy, Esq; With the Lucubrations of Messrs. Francis*

Flimsy, Frederick Florid, and Ben Bombast. To which are added, The Private Opinions of Patty Pout, Lucy Luscious, and Priscilla Positive. Also the Memoirs of a Right Honourable Puppy. Or, the Bon Ton display'd: Together with Anecdotes of a Right Honourable Scoundrel. Conceived By a Celebrated Hen, and laid before the Public by a Famous Cock-Feeder. London, n.d. [ESTC-1772?] (12mo. 3s. Smith) BRITISH LIBRARY

Reviewed: *Monthly Review* 47 (1772): 411
Critical Review 34 (1772): 472
London Magazine 41 (1772): 491
British Magazine & General Review 2 (1772): 556
Universal Catalogue [2] (1772) art. 1278

Eidyllia: or Miscellaneous Poems
See: COLVILL, Robert

The Eighteenth Epistle Of the First Book of Horace
See: NEVILE, Thomas

718 EKINS, J[effery]. *The Loves of Medea and Jason. A Poem, in Three Books: Translated from the Greek of Apollonius Rhodius's Argonautics.* London, 1771 (4to. 3s.6d. Payne. 1774) BRITISH LIBRARY

Reviewed: *Monthly Review* 44 (1771): 344
Critical Review 31 (1771): 165–183
Gentleman's Magazine 41 (1771): 225–227
London Magazine 40 (1771): 370

719 EKINS, J[effery]. *Medea and Jason. A Poem, in Three Books: Translated From The Greek of Apollonius Rhodius's Argonautics, By J. Ekins, M.A. The Second Edition, Corrected.* London, 1772 (12mo. 2s. Payne) BRITISH LIBRARY

Reviewed: *Critical Review* 33 (1772): 489–490

720 *E--l of Ch-----m's Apology, a Poem.* London, 1766 (4to. 1s. Almon) BRITISH LIBRARY

Reviewed: *Monthly Review* 35 (1766): 407
Critical Review 22 (1766): 382–383

721 *An Elegiac Epistle from John Halser, who was impressed on his Return from the East Indies, to Susanna, his Wife. Printed for the Benefit of the Author, now confined on board a Tender. Inscribed to Lieutenant Ayscough*
NOT SEEN (4to. 6d. Wilkie)

Reviewed: *Monthly Review* 44 (1771): 174
Critical Review 31 (1771): 73
London Magazine 40 (1771): 49

722 *An Elegiac Epistle, from Lucy Cooper in the Shades, to The Ravish'd Pomona, Sally Harris.* London, 1774 (4to. 1s. Williams) FOLGER

Reviewed: *Monthly Review* 50 (1774): 232
Critical Review 37 (1774): 236
Universal Catalogue 3 (1774) art. 361

723 *An Elegiac Epistle to his most sacred Majesty King George III*
NOT SEEN (Fol. 1s. Wilkie)

Reviewed: *Monthly Review* 23 (1760): 527

724 *An Elegiac Poem, occasioned by the much lamented Death of the Rev. Mr. Phocion Henley, late Rector of the united Parishes of St.Andrew by the Wardrobe, and St. Anne, Black Friars; and Lecturer of St. Gregory and St. Mary Magdalen, Old Fish-street*
NOT SEEN (4to. 6d. Hood)

Reviewed: *Monthly Review* 31 (1764): 232
Critical Review 18 (1764): 239

725 *An Elegiac Poem on the Death of the Rev. Mr. George Whitefield*
NOT SEEN (4to. 6d. Wills)

Reviewed: *Monthly Review* 44 (1771): 90–91
Critical Review 31 (1771): 76

726 *An Elegiac Poem on the Death of William Beckford, Esq; late Lord-Mayor of the City of London*
NOT SEEN (8vo. 6d. Swan)

Reviewed: *Monthly Review* 43 (1770): 154
Critical Review 30 (1770): 73–74
London Magazine 39 (1770): 426

Elegies I. Morning II. Noon . . .
See: PANTING, Stephen

Elegies on Different Occasions
See: PYE, Henry James

727 *An Elegy on a Drum-head* [*Critical Review* title: *An essay written on a drum-head*]
NOT SEEN (Fol. 6d. Cooke and Coote)

Reviewed: *Monthly Review* 18 (1758): 491
Critical Review 5 (1758): 267

728 *An Elegy on a most excellent Man, and much lamented Friend*
NOT SEEN (Fol. 1s. Walter)

Reviewed: *Monthly Review* 42 (1770): 143
Critical Review 29 (1770): 74

729 *An Elegy on the Approaching Dissolution of Parliament.* London, 1774 (4to. 1s. Almon) NEW YORK PUBLIC LIBRARY

Reviewed: *Monthly Review* 51 (1774): 166
Critical Review 37 (1774): 472
London Magazine 43 (1774): 244
Universal Catalogue 3 (1774) art. 637

730 *An Elegy On the Death of Mr. Bennet and Miss Worsfold.* Oxford, 1769 (4to. 1s. Fletcher) BRITISH LIBRARY

Reviewed: *Monthly Review* 40 (1769): 156–157
Critical Review 27 (1769): 70–71
Critical Memoirs 1 (1769): 162–163 and 523
Town & Country Magazine [1] (1769): 45

731 *An Elegy on the Death of the Guardian Outwitted, An Opera; Written and Composed by Thomas Augustine Arne.* London, 1765 (4to. 1s. Nicoll) BRITISH LIBRARY

Reviewed: *Monthly Review* 32 (1765): 45–47
Critical Review 19 (1765): 155
Candid Review 1 (1765): 37

732 *An Elegy on the Death of the late Rev. Mr. Charles Churchill*
NOT SEEN (4to. 1s. Field)

Reviewed: *Monthly Review* 32 (1765): 76
Critical Review 19 (1765): 72

733 *An Elegy on the Death Of the Late very Celebrated Mr. Charles Churchill.* London, 1765 (4to. 1s. Nicoll) BODLEIAN

Reviewed: *Monthly Review* 31 (1764): 474
Critical Review 18 (1764): 474

734 *An Elegy On the Death of William and Mary, Earl and Countess of Sutherland.* London, 1766 (4to. 6d. Dodsley) BRITISH LIBRARY

Reviewed: *Monthly Review* 35 (1766): 79
Critical Review 22 (1766): 74

An Elegy on the Fears of Death
See: TRUSLER, John

735 *An Elegy on the Late Rt. Hon. W. . . . . . P. . . , Esq.* London, 1766 (4to. 1s.6d. Kearsly) BRITISH LIBRARY

Reviewed: *Monthly Review* 35 (1766): 163–164
Critical Review 22 (1766): 154–155
Gentleman's Magazine 36 (1766): 384

736 *An Elegy on the Much Lamented Death of His Royal Highness Edward, Duke of York, &c.* London, 1767 (Fol. 6d. Becket) BODLEIAN

Reviewed: *Monthly Review* 37 (1767): 395
Critical Review 24 (1767): 314–315
Universal Museum 3 (1767): 541

An Elegy on the Much Lamented Death of William Beckford, Esq.
See: CHATTERTON, Thomas

737 *An Elegy on the unexpected Death of an excellent Physician, the justly admired John Martin Butt, M.D. Inscribed to his afflicted Family. By a sincere Mourner*
NOT SEEN (Fol. 1s. Walter)

Reviewed: *Monthly Review* 42 (1770): 143
Critical Review 29 (1770): 74

738 *Elegy To The Memory of The Right Honourable The Marquis of Granby.* London, 1770 (4to. 6d. Dodsley) YALE (BEINECKE)

Reviewed: *Monthly Review* 44 (1771): 91
Critical Review 31 (1771): 74
London Magazine 39 (1770): 632
Town & Country Magazine 2 (1770): 662

An Elegy to the Memory of the Right Honourable William, late Earl of Bath
See: KELLY, Hugh

An Elegy upon the Death of the late Earl Granville
See: HERVEY, Thomas

An Elegy written among the Ruins of an Abbey
See: JERNINGHAM, Edward

An Elegy written among the Tombs in Westminster-Abbey
See: JERNINGHAM, Edward

Elegy, Written At Amwell
See: SCOTT, John

An Elegy, written in a Quakers Burial Ground
See: WAGSTAFFE, John

An Elegy written in An Empty Assembly-Room
See: CAMBRIDGE, Richard Owen

739 *An Elegy written in Covent-Garden.* London, n.d. [ESTC-1765?] (4to. 1s. Ridley. 1771) BRITISH LIBRARY

Reviewed: *Monthly Review* 44 (1771): 416
Critical Review 31 (1771): 231
Gentleman's Magazine 41 (1771): 229

740 *An Elegy written in Saint Bride's Churchyard, on Tuesday the 3d of January 1769. Humbly inscribed to the Common Council of Farringdon-without*
NOT SEEN (Fol. 6d. Fry)

Reviewed: *Monthly Review* 40 (1769): 157
Critical Review 27 (1769): 72–73
Gentleman's Magazine 39 (1769): 157
Critical Memoirs 1 (1769): 523
Town & Country Magazine [1] (1769): 46

An Elegy, written on Saint Mark's Eve
See: CUMBERLAND, Richard

An Elegy wrote in a Country Church Yard
See: GRAY, Thomas

An Elegy Wrote under a Gallows
See: DOWNMAN, Hugh

741 *Eleutheria: a Poem. Inscribed to Mrs. Macaulay.* London, 1768 (4to. 1s. Cadell) BRITISH LIBRARY

Reviewed: *Monthly Review* 38 (1768): 409–410
Critical Review 25 (1768): 309–310
British Magazine 4 (1763): 158
Universal Museum 4 (1768): 205

742 [ÉLIE DE BEAUMONT, Anne Louise]. *The History of a Young Lady of Distinction. In a Series of Letters.* 2 vols. London, 1754 (12mo. 6s. Noble) BRITISH LIBRARY

Reviewed: *Monthly Review* 10 (1754): 307–308

743 [ÉLIE] DE BEAUMONT, [Anne Louise]. *The History of a Young Lady of Distinction. Translated from the French of Madam de Beaumont.* 2 vols.
NOT SEEN (12mo. 6s. Noble)

Reviewed: *Monthly Review* 35 (1766): 328

744 ÉLIE DE BEAUMONT, [Anne Louise]. *The History of the Marquis de Roselle. In a Series of Letters. By Madam Elie de Beaumont. Translated from the French. In Two Volumes.* London, 1765 (8vo. 6s. Becket) BRITISH LIBRARY

Reviewed: *Monthly Review* 32 (1765): 480
Critical Review 19 (1765): 350–354
Gentleman's Magazine 35 (1765): 125–127
Candid Review 1 (1765): 375–380

745 *Eliza: or, the History of Miss Granville. By the Author of Indiana Danby.* 2 vols. London, 1766 (12mo. 5s. Noble) BRITISH LIBRARY

Reviewed: *Monthly Review* 34 (1766): 82
Critical Review 21 (1766): 156–157

746 ELLIOT, N. *The Atheist. A Poem. By the Author of the Vestry, N. Elliot, Shoe-maker, in St. Ebb's-Lane, Oxford.* Birmingham, 1770 (2s. Fletcher) BRITISH LIBRARY

Reviewed: *Critical Review* 30 (1770): 481
Town & Country Magazine 3 (1771): 44

747 ELLIOT, N. *An Ode to Charity. By the Author of the Atheist, and Vestry, N. Elliot, Shoe-Maker, in St. Ebb's-Lane, Oxford.* Oxford, 1770 (6d. Jackson) BODLEIAN

Reviewed: *Critical Review* 30 (1770): 481

748 [ELLIOT, N.]. *The Vestry, a Poem. By an Overseer of the Poor of the Parish of Saint Peter le Bailey, Oxford*
NOT SEEN (4to. 1s. Jackson at Oxford)

Reviewed: *Critical Review* 23 (1767): 297

749 [ELLIS, John]. *The Canto added by Maphaeus to Virgil's Twelve Books of Aeneas, from the original Bombastic, done into English Hudibrastic; with notes beneath, and Latin Text in ev'ry other page annext.* London, 1758 (12mo. 1s.6d. R. and J. Dodsley) CAMBRIDGE

Reviewed: *Monthly Review* 18 (1758): 527–530
Critical Review 5 (1758): 435–436

The Elopement; or Perfidy Punished
See: COLTON, Henry

750 ELPHINSTON, James (ed.). *A Collection of Poems, From the best Authors: Adapted to every Age, but peculiarly designed to form the Taste of Youth.* London, 1764 (8vo. 3s.6d. Richardson) BRITISH LIBRARY

Reviewed: *Monthly Review* 31 (1764): 231

751 ELPHINSTON, James. *Education, in Four Books.* London, 1763 (8vo. 3s. Owen) BRITISH LIBRARY

Reviewed: *Monthly Review* 28 (1763): 103–108
Critical Review 15 (1763): 214–216

752 [ELPHINSTON, James]. *A Hymn after Sore Eyes. Composed on Easter-Day*
NOT SEEN (Fol. 6d. Owen)

Reviewed: *Monthly Review* 20 (1759): 475

753 [ELPHINSTON, James (trans.)]. *Religion, a Poem: From the French of the Younger Racine.* London, 1754 (8vo. 3s. Hodges, Newbery, Owen, Strahan, and Wilson and Durham) BRITISH LIBRARY

Reviewed: *Monthly Review* 10 (1754): 306–307
Gentleman's Magazine 23 (1753): 592–593

754 ELPHINSTON, James. *Verses, English, French, and Latin, presented to the King of Denmark and Norway, at St. James's*
NOT SEEN (Fol. 6d. Noteman)

Reviewed: *Monthly Review* 39 (1768): 317–318
Critical Review 26 (1768): 316

755 *Elsefair and Evander. A Poem. By S. P. Founded on Fact. Being an Historical Narrative of Two Unfortunate Lovers whom the Author relieved in Carolina in the Year 1766.* London, 1774 (4to. 2s. Snagg. 1774) LIBRARY OF CONGRESS

Reviewed: *Monthly Review* 50 (1774): 316
Critical Review 37 (1774): 474
Universal Catalogue 3 (1774) art. 219

Elvira: A Tragedy
See: MALLET, David

756 *Emendations on An Appeal from the late Dean Swift. Or Right Hon. Earl of Orrery Vindicated.* London, 1752 (6d. Cooper) BRITISH LIBRARY

Reviewed: *Monthly Review* 6 (1752): 238

757 *Emily: or, the History of a Natural Daughter. In Two Volumes.* London, 1756 (12mo. 6s. Noble) UNIVERSITY OF PENNSYLVANIA

Reviewed: *Monthly Review* 14 (1756): 289–292
Critical Review 1 (1756): 122–125

758 *Emma; or, The Unfortunate Attachment. A sentimental Novel.* 3 vols. London, 1773 (12mo. 9s. Hookham. 1773) BRITISH LIBRARY

Reviewed: *Monthly Review* 49 (1773): 69
Critical Review 35 (1773): 475
London Magazine 42 (1773): 249
Town & Country Magazine 5 (1773): 378
Universal Catalogue [2] (1773) art. 733

759 *The Emulation of the Insects: or, A Minister chosen. A Fable*
NOT SEEN (8vo. 6d. Bouquet)

Reviewed: *Monthly Review* 10 (1754): 304

The Enchanter; or, Love and Magic
See: GARRICK, David

760 *England's Tears: a Poem. Inscribed to Britannia. To which is added, Advice to the Voters of Great Britain, at the approaching General Election*
NOT SEEN (4to. 1s.6d. Kearsly. 1774)

Reviewed: *Monthly Review* 51 (1774): 317
Critical Review 38 (1774): 319
Universal Catalogue 3 (1774) art. 1252

761 ENGLISH, John. *Mormo: the British Hero; or, the Mansion-house in Labour. By John English, repugnant to all Confusion*
NOT SEEN (Fol. 1s. Evans)

Reviewed: *Monthly Review* 39 (1768): 318
Critical Review 26 (1768): 316
Political Register 3 (1768): 383

762 ENGLISH, Robert. *The Naval Review. A Poem. Inscribed to the Right Honourable Sir Charles Saunders, Knight of the Bath, and Admiral of the White Squadron of His Majesty's Fleet.* London, 1773 (4to. 1s. Becket. 1773) BODLEIAN

Reviewed: *Monthly Review* 49 (1773): 148
Critical Review 36 (1773): 155
London Magazine 42 (1773): 456
Town & Country Magazine 6 (1774): 437
Universal Catalogue [2] (1773) art. 955

763 ENGLISH, Robert. *The Naval Review; a Poem. The Second Edition.* 2d ed. reviewed; copy seen 3d ed.: London, 1774 (4to. 1s.6d. Becket. 1774) BODLEIAN

Reviewed: *Monthly Review* 51 (1774): 165
Critical Review 37 (1774): 473
Universal Catalogue 3 (1774) art. 774

764 *The English Britons, a Farce, of one Act. Inscribed to John Wilkes, Esq; Written for the Amusement of, and performed by, a select Company at a Seat of Distinction.* London, 1763 (6d. Pridden) BRITISH LIBRARY

Reviewed: *Monthly Review* 29 (1763): 392
Critical Review 16 (1763): 389

765 *The English Theatre: containing twenty Comedies, and twenty Tragedies; being the most valuable Plays which have been acted on the British Stage.* 8 vols.
NOT SEEN (12mo. 24s. Lownds)

Reviewed: *Monthly Review* 23 (1760): 408
Critical Review 10 (1760): 478

The Englishman in Bourdeaux
See: FAVART, Charles Simon

766 *The Entanglement; or, the History of Miss Eleonora Frampton, and Miss Anastasia Shaftoe.* 2 vols.
NOT SEEN (12mo. 5s. Noble)

Reviewed: *Monthly Review* 38 (1768): 499
Critical Review 25 (1768): 59
London Magazine 37 (1768): 47
Universal Museum 4 (1768): 36

767 *The Entertaining Fabulist: Containing A Variety of Diverting Tales and Novels, in Prose and Verse. To which is prefix'd, A Short Tractate of Story-Telling.* London, n.d. [ESTC-1770?] (12mo. 2s.6d.sewed. Bladon) BRITISH LIBRARY

Reviewed: *Monthly Review* 34 (1766): 82

768 *The Entertaining Medley: being a Collection of Genuine Anecdotes, Delightful Stories, Frolicks of Wit and Humour, With other notable Displays of the Force of Human Genius.* London, 1767 (12mo. 3s. Robinson) BRITISH LIBRARY

Reviewed: *Monthly Review* 36 (1767): 400
Critical Review 23 (1767): 218
Gentleman's Magazine 37 (1767): 261

Enthusiasm; a poetical Essay
See: BYROM, John

The Ephesian Matron
See: BICKERSTAFFE, Isaac

The Epigoniad
See: WILKIE, William

An Epistle from Lady Jane Grey to Lord Guilford Dudley
See: KEATE, George

769 *An Epistle from Mr. Banks, Voyager, Monster-hunter, and Amoroso, to Oberea, Queen of Otaheite. Transfused by A. B. C. Esq. Second Professor of the Otaheite, and of every other unknown Tongue. Enriched with the finest Passages of the Queen's Letter to Mr. Banks.* 2d ed. Batavia, n.d. [ESTC: London, 1773; BLC: Batavia imprint fictitious] (4to. 1s. Swan, &c.) BRITISH LIBRARY

Reviewed: *Monthly Review* 50 (1774): 70
Critical Review 37 (1774): 76
Town & Country Magazine 6 (1774): 100
Universal Catalogue [2] (1773) art. 1317

770 *An Epistle from Mrs. B****y, to His R***l H*****ss the D*** of C********d: or, Beauty Scourging Rank.* London, 1772 (4to. 1s. Batteson. 1772) HARVARD (HOUGHTON)

Reviewed: *Monthly Review* 46 (1772): 80
Critical Review 33 (1772): 500
Gentleman's Magazine 42 (1772): 84
Universal Catalogue [1] (1772) art. 91

An Epistle from Oberea, Queen of Otaheite
See: SCOTT, John

An Epistle from the Hon. R--- E---- to his dear Nanny
See: EDGCUMBE, Richard

771 *An Epistle from the Princess F---a, at Naples, to The Countess of -----, in London. Translated from the Italian, And addressed to G. S.--w--n, Esquire.* London, 1771 (4to. 1s. White. 1771) YALE (BEINECKE)

Reviewed: *Monthly Review* 44 (1771): 344
Critical Review 31 (1771): 231

772 *An Epistle from Tully in the Shades, to Orator Ma------n in Covent-Garden.* London, 1755 (8vo. 6d. Cooper) FOLGER

Reviewed: *Monthly Review* 12 (1755): 140

An Epistle from William Lord Russell, to William Lord Cavendish
See: CANNING, George

An Epistle, moral and philosophical, from an Officer at Otaheite
See: COURTENAY, John

An Epistle to a Gentleman of the Temple
See: BYROM, John

An Epistle to a Lady
See: DODD, William

773 *An Epistle to his Grace the Duke of N------e, on his Resignation. By an Independent Whig*
NOT SEEN (4to. 6d. Corbet)

Reviewed: *Monthly Review* 27 (1762): 156–157
Critical Review 14 (1762): 77
British Magazine 3 (1762): 438

An Epistle to Junius
See: HUGHES, Benjamin

774 *An Epistle to Lord Holland. MDCCLXIX.* London, 1770 (4to. 1s. Brown. 1769) BODLEIAN

Reviewed: *Monthly Review* 42 (1770): 144
Critical Review 29 (1770): 146–147

775 *An Epistle to Mr. Hickington. To which is added, A Session of Poets. Written by the Author of Verses on the Approach of Peace*
NOT SEEN (4to. 1s. Sold by the Author in Beverley. 1770)

Reviewed: *Monthly Review* 43 (1770): 484
Critical Review 31 (1771): 73

776 *An Epistle to the Author of Candour. By the Author of The Prospect of Liberty, The Country Spy, &c.* London, 1768 (4to. 1s. Wilkie) YALE (BEINECKE)

Reviewed: *Monthly Review* 38 (1768): 71
Critical Review 25 (1768): 73–74

An Epistle to the Author of The Four Farthing Candles
See: SHIRLEY, William

777 *An Epistle to the Author of the Rosciad and the Apology.* London, 1761 (4to. 6d. Hope) FOLGER

Reviewed: *Monthly Review* 24 (1761): 470
Critical Review 11 (1761): 495

An Epistle to the Hon. Arthur Dobbs
See: STERLING, James

778 *An Epistle to the Irreverend Mr. C-----s. C-------l, In His Own Style and Manner.* London, 1764 (4to. 1s. Nicoll) BRITISH LIBRARY

Reviewed: *Monthly Review* 30 (1764): 67
Critical Review 17 (1764): 77–78

779 *An Epistle to the King*
NOT SEEN (4to. 6d. Waller)

Reviewed: *Monthly Review* 27 (1762): 395
Critical Review 14 (1762): 316

780 *An Epistle To the late Right Honourable Stephen Poyntz, Esq; Occasion'd by the Compleat Victory obtain'd by the Duke Over the Rebels, Written in the Year 1746, and now First published.* London, 1751 (1s. Cooper) BRITISH LIBRARY

Listed: *Monthly Review* 4 (1750–51): 370

781 *An epistle to the rev. dr. Young, occasioned by his new tragedy, the Brothers*
NOT SEEN (4to. 6d. Bouquet)

Reviewed: *Monthly Review* 8 (1753): 238

782 *An Epistle to the Right Hon. Arthur Onslow, on his resigning the Chair of the House of Commons, March 18th, 1761* [*Monthly Review* says by Lockman]
NOT SEEN (Fol. 6d. Dodsley)

Reviewed: *Monthly Review* 24 (1761): 444
Critical Review 11 (1761): 420

783 *An Epistle to the Rt. Hon. the Earl of Chatham, Lord-Keeper of the Privy-Seal, and One of His Majesty's Most Honourable Privy-Council.* London, n.d. (4to. 1s. Bladon) NEWBERRY

Reviewed: *Monthly Review* 35 (1766): 325–326
Critical Review 22 (1766): 319–320

Epistles Philosophical and Moral
See: KENRICK, William

Epistles to Lorenzo
See: KENRICK, William

Epistles to the Great, from Aristippus in Retirement
See: COOPER, John Gilbert

784 *Epistola Politica—An Epistle on the Times, a Poem*
NOT SEEN (4to. 1s. Bladon)

Reviewed: *Monthly Review* 44 (1771): 91
Critical Review 31 (1771): 159

785 *An Epistolary Poem, Humbly Inscribed To The Right Honourable Frederick Lord North, First Lord of the Treasury, Chancellor of the University of Oxford, Knight of the Garter, &c.* London, 1773 (4to. 1s. Wilkie, &c. 1773) BRITISH LIBRARY

Reviewed: *Monthly Review* 48 (1773): 157–158
Critical Review 35 (1773): 70
Universal Catalogue [2] (1773) art. 106

786 *Epithalamion: or, a Bridal Poem on the Marriage of Her Royal Highness The Princess Augusta of England, To His Most Serene Highness The Hereditary Prince of Brunswick-Lunenburgh.* London, 1764 (4to. 6d. Flexney) BRITISH LIBRARY

Reviewed: *Monthly Review* 30 (1764): 158
Critical Review 17 (1764): 79

787 *Epitre de M. Voltaire, au Roi de Prusse. With a Translation*
NOT SEEN (Fol. 6d. Dodsley)

Reviewed: *Monthly Review* 16 (1757): 183

788 *The Epocha; or the Review. M DCC LXII*
NOT SEEN (4to. 1s.6d. Bladon)

Reviewed: *Monthly Review* 46 (1772): 455
Critical Review 33 (1772): 328
Universal Catalogue [1] (1772) art. 581

Epponina: a Dramatic Essay
See: CARR, John

789 [ERBIGNY, Henri Lambert d', Marquis de Thibouville]. *The Danger of the Passions; or, Syrian and Egyptian Anecdotes. Translated from the French of the Author of the School of Friendship.* 2 vols.
NOT SEEN (12mo. 5s.sewed. Evans. 1770)

Reviewed: *Monthly Review* 44 (1771): 173
Critical Review 31 (1771): 160

790 *Ermina; or, the Fair Recluse. In a Series of Letters. By a Lady, Author of Dorinda Catsby, &c.* 2 vols.

NOT SEEN (12mo. 6s. Bladon)

Reviewed: *Monthly Review* 47 (1772): 324
London Magazine 41 (1772): 491
British Magazine & General Review 2 (1772): 372
Universal Catalogue [1] (1772) art. 1207

791 ERSKINE, Andrew. *Town-Eclogues. I. The Hangmen, II. The Harlequins, III. The Street-Walkers, IV. The Undertakers.* London, n.d. [ESTC-1773] (4to. 1s.6d. Cadell. 1773) BRITISH LIBRARY

Reviewed: *Monthly Review* 49 (1773): 148
Critical Review 35 (1773): 316
London Magazine 42 (1773): 196
Universal Catalogue [2] (1773) art. 458

792 *Escapes of a Poetical Genius.* London, 1752 (4to. 1s. Sheepey) BRITISH LIBRARY

Reviewed: *Monthly Review* 6 (1752): 155–156

An Essay on Education. A Poem
See: JOHNSON, Samuel, M.A. of Shrewsbury

793 *An Essay on Friendship, a Poem.* London, 1767 (4to. 1s. Cooke) BRITISH LIBRARY

Reviewed: *Monthly Review* 36 (1767): 408
Critical Review 23 (1767): 225
Gentleman's Magazine 37 (1767): 173

794 *An Essay on Friendship, a Poem.* London, 1767 (4to. 2s. Cooke) NEWBERRY

Reviewed: *Critical Review* 27 (1769): 396

795 *An Essay on Gaming, in An Epistle to a young Nobleman.* London, 1761 (4to. 1s. Field) BODLEIAN

Reviewed: *Monthly Review* 25 (1761): 394–396
Critical Review 12 (1761): 320
British Magazine 2 (1761): 550

An Essay on Happiness, In Four Books
See: DUNCAN, John

796 *An Essay on Immorality. In Three Parts.* London, 1760 (4to. 2s.6d. Hart) BRITISH LIBRARY

Reviewed: *Monthly Review* 24 (1761): 280
Critical Review 11 (1761): 414

797 *An Essay on Patriotism, in the Style and Manner of Mr. Pope's Essay on Man. In Four Epistles. Inscribed to the Rt. Hon. the E----- of C-------. By a Member of a Respectable Society.* London, 1766 (4to. 1s. Wilkie) HARVARD (HOUGHTON)

Reviewed: *Monthly Review* 35 (1766): 325
Critical Review 22 (1766): 226–228
Gentleman's Magazine 36 (1766): 430

An Essay on Sacred Harmony
See: FORTESCUE, James

798 *An Essay on Satyr and Panegyric.* London, 1764 (4to. 1s.6d. Wilson and Fell) UNIVERSITY OF PENNSYLVANIA

Reviewed: *Monthly Review* 30 (1764): 241
Critical Review 17 (1764): 313–314

799 *An Essay on Satirical Entertainments. To which is added, Stevens's new Lecture upon Heads, Now delivering At the Theatre Royal, Hay-Market. With Critical Observations.* 1st ed. reviewed; copy seen 2d ed.: London, 1772 (8vo. 1s.6d. Bell) BRITISH LIBRARY

Reviewed: *Monthly Review* 46 (1772): 542–543
Critical Review 34 (1772): 71
British Magazine & General Review 1 (1772): 457–461
Universal Catalogue [1] (1772) art. 730

An Essay on Woman
See: WILKES, John

800 *An Essay on Woman, a Poem* [*Universal Catalogue* gives author as S. Johnson, A.B.] NOT SEEN (4to. 2s.6d. Baldwin)

Reviewed: *London Magazine* 41 (1772): 542–543
British Magazine & General Review 2 (1772): 560
Universal Catalogue [1] (1772) art. 1297

801 *An Essay on Woman. A Poem. By J. W. Senator. With Notes, by the Bishop of G.* London,

1763 (4to. 1s.6d. Freeman) BRITISH LIBRARY

Reviewed: *Critical Review* 16 (1763): 479

802 *An Essay on Woman. The Fourth Epistle. With Explanatory Notes.* London, n.d. [BODLEIAN CAT.–c. 1763] (4to. 1s. Seymour) BODLEIAN

Reviewed: *Critical Review* 16 (1763): 479

803 *Essays from the Batchelor, in Prose and Verse. By the Authors of the Epistle to Gorges Edmond Howard, Esq.* 2 vols. 1st ed. reviewed; copy seen 2d ed.: Dublin & London, 1773 (12mo. 6s. Becket. 1773) BRITISH LIBRARY

Reviewed: *Monthly Review* 49 (1773): 234
Critical Review 36 (1773): 14–17
Town & Country Magazine 5 (1773): 434
Universal Catalogue [2] (1773) art. 615 [2d ed.]

Essays on Song-Writing
See: AIKIN, John

Essays Pastoral and Elegiac
See: BAKER, Henry

804 *The Essence of Theatrical Wit: being A Select Collection Of the best and most admired Prologues and Epilogues, That have been delivered from the Stage. With the Addition of some that were never made public before.* London, 1768 (8vo. 1s. Wicks) BRITISH LIBRARY

Reviewed: *Monthly Review* 38 (1768): 406

The Estate-Orators, a Town Eclogue
See: WOTY, William

805 *Ethic Epistles upon the Plan of Revealed Religion.* London, 1764 (4to. 1s. Cooke) NEW YORK PUBLIC LIBRARY

Reviewed: *Monthly Review* 30 (1764): 486
Critical Review 17 (1764): 395–396
General Magazine 1 (1764): 244

806 *The Eulogy of Frederic, King of Prussia.* London, 1758 (4to. 6d. Cooper) BRITISH LIBRARY

Reviewed: *Monthly Review* 19 (1758): 588–589
Critical Review 6 (1758): 438

807 *The Eunuch: or, the Northumberland Shepherd. In Four Chapters. Whereon hangs a Tale. Apply it who may.* London, 1752 (8vo. 1s. Cooper) BODLEIAN

Reviewed: *Monthly Review* 6 (1752): 147

808 *Euthemia; or the Power of Harmony. A Poem in Blank Verse. Sacred to the Memory of a Deceased Pair. To which is added, The Court of Discord.* N.p., 1756 (no pub. details) BODLEIAN

Reviewed: *Critical Review* 6 (1758): 344–345

809 [EVANS, Evan]. *The Love Of Our Country, a Poem, With Historical Notes, Address'd To Sir Watkin Williams Wynn of Wynnstay, Bt. Member of Parliament for the County of Salop. By a Curate from Snowdon.* Carmarthen, 1772 (4to. 1s. Carmarthen printed by Ross; sold by Williams, &c in London. 1772) BODLEIAN

Reviewed: *Monthly Review* 48 (1773): 316–317
Critical Review 35 (1773): 316
London Magazine 42 (1773): 196
Universal Catalogue [2] (1773) art. 369

810 EVANS, Evan (ed. & trans.). *Some Specimens of the Poetry of the Antient Welsh Bards. Translated into English, with Explanatory Notes on the Historical Passages, And a short Account of Men and Places mentioned by the Bards, In order to give the Curious some Idea of the Taste and Sentiments of our Ancestors, and their manner of Writing.* London, 1764 (4to. 5s. Dodsley) BRITISH LIBRARY

Reviewed: *Monthly Review* 31 (1764): 22–25
Critical Review 18 (1764): 81–87

An Evening Contemplation in a College
See: DUNCOMBE, John

811 *An Evening Walk, a Poem*
NOT SEEN (8vo. 4d. Lewis)

Reviewed: *Monthly Review* 16 (1757): 363

812 *Eve's Legacy to Her Daughters; A Poem In Two Cantoes. With her Epitaph: and Tiresias.*

London, 1771 (8vo. 1s. Davies) UNIVERSITY OF ILLINOIS

Reviewed: *Monthly Review* 44 (1771): 344
Critical Review 31 (1771): 231
London Magazine 40 (1771): 367

An Exact and Circumstantial History of the Battle of Floddon
See: LAMBE, Robert

813 *Excise Boys, Ha! A new ballad, to the tune of Packington's Pound*
NOT SEEN (Fol. 5pp. 3d. Holden)

Reviewed: *Monthly Review* 5 (1751): 463

The Execution of Sir Charles Bawdin
See: CHATTERTON, Thomas

The Exemplary Mother
See: COOPER, Maria Susanna

814 *The Exhibition in Hell; or, Moloch turn'd Painter.* London, n.d. [HOUGHTON CAT.–1771] (4to. 1s. Organ) HARVARD (HOUGHTON)

Reviewed: *Monthly Review* 44 (1771): 260
Critical Review 31 (1771): 159
Gentleman's Magazine 41 (1771): 132
Town & Country Magazine 3 (1771): 155

815 *The Exhortation. A Poem*
NOT SEEN (4to. 1s. Woodfall)

Reviewed: *Monthly Review* 26 (1762): 233–234
Critical Review 13 (1762): 273
British Magazine 3 (1762): 158

816 *The Exile Triumphant: or, Liberty Appeased. A Poem. Humbly Inscribed to the Worthy Liverymen of the City of London*
NOT SEEN (4to. 1s. Steare)

Reviewed: *Monthly Review* 38 (1768): 245
Critical Review 25 (1768): 227
Universal Museum 4 (1768): 148

817 *The Expedition an Ode, To the Tune of the British Grenadiers.* London, n.d. [ESTC-1759?] (Fol. 6d. Taylor in the Haymarket) BRITISH LIBRARY

Reviewed: *Monthly Review* 20 (1759): 92

The Expedition of Humphry Clinker
See: SMOLLETT, Tobias

818 *The Explanation; or, Agreeable Surprise. By a Young Lady.* 2 vols. London, 1773 (12mo. 5s.sewed. Noble. 1772) BRITISH LIBRARY

Reviewed: *Monthly Review* 47 (1772): 324
Critical Review 34 (1772): 397
London Magazine 41 (1772): 489
Town & Country Magazine 4 (1772): 659–660
British Magazine & General Review 2 (1772): 555
Universal Catalogue [1] (1772) art. 1281

EXPLORALIBUS. *The Invisible Spy*
See: HAYWOOD, Eliza

The Explosion
See: BOWDEN, John

819 *The Expostulation; a Poem.* London, 1768 (4to. 2s.6d. Bingley) UNIVERSITY OF ILLINOIS

Reviewed: *Monthly Review* 38 (1768): 498
Critical Review 25 (1768): 390–391
Gentleman's Magazine 38 (1768): 335–336
Universal Museum 4 (1768): 317

820 *An Extraordinary Ode to an Extraordinary Man, on an Extraordinary Occasion.* London, 1766 (Fol. 6d. Jones) BRITISH LIBRARY

Reviewed: *Monthly Review* 35 (1766): 163
Critical Review 22 (1766): 153–154

The Fable of Jotham
See: CAMBRIDGE, Richard Owen

821 *Fables and Tales for the Ladies. To which are added, Miscellanies, By Another Hand.* London, 1750 (8vo. 3s.6d.bound. Sold by C. Hitch and L. Hawes, in Pater-noster-Row, and H. Whitridge at the Royal Exchange) BRITISH LIBRARY

Reviewed: *Monthly Review* 4 (1750–51): 16–17

822 *Fables and Tales for the World, and Miscellanies for the Country. Patricia's Address. Being fit to be read in all Churches and Chapels throughout England; but not at Berwick upon Tweed, nor in Bedfordshire*

NOT SEEN (8vo. 2s.6d. P. Stevens)

Reviewed: *Monthly Review* 37 (1767): 153
Critical Review 24 (1767): 158–159
Political Register 1 (1767): 179

Fables for grown Gentlemen
See: STEVENSON, John Hall

Fables of Flowers, for the Female Sex
See: WYNNE, John Huddlestone

FAGAN, Christophe Barthélemi (adaptations)
See: GARRICK, David. *The Guardian Three Comedies . . . Freely Translated from Messrs. St Foix and Fagan*

823 [FAGNAN, Marie Antoinette]. *Kanor, a Tale. Translated from the Savage.* London, 1750 (no pub. details) BRITISH LIBRARY

Reviewed: *Monthly Review* 3 (1750): 52–53

824 *The Fair Citizen; or the Real Adventures of Miss Charlotte Bellmour. Written by Herself.* London, 1757 (12mo. 2s. Lownds) NEWBERRY

Reviewed: *Monthly Review* 17 (1757): 82
Critical Review 4 (1757): 95

825 *The Fair Orphan, A Comic Opera, of three acts; As performed at the Theatre in Lynn, by Mr. G. A. Stevens's Company of Comedians.* Lynn, 1771 (8vo. 1s.6d. Nicoll. 1771) BRITISH LIBRARY

Reviewed: *Monthly Review* 44 (1771): 416
Critical Review 31 (1771): 313–314
London Magazine 40 (1771): 274
Town & Country Magazine 3 (1771): 323

The Fair Parricide
See: CRANE, Edward

The Fair Quaker: or, The Humours of the Navy
See: THOMPSON, Edward

826 *Fair Rosamond to the fair Hibernian. An epistle*
NOT SEEN (Fol. 6d. Howard)

Reviewed: *Monthly Review* 6 (1752): 79

827 *The Fair Wanderer: or, the Adventures of Ethelinda, Niece to the late Cardinal B———.* London, 1751 (8vo. 1s. Stamper) BRITISH LIBRARY

Reviewed: *Monthly Review* 5 (1751): 458

828 *The Fair Wanderer: or, the Triumphs of Virtue*
NOT SEEN (8vo. 1s.6d. Brown)

Reviewed: *Critical Review* 27 (1769): 152
Gentleman's Magazine 39 (1769): 158
Critical Memoirs 1 (1769): 525

The Fairies. An Opera
See: GARRICK, David

The Fairy Favour
See: HULL, Thomas

The Fairy Prince: A Masque
See: COLMAN, George (the elder)

The Fairy Tale. In Two Acts
See: COLMAN, George (the elder)

829 *The Fairy's Revel: or, Puck's Trip Thro' London By Moon Light. A Satire.* London, 1770 (4to. 1s.6d. Bladon) FOLGER

Reviewed: *Monthly Review* 43 (1770): 483
Critical Review 31 (1771): 73–74
Town & Country Magazine 3 (1771): 44

Faith. A Poem
See: NUGENT, Robert

830 *The Faithful Fugitives: or, Adventures of Miss Teresa M———. In a Series of Letters to a Friend.* London, 1766 (12mo. 3s. Vernor) UNIVERSITY OF PENNSYLVANIA

Reviewed: *Monthly Review* 34 (1766): 241
Critical Review 21 (1766): 219–221

The Fakeer: A Tale
See: CAMBRIDGE, Richard Owen

831 [FALCONER, William]. *Ode on the Duke of York's Second Departure from England, as Rear Admiral. Written aboard the Royal George. By the Author of the Shipwreck.* London, 1763 (4to. 1s. Millar) BRITISH LIBRARY

Reviewed: *Monthly Review* 28 (1763): 322–323
Critical Review 15 (1763): 324

832 [FALCONER, William]. *The Shipwreck. A Poem. In Three Cantos. By a Sailor.* London, 1762 (4to. 5s. Millar) BRITISH LIBRARY

Reviewed: *Monthly Review* 27 (1762): 197–201
Critical Review 13 (1762): 440
British Magazine 3 (1762): 324

833 FALCONER, W[illiam]. *The Shipwreck. By a Sailor. A New Edition, Corrected and Enlarged.* London, 1764 (8vo. 2s.6d. Millar) BRITISH LIBRARY

Reviewed: *Monthly Review* 30 (1764): 395–399
Critical Review 17 (1764): 294–295

The Fall of Mortimer
See: MOUNTFORT, William

834 *The Fall of Public Spirit. A Dramatic Satire, In Two Acts.* London, 1757 (8vo. 1s. Cook) BRITISH LIBRARY

Reviewed: *Monthly Review* 17 (1757): 87–88
Critical Review 3 (1757): 554

835 [FALQUES, Marianne Agnès]. *Abbassai. An Eastern Novel.* 2 vols.
NOT SEEN (12mo. 6s.6d. Coote)

Reviewed: *Monthly Review* 20 (1759): 380
Critical Review 7 (1759): 460

836 [FALQUES, Marianne Agnès]. *Oriental Anecdotes: Or, the History of Haroun Alrachid. In Two Volumes.* 2 vols.
NOT SEEN (12mo. 6s. Durham and Nicoll)

Reviewed: *Monthly Review* 31 (1764): 160
Critical Review 17 (1764): 296–298

837 [FALQUES, Marianne Agnès]. *The Vizirs: or, the Enchanted Labyrinth. An Oriental Tale. By Made. Fauques de Vaucluse.* 3 vols. London, 1774 (12mo. 9s. Riley) BRITISH LIBRARY

Reviewed: *Monthly Review* 51 (1774): 401
Critical Review 38 (1774): 157
Universal Catalogue 3 (1774) art. 941

838 *False Gratitude. By a Lady.* 2 vols.
NOT SEEN (12mo. 6s. Noble. 1773)

Reviewed: *Monthly Review* 48 (1773): 243–244
Critical Review 34 (1772): 473
London Magazine 42 (1773): 39
Universal Catalogue [1] (1772) art. 1492

839 *The False Step; or The History of Mrs Brudenel.* 2 vols. London, 1771 (12mo. 5s.sewed. Almon) BRITISH LIBRARY

Reviewed: *Monthly Review* 44 (1771): 91–92
Critical Review 31 (1771): 160

840 *Falsehood in Fashion: or, The Vizard Unmask'd: A Satire. To which are added, The Loyal Free Mason, An Ode: and The Choice Of A Wife, in the stile of Lord C--rf--d.* London, 1770 (8vo. 1s. Bladon) YALE (BEINECKE)

Reviewed: *Monthly Review* 43 (1770): 243
Critical Review 30 (1770): 71–72
London Magazine 39 (1770): 426

A Familiar Epistle from A Student of the Middle Temple
See: SPRING, Thomas

841 *A Familiar Epistle to the Author of the Heroic Epistle to Sir William Chambers, and of the Heroic Postscript To The Public.* London, 1774 (4to. 1s.6d. Wilkie. 1774) FOLGER

Reviewed: *Monthly Review* 50 (1774): 317–318
Critical Review 37 (1774): 314
Universal Catalogue 3 (1774) art. 333

842 *A Familiar, Poetical Epistle to Miss Latter, on her Return from London to Reading, Berks*
NOT SEEN (4to. 6d. Nicholl)

Reviewed: *Critical Review* 14 (1762): 155

Family Pictures
See: MINIFIE, Susannah

843 *Family-Prayers, and Moral Essays, In Prose and Verse. By a Merchant.* London, 1769 (8vo. 4s. Buckland, &c. 1769) BRITISH LIBRARY

Reviewed: *Monthly Review* 40 (1769): 439–440
Critical Review 27 (1769): 317–318

844 *Fancy. An Irregular Ode.* London, 1758 (6d. J. Cooke) BRITISH LIBRARY

Reviewed: *Monthly Review* 18 (1758): 491
Critical Review 5 (1758): 162–163

845 *Fanny: or, the Amours of a West-Country young Lady. Contained in a Series of Genuine Letters. Interspersed with some entertaining Particulars during her Travels abroad. In Two Volumes.* London, 1755 (12mo. 6s. Manby) UNIVERSITY OF PENNSYLVANIA

Reviewed: *Monthly Review* 12 (1755): 237

846 *A Farewell to the Fleet at Spithead; describing the wretched Situation of France; concluding with an Address to the Great, by their Example to make Virtue fashionable. Dedicated to Sir George Saville, without his Permission or Knowledge. By a Sea Officer*
NOT SEEN (4to. 1s.6d. Kearsly)

Reviewed: *Monthly Review* 45 (1771): 151
Critical Review 31 (1771): 78

Faringdon Hill. A Poem
See: PYE, Henry James

847 *The Farmer's Journey to London. A Farce, in Three Acts.* Lynn, 1769 (8vo. 1s. Baldwin) BRITISH LIBRARY

Reviewed: *Monthly Review* 40 (1769): 437
Critical Review 27 (1769): 398
Gentleman's Magazine 39 (1769): 261
London Magazine 38 (1769): 376

The Farmer's Return from London
See: GARRICK, David

848 *The Farmer's Son of Kent. A Tale.* 2 vols.
NOT SEEN (12mo. 6s. Noble)

Reviewed: *Monthly Review* 39 (1768): 412
London Magazine 37 (1768): 556

The Fashionable Daughter
See: TURNER, Daniel

The Fashionable Friend
See: BONHOTE, Elizabeth

The Fashionable Lover
See: CUMBERLAND, Richard

849 *The Fatal Affection, or the History of Henry and Caroline.* 2 vols.
NOT SEEN (12mo. 6s. Noble. 1774)

Reviewed: *Monthly Review* 50 (1774): 234
Critical Review 37 (1774): 76
Town & Country Magazine 6 (1774): 101
Universal Catalogue 3 (1774) art. 192

850 *The Fatal Compliance; or, the History of Miss Constantia Pembroke.* 2 vols.
NOT SEEN (12mo. 5s.sewed. Jones)

Reviewed: *Monthly Review* 44 (1771): 499
Critical Review 31 (1771): 483
Town & Country Magazine 3 (1771): 379

The Fatal Discovery. A Tragedy
See: HOME, John

851 *The Fatal Effects of Deception. A Novel. In Three Volumes.* London, 1773 (12mo. 7s.6d.sewed. Jones. 1773) UNIVERSITY OF PENNSYLVANIA

Reviewed: *Monthly Review* 49 (1773): 232
Critical Review 36 (1773): 74
London Magazine 42 (1773): 249

The Fatal effects of Inconstancy
See: DORAT, Claude Joseph

852 *Fatal Friendship. A Novel. By a Lady.* 2 vols. London, 1770 (12mo. 5s.sewed. Lowndes) BRITISH LIBRARY

Reviewed: *Monthly Review* 42 (1770): 488
Critical Review 30 (1770): 397
London Magazine 39 (1770): 212

853 *Fatal Obedience; or, the History of Mr. Freeland.* 2 vols. London, n.d. [ESTC-1780?] (12mo. 6s. Noble) BRITISH LIBRARY

Reviewed: *Monthly Review* 41 (1769): 479
Critical Review 28 (1769): 369–372

A Father's Advice to his Son
See: COOPER, John Gilbert

FAULKNER, George (pseud.)
See: JEPHSON, Robert

854 *The Fault Was All His Own. A Novel. In a Series of Letters. By a Lady.* 2 vols. London, 1771 (12mo. 5s.sewed. Riley) BODLEIAN

Reviewed: *Monthly Review* 44 (1771): 333
Critical Review 31 (1771): 397
London Magazine 40 (1771): 322

FAUQUES DE VAUCLUSE, Mlle.
See: FALQUES, Marianne Agnès

855 FAVART, [Charles Simon]. *The Englishman in Bourdeaux. A Comedy. Written in French, By the celebrated Monsieur Favart. Acted with universal Applause, at the Theatre-Royal, in Paris. Where it has had a more extraordinary Run than any other new Piece, in the Memory of the present Frequenters of the French Stage. Translated by an English Lady now residing in Paris.* London, 1764 (8vo. 1s. Kearsly) UNIVERSITY OF PENNSYLVANIA

Reviewed: *Monthly Review* 29 (1763): 318
Critical Review 16 (1763): 381–383

856 [FAVART, Charles Simon]. *Phillis at Court; a Comic Opera Of Three Acts. As it is now performing, with great Applause, At the Theatre-Royal In Crow-Street, Dublin. The Music by Signior Tomaso Giordani.* [Adaptation of Favart's *Caprice amoureux, ou Ninette à la cour.*] London, 1767 (8vo. 1s. Williams) BRITISH LIBRARY

Reviewed: *Monthly Review* 36 (1767): 238
Critical Review 23 (1767): 229

857 [FAVART, Charles Simon]. *The Reapers: or the Englishman out of Paris. An Opera.* [Adaptation of Favart's *Les Moissoneurs.*] London, 1770 (8vo. 1s.6d. Carnan. 1770) BRITISH LIBRARY

Reviewed: *Monthly Review* 44 (1771): 175
Critical Review 30 (1770): 468–469

FAVART, Charles Simon (further adaptations)
See: GARRICK, David. *A New Dramatic Entertainment called A Christmas Tale*
LLOYD, Robert. *The Capricious Lovers*

858 *The Favourite. A Moral Tale. Written by A Lady of Quality.* 2 vols. London, 1771 (12mo. 5s.sewed. Baldwin) BRITISH LIBRARY

Reviewed: *Monthly Review* 44 (1771): 497
Critical Review 31 (1771): 159

The Favourite, an Historical Tragedy
See: GENTLEMAN, Francis

859 FAWKES, Francis. *A Description of May. From Gawin Douglas, Bishop of Dunkeld.* London, 1752 (4to. 1s.6d. Whiston, &c.) BRITISH LIBRARY

Reviewed: *Monthly Review* 6 (1752): 262–264

860 FAWKES, Francis. *A Description of Winter. From Gawin Douglas, Bishop of Dunkeld.* London, 1754 (4to. 1s. Dodsley, &c.) BRITISH LIBRARY

Reviewed: *Monthly Review* 10 (1754): 384

861 FAWKES, Francis. *The Idylliums of Theocritus. Translated from the Greek, with Notes Critical and Explanatory.* London, 1767 (8vo. 6s. Robinson and Roberts) BRITISH LIBRARY

Reviewed: *Monthly Review* 37 (1767): 206–215
Critical Review 24 (1767): 17–23
Gentleman's Magazine 37 (1767): 314–315
Universal Museum 3 (1767): 372
Political Register 1 (1767): 33–38

862 FAWKES, Francis. *Original Poems and Translations.* London, 1761 (8vo. 5s. Dodsley) BRITISH LIBRARY

Reviewed: *Monthly Review* 25 (1761): 229–231
Critical Review 11 (1761): 485–487
British Magazine 2 (1761): 382

863 FAWKES, Francis. *Partridge-Shooting. An Eclogue. To the Honourable Charles Yorke.* London, 1767 (4to. 1s. Dodsley) BRITISH LIBRARY

Reviewed: *Monthly Review* 37 (1767): 238–239
Critical Review 24 (1767): 74
Universal Museum 3 (1767): 372
Political Register 1 (1767): 250

864 FAWKES, Francis, and William WOTY. *The Poetical Calendar. Containing A Collection Of*

scarce and valuable Pieces Of Poetry: With Variety of Originals and Translations, by the most eminent Hands. Intended as a Supplement to Mr. Dodsley's Collection. Written and Selected By Francis Fawkes, M.A. And William Woty. Vol. I for January. London, 1763 (12mo. 1s.6d. Coote) BRITISH LIBRARY

Reviewed: *Monthly Review* 28 (1763): 160

865 FAWKES, Francis, and William WOTY. *The Poetical Calendar. Containing A Collection Of scarce and valuable Pieces Of Poetry: With Variety of Originals and Translations, by the most eminent Hands. Intended as a Supplement to Mr. Dodsley's Collection. Written and Selected By Francis Fawkes, M.A. And William Woty. Vol. II. for February*. London, 1763 (12mo. 1s. Coote) BRITISH LIBRARY

Reviewed: *Monthly Review* 28 (1763): 239

866 FAWKES, Francis, and William WOTY. *The Poetical Calendar. Containing A Collection Of scarce and valuable Pieces Of Poetry: With Variety of Originals and Translations, by the most eminent Hands. Intended as a Supplement to Mr. Dodsley's Collection. Written and Selected By Francis Fawkes, M.A. And William Woty. Vol. III for March*. London, 1763 (12mo. 1s.6d. Coote) BRITISH LIBRARY

Reviewed: *Monthly Review* 28 (1763): 323

867 FAWKES, Francis, and William WOTY. *The Poetical Calendar. Containing A Collection Of scarce and valuable Pieces Of Poetry: With Variety of Originals and Translations, by the most eminent Hands. Intended as a Supplement to Mr. Dodsley's Collection. Written and Selected By Francis Fawkes, M.A. And William Woty. Vol. IV. for April*. London, 1763 (12mo. 1s.6d. Coote) BRITISH LIBRARY

Reviewed: *Monthly Review* 28 (1763): 488

868 FAWKES, Francis, and William WOTY. *The Poetical Calendar. Containing A Collection Of scarce and valuable Pieces Of Poetry: With Variety of Originals and Translations, by the most eminent Hands. Intended as a Supplement to Mr. Dodsley's Collection. Written and Selected By Francis Fawkes, M.A. And William Woty. Vol. V. for May, Vol. VI. for June, Vol. VII. for July*. London, 1763 (Coote) BRITISH LIBRARY

Reviewed: *Monthly Review* 29 (1763): 156–157

869 FAWKES, Francis, and William WOTY. *The Poetical Calendar. Containing A Collection Of scarce and valuable Pieces Of Poetry: With Variety of Originals and Translations, by the most eminent Hands. Intended as a Supplement to Mr. Dodsley's Collection. Written and Selected By Francis Fawkes, M.A. and William Woty. Vol. VIII. for August*. London, 1763 (12mo. 1s.6d. Coote) BRITISH LIBRARY

Reviewed: *Monthly Review* 29 (1763): 312

870 FAWKES, Francis, and William WOTY. *The Poetical Calendar. Containing A Collection Of scarce and valuable Pieces Of Poetry: With Variety of Originals and Translations, by the most eminent Hands. Intended as a Supplement to Mr. Dodsley's Collection. Written and Selected By Francis Fawkes, M.A. and William Woty. Vol. XI. for November*. London, 1763 (12mo. 1s.6d. Coote) BRITISH LIBRARY

Reviewed: *Monthly Review* 30 (1764): 20–26

871 FAWKES, Francis, and William WOTY. *The Poetical Calendar. Containing A Collection Of scarce and valuable Pieces Of Poetry: With Variety of Originals and Translations, by the most eminent Hands. Intended as a Supplement to Mr. Dodsley's Collection. Written and Selected By Francis Fawkes, M.A. and William Woty. Vol. XII. for December*. London, 1763 (12mo. 1s.6d. Coote) BRITISH LIBRARY

Reviewed: *Monthly Review* 30 (1764): 120–123

872 [FAWKES, Francis (trans.)]. *The Works of Anacreon, Sappho, Bion, Moschus and Musaeus. Translated into English. By a Gentleman of Cambridge*. London, 1760 (12mo. 3s. Newbery) HARVARD (HOUGHTON)

Reviewed: *Monthly Review* 23 (1760): 127–133
Critical Review 9 (1760): 310–314
Gentleman's Magazine 30 (1760): 193–194
British Magazine 1 (1760): 324 [140]

873 *The Feelings of the Heart; or, the History of a Country Girl. Written by Herself, and ad-*

dressed to A Lady of Quality. In Two Volumes. London, 1772 (12mo. 5s. Noble. 1772) HARVARD (HOUGHTON)

Reviewed: *Monthly Review* 46 (1772): 625
Critical Review 33 (1772): 255
Town & Country Magazine 4 (1772): 266
Universal Catalogue [1] (1772) art. 390

Felicia to Charlotte
See: COLLYER, Mary

874 FELL, Miss. *A Poem on the Times. By Miss Fell, of Newcastle*. London, 1774 (4to. 1s. Wilkie) BRITISH LIBRARY

Reviewed: *Monthly Review* 50 (1774): 484
Critical Review 37 (1774): 394
London Magazine 43 (1774): 244
Universal Catalogue 3 (1774) art. 623

875 FELL, Elizabeth. *Fables, Odes, and Miscellaneous Poems*
NOT SEEN (8vo. 3s.bound. Robson. 1771)

Reviewed: *Monthly Review* 45 (1771): 412
Critical Review 32 (1771): 469
Town & Country Magazine 4 (1772): 45

876 FELLOWS, John. *An Elegy on the Death of the Rev. John Gill, D.D. who departed this Life October 14th, 1771, in the Seventy-Fourth Year of his Age*. London, 1771 (8vo. 6d. Robinson) BRITISH LIBRARY

Reviewed: *Monthly Review* 45 (1771): 511
Critical Review 33 (1772): 85
Gentleman's Magazine 41 (1771): 604

877 [FELLOWS, John]. *Grace Triumphant. A Sacred Poem, in Nine Dialogues, Wherein the utmost Power of Nature, Reason, Virtue, and the Liberty of the Human Will, To administer Comfort to the awakened Sinner, are impartially weighed and considered; and The Whole submitted to the serious and candid Perusal of the Reverend Dr. Nowel of Oxford: the Reverend Dr. Adams of Shrewsbury: and the Author of Pietas Oxoniensis. By Philanthropos.* Birmingham, 1770 (8vo. 2s. Johnson) BRITISH LIBRARY

Reviewed: *Monthly Review* 44 (1771): 89–90
Critical Review 30 (1770): 318–319

London Magazine 39 (1770): 580
Town & Country Magazine 2 (1770): 599

878 FELLOWS, John. *Hymns on Believers Baptism*. Birmingham, 1773 (12mo. 1s. Keith, &c. 1773) BRITISH LIBRARY

Reviewed: *Monthly Review* 49 (1773): 505
Universal Catalogue [2] (1773) art. 1203

The Female Adventurers
See: TENCIN, Claudine Alexandrine Guerin de

879 *The Female American; or, the Adventures of Unca Eliza Winkfield. Compiled By Herself*. 2 vols. London, 1767 (12mo. 6s. Noble) BRITISH LIBRARY

Reviewed: *Monthly Review* 36 (1767): 238
Critical Review 23 (1767): 217

880 *Female Artifice; or, Charles F-x outwitted*. 1st ed. reviewed; copy seen 3d ed.: London, 1774 (4to. 1s. Ridley. 1774) BRITISH LIBRARY

Reviewed: *Monthly Review* 50 (1774): 155
Critical Review 37 (1774): 157
Universal Catalogue 3 (1774) art. 230

881 *The Female Barbers, an Irish Tale, after the Manner of Prior*. London, n.d. [BODLEIAN CAT.–c. 1770] (4to. 6d. Williams) BODLEIAN

Reviewed: *Monthly Review* 33 (1765): 248
Critical Review 20 (1765): 235

882 *Female Constancy: or the History of Miss Arabella Waldegrave*. 2 vols.
NOT SEEN (12mo. 5s.sewed. Davies)

Reviewed: *Monthly Review* 41 (1769): 232
Critical Review 27 (1769): 471
Town & Country Magazine [1] (1769): 381

883 *The Female Foundling: or, Virtue, Truth, and Spirit, Opposing every Difficulty. Shewing, The Happy Success of constant Love, in The true and entertaining Life of Mademoiselle D---r. Translated from the French*. 2 vols. London, 1751 (12mo. 5s. Sewed in blue paper. Waller) BRITISH LIBRARY

Reviewed: *Monthly Review* 4 (1750–51): 156

884 *Female Frailty; or, the History of Miss Wroughton.* 2 vols. London, 1772 (12mo. 6s. Noble. 1772) UNIVERSITY OF PENNSYLVANIA

Reviewed: *Monthly Review* 46 (1772): 78–79
Critical Review 32 (1771): 393

885 *Female Friendship: or, the Innocent Sufferer. A Moral Novel.* 2 vols. London, 1770 (12mo. 5s.sewed. Bell) BRITISH LIBRARY

Reviewed: *Monthly Review* 42 (1770): 70
Critical Review 29 (1770): 148

886 *The Female Haberdashers, &c.*
NOT SEEN (8vo. 6d. Wakelin)

Reviewed: *Monthly Review* 5 (1751): 463–464

The Female Pilgrim, or the Travels of Hephzibah
See: MITCHELL, John

The Female Quixote
See: LENNOX, Charlotte

887 *The female rambler, being the adventures of madam Janeton de *****. Taken from the French*
NOT SEEN (12mo. 2s. Reeve)

Reviewed: *Monthly Review* 9 (1753): 315–316

888 *Female Taste: a Satire. In two epistles. Inscribed to a Modern Polite Lady. By a Barrister of the Middle-Temple.* London, 1755 (4to. 1s. Crowder and Woodgate) BRITISH LIBRARY

Reviewed: *Monthly Review* 12 (1755): 510–511

FÉNÉLON, François de
See: SALIGNAC DE LA MOTHE FÉNÉLON, François

889 [FENTON, Richard]. *An Ode addressed To the Savoir Vivre Club.* London, n.d. [ESTC-1772?] (4to. 1s. Newbery. 1772) BRITISH LIBRARY

Reviewed: *Monthly Review* 48 (1773): 317–318
Critical Review 35 (1773): 315
London Magazine 42 (1773): 196
Town & Country Magazine 5 (1773): 266
Universal Catalogue [2] (1773) art. 359

890 FENTON, [Richard]. *Poems. By Mr. Fenton.* London, 1773 (4to. 6s. Kearsly. 1774) BRITISH LIBRARY

Reviewed: *Monthly Review* 50 (1774): 408
Universal Catalogue 3 (1774) art. 363

891 FERGUSSON, Robert. *Poems.* Edinburgh, 1773 (12mo. 2s.6d. Edinburgh printed, sold by Murray in London) BRITISH LIBRARY

Reviewed: *Monthly Review* 51 (1774): 483
Critical Review 39 (1775): 160–161
Universal Catalogue 3 (1774) art. 1249

892 *La Fête Champêtre.* London, 1774 (4to. 1s. Almon. 1774) BRITISH LIBRARY

Reviewed: *Monthly Review* 51 (1774): 68
Critical Review 38 (1774): 76
London Magazine 43 (1774): 451
Town & Country Magazine 6 (1774): 437
Universal Catalogue 3 (1774) art. 904

893 FIELDING, Henry. *Amelia.* 4 vols. London, 1752 [ESTC-1752 {1751}] (12mo. 12s. Millar) BRITISH LIBRARY

Reviewed: *Monthly Review* 5 (1751): 510–515
London Magazine 20 (1751): 531–535 and 592–596

894 FIELDING, Henry. *The Life of Mr. Jonathan Wild The Great. A New Edition, With considerable Corrections and Additions.* London, 1754 (12mo. 3s. Millar) BRITISH LIBRARY

Reviewed: *Monthly Review* 10 (1754): 238

895 FIELDING, Henry. *The Works of Henry Fielding, Esq; With The Life of the Author.* 8 vols. London, 1762 (4to. 4 vols. 5l.5s. bound and gilt, and in 8 vols. 8vo. 2l.12s.6d. in the same binding. Millar) BRITISH LIBRARY

Reviewed: *Monthly Review* 26 (1762): 364–375 and 481–494 and 27 (1762): 49–56
Critical Review 14 (1762): 1–21 [2d ed.]
British Magazine 3 (1762): 438

896 [FIELDING, Sarah]. *The Adventures of David Simple. Volume The Last, in which His History is Concluded.* London, 1753 (12mo. 3s. Millar) BODLEIAN

Reviewed: *Monthly Review* 8 (1753): 143

897 [FIELDING, Sarah]. *The History of Ophelia. Published by the Author of David Simple.* 2 vols. London, 1760 (12mo. 6s. Baldwin) BRITISH LIBRARY

Reviewed: *Monthly Review* 22 (1760): 328
Critical Review 9 (1760): 318
British Magazine 1 (1760): 140 [324]

898 [FIELDING, Sarah]. *The History of the Countess of Dellwyn. By the Author of David Simple.* 2 vols. London, 1759 (8vo. 6s. Millar) BRITISH LIBRARY

Reviewed: *Monthly Review* 20 (1759): 380–381
Critical Review 7 (1759): 377–378

899 [FIELDING, Sarah]. *The Lives of Cleopatra and Octavia. By The Author of David Simple.* London, 1757 (4to. 10s.6d. Printed for the Author, and sold by Millar, &c.) BRITISH LIBRARY

Reviewed: *Monthly Review* 17 (1757): 39–44

900 [FIELDING, Sarah, and Jane COLLIER]. *The Cry. A new Dramatic Fable.* 3 vols. London, 1754 (12mo. 9s. Dodsley) BRITISH LIBRARY

Reviewed: *Monthly Review* 10 (1754): 280–282

901 FIEUX, Charles de, Chevalier de Mouhy. *Female Banishment: or, the Woman Hater. Originally wrote by the Chevalier de Mouhy, Author of the Fortunate Country Maid.* 2 vols. London, 1759 (12mo. 6s. Lownds) BRITISH LIBRARY

Reviewed: *Monthly Review* 21 (1759): 366
Critical Review 8 (1759): 302–307

902 *The Fifteenth Ode of the First Book of Horace Imitated, and Applied to Mr. F----- On his being appointed S----- of S----- And taking on him the Conduct of the --- -----.* 1st ed. reviewed; copy seen 2d ed.: London, 1756 (Fol. 6d. Scott) BRITISH LIBRARY

Reviewed: *Monthly Review* 15 (1756): 655
Critical Review 2 (1756): 476–477

903 *The Fig Leaf*
NOT SEEN (4to. 1s. Tomlinson)

Reviewed: *Monthly Review* 38 (1768): 323
Critical Review 25 (1768): 313–314
London Magazine 37 (1768): 334
Universal Museum (1768): 205

Filial Piety: a Poem
See: CARR, John

The Fine Lady a Novel
See: BRISCOE, Sophia

904 *Fingal, a Poem In Six Books, by Ossian: translated from the Original Galic by Mr. Macpherson; and Rendered into Verse from that Translation.* Oxford, 1772 (8vo. 4s.bound. Rivington. 1772) BRITISH LIBRARY

Reviewed: *Monthly Review* 47 (1772): 71–72

905 *Fingal King of Morven, a Knight-Errant.* London, 1764 (8vo. 6d. Donaldson) BRITISH LIBRARY

Reviewed: *Critical Review* 19 (1765): 155

906 FIORENTINO, Giovanni. *The Novel From which the Play of The Merchant of Venice, Written by Shakespear, Is Taken. Translated from the Italian. To which is added, A Translation of a Novel from the Decamerone of Boccaccio.* London, 1755 (8vo. 6d. Cooper) BRITISH LIBRARY

Reviewed: *Monthly Review* 12 (1755): 389

907 *Fire: A Poem. Occasioned by the Devastations of the destructive Element; as they were found taking Place on the Property, and Manuscript Papers, of the Author*
NOT SEEN (4to. 1s. Bird)

Reviewed: *Monthly Review* 25 (1761): 508
Critical Review 12 (1761): 483
London Magazine 31 (1762): 56

The First Satire of the First Book of Horace imitated
See: NEVILE, Thomas

908 FITZGERALD, Gerald. *The Academick Sportsman; or, a Winter's Day: A Poem.* Dublin, 1773 (4to. 1s. Johnston, reprinted from the Dublin edition. 1773) BRITISH LIBRARY

Reviewed: *Monthly Review* 49 (1773): 226–229
Critical Review 36 (1773): 72
London Magazine 42 (1773): 351–352

909 *Fitz-Gigo, a New English Uproar; with the Way to Make Him; Or, a New Overture upon the Old Score; As it was performed at the Theatre Royal in Covent-Garden, by Mr. Beard, Miss Brent, Sig. Tenducci, Mr. Smith, Mr. Woodward, Pit, Boxes, Galleries, &c. &c. The Words adapted (al Burlesquo) to the favourite Airs in the Opera of Artaxerxes.* 1st ed. reviewed; copy seen 3d ed.: London, n.d. [BODLEIAN CAT.–1763] (4to. 6d. Swingster) BODLEIAN

Reviewed: *Monthly Review* 28 (1763): 239

910 FITZ-JAMES, Oswald. *The Wandsworth Epistle. In Metre. By Oswald Fitz-James, Esq;* London, 1762 (4to. 6d. Finmore) NEWBERRY

Reviewed: *Monthly Review* 27 (1762): 228
Critical Review 14 (1762): 239

Five Pieces of Runic Poetry
See: PERCY, Thomas

911 FLAGELLAN, Christopher (pseud.). *A Funeral Discourse, Occasioned by the much lamented Death of Mr. Yorick, Prebendary of Y--k and Author of the much admired Life and Opinions of Tristram Shandy, Preached before a very mixed Society of Jemmies, Jessamies, Methodists and Christians, at A Nocturnal Meeting in Petticoat Lane, and now published at the unanimous Request of the Hearers, by Christopher Flagellan, A.M. and enriched with the Notes of various Commentators.* London, 1761 (8vo. 1s. Nichols) BRITISH LIBRARY

Reviewed: *Monthly Review* 25 (1761): 320
Critical Review 12 (1761): 317

912 [FLEMING, Francis]. *The Life and extraordinary Adventures, the Perils and Critical Escapes of Timothy Ginnadrake, That Child of chequer'd Fortune. Vol. I.* Bath, n.d. (12mo. 3s.6d. Bath printed, for the Author, and sold by Dodsley, &c. in London) BRITISH LIBRARY

Reviewed: *Monthly Review* 42 (1770): 488

913 [FLEMING, Francis]. *The Life and extraordinary Adventures, the Perils and Critical Escapes of Timothy Ginnadrake, that Child of chequer'd Fortune.* 3 vols. Bath, vol. 3 dated 1771 (12mo. 9s. Bath printed, for the Author; and sold by Dodsley, &c. in London) BRITISH LIBRARY

Reviewed: *Monthly Review* 47 (1772): 239
Critical Review 34 (1772): 51–54
Town & Country Magazine 4 (1772): 359

914 FLETCHER, Phinehas. *Piscatory Eclogues, with other Poetical Miscellanies. Illustrated with Notes, Critical and Explanatory.* Edinburgh, 1771 (8vo. 3s. Cadell) BRITISH LIBRARY

Reviewed: *Monthly Review* 47 (1772): 70–71
Critical Review 34 (1772): 145–147
Universal Catalogue [1] (1772) art. 582

915 FLLOYD, Thomas (trans.). *Tartarian Tales: or, a Thousand and One Quarters of Hours. Written in French by the celebrated Mr. Guelletee, Author of the Chinese, Mogul, and other Tales. The Whole now for the first Time translated into English, By Thomas Flloyd.* [Translation of *Les Milles et Un Quart-d'heure. Contes Tartares* by Thomas Simon GUEULLETTE.] London, 1759 (3s. Tonson) BRITISH LIBRARY

Reviewed: *Monthly Review* 20 (1759): 79–80
Critical Review 7 (1759): 184

916 FOGERTY, Mrs. *The Fatal Connexion.* 2 vols.
NOT SEEN (12mo. 5s. Bladon)

Reviewed: *Monthly Review* 49 (1773): 150
Critical Review 36 (1773): 397
London Magazine 42 (1773): 456
Town & Country Magazine 5 (1773): 669
Universal Catalogue [2] (1773) art. 849

917 FOGERTY, Mrs. *Memoirs of Col. Digby and Miss Stanley. A Narrative founded on Facts. In a Series of Letters.* 2 vols.
NOT SEEN (12mo. 5s. Snagg)

Reviewed: *Monthly Review* 49 (1773): 319
Critical Review 36 (1773): 397

Town & Country Magazine 5 (1773): 669
Universal Catalogue [2] (1773) art. 1127

918 *Folly, a Satire*. London, 1774 (4to. 6d. Payne. 1774) BODLEIAN

Reviewed: *Monthly Review* 51 (1774): 315–316
Critical Review 38 (1774): 152
Town & Country Magazine 6 (1774): 464
Universal Catalogue 3 (1774) art. 1059

919 *Folly, a Satire on the Times. Written by a Fool, and younger Brother to Tristram Shandy*. London, n.d. [HOUGHTON CAT.–1763?] (4to. 2s. Pridden) HARVARD (HOUGHTON)

Reviewed: *Monthly Review* 30 (1764): 69
Critical Review 16 (1763): 478

920 *The Fond Lover: a Poem*. London, 1773 (4to. 1s. Allen. 1773) NEW YORK PUBLIC LIBRARY

Reviewed: *Monthly Review* 49 (1773): 230
Critical Review 36 (1773): 156
Universal Catalogue [2] (1773) art. 950

921 FOOT, James. *Penseroso, or the Pensive Philosopher in his Solitudes, a Poem in Six Books. By the Rev'd. James Foot*. London, 1771 (8vo. 4s.boards. Bathurst. 1771) BRITISH LIBRARY

Reviewed: *Monthly Review* 44 (1771): 417
Critical Review 32 (1771): 150–152

922 FOOTE, [Samuel]. *The Author; a Comedy, of two acts. As it is perform'd at the Theatre Royal in Drury-lane*. London, 1757 (8vo. 1s. Francklin) BRITISH LIBRARY

Reviewed: *Monthly Review* 16 (1757): 361–363
Critical Review 3 (1757): 151–153
Literary Magazine 2 (1757): 76–79

923 FOOTE, Samuel. *The Commissary. A Comedy in Three Acts. As it is Performed at the Theatre in the Hay-Market*. London, 1765 (8vo. 1s.6d. Vaillant) BRITISH LIBRARY

Reviewed: *Monthly Review* 33 (1765): 83
Critical Review 20 (1765): 70–71

924 FOOTE, Samuel. *The Englishman in Paris. A Comedy, in two acts. As it is performed at the Theatre-Royal in Covent-Garden*. London, 1753 (8vo. 1s. Vaillant) BRITISH LIBRARY

Reviewed: *Monthly Review* 8 (1753): 394–395

925 FOOTE, Samuel. *The Englishman return'd from Paris, Being the Sequel to the Englishman in Paris. A Farce in two acts. As it is perform'd at the Theatre-Royal in Covent-Garden*. London, 1756 (1s. Vaillant) BRITISH LIBRARY

Reviewed: *Monthly Review* 14 (1756): 269
Critical Review 1 (1756): 83–85

926 FOOTE, Samuel. *The Knights. A Comedy, in Two Acts. As it is performed at the Theatre-Royal in Drury-Lane*. London, 1754 (8vo. 1s. Vaillant) BRITISH LIBRARY

Reviewed: *Monthly Review* 10 (1754): 239

927 FOOTE, Samuel. *The Lame Lover, a Comedy in Three Acts. As it is Performed at the Theatre-Royal in the Hay-Market*. London, 1770 (8vo. 1s.6d. Elmsley, &c. 1770) BRITISH LIBRARY

Reviewed: *Monthly Review* 43 (1770): 151
Critical Review 30 (1770): 141–143
Gentleman's Magazine 40 (1770): 378–382
London Magazine 39 (1770): 426

928 FOOTE, Samuel. *The Lyar. A Comedy in three acts. As it is Performed at the Theatre in the Hay-Market*. London, 1764 (8vo. 1s.6d. Kearsly) BRITISH LIBRARY

Reviewed: *Monthly Review* 31 (1764): 153–155
Critical Review 18 (1764): 120–124
British Magazine 5 (1764): 433

929 FOOTE, Samuel. *The Mayor of Garret. A Comedy, in Two Acts. As it is Performed at the Theatre-Royal in Drury-Lane*. London, 1764 (8vo. 1s. Vaillant) BRITISH LIBRARY

Reviewed: *Monthly Review* 29 (1763): 463–464
Critical Review 16 (1763): 435–439

930 FOOTE, [Samuel]. *The Minor, A Comedy. As it is now acting at the New Theatre in the Hay-Market. By Authority from the Lord Chamberlain*. London, 1760 (8vo. 1s.6d. Coote) BRITISH LIBRARY

Reviewed: *Monthly Review* 23 (1760): 83
Critical Review 10 (1760): 69–70
British Magazine 1 (1760): 489

931 FOOTE, [Samuel]. *The Orators. As it is now performing at the New Theatre in the Hay-Market.* London, 1762 (8vo. 1s.6d. Coote) BRITISH LIBRARY

Reviewed: *Monthly Review* 26 (1762): 475–476
Critical Review 13 (1762): 520
British Magazine 3 (1762): 324

932 FOOTE, Samuel. *The Patron. A Comedy in three acts. As it is Performed at the Theatre in the Hay-Market.* London, 1764 (8vo. 1s. Kearsly) BRITISH LIBRARY

Reviewed: *Monthly Review* 31 (1764): 153
Critical Review 18 (1764): 53–57
British Magazine 5 (1764): 433
General Magazine 1 (1764): 352–354

933 FOOTE, Samuel. *Taste. A Comedy, Of Two Acts. As it is Acted at the Theatre-Royal in Drury-Lane.* London, 1752 (8vo. 1s. Francklin) BRITISH LIBRARY

Reviewed: *Monthly Review* 6 (1752): 77–78
Gentleman's Magazine 22 (1752): 47

Foote's Prologue Detected
See: HIFFERNAN, Paul

934 ———— *For Ever! A Poem.* London, n.d. (4to. 1s. Newbery) NEW YORK PUBLIC LIBRARY

Reviewed: *Monthly Review* 38 (1768): 335
Critical Review 25 (1768): 227–228
London Magazine 37 (1768): 334

935 *The Force of Nature; or, the History of Charles Lord Sommers: In Two Volumes. By the Editor of the Wanderer.* London, 1768 (12mo. 5s. Noble) BRITISH LIBRARY

Reviewed: *Monthly Review* 38 (1768): 150–151
Critical Review 24 (1767): 430–436
Universal Museum 3 (1767): 652

936 *Fordyce Delineated, a Satire: Occasioned by his Sermons to Young Women.* London, n.d. [IU CAT.–1766?] (4to. 1s. Dingwell) UNIVERSITY OF ILLINOIS

Reviewed: *Monthly Review* 36 (1767): 78–79
Critical Review 23 (1767): 61

937 [FORREST, Frederick]. *A Rattle for Grown Children: containing Odes, Cantatas, Medleys, Songs, and Catches. By Young D'Urfey.* London, 1766 (8vo. 2s. Bladon) BRITISH LIBRARY

Reviewed: *Monthly Review* 34 (1766): 481
Critical Review 22 (1766): 77

938 FORTESCUE, [James]. *Dissertations, Essays, and Discourses, &c. In Prose and Verse. By Dr. Fortescue.* 2 vols. Oxford, 1759 (8vo. 10s. Dodsley) BODLEIAN

Reviewed: *Monthly Review* 21 (1759): 291–296
Critical Review 8 (1759): 137–143

939 [FORTESCUE, James]. *An Essay on Sacred Harmony.* London, 1753 [Included, with its original title page, with his *Essays Moral and Miscellaneous*] (8vo. 6d. Owen) BRITISH LIBRARY

Reviewed: *Monthly Review* 9 (1753): 154

940 FORTESCUE, [James]. *Essays, Moral and Miscellaneous. Viz. An Introductory Speech from Solomon, with an Ode. A Vision on a Plan of the Ancients. A Sketch of Life after the Manners of the Moderns. The State of Man; his Passions, their Objects, and End; their Use, Abuse, Regulation, and Employment. With a Poem Sacred to the Memory of the Princes of Wales and of Orange. Part I.* 1st ed. reviewed; copy seen 2d ed.: London, 1752 (8vo. 1s. Baldwin) BRITISH LIBRARY

Reviewed: *Monthly Review* 6 (1752): 78–79

941 [FORTESCUE, James]. *Pomery-Hill. A Poem. Humbly addressed to his Royal Highness the Prince of Wales. With Other Poems, English and Latin.* London, 1754 (8vo. 1s. Millar) BRITISH LIBRARY

Reviewed: *Monthly Review* 11 (1754): 149–151
Gentleman's Magazine 24 (1754): 245

942 [FORTESCUE, James]. *Science; A Poem, (In a Religious View) on it's Decline and Revival. With a particular regard to the Mission of Moses, And the Coming of the Messiah.* Oxford, 1751 (Oxford: Printed for J. Fletcher in the Turl; and sold by M. Cooper and W. Owen in London, and J. Leake, at Bath) BRITISH LIBRARY

Reviewed: *Monthly Review* 4 (1750–51): 514–519

943 [FORTESCUE, James]. *A View of Life in its several Passions. With a Preliminary Discourse on Moral Writing.* London, 1749 (8vo. 6d. Printed for Cooper and Owen in London, Fletcher at Oxford and Leake at Bath) BRITISH LIBRARY

Reviewed: *Monthly Review* 1 (1749): 408–410

944 *The Fortunate Blue-Coat Boy: or, Memoirs of the Life and Happy Adventures of Mr. Benjamin Templeman; Formerly a Scholar of Christ's-Hospital. By an Orphanotrophian.* 2 vols. London, 1770 (12mo. 6s. Cooke) BRITISH LIBRARY

Reviewed: *Monthly Review* 42 (1770): 71–72
Critical Review 29 (1770): 149–150
Town & Country Magazine 2 (1770): 72

945 *The Fortunate Villager: or, the adventures of Sir Andrew Thomson.* 2 vols.
NOT SEEN (12mo. 6s. Noble)

Reviewed: *Monthly Review* 16 (1757): 284
Critical Review 3 (1757): 187

Fortune, a Rhapsody
See: DERRICK, Samuel

946 *The Fortune-Teller.* 2 vols. London, 1774 (12mo. 6s. Bew. 1774) BRITISH LIBRARY

Reviewed: *Monthly Review* 50 (1774): 326–327
Critical Review 38 (1774): 157
London Magazine 43 (1774): 92
Town & Country Magazine 6 (1774): 464
Universal Catalogue 3 (1774) art. 214

947 *The Fortune-Teller, or footman ennobled. Being the History of the right honourable Earl of R----- and Miss Lucy M–n–y.* 2 vols.
NOT SEEN (12mo. 6s. Noble)

Reviewed: *Monthly Review* 14 (1756): 268–269
Critical Review 1 (1756): 53–56

Forty select Poems on several occasions, by The Right Honourable The Earl of H*******n
See: HAMILTON, Thomas, 6th Earl of Haddington

948 FOSTER, Mrs. *Verses wrote by Mrs Foster. But which never reached the royal hands*
NOT SEEN (4to. 1s. Dodsley)

Reviewed: *Gentleman's Magazine* 39 (1769): 502

949 *The Foundlings. An Elegy.* London, 1763 (4to. 6d. Flexney) HARVARD (HOUGHTON)

Reviewed: *Monthly Review* 28 (1763): 318–320
Critical Review 15 (1763): 239

Four Elegies: Descriptive and Moral
See: SCOTT, John

Four Elegies. I. Morning. II. Noon. III. Evening. IV. Night.
See: PANTING, Stephen

The Four Farthing-Candles
See: SHAW, Cuthbert

950 *Four Hundred and Forty Six Verses, containing Harsh Truths. In which are introduced, A Translation from the High-Dutch: and a Fable.* London, 1757 (4to. 6d. Scott) HARVARD (HOUGHTON)

Reviewed: *Monthly Review* 16 (1757): 603
Critical Review 4 (1757): 90–91

951 *Four Odes. I. To Sleep. II. On Beauty. III. On Taste. IV. To the Right Hon. the Lady **** on the Death of her Son.* London, 1750 (4to. 44pp. 1s.6d. Manby and Cox) BODLEIAN

Reviewed: *Monthly Review* 3 (1750): 47–52

952
Four Pastorals: Morning; Noon; Evening; and Night. Addressed to a Lady. London, 1751 (4to. 1s. Vaillant) BRITISH LIBRARY

Reviewed: *Monthly Review* 5 (1751): 76

953 *Four Pastorals, viz. Hylas, Corydon. 2. Colin Clout, Cuddy. 3. Mopsus, Leander, Argol. 4.*

The Marriage of Zephyr and Flora. By T. S. Esq; Of the Middle Temple. London, 1768 (4to. 2s. Webley) BRITISH LIBRARY

Reviewed: *Monthly Review* 39 (1768): 242
Critical Review 26 (1768): 152–154
Universal Museum 4 (1768): 429
Political Register 3 (1768): 126

954 *The Fourth Grace.* London, 1755 (Fol. 6d. Crowder & Co.) HARVARD (HOUGHTON)

Reviewed: *Monthly Review* 11 (1754): 399
Gentleman's Magazine 24 (1754): 534

955 *The Fourth Satire of Boileau imitated, with a Dedication, to R***** M*rr*s, Esq; of O***l C*ll**e.* London, 1764 (4to. 6d. Flexney) BRITISH LIBRARY

Reviewed: *Monthly Review* 30 (1764): 415
Critical Review 17 (1764): 393

956 FOX, Edmond. *Enthusiasm: A Poem. With Notes variorum. For the Correction of some, and Consolation of Others.* London, 1758 (8vo. 6d. Lewis) BRITISH LIBRARY

Reviewed: *Monthly Review* 19 (1758): 588
Gentleman's Magazine 28 (1758): 599

957 *The Fox; an Elegiac Poem: sacred to the Memory of a late Right H-----ble Personage* NOT SEEN (8vo. 6d. Snagg. 1774)

Reviewed: *Monthly Review* 51 (1774): 245
Critical Review 38 (1774): 152
Town & Country Magazine 6 (1774): 464
Universal Catalogue 3 (1774) art. 1054

Fragments of Ancient Poetry
See: MACPHERSON, James

958 FRANCIS, B. *An Elegy on the Death of the Rev. Mr. George Whitefield*
NOT SEEN (4to. Bristol, printed for the Author, and sold in London by Buckland, &c.)

Reviewed: *Monthly Review* 44 (1771): 174
Critical Review 31 (1771): 475

959 FRANCIS, Philip. *Constantine: a Tragedy. As it is Acted at the Theatre-Royal in Covent-Garden.* London, 1754 (8vo. 1s.6d. Millar) BRITISH LIBRARY

Reviewed: *Monthly Review* 10 (1754): 221–231

960 FRANCIS, Philip. *Eugenia: A Tragedy. As it is Acted at the Theatre-Royal in Drury-Lane. By His Majesty's Servants.* London, 1752 (8vo. 1s.6d. Millar) BRITISH LIBRARY

Reviewed: *Monthly Review* 6 (1752): 238

961 [FRANCIS, Philip]. *A Letter from a Right Honourable Person. And the Answer to it, Translated into Verse, as nearly as the different Idioms of Prose and Poetry will allow. With Notes Historical, Critical, Political, &c.* London, 1761 (4to. 1s. Nichol) BRITISH LIBRARY

Reviewed: *Monthly Review* 25 (1761): 390
British Magazine 2 (1761): 662

962 [FRANCKLIN, Thomas]. *The Earl of Warwick, a Tragedy, As it is perform'd at the Theatre Royal in Drury-Lane.* [From the French original by Jean François de la Harpe.] London, 1766 (8vo. 1s.6d. Davies) BRITISH LIBRARY

Reviewed: *Monthly Review* 35 (1766): 484–485
Critical Review 22 (1766): 425–430
Gentleman's Magazine 36 (1766): 624–625

963 FRANCKLIN, Thomas (trans.). *The Tragedies of Sophocles, From the Greek.* 2 vols. London, 1759 (4to. 1l.1s. Francklin) BRITISH LIBRARY

Reviewed: *Monthly Review* 21 (1759): 417–423
Critical Review 7 (1759): 512–520

964 FRANCKLIN, Thomas. *The Tragedies of Sophocles, translated from the Greek; (With a Dissertation on Antient Tragedy.) By the Rev. Thomas Francklin, M.A. Late Greek Professor in the University of Cambridge. A New Edition, carefully revised and corrected.* 2 vols. London, 1766 (8vo. 10s.bound. Davies) BRITISH LIBRARY

Reviewed: *Critical Review* 23 (1767): 74

965 FRANCKLIN, Thomas. *Translation; a Poem.* London, 1753 (4to. 1s. Dodsley) BRITISH LIBRARY

Reviewed: *Monthly Review* 8 (1753): 507–508

966 FRANCKLIN, Thomas. *Translation, a Poem. By Thomas Francklin, Fellow of Trinity-College, Cambridge. The Second Edition.* London, 1754 (no pub. details) BRITISH LIBRARY

Reviewed: *Literary Magazine* 2 (1757): 31–32

967 [FRANCKLIN, Thomas]. *Truth and Falshood: a Tale.* London, 1755 (Fol. 6d. Cooper) BRITISH LIBRARY

Reviewed: *Monthly Review* 12 (1755): 158

968 *Frederic; or, the Fortunate Beggar. Wherein Is displayed the various Events in Human Life, in A Series of Letters, Copied from Originals.* 2 vols. London, n.d. [BODLEIAN CAT.–c. 1770] (12mo. 6s. Roson) BODLEIAN

Reviewed: *Monthly Review* 47 (1772): 487
Critical Review 35 (1773): 79
London Magazine 41 (1772): 598
Universal Catalogue [1] (1772) art. 1472

969 FREDERICK II, King of Prussia. *Elogy on Prince Henry of Prussia. Composed by His Majesty The King of Prussia; and Read by his Order in an extraordinary Assembly of the Academy of Sciences at Berlin.* Birmingham, 1768 (8vo. 1s.6d. Elmsby) BRITISH LIBRARY

Reviewed: *Monthly Review* 39 (1768): 239–240
Critical Review 26 (1768): 73
London Magazine 37 (1768): 389–390
Political Register 3 (1768): 126

970 FREDERICK II, King of Prussia. *The Seventh Epistle Attempted in English, from the King of Prussia's Oeuvres du Philosophe de Sans Souci. To Maupertuis.* London, 1761 (Fol. 1s. Osborne) BRITISH LIBRARY

Reviewed: *Monthly Review* 24 (1761): 355
Critical Review 11 (1761): 415

FREDERICK II, King of Prussia (adaptation)
See: DERRICK, Samuel. *Sylla*

971 *Frederick the Great. A poem*
NOT SEEN (4to. 6d. Pottinger)

Reviewed: *Monthly Review* 20 (1759): 471–472
Critical Review 7 (1759): 463

972 FREE, John. *An Ode of Consolation Upon the Loss of Minorca. Humbly Address'd to His Royal Highness The Duke of Cumberland, &c. By John Free, D.D. Vicar of East-Coker in Somersetshire; Thursday Lecturer of St. Mary-Hill, London; and Lecturer of Newington in Surry.* London, 1756 (Fol. 6d. Baldwin) HARVARD (HOUGHTON)

Reviewed: *Monthly Review* 15 (1756): 318–319

973 FREE, John. *Poems on Several Occasions, Formerly Written By John Free, D.D. Vicar of East-Coker in Somersetshire, Thursday Lecturer of St. Mary-Hill, London, and Lecturer of Newington in Surry. The Second Edition, With Additions of later Pieces; and an historical and critical Account of the Origin and peculiar Nature of English Poetry, in a Letter to a Member of Parliament.* London, 1757 (12mo. 2s.6d. Owen) UNIVERSITY OF CHICAGO

Reviewed: *Monthly Review* 18 (1758): 185

974 FREE, John. *Stigand: or, the Antigallican. A Poem, in Miltonic Verse.* London, 1750 (4to. 1s. Printed for M. Sheepey) BRITISH LIBRARY

Reviewed: *Monthly Review* 4 (1750–51): 157

975 [FREE, John]. *The Voluntary Exile; or, the English Poet's Sermon in Verse, Written upon divers Important Subjects, Before he embarked for France, and dedicated a La Coterie, or the Society of English Patriots. Part the First. With Variety of Notes, Religious, Historical, and Political.* London, 1765 (4to. 2s.6d. Almon) BODLEIAN

Reviewed: *Monthly Review* 32 (1765): 234
Critical Review 19 (1765): 235

976 *Freedom, a Poem In Two Books: The First, Respecting Man in the general as a Social Creature. The Second, Respecting Man as a Rational Creature. Addressed to the Right Honourable William Pitt, Esquire.* London, 1760 (4to. 2s.6d. Dodsley) BODLEIAN

Reviewed: *Monthly Review* 22 (1760): 516

977 *Freedom; a Poem. Inscribed to John Wilkes, Esq; by a Native of the West Indies*
NOT SEEN (4to. 6d. Plummer)

Reviewed: *Monthly Review* 51 (1774): 69
Critical Review 38 (1774): 76
Town & Country Magazine 6 (1774): 437
Universal Catalogue 3 (1774) art. 767

978 FREEMAN, G. *Day: An Epistle to C. Churchill*
NOT SEEN (8vo. 1s.6d. Williams)

Reviewed: *Monthly Review* 26 (1762): 320
Critical Review 13 (1762): 362
British Magazine 3 (1762): 662

979 FREINSHEMIUS, Jo[annes] (pseud.). *Threnodia: or, an Elegy on The unexpected and unlamented Death of the M----- of B------; Faithfully done into modern English from the Genuine Manuscript in the Grubstreet Vatican. And now publish'd, together with the Original Proeme, and Annotations.* Oxford, 1753 (4to. 6d. Oxford printed) BRITISH LIBRARY

Reviewed: *Monthly Review* 8 (1753): 391

The French Flogged
See: STEVENS, George Alexander

980 *The French Lady. A Novel.* 2 vols.
NOT SEEN (12mo. 6s. Lowndes)

Reviewed: *Monthly Review* 41 (1769): 480
Critical Review 28 (1769): 277–281
Gentleman's Magazine 39 (1769): 549
London Magazine 38 (1769): 537
Town & Country Magazine [1] (1769): 551

The Frenchified Lady Never in Paris
See: DELL, Henry

The Frequented Village
See: KING, Anthony

981 FRIBBLE, Timothy (pseud.). *Tittle Tattle; or, Taste-A-la-Mode. A New Farce. Perform'd with Universal Applause by a Select Company of Belles and Beaux, at the Lady Brilliant's Withdrawing-Room. Pour tuer le Tems.* London, 1749 (8vo. 52pp. 1s. Printed for the Author.) BRITISH LIBRARY

Reviewed: *Monthly Review* 2 (1749–50): 27–28

The Fribbleriad
See: GARRICK, David

982 *The Friendly Rivals; or, Love the best Contriver. A Comedy.* London, 1752 (8vo. 1s.6d. Mechell) BRITISH LIBRARY

Reviewed: *Monthly Review* 6 (1752): 396–397

The Friends. A Sentimental History
See: GUTHRIE, William

983 *The Friends; or, Original Letters of a Person Deceased. Now first published, From The Manuscripts, in his correspondent's hands.* 2 vols. London, 1773 (12mo. 6s. Bell. 1773) BRITISH LIBRARY

Reviewed: *Monthly Review* 48 (1773): 321
Critical Review 36 (1773): 236
London Magazine 42 (1773): 149
Universal Catalogue [2] (1773) art. 341

984 *Friendship: a Poem inscribed to a Friend: to which is added, an Ode.* London, 1769 (4to. 2s.6d. Kearsly. 1769) BRITISH LIBRARY

Reviewed: *Monthly Review* 41 (1769): 57–59
Critical Review 28 (1769): 300–302
Critical Memoirs [2] (1769): 182–183
Political Register 4 (1769): 389

Friendship: a Satire
See: GREENE, Edward Burnaby

985 [FROMAGET, Nicolas]. *The Kinsman of Mahomet; or, Memoirs of a French Slave, During his Eight Years Captivity in Constantinople. Including many Curious Particulars Relative to the Religion, History, Policy, Customs and Manners of the Turks; And Interspersed with A Variety of Adventures in the Seraglios of the East. Written by Himself, And Translated from the Original French.* 2 vols. London, 1774 (12mo. 6s. Culver) BRITISH LIBRARY

Reviewed: *Monthly Review* 50 (1774): 71
Universal Catalogue [2] (1773) art. 1330

986 *The Fruit Shop. A Tale.* 2 vols. London, 1765 (12mo. 4s.sewed. Moran) BRITISH LIBRARY

Reviewed: *Monthly Review* 33 (1765): 86
Critical Review 19 (1765): 475
Candid Review 1 (1765): 441–445

987 *The Fruitless Repentance; or, the History of Miss Kitty Le Fever.* 2 vols. London, 1769 (12mo. 5s.sewed. Newbery) BRITISH LIBRARY

Reviewed: *Monthly Review* 42 (1770): 72
Critical Review 29 (1770): 43–47
London Magazine 38 (1769): 640
Town & Country Magazine 2 (1770): 44

988 *The Fugitive Miscellany. Being a Collection of such Fugitive Pieces, In Prose and Verse, as are not in any other Collection. With many Pieces never before published.* London, 1774 (8vo. 3s. Almon. 1774) BRITISH LIBRARY

Reviewed: *Monthly Review* 51 (1774): 72–73
Critical Review 38 (1774): 240
Gentleman's Magazine 44 (1774): 228
Universal Catalogue 3 (1774) art. 520

989 *Fugitive Pieces. By a Poor Poet.* London, 1767 (4to. 1s. Becket) BRITISH LIBRARY

Reviewed: *Monthly Review* 36 (1767): 329–330
Critical Review 23 (1767): 296

Fugitive Pieces, on Various Subjects. By Several Authors
See: DODSLEY, Robert (ed.)

Fun: A Parodi-tragi-comical Satire
See: KENRICK, William

990 *A Funeral Ode on the Rev. Mr. Adams, who departed this Life, at Rodberow, Gloucestershire, August 10,1770; and on the much lamented Death of the Rev. Mr. George Whitefield.—Together with verses composed in America, by a Negro Girl seventeen years of Age, on Mr. Whitefield*
NOT SEEN (1d.)

Reviewed: *Critical Review* 31 (1771): 76

991 FUNIDOS, Rigdum (pseud.). *Kitty's Stream: or, the Noblemen turned Fisher-Men. A Comic Satire. Addressed to the Gentlemen in the Interest of the Celebrated Miss K----y F---r.* N.p., 1759 [ESTC-London] (4to. 6d. Moore) BRITISH LIBRARY

Reviewed: *Monthly Review* 20 (1759): 476
Critical Review 8 (1759): 176

992 [FURLEY, J. Dennis]. *Choheleth, or The Royal Preacher, a Poem. Most humbly inscribed to the King.* London, 1768 (4to. 6s. Johnston) BRITISH LIBRARY

Reviewed: *Monthly Review* 38 (1768): 246
Critical Review 25 (1768): 191–198
London Magazine 37 (1768): 48
Universal Museum 4 (1768): 148
Political Register 2 (1768): 384

993 [GAILLARD DE LA BATAILLE, Pierre Alexandre]. *The History of Mademoiselle Cronel—&c. Translated from the French*
NOT SEEN (12mo. 1s.6d. Dawe)

Reviewed: *Monthly Review* 17 (1757): 563

994 GALLIARD, Bradshaw. *Odes.* London, 1774 (4to. 2s.6d. Johnson. 1774) BRITISH LIBRARY

Reviewed: *Monthly Review* 51 (1774): 166
Critical Review 38 (1774): 73–74
Town & Country Magazine 6 (1774): 148
Universal Catalogue 3 (1774) art. 655

995 GAMBOLD, John. *The Martyrdom of Ignatius. A Tragedy. Written in the Year 1740. To which is Annexed, The Life of Ignatius, drawn from Authentic Accounts, and from the Epistles written by him from Smyrna and Troas, in his Way to Rome.* London, 1773 (8vo. 2s. Cadell, &c. 1774) BRITISH LIBRARY

Reviewed: *Monthly Review* 50 (1774): 485
Critical Review 36 (1773): 395

The Gamester. A Tragedy
See: MOORE, Edward

The Gamesters. A Poem
See: WILKINSON, Edward

996 GARDINER, Richard. *An elegy on the death of lady Asgill, lady of sir Charles Asgill, knt. and alderman of the city of London. To which

is added, an epitaph on the late sir Edmond Bacon, bart.
NOT SEEN (Fol. 6d. Cooper)

Listed: *Monthly Review* 10 (1754): 157

997 [GARDINER, Richard]. *The History of Pudica, a Lady of N–rf–lk. With an Account of her Five Lovers; Viz. Dick Merryfellow, Count Antiquary, Young 'Squire Fog, of Popgun-hall, Esq; together with Miss Pudica's Sense of the Word Eclaircissement, and an Epithalamium on her Nuptials. By Tom Tenor, Clerk of the Parish. To the Tune of, Green grow the Rushes o'. By William Honeycomb, Esq;* London, 1754 (8vo. 6d. Cooper) BRITISH LIBRARY

Reviewed: *Monthly Review* 10 (1754): 160
Gentleman's Magazine 24 (1754): 194

998 *The Garretteer, a Satire. Inscribed (without Permission) To the Three most distinguished Heroes of the Poem, the Garretteer's Patrons.* London, 1764 (4to. 1s. Hinxman) UNIVERSITY OF PENNSYLVANIA

Reviewed: *Monthly Review* 30 (1764): 158
Critical Review 17 (1764): 77

999 [GARRICK, David]. *Albumazar. A Comedy. As it is now revived at the Theatre-Royal in Drury-Lane. With Alterations.* [Adaptation by Garrick from Thomas Tomkis.] London, 1773 (8vo. 1s. Becket. 1773) BRITISH LIBRARY

Reviewed: *Monthly Review* 49 (1773): 395
Critical Review 36 (1773): 396
Gentleman's Magazine 43 (1773): 509
Universal Catalogue [2] (1773) art. 1196

1000 [GARRICK, David]. *Alfred, a Masque. As it is now revived at the Theatre-Royal in Drury-Lane. By His Majesty's Servants.* [Adapted by Garrick from Mallet and Thomson.] London, 1773 (8vo. 1s.6d. Cadell, &c. 1773) BRITISH LIBRARY

Reviewed: *Monthly Review* 49 (1773): 507–508
Universal Catalogue [2] (1773) art. 1133

1001 [GARRICK, David]. *Catharine and Petruchio. A Comedy in Three Acts. As it is perform'd at the Theatre-Royal in Drury-Lane. Alter'd from Shakespear's Taming of the Shrew.* London, 1756 (8vo. 1s. Tonson) BRITISH LIBRARY

Reviewed: *Monthly Review* 14 (1756): 270
Critical Review 1 (1756): 145–146

1002 [GARRICK, David]. *The Chances. A Comedy. With Alterations.* [Altered by Garrick from Beaumont and Fletcher.] London, 1773 (8vo. 1s.6d. Becket. 1773) BRITISH LIBRARY

Reviewed: *Monthly Review* 48 (1773): 413

GARRICK, David (with George Colman). *The Clandestine Marriage*
See: COLMAN, George (the elder)

1003 [GARRICK, David]. *The Country Girl, a Comedy, (Altered from Wycherley) As it is Acted at the Theatre-Royal in Drury-Lane.* London, 1766 (8vo. 1s.6d. Becket) BRITISH LIBRARY

Reviewed: *Monthly Review* 35 (1766): 405–406
Critical Review 22 (1766): 378–379

1004 [GARRICK, David]. *Cymon. A Dramatic Romance. As it is performed at the Theatre-Royal in Drury-Lane.* London, 1766 (8vo. 1s.6d. Becket) BRITISH LIBRARY

Reviewed: *Monthly Review* 36 (1767): 71
Critical Review 23 (1767): 58–59
Gentleman's Magazine 37 (1767): 28–32

1005 [GARRICK, David]. *The Enchanter; or, Love and Magic. A Musical Drama. As it is performed at the Theatre-Royal in Drury-Lane. The Music composed by Mr. Smith.* London, 1760 (8vo. 6d. Tonson) BRITISH LIBRARY

Reviewed: *Monthly Review* 23 (1760): 527
Critical Review 10 (1760): 483
London Magazine 29 (1760): 672
British Magazine 1 (1760): 714

1006 [GARRICK, David]. *The Fairies. An Opera. Taken from A Midsummer Night's Dream, Written by Shakespear. As it is Perform'd at the Theatre-Royal in Drury-Lane. The Songs from Shakespear, Milton, Waller, Dryden, Lansdown, Hammond, &c. The Music composed by Mr. Smith.* London, 1755 (8vo. 1s. Tonson) BRITISH LIBRARY

Reviewed: *Gentleman's Magazine* 25 (1755): 93–94

Listed: *Monthly Review* 12 (1755): 157

1007 [GARRICK, David]. *The Farmer's Return from London. An Interlude. As it is Performed at the Theatre Royal in Drury Lane.* London, 1762 (4to. 1s. Tonson) BRITISH LIBRARY

Reviewed: *Monthly Review* 26 (1762): 385–386
Critical Review 13 (1762): 362
British Magazine 3 (1762): 213

1008 GARRICK, David. *Florizel and Perdita; or The Winter's Tale. A Dramatic Pastoral, In Three Acts. Altered from Shakespear. As it is performed at the Theatre-Royal in Drury-Lane.* London, 1762 (8vo. 1s.6d. Tonson) BRITISH LIBRARY

Reviewed: *Monthly Review* 26 (1762): 151
Critical Review 13 (1762): 157–158
British Magazine 3 (1762): 158

1009 [GARRICK, David]. *The Fribbleriad.* London, 1761 (4to. 1s. Coote) BRITISH LIBRARY

Reviewed: *Monthly Review* 24 (1761): 444
Critical Review 11 (1761): 494
British Magazine 2 (1761): 382

1010 [GARRICK, David]. *The Guardian. A Comedy of Two Acts. As it is perform'd at the Theatre-Royal in Drury-Lane.* [Adapted from *Le pupille* by Christophe Barthélemi Fagan.] London, 1759 (8vo. 1s. Newbery) BRITISH LIBRARY

Reviewed: *Monthly Review* 20 (1759): 272–273
Critical Review 7 (1759): 171–172
Gentleman's Magazine 29 (1759): 84–86

1011 [GARRICK, David]. *The Irish Widow. In Two Acts. As it is performed at the Theatre-Royal in Drury-Lane.* London, 1772 (8vo. 1s. Becket. 1772) BRITISH LIBRARY

Reviewed: *Monthly Review* 47 (1772): 408
Critical Review 34 (1772): 397
Gentleman's Magazine 42 (1772): 528–532
Universal Catalogue [1] (1772) art. 1371

1012 [GARRICK, David]. *Isabella: or, the Fatal Marriage. A Play. Alter'd from Southern. As it is Now performing at the Theatre-Royal in Drury-Lane.* London, 1757 (8vo. 1s. Tonson) BRITISH LIBRARY

Reviewed: *Critical Review* 5 (1758): 75–76

1013 [GARRICK, David]. *King Arthur: or, the British Worthy. A Masque. By Mr. Dryden. As it is performed at the Theatre-Royal in Drury-Lane, By His Majesty's Company. The Music by Purcell and Dr. Arne.* London, 1770 (8vo. 1s. Davies) BRITISH LIBRARY

Reviewed: *Monthly Review* 43 (1770): 498
Critical Review 30 (1770): 468

1014 [GARRICK, David]. *Lilliput. A Dramatic Entertainment. As it is performed at the Theatre-Royal in Drury-Lane.* London, 1757 (8vo. 1s. Vaillant) BRITISH LIBRARY

Reviewed: *Monthly Review* 16 (1757): 95
Critical Review 2 (1756): 474

1015 [GARRICK, David]. *The Male-Coquette: or, Seventeen Hundred Fifty-Seven. In Two Acts. As it is Performed at the Theatre-Royal in Drury-Lane.* London, 1757 (8vo. 1s. P. Vaillant) BRITISH LIBRARY

Reviewed: *Monthly Review* 17 (1757): 568
Critical Review 5 (1758): 76–79

1016 [GARRICK, David]. *Neck or Nothing, A Farce. In Two Acts. As it is performed at the Theatre Royal in Drury-Lane.* [Adapted from *Crispin, rival de son maître* by Alain René le Sage.] London, 1766 (8vo. 1s. Becket) BRITISH LIBRARY

Reviewed: *Monthly Review* 35 (1766): 483
Critical Review 22 (1766): 468
Gentleman's Magazine 36 (1766): 591

1017 [GARRICK, David]. *A New Dramatic Entertainment, called A Christmas Tale. In Five Parts. As it is performed at the Theatre-Royal in Drury-Lane. Embellished with an Etching, by Mr. Loutherbourg.* [Adapted from *La Fée Urgèle* by Charles Simon Favart.] London, 1774 (8vo. 1s.6d. Becket. 1774) BRITISH LIBRARY

Reviewed: *Monthly Review* 50 (1774): 73

1018 [GARRICK, David]. *An Ode on the Death of Mr. Pelham.* [Also attributed to Edward Moore.] London, 1754 (Fol. 6d. Cooper) BRITISH LIBRARY

Reviewed: *Monthly Review* 10 (1754): 305
Gentleman's Magazine 24 (1754): 145

1019 [GARRICK, David]. *An Ode upon Dedicating A Building, and Erecting A Statue, to Shakespeare, at Stratford Upon Avon. By D. G.* London, 1769 (4to. 1s. Becket) BRITISH LIBRARY

Reviewed: *Monthly Review* 41 (1769): 234–238
Critical Review 28 (1769): 231–233
Gentleman's Magazine 39 (1769): 446–447

1020 [GARRICK, David]. *A Peep Behind The Curtain; or The New Rehearsal. As it is now performed at the Theatre Royal in Drury-Lane.* London, 1767 (8vo. 1s. Becket) BRITISH LIBRARY

Reviewed: *Monthly Review* 37 (1767): 468–469
Critical Review 25 (1768): 143
Gentleman's Magazine 37 (1767): 561–562
Universal Museum 3 (1767): 596
Political Register 2 (1768): 318

1021 [GARRICK, David]. *The Sick Monkey, a Fable.* "Thursday Afternoon David Garrick Esq; arrived at his House in Southampton-street"—*Public Advertiser, April 27, 1765.* London, 1765 (4to. 1s.6d. Fletcher) BRITISH LIBRARY

Reviewed: *Monthly Review* 32 (1765): 394

1022 [GARRICK, David]. *The Songs and Recitative of Orpheus: An English Burletta. Which is introduced in a farce of two acts, called A New Rehearsal: or, A Peep Behind The Curtain. And performed at the Theatre Royal in Drury-Lane.* London, 1767 (8vo. 6d. Becket and DeHondt) BRITISH LIBRARY

Reviewed: *Monthly Review* 37 (1767): 393
Critical Review 24 (1767): 318
Universal Museum 3 (1767): 541

1023 [GARRICK, David]. *The Songs, Choruses, and Serious Dialogue of the Masque called The Institution of the Garter, or, Arthur's Round Table restored.* London, 1771 (8vo. 6d. Becket) BRITISH LIBRARY

Reviewed: *Monthly Review* 45 (1771): 411
Critical Review 32 (1771): 310
London Magazine 40 (1771): 571

1024 [GARRICK, David]. *The Songs, Chorusses, &c. in a new Dramatic Entertainment called A Christmas Tale. In Five Parts. As it is perform'd At the Theatre-Royal in Drury-Lane.* London, n.d. [ESTC-1773] (8vo. 6d. Becket) BRITISH LIBRARY

Reviewed: *Critical Review* 36 (1773): 476

1025 [GARRICK, David]. *Songs, Chorusses, &c. which are introduced in the New Entertainment of the Jubilee, at the Theatre Royal, in Drury-Lane.* London, 1770 (8vo. 6d. Becket) BRITISH LIBRARY

Reviewed: *Monthly Review* 41 (1769): 318

1026 [GARRICK, David]. *The Tempest. An Opera. Taken from Shakespear. As it is Performed at the Theatre-Royal in Drury-Lane. The Songs from Shakespear, Dryden, &c. The Music composed by Mr. Smith.* London, 1756 (8vo. 1s. Tonson) BRITISH LIBRARY

Reviewed: *Monthly Review* 14 (1756): 238
Critical Review 1 (1756): 147–148

1027 *Garrick's Vagary: or, England Run Mad. With Particulars of the Stratford Jubilee.* London, 1769 (8vo. 1s. Bladon) BRITISH LIBRARY

Reviewed: *Monthly Review* 41 (1769): 238
Critical Review 28 (1769): 237
Gentleman's Magazine 39 (1769): 454
London Magazine 38 (1769): 537

Gasconado the Great
See: WORSDALE, James

GAUTIER, J. (translation)
See: MORTIMER, Thomas. *The Life and Military Exploits of Pyrrhus, King of Epire*

GAY, John. *Achilles* (adaptation)
See: COLMAN, George (the elder)

1028 GAY, John. *Fables of Mr. John Gay, with An Italian Translation by Gian Francesco Giorgetti.* London, 1773 (8vo. 6s. Davies. 1773) BRITISH LIBRARY

Reviewed: *Monthly Review* 50 (1774): 231
Universal Catalogue [2] (1773) art. 1111

1029 GAY, John. *The Miscellaneous Works of Mr. John Gay, Vols. III. and IV.*
NOT SEEN (12mo. 6s. Bell)

Reviewed: *Monthly Review* 49 (1773): 337–340
Critical Review 36 (1773): 475
Universal Catalogue [2] (1773) art. 342

1030 GAY, [John]. *The Rehearsal at Goatham.* London, 1754 (8vo. 1s. Baldwin) BRITISH LIBRARY

Reviewed: *Monthly Review* 10 (1754): 312

1031 *The geese in disgrace; a tale*
NOT SEEN (6d. Portsmouth)

Reviewed: *Gentleman's Magazine* 21 (1751): 48

1032 GELLERT, C[hristian] F[ürchtegott]. *The History of the Swedish Countess of G. In Two Parts. By C. F. Gellert, M.A. Professor at the University of Lipsick. Translated from the original German.* London, 1752 (12mo. 3s. Dodsley) BODLEIAN

Reviewed: *Monthly Review* 6 (1752): 231–232

1033 [GÉNARD, François]. *The School of Woman: Or, Memoirs of Constantia. Address'd to the Duchess of *****. By the Author of the School of Man, A Moral Work: Suppress'd at Paris, by Order of the King of France. Translated from the French.* London, 1753 (12mo. 3s. Robinson) BRITISH LIBRARY

Reviewed: *Monthly Review* 9 (1753): 396

The General. A Poem
See: GENTLEMAN, Francis

The Generous Briton
See: KIMBER, Edward

1034 *The Generous Guardian: or, the History of Horatio Saville, Esq; and Miss Louisa C*** In Two Volumes.* London, 1767 (12mo. 5s. Vernor and Chater) HARVARD (HOUGHTON)

Reviewed: *Monthly Review* 38 (1768): 151
Critical Review 24 (1767): 472
Universal Museum 4 (1768): 36

1035 *The generous Husband; or, the History of Lord Lelius and the fair Emilia. Containing likewise the genuine memoirs of Asmodei, the pretended Piedmontese Count, from the time of his birth, to his late ignominious fall in Hyde-Park.* London, 1771 (12mo. 2s.6d. Wheble. 1771) BRITISH LIBRARY

Reviewed: *Monthly Review* 45 (1771): 73
Critical Review 32 (1771): 232
London Magazine 40 (1771): 509

1036 *The Generous Inconstant; a Novel. By a Lady.* 2 vols.
NOT SEEN (12mo. 5s.sewed. Nicoll)

Reviewed: *Monthly Review* 44 (1771): 498
Critical Review 31 (1771): 232
London Magazine 40 (1771): 46

1037 *Genius: a miscellaneous poetical Epistle to the Author of Dido. By a Wappineer.* London, 1767 (4to. 1s. Newbery) UNIVERSITY OF PENNSYLVANIA

Reviewed: *Monthly Review* 36 (1767): 490
Critical Review 23 (1767): 399

Genius and Valour: a Scotch Pastoral
See: LANGHORNE, John

The Genius of Britain
See: CAMBRIDGE, Richard Owen

1038 GENTLEMAN, Francis. *Characters. An Epistle. Inscribed to the Earl of Carlisle.* London, 1766 (4to. 1s.6d. Becket) BRITISH LIBRARY

Reviewed: *Monthly Review* 34 (1766): 404–405
Critical Review 21 (1766): 392–393

1039 [GENTLEMAN, Francis]. *Cupid's Revenge: an Arcadian Pastoral. As it is performed at the Theatre-Royal in the Hay-Market. The Music by Mr. Hook.* London, 1772 (8vo. 1s. Bell) BRITISH LIBRARY

Reviewed: *Monthly Review* 47 (1772): 152
Critical Review 34 (1772): 155
Universal Catalogue [1] (1772) art. 1010

1040 [GENTLEMAN, Francis]. *The Favourite, an Historical Tragedy.* [Adaptation of Ben Jonson's *Sejanus;* first published under that title.] London, 1770 (8vo. 1s.6d. Bell) BRITISH LIBRARY

Reviewed: *Monthly Review* 41 (1769): 478
Critical Review 28 (1769): 461
Gentleman's Magazine 39 (1769): 600
Town & Country Magazine [1] (1769): 661

1041 [GENTLEMAN, Francis]. *The General. A Poem. Respectfully inscribed to the Right Honourable the Marquis of Granby. By the Author of A Trip to the Moon.* London, 1764 (4to. 2s.6d. Bristow) BODLEIAN

Reviewed: *Monthly Review* 31 (1764): 231
Critical Review 18 (1764): 159–160
British Magazine 5 (1764): 433

1042 GENTLEMAN, Francis. *Narcissa and Eliza. A Dramatic Tale.* London, 1754 (4to. 1s.6d. Bouquet) BRITISH LIBRARY

Reviewed: *Monthly Review* 10 (1754): 387–388
Gentleman's Magazine 24 (1754): 245–246

1043 [GENTLEMAN, Francis]. *The Pantheonites. A Dramatic Entertainment. As performed at the Theatre-Royal in the Hay-Market.* London, 1773 (8vo. 1s. Bell. 1773) BRITISH LIBRARY

Reviewed: *Monthly Review* 49 (1773): 232
Critical Review 36 (1773): 235
Universal Catalogue [2] (1773) art. 1037

1044 GENTLEMAN, Francis. *Royal Fables.* London, 1766 (8vo. 2s.6d. Becket) BRITISH LIBRARY

Reviewed: *Monthly Review* 35 (1766): 480–483
Critical Review 21 (1766): 474–476

1045 GENTLEMAN, [Francis]. *Sejanus, a Tragedy. As it was intended for the Stage. With a Preface, wherein the Manager's Reasons for refusing it are set forth.* [Adapted from Ben Jonson's *Sejanus*.] London, 1752 (8vo. 1s.6d. Manby) BRITISH LIBRARY

Reviewed: *Monthly Review* 5 (1751): 464

1046 [GENTLEMAN, Francis]. *The Stratford Jubilee. A New Comedy of Two Acts, as it has been lately exhibited at Stratford Upon Avon, with great applause. To which is prefixed Scrub's Trip to the Jubilee.* London, 1769 (8vo. 1s. Lownds, &c.) BRITISH LIBRARY

Reviewed: *Monthly Review* 41 (1769): 238
Critical Review 28 (1769): 237
Gentleman's Magazine 39 (1769): 454

1047 [GENTLEMAN, Francis]. *The Sultan: or, Love and Fame. A new Tragedy. As it is acted at the Theatre-Royal in the Hay-market.* London, 1770 (8vo. 1s.6d. Bell. 1770) BRITISH LIBRARY

Reviewed: *Monthly Review* 42 (1770): 146
Critical Review 29 (1770): 71–72
London Magazine 39 (1770): 44

1048 [GENTLEMAN, Francis]. *The Theatres. A Poetical Dissection. By Sir Nicholas Nipclose, Baronet.* London, 1772 (4to. 3s. Bell) BRITISH LIBRARY

Reviewed: *Monthly Review* 45 (1771): 508–509
Critical Review 32 (1771): 467–469
Gentleman's Magazine 42 (1772): 29–30
London Magazine 40 (1771): 611
Town & Country Magazine 3 (1771): 657
British Magazine & General Review 1 (1772): 79–80

1049 [GENTLEMAN, Francis]. *The Tobacconist, a Comedy Of Two Acts. Altered from Ben Johnson. Acted at the Theatres Royal in the Hay-Market and Edinburgh. (With universal applause).* London, 1771 (8vo. 1s. Bell. 1771) BRITISH LIBRARY

Reviewed: *Monthly Review* 45 (1771): 151–152
Critical Review 32 (1771): 229
Town & Country Magazine 3 (1771): 437

1050 [GENTLEMAN, Francis]. *A Trip to the Moon. Containing an Account of the Island of Noibla. Its Inhabitants, Religious and Political Customs, &c. By Sir Humphrey Lunatic, Bart.*

York, 1764 (8vo. 2s.6d. Crowder) BRITISH LIBRARY

Reviewed: *Monthly Review* 30 (1764): 354–358
Critical Review 17 (1764): 429–432
General Magazine 1 (1764): 149

1051 [GENTLEMAN, Francis]. *A Trip to the Moon. Containing an Account of the Island of Noibla. Its Inhabitants, Religious and Political Customs, &c. By Sir Humphrey Lunatic, Bart. Volume II.* York, 1765 (12mo. 2s.6d. Crowder) BRITISH LIBRARY

Reviewed: *Monthly Review* 32 (1765): 159
Critical Review 19 (1765): 137–139

1052 *The Gentleman and Lady of Pleasure's Amusement: In Eighty-Eight Questions, with their Answers, on Love and Gallantry. To which are added, The Adventures of Sophia; With the History of Frederick and Caroline.* London, 1759 (12mo. 3s. Thrush) UNIVERSITY OF PENNSYLVANIA

Reviewed: *Monthly Review* 19 (1758): 500–501
Critical Review 6 (1758): 526

1053 *A Genuine Account of the Life and Transactions of Howell ap David Price, Gentleman of Wales. Exhibiting A Series of most remarkable Occurrences during his Seven Years Travels Abroad; Five of which were spent with a Lady he had released from Slavery. With farther Particulars since his Return with her to England. Written by Himself.* London, 1752 (12mo. 3s. Osborn) BRITISH LIBRARY

Reviewed: *Monthly Review* 5 (1751): 459

1054 *Genuine Letters to a Young Lady of Family, Figure, and Fortune: previous to Her Intended Espousals. To which are added, Three Poems, by the same Author: I. Friendship: To Laelius. II. To a Friend: Occasioned by the universally-unwelcome Report of the King of Prussia's being killed, in a Battle with the Austrians. III. To the Memory of the Rev. Mr. Castleman, late Prebendary of Bristol, Vicar of St. Nicholas, in the said City; and also of South Petherton; all in the County of Somerset.* London, 1762 (8vo. 2s. Wilkie) NEWBERRY

Reviewed: *Critical Review* 12 (1761): 401–402

1055 *The genuine Memoirs of Miss Faulkner; otherwise Mrs D***l**n; or, Countess of H*****x, in Expectancy. Containing, the amours and intrigues of several persons of high distinction, and remarkable characters: with some curious political anecdotes, never before published.* London, 1770 (12mo. 3s.sewed. Bingley) BRITISH LIBRARY

Reviewed: *Monthly Review* 42 (1770): 251
Critical Review 30 (1770): 240
London Magazine 39 (1770): 103
Town & Country Magazine 2 (1770): 120

1056 *Genuine Memoirs of Miss Harriet Melvin and Miss Leonora Stanway. In a Series of Letters. By a young Lady of Glocester.* London, 1772 (12mo. 3s. Fuller. 1772) BRITISH LIBRARY

Reviewed: *Monthly Review* 46 (1772): 264–265
Critical Review 33 (1772): 182
British Magazine & General Review 1 (1772): 442
Universal Catalogue [1] (1772) art. 100

1057 *Genuine Memoirs Of the Celebrated Miss Maria Brown. Exhibiting The Life of a Courtezan in the most Fashionable Scenes of Dissipation. Published by the Author of a W** of P***.* 2 vols. London, 1766 (12mo. 6s. Allcock) BRITISH LIBRARY

Reviewed: *Monthly Review* 34 (1766): 406
Critical Review 21 (1766): 395

1058 *Genuine Memoirs of the celebrated Miss Nancy D-----n. Adorned with a beautiful Frontispiece*
NOT SEEN (12mo. 1s. Stevens)

Reviewed: *Monthly Review* 23 (1760): 327
Critical Review 10 (1760): 327
London Magazine 29 (1760): 560
British Magazine 1 (1760): 665

1059 *Genuine Memoirs of the late Celebrated Jane D****s.* London, 1761 (8vo. 2s. Simpson) BRITISH LIBRARY

Reviewed: *Monthly Review* 25 (1761): 229
Critical Review 12 (1761): 158
British Magazine 2 (1761): 495

1060 *George's Coffee-House. A Poem* NOT SEEN (4to. 1s. Osborne)

Reviewed: *Monthly Review* 25 (1761): 78
Critical Review 12 (1761): 76
British Magazine 2 (1761): 437

1061 GERRARD, John. *Poems, by John Gerrard, Curate of Withycombe in the Moor, Devon.* London, 1769 (4to. 5s. Kearsly. 1769) BRITISH LIBRARY

Reviewed: *Monthly Review* 42 (1770): 185–191
Critical Review 29 (1770): 314
London Magazine 39 (1770): 209–210

GESSNER, Salomon. *The Death of Abel [Der Tod Abels]* (translations)
See: COLLYER, Mary (1761)
    NEWCOMB, Thomas (1763)

1062 GESSNER, [Salomon]. *Rural Poems. Translated from the Original German, of M. Gesner.* London, 1762 (8vo. 2s. Becket and De Hondt) BRITISH LIBRARY

Reviewed: *Monthly Review* 27 (1762): 127–134
Critical Review 14 (1762): 21–26
British Magazine 3 (1762): 438

GESSNER, Salomon. *Select Poems*
See: PENNY, Anne

The Ghost (1762)
See: CHURCHILL, Charles

1063 *The Ghost. A Comedy of Two Acts. As it is performed, with great Applause, At the Theatre in Smock-Alley, Dublin.* London, 1767 (8vo. 1s. Williams) BRITISH LIBRARY

Reviewed: *Monthly Review* 36 (1767): 238
Critical Review 23 (1767): 230
Gentleman's Magazine 37 (1767): 172–173

1064 [GIBBES, Phebe]. *The Life and Adventures of Mr. Francis Clive. In Two Volumes.* London, 1764 (12mo. 5s.sewed. Lownds) HARVARD (HOUGHTON)

Reviewed: *Monthly Review* 30 (1764): 243–244
Critical Review 17 (1764): 307
General Magazine 1 (1764): 149

1065 [GIBBES, Phebe]. *The Woman of Fashion: or, the History of Lady Diana Dormer. In Two Volumes.* London, 1767 (12mo. 6s. Wilkie) HARVARD (HOUGHTON)

Reviewed: *Monthly Review* 37 (1767): 151
Critical Review 23 (1767): 465
London Magazine 36 (1767): 262
Universal Museum 3 (1767): 247–250

1066 GIBBONS, Thomas. *The Christian Minister, in three poetic epistles To Philander. To which are added, I. Poetical Versions of several Parts of Scripture. II. Translations of Poems from Greek and Latin Writers. And, III. Original Pieces, chiefly in Verse, on various Occasions.* London, 1772 (8vo. 4s.bound. Buckland, &c. 1772) BRITISH LIBRARY

Reviewed: *Monthly Review* 47 (1772): 151
Critical Review 33 (1772): 408–409
Gentleman's Magazine 42 (1772): 231–232
Universal Catalogue [1] (1772) art. 616

1067 GIBBONS, Thomas. *Juvenilia: Poems on Various Subjects of Devotion and Virtue.* London, 1750 (8vo. 5s. Printed for Buckland in Pater-noster-row, and Ward in Cornhill) BRITISH LIBRARY

Reviewed: *Monthly Review* 3 (1750): 333–341

1068 GIBBONS, Thomas. *An Ode to the Memory of His Grace the Late Duke of Newcastle. By Thomas Gibbons, D.D.* London, 1768 (4to. 6d. Buckland) HARVARD (HOUGHTON)

Reviewed: *Monthly Review* 40 (1769): 87
Critical Review 27 (1769): 70
London Magazine 38 (1769): 104
Town & Country Magazine [1] (1769): 45

1069 GIBBONS, Thomas. *The Tears of Friendship. An Elegiac Ode. Sacred to the Memory of several deceased Friends, and particularly the Rev. Benjamin Grosvenor, D.D. who departed this life Aug. 27, 1758, in the 83d Year of his Age.* London, 1759 (4to. 6d. Buckland) BRITISH LIBRARY

Reviewed: *Monthly Review* 20 (1759): 190–191
Critical Review 7 (1759): 183–184
Gentleman's Magazine 29 (1759): 87

1070 GIBSON, Thomas. *The Birth of Christ, an irregular Ode*
NOT SEEN (4to. 1s. Wilson and Fell)

Reviewed: *Monthly Review* 34 (1766): 165–166
Critical Review 21 (1766): 316

1071 GIBSON, William. *Conscience: a Poetical Essay. By William Gibson, M.A. of Pembroke Hall, Cambridge.* Cambridge, 1772 (4to. 1s. Dodsley, &c. 1772) NEWBERRY

Reviewed: *Monthly Review* 48 (1773): 66
Critical Review 35 (1773): 159
Gentleman's Magazine 43 (1773): 31–32
London Magazine 42 (1773): 41
Universal Catalogue [2] (1773) art. 81

Gideon; or, The Patriot
See: HILL, Aaron

1072 GILES, Joseph. *Miscellaneous Poems: on Various Subjects, and Occasions. Revised and corrected By the late Mr. William Shenstone.* London, 1771 (8vo. 4s.boards. Newbery, &c. 1771) BRITISH LIBRARY

Reviewed: *Monthly Review* 44 (1771): 343

1073 *Gisbal, an Hyperborean Tale: Translated From the Fragments of Ossian The Son of Fingal.* London, 1762 (8vo. 1s. Pridden) HARVARD (HOUGHTON)

Reviewed: *Monthly Review* 27 (1762): 156
Critical Review 14 (1762): 76
British Magazine 3 (1762): 438

1074 GLASSE, John. *Poems on Several Occasions.* London, 1763 (4to. 1s. Lewis) BODLEIAN

Reviewed: *Monthly Review* 29 (1763): 155–156
Critical Review 16 (1763): 150–151

1075 GLOVER, [Richard]. *Boadicia. A Tragedy. As it is acted at the Theatre-Royal in Drury-Lane.* London, 1753 (8vo. 1s.6d. Dodsley) BRITISH LIBRARY

Reviewed: *Monthly Review* 10 (1754): 78

1076 GLOVER, [Richard]. *Leonidas. A Poem. The Fifth Edition.* 2 vols. London, 1770 (12mo. 6s. Cadell, &c. 1770) BRITISH LIBRARY

Reviewed: *Monthly Review* 44 (1771): 341
Critical Review 30 (1770): 378–385

1077 [GLOVER, Richard]. *Medea. A Tragedy.* London, 1761 (4to. 2s.6d. Morgan) BRITISH LIBRARY

Reviewed: *Monthly Review* 25 (1761): 461–465
Critical Review 12 (1761): 296–304
British Magazine 2 (1761): 606

1078 GLYNN, R[obert]. *The Day of Judgment: a Poetical Essay.* Cambridge, 1757 (4to. 1s. Whiston) NEWBERRY

Reviewed: *Monthly Review* 17 (1757): 397–400
Critical Review 4 (1757): 366–368

1079 GODFREY, Thomas. *The Court of Fancy; a Poem. By Thomas Godfrey.* Philadelphia, 1762 (4to. 1s. Philadelphia printed and sold by Becket and De Hondt in London) NEW YORK PUBLIC LIBRARY

Reviewed: *Monthly Review* 29 (1763): 226–227

The Golden Pippin: An English Burletta
See: O'HARA, Kane

1080 [GOLDONI, Carlo]. *The Accomplish'd Maid: A Comic Opera. As it is Performed at the Theatre-Royal in Covent-Garden. The Music by Signr. Niccolo Piccini.* London, 1767 (8vo. 1s.6d. Griffin) BODLEIAN

Reviewed: *Monthly Review* 35 (1766): 483–484
Critical Review 22 (1766): 468
Gentleman's Magazine 36 (1766): 591–592

1081 GOLDONI, Carlo. *Il Padre di Famiglia Commedia Rappresentata per la prima volta in Venezia il Carnevale dell' Anno 1750 di Carlo Goldoni Avvocato Veneziano. The Father of a Family a Comedy Acted for the first time at Venice during the Carnival of 1750 By Charles Goldoni. Translated into English with the Italian Original.* London, 1757 (8vo. 2s.6d. Nourse) BRITISH LIBRARY

Reviewed: *Monthly Review* 17 (1757): 47–50

1082 GOLDONI, Carlo. *Pamela Commedia di Carlo Goldoni Avvocato Veneziano. Pamela a Comedy By Charles Goldoni Translated into*

English With the Italian Original. London, 1756 (8vo. 2s.6d. Nourse) BRITISH LIBRARY

Reviewed: *Monthly Review* 17 (1757): 47–50

1083 GOLDSMITH, Oliver (ed.). *The Beauties of English Poesy. Selected by Oliver Goldsmith.* 2 vols. London, 1767 (12mo. 6s. Griffin) BRITISH LIBRARY

Reviewed: *Monthly Review* 36 (1767): 490–491
Critical Review 23 (1767): 408–411
London Magazine 36 (1767): 206

1084 [GOLDSMITH, Oliver]. *The Bee. Being Essays on the most Interesting Subjects.* London, 1759 (8vo. 2s. Wilkie) BRITISH LIBRARY

Reviewed: *Monthly Review* 22 (1760): 38–45
Critical Review 8 (1759): 499

1085 [GOLDSMITH, Oliver]. *The Citizen of the World; or, Letters from a Chinese Philosopher, Residing in London, to his Friends in the East.* 2 vols. London, 1762 (12mo. 6s. Newbery) BRITISH LIBRARY

Reviewed: *Monthly Review* 26 (1762): 477
Critical Review 13 (1762): 397–400
British Magazine 3 (1762): 324

1086 GOLDSMITH, [Oliver]. *The Deserted Village, a Poem.* London, 1770 (4to. 2s. Griffin. 1770) BRITISH LIBRARY

Reviewed: *Monthly Review* 42 (1770): 440–445
Critical Review 29 (1770): 435–443
Gentleman's Magazine 40 (1770): 271–273
London Magazine 39 (1770): 318
Town & Country Magazine 2 (1770): 268

1087 GOLDSMITH, [Oliver]. *The Good Natur'd Man: a Comedy. As performed at the Theatre-Royal in Covent-Garden.* London, 1768 (8vo. 1s.6d. Griffin) BRITISH LIBRARY

Reviewed: *Monthly Review* 38 (1768): 159–160
Critical Review 25 (1768): 147–148
Gentleman's Magazine 38 (1768): 78–82
Political Register 2 (1768): 187

1088 [GOLDSMITH, Oliver (trans.)]. *The Memoirs of a Protestant, Condemned to the Galleys of France, For His Religion. Written by Himself. Comprehending an Account of the various Distresses he suffered in Slavery; and his Constancy in supporting almost every Cruelty that bigotted Zeal could inflict or Human Nature sustain; also a Description of the Galleys and the Service in which they are employed. The Whole interspersed with Anecdotes relative to the General History of the Times, for a Period of Thirteen Years; during which our Author continued in Slavery, 'till he was at last set free, at the Intercession of the Court of Great Britain. Translated from the Original, just published at the Hague, By James Willington.* [Translated from *Mémoires d'un protestant* by Jean Marteilhé.] 2 vols. London, 1758 (12mo. 6s. Griffiths and Dilly) BRITISH LIBRARY

Reviewed: *Monthly Review* 18 (1758): 445–452
Critical Review 5 (1758): 300–308

1089 [GOLDSMITH, Oliver (ed.)]. *Poems for Young Ladies. In Three Parts. Devotional, Moral, and Entertaining. The Whole being A Collection of the Best Pieces in our Language.* London, 1767 (8vo. 3s.6d. Payne) BRITISH LIBRARY

Reviewed: *Monthly Review* 36 (1767): 240
Critical Review 22 (1766): 469

1090 GOLDSMITH, [Oliver]. *Retaliation: a Poem. Including Epitaphs on the most Distinguished Wits of this Metropolis.* London, 1774 (4to. 1s.6d. Kearsly. 1774) BRITISH LIBRARY

Reviewed: *Monthly Review* 50 (1774): 313–314
Critical Review 37 (1774): 392
Town & Country Magazine 6 (1774): 323
Universal Catalogue 3 (1774) art. 499

1091 GOLDSMITH, [Oliver]. *She Stoops to Conquer: or, The Mistakes of a Night. A Comedy. As it is acted at the Theatre-Royal in Covent-Garden.* London, 1773 (8vo. 1s.6d. Newbery. 1773) BRITISH LIBRARY

Reviewed: *Monthly Review* 48 (1773): 309–314
Critical Review 35 (1773): 229–230
Gentleman's Magazine 43 (1773): 192
Universal Catalogue [2] (1773) art. 377

1092 [GOLDSMITH, Oliver]. *Threnodia Augustalis, sacred to the Memory of her late Royal Highness the Princess Dowager of Wales. Spo-*

ken and sung in the Great Room at Soho Square, on Thursday the 20th of Feb. London, 1772 (4to. 1s. Woodfall. 1772) YALE (BEINECKE)

Reviewed: *Monthly Review* 46 (1772): 260
Critical Review 33 (1772): 173
Town & Country Magazine 4 (1772): 154
Universal Catalogue [1] (1772) art. 266

1093 GOLDSMITH, Oliver. *The Traveller, or a Prospect of Society. A Poem. Inscribed to the Rev. Mr. Henry Goldsmith*. London, 1765 (4to. 1s.6d. Newbery) BRITISH LIBRARY

Reviewed: *Monthly Review* 32 (1765): 47–55
Critical Review 18 (1764): 458–462
Candid Review 1 (1765): 19–25

1094 [GOLDSMITH, Oliver]. *The Vicar of Wakefield: A Tale. Supposed to be written by Himself.* 2 vols. Salisbury, 1766 (12mo. 6s. Newbery) HARVARD (Houghton)

Reviewed: *Monthly Review* 34 (1766): 407
Critical Review 21 (1766): 439–441

1095 GOLDWIN, W[illiam]. *Description of the Antient and Famous City of Bristol. A Poem, by W. Goldwin, A.M. Revised, with large Additions, by I. Smart, A.M.* 2d ed. London, 1751 [Previously published in 1712] (8vo. Robinson &c.) BRITISH LIBRARY

Reviewed: *Monthly Review* 5 (1751): 159–160

GOMEZ, Mmme. de
See: POISSON DE GOMEZ, Madeline Angelique

1096 *Good–Friday, a Poem.* Bath, 1773 (4to. 1s. Bath printed and sold by Dodsley in London 1773) BODLEIAN

Reviewed: *Monthly Review* 48 (1773): 413
Critical Review 35 (1773): 394
London Magazine 42 (1773): 196
Universal Catalogue [2] (1773) art. 368

1097 GOODALL, W[illiam]. *The Adventures of Capt. Greenland. Written In Imitation of all those Wise, Learned, Witty, and Humorous Authors, who either already have, or hereafter may Write in the same Stile and Manner.* 4 vols. London, 1752 (12mo. 12s. Baldwin) BODLEIAN

Reviewed: *Monthly Review* 6 (1752): 310–311

1098 GOODWIN, Simon. *The Messiah. A Poem.* Canterbury, n.d. [ESTC-1770?] (4to. 6d. Baldwin) BRITISH LIBRARY

Reviewed: *Monthly Review* 48 (1773): 70
Critical Review 35 (1773): 159
London Magazine 42 (1773): 41
Universal Catalogue [1] (1772) art. 1508

1099 GORDON, ---- (trans.). *The Comedies of Terence. Translated into English Prose. To which is prefixed, Some Account of the Author, and of the Dramatic Poetry of the Antients. By Mr. Gordon.* London, 1752 (12mo. 3s. Longman, &c.) BRITISH LIBRARY

Reviewed: *Monthly Review* 6 (1752): 311

1100 GORDON, Alexander. *The Prussiad: an Heroick Poem.* London, 1759 (4to. 1s.6d. Burd) BRITISH LIBRARY

Reviewed: *Monthly Review* 21 (1759): 432–434
Critical Review 9 (1760): 149–150
London Magazine 28 (1759): 631
Gentleman's Magazine 29 (1759): 543–544

1101 [GOUGH, James]. *Britannia: A Poem. With Historical Notes. Inscribed to the King, Queen, and Royal Family. The Lords and Commons of Great-Britain and Ireland. The Governors and Members of the British Colonies.* London, 1767 (4to. 1s.6d. Cadell) BRITISH LIBRARY

Reviewed: *Monthly Review* 38 (1768): 70
Critical Review 25 (1768): 72–73
Gentleman's Magazine 38 (1768): 28–29
Universal Museum 4 (1768): 36
Political Register 2 (1768): 64

1102 *Grace, a poem*
NOT SEEN (4to. 6d. Keith)

Reviewed: *Monthly Review* 6 (1752): 240

Grace Triumphant. A Sacred Poem
See: FELLOWS, John

The Graces: a Poetical Epistle
See: WOTY, William

1103 GRAFFIGNY, [Françoise d'Issembourg] d'Happoncourt. *Cenia; or the supposed daughter. Translated from the French of Madam D'Happencourt de Grafigny, by a French Gentleman.* London, 1752 (8vo. 1s. Reeve) BRITISH LIBRARY

Reviewed: *Monthly Review* 6 (1752): 148

1104 GRAHAM, George. *Telemachus. A Mask.* London, 1763 (4to. 2s.6d. Millar) BRITISH LIBRARY

Reviewed: *Monthly Review* 28 (1763): 109–112
Critical Review 15 (1763): 314–318

1105 GRAINGER, James. *A Poetical Translation of the Elegies of Tibullus; and of the Poems of Sulpicia. With The Original Text, and Notes Critical and Explanatory.* 2 vols. London, 1759 (12mo. 6s. Millar) BRITISH LIBRARY

Reviewed: *Monthly Review* 20 (1759): 58–63 and 178–185
Critical Review 6 (1758): 475–482

1106 GRAINGER, James. *The Sugar-Cane: A Poem. In Four Books. With Notes.* London, 1764 (4to. 4s. Dodsley) BRITISH LIBRARY

Reviewed: *Monthly Review* 31 (1764): 105–118
Critical Review 18 (1764): [270]–277

1107 GRANAN, Edward. *The Christiad: An Heroic Poem; in Six Books. Written by Marcus Hieronymus Vida, and translated into English Verse.* London, 1771 (8vo. 5s.sewed. Baldwin. 1771) BRITISH LIBRARY

Reviewed: *Monthly Review* 47 (1772): 70
Critical Review 32 (1771): 443–448

1108 *The Grand Contest; being a Dialogue between James and George, upon a Subject of the Utmost Importance.* London, 1753 (Fol. 6d. Bourn) HARVARD (HOUGHTON)

Reviewed: *Monthly Review* 8 (1753): 472

1109 [GRAVES, Richard (ed.)]. *The Festoon: A Collection of Epigrams, Ancient and Modern. Panegyrical, Satyrical, Amorous, Moral, Humorous, Monumental. With an Essay on that Species of Composition.* London, 1766 (2s.6d. Robinson and Roberts) BRITISH LIBRARY

Reviewed: *Monthly Review* 34 (1766): 83
Critical Review 20 (1765): 457–460
Gentleman's Magazine 35 (1765): 582

1110 [GRAVES, Richard]. *The Love of Order: a Poetical Essay. In Three Cantos.* London, 1773 (4to. 1s.6d. Dodsley. 1773) BRITISH LIBRARY

Reviewed: *Monthly Review* 49 (1773): 121–124
Critical Review 35 (1773): 393
Universal Catalogue [2] (1773) art. 592

1111 [GRAVES, Richard]. *The Progress of Gallantry; A Poetical Essay. In three cantos.* London, 1774 (4to. 1s.6d. Dodsley, 1774) BRITISH LIBRARY

Reviewed: *Monthly Review* 50 (1774): 314
Critical Review 37 (1774): 315
London Magazine 43 (1774): 244
Town & Country Magazine 6 (1774): 268
Universal Catalogue 3 (1774) art. 374

1112 [GRAVES, Richard]. *The Spiritual Quixote: or, the Summer's Ramble of Mr. Geoffry Wildgoose. A Comic Romance.* 3 vols. London, 1773 (12mo. 7s.6d. Dodsley. 1773) BRITISH LIBRARY

Reviewed: *Monthly Review* 48 (1773): 384–388
Critical Review 35 (1773): 275–286
London Magazine 42 (1773): 149
Town & Country Magazine 5 (1773): 266
Universal Catalogue [2] (1773) art. 375

1113 [GRAY, George]. *A Turkish Tale. In Five Cantos.* London, 1770 (12mo. 1s. Becket) BRITISH LIBRARY

Reviewed: *Monthly Review* 42 (1770): 406–407
Critical Review 29 (1770): 314–316
Gentleman's Magazine 40 (1770): 625

1114 GRAY, T[homas]. *Designs by Mr. R. Bentley, for six Poems by Mr. T. Gray.* London, 1753 (Royal 4to. 10s.6d.boards. Dodsley) BRITISH LIBRARY

Reviewed: *Monthly Review* 8 (1753): 477

1115 [GRAY, Thomas]. *An Elegy wrote in a Country Church Yard.* London, 1751 (4to. 7pp. 6d. Dodsley) BRITISH LIBRARY

Reviewed: *Monthly Review* 4 (1750–51): 309

1116 [GRAY, Thomas]. *Ode performed in the Senate-House at Cambridge, July 1, 1769, at the Installation of his Grace Augustus Henry Fitzroy, Duke of Grafton, Chancellor of the University. Set to Music by Dr. Randal, Professor of Music.* 1st ed. reviewed; copy seen 2d ed.: Cambridge, 1769 (4to. 1s. Cambridge printed, and sold by Dodsley, &c. in London) BRITISH LIBRARY

Reviewed: *Monthly Review* 41 (1769): 159–160
Critical Review 28 (1769): 233–234

1117 GRAY, [Thomas]. *Odes by Mr. Gray.* Strawberry-Hill, 1757 (4to. 1s. Dodsley) BRITISH LIBRARY

Reviewed: *Monthly Review* 17 (1757): 239–243
Critical Review 4 (1757): 167–170
Literary Magazine 2 (1757): 422–426 and 466–468

1118 GRAY, [Thomas]. *Poems by Mr. Gray.* London, 1768 (8vo. 2s.6d. Dodsley) BRITISH LIBRARY

Reviewed: *Monthly Review* 38 (1768): 408
Critical Review 25 (1768): 366–371
London Magazine 37 (1768): 157

1119 *The Great Day. A Descriptive Piece. Written abroad*
NOT SEEN (8vo. 1s. Dod)

Reviewed: *Monthly Review* 21 (1759): 352–353

1120 *The Great Shepherd. A Sacred Pastoral, in three parts.* London, 1757 (4to. 1s. Dodsley) BRITISH LIBRARY

Reviewed: *Monthly Review* 16 (1757): 400–402
Critical Review 3 (1757): 381–382

The Grecian Daughter: a Tragedy.
See: MURPHY, Arthur

1121 [GREEN, George Smith]. *The Images of the Ancients, Particularly those in the University of Oxford. With Some Reflections on Virtue, Ancient and Modern: A Poem. To which is added A very friendly Epistle to the Author of the Critical Review: Containing a Key to the Parson's Parlour.* London, 1758 (8vo. 6d. Scott) BODLEIAN

Reviewed: *Monthly Review* 18 (1758): 652

1122 GREEN, G[eorge] S[mith]. *The Life of Mr. John Van, a Clergyman's Son, of Woody, in Hampshire. Being A Series of many extraordinary Events, and surprizing Vicissitudes: In which are shewn, among a great Number of singular and merry Occurrences, his Entrance into the Army as a Trooper; his Bravery against the Rebels; his Marriage with an Heiress of eight hundred Pounds a Year, at St. Ive's in Huntingdonshire; his Conduct in High Life; his Favours from Fortune, and Reduction to Poverty. Written by his Friend and Acquaintance, G. S. Green.* 2 vols. London, n.d. [ESTC-1750?] (12mo. 6s. Noble) BRITISH LIBRARY

Reviewed: *Monthly Review* 16 (1757): 284
Critical Review 3 (1757): 476

1123 [GREEN, George Smith]. *A New Version of the Paradise Lost: or, Milton Paraphrased. In which The Measure and Versification are corrected and harmonized; the Obscurities elucidated; and the Faults of which the Author stands accused by Addison, and other of the Criticks, are removed. With Annotations on the Original Text, to shew The Reasonableness of this New Version. By a Gentleman of Oxford.* Oxford, 1756 (8vo. 1s. Baldwin) BODLEIAN

Reviewed: *Monthly Review* 15 (1756): 653–654
Critical Review 2 (1756): 357–362

1124 GREEN, G[eorge] S[mith]. *The Nice Lady: A Comedy.* London, 1762 (8vo. 1s.6d. Medley) BODLEIAN

Reviewed: *Monthly Review* 26 (1762): 387
Critical Review 13 (1762): 156–157
British Magazine 3 (1762): 158

1125 GREEN, George Smith. *Oliver Cromwell: An Historical Play. To which is Prefix'd an Extract or Journal of the Rise and Progress of Oliver Cromwell.* London, 1752 (8vo. 1s.6d.) BRITISH LIBRARY

Reviewed: *Monthly Review* 5 (1751): 522

1126 GREEN, G[eorge] S[mith]. *The Parson's Parlour. A Poem. By a Tradesman of Oxford.* Oxford, n.d. [ESTC-1756] (8vo. 6d. Baldwin) BRITISH LIBRARY

Reviewed: *Monthly Review* 14 (1756): 574
Critical Review 1 (1756): 481

1127 GREEN, John. *Beauty: A Poem. By John Green, jun. a Student of the honourable Society of Lincoln's Inn*
NOT SEEN (4to. 1s. Reeve)

Reviewed: *Monthly Review* 14 (1756): 558–559
Critical Review 1 (1756): 318–321
Gentleman's Magazine 26 (1756): 198–199

1128 [GREENE, Edward Burnaby]. *Cam. An Elegy.* London, 1764 (4to. 1s.6d. Flexney) BRITISH LIBRARY

Reviewed: *Monthly Review* 30 (1764): 34–36
Critical Review 17 (1764): 72–73

1129 [GREENE, Edward Burnaby]. *The Chaplain. A Poem.* London, 1764 (4to. 1s.6d. Bingley) BRITISH LIBRARY

Reviewed: *Monthly Review* 30 (1764): 157
Critical Review 17 (1764): 238–239
General Magazine 1 (1764): 98

1130 [GREENE, Edward Burnaby]. *Friendship: a Satire.* London, 1763 (4to. 1s.6d. Bingley) BRITISH LIBRARY

Reviewed: *Monthly Review* 29 (1763): 405–407
Critical Review 16 (1763): 385–386

1131 [GREENE, Edward Burnaby]. *Hero, and Leander, a Poem. From the Greek of Musaeus.* London, 1773 (4to. 2s. Ridley. 1774) BRITISH LIBRARY

Reviewed: *Monthly Review* 50 (1774): 483
Critical Review 37 (1774): 315
Town & Country Magazine 6 (1774): 268
Universal Catalogue 3 (1774) art. 494

1132 [GREENE, Edward Burnaby]. *The Laureat. A Poem. Inscribed to the Memory of C. Churchill.* London, 1765 (4to. 1s.6d. Ridley) BRITISH LIBRARY

Reviewed: *Monthly Review* 32 (1765): 153
Critical Review 19 (1765): 87–90
Candid Review 1 (1765): 139–141

1133 [GREENE, Edward Burnaby]. *Poetical Essays.* London, 1772 (12mo. 3s.sewed. Ridley. 1772) BRITISH LIBRARY

Reviewed: *Monthly Review* 47 (1772): 150–151
Critical Review 33 (1772): 173–174

1134 [GREENE, Edward Burnaby]. *The Politician. A Poem. Addressed to Mr. James Scott, Fellow of Trinity College, Cambridge. By the Author of Juvenal's Satires imitated and adapted to the Times.* London, 1766 (4to. 1s.6d. Ridley) BRITISH LIBRARY

Reviewed: *Monthly Review* 34 (1766): 482
Critical Review 21 (1766): 394

1135 [GREENE, Edward Burnaby]. *Privilege. A Poem.* London, 1764 (4to. 1s.6d. Ridley) BRITISH LIBRARY

Reviewed: *Monthly Review* 30 (1764): 323
Critical Review 17 (1764): 292–294
General Magazine 1 (1764): 195

1136 [GREENE, Edward Burnaby]. *The Satires of Juvenal Paraphrastically Imitated, And adapted to the Times. With A Preface.* London, 1763 (8vo. 3s. Ridley) NEWBERRY

Reviewed: *Monthly Review* 28 (1763): 373–376
Critical Review 15 (1763): 310–314

1137 [GREENE, Edward Burnaby]. *The Scourge, a Satire. Part 1.* London, 1765 (4to. 1s.6d. Almon) BRITISH LIBRARY

Reviewed: *Monthly Review* 33 (1765): 488–489
Critical Review 20 (1765): 470
Gentleman's Magazine 35 (1765): 583–584

1138 [GREENE, Edward Burnaby]. *The tenth Epistle of the first book of Horace Imitated.* London, 1756 (4to. 1s. Ross) UNIVERSITY OF ILLINOIS

Reviewed: *Monthly Review* 15 (1756): 653
Critical Review 3 (1757): 87

1139 [GREENE, Edward Burnaby]. *The Tower: A Poetical Epistle, inscribed to John Wilkes,*

Esq; London, 1763 (4to. 6d. Ridley) BRITISH LIBRARY

Reviewed: *Monthly Review* 28 (1763): 487
Critical Review 15 (1763): 407

1140 [GREENE, Edward Burnaby]. *The Works of Anacreon and Sappho, with Pieces from ancient Authors; and Occasional Essays; illustrated by Observations on their Lives and Writings, Explanatory Notes from established Commentators, And additional Remarks by the Editor; With the Classic, an introductory Poem.* London, 1768 (8vo. 3s. Ridley) BRITISH LIBRARY

Reviewed: *Monthly Review* 41 (1769): 426–430
Critical Review 28 (1769): 53–56
Gentleman's Magazine 39 (1769): 453–454
Town & Country Magazine [1] (1769): 435

GRESSET, Jean Baptiste Louis. *Ver-Vert*
See: COOPER, John Gilbert

1141 GREY, Richard. *Of the Immortality of the Soul. A Poem. Translated from the Latin of Isaac Hawkins Browne, Esq;* London, 1754 (4to. 1s.6d. Dodsley) BRITISH LIBRARY

Reviewed: *Monthly Review* 10 (1754): 218–221
Gentleman's Magazine 24 (1754): 147

1142 [GRIFFIN, Philip]. *Juvenile Poems on Several Occasions. By a Gentleman of Oxford.* Oxford, 1764 (12mo. 1s.6d. Fletcher) BRITISH LIBRARY

Reviewed: *Monthly Review* 31 (1764): 230
Critical Review 18 (1764): 118–120
British Magazine 5 (1764): 433

1143 [GRIFFITH, Elizabeth]. *Amana. A Dramatic Poem. By a Lady.* London, 1764 (4to. 2s.6d. Johnston) BRITISH LIBRARY

Reviewed: *Monthly Review* 32 (1765): 233
Critical Review 19 (1765): 235
Gentleman's Magazine 35 (1765): 234
Candid Review 1 (1765): 169–172

1144 [GRIFFITH, Elizabeth]. *The Double Mistake. A Comedy. As it is Performed at the Theatre-Royal in Covent-Garden.* London, 1766 (8vo. 1s.6d. Davies) BRITISH LIBRARY

Reviewed: *Monthly Review* 34 (1766): 78
Critical Review 21 (1766): 55–61

1145 [GRIFFITH, Elizabeth]. *The History of Lady Barton, a Novel, in letters.* 3 vols. London, 1771 (12mo. 7s.6d.sewed. Davis, &c.) BRITISH LIBRARY

Reviewed: *Monthly Review* 46 (1772): 165
Critical Review 32 (1771): 372–377
London Magazine 40 (1771): 569–570
Universal Catalogue [2] (1773) art. 482

1146 [GRIFFITH, Elizabeth]. *The Platonic Wife, a Comedy, As it is Performed at the Theatre-Royal in Drury-Lane. By a Lady.* [Based on *L'heureux divorce* by Jean François Marmontel.] London, 1765 (8vo. 1s.6d. Davies) LIBRARY OF CONGRESS

Reviewed: *Monthly Review* 32 (1765): 155
Critical Review 19 (1765): 153
Gentleman's Magazine 35 (1765): 48
Candid Review 1 (1765): 141–145

1147 [GRIFFITH, Elizabeth]. *The School for Rakes: a Comedy. As it is Performed at the Theatre-Royal in Drury-Lane.* [Adapted from *Eugénie* by Pierre Augustin Caron de Beaumarchais.] London, 1769 (8vo. 1s.6d. Becket) BRITISH LIBRARY

Reviewed: *Monthly Review* 40 (1769): 153–156
Critical Review 27 (1769): 223
Gentleman's Magazine 39 (1769): 157 and 199
Critical Memoirs 1 (1769): 249–255 and 522
Town & Country Magazine [1] (1769): 157

1148 GRIFFITH, [Elizabeth]. *A Wife in the Right: a Comedy.* London, 1772 (8vo. 5s. Printed for the Author, and sold by Dilly, &c. 1772) BRITISH LIBRARY

Reviewed: *Monthly Review* 47 (1772): 152
Critical Review 34 (1772): 58–62
Town & Country Magazine 4 (1772): 358–359
British Magazine & General Review 2 (1772): 77
Universal Catalogue [1] (1772) art. 877

1149 [GRIFFITH, Elizabeth and Richard]. *A Series of Genuine Letters between Henry and Frances.* 2 vols. London, 1757 (12mo. 6s. Johnston) BRITISH LIBRARY

Reviewed: *Monthly Review* 17 (1757): 416–423
Critical Review 3 (1757): 428–432

1150 [GRIFFITH, Elizabeth and Richard]. *A Series of Genuine Letters between Henry and Frances*. Vols. III and IV. London, 1766 (12mo. 6s.bound Johnston) BRITISH LIBRARY

Reviewed: *Monthly Review* 36 (1767): 154–155
Critical Review 23 (1767): 30–36
London Magazine 36 (1767): 47–48

1151 [GRIFFITH, Elizabeth and Richard]. *A Series of Genuine Letters between Henry and Frances*. Vols. V and VI. London, 1770 (12mo. 5s.sewed. Richardson and Urquhart. 1770) BRITISH LIBRARY

Reviewed: *Monthly Review* 43 (1770): 490
Critical Review 30 (1770): 460–461
London Magazine 39 (1770): 631
Town & Country Magazine 3 (1771): 44

1152 [GRIFFITH, Elizabeth and Richard]. *Two Novels. In Letters. By the Authors of Henry and Frances.* [Vols. I and II: *The Delicate Distress, A Novel. In Letters, By Frances.* Vols. III and IV: *The Gordian Knot, or Dignus Vindice Nodus. A Novel. In Letters. By Henry.*] 4 vols. London, 1769 (12mo. 10s.sewed. Becket) BRITISH LIBRARY

Reviewed: *Monthly Review* 41 (1769): 232–233
Critical Review 28 (1769): 132–142

1153 [GRIFFITH, Richard]. *The Posthumous Works of a late celebrated Genius, deceased.* [Spurious Sterne.] 2 vols. London, 1770 (12mo. 5s. Almon, &c. 1770) BRITISH LIBRARY

Reviewed: *Monthly Review* 42 (1770): 360–363
Critical Review 29 (1770): 102–109
Gentleman's Magazine 40 (1770): 80–83
London Magazine 39 (1770): 319

1154 [GRIFFITH, Richard]. *Something New*. 2 vols. London, 1772 (12mo. 6s. Dilly, &c. 1772) BRITISH LIBRARY

Reviewed: *Monthly Review* 46 (1772): 166
Critical Review 33 (1772): 73–75
London Magazine 41 (1772): 88

British Magazine & General Review 1 (1772): 70–75
Universal Catalogue [1] (1772) art. 113

1155 [GRIFFITH, Richard]. *The Triumvirate: or, the Authentic Memoirs of A. B. and C.* 2 vols. London, 1764 (12mo. 6s. Johnston) BRITISH LIBRARY

Reviewed: *Monthly Review* 32 (1765): 316–317
Critical Review 19 (1765): 236–237
Candid Review 1 (1765): 212–216

The Group; composed of The Most Shocking Figures
See: ROSA, Salvator (pseud.)

1156 *The Grove and Clown. A Ludicrous Tale on the Times: or, A Blow on the Other Side.* London, 1769 (4to. 1s. Nicoll) HARVARD (HOUGHTON)

Reviewed: *Monthly Review* 40 (1769): 91
Critical Review 27 (1769): 72
Gentleman's Magazine 39 (1769): 157
London Magazine 38 (1769): 104
Town & Country Magazine [1] (1769): 45

The Guardian. A Comedy
See: GARRICK, David

1157 *The Guardian Angel.* London, 1763 (4to. 2s. Henderson) BODLEIAN

Reviewed: *Monthly Review* 28 (1763): 399–400
Critical Review 15 (1763): 323–324

The Guardian Out-witted
See: ARNE, Thomas Augustine

GUEULLETTE, Thomas Simon (translation)
See: FLLOYD, Thomas. *Tartarian Tales*

1158 [GUICHARD, Éléonore]. *The Bracelet: or, the Fortunate Discovery. Being the History of Miss Polly *****. Translated with some Alterations, from a French work, entituled, Memoires de Cecile.* 2 vols. London, n.d. [ESTC-1759] (12mo. 6s. Noble) BRITISH LIBRARY

Reviewed: *Monthly Review* 20 (1759): 275–276
Critical Review 7 (1759): 382

GUILLARD DE BEAURIEU, Gaspard (translation)
See: BURNE, James

1159 [GUTHRIE, William]. *The Friends. A Sentimental History: Describing Love as a Virtue, As well as a Passion.* 2 vols. London, 1754 (12mo. 6s. Waller) BRITISH LIBRARY

Reviewed: *Monthly Review* 10 (1754): 144

1160 [GUTHRIE, William]. *The Mother: or, the Happy Distress. A Novel.* 2 vols. London, 1759 (12mo. 6s. Baldwin) CAMBRIDGE

Reviewed: *Monthly Review* 20 (1759): 380
Critical Review 7 (1759): 409-413

1161 HACKETT, John. *A Collection of Select Epigrams In which are Many Originals never before printed, by the Most Eminent Hands. Published by Mr. Hackett.* n.p., 1757 [ESTC-London] (12mo. 1s.6d. Hitch) BRITISH LIBRARY

Reviewed: *Monthly Review* 16 (1757): 184

1162 *Hadleigh Grove; or, the History of Sir Charles Davers, and The Fair Jessica. A Novel.* 2 vols. London, n.d. [ESTC-1773] (12mo. 6s. Roson) BRITISH LIBRARY

Reviewed: *Monthly Review* 49 (1773): 508
Critical Review 36 (1773): 397
Town & Country Magazine 6 (1774): 100
Universal Catalogue [2] (1773) art. 1130

1163 HALL, Joseph. *Virgidemiarum. Satires in Six Books. By Joseph Hall, of Emanuel College, Afterwards Bishop of Exeter and of Norwich.* Oxford, 1753 (12mo. 2s.bound. Baldwin in London & Merril in Cambridge) BRITISH LIBRARY

Reviewed: *Monthly Review* 7 (1752): 351-358

1164 HALLER, [Albrecht von,] Baron. *Usong. An Eastern Narrative. Written in German By Baron Haller.* 2 vols. London, 1772 (12mo. 5s. sewed. Newbery. 1772) BRITISH LIBRARY

Reviewed: *Monthly Review* 48 (1773): 160-161
Gentleman's Magazine 43 (1773): 189-191
London Magazine 42 (1773): 91
Universal Catalogue [2] (1773) art. 117

1165 HALLER, Albrecht von, Baron. *Usong. An Oriental History In Four Books. Translated from the German of Baron Albert von Haller, President of the Royal Society at Gottingen, and the Oeconomical Society at Bern, &c.* London, 1773 (12mo. 318pp. 3s.bound. Wilkie) BRITISH LIBRARY

Reviewed: *Critical Review* 35 (1773): 195-198
Universal Catalogue [2] (1773) art. 619

1166 HALLIFAX, Charles. *Miscellanies in prose and verse. Containing, The General Resurrection, a satire,—fables, songs, epitaphs, epigrams, &c.: all entirely new*
NOT SEEN (8vo. 1s. Hooper, &c.)

Reviewed: *Monthly Review* 11 (1754): 464
Gentleman's Magazine 24 (1754): 582-583

1167 HAMILTON, [Anthony]. *Select Tales of Count Hamilton, Author of the Life and Memoirs of the Count de Grammont. Translated from the French.* 2 vols. London, 1760 (12mo. 6s. Burd) BRITISH LIBRARY

Reviewed: *Monthly Review* 22 (1760): 523-524
Critical Review 9 (1760): 413
British Magazine 1 (1760): 378

1168 [HAMILTON, Thomas, 6th Earl of Haddington]. *Forty select Poems on several occasions, by The Right Honourable The Earl of H*******n. To which is added, The Duke of Argyle's Levee: A Poem, Written by the late Lord Binning, and spoken by Colonel Chartres.* 2 vols. London, 1769 (12mo. 4s. Bell) NEW YORK PUBLIC LIBRARY

Reviewed: *Critical Review* 28 (1769): 378
Gentleman's Magazine 39 (1769): 600
London Magazine 38 (1769): 642
Town & Country Magazine [1] (1769): 661

1169 HAMILTON, William. *Poems on several Occasions. By William Hamilton of Bangour, Esquire.* Edinburgh, 1760 (12mo. 3s.6d. Edinburgh, printed by Gordon, and sold by Becket, &c. in London) BRITISH LIBRARY

Reviewed: *Monthly Review* 24 (1761): 162-164
Critical Review 11 (1761): 45-48
London Magazine 30 (1761): 56
British Magazine 2 (1761): 46

Happiness, an Epistle to a Friend
See: COLLIGNON, Charles

Happiness: Characteristic Poem
See: HILTON, William

1170 *The Happy Discovery: or, the History of Miss Emilia Cresswell. In Two Volumes.* London, 1769 (12mo. 5s.sewed. Wilkie, &c.) HARVARD (HOUGHTON)

Reviewed: *Monthly Review* 42 (1770): 70
Critical Review 29 (1770): 475
London Magazine 39 (1770): 379
Town & Country Magazine 2 (1770): 435

1171 *The Happy Extravagant: or, Memoirs of Charles Clairville, Esq. By the Editor of the Wanderer.* 2 vols. London, 1768 (12mo. 6s. Noble) UNIVERSITY OF PENNSYLVANIA

Reviewed: *Monthly Review* 39 (1768): 84
Critical Review 25 (1768): 464
London Magazine 37 (1768): 163
Universal Museum 4 (1768): 316

The Happy Orphans
See: KIMBER, Edward

1172 *Harriet; or, the Innocent Adulteress.* 2 vols. NOT SEEN (12mo. 5s. Baldwin)

Reviewed: *Monthly Review* 44 (1771): 418
Critical Review 31 (1771): 484
Gentleman's Magazine 41 (1771): 278
London Magazine 40 (1771): 226

1173 [HARRIS, James]. *The Spring. A Pastoral. As it is now performing at the Theatre Royal in Drury-Lane. The Music by Mr. Handel, And other Eminent Masters.* London, n.d. [ESTC-1762] (4to. 6d. Davies) BRITISH LIBRARY

Reviewed: *Monthly Review* 27 (1762): 393
Critical Review 14 (1762): 398

1174 [HARRIS, Thomas]. *The Ring. An Epistle, addressed to Mrs. L------m.* London, n.d. [FOLGER CAT.-1768] (4to. 1s. Wilkie) FOLGER

Reviewed: *Monthly Review* 38 (1768): 247
Critical Review 25 (1768): 233

London Magazine 37 (1768): 160
Universal Museum 4 (1768): 149

1175 HARRISON, Elizabeth. *Miscellanies on Moral and Religious Subjects, in Prose and Verse.* London, 1756 (8vo. 5s. Buckland) BRITISH LIBRARY

Reviewed: *Monthly Review* 15 (1756): 537
Literary Magazine 1 (1756): 282–288

1176 HARROD, W[illiam]. *The Patriot: a Tragedy.* London, 1769 (8vo. 2s. Bingley, &c.) BRITISH LIBRARY

Reviewed: *Monthly Review* 41 (1769): 319
Gentleman's Magazine 39 (1769): 500–502
London Magazine 38 (1769): 537

1177 HARROD, W[illiam]. *Sevenoke. A Poem. Humbly Inscribed to His Grace the Duke of Dorset.* London, 1753 (4to. 1s. Fuller) BRITISH LIBRARY

Reviewed: *Monthly Review* 8 (1753): 392

1178 [HART, Charles]. *Herminius and Espasia: a Tragedy. As it was Acted at the Theatre in Edinburgh.* Edinburgh, 1754 (8vo. 1s.6d. Wilson) BRITISH LIBRARY

Reviewed: *Monthly Review* 10 (1754): 386

1179 HART, J[oseph]. *Hymns, &c. composed On various Subjects. With a Preface, containing A Brief and Summary account of the Author's Experience, and The great Things that God hath done for his Soul.* London, 1759 (12mo. 1s.6d. Waller) BRITISH LIBRARY

Reviewed: *Monthly Review* 21 (1759): 351–352

1180 [HARTE, Walter]. *The Amaranth: or, Religious Poems; consisting of Fables, Visions, Emblems, &c. Adorned with Copper-Plates from the Best Masters.* London, 1767 (8vo. 5s. Robinson) BRITISH LIBRARY

Reviewed: *Monthly Review* 37 (1767): 292–295
Critical Review 24 (1767): 121–124
Gentleman's Magazine 37 (1767): 372–373
Universal Museum 3 (1767): 429

1181 HARTSON, Hall. *The Countess of Salisbury. A Tragedy. As it is performed at the Theatre*

Royal in the Hay-Market. London, 1767 (8vo. 1s.6d. Griffin) BODLEIAN

Reviewed: *Monthly Review* 37 (1767): 392–393
Critical Review 24 (1767): 147–152
Gentleman's Magazine 37 (1767): 468
London Magazine 36 (1767): 483
Universal Museum 3 (1767): 429
Political Register 1 (1767): 317–318

1182 HARTSON, Hall. *Youth. A Poem.* London, 1773 (4to. 2s. Griffin. 1773) BRITISH LIBRARY

Reviewed: *Monthly Review* 48 (1773): 159
Critical Review 34 (1772): 396
London Magazine 42 (1773): 40–41
Town & Country Magazine 4 (1772): 602
British Magazine & General Review 2 (1772): 558–559
Universal Catalogue [1] (1772) art. 1378

1183 [HARVEY, John]. *The Bruciad, an Epic Poem, in Six Books.* London, 1769 (8vo. 4s.in boards. Dodsley) BRITISH LIBRARY

Reviewed: *Monthly Review* 41 (1769): 382–390
Critical Review 28 (1769): 142–145
London Magazine 38 (1769): 439

Hau Kiou Choaan
See: PERCY, Thomas (ed.)

1184 HAWKESWORTH, John. *The Adventures of Telemachus, the Son of Ulysses. Translated from the French of Messire François Salignac de la Mothe-Fenelon, Archbishop of Cambray. By John Hawkesworth, L.L.D.* London, 1768 (4to. 1l.1s. Becket) BODLEIAN

Reviewed: *Monthly Review* 39 (1768): 237
Critical Review 27 (1769): 170–178
Gentleman's Magazine 38 (1768): 290–292

1185 HAWKESWORTH, John. *Almoran and Hamet: an Oriental Tale. In Two Volumes.* London, 1761 (8vo. 5s. Payne) BRITISH LIBRARY

Reviewed: *Monthly Review* 24 (1761): 415–435
Critical Review 11 (1761): 469–474
British Magazine 2 (1761): 326

1186 [HAWKESWORTH, John]. *Edgar and Emmeline; a Fairy Tale: In a Dramatic Entertainment of Two Acts; As it is performed at The Theatre-Royal In Drury-Lane.* London, 1761 (8vo. 1s. Payne and Cropley) BRITISH LIBRARY

Reviewed: *Monthly Review* 24 (1761): 159
London Magazine 30 (1761): 112

1187 [HAWKESWORTH, John]. *Oroonoko, a Tragedy, As it is now Acted at the Theatre-Royal In Drury-Lane. By His Majesty's Servants. By Thomas Southern. With Alterations.* London, 1759 (8vo. 1s.6d. Bathurst) BRITISH LIBRARY

Reviewed: *Critical Review* 8 (1759): 480–486
Gentleman's Magazine 29 (1759): 588 [596]
London Magazine 28 (1759): 688

1188 HAWKINS, Thomas (ed.). *The Origin of The English Drama, illustrated in its various species, viz. Mystery, Morality, Tragedy, and Comedy, by specimens from our earliest writers: with Explanatory Notes By Thomas Hawkins, M.A. of Magdalene College, Oxford.* 3 vols. Oxford, 1773 (8vo. 9s.sewed. Oxford printed; and sold by Leacroft in London. 1773) BODLEIAN

Reviewed: *Monthly Review* 48 (1773): 388–390
Critical Review 35 (1773): 349–356
London Magazine 42 (1773): 148

1189 HAWKINS, William. *The Aeneid of Virgil, translated into English Blank Verse*
NOT SEEN (8vo. 2s.6d. Fletcher)

Reviewed: *Monthly Review* 30 (1764): 257–261
Critical Review 17 (1764): 424–429
British Magazine 5 (1764): 376

1190 HAWKINS, William. *Cymbeline. A Tragedy, altered from Shakespeare. As it is perform'd at the Theatre-Royal in Covent-Garden.* London, 1759 (8vo. 1s.6d. Rivington and Fletcher) BRITISH LIBRARY

Reviewed: *Monthly Review* 20 (1759): 462–463

1191 HAWKINS, W[illiam]. *Dramatic and other Poems, Letters, Essays, &c.* [Vol. 2 of 3-vol. collected works; each vol. has separate title.] Oxford, 1758 (8vo. 5s. Dodsley, &c.) BRITISH LIBRARY

Reviewed: *Monthly Review* 21 (1759): 311–312 [3 vols.]
Critical Review 8 (1759): 97–103 [3 vols.]

1192 HAY, William. *Deformity: an Essay.* London, 1754 (1s.6d. Dodsley) BRITISH LIBRARY

Reviewed: *Gentleman's Magazine* 23 (1753): 593

1193 HAY, William. *The Immortality of the Soul. A Poem. Translated from the Latin of Isaac Hawkins Browne, Esq;* London, 1754 (4to. 1s.6d. Dodsley) BRITISH LIBRARY

Reviewed: *Monthly Review* 10 (1754): 218–221
Gentleman's Magazine 24 (1754): 146–147

1194 HAY, William. *Select Epigrams of Martial. Translated and Imitated By William Hay, Esq; with An Appendix Of some by Cowley, and other Hands.* London, 1755 (12mo. 3s. Dodsley) BRITISH LIBRARY

Reviewed: *Monthly Review* 12 (1755): 189–191

1195 HAYES, D[aniel]. *The Authors. A Poem.* London, 1766 (4to. 1s.6d. Griffin) BODLEIAN

Reviewed: *Monthly Review* 35 (1766): 79
Critical Review 21 (1766): 476–478

1196 HAYES, D[aniel]. *An Epistle to C. Churchill, Author of the Rosciad, &c.* London, 1761 (4to. 1s. Bristow) BRITISH LIBRARY

Reviewed: *Monthly Review* 25 (1761): 478
Critical Review 12 (1761): 320
British Magazine 2 (1761): 550

1197 HAYWOOD, Eliza. *Clementina; or, the History of an Italian Lady, who made Her Escape From A Monastery, for the Love Of A Scots Nobleman.* London, 1768 (12mo. 2s.6d. Noble) BRITISH LIBRARY

Reviewed: *Monthly Review* 38 (1768): 412
Critical Review 25 (1768): 59
London Magazine 37 (1768): 47–48

1198 [HAYWOOD, Eliza]. *Dalinda: or, The Double Marriage. Being the Genuine History of a very Recent and Interesting Adventure. Addressed to the Young and Gay of both Sexes.* London, 1749 (In one pocket vol. 3s.bound. Printed for Corbet in Fleet-street and Woodfall near Charing Cross) BRITISH LIBRARY

Reviewed: *Monthly Review* 1 (1749): 238

1199 [HAYWOOD, Eliza]. *The History of Jemmy and Jenny Jessamy.* 3 vols. London, 1753 (12mo. 9s. Gardner) BRITISH LIBRARY

Reviewed: *Monthly Review* 8 (1753): 77

1200 [HAYWOOD, Eliza]. *The History of Miss Betsy Thoughtless.* 4 vols. London, 1751 (12mo. 12s. Gardner) BRITISH LIBRARY

Reviewed: *Monthly Review* 5 (1751): 393–394

1201 [HAYWOOD, Eliza]. *The Invisible Spy. By Exploralibus.* 4 vols. London, 1755 (12mo. 12s. Gardner) BRITISH LIBRARY

Reviewed: *Monthly Review* 11 (1754): 498–502

1202 HAZARD, Joseph. *The Conquest of Quebec. A Poem.* Oxford, 1769 (4to. 1s. Fletcher. 1769) BRITISH LIBRARY

Reviewed: *Monthly Review* 40 (1769): 517–519
Critical Review 27 (1769): 469–471
Critical Memoirs [2] (1769): 216

He Wou'd if he Cou'd
See: BICKERSTAFFE, Isaac

1203 *Health; a Poetical Essay, humbly inscribed to the Right Hon. the Earl of Chatham* NOT SEEN (4to. 1s.6d. Nicoll)

Reviewed: *Monthly Review* 37 (1767): 315–316
Critical Review 24 (1767): 225
Gentleman's Magazine 37 (1767): 468
London Magazine 36 (1767): 482
Universal Museum 3 (1767): 485

1204 [HEARD, William]. *The Tryal of Dramatic Genius: A Poem. To which are added, a Collection of Miscellaneous Pieces. By the same Author.* London, n.d. [ESTC-1773] (8vo. 2s. Goldsmith) BRITISH LIBRARY

Reviewed: *Monthly Review* 48 (1773): 70–71
Critical Review 34 (1772): 471
London Magazine 42 (1773): 40
Universal Catalogue [1] (1772) art. 1460

1205 HEARNE, Erasmus (pseud.). *The Antiquarian School: or The City Latin Electrified. A Ballad. Dedicated by Permission to Sir Nicholas Nemo, Knt.* London, 1761 (Fol. 6d. Stevens) BRITISH LIBRARY

Reviewed: *Monthly Review* 24 (1761): 164–165
Critical Review 11 (1761): 255

1206 *Hébe, an Heroic Poem on her Majesty.* London, 1774 (4to. 1s.6d. Allen. 1774) NEW YORK PUBLIC LIBRARY

Reviewed: *Monthly Review* 51 (1774): 317–318
Universal Catalogue 3 (1774) art. 1256

Hector, a Dramatic Poem
See: SHEPHERD, Richard

Hecuba, a Tragedy
See: DELAP, John

1207 HEDGE, Simon. *The Poor Man's Prayer. Addressed To the Earl of Chatham. An Elegy. By Simon Hedge, a Kentish Labourer.* London, 1766 (4to. 6d. Payne) BRITISH LIBRARY

Reviewed: *Monthly Review* 35 (1766): 323–325
Critical Review 22 (1766): 232–233
Gentleman's Magazine 36 (1766): 430

1208 [HEIDEGGER, John James]. *The artful Priest; or the Virgin Sacrifice; a humorous Tale. By the late celebrated J. J. H--d--g--r, Esq;*
NOT SEEN (4to. 16pp. 6d. John of Gaunt, near Charing Cross)

Reviewed: *Monthly Review* 2 (1749–50): 27

Heliocrene: A Poem
See: MERRICK, James

1209 HELVÉTIUS, [Claude Adrien] (pseud.). *The Child of Nature, improved by Chance. A Philosophical Novel.* 2 vols. London, 1774 (6s.bound. Becket. 1774) BRITISH LIBRARY

Reviewed: *Monthly Review* 51 (1774): 323
Critical Review 38 (1774): 270–274
London Magazine 43 (1774): 449
Universal Catalogue 3 (1774) art. 1040

1210 HENDERSON, Andrew. *Arsinoe; or, the Incestuous Marriage. A Tragedy.* London, n.d. [ESTC-1752] (8vo. 1s. Robinson) BRITISH LIBRARY

Reviewed: *Monthly Review* 6 (1752): 315–316

Henrietta
See: LENNOX, Charlotte

Henry and Emma
See: DUDLEY, Henry Bate

Herminius and Espasia
See: HART, Charles

The Hermit. A Novel
See: ATKYNS, Lady

The Hermit of Warkworth
See: PERCY, Thomas

The Hermitage: a British Story
See: HUTCHINSON, William

Hero, and Leander, a Poem
See: GREENE, Edward Burnaby

An Heroic Epistle to Sir William Chambers
See: MASON, William

An Heroic Postscript to The Public
See: MASON, William

HERVEY, James (adaptations)
See: NEWCOMB, Thomas. *Mr. Hervey's Contemplations on a Flower-Garden*
NEWCOMB, Thomas. *Mr. Hervey's Contemplations on the Night*
NEWCOMB, Thomas. *Mr. Hervey's Meditations and Contemplations*

1211 [HERVEY, Thomas]. *An Elegy upon the Death of the late Earl Granville, Who died the 2d of January, 1763, in the 73d Year of his Age.* London, 1767 (Fol. 6d. R. Davis) BRITISH LIBRARY

Reviewed: *Monthly Review* 36 (1767): 331

1212 HEY, John. *The Redemption: a Poetical Essay.* Cambridge, 1763 (4to. 1s. Beecroft) BRITISH LIBRARY

Reviewed: *Monthly Review* 29 (1763): 470–471
Critical Review 16 (1763): 473–474

1213 *The Hiberniad.* Dublin, 1754 (4to. 1s.6d. Dublin printed, and sold by G. Woodfall in London) BRITISH LIBRARY

Reviewed: *Monthly Review* 10 (1754): 512

1214 [HIFFERNAN, Paul]. *The Earl of Warwick; or, the King and Subject. A Tragedy.* [From the French original by Jean François de la Harpe.] London, 1764 (8vo. 1s.6d. Kearsly) BRITISH LIBRARY

Reviewed: *Monthly Review* 30 (1764): 240
Critical Review 17 (1764): 310–311
General Magazine 1 (1764): 97

1215 [HIFFERNAN, Paul]. *Foote's Prologue Detected; with a Miniature-Prose Epilogue of his Manner in Speaking. By Philo-technicus Misomimides.* London, n.d. [Cropped] [ESTC-1770] (8vo. 1s. Williams) BRITISH LIBRARY

Reviewed: *Monthly Review* 43 (1770): 72
Critical Review 29 (1770): 479

1216 HIFFERNAN, Paul. *The Lady's Choice, a Petite Piece, of Two Acts. As it is performed at the Theatre-Royal in Covent-Garden.* London, n.d. [ESTC-1759] (8vo. 1s. Coote) BRITISH LIBRARY

Reviewed: *Monthly Review* 20 (1759): 463

1217 [HIFFERNAN, Paul]. *The Wishes of a Free People; a Dramatic Poem.* London, 1761 (8vo. 1s. Hooper) BRITISH LIBRARY

Reviewed: *Monthly Review* 25 (1761): 396
Critical Review 12 (1761): 400

1218 [HIGGS, Henry]. *High Life: a Novel. Or, the History of Miss Faulkland.* [Title page says 2 vols., but British Library has only one vol. and story appears to end with this one.] London ed. reviewed; copy seen: Dublin, 1768 (12mo. 6s. Lownds) BRITISH LIBRARY

Reviewed: *Monthly Review* 37 (1767): 394
Critical Review 24 (1767): 350–355
Universal Museum 3 (1767): 394

High Life: A Novel
See: HIGGS, Henry

High Life Below Stairs
See: TOWNLEY, James

1219 *High Taste. A Satire. Addressed to the young Tits of Pleasure*
NOT SEEN (Fol. 1s. Marshall)

Reviewed: *Monthly Review* 26 (1762): 151
Critical Review 13 (1762): 164

1220 HIGHMORE, Elizabeth. *Ambition. A poem, dedicated to the worthy and honourable society of true Britons*
NOT SEEN (Fol. 1s. Cooper)

Reviewed: *Monthly Review* 16 (1757): 461–462
Critical Review 3 (1757): 557

1221 HILL, Aaron. *The Dramatic Works of Aaron Hill, Esq;* 2 vols. London, 1760 (8vo. 10s.6d.boards. Lownds) BRITISH LIBRARY

Reviewed: *Monthly Review* 21 (1759): 545–556
Critical Review 9 (1760): 235–236

1222 [HILL, Aaron]. *Gideon; or, The Patriot. An Epic Poem in Twelve Books. Upon a Hebrew Plan. In Honour of the Two chief Virtues of a People; Intrepidity in Foreign War: and Spirit of Domestic Liberty.* London, 1749 (4to. 147pp., i.e. about 18 sheets) BRITISH LIBRARY

Reviewed: *Monthly Review* 1 (1749): 64–72

1223 HILL, Aaron. *The Insolvent: or, Filial Piety. A Tragedy. Acted at the Theatre in the Haymarket, (by Authority) Under the Direction of Mr. Cibber.* London, 1758 (8vo. 1s.6d. Reeve) BRITISH LIBRARY

Reviewed: *Monthly Review* 18 (1758): 650–651
Critical Review 6 (1758): 17–25

1224 HILL, Aaron. *The Roman Revenge. A Tragedy.* n.p., 1753 [ESTC-London] (8vo. 1s.6d.) BRITISH LIBRARY

Reviewed: *Monthly Review* 10 (1754): 79

1225 [HILL, John]. *The Adventures of Mr George Edwards, a Creole.* London, 1751 (12mo. 3s. Osborn) BRITISH LIBRARY

Reviewed: *Monthly Review* 5 (1751): 237–238
Gentleman's Magazine 21 (1751): 335

1226 [HILL, John]. *The History of a Woman of Quality: or, the Adventures of Lady Frail. By an Impartial Hand.* London, 1751 (12mo. 3s. Cooper and G. Woodfall) BRITISH LIBRARY

Reviewed: *Monthly Review* 4 (1750–51): 307–308
Gentleman's Magazine 21 (1751): 95

1227 [HILL, John (trans.)]. *Memoirs of a Man of Pleasure, or the Adventures of Versorand. Translated from the French.* [From the French original of Henri François de la Solle.] 2 vols. London, 1751 (12mo. 6s. T. Osborne) BRITISH LIBRARY [British Library has vol. 1 only.]

Reviewed: *Monthly Review* 5 (1751): 43–44

1228 [HILL, John]. *The Rout. A Farce of two acts As it is perform'd at the Theatre-Royal in Drury-Lane.* London, 1758 (8vo. 1s. Cooper) BRITISH LIBRARY

Reviewed: *Monthly Review* 19 (1758): 583
Critical Review 7 (1759): 81–82
Gentleman's Magazine 29 (1759): 37

1229 [HILL, John]. *The Smartiad, a Satire, Occasioned by an Epic Poem, intitled The Hilliad.* London, 1753 (Fol. 6d. Job) BRITISH LIBRARY

Reviewed: *Monthly Review* 8 (1753): 151

1230 [HILTON, William]. *Happiness: Characteristic Poem.* London, 1773 (4to. 1s. Murray. 1773) BRITISH LIBRARY

Reviewed: *Monthly Review* 49 (1773): 231
London Magazine 42 (1773): 302
Universal Catalogue [2] (1773) art. 838

1231 *A Hint to such as would be Wise*
NOT SEEN (4to. 5s.sewed. Harrison)

Reviewed: *Monthly Review* 30 (1764): 323
Critical Review 17 (1764): 396–397

1232 *His Majesty King George the Second, His Royal Highness the Prince of Wales, And all the Royal Family. His Grace the Duke of Dorset, And Fairfax, and Watson, for ever: Or,*
Down with the Devil, Pope, and Pretender. An Heroic Poem, with Explanatory Notes suitable to the present Times. By a Freeholder of Kent. London, 1754 (8vo. 6d. Cooper) BRITISH LIBRARY

Reviewed: *Monthly Review* 10 (1754): 305

1233 *The Histories Of Some of the Penitents in the Magdalen-House, as Supposed to be related by Themselves.* 2 vols. London, 1760 (12mo. 6s. Rivington) BRITISH LIBRARY

Reviewed: *Monthly Review* 21 (1759): 449–450
Critical Review 8 (1759): 373–379
London Magazine 28 (1759): 632

1234 *The History and Adventures of a Lady's Slippers and Shoes. Written by Themselves.* London, 1754 (8vo. 1s. Cooper) BRITISH LIBRARY

Reviewed: *Monthly Review* 12 (1755): 237
Gentleman's Magazine 25 (1755): 94

The History and Adventures of an Atom
See: SMOLLETT, Tobias

1235 *The History and Adventures of Frank Hammond.* London, 1754 (12mo. 3s. Griffiths) BRITISH LIBRARY

Reviewed: *Monthly Review* 10 (1754): 391–392

The History of a Woman of Quality
See: HILL, John

The History of a Young Lady of Distinction
See: ÉLIE DE BEAUMONT, Anne Louise

The History of Alicia Montague
See: MARSHALL, Jean

1236 *The History of Amanda. Written by a young Lady*
NOT SEEN (12mo. 3s. Ross)

Reviewed: *Monthly Review* 18 (1758): 182
Critical Review 5 (1758): 172–173

1237 *The History of Amintor and Teresa.* London, 1769 (12mo. 3s. Owen) BRITISH LIBRARY

Reviewed: *Monthly Review* 40 (1769): 86–87
Critical Review 27 (1769): 152
London Magazine 38 (1769): 104

The History of Arsaces
See: JOHNSTONE, Charles

1238 *The History of Barbarossa and Polyana*
NOT SEEN (12mo. 3s. Crowder)

Reviewed: *Monthly Review* 13 (1755): 510

1239 *The History of Benjamin St. Martin, a Fortunate Foundling, Interspersed with Curious Anecdotes and Narratives of the Love-Affairs of some Persons in High Life.* 2 vols. London, 1759 (12mo. 6s. Coote) NEWBERRY

Reviewed: *Monthly Review* 20 (1759): 188
Critical Review 7 (1759): 285

1240 *History of Betty Barnes.* [Has been attributed to Sarah Fielding.] 2 vols. London, 1753 (12mo. 6s. Wilson and Durham) BRITISH LIBRARY

Reviewed: *Monthly Review* 7 (1752): 470

The History of Charles Wentworth
See: BANCROFT, Edward

1241 *The History of Charlotte Summers, the Fortunate Parish Girl.* London, n.d. [ESTC-1750] (6s.bound. Sold by Charles Corbet, in Fleet-street.) BRITISH LIBRARY

Reviewed: *Monthly Review* 2 (1749–50): 352

The History of Charlotte Villars
See: MUKINS Isaac

The history of Cleanthes
See: MEADES, Anna

The History of Cornelia
See: SCOTT, Sarah

1242 *The History of Eliza. Written by a Friend.* 2 vols. London, 1767 (12mo. 6s. Dodsley) BRITISH LIBRARY

Reviewed: *Monthly Review* 36 (1767): 172–173
Critical Review 22 (1766): 434–438

1243 *The History of Eliza Musgrove.* 2 vols. London, 1769 (12mo. 4s.6d.sewed. Johnston) YALE (STERLING)

Reviewed: *Monthly Review* 41 (1769): 73–74
Critical Review 27 (1769): 452–459
London Magazine 38 (1769): 323
Town & Country Magazine [1] (1769): 327

The History of Emily Montague
See: BROOKE, Frances

1244 *The History of Fanny Seymour.* London, 1753 (12mo. 3s. Bathoe) BRITISH LIBRARY

Reviewed: *Monthly Review* 8 (1753): 314

The History of Female Favourites
See: LA ROCHE-GUILHEM, Anne de

1245 *The History of Frederick the Forsaken. Interspersed with Anecdotes relative to several Personages of Rank and Fashion in this Metropolis.* 2 vols.
NOT SEEN (12mo. 6s. Noble)

Reviewed: *Monthly Review* 23 (1760): 408
Critical Review 10 (1760): 280–290
British Magazine 1 (1760): 665

1246 *The History of Honoria, being the Adventures of a Young Lady. Interspersed with the Histories of Emilia, Julia, and Others. By a Young Gentleman.* London, 1754 (12mo. 3s. Bizet) CAMBRIDGE

Reviewed: *Monthly Review* 10 (1754): 480

The History of Indiana Danby
See: *The History of Miss Indiana Danby*

The History of Jack Connor
See: CHAIGNEAU, William

1247 *The History of Jack Wilks, a Lover of Liberty.* 2 vols. London, 1769 (12mo. 6s. Gardner) BRITISH LIBRARY

Reviewed: *Monthly Review* 40 (1769): 258
Critical Review 27 (1769): 151–152
Gentleman's Magazine 39 (1769): 158
Critical Memoirs 1 (1769): 524–525
Town & Country Magazine [1] (1769): 101
Political Register 4 (1769): 389

The History of James Lovegrove
See: RIDLEY, James

1248 *The history of Jasper Banks, commonly call'd, The Handsome Man. In Two Volumes.*

London ed. reviewed; copy seen: Dublin, 1754 (12mo. 6s. Reeve) BODLEIAN

Reviewed: *Monthly Review* 10 (1754): 479–480

The History of Jemmy and Jenny Jessamy
See: HAYWOOD, Eliza

1249 *The History of Joshua Trueman, Esq; and Miss Peggy Williams.* 2 vols. London, 1754 (12mo. 6s. Wilson and Durham) BRITISH LIBRARY

Reviewed: *Monthly Review* 11 (1754): 466

The History of King Lear
See: COLMAN, George (the elder)

The History of Lady Julia Mandeville
See: BROOKE, Frances

1250 *The History of Lady Louisa Stroud, and the honourable Miss Caroline Stretton.* 2 vols. London, 1764 (12mo. 6s.bound. Noble) BRITISH LIBRARY

Reviewed: *Monthly Review* 30 (1764): 244
Critical Review 17 (1764): 307–308

1251 *The History of Lavinia Rawlins. In Two Volumes.* London, 1756 (12mo. 6s. Owen) HARVARD (HOUGHTON)

Reviewed: *Monthly Review* 13 (1755): 398–399

1252 *The History of Lord Aimworth and the Honourable Charles Hartford Esq; in a Series of Letters.* 3 vols.
NOT SEEN (12mo. 9s. Roson, &c. 1773)

Reviewed: *Monthly Review* 48 (1773): 416
London Magazine 42 (1773): 195
Universal Catalogue [2] (1773) art. 479

1253 *The History of Lord Ashborn, and the Honourable Miss Howe; or, the Reclaimed Libertine. In Three Volumes. By the Author of Frederick, or the Fortunate Beggar.* London, n.d. [BEINECKE CAT.–1773] (12mo. 9s. Roson, &c. 1773) YALE (BEINECKE)

Reviewed: *Monthly Review* 49 (1773): 69
Critical Review 36 (1773): 74
Universal Catalogue [2][(1773) art. 763

1254 *The History of Lord Clayton and Miss Meredith.* 2 vols. London ed. reviewed; copy seen: Dublin, 1769 (12mo. 6s. Robinson and Roberts) BRITISH LIBRARY

Reviewed: *Monthly Review* 40 (1769): 259
Critical Review 27 (1769): 310–311
Critical Memoirs 1 (1769): 525

1255 *The History of Lord Stanton. A Novel. By a Gentleman of the Middle Temple, Author of The Trial, or the History of Charles Horton.* 3 vols. London, n.d. [HOUGHTON CAT.–1774] (12mo. 9s. Vernor) HARVARD (HOUGHTON)

Reviewed: *Monthly Review* 50 (1774): 172–176 and 327
Critical Review 37 (1774): 318
London Magazine 43 (1774): 40
Town & Country Magazine 6 (1774): 268
Universal Catalogue 3 (1774) art. 337

The history of Lucy Wellers
See: SMYTHIES, Miss

The History of Mademoiselle Cronel
See: GAILLARD DE LA BATAILLE, Pierre Alexandre

1256 *The History of Major Bromley and Miss Cliffen.* 2 vols. London, 1757 (12mo. 6s. Wilkie) BRITISH LIBRARY

Reviewed: *Monthly Review* 37 (1767): 394
Critical Review 24 (1767): 300–304
Universal Museum 3 (1767): 541
Political Register 1 (1767): 387–388

1257 *The History of Mira, Daughter of Marcio. Interspersed with a Variety of entertaining Subjects relative thereto.* 2 vols.
NOT SEEN (12mo. 6s. Wilkie)

Reviewed: *Monthly Review* 18 (1758): 93

The History of Miss Betsy Thoughtless
See: HAYWOOD, Eliza

1258 *The History of Miss Carolina Manners. In a Series of Genuine Letters to a Friend.* 3 vols.
NOT SEEN (12mo. 7s.6d.sewed. Printed for the Author, and sold by T. Evans. 1772)

Reviewed: *Monthly Review* 46 (1772): 265
Critical Review 33 (1772): 256
British Magazine & General Review 1 (1772): 342
Universal Catalogue [1] (1772) art. 398

1259 *The History of Miss Charlotte Seymour.* 2 vols.
NOT SEEN (12mo. 5s.sewed. Burnet)

Reviewed: *Monthly Review* 30 (1764): 244
Critical Review 17 (1764): 308

The History of Miss Clarinda Cathcart
See: MARISHALL, Jean

1260 *The History of Miss Delia Stanhope. In a Series of Letters to Miss Dorinda Boothby.* 2 vols. Dublin, 1767 (12mo. 6s. Lowndes) BRITISH LIBRARY

Reviewed: *Monthly Review* 35 (1766): 485
Critical Review 22 (1766): 359–362

1261 *The History of Miss Dorinda Catsby, and Miss Emilia Faulkner: In a Series of Letters.* 2 vols. London, 1772 (12mo. 5s.sewed. Bladon) BRITISH LIBRARY

Reviewed: *Monthly Review* 47 (1772): 151
Critical Review 34 (1772): 77
London Magazine 41 (1772): 386
Town & Country Magazine 4 (1772): 490
British Magazine & General Review 2 (1772): 165
Universal Catalogue [1] (1772) art. 981

1262 *The History of Miss Emilia Beville. In Two Volumes.* London, 1768 (12mo. 6s. Noble) HARVARD (HOUGHTON)

Reviewed: *Monthly Review* 37 (1767): 393
Critical Review 24 (1767): 296–300
Universal Museum 3 (1767): 541
Political Register 1 (1767): 388

1263 *The History of Miss Harriot Fitzroy, and Miss Emilia Spencer. By the Author of Lucinda Courtney. In Two Volumes.* London, 1767 (12mo. 6s. F. and J. Noble) UNIVERSITY OF CHICAGO

Reviewed: *Monthly Review* 35 (1766): 407
Critical Review 22 (1766): 354–359

1264 *The History of Miss Harriot Montague.* 2 vols.
NOT SEEN (12mo. 5s. Roson)

Reviewed: *Monthly Review* 42 (1770): 250–251
Critical Review 29 (1770): 149

1265 *History of Miss Indiana Danby. By a Lady.* 2 vols. London, 1765 (12mo. 5s. Dodsley) BRITISH LIBRARY

Reviewed: *Monthly Review* 32 (1765): 480–481
Critical Review 19 (1765): 467–469
London Magazine 36 (1767): 206 [4 vols.]
Universal Museum 1 (1765): 314–320

1266 *The History of Miss Indiana Danby. In Four Volumes. By a Lady. Vols. III and IV.* London, 1767 (12mo. 6s. Lowndes) BRITISH LIBRARY

Reviewed: *Monthly Review* 37 (1767): 77
Critical Review 23 (1767): 278–280
London Magazine 36 (1767): 206 [4 vols.]

1267 *History of Miss Katty N-----. Containing A faithful and particular Relation of her Amours, Adventures, and various Turns of Fortune, in Scotland, Ireland, Jamaica, and in England.* London, n.d. [BLC-1757] (12mo. 3s. Noble) BRITISH LIBRARY

Reviewed: *Monthly Review* 16 (1757): 178–179
Critical Review 3 (1757): 177

1268 *The History of Miss Lucinda Courtney; In a Series of Original Letters, Written by Herself, To her Friend Miss Constantia Bellmour.* 3 vols. London ed. reviewed; copy seen: Dublin, 1764 (12mo. 9s.bound. Noble) BRITISH LIBRARY

Reviewed: *Monthly Review* 31 (1764): 398
Critical Review 18 (1764): 350–353

1269 *The History of Miss Oakley.* London, 1764 (8vo. 2s. Bladon) YALE (BEINECKE)

Reviewed: *Monthly Review* 30 (1764): 488
Critical Review 17 (1764): 400
British Magazine 5 (1764): 377

1270 *The History of Miss Pamela Howard. By the Author of Indiana Danby.* 2 vols. London, 1773 (12mo. 6s. Lowndes. 1773) BRITISH LIBRARY

Reviewed: *Monthly Review* 48 (1773): 154
   Critical Review 34 (1772): 473
   London Magazine 42 (1773): 39
   British Magazine & General Review 2 (1772): 631–632
   Universal Catalogue [1] (1772) art. 1384

1271 *The History of Miss Pittborough. In a Series of Letters. By a Lady.* 2 vols. London, 1767 (8vo. 6s. Cadell) BRITISH LIBRARY

Reviewed: *Monthly Review* 36 (1767): 238
   Critical Review 23 (1767): 131–135
   Universal Museum 3 (1767): 146–147

The History of Miss Sally Sable
See: WOODFIN, A.

1272 *The History of Miss Sommervile. Written by a Lady.* 2 vols. London, 1769 (Small 8vo. 6s. vellum. Newbery and Carnan) BRITISH LIBRARY

Reviewed: *Monthly Review* 41 (1769): 76–77
   Critical Review 27 (1769): 373–382
   London Magazine 38 (1769): 213
   Town & Country Magazine [1] (1769): 269

1273 *The History of Mr. Byron and Miss Greville.* 2 vols. London, 1767 (12mo. 6s. Noble) BRITISH LIBRARY

Reviewed: *Monthly Review* 37 (1767): 151
   Critical Review 23 (1767): 217–218

1274 *The History of Mr. Cecil and Miss Grey. In a Series of Letters.* 2 vols.
NOT SEEN (12mo. 5s.sewed. Richardson and Urquhart)

Reviewed: *Monthly Review* 44 (1771): 262
   Critical Review 31 (1771): 484

The History of Mr. Charles Chance, and Miss Clara Vellum
See: ROBINSON, John

1275 *The History of Mr. Stanly and Miss Temple. A Rural Novel.* 2 vols. London, n.d. [BLC-1780?] (12mo. 5s.sewed. Johnson. 1773) BRITISH LIBRARY

Reviewed: *Monthly Review* 48 (1773): 181–183
   Critical Review 35 (1773): 320

London Magazine 42 (1773): 91
Universal Catalogue [2] (1773) art. 127

1276 *The History of Mrs. Drayton and her Two Daughters.* 3 vols. London, 1767 (12mo. 9s. Noble) BRITISH LIBRARY

Reviewed: *Monthly Review* 36 (1767): 410
   Critical Review 23 (1767): 463–464
   Political Register 1 (1767): 485

The History of My Own Life
See: BANNOC, Adolphus

The History of Nourjahad
See: SHERIDAN, Frances

The History of Ophelia
See: FIELDING, Sarah

The History of Pamela Howard
See: *The History of Miss Pamela Howard*

1277 *The History of Polly Willis. An Orphan.* London, 1755 (12mo. 3s. Reeve) YALE (STERLING)

Reviewed: *Monthly Review* 12 (1755): 235–236

The History of Pompey the little
See: COVENTRY, Francis

1278 *The History of Portia. Written by a Lady.* 2 vols. London, 1759 (12mo. 6s. Withy) BRITISH LIBRARY

Reviewed: *Monthly Review* 20 (1759): 276
   Critical Review 7 (1759): 382

1279 *The History of Reynard the Fox, Bruin the Bear, &c.* London, 1756 (12mo. 3s. Smith) BRITISH LIBRARY

Reviewed: *Monthly Review* 15 (1756): 655

The History of Rhedi
See: DUFF, William

1280 *The History of Sir Charles Beaufort. Containing the Genuine and Interesting Memoirs Of a Family of Distinction in the South of England. Displaying the Miseries that may arise from acting contrary to that peculiar Character which Nature has given both the Sexes. In Two*

Volumes. London, 1766 (12mo. 6s. Lownds) HARVARD (HOUGHTON)

Reviewed: *Monthly Review* 34 (1766): 240–241
Critical Review 21 (1766): 139–140

1281 *The History of Sir Charles Dormer and Miss Harriet Villars: In which are exemplified, from a late Catastrophe in real Life, the Contrast of Virtue and Vice, and the dangerous and fatal Consequences arising from Confidants and Intermeddlers in Family Affairs. By a Lady*. 2 vols.
NOT SEEN (12mo. 5s.sewed. Roson)

Reviewed: *Monthly Review* 42 (1770): 489
Critical Review 30 (1770): 302–305
London Magazine 39 (1770): 580

The History of Sir Charles Grandison
See: RICHARDSON, Samuel

The History of Sir George Ellison
See: SCOTT, Sarah

1282 *The History of Sir Harry Herald and Sir Edward Haunch*. 3 vols. London, 1755 (12mo. 9s. Noble) BRITISH LIBRARY

Reviewed: *Monthly Review* 11 (1754): 467

1283 *The History of Sir Roger and his Son Joe*. 2 vols. London, n.d. (12mo. 6s. Scott) NEWBERRY

Reviewed: *Monthly Review* 17 (1757): 563
Critical Review 4 (1757): 552

The History of Sir William Harrington
See: HULL, Thomas

1284 *The History of Sophia Shakespear*. London, 1753 (12mo. 3s.bound. Reeve, &c.) BRITISH LIBRARY

Reviewed: *Monthly Review* 8 (1753): 230

The History of the Adventures of Arthur O'Bradley
See: POTTER, John

The History of the Chevalier des Grieux
See: PRÉVOST, Antoine François

The History of the Countess of Dellwyn
See: FIELDING, Sarah

1285 *The History of the Gay Bellario and the fair Isabella, Founded on Facts, and illustrated With Adventures in Real Life*. London, 1763 (12mo. 2s.6d.sewed. Cooke) HARVARD (HOUGHTON)

Reviewed: *Monthly Review* 30 (1764): 77–78

The History of the Life and Adventures of Mr. Anderson
See: KIMBER, Edward

The History of the Life of Tamerlane the Great
See: VANE, L. (trans.)

The History of the Marquis de Cressy
See: RICCOBONI, Marie Jeanne

1286 *The History of the War: a new British Medley. In two Parts. Proper to be said or sung in all Companies of True Britons* [*Critical Review* title: *The History of the Present War . . .*]
NOT SEEN (Fol. 6d. Dixwell)

Reviewed: *Monthly Review* 23 (1760): 247
Critical Review 10 (1760): 157
British Magazine 1 (1760): 546

The History of Tom Fool
See: STEVENS, George Alexander

1287 *The History of Tom Jones the Foundling, in his Married State*. London, 1750 (12mo. 2s.6d.sewed. Printed for Jacob Robinson in Ludgate Street) NEWBERRY

Reviewed: *Monthly Review* 2 (1749–50): 25–26

The History of Tom Rigby
See: CHATER, John

1288 *The History of Two Modern Adventurers*. 2 vols. London, 1757 (8vo. 5s. Staples) BRITISH LIBRARY

Reviewed: *Monthly Review* 17 (1757): 477–478
Critical Review 4 (1757): 464

1289 *The History of Wilhelmina Susannah Dormer. Containing A Wonderful Series of Events*. London, n.d. [ESTC-1750?] (8vo. 1s.6d. Cooper) BRITISH LIBRARY

Reviewed: *Monthly Review* 20 (1759): 80
Critical Review 7 (1759): 65–68

1290 *The History of Will Ramble, a Libertine. Compiled from Genuine Materials, and The Several Incidents taken from Real Life*. 2 vols. London, 1755 (12mo. 6s. Woodfall) BRITISH LIBRARY

Reviewed: *Monthly Review* 11 (1754): 466–467

1291 [HITCHCOCK, Robert]. *The Macaroni. A Comedy. As it is performed at the Theatre-Royal in York*. York, 1773 (8vo. Nicoll, &c. 1773) BRITISH LIBRARY

Reviewed: *Monthly Review* 49 (1773): 316
Critical Review 36 (1773): 235
Universal Catalogue [2] (1773) art. 1041 [2d ed.]

The Hobby-Horse: A Characteristical Satire
See: POTTER, John

1292 HODSON, William. *The Dedication of the Temple of Solomon: A Poetical Essay*. Cambridge, 1770 (4to. 1s. Dodsley. 1770) BRITISH LIBRARY

Reviewed: *Monthly Review* 43 (1770): 400
Critical Review 31 (1771): 159
Gentleman's Magazine 41 (1771): 133
London Magazine 39 (1770): 632
Town & Country Magazine 3 (1771): 44

1293 HOGARTH, Theophilus. *Liberty in the Suds; or, Modern Characters. In a Letter to a Friend. By Theophilus Hogarth, Gent*. London, 1764 (4to. 1s.6d. Nicoll) HARVARD (HOUGHTON)

Reviewed: *Monthly Review* 30 (1764): 323
Critical Review 17 (1764): 239–240
General Magazine 1 (1764): 152

1294 HOLLWAY, James. *Merit. A Poem. Inscribed to his Grace the Duke of Grafton*. London, 1768 (4to. 1s. Lewis) BRITISH LIBRARY

Reviewed: *Monthly Review* 38 (1768): 70
Critical Review 24 (1767): 470
Universal Museum 4 (1768): 36

1295 [HOME, John]. *Agis: A Tragedy. As it is acted at the Theatre-Royal in Drury-Lane*. London, 1758 (8vo. 1s.6d. Millar) BRITISH LIBRARY

Reviewed: *Monthly Review* 18 (1758): 275–276
Critical Review 5 (1758): 233–242

1296 [HOME, John]. *Alonzo. A Tragedy. In Five Acts. As it is performed at the Theatre-Royal, Drury-Lane*. London, 1773 (8vo. 1s.6d. Becket) BRITISH LIBRARY

Reviewed: *Monthly Review* 48 (1773): 207–212
Critical Review 35 (1773): 227–229
Gentleman's Magazine 43 (1773): 137–140
Universal Catalogue [2] (1773) art. 346

1297 [HOME, John]. *Douglas: a Tragedy. As it is acted at the Theatre-Royal in Covent-Garden*. London, 1757 (8vo. 1s.6d. Millar) BRITISH LIBRARY

Reviewed: *Monthly Review* 16 (1757): 426–429
Critical Review 3 (1757): 258–268
Literary Magazine 2 (1757): 136–141

1298 [HOME, John]. *The Fatal Discovery. A Tragedy. As it is performed at the Theatre-Royal in Drury-Lane*. London, 1769 (8vo. 1s.6d. Becket) BRITISH LIBRARY

Reviewed: *Monthly Review* 40 (1769): 241–245
Critical Review 27 (1769): 220–223
Gentleman's Magazine 39 (1769): 157–158 and 200
Critical Memoirs 1 (1769): 328–335 and 522
Town & Country Magazine [1] (1769): 157

1299 [HOME, John]. *The Siege of Aquileia. A Tragedy. As it is acted at the Theatre-Royal in Drury-Lane*. London, 1760 (8vo. 1s.6d. Millar) BRITISH LIBRARY

Reviewed: *Monthly Review* 22 (1760): 220–228
Critical Review 9 (1760): 205–214
London Magazine 29 (1760): 167–168

HOMER (burlesques, translations, etc.)
See: BRIDGES, Thomas. *The first Volume of a new Translation* . . .
  BRIDGES, Thomas. *Homer Travestie*
  BRIDGES, Thomas. *A Burlesque Translation of Homer*

LANGLEY, Samuel. *The Iliad of Homer*
SCOTT, Joseph Nicol. *An Essay towards a Translation* . . .

HONEYCOMB, William. *The History of Pudica*
See: GARDINER, Richard

1300 HOOLE, John. *Cyrus: a Tragedy. As it is performed at the Theatre Royal in Covent-Garden.* London, 1768 (8vo. 1s.6d. Davies) BRITISH LIBRARY

Reviewed: *Monthly Review* 39 (1768): 492–493
Critical Review 27 (1769): 80
Gentleman's Magazine 38 (1768): 579–581
London Magazine 38 (1769): 42

1301 HOOLE, John. *Jerusalem Delivered; An Heroic Poem: Translated from the Italian of Torquato Tasso, By John Hoole.* 2 vols. London, 1763 (8vo. 12s. Dodsley) BRITISH LIBRARY

Reviewed: *Monthly Review* 29 (1763): 106–117, 182–193, 251–261, and 321–334
Critical Review 16 (1763): 16–24

1302 [HOOLE, John]. *A Monody: to the Memory of Mrs. Margaret Woffington.* London, 1760 (4to. 1s. Withy) BRITISH LIBRARY

Reviewed: *Monthly Review* 22 (1760): 513–514
Critical Review 10 (1760): 160
British Magazine 1 (1760): 546

1303 HOOLE, John. *Orlando Furioso, translated from the Italian of Ludovico Ariosto. By John Hoole; with explanatory Notes. Vol. I*
NOT SEEN (8vo. 6s.boards. Bathurst, &c. 1773)

Reviewed: *Monthly Review* 48 (1773): 337–344
Gentleman's Magazine 43 (1773): 134–136
London Magazine 42 (1773): 39–40
Universal Catalogue [2] (1773) art. 82

1304 HOOLE, John. *Timanthes: a Tragedy. As it is performed at the Theatre Royal in Covent-Garden.* London, 1770 (8vo. 1s.6d. Becket) BRITISH LIBRARY

Reviewed: *Monthly Review* 42 (1770): 247–248
Critical Review 29 (1770): 209–214
Gentleman's Magazine 40 (1770): 125–126

1305 [HOOLE, John]. *A Translation of Part of the Twenty-third Canto of the Orlando Furioso of Ariosto.* London, 1774 (4to. 1s.6d. Almon. 1774) BRITISH LIBRARY

Reviewed: *Monthly Review* 51 (1774): 244
Universal Catalogue 3 (1774) art. 776

1306 HOOLE, John. *The Works of Metastasio; Translated from the Italian.* 2 vols. London, 1767 (8vo. 6s. Davies) BRITISH LIBRARY

Reviewed: *Monthly Review* 37 (1767): 81–93
Critical Review 24 (1767): 51–56
Gentleman's Magazine 37 (1767): 315–316

1307 HOOPER, William (trans.). *Memoirs of the year Two Thousand Five Hundred. Translated from the French By W. Hooper M.D.* [Translation of *L'An deux mille quatre cent quarante* by Louis Sébastien MERCIER.] 2 vols. London, 1772 (12mo. 6s. Robinson) BODLEIAN

Reviewed: *Monthly Review* 47 (1772): 274–282
Critical Review 33 (1772): 468–476 and 34 (1772): 7–18
London Magazine 41 (1772): 386–387
Universal Catalogue [1] (1772) art. 881
Town & Country Magazine 4 (1772): 323
British Magazine & General Review 1 (1772): 557–560 and 2 (1772): 49–53

1308 [HOOPER, William]. *Psalms and Spiritual Songs. Some according to Portions of Scripture, Some from Texts of Scripture, Some on the scriptural Names, Titles, Characters, and Offices of Christ, And Some Others.* London, 1764 (8vo. 1s.6d. Rivington) BRITISH LIBRARY

Reviewed: *Monthly Review* 32 (1765): 478–479
Critical Review 20 (1765): 79

1309 [HOPE, John]. *Occasional Attempts at Sentimental Poetry, by A Man In Business: with some Miscellaneous Compositions of his Friends.* London, 1769 (8vo. 2s.6d. Durham. 1769) BRITISH LIBRARY

Reviewed: *Monthly Review* 41 (1769): 390–393
Critical Review 27 (1769): 386–388
Critical Memoirs [2] (1769): 128–131
Political Register 4 (1769): 391

1310 [HOPER, Mrs.]. *Queen Tragedy Restor'd: A Dramatick Entertainment.* London, 1749 (8vo. 1s. Owen) BRITISH LIBRARY

Reviewed: *Monthly Review* 2 (1749–50): 90–91

HORACE [Quintus HORATIUS FLACCUS] (allusions, imitations and translations)
See: *An Allusion to the Tenth Ode of the Second Book of Horace*
    CAMBRIDGE, Richard Owen. *A Dialogue* . . .
    CAMBRIDGE, Richard Owen. *The Intruder*
    CANNING, George. *Horace's First Satire Modernised*
    DUNCOMBE, John. *Horace. Book II. Satire VII. Imitated*
    DUNCOMBE, William and John (eds.). *The Works of Horace In English Verse* (2 eds.)
The Fifteenth Ode of the First Book of Horace imitated
    GREENE, Edward Burnaby. *The tenth Epistle of the first book* . . .
An Imitation of The 22d Ode in the First book . . .
Imitations of the Eighteenth Epistle of the first Book, and . . .
    NEVILE, Thomas. *The Eighteenth Epistle Of the First Book of Horace imitated*
    NEVILE, Thomas. *The First Satire of the First book of Horace imitated*
    NEVILE, Thomas. *Imitations of Horace*
    NEVILE, Thomas. *The Seventeenth Epistle Of the First Book* . . .
    POPPLE, William. *Horace's Art of Poetry Translated*
    SMART, Christopher. *The Works of Horace, translated into Verse*
    SMART, Christopher. *The Works of Horace, Translated Literally into English Prose*
    STIRLING, John. *The Works of Horace*
    SWINNEY, Sidney. *The Ninth Satire* . . .

An Hour before Marriage
See: POQUELIN DE MOLIÈRE, Jean Baptiste

1311 *The Hours of Love: in Four Elegies: viz. Night, Morning, Noon, and Evening. By a Student of the Middle Temple. Written in the Year MDCCLII.* London, n.d. [HOUGHTON CAT.–1752?] (Fol. 1s. Cooper) HARVARD (HOUGHTON)

Reviewed: *Monthly Review* 7 (1752): 237

1312 HOWARD, Frederick, 5th Earl of Carlisle. *Poems, consisting of The following Pieces, viz. I. Ode written upon the Death of Mr. Gray. II. For the Monument of a favourite Spaniel. III. Another Inscription for the same. IV. Translations from Dante, Canto xxxiii.* London, 1773 (4to. 1s. Ridley. 1773) BRITISH LIBRARY

Reviewed: *Monthly Review* 48 (1773): 143–145
Critical Review 35 (1773): 314
Gentleman's Magazine 43 (1773): 35
London Magazine 42 (1773): 41
Universal Catalogue [2] (1773) art. 88

1313 HOWARD, Gorges Edmond. *Almeyda, or, the Rival Kings, a Tragedy.* 1st ed. reviewed; copy seen 2d. ed.: Dublin, 1769 (8vo. 1s.6d. Dublin printed, London reprinted Robinson and Roberts) BRITISH LIBRARY

Reviewed: *Monthly Review* 42 (1770): 407–408
Critical Review 28 (1769): 208–212 [3d ed.]
London Magazine 38 (1769): 536 and 39 (1770): 426
Gentleman's Magazine 40 (1770): 625

1314 HOWARD, Gorges Edmond. *The Siege of Tamor. A Tragedy. By Gorges Edmond Howard, Esq;* Dublin, 1773 (8vo. 1s.6d. Dublin printed, London reprinted for G. Robinson. 1773) BRITISH LIBRARY

Reviewed: *Monthly Review* 49 (1773): 246–254
Critical Review 36 (1773): 73
Universal Catalogue [2] (1773) art. 857

1315 HOWARD, Henry. *A Congratulatory and Admonitory Poem: Humbly Address'd to His Most Sacred Majesty George III. King of Great-Britain, France, and Ireland. By H. Howard.* London, 1760 (Fol. 1s. Pridden) HARVARD (HOUGHTON)

Reviewed: *Monthly Review* 23 (1760): 527

1316 HOWARD, H[enry]. *A grand solemn Dirge, in the high burlesque tragi-comic Taste, performed at the Funeral of Old English Liberty, on the same Day as the definitive Treaty of Pease was signed betwixt France, Spain, and Great Britain*
NOT SEEN (4to. 6d. Williams)

Reviewed: *Monthly Review* 28 (1763): 239

1317 HOWARD, Henry. *A visionary interview at the shrine of Shakespeare. Inscribed to Mr. Garrick*
NOT SEEN (4to. 6d. Withy and Ryall)

Reviewed: *Monthly Review* 16 (1757): 183
Critical Review 3 (1757): 176–177

1318 HOWARD, [Leonard]. *The British Genius revived by Success. A poem, humbly addressed to his royal highness prince Edward*
NOT SEEN (Fol. 6d. Hope)

Reviewed: *Monthly Review* 19 (1758): 304
Critical Review 6 (1758): 263

1319 HOWARD, Middleton. *The Conquest of Quebec: a Poem.* Oxford, 1768 (4to. 1s. Fletcher. 1768) BRITISH LIBRARY

Reviewed: *Monthly Review* 40 (1769): 139–140
Critical Review 26 (1768): 472
London Magazine 38 (1769): 104
Universal Museum 4 (1768): 652

1320 HOYLAND, Francis. *Poems and Translations.* London, 1763 (4to. 2s. Bristow) BRITISH LIBRARY

Reviewed: *Monthly Review* 28 (1763): 338–343
Critical Review 16 (1763): 55–58

1321 [HUCKILL, John]. *Avon a Poem in Three Parts.* Birmingham, 1758 (4to. 3s. Birmingham, printed by John Baskerville. Dodsley) BRITISH LIBRARY

Reviewed: *Monthly Review* 19 (1758): 272–276
Critical Review 6 (1758): 83–84
Gentleman's Magazine 28 (1758): 282

1322 HUDSON, [Thomas]. *Four Odes, intended for Choruses to a Tragedy, altered from Shakespeare, on the Death of Julius Caesar. By the Rev. Mr. Hudson*
NOT SEEN (4to. 1s. Davis and Reymers)

Reviewed: *Monthly Review* 21 (1759): 85
Critical Review 7 (1759): 378–379

1323 HUDSON, [Thomas]. *Ode on her Majesty's Birth Day, being kept on the Eighteenth of January*
NOT SEEN (4to. 6d. Davis and Reymers)

Reviewed: *Monthly Review* 32 (1765): 154
Critical Review 19 (1765): 73
Candid Review 1 (1765): 51–52

1324 HUDSON, [Thomas]. *Ode on Masonry, By the Revd. Mr. Hudson, With Annotations By H. Jackson.* London, 1751 (4to. 1s. Griffiths) BRITISH LIBRARY

Reviewed: *Monthly Review* 5 (1751): 396 [N.B. There are two pages 396.]

1325 [HUGGINS, William (trans.)]. *Orlando Furioso, by Ludovico Ariosto. In Italian and English.* [Ed. Temple Henry CROKER.] 2 vols. London, 1755 (4to. 1l.18s.bound, with the annotations) BRITISH LIBRARY

Reviewed: *Critical Review* 3 (1757): 385–398

1326 HUGGINS, W[illiam]. *Part of Orlando Furioso. Translated from the original Italian, By W. Huggins, Esq;* London, 1759 (4to. 6d. Rivington) HARVARD (HOUGHTON)

Reviewed: *Critical Review* 6 (1758): 506–508

1327 [HUGHES, Benjamin]. *An Epistle to Junius.* London, 1774 (4to. 2s.6d. Richardson and Co. 1774) BRITISH LIBRARY

Reviewed: *Monthly Review* 50 (1774): 156
Universal Catalogue 3 (1774) art. 86

1328 [HULL, Thomas]. *The Fairy Favour. As it is performed at the Theatre-Royal in Covent-Garden*
NOT SEEN (8vo. 1s. Griffin) [British Library and Bodleian copies are 1766, pre-performance.]

Reviewed: *Monthly Review* 36 (1767): 164
Critical Review 23 (1767): 139
Gentleman's Magazine 37 (1767): 74–75

1329 HULL, Thomas. *Henry the Second; or, the Fall of Rosamund: A Tragedy; as it is performed at the Theatre-Royal, Covent-Garden.* London, 1774 (8vo. 1s.6d. Bell. 1774) BRITISH LIBRARY

Reviewed: *Monthly Review* 50 (1774): 122–127
Critical Review 37 (1774): 59–62
Universal Catalogue 3 (1774) art. 114

1330 [HULL, Thomas]. *The History of Sir William Harrington. Written some Years since, And revised and corrected By the late Mr. Richardson, Author of Sir Charles Grandison, Clarissa, &c. Now first published, In Four Volumes.* [Also attributed to Anna MEADES.] London, 1771 (12mo. 10s.sewed. Bell. 1771) BRITISH LIBRARY

Reviewed: *Monthly Review* 44 (1771): 262–263
Critical Review 31 (1771): 147–148
Gentleman's Magazine 41 (1771): 229
London Magazine 40 (1771): 101
Town & Country Magazine 3 (1771): 102

1331 [HULL, Thomas]. *The Perplexities: A Comedy. As it is performed at the Theatre Royal in Covent-Garden.* London, 1767 (8vo. 1s. Griffin) BRITISH LIBRARY

Reviewed: *Monthly Review* 36 (1767): 164
Critical Review 23 (1767): 139
Gentleman's Magazine 37 (1767): 84–85

1332 HULL, Thomas. *Pharnaces: An Opera. Altered from the Italian. By Thomas Hull. As it is Performed At the Theatre Royal in Drury-Lane.* [Altered from an Italian alteration of a play by Antonio M. Lucchini.] London, 1765 (8vo. 1s. Tonson) BRITISH LIBRARY

Reviewed: *Monthly Review* 32 (1765): 156
Critical Review 19 (1765): 154
Candid Review 1 (1765): 114

1333 HULL, [Thomas]. *The Prodigal Son; An Oratorio. Set to Music by Mr. Arnold.* London, 1773 (4to. 1s. Bell. 1773) BRITISH LIBRARY

Reviewed: *Monthly Review* 48 (1773): 242
Critical Review 35 (1773): 317
Universal Catalogue [2] (1773) art. 340

1334 HULL, [Thomas]. *Richard Plantagenet a Legendary Tale, Now first Published.* London, n.d. [ESTC-1774] (4to. 2s. Bell. 1774) BRITISH LIBRARY

Reviewed: *Monthly Review* 50 (1774): 315
Critical Review 37 (1774): 235

Town & Country Magazine 6 (1774): 213
Universal Catalogue 3 (1774) art. 339

1335 [HULL, Thomas]. *The Royal Merchant: an Opera. Founded on Beaumont and Fletcher. As it is performed at the Theatre Royal, in Covent-Garden.* London, 1768 (8vo. 1s.6d. Griffin) NEWBERRY

Reviewed: *Monthly Review* 38 (1768): 72
Critical Review 25 (1768): 145
Gentleman's Magazine 38 (1768): 31–32
Political Register 2 (1768): 64

1336 [HULL, Thomas]. *The Spanish Lady, a Musical Entertainment, in two acts; Founded on the Plan of the Old Ballad. As performed at the Theatre-Royal in Covent-Garden.* London, n.d. [BODLEIAN CAT.–1765] (8vo. 6d. Printed for the Author. Sold by Davies, &c.) BODLEIAN

Reviewed: *Monthly Review* 32 (1765): 479
Gentleman's Magazine 35 (1765): 235

1337 [HULL, Thomas]. *The Spanish Lady, a Musical Entertainment, in two acts. Founded on the Plan of the Old Ballad. As perform'd at the Theatre-Royal in Covent-Garden.* London, n.d. [ESTC-1769] (8vo. 1s. Cooper) BRITISH LIBRARY

Reviewed: *Monthly Review* 41 (1769): 479
Critical Review 28 (1769): 463
Gentleman's Magazine 39 (1769): 600

1338 *Humanity: a Poem: Inscribed to George Boden, Esq. By G--- C---.* [Probably by George CASWALL.] London, 1766 (4to. 1s. Marsh) BRITISH LIBRARY

Reviewed: *Monthly Review* 34 (1766): 403
Critical Review 21 (1766): 233
Gentleman's Magazine 36 (1766): 144–145

1339 *Humanity, a Poem. Inscribed to the M--q-s of Gr--by. By a gentleman of 18 years of age. Late of Eton college*
NOT SEEN (4to. 6s. Stamper and Downham)

Listed: *Monthly Review* 5 (1751): 160

1340 HUMDRUM, Humphrey (pseud.). *Mother Midnight's comical Pocket-Book: or, a Bone*

for the Criticks. Being a sure and certain Cure for the Hip. Containing the nicest and largest Dish of Novelties, That ever was Seen– Heard– Smelt– or Tasted; Carefully Cook'd-up by Mother Midnight's merry Grandson; containing Nothing but Originals, all very Humorous, prodigious Satyrical, and quite Uncommon; Informing the Publick, that this Dish of Dishes Was wrote in an uncommon Place, at an uncommon Time, by an uncommon Hand, Humphrey Humdrum, Esq; London, n.d. [ESTC-1760?] (8vo. 1s. Dowse) BRITISH LIBRARY

Reviewed: *Monthly Review* 10 (1754): 74

Humorous Ethics
See: BACON, Phanuel

1341 *A humorous poetical Dialogue, between the once celebrated Miss F---- M------- and the now famed Miss K---- F-----. To which is prefixed, a Dedication, after the manner of modern Dedications, to the venerable Mrs. ****, of Covent-Garden*
NOT SEEN (4to. 1s. Thrush)

Reviewed: *Monthly Review* 22 (1760): 439

The Humorous Quarrel
See: POTTINGER, Israel

1342 *The Humourist.* London, 1763 (12mo. 2s.6d. Coote) BRITISH LIBRARY

Reviewed: *Monthly Review* 28 (1763): 78
Critical Review 14 (1763): 480

The Humours of an Irish Court of Justice
See: STEVENS, George Alexander

1343 *The Humours of Harrogate, Described in a Letter to a Friend. By J. E.* London, 1763 (4to. 1s. Pridden) BODLEIAN

Reviewed: *Monthly Review* 29 (1763): 228–229
Critical Review 16 (1763): 73

1344 [HUMPHREYS, R.]. *The Amusing Instructor: or, Tales and Fables in Prose and Verse, for the Improvement of Youth. With useful and pleasing Remarks on different Branches of Science. Adorned with Cuts.* London, 1769 (12mo. 2s. Harris) BRITISH LIBRARY

Reviewed: *Monthly Review* 42 (1770): 255
Critical Review 27 (1769): 472
Political Register 4 (1769): 387

1345 [HURD, Richard]. *Discord: a Satire.* London, 1773 (4to. 1s. Beecroft, &c. 1773) BRITISH LIBRARY

Reviewed: *Monthly Review* 49 (1773): 504–505
Critical Review 36 (1773): 475
London Magazine 42 (1773): 611–612
Town & Country Magazine 6 (1774): 45
Universal Catalogue [2] (1773) art. 1303

1346 [HUTCHINSON, Benjamin.] *Kimbolton Park: a Poem.* London, 1765 (Fol. 1s. Dodsley) BODLEIAN

Reviewed: *Monthly Review* 33 (1765): 240
Critical Review 20 (1765): 159
Gentleman's Magazine 35 (1765): 384

1347 HUTCHINSON, Benjamin. *Marriage. An Ode.* London, 1765 (Fol. 1s. Dodsley) BRITISH LIBRARY

Reviewed: *Monthly Review* 32 (1765): 233–234
Critical Review 19 (1765): 150
Candid Review 1 (1765): 186–187

1348 [HUTCHINSON, William]. *The Hermitage; a British Story.* York, 1772 (12mo. 3s. Bell) BRITISH LIBRARY

Reviewed: *Monthly Review* 48 (1773): 320
Critical Review 35 (1773): 78–79
Universal Catalogue [1] (1772) art. 1454

1349 [HUTCHINSON, William]. *The Hermitage: a British Story.* 2 vols.
NOT SEEN (12mo. 6s. Bell)

Reviewed: *Critical Review* 36 (1773): 236

A Hymn after Sore Eyes
See: ELPHINSTON, James

A Hymn to May
See: COOKE, Thomas

Hymn to Miss Laurence
See: STEVENSON, John Hall

Hymn to the Power of Harmony
See: CALLANDER, John

The Hypocrite: a Comedy
See: BICKERSTAFFE, Isaac

1350 *Ideal Trifles. Published by a Lady.* London, 1774 (12mo. 3s. Boosey) BRITISH LIBRARY

Reviewed: *Monthly Review* 51 (1774): 487
Critical Review 38 (1774): 474
London Magazine 43 (1774): 608
Universal Catalogue 3 (1774) art. 1255

1351 *The Ides of June. A Poem, to the Fair Sex.* London, 1774 (4to. 6d. Wilkie. 1774) BODLEIAN

Reviewed: *Monthly Review* 51 (1774): 166
Critical Review 37 (1774): 473
London Magazine 43 (1774): 293
Town & Country Magazine 6 (1774): 437
Universal Catalogue 3 (1774) art. 780

1352 *Ierne's Muse to the King*
NOT SEEN (Fol. 6d. Dodsley)

Reviewed: *Monthly Review* 26 (1762): 385
Critical Review 13 (1762): 439
British Magazine 3 (1762): 269

IETRORHAPSODIA: *or, A Physical Rhapsody*
See: SCHOMBERG, Ralph

1353 IGNORAMUS (pseud.). *The World Turn'd Upside Down: or, the Ass not Priest-Ridden, but, the Priest Ass-Ridden. By Ignoramus, Esq;* London, 1754 (4to. 6d. Cooper) BRITISH LIBRARY

Reviewed: *Monthly Review* 10 (1754): 303–304

The Images of the Ancients
See: GREEN, George Smith

1354 *An Imitation of The 22d Ode in the First Book of Horace.* London, n.d. (Fol. 6d. J. M. near St. Paul's) CAMBRIDGE

Reviewed: *Monthly Review* 20 (1759): 279

1355 *Imitations of the Eighteenth Epistle of the first Book, and of the Eighth Ode of the fourth Book of Horace. By the Author of the Eulogy of Frederic King of Prussia*
NOT SEEN (8vo. 1s. Wilkie)

Reviewed: *Monthly Review* 36 (1767): 489
Critical Review 23 (1767): 145
Gentleman's Magazine 37 (1767): 78–79

The Immortality of the Soul. A Poem
See: BROWNE, Isaac Hawkins

Immortality: or, the Consolation of Human Life
See: DENTON, Thomas

1356 *An Impartial Character of the late Doctor Goldsmith; with A Word To His Encomiasts. A Poem.* London, 1774 (4to. 1s. Kearsly. 1774) BRITISH LIBRARY

Reviewed: *Monthly Review* 51 (1774): 68
Critical Review 38 (1774): 76
Town & Country Magazine 6 (1774): 68
Universal Catalogue 3 (1774) art. 902

1357 *The Imperial Russian Miscellany: Containing An Ode on the Birth of the Imperial Prince of Russia; An Epistle to the Czarina; the Czar Peter the Great's Triumph, an Ode; and Several Other Pieces; Occasioned by the Czarina's Bounty to the Sufferers by the late Fires in Muscovy; on the Reduction of the Inland Taxes; the Russian Merchants Acknowledgments; and an Important Conference, in a Discourse between two Russian Noblemen.* London, 1755 (4to. 1s. Cooper) NEW YORK PUBLIC LIBRARY

Reviewed: *Monthly Review* 12 (1755): 158

1358 *The Impetuous Lover, or the Guiltless Parricide. Shewing, To what lengths Love may run, and the extreme Folly of forming Schemes for Futurity. Written under the Instructions, and at the Request of one of the interested Partys. By A. G. Esq;* ["Partys" in title reads "Parties" in title page to vol. 2.] 2 vols. London, 1757 (8vo. 6s. E. Ross) BRITISH LIBRARY

Reviewed: *Monthly Review* 16 (1757): 451–452
Critical Review 4 (1757): 461

1359 *The Impostors Detected: or, the Life of a Portuguese. In which The Artifices and Intrigues of Romish Priests are humorously displayed.* 2 vols. London, 1760 (12mo. 6s. Bristow) BRITISH LIBRARY

Reviewed: *Monthly Review* 23 (1760): 408–409
   Critical Review 10 (1760): 405
   British Magazine 1 (1760): 714

1360 *The Inamorato. A Poem.* London, 1768 (4to. 2s.6d. Dodsley) BRITISH LIBRARY

Reviewed: *Monthly Review* 38 (1768): 335
   Critical Review 25 (1768): 153–154
   Universal Museum 4 (1768): 93
   Political Register 2 (1768): 445

1361 *The Indignant Muse. A Satire. To a Friend.* London, 1755 (4to. 1s. Cooper) UNIVERSITY OF ILLINOIS

Reviewed: *Monthly Review* 12 (1755): 380–381

1362 *The Indiscreet Connection; or, the History of Miss Lester.* 2 vols. London, 1772 (12mo. 5s.sewed. Noble. 1772) BODLEIAN

Reviewed: *Monthly Review* 46 (1772): 539
   Critical Review 33 (1772): 256
   London Magazine 41 (1772): 243
   British Magazine & General Review 1 (1772): 467
   Universal Catalogue [1] (1772) art. 397

Indolence: a Poem
See: CELESIA, Dorothea

The Inefficacy of Satire
See: PARSONS, Philip

1363 INGELDEW, ----. *Free Thoughts on Love and Marriage*
NOT SEEN (4to. 1s. Flexney)

Reviewed: *Monthly Review* 33 (1765): 248
   Critical Review 20 (1765): 159–160

1364 INGELDEW, J. *A Poem On our late Most Gracious Sovereign George II. By Mr. Ingeldew.* London, 1760 (Fol. 6d. Kinnersley) HARVARD (HOUGHTON)

Reviewed: *Monthly Review* 23 (1760): 412
   Critical Review 10 (1760): 408

1365 *Ingratitude. A Poem. Inscribed to the Most Grateful of Mankind.* London, 1764 (8vo. 1s. Williams) BRITISH LIBRARY

Reviewed: *Monthly Review* 30 (1764): 240
   Critical Review 17 (1764): 395
   General Magazine 1 (1764): 150

1366 *Ingratitude: an Epistle to ------ ------, Esq; Occasion'd by the late sad Catastrophe of a Clergyman at Norwich. By a Young Lady, Daughter of the said Clergyman.* [British Library copy cropped] [ESTC: London, 1755] (Fol. 1s. C. Sympson). BRITISH LIBRARY

Reviewed: *Monthly Review* 11 (1754): 476–477

1367 *The injur'd Daughter: or the History of Miss Maria Beaumont.* 2 vols.
NOT SEEN (12mo. 5s.sewed. Noble)

Reviewed: *Monthly Review* 40 (1769): 86
   Critical Review 27 (1769): 151
   London Magazine 37 (1768): 610
   Town & Country Magazine [1] (1769): 101

1368 *The Insects choose a Minister. A Fable*
NOT SEEN (4to. 1s. Owen)

Reviewed: *Monthly Review* 17 (1757): 185–186

The Inspector in the Shades
See: KENNEDY, John

1369 *The Inspector's Rhapsody or Soliloquy on The Loss of his Wigg, in a Scuffle with some Irish Gentlemen at Ranelagh.* London, 1752 (Fol. 6d. Cooper) BRITISH LIBRARY

Reviewed: *Monthly Review* 7 (1752): 475

1370 *The Instructive Novellist:–a Collection of moral, entertaining, and improving Stories, on various Subjects, compiled from the best Authors*
NOT SEEN (12mo. 1s.6d. Noble)

Reviewed: *Monthly Review* 37 (1767): 76

1371 *The Interview; or Jack Falstaff's Ghost. A Poem. Inscribed to David Garrick, Esq;* London, 1766 (4to. 1s. Bladon and Blyth) BRITISH LIBRARY

Reviewed: *Monthly Review* 35 (1766): 79
   Critical Review 22 (1766): 77
   Gentleman's Magazine 36 (1766): 336

1372 *The Intriguing Coxcomb: or the Secret History Of Sir Edmund Godfrey. Illustrated with a Variety of Incidents which happened to himself, and the celebrated Miss L**** C*****, in the Course of their several Years Acquaintance; the Whole calculated to amuse and instruct the attentive Reader.* 2 vols. London, 1759 (12mo. 6s. Scott) BRITISH LIBRARY

Reviewed: *Monthly Review* 20 (1759): 188
Critical Review 7 (1759): 184

Introduction to the School of Shakespeare
See: KENRICK, William

1373 *The Inundation or the life of a Fen-Man, a Poem. With Notes Critical and Explanatory. By a Fen Parson.* Lynn, 1771 (4to. 1s. Baldwin) BRITISH LIBRARY

Reviewed: *Monthly Review* 44 (1771): 491–492
Critical Review 32 (1771): 228
Gentleman's Magazine 41 (1771): 325

1374 *The Invasion, a Farce. Most humbly inscrib'd to the Antigallican Society.* London, 1759 (8vo. 1s. Davis and Reymers) BRITISH LIBRARY

Reviewed: *Monthly Review* 21 (1759): 174
Gentleman's Magazine 29 (1759): 384–385

1375 *Invasion, an occasional Ode. Addressed to the English Nation*
NOT SEEN (4to. 6d. Cooper)

Reviewed: *Monthly Review* 14 (1756): 366

The Invisible Spy
See: HAYWOOD, Eliza

1376 *The Involuntary Inconstant; or the history of Miss Francfort. A Novel. In Two Volumes. By the Editor of the Fatal Compliance.* London, 1772 (12mo. 5s.sewed. Jones. 1772) BRITISH LIBRARY

Reviewed: *Monthly Review* 46 (1772): 456
Critical Review 33 (1772): 256
London Magazine 41 (1772): 243
Universal Catalogue [1] (1772) art. 414

1377 [IRELAND, Stella]. *The Doctor Dissected: or, Willy Cadogan In the Kitchen. Addressed to all Invalids, and Readers of a late Dissertation on the Gout, &c.&c.&c. By a Lady.* London, 1771 (4to. 1s. Davies) BODLEIAN

Reviewed: *Monthly Review* 45 (1771): 236
Critical Review 32 (1771): 153
Gentleman's Magazine 41 (1771): 369–370
London Magazine 40 (1771): 463
Town & Country Magazine 3 (1771): 480

1378 [IRELAND, Stella]. *Modest Exceptions, from the Court of Parnassus, to Mrs. Macaulay's Modest Plea. By the Author of the Doctor Dissected: a Poem.* London, 1774 (4to. 1s. Bew. 1774) BRITISH LIBRARY

Reviewed: *Monthly Review* 51 (1774): 318
Critical Review 38 (1774): 153–154
London Magazine 43 (1774): 451
Town & Country Magazine 6 (1774): 660
Universal Catalogue 3 (1774) art. 901

The Irish Widow
See: GARRICK, David

1379 *The Irishman; or, the Favourite of Fortune: a satirical Novel, founded upon Facts.* 2 vols. NOT SEEN (12mo. 6s.bound. Goldsmith. 1772)

Reviewed: *Monthly Review* 47 (1772): 487
Critical Review 34 (1772): 472
London Magazine 41 (1772): 598
British Magazine & General Review 2 (1772): 631
Universal Catalogue [1] (1772) art. 1383

1380 *An Irregular Ode, occasioned by the Death of Mr. Gray.* London, 1772 (4to. 1s. White. 1772) BRITISH LIBRARY

Reviewed: *Monthly Review* 46 (1772): 168
Critical Review 33 (1772): 85
London Magazine 41 (1772): 31
Town & Country Magazine 4 (1772): 45
British Magazine & General Review 1 (1772): 148
Universal Catalogue [1] (1772) art. 83

1381 [IRWIN, Eyles]. *Saint Thomas's Mount. A Poem. Written by a Gentleman in India.* London, 1774 (4to. 2s.6d. Dodsley. 1774) BRITISH LIBRARY

Reviewed: *Monthly Review* 50 (1774): 311–312
Critical Review 37 (1774): 233–234
London Magazine 43 (1774): 92
Universal Catalogue 3 (1774) art. 218

Isabella: or, the Fatal Marriage
See: GARRICK, David

Islington: A Poem
See: NICHOLS, John

1382 *Israel in Babylon. An Oratorio. The Music selected from the Works of Geo Fr. Handel*
NOT SEEN (4to. 1s. Griffin)

Reviewed: *Monthly Review* 32 (1765): 232

1383 *Israel in Babylon. An Oratorio. The Music selected from the Works of George Frederick Handel, Esq.* London, 1764 (4to. 1s. Griffin) BRITISH LIBRARY

Reviewed: *Monthly Review* 30 (1764): 324–325

1384 *The Israelites on Mount Horeb; an Oratorio. French and English. From a Manuscript of Dr. De Gueldre*
NOT SEEN (4to. 1s. Cadell. 1773)

Reviewed: *Monthly Review* 49 (1773): 504
Universal Catalogue [2] (1773) art. 1043

1385 ITCHENER, George. *Elegiac Tears, or Plaintive Epistles; being a Poetical Translation of the Rev. Mr. Cotton's Elegiacae Lachrymae, Sive Querelae Epistolares.* Chelmsford, 1766 (4to. 1s.6d. Buckland) BRITISH LIBRARY

Reviewed: *Monthly Review* 34 (1766): 167
Critical Review 21 (1766): 155

1386 JACKSON, W. *The Beauties of Nature, displayed in A Sentimental Ramble through Her Luxuriant Fields; with a Retrospective View of Her, and that great Almighty Being Who Gave Her Birth. To which is added, A Choice Collection of Thoughts: concluded with Poems on Various Occasions.* Birmingham, 1769 (8vo. 5s. Longman) BRITISH LIBRARY

Reviewed: *Monthly Review* 42 (1770): 167–173
Critical Review 28 (1769): 398–399

1387 [JACKSON, W.]. *Lycidas: a Musical Entertainment. As it is performed at the Theatre Royal in Covent Garden. The Words altered from Milton.* London, 1767 (8vo. 6d. Griffin) BRITISH LIBRARY

Reviewed: *Monthly Review* 37 (1767): 393

1388 [JACOB, Giles]. *The Rape of the Smock. An Heroi-Comic Poem. In Two Cantos.* London, 1768 (8vo. 6d. Brown) BRITISH LIBRARY

Reviewed: *Critical Review* 25 (1768): 314
Universal Museum 4 (1768): 205

1389 JAGO, Richard. *Edge-Hill, or, The Rural Prospect delineated and moralized. A Poem. In Four Books.* London, 1767 (4to. 10s.6d. Dodsley) BRITISH LIBRARY

Reviewed: *Monthly Review* 37 (1767): 16–21
Critical Review 24 (1767): 166–172
Universal Museum 3 (1767): 484
Political Register 1 (1767): 484

1390 JAGO, Richard. *Labour, and Genius: or, the Mill-Stream, and the Cascade. A Fable. Written in the Year, 1762; and inscribed to The late William Shenstone, Esq;* London, 1768 (4to. 1s. Dodsley) BODLEIAN

Reviewed: *Monthly Review* 39 (1768): 165–166
Critical Review 25 (1768): 392
London Magazine 37 (1768): 554
Universal Museum 4 (1768): 260
Political Register 3 (1768): 382

1391 JANUS, JUNIOR (pseud.). *Miscellaneous Essays in Verse. By Janus, Junior.* London, 1766 (12mo. 3s. Crowder) BRITISH LIBRARY

Reviewed: *Monthly Review* 36 (1767): 162–163
Critical Review 22 (1766): 318–319

Je Ne Sçai Quoi
See: POYNTZ, Anne

1392 *The Jealous Mother; or, Innocence triumphant.* 2 vols.
NOT SEEN (12mo. 6s. Robinson and Roberts)

Reviewed: *Monthly Review* 45 (1771): 152
Critical Review 31 (1771): 480–482

Jean Hennuyer, Bishop of Lizieux
See: MERCIER, Louis Sebastien

1393 JEFFERSON, [Joseph]. *Poems by Mr. Jefferson. The Second Edition.* London, 1773 [First published at York] (8vo. 2s.6d. Griffin, &c. 1773) BRITISH LIBRARY

Reviewed: *Monthly Review* 50 (1774): 316
Critical Review 36 (1773): 394
Town & Country Magazine 5 (1773): 669
Universal Catalogue [2] (1773) art. 1184

1394 JEFFREYS, George. *Miscellanies in Verse and Prose: Containing original Poems, Translations, Imitations, and Plays. To which is added, Three Latin Orations before the University of Cambridge*
NOT SEEN (4to. 10s.6d. Otridge)

Reviewed: *Critical Review* 24 (1767): 203–204

1395 *Jemima and Louisa. In which is contained, several remarkable incidents relating to two ladies of distinguished families and fortunes. In a series of Letters. By a Lady*
NOT SEEN (12mo. 3s. Owen)

Reviewed: *Monthly Review* 21 (1759): 82
Critical Review 8 (1759): 165–166

1396 JENNER, Charles. *The Destruction of Nineveh: a Poem.* Cambridge, 1768 (4to. 1s. Dodsley, &c. 1768) BRITISH LIBRARY

Reviewed: *Monthly Review* 40 (1769): 88–89
Critical Review 26 (1768): 469–470
Universal Museum 4 (1768): 652

1397 JENNER, Charles. *The Gift of Tongues: A Poem.* Cambridge, 1767 (4to. 1s. Johnson) BRITISH LIBRARY

Reviewed: *Monthly Review* 37 (1767): 468
Critical Review 24 (1767): 383–384
Universal Museum 3 (1767): 596

1398 [JENNER, Charles]. *Letters from Altamont in the Capital, to His Friends in the Country.* London, 1767 (8vo. 3s. Becket and DeHondt) BRITISH LIBRARY

Reviewed: *Monthly Review* 37 (1767): 146–147
Critical Review 24 (1767): 63–66

1399 [JENNER, Charles]. *Letters from Lothario to Penelope. To which is added Lucinda, a Dramatic Entertainment Of Three Acts. Inscribed to David Garrick, Esq.* 2 vols. London, 1769 (8vo. 5s. Becket and DeHondt) NEWBERRY

Reviewed: *Monthly Review* 42 (1770): 413
Critical Review 29 (1770): 235

1400 JENNER, Charles. *Louisa: A Tale. To which is added An Elegy to The Memory of Lord Lyttelton.* London, 1774 (4to. 2s. Cadell. 1774) BRITISH LIBRARY

Reviewed: *Monthly Review* 50 (1774): 300–301
Critical Review 37 (1774): 474
Universal Catalogue 3 (1774) art. 373

1401 [JENNER, Charles]. *The Man of Family: a Sentimental Comedy. By the Author of the Placid Man: and Letters from Altamont in the Capital, to his Friends in the Country.* London, 1771 (8vo. 1s.6d. Cadell. 1771) BRITISH LIBRARY

Reviewed: *Monthly Review* 45 (1771): 74
Critical Review 31 (1771): 397

1402 [JENNER, Charles]. *The Placid Man: or, Memoirs of Sir Charles Beville.* 2 vols. London, 1770 (12mo. 6s. Wilkie. 1770) BRITISH LIBRARY

Reviewed: *Monthly Review* 42 (1770): 43–46
Critical Review 29 (1770): 42–43
Town & Country Magazine 2 (1770): 44

1403 JENNER, Charles. *Poems by Charles Jenner, A.M.* Cambridge, 1766 (4to. 3s. Dodsley) BRITISH LIBRARY

Reviewed: *Monthly Review* 35 (1766): 321–322
Critical Review 22 (1766): 72–73
Gentleman's Magazine 36 (1766): 335

1404 JENNER, Charles. *Town Eclogues.* London, 1772 (4to. 2s. Cadell. 1772) BRITISH LIBRARY

Reviewed: *Monthly Review* 47 (1772): 70
Critical Review 34 (1772): 234
Town & Country Magazine 4 (1772): 490

British Magazine & General Review 1 (1772): 444–445
Universal Catalogue [1] (1772) art. 749

1405 JENNINGS, [John]. *An Ode. Occasioned by the Royal Nuptials*
NOT SEEN (Fol. 6d. Cabe)

Reviewed: *Monthly Review* 25 (1761): 240
Critical Review 12 (1761): 231

1406 JENNINGS, John. *An ode on rural pleasures*
NOT SEEN (Fol. 6d. Robinson)

Reviewed: *Monthly Review* 10 (1754): 304

1407 JENNINGS, J[ohn]. *An Ode to Genius*
NOT SEEN (Fol. 6d. Cabe)

Reviewed: *Monthly Review* 36 (1767): 410
Critical Review 23 (1767): 224
Gentleman's Magazine 37 (1767): 261–262

1408 [JENYNS, Soame]. *Miscellaneous Pieces in two Volumes*. London, 1761 (8vo. 6s. Dodsley) BRITISH LIBRARY

Reviewed: *Monthly Review* 25 (1761): 226–227
Critical Review 11 (1761): 417–418

1409 [JENYNS, Soame]. *The Modern Fine Lady*. London, 1751 (Small Fol. About 90ll. 6d. Dodsley) FOLGER

Reviewed: *Monthly Review* 4 (1750–51): 305
Gentleman's Magazine 21 (1751): 95

1410 [JENYNS, Soame]. *Poems. By *****. London, 1752 (8vo. 3s. Dodsley) BRITISH LIBRARY

Reviewed: *Monthly Review* 6 (1752): 211–213

1411 [JENYNS, Soame]. *The 'Squire and the Parson: an Eclogue*. London, n.d. [ESTC-1749] (Fol. 4pp. 6d. Printed for Dodsley) BRITISH LIBRARY

Reviewed: *Monthly Review* 2 (1749–50): 112–113

1412 [JEPHSON, Robert]. *An Epistle to Gorges Edmond Howard, Esq; With Notes Explanatory, Critical, and Historical. By George Faulkner, Esq; and Alderman*. Dublin and London, n.d. [ESTC-1772?] (8vo. 1s. Dublin printed: London reprinted, and sold by Goldsmith, &c. Sixth edition) BRITISH LIBRARY

Reviewed: *Monthly Review* 47 (1772): 150
Critical Review 34 (1772): 236

1413 [JERNINGHAM, Edward]. *Amabella, A Poem*. London, 1768 (4to. 1s. Roson) BODLEIAN

Reviewed: *Monthly Review* 38 (1768): 237–239
Critical Review 25 (1768): 231–232
Gentleman's Magazine 38 (1768): 133
London Magazine 37 (1768): 111
Universal Museum 4 (1768): 93
Political Register 2 (1768): 187

1414 [JERNINGHAM, Edward]. *Andromache to Pyrrhus. An Heroick Epistle*. London, 1761 (4to. 1s. Dodsley) CAMBRIDGE

Reviewed: *Monthly Review* 25 (1761): 508
Critical Review 12 (1761): 483
London Magazine 31 (1762): 56

1415 [JERNINGHAM, Edward]. *The Deserter: A Poem*. London, 1770 (4to. 1s. Roson) BRITISH LIBRARY

Reviewed: *Monthly Review* 42 (1770): 95–97
Critical Review 29 (1770): 148
Gentleman's Magazine 40 (1770): 83

1416 [JERNINGHAM, Edward]. *An Elegy written among the Ruins of an Abbey. By the Author of the Nun*. London, 1765 (4to. 6d. Dodsley) BRITISH LIBRARY

Reviewed: *Monthly Review* 32 (1765): 393
Critical Review 19 (1765): 235–236
Candid Review 1 (1765): 223

1417 [JERNINGHAM, Edward]. *An Elegy written among the Tombs in Westminster-Abbey*. London, 1762 (4to. 6d. Dodsley) BRITISH LIBRARY

Reviewed: *Monthly Review* 26 (1762): 356–358
Critical Review 13 (1762): 364

1418 JERNINGHAM, [Edward]. *Faldoni and Teresa*. London, 1773 (4to. 1s. Robson. 1773) BRITISH LIBRARY

Reviewed: *Monthly Review* 48 (1773): 412
Critical Review 35 (1773): 158–159
Town & Country Magazine 5 (1773): 210
Universal Catalogue [2] (1773) art. 233

1419 JERNINGHAM, [Edward]. *The Funeral of Arabert, Monk of La Trappe; a Poem.* London, 1771 (4to. 1s. Robson. 1771) BRITISH LIBRARY

Reviewed: *Monthly Review* 44 (1771): 488–489
Critical Review 31 (1771): 218–220
Gentleman's Magazine 41 (1771): 325
London Magazine 40 (1771): 275

1420 [JERNINGHAM, Edward]. *Il Latte. An Elegy.* London, 1767 (4to. 1s. Dodsley) BRITISH LIBRARY

Reviewed: *Monthly Review* 36 (1767): 407
Critical Review 23 (1767): 144–145
Gentleman's Magazine 37 (1767): 85

1421 [JERNINGHAM, Edward]. *The Magdalens: An Elegy. By the Author of the Nunnery.* London, 1763 (4to. 6d. Dodsley) BRITISH LIBRARY

Reviewed: *Monthly Review* 28 (1763): 112–114
Critical Review 15 (1763): 76–77
British Magazine 4 (1763): 98

1422 [JERNINGHAM, Edward]. *The Nun: An Elegy. By the Author of the Magdalens.* London, 1764 (4to. 6d. Dodsley) BRITISH LIBRARY

Reviewed: *Monthly Review* 30 (1764): 117–119
Critical Review 17 (1764): 317–318
British Magazine 5 (1764): 377
General Magazine 1 (1764): 97–98

1423 [JERNINGHAM, Edward]. *The Nunnery. An Elegy. In Imitation of the Elegy in a Church-Yard.* London, n.d. [ESTC-1762] (4to. 6d. Dodsley) BRITISH LIBRARY

Reviewed: *Monthly Review* 26 (1762): 358–359
Critical Review 13 (1762): 364

1424 JERNINGHAM, [Edward]. *Poems By Mr. Jerningham.* London, 1774 (8vo. 2s.6d.sewed. Robson. 1774) BRITISH LIBRARY

Reviewed: *Monthly Review* 50 (1774): 408
Critical Review 37 (1774): 313

Gentleman's Magazine 44 (1774): 276–277
Town & Country Magazine 6 (1774): 268

1425 [JERNINGHAM, Edward]. *Poems on various Subjects. Viz. The Nunnery, The Magdalens, The Nun, Ruins of an Abbey, Yarico to Inkle, Il Latte, Fugitive Pieces.* London, 1767 (8vo. 2s. Robson) BRITISH LIBRARY

Reviewed: *Monthly Review* 36 (1767): 406–407
London Magazine 36 (1767): 150
Political Register 1 (1767): 314–315

1426 JERNINGHAM, [Edward]. *The Swedish Curate, a Poem.* London, 1773 (4to. 1s. Robson) BODLEIAN

Reviewed: *Monthly Review* 49 (1773): 148–149
Critical Review 35 (1773): 393–394
London Magazine 42 (1773): 302
Universal Catalogue [2] (1773) art. 631

1427 [JERNINGHAM, Edward]. *Yarico to Inkle, an Epistle. By the Author of the Elegy written among the Ruins of an Abbey.* London, 1766 (4to. 1s. Dodsley) BRITISH LIBRARY

Reviewed: *Monthly Review* 34 (1766): 324
Critical Review 21 (1766): 154–155
Gentleman's Magazine 36 (1766): 143

1428 *Jessy; or, the Bridal Day. A Novel. Written by a Lady, after the Manner of the late Mr. Richardson, (Author of Clarissa, &c.) But not revised by that celebrated Writer.* 2 vols. London, 1771 (12mo. 4s.sewed. Noble) BRITISH LIBRARY

Reviewed: *Monthly Review* 45 (1771): 73
Critical Review 31 (1771): 479–480
London Magazine 40 (1771): 275
Town & Country Magazine 3 (1771): 379

1429 *The Jews Naturalized; or, The English Alienated. A Ballad. To which is added, The Parable of the Chosen and Unjust Servant; Translated from an Original MS. of an Antient Gospel Historian.* London, n.d. [ESTC-1753] (6d. Webb) BRITISH LIBRARY

Reviewed: *Gentleman's Magazine* 23 (1753): 346

1430 *The Jew's Triumph, a Ballad. To be Said or Sung to the Children of Israel, on all Popular*

Occasions, by all Christian People. London, n.d. [HOUGHTON CAT.–1753] (no pub. details) HARVARD (HOUGHTON)

Reviewed: *Monthly Review* 8 (1753): 471

1431 *The Jilts: Or, Female Fortune-Hunters.* 3 vols. London, n.d. [ESTC-1755?] (12mo. 9s. Noble) BRITISH LIBRARY

Reviewed: *Monthly Review* 15 (1756): 535–536
Critical Review 2 (1756): 276

1432 JOEL, Thomas. *Poems and Letters in Prose. Occasionally written by Thomas Joel.* London, 1766 (8vo. 3s.6d. Dodsley) BRITISH LIBRARY

Reviewed: *Monthly Review* 36 (1767): 240
Critical Review 22 (1766): 350–354

1433 *John English's Travels through Scotland. Containing, A curious and entertaining Account of the Manners and strange Customs of the Inhabitants. With many humorous Anecdotes, and Natural Discoveries.* London, n.d. (12mo. 1s.6d. Morgan) BODLEIAN

Reviewed: *Monthly Review* 28 (1763): 77
Critical Review 15 (1763): 77–78

1434 JOHNSON, Charles. *The Song of Solomon paraphrased; in Lyrick Verse. By Mr. Charles Johnson, of Trinity-College, Dublin.* London, 1751 (4to. 1s. Johnston) BODLEIAN

Listed: *Monthly Review* 5 (1751): 76

1435 JOHNSON, S[amuel] (d. 1798). *An Essay on Woman, a Poem.* London, 1772 (4to. 2s.6d. Baldwin. 1772) FOLGER

Reviewed: *Monthly Review* 47 (1772): 410–411

1436 [JOHNSON, Samuel]. *The Prince of Abissinia. A Tale.* 2 vols. London, 1759 (12mo. 5s. Dodsley and Johnston) BRITISH LIBRARY

Reviewed: *Monthly Review* 20 (1759): 428–437
Critical Review 7 (1759): 372–375
Gentleman's Magazine 29 (1759): 184–186
Annual Register 2 (1759): 477–479

1437 [JOHNSON, Samuel (dancing master)]. *Court and Country: a Paraphrase upon Milton. By The Author of Hurlothrumbo.* London, n.d. [FOLGER CAT.–c. 1760] (8vo. 6d. Rivington) FOLGER

Reviewed: *Monthly Review* 20 (1759): 464

1438 JOHNSON, S[amuel], M.A. of Shrewsbury. *An Essay on Education. A Poem. In Two Parts. I. The Pedant. II. The Preceptor.* Shrewsbury, 1771 (4to. 2s.6d. Baldwin) BRITISH LIBRARY

Reviewed: *Monthly Review* 45 (1771): 412
Critical Review 32 (1771): 308–310
Gentleman's Magazine 41 (1771): 514
London Magazine 40 (1771): 570

1439 JOHNSON, S[amuel] (1739?-1798). *Sensibility, a Poem.* London, 1773 (no pub. details) YALE (BEINECKE)

Reviewed: *London Magazine* 42 (1773): 509

1440 [JOHNSTONE, Charles]. *Chrysal: or the Adventures of a Guinea. Wherein are exhibited Views of several striking Scenes, With Curious and interesting Anecdotes of the most Noted Persons of every Rank of Life, whose Hands it passes through in America, England, Holland, Germany, and Portugal. By an Adept.* 2 vols. London, 1760 (12mo. 6s. Becket) BRITISH LIBRARY

Reviewed: *Monthly Review* 23 (1760): 157–158
Critical Review 9 (1760): 419

1441 [JOHNSTONE, Charles]. *Chrysal: or, the Adventures of a Guinea. Wherein are exhibited Views of several striking Scenes, With Curious and interesting Anecdotes of the most Noted Persons in every Rank of Life, whose Hands it passed through, in America, England, Holland, Germany and Portugal. By an Adept. The Second Edition, greatly inlarged and corrected.* 2 vols. London, 1761 [2d ed. of vols. 3 & 4 is dated 1767.] (12mo. 6s. Becket) FOLGER

Reviewed: *Critical Review* 11 (1761): 336

1442 [JOHNSTONE, Charles]. *Chrysal: or the Adventures of a Guinea. Wherein are exhibited Views of several striking Scenes, with Curious and interesting Anecdotes of the most Noted Persons of every Rank of Life, whose Hands it*

passed through, in America, England, Holland, Germany, and Portugal. By an Adept. Vols. III and IV. 2 vols. London, 1765 (12mo. 6s. Becket and De Hondt) BODLEIAN

Reviewed: *Monthly Review* 33 (1765): 87
Critical Review 20 (1765): 120–124
Candid Review 1 (1765): 429–435

1443 [JOHNSTONE, Charles]. *The History of Arsaces, Prince of Betlis. By the Editor of Chrysal.* 2 vols. London, 1774 (12mo. 6s.bound. Becket. 1774) BRITISH LIBRARY

Reviewed: *Monthly Review* 51 (1774): 237–238
Critical Review 38 (1774): 274–277
London Magazine 43 (1774): 501
Universal Catalogue 3 (1774) art. 1039

1444 [JOHNSTONE, Charles]. *The Reverie; or, a Flight to the Paradise of Fools. By the Editor of the Adventures of a Guinea.* 2 vols. London, 1762 (12mo. 5s.boards. Becket and De Hondt) BRITISH LIBRARY

Reviewed: *Monthly Review* 27 (1762): 471–472
Critical Review 14 (1762): 440–445
British Magazine 4 (1763): 46

Joineriana: or the Book of Scraps
See: PATERSON, Samuel

1445 [JOLYOT DE CRÉBILLON, Claude Prosper (le fils)]. *The Secret History of Zeokinisul, King of the Kofirans. Being an authentic Account of the Amours of Lewis XV. and Interspersed with several curious Anecdotes. Translated from the Arabian Manuscript of the learned Krinelbol. With a Key, explaining the fictitious Names used in this History.* London, 1761 (8vo. 2s. Thrush) BODLEIAN

Reviewed: *Critical Review* 11 (1761): 500

JOLYOT DE CRÉBILLON, Claude Prosper (le fils) (translation)
See: CLANCY, Michael. *Memoirs of M. de Meilcour*

JOLYOT DE CRÉBILLON, Prosper (le père) (translation)
See: KIMBER, Edward. *The Happy Orphans*

1446 JONES, Charles. *A Congratulatory Ode to Ireland. -Non deficit alter Aureus-* NOT SEEN (Fol. 6d. Williams)

Reviewed: *Critical Review* 16 (1763): 151

1447 JONES, Henry. *The Earl of Essex. A Tragedy. As it is Acted at the Theatre Royal in Covent-Garden.* London, 1753 (8vo. 1s.6d. Dodsley) BRITISH LIBRARY

Reviewed: *Monthly Review* 8 (1753): 225–229

1448 JONES, Henry. *An Epistle To the Right Honourable The Earl of Orrery, Occasion'd by reading his Lordship's Translation of Pliny's Epistles.* London, 1751 (Fol. 1s. Owen) BRITISH LIBRARY

Reviewed: *Monthly Review* 5 (1751): 76–77

1449 JONES, Henry. *Kew Garden. A Poem. In Two Cantos.* London, 1767 (4to. 2s.6d. Dodsley) BRITISH LIBRARY

Reviewed: *Monthly Review* 37 (1767): 152
Critical Review 24 (1767): 315–316
Universal Museum 3 (1767): 541

1450 JONES, Henry. *Merit. A Poem: inscribed to the Right Honourable Philip Earl of Chesterfield.* London, 1753 (4to. 1s. Dodsley) BRITISH LIBRARY

Reviewed: *Monthly Review* 8 (1753): 471–472

1451 JONES, [Henry]. *The Patriot Enterprize: or An Address to Britain. A Poem. Inscribed to the Right Hon. William Pitt, &c. &c. By Mr. Jones, Author of the Earl of Essex. To which is added, the Prussian Campaign, A Poem. Celebrating The Atchievements of Frederick the Great, In the Years 1756–57. By William Dobson, L.L.B.* London & Dublin, 1758 (4to. 6d. Cooper) BODLEIAN

Reviewed: *Monthly Review* 18 (1758): 624
Gentleman's Magazine 28 (1758): 282

1452 [JONES, Henry]. *The Relief, or, Day Thoughts: a Poem. Occasioned by the Complaint, or Night Thoughts.* London, 1754 (4to. 1s. Robinson) BRITISH LIBRARY

Reviewed: *Monthly Review* 10 (1754): 304

1453 JONES, Henry. *Vectis. The Isle of Wight: a Poem. In Three Cantos.* London, 1766 (4to. 2s.6d. Flexney) BRITISH LIBRARY

Reviewed: *Monthly Review* 34 (1766): 349–351
Critical Review 21 (1766): 317–318
Gentleman's Magazine 36 (1766): 190

1454 JONES, Henry. *Verses To His Grace The Duke of Newcastle, On The Death of the Right Honourable Henry Pelham.* London, 1754 (4to. 6d. Cooper) BRITISH LIBRARY

Listed: *Monthly Review* 10 (1754): 305
Reviewed: *Gentleman's Magazine* 24 (1754): 193–194

1455 JONES, Lewis. *Alpha and Omega, a Poem, In Five Cantoes: Addressed to Alphonso, A Young Gentleman Atheistically inclined. To which are added, The Third Chapter of Habbakuk, Reflections on the Sea-Side, &c.* Glocester, 1758 (4to. 2s. Davy and Law, &c.) BRITISH LIBRARY

Reviewed: *Monthly Review* 19 (1758): 589–590

1456 [JONES, Lindesius]. *The Authors a Dramatic Satyr In Two Acts. As it has been frequently Acted with great Applause in this, and the other end of the Town; by the Public's Company of Dunces.* London, 1755 (8vo. 1s. Typus) BRITISH LIBRARY

Reviewed: *Monthly Review* 12 (1755): 384

1457 JONES, Mary. *Miscellanies in Prose and Verse.* Oxford, 1750 (8vo. 5s. Dodsley) BRITISH LIBRARY

Reviewed: *Monthly Review* 6 (1752): 213–23 and 470–481

1458 [JONES, Sir William]. *Poems consisting chiefly of Translations from the Asiatick Languages. To which are added, Two Essays, I. On the Poetry of the Eastern nations. II. On the Arts, commonly called Imitative.* Oxford, 1772 (8vo. 4s.sewed. Elmsley. 1772) BRITISH LIBRARY

Reviewed: *Monthly Review* 46 (1772): 508–517
Critical Review 33 (1772): 314–318
London Magazine 41 (1772): 189
British Magazine & General Review 1 (1772): 456–457
Universal Catalogue [1] (1772) art. 586

1459 JONSON, Ben. *The Works of Ben. Jonson. In Seven Volumes. Collated with All the former Editions, and Corrected; with Notes Critical and Explanatory. By Peter Whalley, Fellow of St. John's College in Oxford.* 7 vols. London, 1756 (8vo. 1l.15s.bound. Midwinter) BRITISH LIBRARY

Reviewed: *Monthly Review* 15 (1756): 198
Critical Review 1 (1756): 462 472
Literary Magazine 1 (1756): 169–171

JONSON, Ben (adaptations)
See: *Airs, Duets, Chorusses, &c. in the New Masque called the Druids*
COLMAN, George (the elder). *The Fairy Prince*
GENTLEMAN, Francis. *The Favourite*
GENTLEMAN, Francis. *Sejanus, a Tragedy*
GENTLEMAN, Francis. *The Tobacconist*

A Journey through Every Stage of Life
See: SCOTT, Sarah

1460 *The Journey to Emmaus. A Sacred Eclogue.* Dublin printed, London reprinted, 1751 (4to. 1s. Noon) BRITISH LIBRARY

Reviewed: *Monthly Review* 5 (1751): 160

1461 *The Journey to London: or, the History of the Selby-Family.* 2 vols. London, 1774 (12mo. 6s. Noble. 1774) UNIVERSITY OF PENNSYLVANIA

Reviewed: *Monthly Review* 50 (1774): 233–234
Critical Review 37 (1774): 77
Town & Country Magazine 6 (1774): 155
Universal Catalogue 3 (1774) art. 195

1462 *The Joys of Hymen, or, the Conjugal Directory: a Poem In Three Books.* London, 1768 (8vo. 2s. D. Davis. 1768) BRITISH LIBRARY

Reviewed: *Monthly Review* 40 (1769): 156
Critical Review 26 (1768): 152
Universal Museum 4 (1768): 429
Political Register 3 (1768): 189

The Judgment of Paris. An English Burletta.
See: SCHOMBERG, Ralph

Julia, a poetical Romance
See: RUSSELL, William

Julia to Pollio
See: NELTHORPE, George

1463 *The Jumble: a Satire. Addressed to the Revd. Mr. C. Ch–rch–ll.* London, 1763 (4to. 1s. Johnston) BODLEIAN

Reviewed: *Monthly Review* 30 (1764): 67
Critical Review 16 (1763): 476–478

1464 JUNIUS (pseud.). *Political Poems: a Compilation. By Junius*
NOT SEEN (8vo. 1s. Crowder. 1772)

Reviewed: *Monthly Review* 46 (1772): 455
Critical Review 33 (1772): 329
Town & Country Magazine 4 (1772): 266

1465 [JUSTICE, Elizabeth]. *Amelia: or, The Distress'd Wife. A History Founded on Real Circumstances. By a Private Gentlewoman.* London, 1751 (8vo. 5s.sewed. To be had of J. Swan, and other booksellers) BRITISH LIBRARY

Reviewed: *Monthly Review* 5 (1751): 72–73

1466 *Justice a Poem.* London, 1774 (4to. 1s.6d. Kearsly. 1774)

Reviewed: *Monthly Review* 51 (1774): 394
Critical Review 38 (1774): 392
London Magazine 43 (1774): 608

1467 *The Justification, a Satire. Vindicating the Character of a Much-Injur'd Nobleman. To which is annex'd a Letter to a certain great D-----; Interspersed with Reflections on the Love of our Country, And Private Pique and Resentment. By a Gentleman of the Middle-Temple.* London, n.d. [ESTC-1760?] (4to. 1s. Anderson and Burd) BRITISH LIBRARY

Reviewed: *Monthly Review* 21 (1759): 269
Critical Review 8 (1759): 259

1468 JUSTITIA (pseud.). *The Lap-Dog or, Truth in a Fable: Dedicated to the celebrated Actress Mrs. Cibber.* London, 1753 (Fol. 6d. Doughty) HARVARD (PUSEY)

Reviewed: *Gentleman's Magazine* 23 (1753): 203
Listed: *Monthly Review* 8 (1753): 393

JUVENAL (Decimus Junius JUVENALIS) (translations and imitations)
See: DERRICK, Samuel. *The Third Satire of Juvenal . . .*
GREENE, Edward Burnaby. *The Satires of Juvenal Paraphrastically Imitated*
NEVILE, Thomas. *The Fourteenth Satire . . .*
NEVILE, Thomas. *Imitations of Juvenal and Persius*
The Subscription Soldier

The Juvenaliad. A Satire
See: WALLIS, George

The Juvenile Adventures of David Ranger
See: KIMBER, Edward

1469 *The Juvenile Adventures of Miss Kitty F-----r.* 2 vols. London, 1759 (12mo. 3s.sewed. Smith) UNIVERSITY OF ILLINOIS

Reviewed: *Monthly Review* 20 (1759): 276 and 379
Critical Review 8 (1759): 176

Juvenile Poems on Several Occasions. By a Gentleman of Oxford
See: GRIFFIN, Philip

1470 *The Juverniad; or, exploits of Richard Strongbow, earl of Pembroke, in the war of Ireland. An essay on epic poetry. Canto 1*
NOT SEEN (8vo. 6d. Owen)

Reviewed: *Monthly Review* 10 (1754): 385

Kanor, a Tale
See: FAGNAN, Marie Antoinette

1471 KEATE, George. *The Alps. A Poem.* London, 1763 (4to. 1s.6d. Dodsley) BRITISH LIBRARY

Reviewed: *Monthly Review* 28 (1763): 376–383
Critical Review 15 (1763): 390–391

1472 [KEATE, George]. *Ancient and modern Rome, a Poem. Written at Rome in the Year*

1755. London, 1760 (4to. 1s.6d. Dodsley) BRITISH LIBRARY

Reviewed: *Monthly Review* 22 (1760): 145–149
Critical Review 9 (1760): 130–133.
London Magazine 29 (1760): 111

1473 [KEATE, George]. *An Epistle from Lady Jane Grey to Lord Guilford Dudley. Supposed to have been written in the Tower, a few Days before they suffered*. London, 1762 (4to. 1s. Dodsley) BRITISH LIBRARY

Reviewed: *Monthly Review* 26 (1762): 224–227
Critical Review 13 (1762): 271
London Magazine 31 (1762): 112

1474 KEATE, George. *Ferney: an Epistle to Monsr. De Voltaire*. London, 1768 (4to. 1s. Dodsley) BRITISH LIBRARY

Reviewed: *Monthly Review* 38 (1768): 138–141
Critical Review 25 (1768): 152–153
Gentleman's Magazine 38 (1768): 85
London Magazine 37 (1768): 105
Universal Museum 4 (1768): 93
Political Register 2 (1768): 318

1475 KEATE, George. *The Monument in Arcadia: a Dramatic Poem, In Two Acts*. London, 1773 (4to. 2s. Dodsley. 1773) BRITISH LIBRARY

Reviewed: *Monthly Review* 49 (1773): 130–133
Critical Review 35 (1773): 392
London Magazine 42 (1773): 302
Universal Catalogue [2] (1773) art. 617

1476 KEATE, George. *Netley Abbey. An Elegy. The Second Edition, corrected and enlarged.* ["Corrected and enlarged" edition of *The Ruins of Netley Abbey*.] London, 1769 (1s. Dodsley) BRITISH LIBRARY

Reviewed: *Critical Review* 27 (1769): 153–154
Town & Country Magazine [1] (1769): 101

1477 [KEATE, George]. *A Poem to the Memory of the Celebrated Mrs. Cibber*. London, 1766 (4to. 6d. Dodsley) BRITISH LIBRARY

Reviewed: *Monthly Review* 34 (1766): 243–244
Critical Review 21 (1766): 155–156

1478 KEATE, George. *The Ruins of Netley Abbey. A Poem*. London, 1764 (4to. 6d. Dodsley) BRITISH LIBRARY

Reviewed: *Monthly Review* 30 (1764): 322–323
Critical Review 17 (1764): 472
British Magazine 5 (1764): 376
General Magazine 1 (1764): 197

1479 [KEATE, George]. *The Temple-Student: an epistle to a friend, Who had requested the Author's Opinion of some Verses*. London, 1765 (4to. 1s. Dodsley) BRITISH LIBRARY

Reviewed: *Monthly Review* 33 (1765): 86
Critical Review 19 (1765): 392
Candid Review 1 (1765): 365–368

1480 KEENE, Elizabeth Carolina. *Dido to Aeneas From Ovid*
NOT SEEN (4to. 6d. Kinnersley)

Reviewed: *Monthly Review* 18 (1758): 651

1481 KEENE, Elizabeth Carolina. *Miscellaneous Poems*. London, 1762 (8vo. 5s.sewed. Hooper) BRITISH LIBRARY

Reviewed: *Monthly Review* 27 (1762): 75–76

1482 KELLY, D. *Molly White: or the Bride Bewitched. A Tale*. London, 1767 (4to. 1s.6d. Griffin) BRITISH LIBRARY

Reviewed: *Monthly Review* 36 (1767): 78
Critical Review 22 (1766): 469
Gentleman's Magazine 36 (1766): 591

1483 [KELLY, Hugh]. *L'Amour A-la-Mode: Or, Love A-la-Mode. A Farce in three Acts*. London, 1760 (8vo. 1s. Williams) BRITISH LIBRARY

Reviewed: *Monthly Review* 22 (1760): 257
Critical Review 9 (1760): 236–237

1484 [KELLY, Hugh]. *Clementina, a Tragedy, As it is perform'd with universal Applause at the Theatre-Royal in Covent-Garden*. London, 1771 (8vo. 1s.6d. Dilly, &c. 1771) BRITISH LIBRARY

Reviewed: *Monthly Review* 44 (1771): 244–254
Critical Review 31 (1771): 311–313
London Magazine 40 (1771): 162–163

1485 [KELLY, Hugh]. *An Elegy to the Memory of the Right Honourable William, late Earl of Bath.* London, 1765 (4to. 1s.6d. Nicoll) HARVARD (HOUGHTON)

Reviewed: *Monthly Review* 32 (1765): 75-76
Critical Review 19 (1765): 69-70
Candid Review 1 (1765): 44-45

1486 KELLY, Hugh. *False Delicacy: a Comedy; as it is performed at the Theatre-Royal in Drury-Lane. By His Majesty's Servants.* London, 1768 (8vo. 1s.6d. Johnson) BRITISH LIBRARY

Reviewed: *Monthly Review* 38 (1768): 159
Critical Review 25 (1768): 145-147
Gentleman's Magazine 38 (1768): 78-82
Political Register 2 (1768): 186-187

1487 [KELLY, Hugh]. *Memoirs of a Magdalen: or, the History of Louisa Mildmay. Now first published from a Series of Original Letters.* 2 vols. London, 1767 (12mo. 6s. Griffin) BRITISH LIBRARY

Reviewed: *Monthly Review* 36 (1767): 238
Critical Review 22 (1766): 373-375
Gentleman's Magazine 36 (1766): 542

1488 KELLY, Hugh. *The Romance of an Hour, a Comedy of Two Acts, As it is performed, with Universal Applause, at The Theatre Royal in Covent-Garden.* [Based on *L'amitié à l'épreuve* by Jean François Marmontel.] London, 1774 (8vo. 1s. Kearsly) BRITISH LIBRARY

Reviewed: *Monthly Review* 52 (1775): 91-92
Critical Review 38 (1774): 480

1489 [KELLY, Hugh]. *The School for Wives. A Comedy. As it is performed at the Theatre-Royal in Drury-Lane.* London, 1774 (8vo. 1s.6d. Becket. 1774) LIBRARY OF CONGRESS

Reviewed: *Monthly Review* 50 (1774): 34-42
Critical Review 37 (1774): 56-59
Universal Catalogue [3] (1774) art. 123

1490 [KELLY, Hugh]. *Thespis: or, a Critical Examination into the Merits of all the Principal Performers belonging to Drury-Lane Theatre.* London, 1766 (4to. 2s. Kearsly) BODLEIAN

Reviewed: *Monthly Review* 35 (1766): 388-390

1491 KELLY, Hugh. *Thespis: or, a Critical Examination into the Merits of all the Principal Performers belonging to Covent-Garden Theatre. Book the Second.* London, 1767 (4to. 1s.6d. Williams) BRITISH LIBRARY

Reviewed: *Monthly Review* 36 (1767): 162

1492 KELLY, Hugh. *Thespis: or, a Critical Examination into the Merits of all the Principal Performers belonging to Drury-Lane Theatre. The Second Edition, with Corrections and Additions.* London, 1766 (4to. 2s.6d. Kearsly) BRITISH LIBRARY

Reviewed: *Critical Review* 23 (1767): 60

1493 [KELLY, Hugh]. *The Tutor; or, The History of George Wilson and Lady Fanny Melfont.* 2 vols. London, 1771 (12mo. 5s.sewed. Vernor) UNIVERSITY OF CHICAGO

Reviewed: *Monthly Review* 45 (1771): 232
Critical Review 32 (1771): 153-154

1494 KELLY, Hugh. *A Word to the Wise, a Comedy, as it was performed at the Theatre Royal, in Drury-Lane.* London, 1770 (8vo. 5s. Dodsley, &c. 1770) BRITISH LIBRARY

Reviewed: *Monthly Review* 43 (1770): 150-151
Critical Review 30 (1770): 230-231
Gentleman's Magazine 40 (1770): 225-227
London Magazine 39 (1770): 265-267

1495 [KENNEDY, John]. *The Inspector in the Shades. A New Dialogue In the Manner of Lucian.* London, 1752 (8vo. 6d. Swan) HARVARD (HOUGHTON)

Reviewed: *Monthly Review* 7 (1752): 75

1496 KENRICK, W[illiam]. *The Duellist, a Comedy. As it is acted at the Theatre Royal in Covent Garden. Written by W. Kenrick, LL.D.* London, n.d. [ESTC-1773] (8vo. 1s.6d. Evans. 1773) BRITISH LIBRARY

Reviewed: *Monthly Review* 49 (1773): 396
Critical Review 36 (1773): 476
Gentleman's Magazine 43 (1773): 610-611

1497 [KENRICK, William (trans.)]. *Eloisa: Or, a Series of Original Letters Collected and Published By J. J. Rousseau. Translated from the*

French. In Four Volumes. London, 1761 (8vo. 12s. Becket) HARVARD (HOUGHTON)

Reviewed: *Monthly Review* 24 (1761): 227–235 and 25 (1761): 192–214 and 241–260
Critical Review 12 (1761): 203–211

1498 [KENRICK, William (trans.)]. *Emilius and Sophia: or, A New System of Education. Translated from the French of J. J. Rousseau, Citizen of Geneva. By the Translator of Eloisa.* 2 vols. London, 1762 (5s.sewed. Becket, &c.) BRITISH LIBRARY

Reviewed: *Monthly Review* 27 (1762): 212–217, 258–269, and 342–358
Critical Review 14 (1762): 250–270, 336–346, and 426–440 and 15 (1763): 21–34 [4 vols.]
British Magazine 3 (1762): 606
Annual Register 5 (1762): 225–237 [4 vols.]

1499 [KENRICK, William (trans.)]. *Emilius and Sophia: or, A New System of Education. Translated from the French of Mr. J. J.Rousseau, Citizen of Geneva. By the Translator of Eloisa. Vols. III and IV.* London, 1763 (5s.sewed. Becket and DeHondt) BRITISH LIBRARY

Reviewed: *Monthly Review* 28 (1763): 1–14 and 81–96
Critical Review 14 (1762): 250–270, 336–346, and 426–440, and 15 (1763): 21–34 [4 vols.]
Annual Register 5 (1762): 225–237 [4 vols.]

1500 KENRICK, W[illiam]. *An Epistle to G. Colman, from W. Kenrick.* London, 1768 (4to. 1s. Fletcher) BRITISH LIBRARY

Reviewed: *Monthly Review* 38 (1768): 149
Critical Review 25 (1768): 150–151
London Magazine 37 (1768): 112

1501 [KENRICK, William]. *Epistles Philosophical and Moral.* [Revised version of *Epistles to Lorenzo.*] London, 1759 (8vo. 6s. Wilcox) BRITISH LIBRARY

Reviewed: *Monthly Review* 20 (1759): 1–17
Critical Review 6 (1758): 439–453

1502 [KENRICK, William]. *Epistles to Lorenzo.* London, 1756 (8vo. 1s.6d. Whiston) YALE (STERLING)

Reviewed: *Monthly Review* 16 (1757): 226–230
Critical Review 3 (1757): 162–167

1503 KENRICK, W[illiam]. *Falstaff's Wedding, a Comedy: as it is acted at the Theatre Royal in Drury-Lane. Being a Sequel to the Second Part of the Play of King Henry the Fourth. Written in imitation of Shakespeare.* London, 1766 (8vo. 1s.6d. Davis and Reymers) BRITISH LIBRARY

Reviewed: *Monthly Review* 34 (1766): 320–321
Critical Review 21 (1766): 319

1504 KENRICK, [William]. *Falstaff's Wedding: a Comedy. Being a Sequel to the Second Part of the Play of King Henry the Fourth. Written in imitation of Shakespeare, by Mr. Kenrick.* London, 1760 [1766] [ESTC-1760? Preface dated Jan. 1, 1766] (8vo. 1s.6d. Wilkie) BRITISH LIBRARY

Reviewed: *Monthly Review* 34 (1766): 240
Critical Review 21 (1766): 149–150

1505 [KENRICK, William]. *Fun: A Parodi-tragi-comical Satire. As it was to have been performed at the Castle-Tavern, Pater-noster-Row, on Thursday, February 13th, 1752, but Suppressed, by A Special Order from the Lord-Mayor and Court of Aldermen.* London, 1752 (8vo. 1s. Stamper) BRITISH LIBRARY

Reviewed: *Monthly Review* 6 (1752): 238

1506 [KENRICK, William]. *Introduction to the School of Shakespeare; held on Wednesday Evenings, In the Apollo, at the Devil Tavern, Temple Bar. To which is added a Retort Courteous on the Criticks, As delivered at the Second and Third Lectures.* London, n.d. [ESTC-1774] (8vo. 1s. Sold by all the Booksellers, &c.) BRITISH LIBRARY

Reviewed: *Monthly Review* 50 (1774): 218–219
Universal Catalogue 3 (1774) art. 229

1507 [KENRICK, William]. *Love in the Suds; a Town Eclogue. Being the Lamentations of Roscius for the Loss of his Nyky.* [Published with *A Letter to David Garrick, Esq. from William Kenrick, LL.D.* but has its own title page.] London, 1772 (Fol. 2s.6d. Wheble) BRITISH LIBRARY

Reviewed: *Monthly Review* 47 (1772): 71
Critical Review 34 (1772): 155
London Magazine 41 (1772): 337
British Magazine & General Review 2 (1772): 156–157
Universal Catalogue [1] (1772) art. 977

1508 [KENRICK, William]. *The Pasquinade. With Notes Variorum. Book the First.* London, 1753 (4to. 1s. Mountfort) BRITISH LIBRARY

Reviewed: *Monthly Review* 8 (1753): 80

1509 KENRICK, W[illiam]. *Poems; Ludicrous, Satirical, and Moral.* London, 1768 (8vo. 4s. Fletcher) BRITISH LIBRARY

Reviewed: *Monthly Review* 38 (1768): 334
London Magazine 37 (1768): 113
Political Register 2 (1768): 320

KENRICK, William. *A Poetical Epistle to G. Colman*
See: KENRICK, William. *An Epistle to G. Colman*

1510 [KENRICK, William]. *A Whipping for the Welch Parson. Being A Comment on The Rev. Mr. Evan Lloyd's Epistle to David Garrick, Esq. By Scriblerus Flagellarius. To which is superadded The Parson's Text.* London, 1773 (Fol. 1s.6d. Evans. 1773) BRITISH LIBRARY

Reviewed: *Monthly Review* 48 (1773): 160
Critical Review 35 (1773): 71
Universal Catalogue [2] (1773) art. 120

1511 KENRICK, W[illiam]. *The Widow'd Wife. A Comedy: as it is acted at the Theatre Royal in Drury Lane. By His Majesty's Servants.* London, 1767 (8vo. 1s.6d. Davies) BRITISH LIBRARY

Reviewed: *Monthly Review* 38 (1768): 72
Critical Review 25 (1768): 143–145
Gentleman's Magazine 37 (1767): 599–600
Political Register 2 (1768): 64

The Kenrickad
See: ARIEL (pseud.)

1512 *The Kentish Candidates. D--r--g, W--t--n, and F--r--x. As Sung at Both Ends of the Town of Maidstone, The Day the Grand Jury met.* London, n.d. [ESTC-1754] (6d. Carpenter) BRITISH LIBRARY

Listed: *Monthly Review* 9 (1753): 236

The Kentish Cricketers
See: BURNBY, John

1513 *The Kept Mistress.* London, 1761 (8vo. 2s. Morgan) BRITISH LIBRARY

Reviewed: *Monthly Review* 25 (1761): 393
Critical Review 12 (1761): 310–311
British Magazine 2 (1761): 550

1514 KIDDELL, Henry. *Stanzas on Religion* NOT SEEN (Fol. 6d. Owen)

Reviewed: *Monthly Review* 5 (1751): 397

1515 KIDDELL, Henry. *Tiverton: a Poem.* London, n.d. [British Library copy cropped; ESTC-1753] (4to. 6d. Griffiths) BRITISH LIBRARY

Reviewed: *Monthly Review* 10 (1754): 78
Gentleman's Magazine 24 (1754): 50

1516 [KIDGELL, John]. *The Card.* 2 vols. London, 1755 (12mo. 6s. Newbery) BRITISH LIBRARY

Reviewed: *Monthly Review* 12 (1755): 117–121
Gentleman's Magazine 25 (1755): 94–95

1517 [KIMBER, Edward]. *The Generous Briton; or, the Authentic Memoirs of William Goldsmith, Esq;* 2 vols. London, 1765 (Two pocket vols. 5s. Henderson) BRITISH LIBRARY

Reviewed: *Monthly Review* 33 (1765): 86
Critical Review 19 (1765): 466–467

1518 [KIMBER, Edward]. *The Happy Orphans: an authentic History of Persons in High Life. With A Variety of uncommon Events and surprizing Turns of Fortune.* [Translation from Crébillon père.] 2 vols. London, 1759 (12mo. 6s. Woodgate and Brooks) BRITISH LIBRARY

Reviewed: *Monthly Review* 19 (1758): 580
Critical Review 7 (1759): 174–175

1519 [KIMBER, Edward]. *The History of the Life and Adventures of Mr. Anderson. Containing His strange Varieties of Fortune in Europe and America. Compiled from his Own Papers.* London, 1754 (12mo. 3s. Owen) LIBRARY OF CONGRESS

Reviewed: *Monthly Review* 10 (1754): 147

1520 [KIMBER, Edward]. *The Juvenile Adventures of David Ranger, Esq; From An original Manuscript found in the Collections of a late Noble Lord.* 2 vols. London, 1757 (12mo. 6s. Stevens) NEWBERRY

Reviewed: *Monthly Review* 15 (1756): 655–656
Critical Review 2 (1756): 379

1521 [KIMBER, Edward]. *The Life and Adventures of James Ramble, Esq; Interspersed, With the various Fortunes of certain noble Personages Deeply concerned in the Northern Commotions in the Year 1715. From his own Manuscript.* 2 vols. London, 1755 (12mo. 6s. Baldwin) BODLEIAN

Reviewed: *Monthly Review* 12 (1755): 144–145
Gentleman's Magazine 24 (1754): 581

1522 [KIMBER, Edward]. *The Life and Adventures of Joe Thompson. A Narrative founded on Fact. Written by Himself.* 2 vols. London, 1750 (6s. Printed for J. Hinton) BRITISH LIBRARY

Reviewed: *Monthly Review* 3 (1750): 366–367

1523 [KIMBER, Edward]. *The Life, extraordinary Adventures, Voyages, and surprizing Escapes of Capt. Neville Frowde, of Cork. In four parts. Written by himself, and now first published from his own Manuscript.* London, 1708 [1758] [ESTC-1708, i.e. {1758}] (12mo. 3s. Wren) BRITISH LIBRARY

Reviewed: *Monthly Review* 19 (1758): 311
Critical Review 6 (1758): 261–262

1524 [KIMBER, Edward]. *Maria; the Genuine Memoirs of a Young Lady of Rank and Fortune. By the author of The Life and Adventures of Joe Thompson.* 2 vols. 1st ed. reviewed; copy seen 2d ed.: London, 1765 (8vo. 6s. Baldwin) BRITISH LIBRARY

Reviewed: *Monthly Review* 30 (1764): 243
Critical Review 18 (1764): 313
General Magazine 1 (1764): 96

Kimbolton Park: a Poem
See: HUTCHINSON, Benjamin

1525 [KING, Anthony]. *The Frequented Village. A Poem. By a Gentleman of the Middle Temple.* London, n.d. [BLC-1771?] (4to. 2s. Godwin) BRITISH LIBRARY

Reviewed: *Monthly Review* 45 (1771): 509–510
Critical Review 32 (1771): 391
Gentleman's Magazine 41 (1771): 560
London Magazine 40 (1771): 613–614
Town & Country Magazine 3 (1771): 657

1526 KING, George. *The Button-Maker's Jests. By George King, of St. James's, Button-maker. Containing The Cream, Marrow and Fatness of every witty Thing he either hath, or ever shall say during his Life. Calculated to make the Countryman stare, the Citizen laugh, and the Courtier grin; adapted both to the sultry Days of Autumn, or the gloomy Nights of Winter. Embellished with a curious Copper Plate, finely engraved.* N.p, n.d. [ESTC: London, 1780?] (8vo. 1s. Frederick) BRITISH LIBRARY

Reviewed: *Critical Review* 30 (1770): 311
Town & Country Magazine 2 (1770): 598

1527 KING, John Glen. *Poems on Several Occasions. By John Glen King, B.A. Of Gonville and Caius College, Cambridge.* London, 1753 (8vo. 2s. Bourn) HARVARD (HOUGHTON)

Reviewed: *Monthly Review* 9 (1753): 154

1528 [KING, Thomas]. *Love at First Sight: a Ballad Farce, of Two Acts. As performed at the Theatre-Royal in Drury-Lane.* London, 1763 (8vo. 1s. Becket and DeHondt) BRITISH LIBRARY

Reviewed: *Monthly Review* 29 (1763): 464
Critical Review 16 (1763): 316–317

1529 KING, Thomas. *Wit's Last Stake. A Farce. As it is performed at the Theatre Royal, Drury-Lane.* [Adaptation of *Le Légataire universel* by Jean François Regnard.] London, 1769 (8vo. 1s. Becket) BRITISH LIBRARY

Reviewed: *Monthly Review* 40 (1769): 158–159
Critical Review 27 (1769): 80
Gentleman's Magazine 39 (1769): 157 and 199
London Magazine 38 (1769): 102
Critical Memoirs 1 (1769): 159–160 and 521–522

The Kinsman of Mahomet
See: FROMAGET, Nicolas

1530 KIRKPATRICK, J[ames]. *The Sea-Piece A narrative, philosophical and descriptive Poem. In Five Cantos.* London, 1750 (8vo. 3s.6d.bound. Printed for Robinson in Ludgate-street) BODLEIAN

Reviewed: *Monthly Review* 2 (1749–50): 257–263

1531 KLOPSTOCK, [Friedrich Gottlieb]. *The third Volume of the Messiah, attempted from the German of Mr. Klopstock*
NOT SEEN (12mo. 3s. Dodsley)

Reviewed: *Monthly Review* 46 (1772): 467
Critical Review 32 (1771): 393–395
Gentleman's Magazine 41 (1771): 561

KLOPSTOCK, Friedrich Gottlieb (translations)
See: COLLYER, Joseph. *The Messiah*
LLOYD, Robert. *The Death of Adam*

1532 *The Ladies Miscellany. A New Work. Containing, I. Entertaining Novels. II. Family-Pictures: or, Domestic Life exhibited and contrasted in various Situations. III. Flights of Fancy: or, Original Essays in Prose and Verse. IV. Modern Characters displayed: or, Dialogues of the Living. The Whole calculated for the Amusement and Instruction of the Female World.* 2 vols. London ed. reviewed; copy seen: Dublin, 1770 (12mo. 6s. Lowndes) BRITISH LIBRARY

Reviewed: *Monthly Review* 41 (1769): 480
Gentleman's Magazine 39 (1769): 549

1533 LA FONTAINE, [Jean de]. *The Lion A Whelp, and at full Age; A Fable, From the French of La Fontaine, which has been suppressed in most of the modern Editions. Dedicated to the Right Hon. the Earl of Granville, President of his Majesty's Privy Council.* London, 1755 (Fol. 6d. Cooper) FOLGER

Reviewed: *Monthly Review* 12 (1755): 231–232
Gentleman's Magazine 25 (1755): 142

1534 LA FONTAINE, Jean de. *The Spectacles. A Tale. From the French of Mons. de la Fontaine.* London, 1753 (4to. 6d. Goringe) BRITISH LIBRARY

Reviewed: *Monthly Review* 8 (1753): 51

LA FONTAINE (translation)
See: RUGELEY, Rowland. *Miscellaneous Poems*

LA HARPE, Jean François de (translations/adaptations)
See: FRANCKLIN, Thomas. *The Earl of Warwick*
HIFFERNAN, Paul. *The Earl of Warwick*

1535 LAMBE, Robert (ed.). *An Exact and Circumstantial History of the Battle of Floddon. In Verse. Written about the time of Queen Elizabeth. In which are related many particular Facts not to be found in the English History. Published from a curious Manuscript in the Possession of John Askew, of Palins-burn, in Northumberland, Esq; with Notes, by Robert Lambe, Vicar of Norham Upon Tweed.* Berwick upon Tweed, 1774 (8vo. 4s.sewed. Berwick upon Tweed printed, and sold by Dilly, &c. in London. 1774) BODLEIAN

Reviewed: *Monthly Review* 51 (1774): 333–340
Critical Review 39 (1775): 112–116
London Magazine 43 (1774): 244

1536 [LAMBE, Thomas]. *Lycidas, a Masque. To which is added Delia, a Pastoral Elegy; and Verses On the Death of the Marquis of Carmarthen.* London, 1762 (4to. 1s. Pote) BRITISH LIBRARY

Reviewed: *Monthly Review* 26 (1762): 154
Critical Review 13 (1762): 166

1537 *The Lamentable and True Tragedie of M. Arden, of Feversham, in Kent. Who was Most wickedlye murdered, by the Means of his disloyall and wanton Wyfe, who for the Love she bare to one Mosbie, hyred two desperat Ruffins, Blackwill and Shagbag, to kill him. Wherein is shewed, The great Malice and Discimulation of a wicked Woman, the unsatiable desire of filthie lust, and the shamefull End of all Murderers.*

With a Preface; in which some Reasons are offered, in favour of its being the earliest dramatic Work of Shakespear now remaining; and a genuine Account given of the Murder from authentic Papers of the Time. Feversham, 1770 (8vo. 1s.6d. Printed for Stephen Doorne, at Feversham; and sold in London by Hawes and Co. 1770) BRITISH LIBRARY

Reviewed: *Monthly Review* 43 (1770): 493–497
Town & Country Magazine 2 (1770): 436

1538 *A Lamentation for the Departure of the Hanoverians. Being An Epistle from an English Maiden to her German Sweetheart.* London, n.d. (Fol. 6d. Morgan) YALE (BEINECKE)

Reviewed: *Monthly Review* 16 (1757): 580 [570]
Critical Review 3 (1757): 556–557

1539 LA MOTHE, Marie Catherine, Comtesse d'Aulnoy. *The court of Queen Mab; containing a select collection of only the most instructive and entertaining tales of the Fairies. Written by the countess d'Aulnoy. To which are added, a fairy tale in the ancient English stile, by Dr. Parnel, and queen Mab's song* NOT SEEN (12mo. 3s. Cooper)

Listed: *Monthly Review* 6 (1752): 145

1540 LA MOTHE, Marie Catherine, Comtesse d'Aulnoy. *The Earl of Douglas, an English Story. From the French of the Countess D'Anois. In Three Volumes. By the translator of Dorval; Observations on the Greeks; Christiana, Queen of Sweden, &c. &c.* 3 vols. Lynn, 1774 (12mo. 7s.6d. Baldwin. 1774) BODLEIAN

Reviewed: *Monthly Review* 51 (1774): 322
Critical Review 37 (1774): 112–115
London Magazine 43 (1774): 92

1541 [LANCASTER, Nathaniel]. *Methodism Triumphant, or, the Decisive Battle between the Old Serpent and the Modern Spirit.* London, 1767 (4to. 2s.6d. Wilkie.) BRITISH LIBRARY

Reviewed: *Monthly Review* 37 (1767): 394–395
Critical Review 25 (1768): 66–67
Universal Museum 3 (1767): 596

1542 [LANGHORNE, John]. *The Correspondence of Theodosius and Constantia, From their first acquaintance to the departure of Theodosius. Now first published from the Original Manuscripts. By the Editor of the Letters that passed between Theodosius and Constantia, after she had taken the Veil.* London, 1765 (12mo. 2s.6d.sewed. Becket and Co.) BRITISH LIBRARY

Reviewed: *Monthly Review* 32 (1765): 19–29
Critical Review 19 (1765): 169–173
Candid Review 1 (1765): 33–35

1543 [LANGHORNE, John]. *The Country Justice. A Poem. By one of his Majesty's Justices of the Peace for the County of Somerset. Part the first.* London, 1784 [Misprint for 1774; part 2 is dated 1775.] [ESTC: Misprinted date] (4to. 1s.6d. Becket. 1774) BRITISH LIBRARY

Reviewed: *Monthly Review* 51 (1774): 45–49
Critical Review 38 (1774): 76
Gentleman's Magazine 44 (1774): 430–431
London Magazine 43 (1774): 449–450
Town & Country Magazine 6 (1774): 437
Universal Catalogue 3 (1774) art. 798

1544 LANGHORNE, John. *The Death of Adonis. A pastoral Elegy. From the Greek of Bion.* London, 1759 (4to. 6d. Griffiths) BRITISH LIBRARY

Reviewed: *Monthly Review* 20 (1759): 570–572
Critical Review 7 (1759): 260–263

1545 [LANGHORNE, John]. *The Effusions of Friendship and Fancy. In several Letters to and from Select Friends.* 2 vols. London, 1763 (12mo. 5s. Becket & De Hondt) BRITISH LIBRARY

Reviewed: *Monthly Review* 28 (1763): 481–483
Critical Review 16 (1763): 6–11

1546 [LANGHORNE, John]. *The Effusions of Friendship and Fancy. In several Letters to and from Select Friends. The Second Edition.* 2 vols. London, 1766 (8vo. 6s. Becket and De Hondt) BRITISH LIBRARY

Reviewed: *Monthly Review* 34 (1766): 313–314
Critical Review 22 (1766): 316

1547 LANGHORNE, J[ohn]. *The Enlargement of the Mind. Epistle I. To General Craufurd. Written at Belvidere, 1763*. London, 1763 (4to. 1s. Becket and De Hondt) BRITISH LIBRARY

Reviewed: *Monthly Review* 29 (1763): 229
Critical Review 16 (1763): 314–315

1548 LANGHORNE, J[ohn]. *The Enlargement of the Mind. Epistle II. To William Langhorne, M.A.* London, 1765 (4to. 1s. Becket) BRITISH LIBRARY

Reviewed: *Monthly Review* 32 (1765): 313–315
Critical Review 19 (1765): 233–234
Candid Review 1 (1765): 189–190

1549 LANGHORNE, [John]. *The Fables of Flora*. London, 1771 (4to. 3s.sewed. Murray. 1771) BRITISH LIBRARY

Reviewed: *Monthly Review* 44 (1771): 225–230
Critical Review 31 (1771): 55–58
London Magazine 40 (1771): 49
Town & Country Magazine 3 (1771): 44

1550 LANGHORNE, John. *Frederic and Pharamond, or the Consolations of Human Life*. London, 1769 (8vo. 2s.6d. Becket and DeHondt) BRITISH LIBRARY

Reviewed: *Monthly Review* 40 (1769): 177–185
Critical Review 27 (1769): 146–149
Gentleman's Magazine 39 (1769): 150–152
London Magazine 38 (1769): 41–42
Critical Memoirs 1 (1769): 149–152
Political Register 4 (1769): 389

1551 [LANGHORNE, John]. *Genius and Valour: a Scotch Pastoral*. London, 1763 (4to. 1s.6d. Becket and DeHondt) UNIVERSITY OF PENNSYLVANIA

Reviewed: *Monthly Review* 28 (1763): 398–399
Critical Review 15 (1763): 392–393

1552 LANGHORNE, J[ohn]. *A Hymn to Hope*. London, 1761 (4to. 6d. Griffiths) BRITISH LIBRARY

Reviewed: *Monthly Review* 25 (1761): 150–151
Critical Review 11 (1761): 420

1553 [LANGHORNE, John]. *Letters Supposed to have passed between M. De St. Evremond and Mr. Waller. Collected and published By the Editor of the Letters between Theodosius and Constantia*. 2 vols. London, 1769 (12mo. 5s.sewed. Becket and Co. 1769) BRITISH LIBRARY

Reviewed: *Monthly Review* 41 (1769): 304–309
Critical Review 28 (1769): 110–115
London Magazine 38 (1769): 437–438
Town & Country Magazine [1] (1769): 435

1554 [LANGHORNE, John]. *The Letters that passed between Theodosius and Constantia; after she had taken the Veil. Now first published from the Original Manuscripts*. London, 1763 (Small 8vo. 2s.6d. Becket and DeHondt) BRITISH LIBRARY

Reviewed: *Monthly Review* 29 (1763): 147–153
Critical Review 16 (1763): 11–16

1555 [LANGHORNE, John]. *The Letters that passed between Theodosius and Constantia; after She had Taken the Veil. The second Edition*. London, 1764 (12mo. 2s.sewed. Becket and DeHondt) BRITISH LIBRARY

Reviewed: *Monthly Review* 29 (1763): 477
Critical Review 17 (1764): 80

1556 [LANGHORNE, John]. *Letters to Eleonora*. 2 vols. NOT SEEN (12mo. 5s.sewed. Bladon)

Reviewed: *Monthly Review* 45 (1771): 73
Critical Review 32 (1771): 230–231

1557 LANGHORNE, [John]. *The Origin of the Veil. A Poem*. London, 1773 (4to. 1s. Becket. 1773) BRITISH LIBRARY

Reviewed: *Monthly Review* 48 (1773): 69–70
Critical Review 35 (1773): 70
London Magazine 42 (1773): 41
Universal Catalogue [2] (1773) art. 80

1558 LANGHORNE, John. *The Poetical Works of John Langhorne. In Two Volumes*. London, 1766 (8vo. 6s. Becket and DeHondt) BRITISH LIBRARY

Reviewed: *Monthly Review* 35 (1766): 76
Critical Review 22 (1766): 291–299

1559 LANGHORNE, John. *Precepts of Conjugal Happiness. Addressed to a Lady on her Mar-*

riage. London, 1767 (4to. 1s. Becket) BRITISH LIBRARY

Reviewed: *Monthly Review* 38 (1768): 406–407
Critical Review 25 (1768): 230–231
London Magazine 37 (1768): 221
Political Register 2 (1768): 384

1560 [LANGHORNE, John]. *Solyman and Almena*. London, 1762 (12mo. 3s. Payne) NEWBERRY

Reviewed: *Monthly Review* 26 (1762): 254–264
Critical Review 13 (1762): 148–154
London Magazine 31 (1762): 112
British Magazine 3 (1762): 158

1561 LANGHORNE, J[ohn]. *The Tears of Music. A Poem, to the Memory of Mr. Handel. With an Ode to the River Eden*. London, 1760 (4to. 1s. Griffiths) BRITISH LIBRARY

Reviewed: *Monthly Review* 22 (1760): 261–262
Critical Review 9 (1760): 323–324
British Magazine 1 (1760): 324 [140]

1562 [LANGHORNE, John]. *Verses in Memory of a Lady. Written at Sandgate Castle, MDCCLXVIII*. London, 1768 (4to. 6d. Becket) BRITISH LIBRARY

Reviewed: *Monthly Review* 39 (1768): 489–490
Critical Review 26 (1768): 471–472
Gentleman's Magazine 39 (1769): 100–101
London Magazine 37 (1768): 666
Universal Museum 4 (1768): 652

1563 [LANGHORNE, John]. *The Viceroy: A Poem. Addressed to the Earl of Halifax*. London, 1762 (4to. 5s. Payne) BRITISH LIBRARY

Reviewed: *Monthly Review* 27 (1762): 75
Critical Review 13 (1762): 499–500
British Magazine 3 (1762): 382

1564 LANGHORNE, J[ohn]. *The Visions of Fancy. In Four Elegies*. London, 1762 (8vo. 1s. Payne and Cropley) BRITISH LIBRARY

Reviewed: *Monthly Review* 27 (1762): 394
Critical Review 14 (1762): 480

1565 LANGHORNE, William. *Job. A Poem. In Three Books*. London, 1760 (4to. 2s.6d. Griffiths) BRITISH LIBRARY

Reviewed: *Monthly Review* 22 (1760): 242–246
Critical Review 9 (1760): 150–151

1566 LANGHORNE, William. *A Poetical Paraphrase On Part of the Book of Isaiah*. London, 1761 (4to. 2s.6d. Griffiths) BRITISH LIBRARY

Reviewed: *Monthly Review* 25 (1761): 146–149
Critical Review 11 (1761): 456–469
British Magazine 2 (1761): 382

1567 LANGLEY, Samuel. *The Iliad of Homer, Translated from the Greek into Blank Verse. With Notes, Pointing out the peculiar Beauties of the Original, and the Imitations of it by succeeding Poets. With Remarks on Mr. Pope's admired Version. Being a Specimen of the Whole, which is to follow*. London, 1767 (4to. 3s. Dodsley) BRITISH LIBRARY

Reviewed: *Monthly Review* 36 (1767): 163
Critical Review 23 (1767): 36–41

The Lap-Dog or, Truth in a Fable
See: JUSTITIA (pseud.)

1568 [LA ROCHE-GUILHEM, Anne de]. *The History of Female Favourites. Of Mary de Padilla, under Peter the Cruel, King of Castile; Livia, under the Emperor Augustus; Julia Farnesa, under Pope Alexander the Sixth; Agnes Soreau, under Charles VII. King of France; and Nantilda, under Dagobert, King of France*. London, 1772 (8vo. 5s. bound. Parker. 1772) BRITISH LIBRARY

Reviewed: *Monthly Review* 46 (1772): 265
Critical Review 33 (1772): 218–221
London Magazine 41 (1772): 88
British Magazine & General Review 1 (1772): 455
Universal Catalogue [1] (1772) art. 234

1569 *The late Administration Epitomized; an Epistle in Verse To the Right Honourable William Pitt, Esq*. London, 1763 (4to. 1s. Bathoe) NEW YORK PUBLIC LIBRARY

Reviewed: *Monthly Review* 28 (1763): 320
Critical Review 15 (1763): 69–70

Il Latte. An Elegy
See: JERNINGHAM, Edward

1570 [LATTER, Mary]. *Liberty and Interest. A Burlesque Poem on the Present Times.* London, 1764 (4to. 1s. Fletcher) BRITISH LIBRARY

Reviewed: *Monthly Review* 30 (1764): 69
Critical Review 17 (1764): 76

1571 LATTER, [Mary]. *A Miscellaneous Poetical Essay; In Three Parts: Part I. Authors considered: Pope, Swift, Milton, Dryden, Butler, &c. Part II. Content, a Vision. Part III. The Vision continued; Contemplation. By Mrs Latter of Reading.* [Title given incorrectly in *Monthly Review* as *Poems, by Mrs. Latter of Reading.*] London, 1761 (8vo. 1s. Sandby) LIBRARY OF CONGRESS

Reviewed: *Monthly Review* 24 (1761): 444

1572 LATTER, Mary. *The Miscellaneous Works, in Prose and Verse, of Mrs. Mary Latter, Of Reading, Berks. In Three Parts.* Reading, 1759 (8vo. 3s.sewed. Wilkie) BRITISH LIBRARY

Reviewed: *Monthly Review* 21 (1759): 82
Critical Review 8 (1759): 171

LATTER, Mary. *Poems by Mrs. Latter of Reading*
See: LATTER, Mary. *A Miscellaneous Poetical Essay*

1573 LATTER, [Mary]. *Pro & Con; or, The Opinionists: An Ancient Fragment. Published for the Amusement of the Curious in Antiquity.* London, 1771 (12mo. 2s. Lowndes) BRITISH LIBRARY

Reviewed: *Monthly Review* 45 (1771): 156
Critical Review 32 (1771): 240
London Magazine 40 (1771): 463

The Laureat. A Poem
See: GREENE, Edward Burnaby

1574 *The Laurel: Containing Various Branches of Poetry.* London, n.d. [ESTC-1750?] (8vo. 2s. Woodfall) BRITISH LIBRARY

Reviewed: *Monthly Review* 4 (1750–51): 376

1575 [LAWRENCE, Herbert]. *The Contemplative Man, or the History of Christopher Crab, Esq; of North Wales.* 2 vols. London, 1771 (12mo. 5s.sewed. Whiston. 1771) BRITISH LIBRARY

Reviewed: *Monthly Review* 46 (1772): 263–264
Critical Review 32 (1771): 448–453
Town & Country Magazine 4 (1772): 45

1576 [LAWRENCE, Herbert]. *The Life and Adventures of Common Sense: An Historical Allegory.* London, 1769 (12mo. 2s.6d. Lawrence) BRITISH LIBRARY

Reviewed: *Monthly Review* 40 (1769): 344
Critical Review 27 (1769): 217–219
Critical Memoirs 1 (1769): 527
Town & Country Magazine [1] (1769): 157

1577 [LAWRENCE, Herbert]. *The Life and Adventures of Common Sense: An Historical Allegory. Vol. II.* London, 1769 (8vo. 2s.6d. Lawrence. 1769) BODLEIAN

Reviewed: *Monthly Review* 42 (1770): 135–142

1578 LAYARD, Charles Peter. *Charity: A Poetical Essay.* Cambridge, 1773 (Cambridge printed, and sold by Beecroft, &c. in London. 1773) BRITISH LIBRARY

Reviewed: *Monthly Review* 50 (1774): 70
Critical Review 36 (1773): 475
Town & Country Magazine 6 (1774): 45
Universal Catalogue [2] (1773) art. 1306

1579 LAZARUS (pseud.). *An irregular Pindaric Ode, to his Majesty's Ship Deptford; occasioned by her bringing home his Excellency the brave Gen. Blakeney. By Lazarus, one of the correspondents of the Westminster Journal* NOT SEEN (4to. 6d. Mechell)

Reviewed: *Monthly Review* 16 (1757): 286
Critical Review 3 (1757): 288

1580 LEA, Charles Augustine. *Eliza to Comus. An Epistle. In Imitation of Mr. Pope's Eloisa to Abelard.* London, 1753 (4to. 6d. Bouquet) BRITISH LIBRARY

Reviewed: *Monthly Review* 8 (1753): 151

1581 LEAPOR, [Mary]. *Poems upon several Occasions. By Mrs. Leapor of Brackley in Northamptonshire.* London, 1748 (8vo. 5s. Published for the Benefit of the Author's Father. Sold by

J. Roberts in Warwick Lane) BRITISH LIBRARY

Reviewed: *Monthly Review* 2 (1749–50): 14–25

1582 LEAPOR, [Mary]. *Poems upon Several Occasions. By the late Mrs Leapor, of Brackley in Northamptonshire. The Second and Last Volume.* London, 1751 (8vo. 5s. Roberts) BRITISH LIBRARY

Reviewed: *Monthly Review* 5 (1751): 23–32

LE BOVIER DE FONTANELLE, Bernard (adaptation)
See: WHITEHEAD, William. *The School for Lovers*

1583 [LECHMERE, Edward]. *Poems and Translations, by A Young Gentleman of Oxford.* London, 1770 (4to. 2s. Robinson and Roberts. 1770) BRITISH LIBRARY

Reviewed: *Monthly Review* 43 (1770): 152–153
Critical Review 29 (1770): 446–449
Town & Country Magazine 2 (1770): 324

1584 LEE, Francis Bacon. *The Debauchee, a Poem, In Six Cantos. With An Elegy On the Death of a Libertine.* London, n.d. (4to. 2s. Cooke) NEW YORK PUBLIC LIBRARY

Reviewed: *Monthly Review* 45 (1771): 235
Critical Review 32 (1771): 152
Gentleman's Magazine 41 (1771): 370
London Magazine 40 (1771): 414
Town & Country Magazine 3 (1771): 437

1585 [LEE, John]. *The Country Wife, a Comedy in Two Acts. As it is performed at the Theatre-Royal in Drury-Lane. (Altered from Wycherley).* London, n.d. [ESTC-1765] (8vo. 1s. For the Editor.) BRITISH LIBRARY

Reviewed: *Monthly Review* 32 (1765): 479
Critical Review 19 (1765): 480
Candid Review 1 (1765): 368

1586 [LELAND, Thomas]. *Longsword, Earl of Salisbury. An Historical Romance.* 2 vols. London, 1762 (12mo. 6s.bound. Johnston) BRITISH LIBRARY

Reviewed: *Monthly Review* 26 (1762): 236–237
Critical Review 13 (1762): 252–257

1587 LEMAISTRE, Stephen Caesar. *Spring. An Ode to Nerissa*
NOT SEEN (Fol. 6d. Cooper)

Reviewed: *Monthly Review* 15 (1756): 201–202

1588 [LENNOX, Charlotte]. *The Female Quixote; or, the Adventures of Arabella.* 2 vols. London, 1752 (12mo. 6s. Millar) BRITISH LIBRARY

Reviewed: *Monthly Review* 6 (1752): 249–262
Gentleman's Magazine 22 (1752): 146

1589 [LENNOX, Charlotte]. *Henrietta. By the Author of the Female Quixote.* 2 vols. London, 1758 (12mo. 6s. Millar) BRITISH LIBRARY

Reviewed: *Monthly Review* 18 (1758): 273
Critical Review 5 (1758): 122–130

1590 [LENNOX, Charlotte]. *The Life of Harriot Stuart. Written by Herself.* 2 vols. London, 1751 (12mo. 5s. Payne and Bouquet) BRITISH LIBRARY

Reviewed: *Monthly Review* 4 (1750–51): 160
Gentleman's Magazine 20 (1750): 575

1591 [LENNOX, Charlotte (trans.)]. *The Memoirs of the Countess of Berci. Taken from the French By the Author of the Female Quixote.* 2 vols. London, 1756 (12mo. 6s. Millar) BRITISH LIBRARY

Reviewed: *Monthly Review* 14 (1756): 516–520
Critical Review 1 (1756): 312–314

1592 [LENNOX, Charlotte]. *Philander. A Dramatic Pastoral. By the Author of the Female Quixote.* London, 1758 (8vo. 1s. Millar) BRITISH LIBRARY

Reviewed: *Monthly Review* 17 (1757): 568
Critical Review 4 (1757): 468

1593 [LENNOX, Charlotte]. *Shakespear Illustrated: or the Novels and Histories, On which the Plays of Shakespear Are Founded, Collected and Translated from the Original Authors. With Critical Remarks. By the Author of the Female Quixote.* 2 vols. London, 1753 (12mo. 6s. Millar) BRITISH LIBRARY

Reviewed: *Monthly Review* 9 (1753): 145
Gentleman's Magazine 23 (1753): 250

1594 [LENNOX, Charlotte]. *Shakespear Illustrated: or the Novels and Histories, On which the Plays of Shakespear Are Founded, Collected and Translated from the Original Authors. With Critical Remarks. The Third and Last Volume. By the Author of the Female Quixote.* London, 1754 (12mo. 3s. Millar) BRITISH LIBRARY

Reviewed: *Monthly Review* 10 (1754): 309
Gentleman's Magazine 24 (1754): 99

1595 LENNOX, Charlotte. *The Sister: A Comedy.* London, 1769 (8vo. 1s.6d. Dodsley, &c. 1769) BRITISH LIBRARY

Reviewed: *Monthly Review* 40 (1769): 245–249
Critical Review 27 (1769): 223–224
Gentleman's Magazine 39 (1769): 157 and 199–200
Critical Memoirs 1 (1769): 326–328 and 522
Town & Country Magazine [1] (1769): 157

1596 LENNOX, Charlotte. *Sophia.* 2 vols. London, 1762 (12mo. 6s. Fletcher) BRITISH LIBRARY

Reviewed: *Monthly Review* 27 (1762): 73–74
Critical Review 13 (1762): 434–435
Gentleman's Magazine 32 (1762): 295
British Magazine 3 (1762): 324

Leonidas. A Poem
See: GLOVER, Richard

1597 LE PRINCE DE BEAUMONT, Jeanne Marie. *Letters from Emerance to Lucy. Translated from the French of Madame Le Prince de Beaumont.* 2 vols. London, 1766 (12mo. 5s. Nourse) BRITISH LIBRARY

Reviewed: *Monthly Review* 35 (1766): 147
Critical Review 21 (1766): 432–438

1598 LE PRINCE DE BEAUMONT, Jeanne Marie. *The New Clarissa: a True History.* 2 vols. London, 1768 (12mo. 6s. Nourse) BRITISH LIBRARY

Reviewed: *Monthly Review* 39 (1768): 82–83
Critical Review 26 (1768): 355–359
London Magazine 37 (1768): 276
Universal Museum 4 (1768): 429

1599 LE PRINCE DE BEAUMONT, Jeanne Marie. *The Virtuous Widow: or, Memoirs of the Baroness de Batteville. Translated from the French of Madame Le Prince De Beaumont.* London ed. reviewed; copy seen: Dublin, 1767 (12mo. 3s. Nourse) BRITISH LIBRARY

Reviewed: *Monthly Review* 35 (1766): 27–30
Critical Review 21 (1766): 438–439

LE SAGE, Alain René (adaptation)
See: GARRICK, David. *Neck or Nothing*

1600 *Lesbia: A Tale. In Two Cantos.* London, 1756 (4to. 6d. Withy) BRITISH LIBRARY

Reviewed: *Monthly Review* 14 (1756): 575

1601 LESLIE, John. *Killarney: a Poem.* London, 1772 (4to. 6s.boards. Robinson. 1772) BRITISH LIBRARY

Reviewed: *Monthly Review* 47 (1772): 216–218
Critical Review 33 (1772): 328
Universal Catalogue [1] (1772) art. 603

1602 LESLIE, John. *Phoenix Park: a Poem. By the Author of Killarney.* London, 1772 (4to. 2s. Robinson. 1772) BRITISH LIBRARY

Reviewed: *Monthly Review* 48 (1773): 160
Critical Review 35 (1773): 158
Town & Country Magazine 5 (1773): 210
Universal Catalogue [2] (1773) art. 118

1603 [LESUIRE, Robert Martin, and ––– LOUVEL]. *The Savages of Europe. From the French.* London, 1764 (12mo. 2s. Davies) BRITISH LIBRARY

Reviewed: *Monthly Review* 30 (1764): 330–331
Critical Review 17 (1764): 267–271
General Magazine 1 (1764): 144–146

1604 [LETCHWORTH, Thomas]. *Miscellaneous Reflections: or, An Evening's Meditation. A Poem. Addressed to the Youth. By T. L.* London, 1765 (4to. 1s. Richardson and Urquhart) BRITISH LIBRARY

Reviewed: *Monthly Review* 32 (1765): 75
Critical Review 18 (1764): 474

1605 [LETCHWORTH, Thomas]. *A Morning's Meditation, or, a Descant on the Times. A*

Poem. By T. L. London, 1765 (4to. 1s.6d. Richardson and Urquhart) BRITISH LIBRARY

Reviewed: *Monthly Review* 32 (1765): 479
Critical Review 19 (1765): 313
Candid Review 1 (1765): 275–276

A Letter from a Gentleman in London to his friend in Pennsylvania
See: SMITH, William

A Letter from a Right Honourable Person
See: FRANCIS, Philip

1606 *A Letter from Alma Mater to her beloved Son Jemmy Twitcher*
NOT SEEN (4to. 1s. Pottinger)

Reviewed: *Critical Review* 17 (1764): 237

1607 *A Letter of Expostulation from the Manager of the Theatre in Tottenham-Court, to the Manager of the Theatre in the Hay-Market. Relative to A New Comedy, called the Minor.* London, n.d. [ESTC-1760] (Fol. 1s. Stevens) BRITISH LIBRARY

Reviewed: *Monthly Review* 23 (1760): 246–247
Critical Review 10 (1760): 238

A Letter to a Friend in Italy
See: CLARKE, Edward

1608 *Letters between An English Lady and Her Friend at Paris. In which are contained The Memoirs of Mrs. Williams. By a Lady. In Two Volumes.* London, 1770 (12mo. 5s.sewed. Becket) YALE (STERLING)

Reviewed: *Monthly Review* 42 (1770): 330
Critical Review 29 (1770): 294–299
London Magazine 39 (1770): 211
Town & Country Magazine 2 (1770): 214

Letters between Emilia and Harriet
See: COOPER, Maria Susanna

Letters between Henry and Frances
See: GRIFFITH, Elizabeth and Richard. *A Series of Genuine Letters between Henry and Frances*

Letters from Altamont in the Capital
See: JENNER, Charles

1609 *Letters from Clara; or, the Effusions of the Heart.* 2 vols.
NOT SEEN (12mo. 5s.sewed. Wilkie)

Reviewed: *Monthly Review* 44 (1771): 418
Critical Review 31 (1771): 484
London Magazine 40 (1771): 226
Town & Country Magazine 3 (1771): 213

1610 *Letters from Julia, the Daughter of Augustus, to Ovid. A manuscript discovered at Herculaneum. Translated from the original. To which is annexed, The Lady and the Sylph, a visionary tale*
NOT SEEN (12mo. 2s. L. Davis)

Reviewed: *Monthly Review* 9 (1753): 145

Letters from Lothario to Penelope
See: JENNER, Charles

1611 *Letters from Sophia to Mira: containing the Adventures of a Lady; in which The several Situations, most common in Female Life, are naturally described.* London, 1763 (12mo. 3s. Dodsley) BRITISH LIBRARY

Reviewed: *Monthly Review* 27 (1762): 472–473
Critical Review 15 (1763): 77

Letters Supposed to have passed between M. de St. Evremond and Mr. Waller
See: LANGHORNE, John

The Letters that passed between Theodosius and Constantia
See: LANGHORNE, John

Letters to Eleonora
See: LANGHORNE, John

1612 LETTICE, John. *The Conversion of St. Paul: A Poetical Essay.* Cambridge, 1765 (4to. 1s. Whiston and White) BRITISH LIBRARY

Reviewed: *Monthly Review* 32 (1765): 146–148
Critical Review 19 (1765): 73–74
Candid Review 1 (1765): 39

1613 [LETTICE, John]. *Love Elegies.* London, 1760 (4to. 1s. Dodsley) BRITISH LIBRARY

Reviewed: *Monthly Review* 23 (1760): 167–168
Critical Review 10 (1760): 245–246
British Magazine 1 (1760): 602

Leucothoe. A Dramatic Poem
See: BICKERSTAFFE, Isaac

1614 *The Levee: a Poem. Occasion'd by the Number of Clergy at the Duke of N----le's last Levee.* London, 1756 (Fol. 6d. Cooper) BRITISH LIBRARY

Reviewed: *Monthly Review* 15 (1756): 654–655
Critical Review 2 (1756): 479–480

1615 LEWIS, Edward. *The Italian Husband: or, the Violated Bed Avenged. A Moral Drama.* London, 1754 (8vo. 1s. Cooper) BRITISH LIBRARY

Reviewed: *Monthly Review* 11 (1754): 398–399

1616 LEWIS, Richard. *The Robin-Hood Society: a Satire. With Notes Variorum. By Peter Pounce, Esq;* London, 1756 (8vo. 2s. Withers) BRITISH LIBRARY

Reviewed: *Monthly Review* 15 (1756): 86–88
Critical Review 2 (1756): 286–287

1617 [LEWIS, Richard]. *The Spouting-Club. A mock heroic, comico, farcico, tragico, burlesque poem. By the Author of the Robin Hood Society, a Satire*
NOT SEEN (8vo. 6d. Withy)

Reviewed: *Monthly Review* 19 (1758): 589

1618 LEWIS, R[obert]. *The Adventures of a Rake. In the Character of a Public Orator. Interspersed with several Serious and Comic Pieces, pronounced before some polite Audiences with great Applause, and published at their request.* 2 vols. London, 1759 (12mo. 6s. Withy, &c.) BODLEIAN

Reviewed: *Monthly Review* 21 (1759): 451
Critical Review 8 (1759): 408–409
London Magazine 28 (1759): 632

1619 LEWIS, Will[iam] Lillington. *The Thebaid of Statius, translated into English Verse, with Notes and Observations; and a Dissertation upon the whole by Way of Preface.* Oxford, 1767 (8vo. 10s. Fletcher) BODLEIAN

Reviewed: *Monthly Review* 37 (1767): 175–185
Critical Review 23 (1767): 360–368
Political Register 1 (1767): 485

1620 *The Liar, a Comedy. In Three Acts.* London, 1763 (8vo. 1s. Cooke) LIBRARY OF CONGRESS

Reviewed: *Monthly Review* 29 (1763): 464

1621 *The Libertine Husband Reclaimed; and Virtuous Love Rewarded.* 2 vols. London, 1774 (12mo. 5s.sewed. Bew) BRITISH LIBRARY

Reviewed: *Monthly Review* 52 (1775): 360–361
Critical Review 38 (1774): 455–460

1622 *Liberty. A Poem*
NOT SEEN (4to. 1s. Hood)

Reviewed: *Critical Review* 16 (1763): 240

1623 *Liberty, a Poem. Inscribed to John Wilkes, Esq;*
NOT SEEN (4to. 1s. Flexney)

Reviewed: *Monthly Review* 39 (1768): 316
Critical Review 26 (1768): 69
London Magazine 37 (1768): 445
Universal Museum 4 (1768): 372
Political Register 3 (1768): 128

Liberty and Interest
See: LATTER, Mary

1624 *Liberty Deposed, or the Western Election. A Satirical Poem. In Three Books.* London, n.d. [ESTC-1770?] (8vo. 1s.6d. Alman) BRITISH LIBRARY

Reviewed: *Monthly Review* 38 (1768): 334
Critical Review 25 (1768): 227
Universal Museum 4 (1768): 148

1625 *Liberty Regain'd: Set forth in the Remarkable Life and Actions of W**** S****, Written by Himself. With the Particulars of his being transported from Liverpool, in Lancashire, (into the West Indies) for five Years; his Return to England, in November last; and a remarkable Account of his Transactions, Intrigues, &c. from fifteen Years of Age. Being A proper Warn-*

ing for Youth to follow the Steps of Virtue, whilst Young, and to shun Bad Company, Loose and Inordinate Desires, of Sinful and Forbidden Pleasures. London, 1755 (8vo. 6d. Crowder and Co.) BRITISH LIBRARY

Reviewed: *Monthly Review* 12 (1755): 80

The Library: An Epistle From a Bookseller
See: MARSH, Charles

1626 *A Lick at the Country C-----y. A Satire on the Tythe-Pig*. London, 1752 (4to. 6d. Dickinson) BRITISH LIBRARY

Reviewed: *Monthly Review* 6 (1752): 239

1627 *The Life, Adventures and Amours, of Sir R-- P---, who so recently had the honour to present the F--- Address at the English Court*. London, 1770 (8vo. 1s.6d. Brough) BRITISH LIBRARY

Reviewed: *Monthly Review* 42 (1770): 251
Town & Country Magazine 2 (1770): 120

1628 *The Life, Adventures, Intrigues, and Amours of the celebrated Jemmy Twitcher. Exhibiting Many Striking Proofs To what Baseness the Human Heart is capable of Descending. The whole Faithfully compiled from Authentick Materials*. London, n.d. [ESTC-1770?] (8vo. pamphlet. 2s. Brough) BRITISH LIBRARY

Reviewed: *Monthly Review* 43 (1770): 151–152
London Magazine 39 (1770): 481
Town & Country Magazine 2 (1770): 491

The Life and Actions of Jesus Christ
See: RYLAND, John Collett

1629 *The Life and Adventures of a Cat*. London, 1760 (12mo. 2s.6d.bound. Minors) BRITISH LIBRARY

Reviewed: *Monthly Review* 22 (1760): 435–436
Critical Review 9 (1760): 420
London Magazine 29 (1760): 224

1630 *The Life and Adventures of a Reformed Magdalen. In a Series of Letters to Mrs. B***, of Northampton. Written by Herself*. 2 vols. London, 1763 (12mo. 5s. Nicholl) BRITISH LIBRARY

Reviewed: *Monthly Review* 30 (1764): 77
Critical Review 17 (1764): 36–37

1631 *The Life and Adventures of an Animal: Or, the secret History of the Count de M---p---n; with his Politica and Intrigues in France, Germany, Holland, Spain, and particularly England; in which last Country he passed the most agreeable, and the greatest Part of his Days. Wherein are introduced several modern Characters, never before delineated*
NOT SEEN (12mo. 2s.)

Reviewed: *Critical Review* 11 (1761): 78
London Magazine 29 (1760): 672
British Magazine 2 (1761): 98

The Life and Adventures of Benjamin Brass
See: OAKMAN, John

The Life and Adventures of Christopher Wagstaffe
See: *The Life, Travels, and Adventures, of Christopher Wagstaffe*

The Life and Adventures of Common Sense
See: LAWRENCE, Herbert

The Life and Adventures of James Ramble
See: KIMBER, Edward

The Life and Adventures of Joe Thompson
See: KIMBER, Edward

The Life and Adventures of Mademoiselle de la Sarre
See: CROWLEY, Thomas

The Life and Adventures of Mr. Francis Clive
See: GIBBES, Phebe

The Life and Adventures of Peter Wilkins
See: PALTOCK, Robert

The Life and Adventures of Sir Bartholomew Sapskull
See: DONALDSON, William

The Life and Amours of Count de Turenne
See: BOYER, Jean Baptiste de, Marquis d'Argens

1632 *The Life and Amours of Hafen Slawkenbergius; Author of the Institute of Noses. Compiled from authentic Materials, communicated to the Editor, by the learned Mr. Heydegger, of Strasburg*
NOT SEEN (8vo. 1s. Flexney)

Reviewed: *Monthly Review* 25 (1761): 503
Critical Review 13 (1762): 76
London Magazine 31 (1762): 56
British Magazine 3 (1762): 102

The Life and extraordinary Adventures, the Perils and Critical Escapes of Timothy Ginnadrake
See: FLEMING, Francis

The Life and Heroic Actions of Balbe Berton
See: LUSSAN, Marguerite de

The Life and History of a Pilgrim
See: WOLLASTON, George

1633 *The Life and Memoirs of Mr. Ephraim Tristram Bates, commonly called Corporal Bates, A broken-hearted Soldier: who, From a private Centinel in the Guards, was, from his Merits, advanced, regularly, to be Corporal, Serjeant, and Paymaster Serjeant; and had he lived a few Days longer, might have died a Commission-Officer, to the great Loss of his lamentable Lady, whose Marriage he had intended to declare as soon as his Commission was signed; and who, to make up for the Loss of so dear an Husband, and her Pension, which then no Duke on Earth could have hindered, in order to put Bread into the Mouths of seven small Children, the youngest now at her breast, the sweet Creatures being two Twins, publishes these Memoirs from the Original Papers, sealed up with the Seal of dear Mr. Bates, and found, exactly as he mentioned in his last Will and Testament, in an Oven, never used, where, in his Life time, he secreted many State Papers, &c. &c. &c.* London, 1756 (12mo. 3s. Owen) BRITISH LIBRARY

Reviewed: *Monthly Review* 15 (1756): 426–427
Critical Review 2 (1756): 138–143

1634 *The Life and Opinions of Bertram Montfichet, Esq; Written by Himself.* 2 vols. London, n.d. [ESTC-1761?] (8vo. 5s. Seyffert) BRITISH LIBRARY

Reviewed: *Monthly Review* 24 (1761): 276
Critical Review 11 (1761): 393–395
London Magazine 30 (1761): 168
British Magazine 2 (1761): 161

1635 *The Life and Opinions of Jeremiah Kunastrokius, Doctor of Physick, &c.*
NOT SEEN (12mo. 2s.6d. Cabe)

Reviewed: *Critical Review* 10 (1760): 79
British Magazine 1 (1760): 433

1636 *The Life and Opinions of Miss Sukey Shandy, of Bow-Street, Gentlewoman. In a Series of Letters To her Dear Brother Tristram Shandy, Gent.* London, 1760 (12mo. 2s. Stevens) HARVARD (HOUGHTON)

Reviewed: *Monthly Review* 23 (1760): 83
Critical Review 10 (1760): 72
London Magazine 29 (1760): 328

The Life and Opinions of Tristram Shandy
See: STERNE, Laurence

The Life and Opinions of Tristram Shandy (spurious vol. 3)
See: CARR, John

1637 *The Life and Opinions of Tristram Shandy, Gent. Vol. IX.* [Spurious; not by Sterne]
NOT SEEN (8vo. 2s.6d. Durham)

Reviewed: *Monthly Review* 34 (1766): 168
Critical Review 21 (1766): 141

1638 *The Life and Real Adventures of Hamilton Murray. Written by himself.* 3 vols. London, 1759 (12mo. 9s. Burd) BRITISH LIBRARY

Reviewed: *Monthly Review* 20 (1759): 188
Critical Review 7 (1759): 282–283

1639 *The life and surprizing Adventures of Crusoe Richard Davis.* 2 vols.
NOT SEEN (12mo. 6s. bound. Noble)

Reviewed: *Monthly Review* 15 (1756): 656
Critical Review 2 (1756): 351–357

1640 *The Life and surprising Adventures of Don Antonio de Trezanio, who was self-educated,*

and lived forty-five Years on an uninhabited Island in the East Indies
NOT SEEN (12mo. 2s.6d. Serjeant)

Reviewed: *Monthly Review* 25 (1761): 472
Critical Review 13 (1762): 168

The Life, extraordinary Adventures, Voyages, and surprizing Escapes of Capt. Neville Frowde
See: KIMBER, Edward

The Life of Harriot Stuart
See: LENNOX, Charlotte

The Life of John Buncle, Esq;
See: AMORY, Thomas

The Life of Lamenther
See: WALL, Anne

1641 *The Life of Patty Saunders. Written by Herself.* London, 1752 (12mo. 3s. Owen) CAMBRIDGE

Reviewed: *Monthly Review* 6 (1752): 77

1642 *The Life, Opinions and Sentimental Journal of George Noel*
NOT SEEN (12mo. 1s. Woodgate)

Reviewed: *Gentleman's Magazine* 39 (1769): 454

1643 *The Life, Travels, and Adventures, of Christopher Wagstaff, Gentleman, Grandfather to Tristram Shandy. Originally published In the latter End of the last Century. Interspersed with A suitable Variety of Matter, By the Editor. The whole being intended as a full and final Answer to every thing that has been, or shall be, written in the out-of-the-way Way.* 2 vols. London, 1762 (12mo. 6s. Hinxman) BRITISH LIBRARY

Reviewed: *Monthly Review* 26 (1762): 474
Critical Review 13 (1762): 519
British Magazine 3 (1762): 382

1644 *Light Summer Reading for Ladies: or, the History of Lady Lucy Fenton.* 3 vols.
NOT SEEN (Small 8vo. 7s.6d. Robinson and Roberts)

Reviewed: *Monthly Review* 39 (1768): 82
Critical Review 25 (1768): 462–466

London Magazine 37 (1768): 276
Universal Museum 4 (1768): 259

Lilliput. A Dramatic Entertainment
See: GARRICK, David

1645 LILLO, George. *Arden of Feversham. An historical Tragedy: taken from Holingshead's Chronicle, In the Reign of King Edward VI. Acted at the Theatre-Royal, in Drury-Lane. By the late Mr. Lillo.* London, 1762 (8vo. 1s.6d. Printed for Stephen Doorne, at Feversham; and sold in London by Hawes and Co. 1770) BODLEIAN

Reviewed: *Monthly Review* 27 (1762): 473–474
Critical Review 15 (1763): 133–139
British Magazine 4 (1763): 158

1646 LILLO, George. *The Works of Mr. George Lillo; with Some Account Of His Life.* 2 vols. London, 1775 (8vo. 6s.boards. Davies) BRITISH LIBRARY

Reviewed: *Monthly Review* 52 (1775): 54–57
Critical Review 38 (1774): 477–479
London Magazine 44 (1775): 91

1647 *The Lion, the Leopard, and the Badgers. A Fable*
NOT SEEN (4to. 6d. Cooper)

Reviewed: *Monthly Review* 15 (1756): 424–425

Lionel and Clarissa
See: BICKERSTAFFE, Isaac

1648 *Lisbon restored, a Vision. (On the First of November, 1756) Addressed to the Sons of Commerce, With an Ode to Britannia, Found among the Papers of a Portuguese Gentleman lately Deceased.* London, 1757 (4to. 6d. Reeve) BRITISH LIBRARY

Reviewed: *Monthly Review* 16 (1757): 463
Critical Review 3 (1757): 472

The Lives of Cleopatra and Octavia
See: FIELDING, Sarah

1649 LLOYD, E[van]. *Conversation. A Poem.* London, 1767 (4to. 2s.6d. Richardson and Urquhart) BRITISH LIBRARY

Reviewed: *Monthly Review* 37 (1767): 394
Critical Review 24 (1767): 341–344
Gentleman's Magazine 38 (1768): 28
Universal Museum 3 (1767): 596
Political Register 1 (1767): 484

1650 LLOYD, E[van]. *The Curate. A Poem. Inscribed to all the Curates in England and Wales. By E. Lloyd Author of the Powers of the Pen.* London, 1766 (4to. 2s.6d. Richardson and Urquhart) BRITISH LIBRARY

Reviewed: *Monthly Review* 34 (1766): 405–406
Critical Review 21 (1766): 316
Gentleman's Magazine 36 (1766): 191

1651 LLOYD, Evan. *An Epistle to David Garrick, Esq.* London, 1773 (4to. 2s. Richardson and Urquhart. 1773) BRITISH LIBRARY

Reviewed: *Monthly Review* 48 (1773): 70
Critical Review 35 (1773): 70–71
London Magazine 42 (1773): 41
Universal Catalogue [2] (1773) art. 105

1652 LLOYD, E[van]. *The Methodist. A Poem. By E. Lloyd, Author of the Powers of the Pen, and the Curate.* London, 1768 (4to. 2s.6d. Urquhart) BRITISH LIBRARY

Reviewed: *Monthly Review* 35 (1766): 319–321
Critical Review 22 (1766): 75–77
Gentleman's Magazine 36 (1766): 335

1653 [LLOYD, Evan]. *The Powers of the Pen. Addressed to John Curre, Esqr.* London, 1766 (4to. 2s. Richardson) BRITISH LIBRARY

Reviewed: *Monthly Review* 34 (1766): 165
Critical Review 21 (1766): 153–154
Gentleman's Magazine 36 (1766): 37

1654 LLOYD, E[van]. *The Powers of the Pen. A Poem. Addressed to John Curre, Esq. By E. Lloyd, M.A. The Second Edition, With Large Additions.* London, 1768 (4to. 2s.6d. Richardson and Urquhart) FOLGER

Reviewed: *Critical Review* 26 (1768): 314

1655 [LLOYD, Robert]. *The Actor, a Poetical Epistle to Bonnell Thornton, Esq;* London, 1760 (4to. 1s. Dodsley) BRITISH LIBRARY

Reviewed: *Monthly Review* 22 (1760): 516–518
Critical Review 9 (1760): 302–306
British Magazine 9 (1760): 324 [140]

1656 [LLOYD, Robert]. *Arcadia: or, the Shepherd's Wedding. A Dramatic Pastoral. As it is Performed at the Theatre-Royal in Drury-Lane.* London, 1761 (8vo. 6d. Tonson) BRITISH LIBRARY

Reviewed: *Monthly Review* 25 (1761): 398
Critical Review 12 (1761): 403–404

1657 LLOYD, Robert. *The Capricious Lovers; A Comic Opera. As it is performed at the Theatre Royal in Drury-Lane. The Music composed by Mr. Rush.* [Adaptation from Charles Simon Favart.] London, 1764 (8vo. 1s.6d. Griffin) BRITISH LIBRARY

Reviewed: *Monthly Review* 31 (1764): 474
Critical Review 18 (1764): 475–476
General Magazine 1 (1764): 554–555

1658 [LLOYD, Robert]. *The Death of Adam. A Tragedy. In Three Acts. From the German of Mr. Klopstock.* London, 1763 (8vo. 1s.6d. Becket and De Hondt) BRITISH LIBRARY

Reviewed: *Monthly Review* 29 (1763): 95–99
Critical Review 16 (1763): 38–41

1659 LLOYD, R[obert]. *An Epistle to C. Churchill, Author of the Rosciad.* London, 1761 (4to. 1s. Flexney) BRITISH LIBRARY

Reviewed: *Monthly Review* 25 (1761): 78
Critical Review 12 (1761): 160
British Magazine 2 (1761): 495

LLOYD, Robert. *The Moral Tales of M. Marmontel*
See: DENIS, Charles

1660 LLOYD, Robert. *The New-River Head. A Tale. Attempted in the Manner of Mr. C. Denis. And Inscribed to John Wilkes, Esq.* London, 1763 (4to. 1s. Kearsly) BODLEIAN

Reviewed: *Monthly Review* 29 (1763): 228
Critical Review 16 (1763): 72

1661 LLOYD, Robert. *Poems.* London, 1762 (4to. 10s.6d. Davies) BRITISH LIBRARY

Reviewed: *Monthly Review* 26 (1762): 385
Critical Review 13 (1762): 244–249
British Magazine 3 (1762): 213

1662 LLOYD, Robert. *The Poetical Works of Robert Lloyd, A.M. To which is prefixed an Account of the Life and Writings of the Author. By W. Kenrick, LL.D.* 2 vols. London, 1774 (8vo. 6s.sewed. Evans. 1774) BRITISH LIBRARY

Reviewed: *Monthly Review* 51 (1774): 317
Universal Catalogue 3 (1774) art. 1047

1663 [LLOYD, Robert]. *The Progress of Envy a Poem, in Imitation of Spenser. Occasioned by Lauder's Attack on the Character of Milton. Inscribed to the Right Honourable The Earl of Bath.* London, 1751 (4to. 1s. Newbery) BRITISH LIBRARY

Reviewed: *Monthly Review* 4 (1750–51): 375–376

1664 [LLOYD, Robert]. *Shakespeare: An Epistle to Mr. Garrick; with An Ode to Genius.* London, 1760 (Fol. 1s. Davies) HARVARD (PUSEY)

Reviewed: *Monthly Review* 23 (1760): 371–375
Critical Review 10 (1760): 408
British Magazine 1 (1760): 714

1665 [LLOYD, Robert]. *The Tears and Triumphs of Parnassus: an Ode for Musick, As it is perform'd at the Theatre-Royal in Drury-Lane.* London, 1760 (4to. 6d. Vaillant) BRITISH LIBRARY

Reviewed: *Monthly Review* 23 (1760): 410
Critical Review 10 (1760): 407

1666 [LLOYD, Robert]. *Two Epistles on Happiness: To a Young Lady.* London, 1754 (4to. 1s. Knapton) BRITISH LIBRARY

Reviewed: *Monthly Review* 11 (1754): 309–313
Gentleman's Magazine 24 (1754): 343

LLOYD, Robert. *Two Odes* (with George COLMAN [the elder])
See: COLMAN, George (the elder)

1667 LLOYD, Robert (pseud.). *The Triumph of Genius, a Dream; Sacred to the Memory of The late Mr. Charles Churchill.* London, 1764 (4to. 1s. Jones) BRITISH LIBRARY

Reviewed: *Monthly Review* 31 (1764): 398
Critical Review 18 (1764): 400

1668 *The Locket; or, the History of Mr. Singleton. By the Author of Emily; Or, the History Of a Natural Daughter.* 2 vols. London, 1774 (12mo. 6s. Snagg. 1774) NEWBERRY

Reviewed: *Monthly Review* 51 (1774): 72

1669 LOCKMAN, John. *Business, Pleasure, and Prudence: a Fable. Inscribed to the Right Honourable William, Lord Boston. By John Lockman.* London, 1769 (Fol. 6d. Dodsley) HARVARD (HOUGHTON)

Reviewed: *Monthly Review* 41 (1769): 72
Critical Review 28 (1769): 74
Gentleman's Magazine 39 (1769): 357

1670 LOCKMAN, John. *An Ode on the Birth-Day of his Royal Highness George, Prince of Wales. 4th June, 1760.* London, 1760 (4to. 6d.) BODLEIAN

Reviewed: *Critical Review* 9 (1760): 500

1671 LOCKMAN, [John] (trans.). *Pharsamond: or, the New Knight-Errant. In which is introduced The Story of the Fair Anchoret, With that of Tarmiana and her unfortunate Daughter. Written originally in French, By Monsieur de Marivaux, Member of the French Academy in Paris: Author of the Life of Marianne, &c. Translated by Mr. Lockman.* 2 vols. London, 1750 (12mo. 6s.bound. Davis) UNIVERSITY OF PENNSYLVANIA

Reviewed: *Monthly Review* 2 (1749–50): 91–92

1672 LOCKMAN, John. *The Shetland Herring, and Peruvian Gold-Mine. A Fable. Most humbly inscribed to his Royal Highness Frederick Prince of Wales: On his graciously condescending to be Governor of the Society of the Free British Fishery.* London, 1751 (Fol. 6d. Owen) BRITISH LIBRARY

Reviewed: *Monthly Review* 5 (1751): 77

1673 LOCKMAN, John. *Time, wisdom, and glory, a poem. Addressed to the Pr. of Wales, on account of his birthday*
NOT SEEN (6d. Dodsley)

Reviewed: *Gentleman's Magazine* 29 (1759): 287

1674 LOCKMAN, John. *Truth: a Vision. Most humbly addressed to the Prince of Wales: On His Royal Highness's Birth-Day, June 4, 1758.* London, 1758 (Fol. 6d. Dodsley) BRITISH LIBRARY

Reviewed: *Monthly Review* 19 (1758): 303

1675 [LOCKMAN, John]. *Verses on The Demise of the late King, and the Accession of His Present Majesty. Most humbly addressed and presented to His Majesty, at St. James's. To which is prefix'd, An Epistle to the Most Noble the Marquis of Caernarvon, on the above Occasion.* London, 1760 (Fol. 6d. Dodsley) YALE (BEINECKE)

Reviewed: *Monthly Review* 24 (1761): 164
Critical Review 10 (1760): 483

1676 *London: a Satire.* Portsmouth, 1751 (Fol. 6d. Owen) FOLGER

Reviewed: *Monthly Review* 5 (1751): 397

1677 [LONG, Edward]. *The Anti-Gallican; or, the History and Adventures of Harry Cobham, Esquire. Inscribed to Louis the XVth, by the Author.* London, 1757 (12mo. 3s. Lownds) PRIVATE COLLECTION

Reviewed: *Critical Review* 3 (1757): 477

1678 *Long Life to their most excellent Britannic Majesties, King George III. and Queen Charlotte: or, Down with the Devil, Pope, French King, and Pretender. An heroic Poem. By a Freeholder of Kent*
NOT SEEN (8vo. 6d. Corbet)

Reviewed: *Critical Review* 12 (1761): 316

Longsword, Earl of Salisbury
See: LELAND, Thomas

1679 *Louisa. A Sentimental Novel.* London, 1771 (12mo. 3s. Lowndes) BRITISH LIBRARY

Reviewed: *Monthly Review* 44 (1771): 173
Town & Country Magazine 3 (1771): 155

1680 *Louisa: or, Virtue in Distress. Being the History of a natural Daughter of Lady ****.* London, 1760 (12mo. 3s. Corbet) BRITISH LIBRARY

Reviewed: *Monthly Review* 22 (1760): 329
Critical Review 9 (1760): 318–319
British Magazine 1 (1760): 324 [140]

1681 LOVE, James. *Cricket. An Heroic Poem: illustrated With the Critical Observations of Scriblerus Maximus. To which is added An Epilogue, call'd Bucks Have at Ye All. Spoken by Mr. King, at the Theatre Royal in Dublin, in the Character Of Ranger in the Suspicious Husband.* London, 1770 (4to. 1s. Davies) BRITISH LIBRARY

Reviewed: *Monthly Review* 44 (1771): 343
Critical Review 31 (1771): 230–231
Gentleman's Magazine 41 (1771): 228
London Magazine 40 (1771): 226
Town & Country Magazine 3 (1771): 213

1682 LOVE, J[ames]. *Timon of Athens. As it is acted at the Theatre-Royal on Richmond-Green. Altered from Shakespear and Shadwell.* London, 1768 (8vo. 1s.6d. Hingeston) NEWBERRY

Reviewed: *Monthly Review* 39 (1768): 81

1683 [LOVE, James]. *The Village Wedding: or, the Faithful Country Maid. A pastoral entertainment of Music. As it is performed at the Theatre-Royal at Richmond.* London, 1767 (8vo. 1s. Hingeston) BRITISH LIBRARY

Reviewed: *Monthly Review* 37 (1767): 152
Gentleman's Magazine 37 (1767): 411
London Magazine 36 (1767): 424

1684 *Love and Beauty. A Collection of Poems. Containing A Variety of the most approved pieces of Poetry on those Subjects, written by the best Authors. To which are added some choice Originals, with a suitable Dedication.* London, 1769 (8vo. 2s.6d. Wilkie) BRITISH LIBRARY

Reviewed: *Monthly Review* 40 (1769): 156
Critical Review 27 (1769): 71
Gentleman's Magazine 39 (1769): 157
Critical Memoirs 1 (1769): 160–162
Political Register 4 (1769): 391

1685 *Love and Friendship: or, The Fair Fugitive. Exemplified In the Histories of Families of Distinction, in the West of England; and interspers'd With a Variety of Characters, and several pleasing and interesting Incidents.* London, 1757 (12mo. 3s. Reeve) BRITISH LIBRARY

Reviewed: *Monthly Review* 16 (1757): 285
Critical Review 3 (1757): 476–477

1686 *Love and Friendship; or, The Lucky Recovery. A comedy. By the author of Alfred the Great, a tragedy.* London, 1754 (8vo. 1s. Mechell) BRITISH LIBRARY

Reviewed: *Monthly Review* 10 (1754): 312

1687 *Love and Innocence, a Pastoral Serenata. As performed at Marybone-Gardens. Set to Music by Mr. Hook.* London, 1769 (8vo. 1s. Becket) BRITISH LIBRARY

Reviewed: *Monthly Review* 41 (1769): 319
Critical Review 28 (1769): 237
London Magazine 38 (1769): 439–440

1688 *Love and Wine; or, the sequel to the comedy of Love and Friendship. By the author of Alfred the Great, a tragedy*
NOT SEEN (8vo. 6d. Mechell)

Reviewed: *Monthly Review* 11 (1754): 467

1689 *Love at Cross Purposes: exemplified in two sentimental and connected Histories from real Life. viz. I. The forced Marriage; or the History of Sir George Freemore and Miss Emily Menel, in two Volumes. II. Memoirs of Lady Frances Freemore and her Family, in two Volumes.* 4 vols.
NOT SEEN (12mo. 10s.sewed. Noble)

Reviewed: *Monthly Review* 39 (1768): 501–503
Critical Review 28 (1769): 375–376
London Magazine 37 (1768): 667

Love at First Sight: A Ballad Farce
See: KING, Thomas

1690 *Love at First Sight: or the History of Miss Caroline Stanhope.* 3 vols. London, 1773 (12mo. 7s.6d.sewed. Jones. 1773) BRITISH LIBRARY

Reviewed: *Monthly Review* 48 (1773): 155
Critical Review 35 (1773): 78
Town & Country Magazine 5 (1773): 210
Universal Catalogue [1] (1772) art. 1491

Love Elegies
See: LETTICE, John

1691 *Love Elegies: and other Poems.* London, 1761 (4to. 1s. Davies) BRITISH LIBRARY

Reviewed: *Monthly Review* 25 (1761): 79
Critical Review 12 (1761): 56–57

1692 *The Love Encounter*
NOT SEEN (6d. Cooper)

Reviewed: *Gentleman's Magazine* 25 (1755): 143

A Love Epistle, in Verse
See: SHEBBEARE, John

The Love Epistles of Aristaenetus
See: SHERIDAN, Richard Brinsley

1693 *Love, Friendship, and Charity; A Poem. Written by A Gentleman, for his Amusement.* London, n.d. [ESTC-1774?] (4to. 1s.6d. Shropshire, &c. 1774) BRITISH LIBRARY

Reviewed: *Monthly Review* 50 (1774): 483
Critical Review 37 (1774): 394–395

1694 *Love in a Nunnery; or, the secret History of Miss Charlotte Hamilton, a young Lady; who, after a variety of uncommon Incidents, was forced into a Convent, &c. &c.* 2 vols.
NOT SEEN (12mo. 5s. Roson)

Reviewed: *Monthly Review* 46 (1772): 78
Gentleman's Magazine 42 (1772): 85

Love in a Village
See: BICKERSTAFFE, Isaac

1695 *Love in High Life; or the Amours of a Court.* London, n.d. [ESTC-1760?] (12mo. 2s.6d. Knowles) BRITISH LIBRARY

Reviewed: *Monthly Review* 32 (1765): 235
Critical Review 19 (1765): 476

Love in the City
See: BICKERSTAFFE, Isaac

Love in the Suds
See: KENRICK, William

1696 *The Love of Money. A Satire.* London, 1771 (4to. 2s. Evans. 1771) BRITISH LIBRARY

Reviewed: *Monthly Review* 44 (1771): 342–343
Critical Review 31 (1771): 231
Gentleman's Magazine 41 (1771): 228
London Magazine 40 (1771): 226

The Love of Order
See: GRAVES, Richard

The Love of our Country
See: EVANS, Evan

1697 *The Love Plea. Ode to Sylvia*
NOT SEEN (Townshend)

Reviewed: *Critical Review* 9 (1760): 244

1698 *Love Verses. Consisting of, I. An Elegy to Damon. II. An Elegy, in Answer to the foregoing. III. The Recantation. An Ode.*
NOT SEEN (4to. 1s. Davies)

Reviewed: *Monthly Review* 25 (1761): 507
Critical Review 12 (1761): 401
British Magazine 2 (1761): 606

1699 *The Lover's Manual. Being A Choice Collection of Poems from the Most approv'd Modern Authors. With several Original Pieces. In Five Books. Containing I. Love Epistles in Verse. II. Love Epistles in Prose. III. Epistolary Panegyrics. IV. Acrostics. V. Select Pieces of Poetry.* London, 1753 (12mo. 3s. Hitch and Hawes) BRITISH LIBRARY

Listed: *Monthly Review* 9 (1753): 477

The Lovers: or, the Memoirs of Lady Mary Sc-----, and the Hon. Miss Amelia B-----
See: TREYSSAC DE VERGY, Pierre Henri

1700 *The Loves of Carmi and Iphis; a Novel Founded on the Story of Jephtha's Vow.* London, 1762 (12mo. 1s.6d. Field) HARVARD (HOUGHTON)

Reviewed: *Monthly Review* 28 (1763): 245–246

1701 *The Loves of Mirtil Son of Adonis A Pastoral.* London, 1770 (8vo. 3s.sewed. Evans. 1770) BRITISH LIBRARY

Reviewed: *Monthly Review* 43 (1770): 326
Critical Review 30 (1770): 67–68
Town & Country Magazine 2 (1770): 435

The Loves of Othniel and Achsah
See: TOOKE, William

1702 *Low Life Above Stairs. A Farce. As it is Acted In most Families of Distinction Throughout the Kingdom.* London, 1759 (8vo. 1s. Williams) BRITISH LIBRARY

Reviewed: *Monthly Review* 21 (1759): 449
Critical Review 8 (1759): 420
London Magazine 28 (1759): 631

Lucilla: or the Progress of Virtue
See: RESTIF DE LA BRETONNE, Nicolas Anne Edmé

1703 LUMLEY, Thomas. *Bribery: A Poem.* London, 1765 (4to. 1s.6d. Flexney) BODLEIAN

Reviewed: *Monthly Review* 33 (1765): 85
Critical Review 20 (1765): 72

LUNATIC, Sir Humphrey (pseud.)
See: GENTLEMAN, Francis

1704 [LUSSAN, Marguerite de]. *The Life and Heroic Actions of Balbe Berton, Chevalier de Grillon. Translated from the French by a Lady, and revised by Mr. Richardson, Author of Clarissa, Grandison, &c.* 2 vols. London, n.d. [ESTC-1760?] (12mo. 6s. Woodgate and Co.) BRITISH LIBRARY

Reviewed: *Monthly Review* 23 (1760): 156–157
Critical Review 9 (1760): 342–353
British Magazine 1 (1760): 140 [324]

1705 *Lusus Poetici*
NOT SEEN (4to. 1s.6d. T. Lewis)

Reviewed: *Monthly Review* 52 (1775): 273–274
Critical Review 38 (1774): 236
Town & Country Magazine 6 (1774): 448

Lycidas, a Masque
See: LAMBE, Thomas

Lycidas: a Musical Entertainment
See: JACKSON, W.

Lycoris: or, the Grecian Courtesan
See: BRET, Antoine

Lydia, or Filial Piety
See: SHEBBEARE, John

Lyric Consolations
See: STEVENSON, John Hall

The Macaroni. A Comedy
See: HITCHCOCK, Robert

1706 *The Macaroni. A Satire*
NOT SEEN (4to. 1s. Almon)

Reviewed: *Critical Review* 35 (1773): 315

1707 MacDONALD, Donald. *Three Beautiful and Important Passages Omitted by the Translator of Fingal. Translated and Restored by Donald MacDonald.* London, 1762 (4to. 6d. Hinxman) BODLEIAN

Reviewed: *Monthly Review* 25 (1761): 504–505
Critical Review 13 (1762): 75
British Magazine 3 (1762): 102

1708 MACEUEN, ———— (trans.). *Letters from Elizabeth Sophia de Valiere to her Friend Louisa Hortensia de Canteleu. By Madam Riccoboni. Translated from the French by Mr. Maceuen.* 2 vols. London, 1772 (12mo. 6s. Becket. 1772) BRITISH LIBRARY

Reviewed: *Monthly Review* 47 (1772): 8–13
Critical Review 34 (1772): 62–65
London Magazine 41 (1772): 287
Town & Country Magazine 4 (1772): 414
British Magazine & General Review 2 (1772): 163–165

1709 [MACKENZIE, Henry]. *The Man of Feeling.* London, 1771 (12mo. 2s.6d.sewed. Cadell. 1771) BRITISH LIBRARY

Reviewed: *Monthly Review* 44 (1771): 418
Critical Review 31 (1771): 482–483
London Magazine 40 (1771): 411–413
Town & Country Magazine 3 (1771): 436

1710 [MACKENZIE, Henry]. *The Man of the World. In Two Parts.* 2 vols. London, 1773 (12mo. 5s.sewed. Cadell. 1773) BRITISH LIBRARY

Reviewed: *Monthly Review* 48 (1773): 268–269
Critical Review 35 (1773): 269–274
London Magazine 42 (1773): 149
Town & Country Magazine 5 (1773): 266
Universal Catalogue [2] (1773) art. 259

1711 [MACKENZIE, Henry]. *The Prince of Tunis. A Tragedy. As performed at the Theatre-Royal of Edinburgh.* Edinburgh, 1773 (8vo. 1s.6d. Cadell, &c. 1773) HARVARD (HOUGHTON)

Reviewed: *Monthly Review* 48 (1773): 436–439
Critical Review 35 (1773): 474–475
Town & Country Magazine 5 (1773): 378

1712 [MACKENZIE, Henry]. *The Pursuits of Happiness. Inscribed to a Friend.* London, 1771 (4to. 1s.6d. Cadell. 1771) BRITISH LIBRARY

Reviewed: *Monthly Review* 45 (1771): 150–151
Critical Review 31 (1771): 395–396
London Magazine 40 (1771): 323
Town & Country Magazine 3 (1771): 379 and 436 [different reviews]

1713 *M--ckl–n's Answer to Tully.* London, 1755 (8vo. 6d. Cooper) BRITISH LIBRARY

Reviewed: *Monthly Review* 12 (1755): 140

1714 MACPHERSON, James. *Fingal, an Ancient Epic Poem, In Six Books: Together with several other Poems, composed by Ossian the Son of Fingal. Translated from the Galic Language, By James Macpherson.* London, 1762 [BLC-1762 {1761}] (4to. 12s. Becket and Hondt) BRITISH LIBRARY

Reviewed: *Monthly Review* 26 (1762): 41–57 and 130–141
Critical Review 12 (1761): 405–418 and 13 (1762): 45–53
British Magazine 2 (1761): 662
Universal Catalogue [1] (1772) art. 598
Annual Register 4 (1761): 276–286

1715 [MACPHERSON, James]. *Fragments of Ancient Poetry, Collected in the Highlands of Scotland, and Translated from the Galic or Erse*

Language. Edinburgh, 1760 (12mo. 1s. Edinburgh) BRITISH LIBRARY

Reviewed: *Monthly Review* 23 (1760): 204–211
Critical Review 10 (1760): 28–30
Gentleman's Magazine 30 (1760): 407–409
British Magazine 1 (1760): 433
Annual Register 3 (1760): 253–256

1716 MACPHERSON, James. *The Iliad of Homer.* 2 vols. London, 1773 (4to. 1l.11s.6d.boards. Becket. 1773) BRITISH LIBRARY

Reviewed: *Monthly Review* 48 (1773): 393–397
Critical Review 35 (1773): 161–176
London Magazine 42 (1773): 148
Town & Country Magazine 5 (1773): 267
Universal Catalogue [2] (1773) art. 350

1717 [MACPHERSON, James]. *The Songs of Selma. From the Original of Ossian the Son of Fingal.* London, 1762 (4to. 1s. Griffiths) BRITISH LIBRARY

Reviewed: *Monthly Review* 26 (1762): 79–80
Critical Review 13 (1762): 78–79
British Magazine 3 (1762): 102

1718 MACPHERSON, James. *Temora, an Ancient Epic Poem, in Eight Books: Together with several other Poems, composed by Ossian, the Song of Fingal. Translated from the Galic Language, By James Macpherson.* London, 1763 (4to. 10s.6d. Becket) BRITISH LIBRARY

Reviewed: *Monthly Review* 28 (1763): 274–281
Critical Review 15 (1763): 200–209
British Magazine 4 (1763): 158

1719 MacWHIM, Caleb. *A Shandean Essay on Human Passions; with a Smack here and there of Butler, Prior, Swift, Pope, &c.* NOT SEEN (4to. 1s. Coote)

Reviewed: *Monthly Review* 23 (1760): 527
Critical Review 11 (1761): 80

1720 MADDEN, William Balfour. *Bellisle, a Poem: Inscribed to Sir Ralph Gore, Bart.* London, 1761 (4to. 1s. Millar) BODLEIAN

Reviewed: *Monthly Review* 24 (1761): 355
Critical Review 11 (1761): 416
London Magazine 30 (1761): 168

1721 *The Mad Man, a Burletta, performed at Marybone Gardens.* London, 1770 (4to. Piguenit) BRITISH LIBRARY

Reviewed: *Town & Country Magazine* 2 (1770): 491

1722 *The Madman. A Satire.* London, 1754 (Fol. 6d. Swan) HARVARD (HOUGHTON)

Reviewed: *Monthly Review* 10 (1754): 305
Gentleman's Magazine 24 (1754): 305

The Magdalens: An Elegy
See: JERNINGHAM, Edward

The Magic Girdle: a Burletta
See: CAREY, George Savile

1723 *The Magnet. A Musical Entertainment, as sung at Marybone Gardens.* London, 1771 (4to. 1s. Becket) BRITISH LIBRARY

Reviewed: *Monthly Review* 45 (1771): 236
Critical Review 32 (1771): 310
Gentleman's Magazine 41 (1771): 514
London Magazine 40 (1771): 414
Town & Country Magazine 3 (1771): 436

1724 *The Maid of Quality: or, the History of Lady Lucy Layton.* 2 vols. London ed. reviewed; copy seen: Dublin, 1770 (12mo. 6s. Verner) BRITISH LIBRARY

Reviewed: *Monthly Review* 42 (1770): 487
Critical Review 29 (1770): 47–49
London Magazine 39 (1770): 104
Town & Country Magazine 2 (1770): 44

The Maid of the Mill
See: BICKERSTAFFE, Isaac

The Maid of the Oaks
See: BURGOYNE, John

1725 [MAINVILLERS, Genu Soalhat de]. *The Beau-Philosopher; or, the History of the Chevalier de Mainvillers. Translated from the French Original.* London, 1751 (12mo. 3s. Freeman) BRITISH LIBRARY

Reviewed: *Monthly Review* 5 (1751): 385–403

1726 *Majesty Misled: a Tragedy.* London, 1769 (8vo. 1s.6d. Jordan) BRITISH LIBRARY

Reviewed: *Monthly Review* 43 (1770): 244–245
Critical Review 30 (1770): 310–311

Makarony Fables
See: STEVENSON, John Hall

The Male-Coquette: or, Seventeen Hundred Fifty-Seven
See: GARRICK, David

The Male-Coquette: or, the History of the Hon. Edward Astell
See: TIMBURY, Jane

1727 MALLET, David. *Alfred: a Masque. Acted at the Theatre-Royal in Drury-Lane, By His Majesty's Servants.* London, 1751 (1s.6d. Millar) BRITISH LIBRARY

Reviewed: *Monthly Review* 4 (1750–51): 366–370

1728 [MALLET, David]. *Britannia: A Masque. Acted at the Theatre-Royal in Drury-Lane.* London, 1755 (8vo. 6d. Millar) BRITISH LIBRARY

Reviewed: *Monthly Review* 12 (1755): 383

1729 [MALLET, David]. *Edwin and Emma.* Birmingham, 1760 (4to. 1s. Elegantly printed at Birmingham, by Baskerville; and sold by Millar in London) BRITISH LIBRARY

Reviewed: *Monthly Review* 22 (1760): 514
Critical Review 9 (1760): 244

1730 [MALLET, David]. *Elvira: A Tragedy. Acted at the Theatre Royal in Drury-Lane.* London, 1763 (8vo. 1s.6d. Millar) BRITISH LIBRARY

Reviewed: *Monthly Review* 28 (1763): 67–68
Critical Review 15 (1763): 90–96
British Magazine 4 (1763): 98

1731 MALLET, David. *Poems on Several Occasions.* London, 1762 (8vo. 2s. Millar) BRITISH LIBRARY

Reviewed: *Monthly Review* 26 (1762): 360–364
Critical Review 13 (1762): 353–355
British Magazine 3 (1762): 213

1732 [MALLET, David]. *Truth, in Rhyme: addressed to a certain Noble Lord.* London, 1761 (4to. 1s. Millar) BRITISH LIBRARY

Reviewed: *Monthly Review* 25 (1761): 79
Critical Review 11 (1761): 492
British Magazine 2 (1761): 382

1733 [MALLET, David]. *Tyburn to the Marine Society. A Poem.* London, 1759 (8vo. 1s. Cooper) BRITISH LIBRARY

Reviewed: *Monthly Review* 20 (1759): 472–474
Critical Review 7 (1759): 465
Gentleman's Magazine 29 (1759): 233

1734 MALLET, David. *The Works of David Mallet, Esq; In Three Volumes. A New Edition corrected.* London, 1759 (12mo. 9s. Millar and Vaillant) BRITISH LIBRARY

Reviewed: *Monthly Review* 20 (1759): 464
Critical Review 7 (1759): 276

Man and Wife; or, the Shakespeare Jubilee
See: COLMAN, George (the elder)

The Man of Family: a Sentimental Comedy
See: JENNER, Charles

The Man of Feeling
See: MACKENZIE, Henry

1735 *The Man of Honour; or the History of Harry Waters, Esq.*
NOT SEEN (12mo. 2s.6d.sewed. Noble)

Reviewed: *Monthly Review* 45 (1771): 503
Critical Review 32 (1771): 311
London Magazine 40 (1771): 571

1736 *The Man Of Honour; or the History of Harry Waters Esq; Vol. 2 and 3*
NOT SEEN (12mo. 5s.sewed. Noble)

Reviewed: *Monthly Review* 48 (1773): 71
Critical Review 34 (1772): 473
London Magazine 41 (1772): 599
Town & Country Magazine 3 (1771): 602
Universal Catalogue [1] (1772) art. 1504

1737 *The Man of the Mill. A New Burlesque Tragic Opera. The Musick compiled, and the*

Words written, by Seignior Squallini. London, 1765 (8vo. 1s. Cooke) BRITISH LIBRARY

Reviewed: *Monthly Review* 32 (1765): 156
Critical Review 19 (1765): 154

The Man of the World
See: MACKENZIE, Henry

1738 *The Managers: a Comedy: As it is Acted in Covent-Garden.* London, 1768 (4to. 1s. Nokes) BRITISH LIBRARY

Reviewed: *Monthly Review* 38 (1768): 242
Critical Review 25 (1768): 151

1739 *The Managers Managed: or, the Characters of the Four Kings of Brentford.* London, 1768 (4to. 1s. Nicoll) FOLGER

Reviewed: *Critical Review* 25 (1768): 228
London Magazine 37 (1768): 334

1740 MANDEY, ----. *An Occasional Ode, by Capt. Mandey*
NOT SEEN (4to. printed entirely on blue paper. 1s. All the shops)

Reviewed: *Monthly Review* 2 (1749–50): 133

1741 *Margaretta, Countess of Rainsford. A Sentimental Novel. In Two Volumes.* London, 1769 (12mo. 6s. Johnson and Payne) UNIVERSITY OF PENNSYLVANIA

Reviewed: *Monthly Review* 40 (1769): 345
Critical Review 27 (1769): 370–373
Gentleman's Magazine 39 (1769): 158
London Magazine 38 (1769): 213
Critical Memoirs 1 (1769): 525
Town & Country Magazine [1] (1769): 269

1742 *Margate in Miniature; or, the New Margate Guide*
NOT SEEN (8vo. 1s.6d. Roson)

Reviewed: *Monthly Review* 43 (1770): 326
Critical Review 30 (1770): 232
Town & Country Magazine 2 (1770): 548

Maria; the Genuine Memoirs of a Young Lady
See: KIMBER, Edward

1743 MARINI, Giovanni Battista. *Cynthia and Daphne. Translated from the Italian of Il Cavalier Marino. With a Dedication In Blank Verse, to the Duke of York.* London, 1766 (4to. 2s. Almon) BRITISH LIBRARY

Reviewed: *Monthly Review* 35 (1766): 322
Critical Review 22 (1766): 74

1744 [MARISHALL, Jean]. *The History of Alicia Montague. By the Author of Clarinda Cathcart.* 2 vols. London, 1767 (12mo. 6s. Robinson and Roberts) BRITISH LIBRARY

Reviewed: *Monthly Review* 37 (1767): 76
Critical Review 23 (1767): 210–214

1745 [MARISHALL, Jean]. *The History of Miss Clarinda Cathcart, and Miss Fanny Renton.* 2 vols. London, 1766 (12mo. 6s. Noble) BRITISH LIBRARY

Reviewed: *Monthly Review* 33 (1765): 405
Critical Review 20 (1765): 288–292

1746 [MARISHALL, Jean]. *Sir Harry Gaylove; or, Comedy in Embryo. In Five Acts. By the Author of Clarinda Cathcart, and Alicia Montague.* Edinburgh, 1772 (8vo. 2s.6d. Edinburgh, printed for the Author and sold by Dilly &c. in London, 1772) BRITISH LIBRARY

Reviewed: *Monthly Review* 48 (1773): 72–73
Critical Review 35 (1773): 230–232
Universal Catalogue [2] (1773) art. 167

MARIVAUX
See: CARLET DE CHAMBLAIN DE MARIVAUX, Pierre

1747 MARMONTEL, [Jean François]. *Belisarius.* London, 1767 (12mo. 3s. Vaillant) BRITISH LIBRARY

Reviewed: *Monthly Review* 36 (1767): 290–298
Critical Review 23 (1767): 168–179
Gentleman's Magazine 37 (1767): 178–180

1748 MARMONTEL, [Jean François]. *Moral Tales, by M. Marmontel.* 2 vols. London, 1764 (12mo. 6s. Becket and De Hondt) BRITISH LIBRARY

Reviewed: *Monthly Review* 30 (1764): 59–61
Critical Review 17 (1764): 43–49

1749 MARMONTEL, [Jean François]. *Moral Tales. By M. Marmontel. Vol. III*. London, 1766 (8vo. 3s. Becket) BRITISH LIBRARY

Reviewed: *Monthly Review* 34 (1766): 234
Critical Review 20 (1765): 448–450

MARMONTEL, Jean François (translations and adaptations)
See: DENIS, Charles, and Robert LLOYD. *Moral Tales*
GRIFFITH, Elizabeth. *The Platonic Wife*
KELLY, Hugh. *The Romance of an Hour*
TRAPAUD, Elisha. *Aglaura*

The Marriage-act. A Novel
See: SHEBBEARE, John

Marriage. An Ode
See: HUTCHINSON, Benjamin

1750 *The married Victim; or, the History of Lady Villars. A Narrative founded on Facts*. 2 vols. NOT SEEN (12mo. 5s.sewed. Hookham. 1772)

Reviewed: *Monthly Review* 46 (1772): 79
Critical Review 32 (1771): 47

1751 MARRIOTT, George. *The Birth of the Jesuit. A Poem. In Three Books*. London, 1768 (4to. 2s.6d. Flexney) BODLEIAN

Reviewed: *Monthly Review* 38 (1768): 247–248
Critical Review 25 (1768): 70–72
London Magazine 37 (1768): 43
Universal Museum 4 (1768): 93
Political Register 2 (1768): 445

1752 MARRIOTT, George. *The Jesuit. An Allegorical Poem. With Airs and Choruses, as rehearsed after the example of ancient Bards and Minstrels*. London, 1773 (4to. 2s.6d. Leacroft) BRITISH LIBRARY

Reviewed: *Monthly Review* 49 (1773): 46–49
Critical Review 36 (1773): 71–72
Gentleman's Magazine 43 (1773): 237–240
London Magazine 42 (1773): 249
Universal Catalogue [2] (1773) art. 604

1753 MARRIOTT, George. *The Primate, an Ode, written in Sweden*
NOT SEEN (4to. 1s. Flexney)

Reviewed: *Monthly Review* 37 (1767): 315
Critical Review 24 (1767): 159
Universal Museum 3 (1767): 429

1754 [MARRIOTT, Sir James]. *Poems. Laura, or, The Complaint: Ode on the Power of Music: The Valetudinarian: On the Death of his Royal Highness Frederick Prince of Wales. By a Gentleman of Cambridge*. London, 1753 (4to. 1s. Whiston and White) BRITISH LIBRARY

Reviewed: *Monthly Review* 8 (1753): 157–158

1755 MARRIOTT, Thomas. *Female Conduct: Being an Essay on the Art of Pleasing. To be practised by the Fair Sex, Before, and After Marriage. A Poem, in Two Books. Inscribed to Plautilla*. London, 1759 (8vo. 4s. Owen) BRITISH LIBRARY

Reviewed: *Monthly Review* 20 (1759): 135–141
Critical Review 7 (1759): 26–30

1756 [MARRIOTT, Thomas]. *The Twentieth Epistle of Horace To His Book, Modernized by the Author of Female Conduct, and applied to his own Book. And Intended as an Answer to the Remarks on his Book, made by the Writer of the Critical Review, and by the Writer of the Monthly Review*. London, 1759 (8vo. 6d. Owen) BRITISH LIBRARY

Reviewed: *Monthly Review* 20 (1759): 604
Critical Review 8 (1759): 84–86

1757 MARSH, Charles. *Cymbeline: King of Britain. A Tragedy, Written by Shakespear. With some alterations, By Charles Marsh. As it was agreed to be acted at the Theatre-Royal in Covent-Garden*. London, n.d. [ESTC-1758?] (8vo. 1s.6d. Marsh) BRITISH LIBRARY

Reviewed: *Monthly Review* 20 (1759): 463

1758 [MARSH, Charles]. *The Library: An Epistle From a Bookseller, to A Gentleman, his Customer; Desiring him to discharge his Bill*. [FOLGER CAT.: A reworking and expansion of his 1741 *A Poetical Epistle Humbly Inscrib'd to ------ Anybody*.] London, 1761 (4to. 1s. Marsh) FOLGER

Reviewed: *Monthly Review* 34 (1766): 480
Critical Review 21 (1766): 478–479

1759 MARSH, Charles. *The Winter's Tale. A Play. Alter'd from Shakespear.* London, 1756 (8vo. 1s. Marsh) BRITISH LIBRARY

Reviewed: *Monthly Review* 14 (1756): 270
Critical Review 1 (1756): 144–145

MARSHAL, William (pseud.)
See: WALPOLE, Horace

MARTEILHÉ, Jean. *The Memoirs of a Protestant*
See: GOLDSMITH, Oliver (trans.)

1760 MARTEN, Thomas. *The Marriage: or, History of four well-known Characters. Translated from the celebrated French novel of the same Title.* 2 vols.
NOT SEEN (12mo. 5s.sewed. Wheble. 1771)

Reviewed: *Monthly Review* 45 (1771): 73
Critical Review 32 (1771): 231
London Magazine 40 (1771): 274

MARTIAL (Marcus Valerius MARTIALIS) (translation)
See: SCOTT, William. *Epigrams of Martial*

1761 MARVELL, Andrew. *The Works of Andrew Marvell, Esq.* 2 vols. London, 1772 (12mo. 5s. Davies) BRITISH LIBRARY

Reviewed: *Monthly Review* 48 (1773): 241–242
Critical Review 33 (1772): 174
Universal Catalogue [1] (1772) art. 109

1762 [MASON, William]. *Caractacus, a Dramatic Poem: Written on the Model of the Ancient Greek Tragedy. By the Author of Elfrida.* London, 1759 (4to. 2s.6d. Knapton) BRITISH LIBRARY

Reviewed: *Monthly Review* 20 (1759): 507–512
Critical Review 8 (1759): 11–16

1763 [MASON, William]. *Chorus of the Dramatic Poem of Elfrida. As performed at the Theatre-Royal in Covent-Garden.* London, 1772 (4to. 6d. Horsfield, &c. 1772) BRITISH LIBRARY

Reviewed: *Monthly Review* 47 (1772): 486
Critical Review 35 (1773): 71

1764 MASON, William. *Elegies.* London, 1763 (4to. 1s. Dodsley) BRITISH LIBRARY

Reviewed: *Monthly Review* 27 (1762): 485–492
Critical Review 14 (1762): 447–450
British Magazine 4 (1763): 46

1765 MASON, [William]. *Elfrida, a Dramatic Poem. Written on the Model of The Antient Greek Tragedy.* London, 1752 (1st ed. 4to. 2s.6d.; 2nd ed. 8vo. 1s.6d. Knapton) BRITISH LIBRARY

Reviewed: *Monthly Review* 6 (1752): 387–393

1766 MASON, W[illiam]. *The English Garden: a Poem. Book the First.* London, 1772 (4to. 2s. Horsfield. 1772) BRITISH LIBRARY

Reviewed: *Monthly Review* 46 (1772): 219–226
Critical Review 33 (1772): 171–173
Gentleman's Magazine 42 (1772): 78–80
London Magazine 41 (1772): 88
Town & Country Magazine 4 (1772): 99
British Magazine & General Review 1 (1772): 168–169
Universal Catalogue [1] (1772) art. 237

1767 [MASON, William]. *An Heroic Epistle to Sir William Chambers, Knight, Comptroller General of his Majesty's Works, And Author of a late Dissertation on Oriental Gardening. Enriched with explanatory Notes, chiefly extracted from that elaborate Performance.* London, 1773 (4to. 1s. Almon. 1773) HARVARD (HOUGHTON)

Reviewed: *Monthly Review* 48 (1773): 314–315
Critical Review 35 (1773): 465–470
Gentleman's Magazine 43 (1773): 290–291
London Magazine 42 (1773): 196–197

1768 [MASON, William]. *An Heroic Postscript to The Public, Occasioned by their favourable Reception of a late Heroic Epistle To Sir William Chambers, Knt. &c. By the Author of that Epistle.* London, 1774 (4to. 1s. Almon. 1774) BRITISH LIBRARY

Reviewed: *Monthly Review* 50 (1774): 154–155
Critical Review 37 (1774): 313–314
Gentleman's Magazine 44 (1774): 85
Universal Catalogue 3 (1774) art. 207

1769 MASON, [William]. *An Ode Performed on the Senate-House at Cambridge July 1, 1749. At the Installation of His Grace Thomas Holles*

Duke of Newcastle Chancellor of the University. Cambridge, 1749 (4to. 8pp.) BRITISH LIBRARY

Reviewed: *Monthly Review* 1 (1749): 238

1770 MASON, [William]. *Odes By Mr. Mason.* Cambridge, 1756 (4to. 1s. Dodsley) BRITISH LIBRARY

Reviewed: *Monthly Review* 14 (1756): 434–441
Critical Review 1 (1756): 208–214

1771 MASON, William. *Poems by William Mason, M.A.* London, 1764 (8vo. 5s. Horsfield) BRITISH LIBRARY

Reviewed: *Monthly Review* 30 (1764): 66–67
Critical Review 17 (1764): 237

1772 *The Masque. A new and select Collection of the best English, Scotch, and Irish Songs, Catches, Duets, and Cantatas, in the true Spirit and Taste of the three different Nations. Collected from all the numerous Books of this Kind that have been published from the first Appearance of such Works to the present Time; including every celebrated Song that has been sung at the public Gardens and Theatres, either the last or any preceding Season. With a great Number of Valuable Originals. Being an Attempt to improve upon others in the true Spirit of Social Mirth and good Fellowship, without forgetting the Respect that is due to the Public. To which is added, A complete Collection of the various Toasts, Sentiments, and Hob-Nobs that are now in vogue.* 1st ed. reviewed; copy seen 2d ed.: London, 1768 (12mo. 3s. Richardson and Urquhart) BRITISH LIBRARY

Reviewed: *Monthly Review* 36 (1767): 410

1773 *The Masquerade; a Poem. Inscribed to the King of Denmark.* London, 1768 (4to. 1s.6d. Evans) BRITISH LIBRARY

Reviewed: *Monthly Review* 39 (1768): 401
Critical Review 26 (1768): 381–382
Gentleman's Magazine 38 (1768): 621
Universal Museum 4 (1768): 597
Political Register 3 (1768): 384

1774 *The Masquerade; or, the History of Lord Avon and Miss Tameworth. In a Series of Letters.* 2 vols. London, 1769 (12mo. 6s. Robinson and Roberts) BODLEIAN

Reviewed: *Monthly Review* 42 (1770): 71
Critical Review 28 (1769): 453–455
London Magazine 38 (1769): 640

1775 *The Massacre*
NOT SEEN (4to. 1s. Hanson, near St. Paul's)

Reviewed: *Monthly Review* 40 (1769): 250–251
Gentleman's Magazine 39 (1769): 158
Critical Memoirs 1 (1769): 523

1776 MASSEY, William. *Ovid's Fasti, or the Romans Sacred Calendar, Translated into English Verse. With Explanatory Notes.* London, 1757 (8vo. 4s. Keith) BRITISH LIBRARY

Reviewed: *Monthly Review* 18 (1758): 127–129
Critical Review 4 (1757): 402–409

1777 MASSINGER, Philip. *The Dramatic Works of Mr. Philip Massinger, compleat. In Four Volumes. Revised, Corrected, and all the Various Editions Collated, By Mr. Coxeter. With Notes Critical and Explanatory, By the Editor, And by Various Authors.* London, 1759 (8vo. 1l.4s. Dell) BRITISH LIBRARY

Reviewed: *Monthly Review* 21 (1759): 176–177
Critical Review 8 (1759): 86–87

1778 MASTERS, Mary. *Familiar Letters and Poems on Several Occasions.* London, 1755 (8vo. 5s.sheets. Henry and Cave) BRITISH LIBRARY

Reviewed: *Monthly Review* 13 (1755): 155–157
Gentleman's Magazine 25 (1755): 190–191

1779 *The Matron. An Elegy.* London, 1774 (4to. 6d. Johnson) BRITISH LIBRARY

Reviewed: *Monthly Review* 51 (1774): 483
Critical Review 38 (1774): 151
Gentleman's Magazine 44 (1774): 377

The Matrons. Six Short Histories
See: PERCY, Thomas

1780 MATTHEWS, John. *An Address to the Victuallers of this Kingdom in General. To which is prefixed, A Poem upon Liberty.* London, 1761 (8vo. 6d. Thrush) BRITISH LIBRARY

Reviewed: *Critical Review* 12 (1761): 482

1781 MAUDE, Thomas. *Wensleydale: or, Rural Contemplations, a Poem.* London, 1771 (4to. 2s.6d. Davies. 1772) HARVARD (HOUGHTON)

Reviewed: *Monthly Review* 47 (1772): 114–118
Critical Review 33 (1772): 381–384
Gentleman's Magazine 42 (1772): 232–233
Town & Country Magazine 4 (1772): 267

1782 MAXWELL, Archibald. *Portsmouth. A Descriptive Poem, in Two Books.* Portsmouth, 1755 (8vo. 1s. Owen) BRITISH LIBRARY

Reviewed: *Monthly Review* 13 (1755): 297

1783 MAXWELL, James. *Divine Miscellanies; or, Sacred Poems.* Birmingham, 1756 (12mo. 2s.6d. Dilly) BRITISH LIBRARY

Reviewed: *Monthly Review* 16 (1757): 286

1784 MAXWELL, James. *Hymns and Spiritual Songs, adapted to the various Cases, I. Of Unregenerate Sinners, II. Of those who are Convinced, III. Of true Believers.*
NOT SEEN (12mo. 1s. Fuller)

Reviewed: *Monthly Review* 21 (1759): 352

1785 MAY, Henry. *Poetic Essays on Several Affecting Subjects: By Henry May.* London, 1761 (8vo. 1s. Keith) JOHNS HOPKINS

Reviewed: *Monthly Review* 24 (1761): 356
Critical Review 11 (1761): 75–76
British Magazine 2 (1761): 46

1786 [MEADES, Anna]. *The history of Cleanthes, an Englishman of the highest Quality, and Celemene, the Illustrious Amazonian Princess: Interspersed With a Variety of most entertaining Incidents and surprizing Turns of Fortune; and a particular Account of that famous Island, so much talk'd of, but hitherto so little known. Written by a Person well acquainted with all the Principal Characters from their Original.* 2 vols. London, 1757 (8vo. 6s. J. Scott) BRITISH LIBRARY

Reviewed: *Monthly Review* 16 (1757): 567–568
Critical Review 4 (1757): 461

Medea. A Tragedy
See: GLOVER, Richard

1787 *Medea to Jason. An Epistle. By a Gentleman*
NOT SEEN (Fol. 1s. Hitch)

Reviewed: *Monthly Review* 23 (1760): 410–411
Critical Review 10 (1760): 159–160
British Magazine 1 (1760): 546

Medico Mastix
See: SCHOMBERG, Ralph

1788 MEEN, [Henry]. *Happiness: A Poetical Essay. By Mr. Meen, of Emmanuel-College, Cambridge.* London, 1766 (4to. 1s.6d. Dodsley) BRITISH LIBRARY

Reviewed: *Monthly Review* 34 (1766): 479–480
Critical Review 22 (1766): 73

1789 MEILAN, Mark Anthony. *The Dramatic Works of Mark Anthony Meilan; consisting of Three Tragedies, Emilia, Northumberland, the Friends. As they were presented to the Managers of both our Theatres, but Refused. Published by way of an appeal from the arbitrary decisions of the Despots of the Drama, to Candour and the Lovers of Theatrical Amusements, Whose Liberality so amply aggrandizes those Defaulters.* London, n.d. (8vo. 6s. White, &c.) BODLEIAN

Reviewed: *Monthly Review* 44 (1771): 343
Critical Review 31 (1771): 228–229
Gentleman's Magazine 41 (1771): 228
Town & Country Magazine 3 (1771): 261

The Melancholy Student
See: BROMEHEAD, Joseph

MELMOTH, Courtney (pseud.)
See: PRATT, Samuel Jackson

Melpomene: or The Regions of Terror and Pity
See: DODSLEY, Robert

1790 *Memoirs of a Coquet; or, the History of Miss Harriot Airy. By the Author of Emily Willis; or, the History of a Natural Daughter.* London, 1765 (12mo. 3s. Noble) BRITISH LIBRARY

Reviewed: *Monthly Review* 32 (1765): 394
Critical Review 19 (1765): 236

Candid Review 1 (1765): 190

Memoirs of a Coxcomb
See: CLELAND, John

1791 *Memoirs of a Gentleman, who Resided Several Years in the East Indies During the late Revolutions, and Most Important Events in that Part Of The World; containing, several anecdotes of a public as well as of a private nature, never before published. Written by Himself.* London, 1774 (12mo. 3s. Donaldson. 1774) BRITISH LIBRARY

Reviewed: *Monthly Review* 50 (1774): 71
Critical Review 36 (1773): 477
Town & Country Magazine 6 (1774): 45
Universal Catalogue [2] (1773) art. 1305

Memoirs of a Magdalen
See: KELLY, Hugh

Memoirs of a Man of Pleasure
See: HILL, John

1792 *Memoirs of a Scoundrel. By an Injured Fair.* 2 vols.
NOT SEEN (12mo. 6s. Cooke)

Reviewed: *Monthly Review* 39 (1768): 85
Universal Museum 4 (1768): 429

1793 *Memoirs of a Young Lady of Family. Being A succinct account of the capriciousness of fortune, and an accurate survey of the heart of that incomprehensible animal, called Man.* London, 1758 (12mo. 3s. Scott) BRITISH LIBRARY

Reviewed: *Monthly Review* 18 (1758): 182–183
Critical Review 5 (1758): 170

1794 *The Memoirs of a Young Lady of Quality, a Platonist.* 3 vols. London, 1756 (8vo. 9s. Baldwin) BRITISH LIBRARY

Reviewed: *Monthly Review* 16 (1757): 178
Critical Review 3 (1757): 252–258

1795 *The Memoirs of an American. With a Description of the Kingdom of Prussia, and the Island of St. Domingo. Translated from the French.* 2 vols. London, 1773 (12mo. 5s.sewed. Noble) BRITISH LIBRARY

Reviewed: *Monthly Review* 47 (1772): 411
Critical Review 34 (1772): 397
London Magazine 41 (1772): 489
Town & Country Magazine 5 (1773): 31
British Magazine & General Review 2 (1772): 555
Universal Catalogue [1] (1772) art. 1282

1796 *Memoirs of an Hermaphrodite. Inscribed to the Chevalier D'Eon*
NOT SEEN (12mo. 2s. Roson)

Reviewed: *Monthly Review* 46 (1772): 265
Critical Review 33 (1772): 336
British Magazine & General Review 1 (1772): 257–258
Universal Catalogue [1] (1772) art. 383

1797 *Memoirs of an Oxford Scholar. Containing, His Amour with the beautiful Miss L——— of Essex; And interspers'd with Several Entertaining Incidents. Written by Himself.* London, 1756 (12mo. 3s. Reeve) BRITISH LIBRARY

Reviewed: *Monthly Review* 13 (1755): 510

1798 *Memoirs of an Unfortunate Lady of Quality.* 3 vols. London, 1774 (12mo. 7s.6d. Snagg. 1774) HARVARD (HOUGHTON)

Reviewed: *Monthly Review* 51 (1774): 322–323

1799 *Memoirs of B——— Tracey.* London, n.d. [ESTC-1757] (12mo. 3s. J. King) BRITISH LIBRARY

Reviewed: *Monthly Review* 17 (1757): 478

Memoirs of Fanny Hill
See: CLELAND, John

1800 *The Memoirs of Fidelio and Harriot: wherein The Contrast between Virtue and Vice is fully exhibited from a real Fact, Transacted in the Year 1720. Preserved in the original Manuscript of Mrs. Harvey.* London, 1753 (12mo. 3s. Manby) UNIVERSITY OF PENNSYLVANIA

Reviewed: *Monthly Review* 7 (1752): 470

1801 *Memoirs of Francis Dillon, Esq; In a Series Of Letters written by himself.* 2 vols. London,

1772 (12mo. 6s. Hookham. 1772) UNIVERSITY OF CHICAGO

Reviewed: *Monthly Review* 46 (1772): 457
Critical Review 33 (1772): 327

1802 *The Memoirs of George Tudor, wrote originally by several Hands, but revised and set in order wholly by himself.* 2 vols.
NOT SEEN (12mo. 5s. Pridden)

Reviewed: *Monthly Review* 37 (1767): 314
Critical Review 24 (1767): 205–212
London Magazine 36 (1767): 425

1803 *The memoirs of Harriot and Charlotte Meanwell. Who from a State of Affluence are reduced to the greatest Distress. Written by themselves*
NOT SEEN (12mo. 3s. Owen)

Reviewed: *Monthly Review* 16 (1757): 578
Critical Review 4 (1757): 95

1804 *Memoirs of Lady Harriot Butler: now first published From Authentic Papers, in the Lady's own Hand-writing.* 2 vols. London, 1741 [1761], 1762 (12mo. 6s. Freeman) BRITISH LIBRARY

Reviewed: *Monthly Review* 25 (1761): 472
Critical Review 12 (1761): 363–370
British Magazine 2 (1761): 662

1805 *Memoirs of Lady Woodford. Written By Herself, and addressed to a friend. In Two Volumes.* London, 1771 (12mo. 5s.sewed. Noble) BODLEIAN

Reviewed: *Monthly Review* 44 (1771): 498
Critical Review 31 (1771): 482

1806 *Memoirs of Lydia Tongue-Pad and Juliana Clackit.* London, n.d. [ESC-1760?] (12mo. 2s.6d. Coote) BRITISH LIBRARY

Reviewed: *Monthly Review* 38 (1768): 249
Critical Review 26 (1768): 376

1807 *Memoirs of Madame de Stahl. Translated from the French*
NOT SEEN (12mo. 3s. Reeve)

Reviewed: *Monthly Review* 20 (1759): 188–189

1808 *Memoirs of Miss Arabella Bolton. Containing A Genuine Account of her Seduction, and the barbarous Treatment she afterwards received from the Honourable Colonel L—–l, the present supposed M—–r for the County of Middlesex. With various other Misfortunes and Embarrassments, into which this unhappy young Woman has been cruelly involved thro' the Vicissitudes of Life, and the Villainy of her Seducer. The whole taken From the Original Letters of the said C—–l L—–l to Dr. Kelly, who attended her in the greatest Misfortunes and Distresses under which she laboured; And Also From several Original Letters from Doctor Kelly and Miss Bolton, and from other authenticated Papers in the Hands of the Publisher.* London, 1770 (12mo. 2s.6d. Fell) BRITISH LIBRARY

Reviewed: *Monthly Review* 42 (1770): 251
Critical Review 30 (1770): 240
London Magazine 39 (1770): 104

1809 *Memoirs of Miss Arabella Bolton. Containing A Genuine Account of her Seduction, and the barbarous Treatment she afterwards received from the Honourable Colonel L—–l, the present supposed M—–r for the County of Middlesex. Vol. II*
NOT SEEN (12mo. 2s.6d. Fell)

Reviewed: *Monthly Review* 43 (1770): 65
Critical Review 30 (1770): 240 [2 vols.]

1810 *The Memoirs of Miss Betsey F.T. Author of the Address to old Maids and Batchelors, &c. Containing a Series of Adventures, as well Tragical as Comical, Gay and Amorous, Serious and Jocose. Intermixed with the Characters of some of the most eminent Beaux and Belles of the present Age. Being a real History. Written by Herself.* 2 vols.
NOT SEEN (12mo. 6s. Withy)

Reviewed: *Monthly Review* 24 (1761): 351
Critical Review 11 (1761): 335
British Magazine 2 (1761): 265

1811 *The Memoirs of Miss D'Arville; or, the Italian Female Philosopher: in a Series of Adventures, founded on Fact. Translated from the Italian.* 2 vols.
NOT SEEN (12mo. 5s. Pridden)

Reviewed: *Monthly Review* 30 (1764): 243
   Critical Review 19 (1765): 160
   General Magazine 1 (1764): 96

Memoirs of Miss Harriet Melvin
See: *Genuine Memoirs of Miss Harriet Melvin*

Memoirs of Miss Katty N---.
See: *History of Miss Katty N---*

1812 *The memoirs of Miss M--- P---, a celebrated British toast*
NOT SEEN (8vo. 1s. Sold at all the pamphlet shops)

Reviewed: *Monthly Review* 6 (1752): 146

Memoirs of Miss Sidney Bidulph
See: SHERIDAN, Frances

1813 *The Memoirs of Miss Williams: A History founded on Facts.* 2 vols.
NOT SEEN (12mo. 5s.sewed. Johnson. 1772)

Reviewed: *Monthly Review* 46 (1772): 457
   Critical Review 33 (1772): 498
   London Magazine 41 (1772): 386

1814 *Memoirs of Mr. Charles Guildford. In a regular Series of Letters, Wrote by Himself to a Friend. The whole founded on real Facts.* 2 vols. London, 1761 (12mo. 6s. Withy) BRITISH LIBRARY

Reviewed: *Monthly Review* 25 (1761): 503
   Critical Review 12 (1761): 480
   British Magazine 3 (1762): 44

1815 *Memoirs of Mr. Walcott, a Gentleman of Yorkshire, and his Family. A Narrative founded on real Facts.* 2 vols.
NOT SEEN (12mo. 5s. Jones)

Reviewed: *Monthly Review* 34 (1766): 241
   Critical Review 21 (1766): 157

1816 *Memoirs of Mr. Wilson: or, the Providential Adultery.* 2 vols. London, 1771 (12mo. 5s.sewed. Hall) BRITISH LIBRARY

Reviewed: *Monthly Review* 44 (1771): 92

1817 *Memoirs of Mrs. Arabella W---t, shewing the unkind Usage she received from an only Brother. The Cause of her coming to London. The Manner in which she was seduced from the Inn to a house of ill Fame. How she was there debauched, and confined two Years; and how dispos'd of since*
NOT SEEN (8vo. 1s. Printed for W. Reeve)

Reviewed: *Monthly Review* 2 (1749–50): 114–115

Memoirs of Several Ladies of Great Britain
See: AMORY, Thomas

1818 *Memoirs of Sir Charles Goodville and his Family: in a Series of Letters to a Friend.* 2 vols. London, 1753 (12mo. 6s. Browne, &c.)
BRITISH LIBRARY

Reviewed: *Monthly Review* 8 (1753): 187–189

Memoirs of Sir Roger and his Son Joe
See: *History of Sir Roger and his Son Joe*

1819 *Memoirs of Sir Thomas Hughson and Mr Joseph Williams, With the remarkable History, Travels, and Distresses, of Telemachus Lovet. The Whole calculated For the Improvement of the Mind and Manners; and for a becoming and useful Entertainment for the Youth of both Sexes. In Four Volumes.* London, 1757 (8vo. 12s. Printed for the author and sold by L. Davis)
YALE (BEINECKE)

Reviewed: *Monthly Review* 16 (1757): 452
   Critical Review 4 (1757): 460–461

1820 *Memoirs of the Bedford Coffee-House. By a Genius.* London, 1763 (12mo. 2s. Single)
BRITISH LIBRARY

Reviewed: *Monthly Review* 27 (1762): 478
   Critical Review 14 (1762): 479

1821 *Memoirs of the celebrated Miss Ann C----y; containing a succinct Narrative of the most remarkable Incidents of that Lady's Life; with many curious Anecdotes, never before made public.* 2 vols.
NOT SEEN (12mo. 5s. Roson. 1773)

Reviewed: *Monthly Review* 48 (1773): 417
   Critical Review 36 (1773): 396–397
   Town & Country Magazine 5 (1773): 669
   Universal Catalogue [2] (1773) art. 481

1822 *Memoirs of the celebrated Miss Fanny M-----.* 1st ed. reviewed; copy seen 2d ed.: London, 1759 (12mo. 3s. Scott) BRITISH LIBRARY

Reviewed: *Monthly Review* 19 (1758): 580
Critical Review 7 (1759): 87

1823 *Memoirs of the Celebrated Miss Fanny M-----. Vol. II.* London, 1759 (12mo. 3s. Thrush) HARVARD (HOUGHTON)

Reviewed: *Critical Review* 7 (1759): 288

1824 *Memoirs of the Chevalier de **** A Novel. Translated from the French.* London, 1760 (12mo. 3s. Cooke) BRITISH LIBRARY

Reviewed: *Monthly Review* 22 (1760): 156–157
Critical Review 9 (1760): 77

1825 *Memoirs of the Chevalier Pierpoint. In Two Volumes.* London, 1763 (12mo. 4s. Dodsley) BODLEIAN

Reviewed: *Monthly Review* 28 (1763): 78
Critical Review 15 (1763): 11–13
British Magazine 4 (1763): 46

1826 *Memoirs of the Chevalier Pierpoint. Vols. III and IV.* London, 1763 (12mo. 5s. Dodsley) BODLEIAN

Reviewed: *Monthly Review* 30 (1764): 244
Critical Review 17 (1764): 478–479

The Memoirs of the Countess of Berci
See: LENNOX, Charlotte

1827 *Memoirs of the Life and Actions of Charles Osborn, Esq; Natural Son to the E--l of A--e. Containing An Account of his polite Education; his Loss of a vast Estate left him by his Father; his Distress, till relieved by an unknown Lady, by whom he had seven Children before he ever saw her; his Extravagancies; his eight several Marriages; his Intrigues; his turning Priest; with the vast Fluctuation of his Fortune, till resolving to live soberly, he not only married the unknown Lady, but became possessed of the great Estate he had lost; and made Restitution. Written by himself in the decline of life.* London, 1752 (12mo. 3s. Cooper) UNIVERSITY OF PENNSYLVANIA

Reviewed: *Monthly Review* 5 (1751): 460

1828 *Memoirs of the Life and Adventures of Sobrina.* 2 vols. London, 1755 (6s. Woodyer) BRITISH LIBRARY

Reviewed: *Monthly Review* 12 (1755): 383

1829 *Memoirs of the Life and Adventures of Tsonnonthouan, a King Of the Indian Nation called Roundheads. Extracted from Original Papers and Archives.* 2 vols. London, 1763 (12mo. 6s.bound. Knox) BRITISH LIBRARY

Reviewed: *Monthly Review* 28 (1763): 492–493
Critical Review 15 (1763): 378–388

Memoirs of the life of Parnese
See: PALTOCK, Robert

1830 *Memoirs of the Life, Sufferings, and Surprising Adventures Of a Noble Foreigner at *******. To which are added, Some Instructive Remarks on the Vicissitudes of Fortune. Written by Himself.* London, 1752 (12mo. 1s. Corbet) BODLEIAN

Reviewed: *Monthly Review* 6 (1752): 77

Memoirs of the Noted Buckhorse
See: ANSTEY, Christopher

1831 *Memoirs of the Princess of Montpensier, and the Duke of Balastre. Translated from the French*
NOT SEEN (12mo. 2s.sewed. Wilkie)

Reviewed: *Monthly Review* 30 (1764): 489

1832 *Memoirs of the Shakespear's-Head In Covent-Garden: In which are introduced Many entertaining Adventures, And several remarkable Characters. By the Ghost of Shakespear.* 2 vols. London, 1755 (12mo. 6s. Noble) BRITISH LIBRARY

Reviewed: *Monthly Review* 11 (1754): 319
Gentleman's Magazine 24 (1754): 486

1833 [MENDEZ, Moses]. *The Battiad, Canto the First and The Battiad. Canto the Second.* London, 1750 [Published separately] (Fol. 6d.each) BODLEIAN

Reviewed: *Monthly Review* 4 (1750–51): 44–51

1834 MENDEZ, Moses, and others. *A Collection of the Most esteemed Pieces of Poetry, That have appeared for several Years. With Variety of Originals, By the Late Moses Mendez, Esq; And other Contributors to Dodsley's Collection. To which this is intended as a Supplement.* London, 1767 (8vo. 3s. Richardson) BRITISH LIBRARY

Reviewed: *Monthly Review* 38 (1768): 71–72
Critical Review 24 (1767): 357–361
Gentleman's Magazine 37 (1767): 640
London Magazine 37 (1768): 48
Universal Museum 3 (1767): 596
Political Register 1 (1767): 463

1835 MENDEZ, Moses. *The Double Disappointment; a Farce. As it is acted at the Theatre Royal in Covent Garden.* London, 1760 (8vo. 1s. Noble) BRITISH LIBRARY

Reviewed: *Monthly Review* 21 (1759): 453

1836 [MENDEZ, Moses]. *The Seasons. In Imitation of Spenser.* London, 1751 (Fol. 1s. Baker) HARVARD (HOUGHTON)

Reviewed: *Monthly Review* 4 (1750–51): 519–523
Gentleman's Magazine 21 (1751): 238–239

1837 [MENDEZ, Moses]. *The Shepherds Lottery. A Musical Entertainment. As it is perform'd by His Majesty's Company of Comedians at the Theatre-Royal in Drury-Lane. The Music Compos'd by Dr. Boyce.* London, 1751 (8vo. 6d. Cooper) BRITISH LIBRARY

Listed: *Monthly Review* 5 (1751): 464

1838 MENNELL, G. *Religion, a Poem. Inscribed to Walter Griffith Esq.* Portsmouth, 1771 (4to. 1s. Printed for the Author) BODLEIAN

Reviewed: *Monthly Review* 45 (1771): 412
Critical Review 32 (1771): 470
London Magazine 40 (1771): 413

1839 *The Mercenary Marriage; or, the History of Miss Shenstone.* 2 vols. London, 1773 (12mo. 6s. Noble. 1773) BODLEIAN

Reviewed: *Monthly Review* 48 (1773): 154
Critical Review 35 (1773): 78
London Magazine 42 (1773): 91
Town & Country Magazine 5 (1773): 210
Universal Catalogue [2] (1773) art. 133

1840 [MERCER, Thomas]. *Poems. By the Author of the Sentimental Sailor.* London, 1774 (4to. 3s.6d.boards. Dilly. 1774) BRITISH LIBRARY

Reviewed: *Monthly Review* 51 (1774): 340–344
Critical Review 38 (1774): 215–218
London Magazine 43 (1774): 197
Universal Catalogue 3 (1774) art. 769

1841 [MERCER, Thomas]. *The Sentimental Sailor or St. Preux to Eloisa An Elegy In Two Parts, with Notes.* Edinburgh, 1772 (4to. 2s. Edinburgh printed, and sold by Dilly in London. 1772) BRITISH LIBRARY

Reviewed: *Monthly Review* 48 (1773): 68–69
Critical Review 35 (1773): 232
London Magazine 41 (1772): 598
Universal Catalogue [1] (1772) art. 1459

1842 [MERCIER, Louis Sébastien]. *Jean Hennuyer, Bishop of Lizieux or, the Massacre of St. Bartholomew; a Dramatic Entertainment, in Three Acts. Translated from the French.* London, 1773 (8vo. 1s.6d. Leacroft. 1773) BRITISH LIBRARY

Reviewed: *Monthly Review* 49 (1773): 43–46
London Magazine 42 (1773): 249
Universal Catalogue [2] (1773) art. 612

MERCIER, Louis Sébastien (additional translation)
See: HOOPER, William

The Meretriciad
See: THOMPSON, Edward

1843 [MERRICK, James]. *Heliocrene: A Poem, in Latin and English, on the Chalybeate Well, at Sunning-Hill, in Windsor Forest.* London, 1756 (4to. 6d. No publisher's name) BRITISH LIBRARY

Reviewed: *Monthly Review* 14 (1756): 577–579
Critical Review 2 (1756): 88–89

1844 MERRICK, James. *Poems on Sacred Subjects.* Oxford, 1763 (4to. 1s. Dodsley) BRITISH LIBRARY

Reviewed: *Monthly Review* 28 (1763): 318
Critical Review 15 (1763): 156
British Magazine 4 (1763): 98

1845 MERRICK, James. *The Psalms, Translated or Paraphrased In English Verse.* Reading, 1765 (4to. 10s.6d. Newbery) BRITISH LIBRARY

Reviewed: *Monthly Review* 33 (1765): 230–235
Critical Review 20 (1765): 208–216

1846 *The Merry Fellow. A Collection Of the best Modern Jests Comic Tales, Poems, Fables, Epigrams, Epitaphs, and Riddles.* London, 1754 (12mo. 3s. Owen) BRITISH LIBRARY

Reviewed: *Monthly Review* 9 (1753): 473

The Merry Miller
See: SADLER, Thomas

The Messiah, a Sacred Poem [Four separately published books: *The Nativity, The Temptation, The Crucifixion,* and *The Resurrection*]
See: WEEKES, Nathaniel

1847 *Messiah, a Sacred Poem.* Cambridge, 1763 (4to. 2s.6d. Beecroft) BRITISH LIBRARY

Reviewed: *Critical Review* 16 (1763): 393–394

1848 *The Metamorphosis of a Prude*
NOT SEEN (no pub. details)

Reviewed: *Monthly Review* 15 (1756): 653

1849 [METASTASIO, Pietro Antonio Domenico Bonaventura]. *Artaxerxes. An English Opera. As it is Performed At the Theatre-Royal in Covent-Garden. The Music composed by Tho. Aug. Arne, Mus. Doc.* London, 1761 (8vo. 1s. Tonson) BRITISH LIBRARY

Reviewed: *Monthly Review* 26 (1762): 149
Critical Review 13 (1762): 158

METASTASIO, Pietro Antonio Domenico Bonaventura (translations and adaptations)
See: HOOLE, John. *The Works of Metastasio*
ROLT, Richard. *The Royal Shepherd*

Methodism Triumphant
See: LANCASTER, Nathaniel

The Methodist, a Comedy
See: POTTINGER, Israel

1850 MICHELL, Richard. *Hackwood Park, a Poem.* N.p., 1765 (4to. 1s.6d. Hawes) BODLEIAN

Reviewed: *Monthly Review* 34 (1766): 324
Critical Review 21 (1766): 318

1851 [MICKLE, William Julius]. *The Concubine: a Poem, in two Cantos. In the Manner of Spenser.* Oxford, 1767 (4to. 2s.6d. Dodsley) BRITISH LIBRARY

Reviewed: *Monthly Review* 36 (1767): 352–355
Critical Review 23 (1767): 398–399
Political Register 1 (1767): 484

1852 [MICKLE, William Julius]. *The Concubine: a Poem, in two Cantos. In the Manner of Spenser. A New Edition, with Alterations.* London, 1769 (4to. 2s.6d. Davies) BRITISH LIBRARY

Reviewed: *Critical Review* 28 (1769): 206–208

1853 MICKLE, William Julius. *The First Book of the Lusiad, published as A Specimen of a Translation of that celebrated Epic Poem.* Oxford, n.d. [BODLEIAN CAT.–1771] (8vo. 1s. Oxford printed, and sold by Cadell, &c. in London) BODLEIAN

Reviewed: *Monthly Review* 45 (1771): 182–188
Critical Review 32 (1771): 106–109
Gentleman's Magazine 41 (1771): 323–325
Town & Country Magazine 3 (1771): 437
British Magazine & General Review 1 (1771): 175–176

1854 [MICKLE, William Julius]. *Pollio: an Elegiac Ode. Written in the Wood near R--- Castle, 1762.* Oxford, 1766 (4to. 1s. Payne) BRITISH LIBRARY

Reviewed: *Monthly Review* 33 (1765): 486–487
Critical Review 20 (1765): 467–468
Gentleman's Magazine 35 (1765): 584

1855 [MICKLE, William Julius]. *Providence: or, Arandus and Emilec. A Poem.* London, 1762 (4to. 2s. Becket) BRITISH LIBRARY

Reviewed: *Monthly Review* 27 (1762): 394–395
Critical Review 14 (1762): 276–280
British Magazine 3 (1762): 606

Midas; an English Burletta
See: O'HARA, Kane

1856 *The Middlesex Freeholder; or, the Triumph of Liberty. Addressed to the Leading Members of the Society at the London Tavern, Supporters of the Bill of Rights. By a Gentleman of Middlesex.* London, 1769 (4to. 1s. Bladon) HARVARD (HOUGHTON)

Reviewed: *Monthly Review* 40 (1769): 251
Critical Review 27 (1769): 234
Critical Memoirs 1 (1769): 524
Town & Country Magazine (1769): 157
Political Register 4 (1769): 391

1857 *The Middlesex Petition Inversed.* London, 1769 (4to. 1s. Bladon) BODLEIAN

Reviewed: *Monthly Review* 41 (1769): 160
Critical Review 28 (1769): 71
Gentleman's Magazine 39 (1769): 405

1858 *A mid-night contemplation in the country* NOT SEEN (Fol. 6d. Owen)

Reviewed: *Monthly Review* 6 (1752): 397

1859 *The Midnight Spy, or, a View of the Transactions of London and Westminster, from The Hours of Ten in the Evening, till Five in the Morning; Exhibiting a great Variety of Scenes in High and Low Life, With the Characters of some Well Known Nocturnal Adventurers. Also the Humours of Round Houses, Night Houses, Bagnios, Jelly Houses, Gaming Tables, Routes, and other Places of Midnight Resort. With General and Particular Descriptions of Women of the Town.* London, 1766 (12mo. 2s. Cooke) BODLEIAN

Reviewed: *Monthly Review* 34 (1766): 315
Critical Review 21 (1766): 313

1860 MILLER, J[ohn]. *Poems on Several Occasions. To which are added, Dramatic Epistles from the Principal Characters in some of our most approved English Tragedies.* London, 1754 (8vo. 5s. Dodsley, Owen &c.) BRITISH LIBRARY

Reviewed: *Monthly Review* 10 (1754): 512

1861 [MILLS, Andrew Hervey]. *Bagatelles. In this Collection is reprinted the Fragment: or, Allen and Ella. Which (Unknown to the Author) Appeared some Years since under the Title of Collin and Lucy. To which is subjoined, a Journey to, and Description of, the Paraclete, near the city of Troyes, in Champagne, where Abelard and Eloisa were buried. All By the Same Hand.* London, 1767 (12mo. 3s. Dodsley, &c.) BRITISH LIBRARY

Reviewed: *Monthly Review* 37 (1767): 152
Critical Review 24 (1767): 58–63
Gentleman's Magazine 37 (1767): 411
London Magazine 36 (1767): 424

1862 [MILLS, Andrew Hervey]. *Colin and Lucy. A Fragment. Dated in the year 1564, being in or about the Sixth Year of the Reign of Queen Elizabeth.* London, n.d. [ESTC-1755] (4to. 6d. Owen) BRITISH LIBRARY

Reviewed: *Monthly Review* 12 (1755): 157–158

1863 MILTON, John. *Paradise Lost. A Poem, in Twelve Books. The Author John Milton. A New Edition, With Notes of various Authors, By Thomas Newton, D.D.* 2 vols. London, 1749 (In two large Volumes 4to. with Cuts, designed by Hayman, and engraved by Grignion and Ravenet, at the Expence of the Earl of Bath, to whom the Book is dedicated. It is now sold, by Mess. Tonson and Draper, for 1l.1s.6d. in Sheets, which was the Subscription Price; and will come to about 2l. handsomely bound.) BRITISH LIBRARY

Reviewed: *Monthly Review* 2 (1749–50): 188–212

1864 MILTON, John. *Paradise Regain'd. A Poem, in Four Books. To which is added Samson Agonistes: and Poems upon Several Occasions. The Author John Milton. A New Edition, With Notes of various Authors, By Thomas Newton, D.D.* London, 1752 (4to. 1l.5s.bound. Tonson, &c.) BRITISH LIBRARY

Reviewed: *Monthly Review* 8 (1753): 21–23

MILTON, John (adaptations)

Comus
See: COLMAN, George. *Comus, a Masque*

Lycidas
See: JACKSON, W. *Lycidas: a Musical Entertainment*
LAMBE, Thomas. *Lycidas. a Masque*

Paradise Lost
See: GREEN, George Smith. *A New Version of the Paradise Lost*
STILLINGFLEET, Benjamin. *Paradise Lost*

1865 MILWARD, Thomas. *Peleia; or, the Old Woman. A Mythological Eclogue.* London, 1763 (4to. 1s. Dodsley) BRITISH LIBRARY

Reviewed: *Monthly Review* 28 (1763): 238–239
Critical Review 15 (1763): 156
British Magazine 4 (1763): 98

1866 *The Mimic: a Poem. By the Author.* London, 1761 (4to. 1s. Scott) HARVARD (HOUGHTON)

Reviewed: *Monthly Review* 24 (1761): 356
Critical Review 11 (1761): 419

1867 MINIFIE, [Margaret and Susannah]. *The Histories of Lady Frances S———, and Lady Caroline S———. Written by the Miss Minifies, Of Fairwater, in Somersetshire.* 3 vols. London, 1763 (12mo. 9s. Dodsley) BRITISH LIBRARY

Reviewed: *Monthly Review* 29 (1763): 160
Critical Review 16 (1763): 108–117

1868 MINIFIE, [Margaret and Susannah]. *The Histories of Lady Frances S———, and Lady Caroline S———. Written by the Miss Minifies, Of Fairwater, in Somersetshire. Vol. IV.* London, 1763 (12mo. 3s. Dodsley) BRITISH LIBRARY

Reviewed: *Monthly Review* 31 (1764): 74
Critical Review 18 (1764): 158

1869 MINIFIE, [Margaret and Susannah]. *The Picture. A Novel. By the Miss Minifies, of Fairwater in Somersetshire.* 3 vols. London, 1766 (12mo. 9s. bound. Johnson) BRITISH LIBRARY

Reviewed: *Monthly Review* 34 (1766): 406
Critical Review 21 (1766): 288–291

1870 [MINIFIE, Susannah]. *Barford Abbey, a Novel. In a Series of Letters.* 2 vols. London, 1768 (12mo. 6s. Cadell) BRITISH LIBRARY

Reviewed: *Monthly Review* 38 (1768): 335
Critical Review 24 (1767): 422–430
Universal Museum 3 (1767): 652
Town & Country Magazine (1769): 551

1871 MINIFIE, [Susannah]. *The Cottage; a Novel: In a Series of Letters.* 3 vols. London, 1769 (12mo. 7s.6d. Durham &c.) BRITISH LIBRARY

Reviewed: *Monthly Review* 40 (1769): 519
Critical Review 28 (1769): 247–257
London Magazine 38 (1769): 379

1872 [MINIFIE, Susannah]. *Family Pictures, a Novel. Containing Curious and Interesting Memoirs of several Persons of Fashion, in W———re. By a Lady.* 2 vols. London, 1764 (12mo. 5s. Nicoll) BRITISH LIBRARY

Reviewed: *Monthly Review* 30 (1764): 243
Critical Review 18 (1764): 313
General Magazine 1 (1764): 96

1873 *The Minister of State, A Satire.* London, 1762 (4to. 1s.6d. Wilson and Fell) BRITISH LIBRARY

Reviewed: *Monthly Review* 27 (1762): 390–391
Critical Review 14 (1762): 316

The Minor
See: FOOTE, Samuel

Minorca A Tragedy
See: DELL, Henry

The Minstrel; or, The Progess of Genius
See: BEATTIE, James

The Mirrour. A Comedy
See: DELL, Henry

1874 *A Mirrour for the Critics, &c. &c. Written in the Year 1759. By an Oxfordshire Ploughman. To which are added, Female Volunteers, or Miscellaneous Pieces. Spoken Extempore on several Occasions, by a Sister of the Oxfordshire Ploughman*
NOT SEEN (8vo. 6d. Whiteridge)

Reviewed: *Monthly Review* 27 (1762): 393–394
Critical Review 14 (1762): 319

1875 *Mirth, a Poem in Answer to Warton's Pleasures of Melancholy By a Gentleman of Cambridge.* [Has been attributed to William Mason; ESTC says attribution probably false.] N.p., 1774 [ESTC-London] (4to. 1s.6d. Johnson. 1774) BRITISH LIBRARY

Reviewed: *Monthly Review* 51 (1774): 318
Critical Review 37 (1774): 313–314
Universal Catalogue 3 (1774) art. 511

Mirza and Fatima
See: SAURIN, Bernard Joseph

1876 *The miscellaneous and whimsical lucubrations of Lancelot Poverty-struck, an unfortunate son of Apollo*
NOT SEEN (2s. J. Cooke)

Reviewed: *Gentleman's Magazine* 28 (1758): 135

1877 *Miscellaneous Devotions in Prose and Verse. By a Convert from Infidelity.* London, 1757 (8vo. 6d. Lewis) BRITISH LIBRARY

Reviewed: *Monthly Review* 17 (1757): 381–382

1878 *Miscellaneous Odes I. The Fifth Ode of the Fourth Book of Horace to Augustus when abroad, imitated. II. An Ode to Friendship. III. An Ode to the Right Honble the Earl H----t. IV. An Ode to the Lord Bishop of N------h. V. An Ode to Virtue.* London, 1753 (4to. 1s. Reeve) UNIVERSITY OF ILLINOIS

Reviewed: *Monthly Review* 8 (1753): 238

Miscellaneous Pieces in two Volumes
See: JENYNS, Soame

1879 *Miscellaneous Pieces of Antient English Poesie. Viz. The Troublesome Raigne of King John, Written by Shakespeare, Extant in no Edition of his Writings. The Metamorphosis of Pigmalion's Image, and certain Satyres. By John Marston. The Scourge of Villanie. By the same. All printed before the Year 1600.* London, 1764 (12mo. 2s.6d. Horsfield) UNIVERSITY OF PENNSYLVANIA

Reviewed: *Monthly Review* 32 (1765): 315
Critical Review 19 (1765): 211–214

Miscellaneous Pieces of Poetry. Selected from Various Eminent Authors
See: STUART, Charles, and John BONAR (eds.)

Miscellaneous Poems: on Various Subjects, and Occasions
See: GILES, Joseph

Miscellaneous Poems, written By a Lady
See: BURTON, Philippina

Miscellaneous Reflections: or, An Evening's Meditation
See: LETCHWORTH, Thomas

1880 *Miscellanies. The Lion, Cock, and Peacock; a Fable. And an Essay on the ever-glorious Peace! concluded at Paris, in 1763*
NOT SEEN (4to. 2s.6d. Williams)

Reviewed: *Monthly Review* 37 (1767): 468
Critical Review 24 (1767): 226
London Magazine 36 (1767): 482
Universal Museum 3 (1767): 485

Miss Melmoth: or, The New Clarissa
See: BRISCOE, Sophia

1881 *The Mistakes of Men in Search of Happiness. An Ethic Epistle, to Mrs. *******.* London, 1761 (4to. 1s. Dodsley) BRITISH LIBRARY

Reviewed: *Monthly Review* 24 (1761): 444
Critical Review 11 (1761): 419

1882 [MITCHELL, John]. *The Female Pilgrim, or the Travels of Hephzibah, Under the Similitude of a Dream: In which is given, An historical Account of the Pilgrim's Extract, and a Description of her native Country, with the State of the Inhabitants thereof. –The Reason why, and Manner how she left the Place of her Nativity, in Search of a better Country.– The kind Entertainment she met with on the Road –The Dangers she went thro', with her Safe Arrival at the Country she travelled in Search of. Interspersed with Variety of Reflections, Dialogues, Songs, &c. The Whole calculated equally for Instruction and Entertainment, and suited to all Capacities.* London, 1762 (8vo. 7s. Johnston) BRITISH LIBRARY

Reviewed: *Monthly Review* 27 (1762): 219
Critical Review 14 (1762): 153

1883 *A Mob in the Pit: or, Lines addressed to the D--ch-ss of A---------ll.* London, 1773 (4to. 1s. Bladon. 1773) BRITISH LIBRARY

Reviewed: *Monthly Review* 48 (1773): 413
London Magazine 42 (1773): 249
Universal Catalogue [2] (1773) art. 590

1884 *The Mock Monarchs: or, the Benefits of High Blood.* 2 vols. London, n.d. [ESTC-1754?] (12mo. 6s. Crowder, &c.) BRITISH LIBRARY

Reviewed: *Monthly Review* 11 (1754): 471

1885 MOCULLOCH, Philim. *The Murphiad. A Mock Heroic Poem.* London, 1761 (8vo. 1s. Williams) BRITISH LIBRARY

Reviewed: *Monthly Review* 25 (1761): 78
Critical Review 12 (1761): 229–230
British Magazine 2 (1761): 550

1886 *Modern Characters: illustrated by Histories in Real Life, and Address'd to the Polite World.* 2 vols. London, 1753 (12mo. 6s. Gardner) BRITISH LIBRARY

Reviewed: *Monthly Review* 9 (1753): 144

Modern Chastity: or, the Agreeable Rape
See: ALLEN, Bennet

1887 *The Modern Couple, or the History of Miss Davers. In a Series of Letters.* 2 vols.
NOT SEEN (12mo. 5s.sewed. Noble)

Reviewed: *Monthly Review* 43 (1770): 500
Critical Review 31 (1771): 76

1888 *The Modern Courtezan, an Heroic Poem. Inscrib'd to Miss F---y M----y. With Notes, Critical, Historical, Explanatory, and Comical, prefix'd.* London, n.d. [ESTC-1750?] (4to. 1s. Carpenter) BRITISH LIBRARY

Reviewed: *Monthly Review* 5 (1751): 77

1889 *Modern Extravagance. A poetical Essay*
NOT SEEN (4to. 1s. Cooke)

Reviewed: *Monthly Review* 27 (1762): 219

Reviewed: *Monthly Review* 37 (1767): 315
Critical Review 24 (1767): 225–226
Universal Museum 3 (1767): 484

1890 *The Modern Fine Gentleman, A Novel, In Two Volumes.* 2 vols. London, 1774 (12mo. 5s.sewed. Lowndes) BRITISH LIBRARY

Reviewed: *Monthly Review* 52 (1775): 275–276
Critical Review 38 (1774): 473

The Modern Fine Lady
See: JENYNS, Soame

1891 *Modern Gallantry display'd; or, the Courtezan delineated; in the authentic Memoirs of several celebrated Ladies of high Taste, who are equally distinguished for their Beauties and Blemishes; interspersed with Variety of real Characters drawn from the Life, and now existing in this Metropolis. By the Author of the Midnight Spy*
NOT SEEN (12mo. 3s. Cooke)

Reviewed: *Monthly Review* 36 (1767): 400
Critical Review 23 (1767): 311

1892 *Modern Gallantry; or the New Art of Love. By a Lady, well-known for her literary Acquisitions, and Amorous Intrigues*
NOT SEEN (4to. 1s. Roson)

Reviewed: *Monthly Review* 39 (1768): 401–402
Critical Review 26 (1768): 315–316
Gentleman's Magazine 38 (1768): 533
London Magazine 37 (1768): 553–554

1893 *Modern Honour: a Poem, in Two Cantos. Supposed to be Written by Dean Swift, in 1740, And Addressed to Mr. P***.* London, 1760 (4to. 2s.6d. Baldwin) HARVARD (HOUGHTON)

Reviewed: *Monthly Review* 23 (1760): 85–86
Critical Review 10 (1760): 72–74
British Magazine 1 (1760): 489

1894 *Modern humour. An entire new collection of tales, allegories, fables, maxims, remarks, and repartees, instructive and entertaining*
NOT SEEN (12mo. 3s. Cooper)

Reviewed: *Monthly Review* 10 (1754): 237–238

1895 *The Modern Lovers: or, the Adventures of Cupid, the God of Love: a Novel.* London, 1756 (12mo. 3s. Cooke) BRITISH LIBRARY

Reviewed: *Monthly Review* 15 (1756): 536

Modern Matrimony. A Poem
See: DOBBS, Francis

1896 *The Modern Wife. A Novel.* 2 vols. London, 1769 (12mo. 6s. Lownds) BRITISH LIBRARY

Reviewed: *Monthly Review* 39 (1768): 411
Critical Review 26 (1768): 452–457
London Magazine 37 (1768): 552
Political Register 3 (1768): 383

Modest Exceptions, from the Court of Parnassus
See: IRELAND, Stella

1897 MOFFET, William. *The Irish Hudibras. Hesperi-neso-graphia: or, a Description of the Western Isle. In Eight Cantos. With Annotations.* London, 1755 (8vo. 1s. Reason) BRITISH LIBRARY

Reviewed: *Monthly Review* 12 (1755): 378

MOLIÈRE
See: POQUELIN DE MOLIÈRE, Jean Baptiste

Momus, a Poem
See: CAREY, George Savile

1898 MONCREIFF, John. *Appius: a Tragedy. As it is Acted at the Theatre-Royal, in Covent-Garden.* London, 1755 (8vo. 1s.6d. Millar) BRITISH LIBRARY

Reviewed: *Monthly Review* 12 (1755): 232

1899 [MONCREIFF, John]. *Themistocles, a Satire on Modern Marriage.* 1st ed. reviewed; copy seen 2d ed.: London, 1759 (4to. 6d. Morley) BRITISH LIBRARY

Reviewed: *Monthly Review* 22 (1760): 167
Critical Review 8 (1759): 500
London Magazine 28 (1759): 688

1900 *A Monody on the Death of Dr. Oliver Goldsmith.* London, 1774 (4to. 1s.6d. Davies. 1774) BRITISH LIBRARY

Reviewed: *Monthly Review* 51 (1774): 164–165
Critical Review 38 (1774): 76
Town & Country Magazine 6 (1774): 437
Universal Catalogue 3 (1774) art. 927

1901 *A Monody on the Death of General Wolfe*
NOT SEEN (4to. 1s. Thrush)

Reviewed: *Monthly Review* 21 (1759): 456
Critical Review 8 (1759): 412–413
London Magazine 28 (1759): 631

1902 *A Monody on the Death of his Most Sacred Majesty, George II. King of Great-Britain, France and Ireland, Defender of the Faith, &c. Who departed this Life October the 25th, 1760.* London, 1760 (1s. Pottinger) BRITISH LIBRARY

Reviewed: *Monthly Review* 23 (1760): 412
Critical Review 10 (1760): 327
British Magazine 1 (1760): 665

1903 *A Monody on the Death of the Reverend Mr. George Whitefield*
NOT SEEN (4to. 6d. Miller)

Reviewed: *Monthly Review* 44 (1771): 90
Critical Review 31 (1771): 74–75
Town & Country Magazine 2 (1770): 599

1904 *A Monody on the Decease of His Royal Highness William Augustus, Duke of Cumberland, Addressed to the Honourable -----.* London, 1765 (4to. 1s. Becket) BRITISH LIBRARY

Reviewed: *Monthly Review* 33 (1765): 405
Critical Review 20 (1765): 395–396
Gentleman's Magazine 35 (1765): 529

Monody to the Memory of a Young Lady who died in Child-bed
See: SHAW, Cuthbert

A Monody: to the Memory of Mrs. Margaret Woffington
See: HOOLE, John

1905 *A Monody. Written by an absent Husband.* London, 1769 (4to. 1s.6d. Griffin) YALE (BEINECKE)

Reviewed: *Monthly Review* 42 (1770): 142–143
Critical Review 28 (1769): 71–72
Gentleman's Magazine 39 (1769): 357

1906 *Monopoliza: or, Craesus turn'd Poulterer. An Epic Poem. Book the First.* London, 1753 (Fol. 1s. Cooper) NEWBERRY

Reviewed: *Monthly Review* 8 (1753): 391

1907 M[ONTAGU], Lady M[ary] W[ortley]. *The Poetical Works Of the Right Honourable Lady M--y W--y M--------e.* London, 1768 (8vo. 2s.sewed. Williams) BRITISH LIBRARY

Reviewed: *Monthly Review* 38 (1768): 149
Critical Review 25 (1768): 228–230
Gentleman's Magazine 38 (1768): 133
Political Register 2 (1768): 121

1908 [MONTAGUE, Mary Seymour]. *An Original Essay on Woman, in Four Epistles. Written by a Lady.* London, 1771 (4to. 2s.6d. Swan) BRITISH LIBRARY

Reviewed: *Monthly Review* 44 (1771): 489–490
Critical Review 31 (1771): 396–397

1909 MONTESQUIEU, Charles de Secondat, Baron de. *The Temple of Gnidus. A Poem from the French Prose of M. Secondat, Baron de Montesquieu*
NOT SEEN (4to. 1s.6d. Hooper)

Reviewed: *Monthly Review* 29 (1763): 154–155
Critical Review 15 (1763): 389–390

MONTESQUIEU, Charles de Secondat, Baron de.
The Temple of Gnidus (1765)
See: SAYER, John

1910 MONTESQUIEU, Charles de Secondat, Baron de. *The Temple of Gnidos. Translated a Second Time from the French of Mons. De Secondat, Baron de Montesquieu.* London, 1767 (8vo. 1s.6d. Kearsly) BODLEIAN

Reviewed: *Monthly Review* 38 (1768): 239–240
Critical Review 25 (1768): 216
Gentleman's Magazine 38 (1768): 35–36
Political Register 2 (1768): 282

1911 MOORE, Rev. Mr. *A Sea-piece, written on the Coast near Mounts-Bay in Cornwal*
NOT SEEN (4to. 6d. Baldwin)

Reviewed: *Monthly Review* 22 (1760): 512–513
Critical Review 10 (1760): 78
British Magazine 1 (1760): 490

1912 MOORE, Anthony. *An Essay on the Art of Preaching, Addressed to the Clergy.* Falmouth, 1758 (8vo. 1s.6d. Cave) BRITISH LIBRARY

Reviewed: *Monthly Review* 19 (1758): 585–586
Critical Review 6 (1758): 330–332
Gentleman's Magazine 28 (1758): 490–492

1913 [MOORE, Edward]. *The Gamester. A Tragedy. As it is Acted at the Theatre-Royal in Drury-Lane.* London, 1753 (8vo. 1s.6d. Franklin) BRITISH LIBRARY

Reviewed: *Monthly Review* 8 (1753): 146–147

1914 MOORE, [Edward]. *Gil Blas. A Comedy. As it is Acted at the Theatre-Royal in Drury-lane.* London, 1751 (1s.6d. Franklin) BRITISH LIBRARY

Reviewed: *Monthly Review* 4 (1750–51): 295–297

1915 [MOORE, Henry]. *A Poem Sacred to the Memory Of the late Reverend P. Doddridge, D.D. By H---. M---.* London, 1752 (4to. 6d. Buckland) BRITISH LIBRARY

Reviewed: *Monthly Review* 6 (1752): 156

1916 *A Moral and Descriptive Epistle, Inscribed To the Honourable Miss *****. With A Cerealian Hymn for 1758. Set to Music.* London, 1761 (4to. 2s. Stuart) NEW YORK PUBLIC LIBRARY

Reviewed: *Monthly Review* 24 (1761): 355
Critical Review 11 (1761): 299–300
British Magazine 2 (1761): 265

1917 MORE, Hannah. *The Inflexible Captive: a Tragedy.* Bristol, 1774 (8vo. 1s.6d. Cadell, &c. 1774) BRITISH LIBRARY

Reviewed: *Monthly Review* 50 (1774): 243–251
Critical Review 37 (1774): 396–397 [2d ed.]
Universal Catalogue 3 (1774) art. 329

1918 MORE, Hannah. *The Search after Happiness: a Pastoral. In Three Dialogues. By a Young Lady*. Bristol, n.d. [IU CAT–1766?] (8vo. 1s.6d. Cadell, &c. 1773) UNIVERSITY OF ILLINOIS

Reviewed: *Monthly Review* 49 (1773): 202–204
Critical Review 35 (1773): 474
London Magazine 42 (1773): 302
Universal Catalogue [2] (1773) art. 736

1919 MORE, Hannah. *The Search after Happiness: a Pastoral Drama. The Third Edition*. Bristol, 1774 (8vo. 1s.6d. Cadell. 1773) BRITISH LIBRARY

Reviewed: *Monthly Review* 50 (1774): 155–156
Gentleman's Magazine 44 (1774): 225

1920 MORELL, [Thomas]. *Eschylus's Prometheus Captivus*
NOT SEEN (4to. 10s.6d.sewed. Longman. 1774)

Reviewed: *Monthly Review* 50 (1774): 326

1921 [MORELL, Charles]. *The Contrast. A Familiar Epistle to Mr. C. Churchill, on reading His Poem called Independence. By a Neighbour*. London, 1764 (4to. 1s. Rivington) BODLEIAN

Reviewed: *Monthly Review* 31 (1764): 318
Critical Review 18 (1764): 318

MORELL, Sir Charles (pseud.)
See: RIDLEY, James

1922 MOREY, Thomas. *On the Birth-Day of his Royal Highness George Prince of Wales, a Poem. Written on the 4th of June, 1759. By Mr. Thomas Morey*
NOT SEEN (Fol. 1s. Cabe)

Reviewed: *Monthly Review* 21 (1759): 455–456
Critical Review 8 (1759): 410

1923 MOREY, Thomas. *The Retrospect: Or a View of Things past*
NOT SEEN (Fol. 1s. Cabe)

Reviewed: *Monthly Review* 22 (1760): 77

1924 MORGAN, McNamara. *Philoclea. A Tragedy. As it is Acted at the Theatre Royal in Covent-Garden*. London, 1754 (8vo. 2s.6d. Dodsley) BRITISH LIBRARY

Reviewed: *Monthly Review* 10 (1754): 157

1925 [MORGAN, Macnamara]. *The Scandalizade, a Panegyri-Satiri-Serio-Comic-Dramatic Poem. By Porcupinus Pelagius, Author of the Causicade*. London, 1750 (4to. 37pp. 1s.6d. Printed for G. Smith) BRITISH LIBRARY

Reviewed: *Monthly Review* 2 (1749–50): 450–451

The Morning Walk; or, City Encompass'd
See: DRAPER, W. H.

A Morning's Meditation, or, a Descant on the Times
See: LETCHWORTH, Thomas

1926 MORRIS, Ralph. *A Narrative of the Life and astonishing Adventures of John Daniel, A Smith at Royston in Hertfordshire, For a Course of seventy Years. Containing, The melancholy Occasion of his Travels. His Shipwreck with one Companion on a desolate Island. Their way of Life. His accidental discovery of a Woman for his Companion. Their peopling the Island. Also, A Description of a most surprising Engine, invented by his Son Jacob, on which he flew to the Moon, with some Account of its Inhabitants. His return, and accidental Fall into the Habitation of a Sea-Monster, with whom he lived two Years. His further Excursions in Search of England. His Residence in Lapland, and Travels to Norway, from whence he arrived at Aldborough, and further Transactions till his death, in 1711. Aged 97. Illustrated with several Copper Plates, Engraved by Mr. Boitard. Taken from his own Mouth, By Mr. Ralph Morris*. London, 1751 (12mo. 3s. Cooper) BRITISH LIBRARY

Reviewed: *Monthly Review* 5 (1751): 518

1927 MORTIMER, Thomas. *The Life and Military Exploits of Pyrrhus, King of Epire. In Six Books. Written Originally in French by M. Gautier. And now Render'd into English, By Thomas Mortimer*. [Translation of *Les Voyages et les expéditions de Pirrhus Roi d' Épire* by J. Gautier.] London, 1751 (8vo. 5s.boards. Buckland, Griffiths, &c. &c.) BRITISH LIBRARY

Reviewed: *Monthly Review* 5 (1751): 369–370

1928 MORTON, [John]. *Ode, Inscrib'd To The Reverend Dr. Watts: upon his promoting a Plan for a Country Infirmary at Leicester*. Leicester, 1766 (4to. 1s. Flexney) BRITISH LIBRARY

Reviewed: *Monthly Review* 36 (1767): 162
Critical Review 22 (1766): 381–382

1929 [MOSS, Thomas]. *Poems on several Occasions*. Wolverhampton, 1769 (4to. 2s.6d. Longman. 1769) BRITISH LIBRARY

Reviewed: *Monthly Review* 42 (1770): 145
Critical Review 29 (1770): 207–208

1930 *The Mother-in-Law: or, the Innocent Sufferer. Interspersed with the Uncommon and Entertaining Adventures of Mr. Hervey Falconer. In Two Volumes*. London, 1757 (12ves. 6s. Noble) HARVARD (HOUGHTON)

Reviewed: *Monthly Review* 17 (1757): 81
Critical Review 4 (1757): 95

Mother Midnight's comical Pocket-Book
See: HUMDRUM, Humphrey (pseud.)

The Mother: or, the Happy Distress. A Novel
See: GUTHRIE, William

1931 *The Motto, or, An Inscription for his Majesty's Wedding-Ring; a Poem: Humbly addressed to the King*
NOT SEEN (4to. 1s. Pottinger)

Reviewed: *Monthly Review* 25 (1761): 319
Critical Review 12 (1761): 236

MOUHY, Chevalier de. *Female Banishment*
See: FIEUX, Charles de, Chevalier de Mouhy

1932 [MOUNTFORT, William]. *The Fall of Mortimer. An Historical Play. Dedicated to the Right Honourable John Earl of Bute, &c. &c. &c.* London, 1763 (8vo. 2s. Kearsly) BRITISH LIBRARY

Reviewed: *Monthly Review* 28 (1763): 241–242
Critical Review 15 (1763): 234–235
British Magazine 4 (1763): 158

1933 MOZEEN, T[homas]. *A Collection of Miscellaneous Essays*. London, 1762 (8vo. 5s. Stuart) BRITISH LIBRARY

Reviewed: *Monthly Review* 27 (1762): 160
Critical Review 14 (1762): 47–49
British Magazine 3 (1762): 269

1934 MOZEEN, T[homas]. *Fables in Verse*. 2 vols. London, 1765 (8vo. 1s. Bladon) BRITISH LIBRARY

Reviewed: *Monthly Review* 33 (1765): 241
Critical Review 20 (1765): 171–176

1935 MOZEEN, T[homas]. *The Lyric Pacquet. Containing most of the Favourite Songs, serious and comic, that have been performed for three Seasons past at Sadler's Wells, &c.*
NOT SEEN (8vo. 2s.6d. Dixwell)

Reviewed: *Monthly Review* 31 (1764): 317–318
Critical Review 18 (1764): 238

1936 [MOZEEN, Thomas]. *Young Scarron*. London, 1752 (12mo. 3s. Trye) BRITISH LIBRARY

Reviewed: *Monthly Review* 5 (1751): 518–519

1937 MUKINS, Isaac. *The History of Charlotte Villars: A Narrative founded on Truth, Interspersed with Variety of Incidents Instructive and Entertaining*. London, 1756 (12mo. 3s. Crowder) BRITISH LIBRARY

Reviewed: *Monthly Review* 13 (1755): 510

1938 MULSO, Thomas. *Callistus; or, the Man of Fashion. And Sophronius; or, the Country Gentleman. In Three Dialogues*. London, 1768 (8vo. 2s.6d. White) BRITISH LIBRARY

Reviewed: *Monthly Review* 38 (1768): 347–355
Critical Review 25 (1768): 213
Universal Museum 4 (1768): 148

1939 *Mumbo Chumbo: A Tale. Written in antient manner. Recommended to Modern Devotees.* London, 1765 (4to. 1s. Becket) BRITISH LIBRARY

Reviewed: *Monthly Review* 32 (1765): 232–233
Critical Review 19 (1765): 149–150
Candid Review 1 (1765): 185–186

1940 *Mundus Muliebris: Or, An Essay on Woman* NOT SEEN (4to. 6d. Jackson)

Reviewed: *Monthly Review* 29 (1763): 465
Critical Review 16 (1763): 479

1941 [MUNDY, Francis Noel Clarke]. *Poems.* Oxford, 1768 (4to. 2s.6d. Printed at Oxford, by Jackson; and sold by Becket in London. 1768) BRITISH LIBRARY

Reviewed: *Monthly Review* 40 (1769): 306–310
Critical Review 27 (1769): 66–67
Gentleman's Magazine 39 (1769): 157
London Magazine 38 (1769): 43–44
Critical Memoirs 1 (1769): 34–37 and 523
Town & Country Magazine [1] (1769): 45

1942 MURDOCH, John (trans.). *The Tears of Sensibility. Translated from the French of Mons. D'Arnaud.* 2 vols. NOT SEEN (12mo. 5s.bound. Dilly. 1773)

Reviewed: *Monthly Review* 48 (1773): 319–320
Critical Review 35 (1773): 233
London Magazine 42 (1773): 39
Universal Catalogue [2] (1773) art. 111

The Murphiad
See: MOCULLOCH, Philim

1943 MURPHY, [Arthur]. *All in the Wrong. A Comedy. As it is Acted at the Theatre-Royal in Drury-Lane.* London, 1761 (8vo. 1s.6d. Vaillant) BRITISH LIBRARY

Reviewed: *Monthly Review* 25 (1761): 472–473
Critical Review 12 (1761): 431–437
British Magazine 2 (1761): 662

1944 [MURPHY, Arthur]. *Alzuma, a Tragedy. As performed at the Theatre Royal in Covent-Garden.* [Adaptation of Voltaire.] London, 1773 (8vo. 1s.6d. Lowndes. 1773) BRITISH LIBRARY

Reviewed: *Monthly Review* 48 (1773): 212–215
Critical Review 35 (1773): 229
Universal Catalogue [2] (1773) art. 362

1945 MURPHY, Arthur. *The Apprentice. A Farce, in two acts, As it is Perform'd at the Theatre-Royal in Drury-Lane.* London, 1756 (8vo. 1s. Vaillant) BRITISH LIBRARY

Reviewed: *Monthly Review* 14 (1756): 78
Critical Review 1 (1756): 78–82
Gentleman's Magazine 26 (1756): 47

1946 MURPHY, Arthur. *The Citizen. A Farce. As it is performed at the Theatre Royal, in Covent Garden.* London, 1763 (8vo. 1s. Kearsly) BRITISH LIBRARY

Reviewed: *Monthly Review* 28 (1763): 166–167
Critical Review 15 (1763): 113–119
British Magazine 4 (1763): 98

1947 [MURPHY, Arthur]. *The Desert Island, a Dramatic Poem, in Three Acts. As it is Acted at the Theatre-Royal in Drury-Lane.* London, 1760 (8vo. 1s. Vaillant) BRITISH LIBRARY

Reviewed: *Monthly Review* 22 (1760): 135–140
Critical Review 9 (1760): 133–140
British Magazine 1 (1760): 155

1948 MURPHY, Arthur. *The Examiner. A Satire.* London, 1761 (4to. 1s.6d. Coote) BRITISH LIBRARY

Reviewed: *Monthly Review* 25 (1761): 398
Critical Review 12 (1761): 400

1949 [MURPHY, Arthur]. *The Grecian Daughter: a Tragedy: As it is acted at the Theatre-Royal in Drury-lane.* London, 1772 (8vo. 1s.6d. Griffin. 1772) BRITISH LIBRARY

Reviewed: *Monthly Review* 46 (1772): 259–260
Critical Review 33 (1772): 224–229
Gentleman's Magazine 42 (1772): 137–139

1950 MURPHY, Arthur. *No One's Enemy but His Own. A Comedy In Three Acts, As it is Performed at the Theatre-Royal in Covent-Garden.* [Adaptation of Voltaire's *L'indiscret.*] London, 1764 (8vo. 1s.6d. Vaillant) BRITISH LIBRARY

Reviewed: *Monthly Review* 30 (1764): 70
Critical Review 17 (1764): 49–51

1951 MURPHY, Arthur. *An Ode to the Naiads of Fleet-Ditch.* London, 1761 (4to. 1s. Cooper) BRITISH LIBRARY

Reviewed: *Monthly Review* 24 (1761): 444
Critical Review 11 (1761): 495
British Magazine 2 (1761): 382

1952 MURPHY, [Arthur]. *The Old Maid. A Comedy In Two Acts, As it is Performed at the Theatre-Royal in Drury-Lane.* London, 1761 (8vo. 1s. Vaillant) BRITISH LIBRARY

Reviewed: *Monthly Review* 25 (1761): 473
Critical Review 12 (1761): 437–438
British Magazine 2 (1761): 662

1953 MURPHY, Arthur. *The Orphan of China, a Tragedy, As it is perform'd at the Theatre-Royal in Drury-Lane.* [Adaptation of Voltaire.] London, 1759 (8vo. 1s.6d. Vaillant) BRITISH LIBRARY

Reviewed: *Monthly Review* 20 (1759): 575–576
Critical Review 7 (1759): 434–440

1954 MURPHY, [Arthur]. *A Poetical Epistle to Mr. Samuel Johnson, A.M. By Mr. Murphy.* London, 1768 (Fol. 1s. Vaillant) FOLGER

Reviewed: *Monthly Review* 23 (1760): 412
Critical Review 10 (1760): 319–320
London Magazine 29 (1760): 560
British Magazine 1 (1760): 602

1955 [MURPHY, Arthur]. *The School for Guardians. A Comedy. As it is Performing at the Theatre-Royal in Covent-Garden.* [Adaptation of Molière's *L'école des femmes*.] London, 1767 (8vo. 1s.6d. Becket) BRITISH LIBRARY

Reviewed: *Monthly Review* 36 (1767): 71–72
Critical Review 23 (1767): 59–60
Gentleman's Magazine 37 (1767): 34

1956 [MURPHY, Arthur]. *The Spouter: or, the Triple Revenge. A Comic Farce, in Two Acts. As it was intended to be perform'd. With the Original Prologue. Written by the Author; and intended to be spoke by Mr. Garrick, dress'd in Black.* London, 1756 (8vo. 1s. Reeve) BRITISH LIBRARY

Reviewed: *Monthly Review* 14 (1756): 67
Critical Review 1 (1756): 146–147

1957 [MURPHY, Arthur]. *The Upholsterer, or What News? A Farce, In Two Acts. As it is Performed at the Theatre Royal, in Drury-Lane. By the Author of the Apprentice.* London, 1758 (8vo. 1s. Vaillant) LIBRARY OF CONGRESS

Reviewed: *Monthly Review* 18 (1758): 415–420
Critical Review 5 (1758): 330–333
Literary Magazine 3 (1758): 170–173

1958 MURPHY, [Arthur]. *The Way to Keep Him, a Comedy In Five Acts, As it is performed at the Theatre-Royal in Drury-Lane. By Mr. Murphy. The Fourth Edition.* London, 1761 (8vo. 1s.6d. Vaillant) BRITISH LIBRARY

Reviewed: *Monthly Review* 24 (1761): 158–159
Critical Review 11 (1761): 48–52
Gentleman's Magazine 31 (1761): 46
London Magazine 30 (1761): 56
British Magazine 2 (1761): 46

1959 MURPHY, Arthur. *The Way to Keep Him, a Comedy In Three Acts: As it is perform'd at the Theatre-Royal in Drury-Lane.* London, 1760 (8vo. 1s.6d. Vaillant) BRITISH LIBRARY

Reviewed: *Monthly Review* 22 (1760): 140–145
Critical Review 9 (1760): 141–143
British Magazine 1 (1760): 156

1960 [MURPHY, Arthur]. *What we must All come to. A Comedy In Two Acts, As it was intended to be Acted at the Theatre-Royal in Covent-Garden.* London, 1764 (8vo. 1s. Vaillant) BRITISH LIBRARY

Reviewed: *Monthly Review* 30 (1764): 70
Critical Review 17 (1764): 51–52

1961 [MURPHY, Arthur]. *Zenobia: a Tragedy. As it is performed at the Theatre Royal in Drury-Lane. By the Author of the Orphan of China.* London, 1768 (8vo. 1s. Griffin) BRITISH LIBRARY

Reviewed: *Monthly Review* 38 (1768): 244
Critical Review 25 (1768): 314
Political Register 2 (1768): 320

1962 [MURRAY, James]. *The Travels of the Imagination; A true Journey from Newcastle to London, in a Stage-Coach. With Observations upon the Metropolis. By J. M.* London, 1773 (8vo. 1s.6d. Dilly) BODLEIAN

Reviewed: *Monthly Review* 48 (1773): 329–330
Critical Review 36 (1773): 79
London Magazine 42 (1773): 195

1963 MURRAY, Oliver James. *The Candid Inquisitor; or, Mock Patriotism Displayed; a Poem*
NOT SEEN (4to. 1s.6d. Shatwell)

Reviewed: *Monthly Review* 45 (1771): 412
Critical Review 32 (1771): 392
Gentleman's Magazine 41 (1771): 560

Musae Seatoniae
See: REED, Isaac (ed.)

MUSAEUS (translations)
See: GREENE, Edward Burnaby. *Hero and Leander*
SLADE, John. *The Loves of Hero and Leander*

1964 *The Muse in a Fright; or, Britannia's Lamentation: A Rhapsody. Containing a Succinct Account of the Rise and Progress of British Liberty, and the Establishment of the Press; with the Methods now taking to Destroy it. In which will be displayed, A Number of Whole Length Characters, &c.* London, n.d. (4to. 1s.6d. Bew) NEWBERRY

Reviewed: *Monthly Review* 50 (1774): 316
Critical Review 37 (1774): 314
Universal Catalogue 3 (1774) art. 372

1965 *The Muse in a Moral Humour: being, a Collection Of Agreeable and Instructive Tales, Fables, Pastorals, &c. By Several Hands.* London, 1757 (8vo. 3s. Noble) BRITISH LIBRARY

Reviewed: *Critical Review* 3 (1757): 477

1966 *The Muse in Miniature, a series of Moral Miscellanies, Humbly attempted by The Trifler.* London, 1771 (no pub. details) BRITISH LIBRARY

Reviewed: *London Magazine* 40 (1771): 274

1967 *The Muses Address to David Garrick, Esq; with Harlequin's Remonstrance, In Answer to the said Address.* London, 1761 (8vo. 6d. Nicoll) BODLEIAN

Reviewed: *Monthly Review* 25 (1761): 392
Critical Review 12 (1761): 316
British Magazine 2 (1761): 550

1968 *The Muse's Blossoms: or, Juvenile Poems.* London, 1769 (8vo. 1s. Printed at Bath; sold by Robinson and Co. in London) BRITISH LIBRARY

Reviewed: *Monthly Review* 40 (1769): 302–306
Critical Review 27 (1769): 153
Gentleman's Magazine 39 (1769): 158
London Magazine 38 (1769): 268
Critical Memoirs 1 (1769): 433–436 and 522
Town & Country Magazine [1] (1769): 101

1969 *The Muses choice; or, best collection of humorous tales, epigrams, &c.*
NOT SEEN (1s.6d. Stamper)

Reviewed: *Monthly Review* 5 (1751): 463

1970 *The Muse's Recreation, in Four Poems, viz. The Farewell to Summer, a Pastoral Elegy. The Queen's Arrival, a Pastoral. Silence, a Poem. Devotion, a Rhapsody.* London, 1762 (4to. 1s. Johnston) BRITISH LIBRARY

Reviewed: *Monthly Review* 26 (1762): 151
Critical Review 13 (1762): 80
British Magazine 3 (1762): 102

The Musical Lady
See: COLMAN, George (the elder)

1971 *The Mystic Miracle; or, Living Grave: a Poem. Inscribed to the Rev. Mr. Lindsey*
NOT SEEN (8vo. 1s. French)

Reviewed: *Monthly Review* 51 (1774): 318
Critical Review 38 (1774): 153
Town & Country Magazine 6 (1774): 660
Universal Catalogue 3 (1774) art. 1050

1972 [MYTTON, Thomas]. *A Poem on the Pomfret Statues. To which is added another on Laura's Grave.* Oxford, 1758 (4to. 6d. Oxford printed for Daniel Prince. Sold also by Rivington and Fletcher in London) BRITISH LIBRARY

Reviewed: *Monthly Review* 19 (1758): 206

The Nabob: or, Asiatic Plunderers
See: CLARKE, Richard

1973 *Nancy to John; or the Whore to the Justice. A Ballad*
NOT SEEN (Fol. 6d. Wicks)

Reviewed: *Monthly Review* 23 (1760): 411–412

A Narrative of the Life and astonishing Adventures of John Daniel
See: MORRIS, Ralph

1974 *Nature. A Novel. In a Series of Letters*
NOT SEEN (12mo. 3s. Murdoch)

Reviewed: *Monthly Review* 42 (1770): 250

1975 *Nature: an Ethic Epistle, Inscribed to the Honourable Mrs. D-----y.* London, 1764 (4to. 1s. Flexney) UNIVERSITY OF ILLINOIS

Reviewed: *Monthly Review* 30 (1764): 241–242
Critical Review 17 (1764): 238

1976 *The Navy Leeches: a Poem*
NOT SEEN (4to. 1s.6d. Richardson and Urquhart)

Reviewed: *Monthly Review* 40 (1769): 176
Critical Review 27 (1769): 154
Gentleman's Magazine 39 (1769): 157
Critical Memoirs 1 (1769): 522

Neck or Nothing, A Farce
See: GARRICK, David

1977 [NELTHORPE, George]. *A Crust for the Critics. Inscribed to the Most Impertinent Puppy on Earth.* London, 1762 (4to. 6d. Grinsel) NEW YORK PUBLIC LIBRARY

Reviewed: *Monthly Review* 26 (1762): 150

1978 [NELTHORPE, George]. *Julia to Pollio. Upon his leaving her abroad. Written some Years ago. And now first published from the Original Manuscript.* London, 1770 (4to. 2s. Robinson and Co.) BRITISH LIBRARY

Reviewed: *Monthly Review* 42 (1770): 486
Critical Review 30 (1770): 227–230
London Magazine 39 (1770): 580
Town & Country Magazine 2 (1770): 548

NEMO, Sir Nicholas (pseud.)
See: DUNCOMBE, John

1979 [NEVILE, Thomas]. *The Eighteenth Epistle Of the First Book of Horace Imitated.* London, 1756 (4to. 1s. Dodsley) NEWBERRY

Reviewed: *Monthly Review* 14 (1756): 454

1980 [NEVILE, Thomas]. *The First Satire of the First Book of Horace imitated.* London, 1755 (4to. 1s. Dodsley) BRITISH LIBRARY

Reviewed: *Monthly Review* 12 (1755): 230–231
Gentleman's Magazine 25 (1755): 142

1981 NEVILE, Thomas. *The Fourteenth Satire of Juvenal Imitated By Thomas Nevile, A.M. Fellow of Jesus College, Cambridge.* London, 1769 (4to. 1s. Beecroft. 1769) YALE (BEINECKE)

Reviewed: *Monthly Review* 40 (1769): 136–137
Critical Review 27 (1769): 152–153
Town & Country Magazine [1] (1769): 101

1982 NEVILE, Thomas. *The Georgics of Virgil Translated.* Cambridge, 1767 (8vo. 2s. Cadell) BRITISH LIBRARY

Reviewed: *Monthly Review* 36 (1767): 337–340
Critical Review 23 (1767): 282–284
Political Register 1 (1767): 486

1983 NEVILE, Thomas. *Imitations of Horace.* London, 1758 (12mo. 2s. Dodsley, &c.) BRITISH LIBRARY

Reviewed: *Monthly Review* 18 (1758): 538–541

1984 NEVILE, Thomas. *Imitations of Juvenal and Persius.* London, 1769 (Small 8vo. 2s. Beecroft, &c. 1769) BRITISH LIBRARY

Reviewed: *Monthly Review* 42 (1770): 46–52

1985 [NEVILE, Thomas]. *The Seventeenth Epistle Of the First Book of Horace Imitated.* London, 1756 (4to. 1s. Dodsley) BRITISH LIBRARY

Reviewed: *Monthly Review* 14 (1756): 259–260
Critical Review 1 (1756): 164

1986 NEVILL, Valentine. *The Reduction of Louisbourg. A Poem, Wrote on board His Majesty's Ship Orford, in Louisbourg Harbour. By Valentine Nevill, Esquire, of Greenwich in Kent, Secretary to the Honourable Admiral Townsend.* Portsmouth, 1758 (Fol. 1s. Owen) LIBRARY OF CONGRESS

Reviewed: *Monthly Review* 20 (1759): 90–91
  Critical Review 6 (1758): 522
  Gentleman's Magazine 28 (1758): 600

1987 *A New Ballad on Subsidy Treaties. To the Tune of Packington's Pound.* London, n.d. [ESTC-1760?] (Fol. 6d. Web) BRITISH LIBRARY

Listed: *Monthly Review* 6 (1752): 155

The New Bath Guide
See: ANSTEY, Christopher

1988 *A New Birth-day Ode for 1758, as it was presented to his Royal Highness George-William-Frederic, Prince of Wales. By the Author of Mattins; or, an Universal Hymn to the Great Creator. A Pindaric Ode, now on Subscription, and which will speedily be published* NOT SEEN (Fol. 6d. Cooper)

Reviewed: *Monthly Review* 19 (1758): 303

1989 *The New Boghouse Miscellany: or, a Companion for the Close-stool. Consisting of Original Pieces In Prose and Verse By several Modern Authors. Printed on an excellent soft Paper; and absolutely necessary for all those, who read with a View to Convenience, as well as Delight. Revised and corrected by a Gentleman well skilled in the Fundamentals of Literature, near Privy-Garden.* London, 1761 (2s.6d. Cabe) FOLGER

Reviewed: *London Magazine* 29 (1760): 672

A New Book of the Dunciad
See: DODD, William

1990 *The new Brighthelmstone Directory: or, Sketches in Miniature of the British Shore.* London, 1770 (Small 8vo. 1s.6d. Durham. 1770) BRITISH LIBRARY

Reviewed: *Monthly Review* 42 (1770): 250
  Critical Review 29 (1770): 117–119
  London Magazine 39 (1770): 104
  Town & Country Magazine 2 (1770): 120

1991 *The New Circuit Companion; or a Mirror for Grand-Juries: a Familiar Epistle.* London, 1769 (8vo. 1s. Ireland printed. London reprinted for Bingley. 1769) BRITISH LIBRARY

Reviewed: *Monthly Review* 42 (1770): 74–75
  Critical Review 28 (1769): 464–465
  Gentleman's Magazine 39 (1769): 600
  London Magazine 38 (1769): 640

A New Collection of Fairy Tales
See: BROOKE, Henry

A New Dramatic Entertainment, called A Christmas Tale
See: GARRICK, David

1992 *The New Foundling Hospital for Wit. Being A Collection of Several Curious Pieces, in Verse and Prose: written by Lord Chesterfield, Lord Hardwicke, Lord Lyttelton, Sir C. H. Williams, Mr. Wilkes, Mr. Churchill, Mr. Garrick, Mr. Potter, Dr. Akenside, And Other Eminent Persons.* 1st ed. reviewed; copy seen 2d ed.: London, 1768 (8vo. 1s. Almon) BRITISH LIBRARY

Reviewed: *Monthly Review* 38 (1768): 404–405
  Critical Review 25 (1768): 314
  London Magazine 37 (1768): 276
  Political Register 2 (1768): 383

1993 *The New Foundling Hospital for Wit. Being A Collection of Curious Pieces In Verse and Prose. By several eminent persons. Part the second.* London, 1768 (8vo. 2s.6d. Almon) BRITISH LIBRARY

Reviewed: *Monthly Review* 39 (1768): 485
  Political Register 3 (1768): 381–382

1994 *The New Foundling Hospital for Wit. Being A Collection of Several Curious Pieces In Verse and Prose. Many of which were never before Printed. Written by the Earl of Chesterfield, Earl of Carlisle, Earl Delawarr, Lord Lyttelton, Lord Harvey, Lord Capel, Lady M. W. Montague, Sir Charles Hanbury Williams, Sir Walter Raleigh, Rt. Hon. Ch. Townshend, John Wilkes, Esq; D. Garrick, Esq; B. Thornton, Esq; Mrs Lenox, Mr. Rt. Lloyd, Mr. W. Kenrick, Mr. J. Cunningham; And other Eminent*

Persons. Part The Third. London, 1769 (8vo. 2s.6d. Almon) BRITISH LIBRARY

Reviewed: *Monthly Review* 41 (1769): 156
London Magazine 38 (1769): 379

1995 *The New Foundling Hospital for Wit. Being A Collection Of Curious Pieces In Verse and Prose. By Sir C. Hanbury Williams, Earl of Chesterfield, Earl of Hardwicke, Earl of Carlisle, Lords Lyttelton, Harvey, Capel, Lady M. W. Montague, T. Potter, C. Townshend, J. S. Hall, J. Wilkes, D. Garrick, B. Thornton, G. Colman, R. Lloyd, &c. &c. Adorned with a curious Frontispiece. Part the Fourth.* London, 1771 (12mo. 2s.6d.sewed. Almon. 1771) BRITISH LIBRARY

Reviewed: *Monthly Review* 44 (1771): 344

1996 *The New Foundling Hospital for Wit. Being A Collection of Curious Pieces in verse and prose, several of which were never before printed. By Sir C. Hanbury Williams, Earl of Chesterfield, Earl of Delawarr, Earl of Bath, Earl of Hardwicke, Earl of Carlisle, Lords Lyttelton, Harvey, Capel, Lady M. W. Montague, Hon. C. Yorke, Hon. H. Walpole, Hon. C. Morris, Sir J. Mawbey, T. Potter, C. Townshend, Soame Jenyns, Dr. King, Dr. Armstrong, C. Anstey, T. Edwards, C. Churchill, J. Thomson, J. S. Hall, J. Wilkes, D. Garrick, R. Bentley, S. Johnson, B. Thornton, G. Colman, R. Lloyd, &c. &c. Adorned with a curious Frontispiece. Part the Fifth.* London, 1722 [1772] (12mo. 2s.6d. Almon. 1772) BRITISH LIBRARY

Reviewed: *Monthly Review* 47 (1772): 325
Universal Catalogue [1] (1772) art. 998

1997 *A New Historical, Political, Satyrical, Burlesque Ode, on that most Famous Expedition, of all Expeditions, Commonly called, The Grand Secret Expedition, As it was Performed By the Author, At a late High Borlace.* London, 1757 (Fol. 6d. Graffenheim) BRITISH LIBRARY

Reviewed: *Monthly Review* 17 (1757): 479

A new Musical Interlude called The Election
See: ANDREWS, Miles Peter

1998 *A new Receipt to tame a Shrew. A Tale* NOT SEEN (4to. 11pp. 6d. Printed for D. Henry in Wine-Office Court, Fleet-street)

Reviewed: *Monthly Review* 1 (1749): 424

1999 *A new Scene for the Comedy called The Knights. Or, Fresh Tea for Mr. Foote.* London, 1758 (8vo. 6d. Wilkie) BRITISH LIBRARY

Reviewed: *Monthly Review* 18 (1758): 183
Critical Review 5 (1758): 170

A New Version of the Paradise Lost
See: GREEN, George Smith

2000 *The new-year's gift. A poem: presented with a pair of silk stockings, to miss *****
NOT SEEN (6d. Robinson)

Listed: *Monthly Review* 10 (1754): 78

2001 [NEWBY, Peter]. *Six Pastorals. The Elegy. The Happy Couple. The Rivals. The Artless Lovers. The Unexpected Bliss. The Farewell. By P----- N-----.* London, 1773 (8vo. 1s. Allen. 1773) YALE (BEINECKE)

Reviewed: *Monthly Review* 48 (1773): 319
Critical Review 35 (1773): 393
Universal Catalogue [2] (1773) art. 232

2002 NEWCOMB, [Thomas]. *A congratulatory Ode to the Queen, on her Voyage to England*
NOT SEEN (4to. 6d. Seymour)

Reviewed: *Monthly Review* 25 (1761): 318

2003 NEWCOMB, Thomas. *The Consummation. A Sacred Ode, on the Final Dissolution of the World: Inscribed to his Grace The Archbishop of Canterbury.* London, 1752 (4to. 1s. Owen) BRITISH LIBRARY

Reviewed: *Monthly Review* 6 (1752): 156

2004 NEWCOMB, Thomas. *The Death of Abel. A Sacred Poem. Written originally in the German Language. Attempted in the Stile of Milton.* [Translation/adaptation of *Der Tod Abels* by Salomon Gessner.] London ed. reviewed; copy seen: Dublin, 1763 (8vo. 3s.sewed. Davis and Reymers) BRITISH LIBRARY

Reviewed: *Monthly Review* 28 (1763): 295–297
Critical Review 16 (1763): 50–55

2005 NEWCOMB, T[homas]. *Mr. Hervey's Contemplations on a Flower-Garden, done into Blank Verse (After the Manner of Dr. Young).* London, 1757 (8vo. 1s.6d. Rivington and Fletcher) CAMBRIDGE

Reviewed: *Monthly Review* 17 (1757): 459–461
Critical Review 4 (1757): 62–67

2006 NEWCOMB, T[homas]. *Mr. Hervey's Contemplations on the Night, done into blank Verse, (after the Manner of Dr. Young)*
NOT SEEN (8vo. 1s.6d. Rivington)

Reviewed: *Monthly Review* 16 (1757): 289–298
Critical Review 3 (1757): 118–124

2007 NEWCOMB, T[homas]. *Mr. Hervey's Meditations and Contemplations. In Two Volumes. Containing, Vol. I Meditations among the Tombs. Reflections on a Flower-Garden. A Descant on Creation. Vol. II. Contemplations on the Night. Contemplations on the Starry Heavens. A Winter Piece. Attempted in Blank Verse, (after the Manner of Dr. Young).* London, 1764 (8vo. 1s.6d. Rivington) BRITISH LIBRARY

Reviewed: *Monthly Review* 30 (1764): 488–64
Critical Review 18 (1764): 63–64
British Magazine 5 (1764): 377
General Magazine 1 (1764): 242

2008 [NEWCOMB, Thomas]. *Novus Epigrammatum Delectus: or, Original State Epigrams, and Minor Odes: Suited to the Times. All Written by the same Author.* London, 1760 (8vo. 2s. Kearsley, &c.) BRITISH LIBRARY

Reviewed: *Monthly Review* 22 (1760): 514–515

2009 [NEWCOMB, Thomas]. *An ode to the king of Prussia. Occasioned by his late victories in Germany. By the author of a poetical version of Mr. Hervey's contemplations*
NOT SEEN (Fol. 6d. Baldwin)

Reviewed: *Monthly Review* 18 (1758): 489–490
Critical Review 5 (1758): 164

2010 NEWCOMB, Thomas. *On the Successes of the British Arms, a congratulatory Ode. Addressed to his Majesty*
NOT SEEN (4to. 6d. Davis)

Reviewed: *Monthly Review* 28 (1763): 160–161
Critical Review 15 (1763): 154–156

2011 NEWCOMB, [Thomas]. *The Retired Penitent. Being a Poetical Version of the Rev. Dr. Young's Moral Contemplations. Revised, approved, and published with the Consent of that learned and eminent Writer*
NOT SEEN (8vo. 6d. Buckland)

Reviewed: *Monthly Review* 23 (1760): 330–331
Critical Review 10 (1760): 159
British Magazine 1 (1760): 546

2012 NEWCOMB, [Thomas]. *Vindicta Britannica, an Ode on the Royal Navy. Inscribed to the King.* London, 1758 (4to. 6d. Scott) BRITISH LIBRARY

Reviewed: *Monthly Review* 20 (1759): 89–90
Critical Review 6 (1758): 521–522
Gentleman's Magazine 28 (1758): 601

New-market. A Satire
See: WARTON, Thomas

2013 *The News-Paper Wedding; or, an Advertisement for a Husband. A Novel; Founded on Incidents which arose in Consequence of an Advertisement that appeared in the Daily Advertiser of July 29, 1772. Including A Number of original Letters on the Subject of Love and Marriage.* 2 vols. London, 1774 (12mo. 6s. Snagg. 1774) BODLEIAN

Reviewed: *Monthly Review* 50 (1774): 327
Critical Review 37 (1774): 318–319
London Magazine 43 (1774): 198
Universal Catalogue 3 (1774) art. 353

The Nice Lady: A Comedy
See: GREEN, George Smith

2014 [NICHOLS, John]. *The Buds of Parnassus: a Collection of Original Poems. Containing, An Ode to Scandal. An Epistle to a Lady, on the Birth of her Daughter. Stanzas to Liberty, occasioned by a Verdict lately given in the Court of Common Pleas, Guildhall. The Laurel and*

Tulip. A Fable. The State of the Drunkard (Imitated from Prov. xxiii.29. et. seq.) And An Epistle to George Onslow, Esq. on his spirited Answer to the Thanks given him by his Constituents. London, 1763 (4to. 1s. Wilkie) BODLEIAN

Reviewed: *Monthly Review* 29 (1763): 229
Critical Review 16 (1763): 151

2015 [NICHOLS, John]. *Islington: A Poem. Addressed to Mr. Benjamin Stapp. To which are subjoined several other Poetical Essays by the same Author*
NOT SEEN (4to. 1s. Flexney)

Reviewed: *Monthly Review* 29 (1763): 227
Critical Review 16 (1763): 316

2016 NICKLIN, Edward. *Pride and Ignorance, A Poem*. Birmingham, 1770 (4to. 2s.6d. Baldwin) BRITISH LIBRARY

Reviewed: *Monthly Review* 42 (1770): 406
Critical Review 29 (1770): 393–394
London Magazine 39 (1770): 319

Night: An Epistle to Robert Lloyd
See: CHURCHILL, Charles

The Ninth Satire of Horace
See: SWINNEY, Sidney

NIPCLOSE, Sir Nicholas (pseud.)
See: GENTLEMAN, Francis

No One's Enemy but His Own
See: MURPHY, Arthur

2017 *No Rape: an Epistle from a Lord's Favourite Mistress to Miss *******, in the City*. London, 1768 (4to. 1s. Bingley) NEWBERRY

Reviewed: *Monthly Review* 38 (1768): 148
Gentleman's Magazine 38 (1768): 133

2018 *The Noble Cuckolds; or the Pleasures of a Single Life, and the Miseries of Matrimony. Occasionally Published upon the Many Divorces lately granted by Parliament betwixt Noble Personages. By the Right Hon. Lord------To which is added, Address'd to the Unmarried of both Sexes, The Contrast. Being a Parallel between Courtship and Matrimony*. [New edition of much-republished 1701 poem, *The Pleasures of a Single Life*.] London, 1772 (8vo. Bladon) BRITISH LIBRARY

Reviewed: *Town & Country Magazine* 4 (1772): 490

2019 *The Noble Family: a Novel. In a Series of Letters*. 2 vols.
NOT SEEN (5s. Pearch)

Reviewed: *Critical Review* 31 (1771): 482

2020 *The Noble Lovers; or, the History of Lord Emely and Miss Villars; containing some Characters of the most celebrated Persons in High Life*. 3 vols.
NOT SEEN (12mo. 7s.6d. Bladon. 1772)

Reviewed: *Monthly Review* 47 (1772): 151
Critical Review 34 (1772): 76–77
London Magazine 41 (1772): 386
British Magazine & General Review 2 (1772): 165
Universal Catalogue [1] (1772) art. 980

The Noble Pedlar
See: CAREY, George Saville

2021 *The Noctuary: or, an Address from the Tombs. A Poem in Blank Verse. To which is added, An Ode on the last Day*. London, 1752 (8vo. 1s. Owen) BRITISH LIBRARY

Reviewed: *Monthly Review* 6 (1752): 155
Gentleman's Magazine 22 (1752): 95

2022 NO-HEAD, Peter (pseud.). *An Irregular Balladistical Ode, Composed in order to be set to Musick, and annually performed, in Commemoration of the Resolution entered into by the C-mm-n C------l of London, to invite his Majesty the King of Denmark to Dine with the Lord M---r, &c. &c. Humbly dedicated To the Right Honourable the L--d M---r, The Right Worshipful the Court of A------n, And the Right Elegant, and well-bred Gentlemen of the Mazarine Robe. By Peter No-Head, Esq; Candidate for the Place of City Poet Laureat*. London, 1768 (4to. 1s. Nicoll) NEWBERRY

Reviewed: *Monthly Review* 39 (1768): 401
Critical Review 26 (1768): 382
Universal Museum 4 (1768): 597

2023 NORRIS, Henry. *Aracyntha: an Elegy*
NOT SEEN (4to. 1s. Caston)

Reviewed: *Critical Review* 33 (1772): 328
Universal Catalogue [1] (1772) art. 614

North America, a Descriptive Poem
See: DONALDSON, William

2024 *The North Briton: an Elegy*. London, 1764 (Fol. 6d. Nicoll) BRITISH LIBRARY

Reviewed: *Monthly Review* 29 (1763): 398
Critical Review 16 (1763): 391

2025 *A Northern Circuit: Described, in a Letter to a Friend: a Poetical Essay. To which is prefixed, An Introductory Dialogue, between Bayes and his Muse. By a Gentleman of the Middle Temple*. London, 1751 (8vo. 1s. Payne and Bouquet) BRITISH LIBRARY

Reviewed: *Gentleman's Magazine* 21 (1751): 48
Listed: *Monthly Review* 4 (1750–51): 304

Northern Memoirs
See: WOODFIN, A.

A Nosegay and a Simile for the Reviewers
See: STEVENSON, John Hall

The Note of Hand; or, Trip to Newmarket
See: CUMBERLAND, Richard

2026 [NOTT, John]. *Alonzo; or, the youthful Solitaire. A Tale*. London, 1772 (4to. 1s.6d. Robson, &c. 1772) BRITISH LIBRARY

Reviewed: *Monthly Review* 46 (1772): 537
Critical Review 33 (1772): 328
British Magazine & General Review 1 (1772): 464
Universal Catalogue [1] (1772) art. 562

2027 *The Novelist: or, Tea-Table Miscellany. Containing the Select Novels of Dr. Croxall; With other Polite Tales, and Pieces of Modern Entertainment*. 2 vols. London, 1766 (12mo. 6s. Lowndes) BRITISH LIBRARY

Reviewed: *Monthly Review* 33 (1765): 491
Critical Review 20 (1765): 400

2028 *The Noviciate of the Marquis de ———— or, the Apprentice turned Master. Translated from the French*
NOT SEEN (12mo. 3s. Pottinger and Cooke)

Reviewed: *Monthly Review* 20 (1759): 188
Critical Review 7 (1759): 278–279

Novus Epigrammatum Delectus
See: NEWCOMB, Thomas

2029 *The Nowiad: An Heroic Poem. Humbly Inscrib'd to the Most Renown'd Tom Thumb the Great, Patentee and Grand Manager of the Old-New-English-French Theatre. In which due Honour will be paid to his most noble Allies, our truly British spirited Sons of Mars. With Notes historical and critical. By a Spectator.* [British Library copy cropped; ESTC-1755.] (Fol. 6d. Cooper) BRITISH LIBRARY

Reviewed: *Monthly Review* 13 (1755): 459–460

2030 [NUGENT, Robert]. *Faith. A Poem*. London, 1774 (4to. 1s. Becket. 1774) BRITISH LIBRARY

Reviewed: *Monthly Review* 50 (1774): 232
Critical Review 37 (1774): 234–235
Gentleman's Magazine 44 (1774): 276
Universal Catalogue [3] (1774) art. 362

2031 [NUGENT, Robert]. *The Oppressed Captive. Being An Historical Novel, deduced from the Distresses of real Life, in an impartial and candid Account of the unparalleled sufferings of Caius Silius Nugenius, now under Confinement in the Fleet Prison, at the Suit of an implacable and relentless Parent*. London, 1757 (12mo. 3s. Sold by the Author in the Fleet-Prison) BRITISH LIBRARY

Reviewed: *Monthly Review* 16 (1757): 363

2032 NUGENT, [Thomas] (trans.). *Emilius; or, an Essay on Education. By John James Rousseau, Citizen of Geneva. Translated from the French By Mr. Nugent.* 2 vols. London, 1763 (8vo. 10s. Nourse and Vaillant) BRITISH LIBRARY

Reviewed: *Monthly Review* 28 (1763): 137–138

The Nun: An Elegy
See: JERNINGHAM, Edward

2033 *The Nun; or, the Adventures of the Marchioness of Beauville.* London, 1771 (12mo. 2s.6d. Roson) BRITISH LIBRARY

Reviewed: *Monthly Review* 44 (1771): 262
Critical Review 31 (1771): 315–316
Gentleman's Magazine 41 (1771): 229
London Magazine 40 (1771): 274
Town & Country Magazine 3 (1771): 323

The Nunnery. An Elegy
See: JERNINGHAM, Edward

2034 *The Nunnery for Coquettes.* London, 1771 (12mo. 3s. Lowndes) BRITISH LIBRARY

Reviewed: *Monthly Review* 43 (1770): 489
Critical Review 30 (1770): 476–477
London Magazine 39 (1770): 530
Town & Country Magazine 2 (1770): 547

2035 *The Nunnery; or, the History of Miss Sophia Howard.* 2 vols. London, 1767 (12mo. 6s. Noble) NEWBERRY

Reviewed: *Monthly Review* 36 (1767): 171–172
Critical Review 23 (1767): 146

Nuptial Elegies
See: PORTAL, Abraham

The Nuptials. A Didactick Poem
See: SHEPHERD, Richard

2036 [OAKMAN, John]. *The Life and Adventures of Benjamin Brass. An Irish Fortune-Hunter.* 2 vols. London, 1765 (12mo. 5s. Nicoll) BRITISH LIBRARY

Reviewed: *Monthly Review* 32 (1765): 76–77
Critical Review 19 (1765): 74–75

2037 OBRIEN, Charles. *A Dialogue between the Poet and his Friend. A Satire.* London, 1755 (4to. 6d. Carpenter) BRITISH LIBRARY

Reviewed: *Monthly Review* 13 (1755): 454

2038 [O'BRIEN, William]. *Cross Purposes: a Farce of Two Acts, As it is performed at the Theatre-Royal in Covent-Garden.* London, 1772 (8vo. 1s. Davies. 1772) BRITISH LIBRARY

Reviewed: *Monthly Review* 47 (1772): 486
Critical Review 34 (1772): 471
Gentleman's Magazine 42 (1772): 577–580
Universal Catalogue [1] (1772) art. 1494

2039 [O'BRIEN, William]. *The Duel. A Play. As Performed at the Theatre-Royal in Drury-Lane.* [Translation of *Le Philosophe sans le savoir* by Michel Jean SEDAINE.] London, 1772 (8vo. 1s.6d. Davies. 1772) BRITISH LIBRARY

Reviewed: *Monthly Review* 48 (1773): 39–42
Critical Review 35 (1773): 71
Universal Catalogue [2] (1773) art. 93

Occasional Attempts at Sentimental Poetry
See: HOPE, John

2040 *An occasional Ode*
NOT SEEN (6d. Comyns)

Reviewed: *Monthly Review* 14 (1756): 59 Listed: *Critical Review* 1 (1756): 291

2041 *Occasional Verses on the Death of Mr. Sterne. To which is added, An Epistle to a Young Lady, on the Taste and Genius of the Times.* London, 1768 (4to. 1s. Murdoch) BODLEIAN

Reviewed: *Monthly Review* 39 (1768): 165
Critical Review 25 (1768): 312–313
Universal Museum 4 (1768): 205

2042 *The Ocean: a Poem, In Blank Verse, Wrote by the Sea-Side.* London, 1766 (4to. 6d. Walter) BODLEIAN

Reviewed: *Monthly Review* 34 (1766): 324
Critical Review 21 (1766): 151–152
Gentleman's Magazine 36 (1766): 143

The Oculist
See: BACON, Phanuel

An Ode addressed To the Savoir Vivre Club
See: FENTON, Richard

2043 *An Ode, as presented to the Right Hon. William Pitt. Published by order of the Managers and Proprietors of the Antigallican private Ship*

of War, and laudable society of Antigallicans, held at the Lebeck's Head in the Strand. By a member of the said Association
NOT SEEN (4to. 6d. Reeve)

Reviewed: *Monthly Review* 16 (1757): 462

An Ode consecrated to the Memory of his Grace the Duke of Newcastle
See: SWINNEY, Sidney

2044 *An Ode, design'd for the anniversary of the most noble Order of Bucks; and to them inscrib'd by a Brother. To which is added, a Song, call'd, The Visit*
NOT SEEN (4to. 6d. Williams)

Reviewed: *Critical Review* 24 (1767): 316
Universal Museum 3 (1767): 541

An Ode In Honour of his Royal Highness the Prince of Wales's Birth-Day
See: SCOTT, William

2045 *Ode inscribed to The Right Honourable Spencer Earl Of Northampton.* Northampton, 1774 (4to. 6d. Robinson, &c. 1774) BODLEIAN

Reviewed: *Monthly Review* 50 (1774): 155
Critical Review 37 (1774): 235–236
London Magazine 43 (1774): 39
Town & Country Magazine 6 (1774): 213
Universal Catalogue [2] (1773) art. 1335

2046 *An Ode: occasioned by the Success of Admiral Boscawen. By a Gentleman of the University of Oxford.* London, 1759 (4to. 6d. Baldwin) BRITISH LIBRARY

Reviewed: *Monthly Review* 21 (1759): 351
Critical Review 8 (1759): 330

2047 *Ode on an Evening View of the Crescent at Bath. Inscribed to the Rev. Sir Peter Rivers Gay, Bart.* N.p., 1773 [ESTC-London] (4to. 6d. Dodsley, &c. 1773) BRITISH LIBRARY

Reviewed: *Monthly Review* 49 (1773): 229

2048 *An Ode on Beauty. To Stella*
NOT SEEN (4to. 6d. Comyns)

Reviewed: *Monthly Review* 12 (1755): 232

An Ode on Beauty, To which are prefixed . . .
See: COOKE, Thomas

An Ode on Benevolence
See: COOKE, Thomas

2049 *The Ode On dedicating a Building, and Erecting a Statue, to Le Stue, Cook to the Duke of Newcastle At Clermont; With Notes, By Martinus Scriblerus, To which are prefixed, Testimonies to the Genius and Merits of Le Stue.* Oxford, 1769 (4to. 1s.6d. Nicoll) FOLGER

Reviewed: *Monthly Review* 41 (1769): 318–319
Critical Review 28 (1769): 308
London Magazine 38 (1769): 537

2050 *An ode on his august Majesty Frederic King of Prussia. Humbly dedicated to the Right Honourable W----- P---, Esq;*
NOT SEEN (Fol. 1s. Woodgate and Co.)

Reviewed: *Monthly Review* 18 (1758): 490

An Ode on Pleasure
See: COOKE, Thomas

An Ode on Poetry, Painting, and Sculpture
See: COOKE, Thomas

An Ode on the Death of Mr. Pelham
See: GARRICK, David

Ode on the Duke of York's Second Departure
See: FALCONER, William

2051 *An Ode on the Expedition. Inscribed to the Right Honourable W-- P--t, Esquire.* London, 1757 (4to. 6d. Cooke) CAMBRIDGE

Reviewed: *Monthly Review* 17 (1757): 379
Critical Review 4 (1757): 467

2052 *Ode on the glorious Victory obtained by the Allied Army, in Germany, over the French, in the Plains near Minden*
NOT SEEN (4to. 1s. Dodsley)

Reviewed: *Monthly Review* 21 (1759): 269
Critical Review 8 (1759): 246–248

2053 *Ode on the Institution of a Society in Liverpool, for the Encouragement of Designing,*

Drawing, Painting, &c. Read before the Society, Dec. 13, 1773
NOT SEEN (4to. Liverpool printed, no bookseller's name. 1774)

Reviewed: *Monthly Review* 51 (1774): 482
Critical Review 39 (1775): 160

An Ode on the Powers of Poetry
See: COOKE, Thomas

2054 *An Ode on the present Times*
NOT SEEN (Fol. 6d. Dodsley)

Reviewed: *Monthly Review* 14 (1756): 63
Critical Review 2 (1756): 87

2055 *Ode on the Return of Peace. Also The Speech of Europa.* London, 1763 (4to. 6d. Becket and DeHondt) UNIVERSITY OF ILLINOIS

Reviewed: *Monthly Review* 28 (1763): 400
Critical Review 15 (1763): 394

Ode performed in the Senate-House at Cambridge
See: GRAY, Thomas

2056 *An Ode, Sacred to the Memory Of a late Eminently Distinguish'd Placeman, On his retiring from Business.* London, 1763 (4to. 1s. Woodfall) BRITISH LIBRARY

Reviewed: *Monthly Review* 28 (1763): 238
Critical Review 15 (1763): 239

2057 *An Ode, sacred to the Memory of General Wolfe*
NOT SEEN (Fol. 6d. Millan)

Reviewed: *Monthly Review* 21 (1759): 455
Critical Review 8 (1759): 409

2058 *An Ode, Sacred to the Memory of The Late Right Honourable George Lord Lyttelton.* London, 1773 (4to. 1s. Dodsley. 1773) BRITISH LIBRARY

Reviewed: *Monthly Review* 49 (1773): 317–318
Critical Review 36 (1773): 234
London Magazine 42 (1773): 456

2059 *An Ode to a Player. Written Extempore by an Antigallican.* London, 1755 (Fol. 6d. Moore) FOLGER

Reviewed: *Monthly Review* 13 (1755): 459

Ode to Criticism
See: WODHULL, Michael

2060 *An Ode to Duke Humphry, imitated from Horace.* London, 1763 (4to. 1s. Hinxman) BRITISH LIBRARY

Reviewed: *Monthly Review* 28 (1763): 69–70
Critical Review 15 (1763): 77
British Magazine 4 (1763): 46

2061 *Ode to his Grace the D. of B----, on a late very particular address from the kingdom of Ireland; being an allusion to the tenth ode of the second book of Horace*
NOT SEEN (Fol. 6d. Scott)

Reviewed: *Monthly Review* 18 (1758): 186

2062 *An Ode to Liberty, inscribed to The Right Hon. Thomas Harley, the Lord Mayor of the City of London.* London, 1768 (4to. 6d. Wilkie) BRITISH LIBRARY

Reviewed: *Monthly Review* 38 (1768): 334
Critical Review 25 (1768): 309
Universal Museum 4 (1768): 205

2063 *An Ode to Lord B***, on the Peace. By the Author of the Minister of State, a Satire.* London, 1762 (4to. 1s. Howard) BRITISH LIBRARY

Reviewed: *Monthly Review* 27 (1762): 460
Critical Review 14 (1762): 395
British Magazine 3 (1762): 606

An Ode to Love
See: SHEPHERD, Richard

2064 *An Ode to Palinurus.* London, 1770 (4to. 1s. Wilkie) BRITISH LIBRARY

Reviewed: *Monthly Review* 42 (1770): 250
Critical Review 29 (1770): 233
London Magazine 39 (1770): 212
Town & Country Magazine 2 (1770): 120

2065 *An ode to Sir John T--r---no, knt. late one of the sheriffs of the city of London*
NOT SEEN (Fol. 6d. Cooper)

Reviewed: *Monthly Review* 13 (1755): 297

2066 *An Ode to the Duke of Newcastle. By a Shepherd.* London, 1754 (4to. 1s.6d. Millan, &c.) BRITISH LIBRARY

Reviewed: *Monthly Review* 11 (1754): 384–387
Gentleman's Magazine 24 (1754): 534

2067 *An Ode to the Earl of Ch-----m. By the Author of the E--l of Ch-----m's Apology.* London, 1767 (Fol. 6d. Alman) BRITISH LIBRARY

Reviewed: *Monthly Review* 36 (1767): 331–332
Critical Review 23 (1767): 297–298

An Ode to the king of Prussia
See: NEWCOMB, Thomas

2068 *Ode to the Legislator Elect of Russia, On his being prevented from entering on his high Office of Civilization, by a Fit of the Gout.* London, 1766 (4to. 1s. Nicoll) HARVARD (HOUGHTON)

Reviewed: *Monthly Review* 35 (1766): 322
Critical Review 22 (1766): 155

2069 *An Ode to the Most Unpopular Man Living.* N.p., 1753 (4to. 6d. No publisher's name) NEWBERRY

Reviewed: *Monthly Review* 8 (1753): 238

2070 *An Ode to the People of England.* London, 1765 (4to. 6d. Langford) BRITISH LIBRARY

Reviewed: *Monthly Review* 33 (1765): 165
Critical Review 20 (1765): 154

2071 *An Ode to the People of England.* London, 1769 (4to. 1s. Kearsley. 1769) BODLEIAN

Reviewed: *Monthly Review* 42 (1770): 75
Critical Review 28 (1769): 460
London Magazine 38 (1769): 642

An Ode to the Right Honourable the Earl of Lincoln
See: BISHOP, Samuel

2072 *An Ode To the Right Honourable the Marchioness of Granby In the Year 1758.* London, n.d. [BEINECKE CAT.–1759] (4to. 1s. Newbery) YALE (BEINECKE)

Reviewed: *Monthly Review* 21 (1759): 353–354
Critical Review 8 (1759): 330–332

2073 *An Ode to Virtue. In Blank Lyric Verse.* London, 1767 (4to. 1s. Nicoll) NEW YORK PUBLIC LIBRARY

Reviewed: *Monthly Review* 36 (1767): 490
Critical Review 24 (1767): 316
Universal Museum 3 (1767): 541

An Ode upon Dedicating A Building, and Erecting A Statue, to Shakespeare
See: GARRICK, David

2074 *An Ode upon the Fleet and Royal Yatch, going to conduct The Princess of Mecklenburg to be Queen of Great Britain.* Birmingham, 1761 (4to. 1s. Dodsley) YALE (BEINECKE)

Reviewed: *Monthly Review* 25 (1761): 229
Critical Review 12 (1761): 320

2075 *An Ode upon the present period of time; with A Letter, addressed to The Right Honourable George Grenville.* London, 1769 (4to. 6d. Alman) BRITISH LIBRARY

Reviewed: *Monthly Review* 40 (1769): 87
Critical Review 27 (1769): 72
Gentleman's Magazine 39 (1769): 157
London Magazine 38 (1769): 104
Critical Memoirs 1 (1769): 37–38
Town & Country Magazine [1] (1769): 45
Political Register 4 (1769): 391

Odes Descriptive and Allegorical
See: SHEPHERD, Richard

Odes, on the Four Seasons
See: SHAW, Cuthbert

The Oeconomy of Beauty
See: COSENS, --

The Oeconomy of Happiness
See: TRAPAUD, Elisha

2076 *The Oeconomy of the Mind*
NOT SEEN (8vo. 1s. Bladon)

Reviewed: *Monthly Review* 36 (1767): 489

Of Benevolence: an Epistle to Eumenes
See: ARMSTRONG, John

2077 *Of the Characters of Men. An Epistle to Ralph Allen, Esq;* London, 1750 (4to. 1s. Cooper) BRITISH LIBRARY

Reviewed: *Monthly Review* 2 (1749–50): 331

2078 OGBORNE, David. *The Merry Midnight Mistake, or Comfortable Conclusion. A new Comedy.* Chelmsford, 1765 (8vo. 1s. Chelmsford printed; and sold by Williams in London) BRITISH LIBRARY

Reviewed: *Monthly Review* 33 (1765): 327
Critical Review 20 (1765): 316
Gentleman's Magazine 35 (1765): 483

2079 OGDEN, James. *The British Lion Rous'd; Or, Acts of the British Worthies, a Poem, in Nine Books.* Manchester, 1762 (8vo. 5s. Printed at Manchester) BRITISH LIBRARY

Reviewed: *Monthly Review* 26 (1762): 316–317

2080 OGDEN, James. *An Epistle on Poetical Composition*
NOT SEEN (4to. 1s. Hinxman)

Reviewed: *Monthly Review* 27 (1762): 227–228
Critical Review 13 (1762): 363

2081 OGDEN, James. *On the Crucifixion and Resurrection. A Poem*
NOT SEEN (4to. 1s. Hinxman)

Reviewed: *Monthly Review* 27 (1762): 227–228
Critical Review 13 (1762): 363–364

2082 OGILVIE, John. *The Day of Judgment. A Poem. In Two Books. The Second Edition, Corrected and Enlarged.* London, 1759 (8vo. 1s. Keith) BRITISH LIBRARY

Reviewed: *Monthly Review* 20 (1759): 141–150

2083 OGILVIE, John. *The Day of Judgment. A Poem. In Two Books. The Third Edition, corrected. To which are now added, I. An Ode to Melancholy. II. Ode on Sleep. III. Ode on Time. IV. To the Memory of Mr. H** M***. an Elegy. V. To the Memory of the late pious and ingenious Mr. Hervey. VI. The Third Chapter of Habakkuk paraphrased. By John Ogilvie, A.M.* London, 1759 (8vo. 2s. Keith) FOLGER

Reviewed: *Monthly Review* 21 (1759): 467–469

2084 [OGILVIE, John]. *Paradise: a Poem.* London, 1769 (4to. 1s.6d. Pearch. 1769) BRITISH LIBRARY

Reviewed: *Monthly Review* 40 (1769): 115–117
Critical Review 26 (1768): 470–471
London Magazine 37 (1768): 666
Universal Museum 4 (1768): 652

2085 OGILVIE, John. *Philosophical and Critical Observations on the Nature, Characters, and Various Species of Composition.* 2 vols. London, 1774 (8vo. 12s.bound. Robinson. 1774) BRITISH LIBRARY

Reviewed: *Monthly Review* 51 (1774): 249–254

2086 OGILVIE, John. *Poems on several Subjects.* 2 vols. London, 1769 (8vo. 10s.6d.sewed. Pearch. 1769) BRITISH LIBRARY

Reviewed: *Monthly Review* 42 (1770): 114–124
Critical Review 29 (1770): 72

2087 OGILVIE, John. *Poems on Several Subjects. To which is prefix'd, An Essay on Lyric Poetry of the Ancients; In Two Letters inscribed to The Right Honourable James Lord Deskfoord.* London, 1762 (4to. 10s.6d. Keith) BRITISH LIBRARY

Reviewed: *Monthly Review* 27 (1762): 239–254
Critical Review 14 (1762): 293–301
British Magazine 3 (1762): 606

2088 OGILVIE, John. *Providence. An Allegorical Poem. In Three Books.* London, 1764 (4to. 8s.sewed. Burnet) BRITISH LIBRARY

Reviewed: *Monthly Review* 30 (1764): 130–131 and 217–236
Critical Review 17 (1764): 172–180

2089 [OGILVIE, John]. *Solitude: or, the Elysium of the Poets, a Vision; to which is subjoined An Elegy.* London, 1765 (4to. 2s.6d. Burnet) BRITISH LIBRARY

Reviewed: *Monthly Review* 34 (1766): 116–124
Critical Review 21 (1766): 363–369

2090 [O'HARA, Kane]. *The Golden Pippin: An English Burletta, in Three Acts. As it is performed at the Theatre-Royal, Covent-Garden. By the Author of Midas*. London, 1773 (8vo. 1s.6d. Becket. 1773) BRITISH LIBRARY

Reviewed: *Monthly Review* 48 (1773): 153–154
Universal Catalogue [2] (1773) art. 223

2091 [O'HARA, Kane]. *The Golden Pippin: An English Burletta, in two Acts, as it is performed at Covent Garden. By the Author of Midas* NOT SEEN (8vo. 1s. Becket)

Reviewed: *Monthly Review* 48 (1773): 154
Critical Review 35 (1773): 159–160

2092 [O'HARA, Kane]. *Midas; an English Burletta. As it is performed, at the Theatre-Royal, in Covent-Garden*. London, 1764 (8vo. 1s.6d. Kearsly) BRITISH LIBRARY

Reviewed: *Monthly Review* 30 (1764): 244–245
Critical Review 17 (1764): 312

2093 [O'HARA, Kane]. *Songs in the new Burletta of Midas. As it is performed at the Theatre-Royal in Crow-street, Dublin* NOT SEEN (8vo. 1s. London, reprinted by Nicoll)

Reviewed: *Monthly Review* 26 (1762): 232

2094 *Oithona: A Dramatic Poem, taken from The Prose Translation of The Celebrated Ossian. As performed At the Theatre Royal in the Hay Market. Set to Musick by Mr. Barthelemon*. London, 1768 (8vo. 6d. Becket) BRITISH LIBRARY

Reviewed: *Monthly Review* 38 (1768): 335

2095 [O'KEEFE, John]. *The She Gallant: or, Square Toes Outwitted. A New Comedy of Two Acts. As now performing, with great Applause, At the Theatre in Smock-Alley, Dublin*. London, 1767 (8vo. 1s. Lowndes) BRITISH LIBRARY

Reviewed: *Monthly Review* 36 (1767): 163
Critical Review 23 (1767): 140–141

The Old Women Weatherwise
See: CAREY, George Saville

2096 OLDHAM, John. *The Compositions in Prose And Verse of Mr. John Oldham. To which are added Memoirs Of His Life, and Explanatory Notes upon some Obscure Passages Of His Writings. By Edward Thompson*. 3 vols. London, 1770 (12mo. 9s. Flexney) BRITISH LIBRARY

Reviewed: *Town & Country Magazine* 3 (1771): 102

2097 *The Olympiade. Address'd To Stella, on the Birth of her Son*. London, 1752 (4to. 24 pp. Owen) NEWBERRY

Reviewed: *Monthly Review* 5 (1751): 463

2098 *On Beneficence. A Poetical Essay*. London, 1764 (4to. 2s. Wilson and Fell) YALE (BEINECKE)

Reviewed: *Monthly Review* 30 (1764): 242–243
Critical Review 17 (1764): 80

On the Abuse of Poetry
See: WEEKES, Nathaniel

On the much lamented Death of the Marquis of Tavistock
See: ANSTEY, Christopher

2099 *One Thousand, Seven Hundred, and Fifty-nine: A Poem, inscribed to every Briton who bore a part in the Service of that distinguished Year*
NOT SEEN (Fol. 6d. Baldwin)

Reviewed: *Monthly Review* 22 (1760): 516
Critical Review 9 (1760): 495

2100 *One Thousand Seven hundred and Fifty Six. A Dialogue*. London, 1756 (8vo. 1s. Withy) INDIANA UNIVERSITY [Microfilm copy only; source unknown]

Reviewed: *Monthly Review* 15 (1756): 425
Critical Review 2 (1756): 282

2101 *One thousand Seven Hundred, Sixty-Eight: or, Past 12 o'Clock, and a Cloudy Morning. In Two Cantos. Canto 1*. London, 1768 (4to. 1s.6d. Bingley) BRITISH LIBRARY

Reviewed: *Monthly Review* 39 (1768): 81
Critical Review 26 (1768): 69

London Magazine 37 (1768): 390
Political Register 3 (1768): 251

2102 ONELY, Richard. *The Charge of Cyrus the Great. A Poetical Essay.* N.p., 1756 [ESTC-London?] (4to. 1s. Whiston) BRITISH LIBRARY

Reviewed: *Monthly Review* 14 (1756): 520–525

2103 *The Opera: A Poem. By the Author of the Coach Drivers.* London, 1767 (4to. 1s. Flexney) BRITISH LIBRARY

Reviewed: *Monthly Review* 36 (1767): 78
Critical Review 22 (1766): 469–470

The Oppressed Captive
See: NUGENT, Robert

2104 *Oppression. A Poem. By an American. With Notes, by a North Briton.* London, 1765 (4to. 2s. Moran) BODLEIAN

Reviewed: *Monthly Review* 32 (1765): 392
Critical Review 19 (1765): 315–316
Candid Review 1 (1765): 277–279

2105 *Oppression Display'd; or, The Baronet and Miller. A tale. In Four Cantos. By a Trueborn Englishman.* London, 1758 (4to. 1s. Wilkie) UNIVERSITY OF ILLINOIS

Reviewed: *Monthly Review* 18 (1758): 279
Critical Review 5 (1758): 268

2106 *The Optimist: or Satire in Good-Humour.* London, 1774 (4to. 1s. Alman. 1774) BRITISH LIBRARY

Reviewed: *Monthly Review* 51 (1774): 166
Critical Review 38 (1774): 237
Town & Country Magazine 6 (1774): [548]
Universal Catalogue 3 (1774) art. 644

2107 *The Orange-Girl at Foote's to Sally Harris: or, The Town to the Country Pomona.* London, 1773 (4to. 1s. Bladon) BRITISH LIBRARY

Reviewed: *Monthly Review* 49 (1773): 65
Critical Review 36 (1773): 72–73
London Magazine 42 (1773): 351
Universal Catalogue [2] (1773) art. 837

Oriental Anecdotes
See: FALQUES, Marianne Agnès

Oriental Apologues
See: BILLARDON DE SAUVIGNY, Louis Edmé

Oriental Eclogues
See: COLLINS, William

The Origin of the Newcastle Burr
See: DAWES, Richard

An Original Essay on Woman
See: MONTAGUE, Mary Seymour

Original Poems on several Occasions. By C. R.
See: REEVE, Clara

Original Poems on various Subjects, By a Young Lady, Eighteen Years of Age
See: PORTER, Anna Maria

2108 *Original Poems, Translations, and Imitations, From the French, &c. By a Lady.* London, 1773 (8vo. 2s.6d.sewed. Robinson. 1773) BRITISH LIBRARY

Reviewed: *Monthly Review* 50 (1774): 70
Critical Review 37 (1774): 133–134
Universal Catalogue [2] (1773) art. 1302

Oroonoko, a Tragedy
See: HAWKESWORTH, John

2109 *The Orphan Daughter. A moral Tale.* 2 vols. NOT SEEN (12mo. 6s. Noble)

Reviewed: *Monthly Review* 39 (1768): 84
Critical Review 26 (1768): 376
London Magazine 37 (1768): 276
Universal Museum 4 (1768): 429

The Orphan of China, a Tragedy
See: MURPHY, Arthur

2110 *The Orphan Swains; or, London contagious to the Country. A Novel. By a young Libertine Reformed.* 2 vols.
NOT SEEN (12mo. 5s. Snagg)

Reviewed: *Monthly Review* 50 (1774): 327
Critical Review 37 (1774): 318
Town & Country Magazine 6 (1774): 268
Universal Catalogue 3 (1774) art. 371

2111 *Osro and Tylo. A poem. Written some years ago near Raby, in the county of Durham* NOT SEEN (4to. 1s. Hitch)

Reviewed: *Monthly Review* 12 (1755): 230

OSSIAN
See: MACPHERSON, James [In addition, for non-"genuine" (i.e., non-Macpherson) items, see: *Gisbal, an Hyperborean Tale;* and MacDONALD, Donald. *Three Beautiful and Important Passages.*]

OSSIAN (adaptation)
See: *Oithona: a Dramatic Poem*

2112 *Otaheite: a Poem.* London, 1774 (4to. 1s. Bathurst. 1774) BRITISH LIBRARY

Reviewed: *Monthly Review* 50 (1774): 310–311
Critical Review 37 (1774): 235
Town & Country Magazine 6 (1774): 213
Universal Catalogue 3 (1774) art. 228

2113 OVERBURY, Sir Thomas. *The Miscellaneous Works In Verse and Prose of Sir Thomas Overbury, Knt. with Memoirs of his Life. The Tenth Edition.* London, 1753 (3s.bound. Bouquet) CAMBRIDGE

Reviewed: *Monthly Review* 8 (1753): 465–466

2114 OVID (Publius OVIDIUS NASO). *Ovid's Metamorphoses Epitomized in an English Poetical Style. For the Use and Entertainment of the Ladies of Great Britain.* London, 1760 (8vo. 3s. Horsfield) BRITISH LIBRARY

Reviewed: *Monthly Review* 24 (1761): 154–156
Critical Review 10 (1760): 385–386
British Magazine 1 (1760): 713–714

2115 OVID (Publius OVIDIUS NASO). *Penelope to Ulysses, from Ovid. Being a specimen of a new translation of Ovid's epistles* NOT SEEN (4to. 6d. Bathurst)

Reviewed: *Monthly Review* 6 (1752): 314–315

OVID (Publius OVIDUS NASO) (translations)
See: BARRETT, Stephen. *Ovid's Epistles*
MASSEY, William. *Ovid's Fasti*

The Oxford Sausage
See: WARTON, Thomas (ed.)

The Oxonian in Town
See: COLMAN, George (the elder)

2116 *The Oxonian: or, the Adventures of Mr. G. Edmunds, Student of Brazen-Nose College, Oxford. Dedicated, by his Lordship's Permission, To the Right Hon. the Earl of ----. By a Member of the University.* 2 vols. London, 1771 (12mo. 5s. Roson) NEWBERRY

Reviewed: *Monthly Review* 46 (1772): 78
Critical Review 32 (1771): 154

The Padlock: a Comic Opera
See: BICKERSTAFFE, Isaac

2117 *Palladias and Irene, a Drama, in Three Acts* NOT SEEN (8vo. 1s.6d. Dodsley)

Reviewed: *Monthly Review* 50 (1774): 74
Critical Review 36 (1773): 476
Universal Catalogue [2] (1773) art. 1295

2118 [PALTOCK, Robert]. *The Life and Adventures of Peter Wilkins, a Cornish man: Relating particularly His Shipwreck near the South Pole; his wonderful Passage thro' a subterraneous Cavern into a kind of new World; his there meeting with a Gawry or flying Woman, whose Life he preserv'd, and afterwards married her; his extraordinary Conveyance to the Country of Glums and Gawrys, or Men and Women that fly. Likewise a Description of this strange Country, with the Laws, Customs, and Manners of its Inhabitants, and the Author's remarkable Transactions among them. Taken from his own Mouth, in his Passage to England, from off Cape Horn in America, in the Ship Hector. With an Introduction, giving an Account of the surprizing Manner of his coming on board that Vessel, and his Death on his landing at Plymouth in the Year 1739. Illustrated with several Cuts, clearly and distinctly representing the Structure and Mechanism of the Wings of the Glums and Gawrys, and the Manner in which they use them either to swim or fly. By R. S. a Passenger in the Hector.* London, 1751 (Printed for J. Robinson and R. Dodsley) BRITISH LIBRARY

Reviewed: *Monthly Review* 4 (1750–51): 157

2119 [PALTOCK, Robert]. *Memoirs of the life of Parnese, A Spanish Lady of vast Fortune. Written by Herself: Shewing the irresistable Force of Education: With A True Account of the Hardships she suffered, in Man's Apparel, for eight Years, in different Countries, in the Prosecution of a virtuous Amour with Rockbartez; her Escape from Slavery with Sarpeta, her Master's Daughter; their Flight into Persia; her accidental Marriage there to Rockbartez; and Return. Interspersed with the Story of Beaumont and Sarpeta. Translated from the Spanish Manuscript, By R. P. Gent.* London, 1751 (In one pocket vol. 3s. Printed for W. Owen, and W. Clark) BRITISH LIBRARY

Reviewed: *Monthly Review* 4 (1750–51): 156–157

Pandaemonium: or, a new Infernal Expedition
See: PHILALETHES

2120 *The Pantheon, a Poem.* London, 1773 (4to. 2s.6d. Williams. 1773) BRITISH LIBRARY

Reviewed: *Monthly Review* 49 (1773): 230
Critical Review 36 (1773): 234
London Magazine 42 (1773): 456
Universal Catalogue [2] (1773) art. 967

2121 *The Pantheon Rupture; or, a dispute between Elegance and Reason, with their Final Separation. To which are added, Pantheon Epistles; or, the modern art of Polite Letter-Writing.* London, 1772 (4to. 1s.6d. Roson. 1772) BRITISH LIBRARY

Reviewed: *Monthly Review* 46 (1772): 455
Critical Review 33 (1772): 329
Universal Catalogue [1] (1772) art. 567

The Pantheonites
See: GENTLEMAN, Francis

2122 PANTING, Stephen. *Four Elegies. I. Morning. II. Noon. III. Evening. IV. Night.* London, 1761 (4to. 1s. Bristow) BRITISH LIBRARY

Reviewed: *Monthly Review* 26 (1762): 152–153
Critical Review 11 (1761): 167
British Magazine 2 (1761): 161

Paradise: a Poem
See: OGILVIE, John

Paradise Lost. An Oratorio
See: STILLINGFLEET, Benjamin

PARAGRAPH, Peter (pseud.)
See: ADAIR, James Makittrick

2123 *A Paraphrase of Eight of the Psalms of David* NOT SEEN (4to. 1s. Becket and DeHondt)

Reviewed: *Monthly Review* 37 (1767): 395
Critical Review 24 (1767): 317–318
Gentleman's Magazine 37 (1767): 553–554
Universal Museum 3 (1767): 541

2124 *The Parasite.* 2 vols. London ed. reviewed; copy seen: Dublin, 1765 (8vo. 6s.6d. Burnet) BRITISH LIBRARY

Reviewed: *Monthly Review* 32 (1765): 235
Critical Review 19 (1765): 236
Candid Review 1 (1765): 204–205

2125 PARISH, Henry. *Pentecost. A Poetical Fragment.* London, 1761 (4to. 1s. Walter) BRITISH LIBRARY

Reviewed: *Monthly Review* 24 (1761): 470
Critical Review 11 (1761): 420

2126 PARNELL, Thomas. *Poems on several Occasions. Written by Dr. Thomas Parnell, Late Archdeacon of Clogher: And published by Mr. Pope. With The Life of Zoilus: And his Remarks on Homer's Battle of the Frogs and Mice. A new Edition. To which is prefixed, the Life of Dr. Parnell, written by Dr. Goldsmith.* London, 1770 (8vo. 3s.6d.sewed. Davies. 1770) BRITISH LIBRARY

Reviewed: *Monthly Review* 43 (1770): 326
Critical Review 30 (1770): 44–50
London Magazine 39 (1770): 319
Town & Country Magazine 2 (1770): 325

2127 PARNELL, Thomas. *The Posthumous Works of Dr. Thomas Parnell, late Archdeacon of Clogher; containing Poems Moral and Divine: and On Various other Subjects.* London, 1758 (8vo. 5s. Johnston) BRITISH LIBRARY

Reviewed: *Monthly Review* 19 (1758): 380–385
Critical Review 6 (1758): 118–121
Gentleman's Magazine 28 (1758): 282–284

The Parson's Parlour
See: GREEN, George Smith

2128 PARSONS, James. *Life. A Poem. To The Reverend J*** C******, M.A. Student of Christ Church, Oxford.* Oxford, 1768 (4to. 1s.6d. Fletcher) BRITISH LIBRARY

Reviewed: *Monthly Review* 38 (1768): 408
Critical Review 25 (1768): 233
Universal Museum 4 (1768): 204

2129 [PARSONS, Philip]. *The Inefficacy of Satire. A Poem, Occasioned by the Death of Mr. Churchill.* London, 1765 (4to. 6d. Hawes) BODLEIAN

Reviewed: *Monthly Review* 32 (1765): 153
Critical Review 19 (1765): 151
Candid Review 1 (1765): 139

2130 *Parthenia; or the Lost Shepherdess. An Arcadian Drama.* London, 1764 (8vo. 1s. Newbery) BRITISH LIBRARY

Reviewed: *Monthly Review* 32 (1765): 233
Critical Review 19 (1765): 152–153
Candid Review 1 (1765): 135–137

2131 PARTRIDGE, Solomon, jnr. *The Cobler's End. A Tale. Addressed to a Friend.* London, 1769 (8vo. 1s. Fell, &c.) BRITISH LIBRARY

Reviewed: *Monthly Review* 42 (1770): 77
Critical Review 29 (1770): 74
Town & Country Magazine 2 (1770): 72

2132 *Party Dissected: or Plain Truth. A Poem. By a Plain Dealer.* London, 1770 (4to. 2s. Bell, &c. 1770) HARVARD (HOUGHTON)

Reviewed: *Monthly Review* 42 (1770): 486
Critical Review 30 (1770): 68–71

The Pasquinade
See: KENRICK, William

2133 *The Passion; an Oratorio: As performed at the Theatre-Royal in Covent-Garden* NOT SEEN (8vo. 1s. Griffin)

Reviewed: *Monthly Review* 42 (1770): 331
Critical Review 29 (1770): 480
Town & Country Magazine 2 (1770): 214

2134 *The Passions Personify'd, in Familiar Fables.* [ESTC: attributed to Herbert Lawrence; formerly ascribed to Edward Young.] London, n.d. [ESTC-1773] (8vo. 5s. Whiston. 1773) BRITISH LIBRARY

Reviewed: *Monthly Review* 48 (1773): 406–408
Critical Review 36 (1773): 73
London Magazine 42 (1773): 195–196
Universal Catalogue [2] (1773) art. 378

2135 *Past Twelve o'Clock, or Byng's Ghost, an Ode, Inscribed to the Triumvirate; more particularly his Grace of N********.* 1st ed. reviewed; copy seen 2d ed.: London, 1757 (Fol. 6d. Scott) BRITISH LIBRARY

Reviewed: *Monthly Review* 16 (1757): 286
Critical Review 3 (1757): 286–287

2136 *The Pastor, a Poem: or, A Caution against Error and Delusion. With a Remark on the Doctrine of Perfection. Recommended to the World in general; the Methodists in particular: and dedicated to the Rev. Mr. Whitefield* NOT SEEN (4to. 1s. Tilly on Fishstreet-hill)

Reviewed: *Monthly Review* 39 (1768): 78–80
Critical Review 25 (1768): 312
Universal Museum 4 (1768): 205

2137 *A Pastoral Ballad In Four Parts: Admiration, Hope, Disappointment, Success.* London, 1774 (4to. 1s. Longman. 1774) BRITISH LIBRARY

Reviewed: *Monthly Review* 50 (1774): 484
Critical Review 38 (1774): 76
Universal Catalogue 3 (1774) art. 643

A Pastoral Cordial
See: STEVENSON, John Hall

2138 *A Pastoral Elegy.* London, 1759 (4to. 6d. Dodsley) BRITISH LIBRARY

Reviewed: *Monthly Review* 20 (1759): 383

2139 *Pastoral poems on various subjects* NOT SEEN (8vo. 1s. Cooper)

Reviewed: *Monthly Review* 5 (1751): 396

A Pastoral Puke
See: STEVENSON, John Hall

2140 [PATERSON, Samuel]. *Joineriana: or the Book of Scraps.* 2 vols. London, 1772 (12mo. 5s.sewed. Johnson. 1772) BRITISH LIBRARY

Reviewed: *Monthly Review* 48 (1773): 49–54
Critical Review 34 (1772): 449–451
London Magazine 41 (1772): 597
Town & Country Magazine 5 (1773): 31
British Magazine & General Review 2 (1772): 634–636
Universal Catalogue [1] (1772) art. 1469

2141 *A Pathetick Address to all True Britons.* London, n.d. [ESTC-1756] (Fol. 6d. Scott) BRITISH LIBRARY

Reviewed: *Monthly Review* 15 (1756): 318
Critical Review 2 (1756): 188

The Paths of Virtue delineated
See: RICHARDSON, Samuel

The Patricians: or, A Candid Examination
See: DELAMAYNE, Thomas Hallie

2142 [PATRICK, J.]. *Quebec: A poetical Essay, in Imitation of the Miltonic Stile: Being a regular Narrative of the Proceedings and Capital Transactions performed by the British Forces under the Command of Vice-Admiral Saunders and Major-General Wolf, in the Glorious Expedition against Canada, in the year 1759. The Performance of a Volunteer on board his Majesty's Ship Somerset, during the Passage home from Quebec. The Whole embellished with entertaining and explanatory Notes*
NOT SEEN (4to. 1s.6d. Whitridge)

Reviewed: *Monthly Review* 22 (1760): 510–512
Critical Review 10 (1760): 79
British Magazine 1 (1760): 490

The Patriot: A Pindaric Address to Lord Buckhorse
See: ANSTEY, Christopher

2143 *The Patriot. A Poem. Inscribed to the Supporters of the Bill of Rights.* London, n.d. [ESTC-1773] (4to. 1s.6d. Evans. 1772) BRITISH LIBRARY

Reviewed: *Monthly Review* 48 (1773): 70
Critical Review 34 (1772): 470–471

British Magazine & General Review 2 (1772): 631
Universal Catalogue [1] (1772) art. 1507

The Patriot Muse
See: PRIME, Benjamin Young

2144 *The Patriot Poet, a Satire. Inscribed to the Reverend Mr. Ch-----ll. By a Country Curate.* London, 1764 (4to. 1s. Burnet) BRITISH LIBRARY

Reviewed: *Monthly Review* 30 (1764): 240
Critical Review 17 (1764): 314–316

2145 *Patriotism! A Farce. As it is Acted by his Majesty's Servants.* London, 1764 (8vo. 6d. Nicoll) BRITISH LIBRARY [Has been attributed to --- Baillie.]

Reviewed: *Monthly Review* 30 (1764): 70
Critical Review 16 (1763): 479

Patriotism, a Mock-Heroic
See: BENTLEY, Richard (the younger)

2146 *The Patriot's Guide; a Poem. Inscribed to the Earl of C----m, Junius, and John Wilkes, Esq;*
NOT SEEN (4to. 2s.6d. Wheble)

Reviewed: *Monthly Review* 45 (1771): 510
Critical Review 33 (1772): 85
Gentleman's Magazine 41 (1771): 604

2147 *The Patron a Satire.* London, 1774 (4to. 1s. Flexney. 1774) BRITISH LIBRARY

Reviewed: *Monthly Review* 50 (1774): 312–313
Critical Review 37 (1774): 314
London Magazine 43 (1774): 244
Universal Catalogue 3 (1774) art. 347

2148 *Peace. A Poem.* London, 1774 (4to. 1s. Becket. 1774) BRITISH LIBRARY

Reviewed: *Monthly Review* 50 (1774): 484
Critical Review 37 (1774): 473
Town & Country Magazine 6 (1774): 437
Universal Catalogue 3 (1774) art. 768

2149 PEACOCK, James. *The First Pastoral of Virgil in English Verse; attempted by James Peacock*

NOT SEEN (4to. 6d. Cooper)

Reviewed: *Monthly Review* 23 (1760): 247
Critical Review 10 (1760): 159
British Magazine 1 (1760): 546

2150 PEAKE, John. *Brown Beer: A Poem*. London, [1762] (4to. 6d. Williams) BRITISH LIBRARY

Reviewed: *Monthly Review* 26 (1762): 150
Critical Review 13 (1762): 166

2151 *The Pedagogue: or, Strictures on Tuition* NOT SEEN (4to. 1s. Clarke)

Reviewed: *Monthly Review* 39 (1768): 399–400

A Peep Behind the Curtain
See: GARRICK, David

2152 *Peeping Tom to the Countess of Coventry. An Epithalamium*. London, 1752 (Fol. 6d. Robinson) FOLGER

Reviewed: *Monthly Review* 6 (1752): 239

PELAGIUS, Porcupinus (pseud.)
See: MORGAN, Macnamara

2153 PENN, James. *The Farmer's Daughter of Essex*. London, 1767 (12mo. 3s. Bladon) BRITISH LIBRARY

Reviewed: *Monthly Review* 37 (1767): 76
Critical Review 23 (1767): 464
London Magazine 36 (1767): 310–311
Political Register 1 (1767): 177–178

2154 [PENNY, Anne Christian]. *Anningait and Ajutt; a Greenland Tale. Inscribed to Mr. Samuel Johnson, A.M. Taken from the IVth Volume of his Ramblers, versified By a Lady*. London, 1761 (4to. 1s. Dodsley) BRITISH LIBRARY

Reviewed: *Monthly Review* 24 (1761): 315–316
Critical Review 11 (1761): 291–293
British Magazine 2 (1761): 265

2155 [PENNY, Anne Christian]. *Poems, with a Dramatic Entertainment. By **** *****.* London, n.d. [ESTC-1771] (4to. 10s.6d. Dodsley) BRITISH LIBRARY

Reviewed: *Monthly Review* 47 (1772): 70
Universal Catalogue [1] (1772) art. 1023

2156 [PENNY, Anne]. *Select Poems from M. Gesner's Pastorals. By the Versifier of Anningait and Ajutt*. London, 1762 (4to. 1s. Newbery) BRITISH LIBRARY

Reviewed: *Monthly Review* 27 (1762): 393
Critical Review 14 (1762): 318 [2d ed.]

2157 PENNYLESS, Peter (pseud.). *Sentimental Lucubrations*. London, 1770 (12mo. 2s.6d. sewed. Becket and DeHondt. 1770) BRITISH LIBRARY

Reviewed: *Monthly Review* 42 (1770): 180–185
Critical Review 29 (1770): 110–113
Town & Country Magazine 2 (1770): 72

Il Penseroso
See: COWPER, William

Penshurst
See: COVENTRY, Francis

PENTWEAZEL, Ebenezer
See: *A Satirical Dialogue between A Sea Captain and his Friend in Town*

2158 [PERCY, Thomas]. *Five Pieces of Runic Poetry Translated from the Islandic Language*. London, 1763 (8vo. 1s.6d. Dodsley) BRITISH LIBRARY

Reviewed: *Monthly Review* 28 (1763): 281–286
Critical Review 15 (1763): 307–310

2159 [PERCY, Thomas (ed.)]. *Hau Kiou Choaan or The Pleasing History. A Translation from the Chinese Language. To which are added, I. The Argument or Story of a Chinese Play, II. A Collection of Chinese Proverbs, and, III. Fragments of Chinese Poetry. In Four Volumes. With Notes*. London, 1761 (Small 8vo. 10s. Dodsley) BRITISH LIBRARY

Reviewed: *Monthly Review* 25 (1761): 427–436
Critical Review 12 (1761): 373–381
British Magazine 2 (1761): 662

2160 [PERCY, Thomas]. *The Hermit of Warkworth. A Northumberland Ballad. In Three Fits*

Or Cantos. London, 1771 (4to. 2s.6d. Davies, &c. 1771) BRITISH LIBRARY

Reviewed: *Monthly Review* 45 (1771): 96–103
Critical Review 31 (1771): 390–395
Gentleman's Magazine 41 (1771): 363–366

2161 [PERCY, Thomas]. *The Matrons. Six Short Histories*. London, 1762 (8vo. 3s. Dodsley) BRITISH LIBRARY

Reviewed: *Monthly Review* 26 (1762): 509–510
Critical Review 14 (1762): 153–154

2162 PERCY, Thomas. *Reliques of Ancient English Poetry: consisting of Old Heroic Ballads, Songs, and other Pieces of our earlier Poets, (Chiefly of the Lyric kind.) Together with some few of later Date*. 3 vols. London, 1765 (8vo. 10s.6d. Dodsley) BRITISH LIBRARY

Reviewed: *Monthly Review* 32 (1765): 241–253
Critical Review 19 (1765): 119–130
Annual Register 8 (1765): 310–311
Candid Review 1 (1765): 99–109 and 177–182

2163 *The Peregrinations of Jeremiah Grant, Esq; The West Indian*. London, 1763 (12mo. 3s. Burnet) UNIVERSITY OF PENNSYLVANIA

Reviewed: *Monthly Review* 28 (1763): 162
Critical Review 15 (1763): 13–21
British Magazine 4 (1763): 46

2164 [PERFECT, W.]. *A Bavin of Bays: Containing Various Original Essays in Poetry. By a Minor Poet*. London, 1763 (12mo. 3s.sewed. Oliver) BRITISH LIBRARY

Reviewed: *Monthly Review* 29 (1763): 312
Critical Review 16 (1763): 285–289

2165 *The Perplexed Lovers: Or, the History of Sir Edward Balchen, Bart*. 3 vols. London, 1768 (12mo. 7s.6d. Noble) BRITISH LIBRARY

Reviewed: *Monthly Review* 37 (1767): 469–470
Critical Review 24 (1767): 355–356
Universal Museum 3 (1767): 596

The Perplexities: A Comedy
See: HULL, Thomas

2166 *The Perplexities of Riches*
NOT SEEN (12mo. 5s.sewed. Robinson and Roberts. 1771)

Reviewed: *Monthly Review* 46 (1772): 79
Critical Review 33 (1772): 84

2167 *Phil and Harriet: A true Tale. With Instructions to a Rose: An Ode. In Paraphrase on Waller and Crudeli*
NOT SEEN (4to. 6d. Morley)

Reviewed: *Monthly Review* 22 (1760): 167
Critical Review 9 (1760): 80

2168 PHILALETHES. *Pandaemonium: or, a new Infernal Expedition. Inscrib'd to a Being who calls himself William Lauder. By Philalethes*. London, 1750 (4to. 6d.) BRITISH LIBRARY

Reviewed: *Monthly Review* 4 (1750–51): 160

Philander. A Dramatic Pastoral
See: LENNOX, Charlotte

PHILANTHROPOS (pseud.)
See: FELLOWS, John

Philaster, a Tragedy
See: COLMAN, George (the elder)

2169 PHILATER (pseud.). *Silenus: an Elegy. Upon the Death of Dr. Slop. By Way of Dialogue Between a Curate and a Sexton; The Doctor's Butler, and a Livery Servant. By Philater*. London, 1773 (8vo. 6d. Bladon. 1773) BRITISH LIBRARY

Reviewed: *Monthly Review* 48 (1773): 412
London Magazine 42 (1773): 92
Universal Catalogue [2] (1773) art. 226

2170 PHILIPS, John. *Poems attempted in the Style of Milton. By Mr. John Philips. With a new Account of his Life and Writings*. London, 1762 (8vo. 2s.6d. Tonson) BRITISH LIBRARY

Reviewed: *Monthly Review* 27 (1762): 227
Critical Review 14 (1762): 154

Phillis at Court; a Comic Opera Of Three Acts
See: FAVART, Charles Simon

Philodamus. A Tragedy
See: BENTLEY, Richard (the younger)

2171 PHILOLETHES (pseud.). *The Pluralist, a Poem; or, the Poor Curate's Appeal to all Reasonable and well-disposed Christians, wheresoever dispersed, throughout his Majesty's Dominions, or elsewhere.* London, 1769 (4to. 1s. Dodsley) BRITISH LIBRARY

Reviewed: *Monthly Review* 42 (1770): 77
Critical Review 28 (1769): 463–464
Gentleman's Magazine 39 (1769): 600
London Magazine 38 (1769): 642
Town & Country Magazine [1] (1769): 661

2172 [PHIPPS, Joseph]. *The Winter-Piece. A Poem.* London, 1763 (4to. 1s. Bristow) HARVARD (HOUGHTON)

Reviewed: *Monthly Review* 28 (1763): 161–162
Critical Review 15 (1763): 154

The Phoenix; or, the History of Polyarchus and Argenis
See: REEVE, Clara (trans.)

Phoenix Park: a Poem
See: LESLIE, John

2173 *The Physicians. A Satire. With other Poems. To which is added, a Specimen of an Enquiry concerning the Mind*
NOT SEEN (8o. 1s.6d. Bladon. 1773)

Reviewed: *Monthly Review* 49 (1773): 314
Critical Review 36 (1773): 315
London Magazine 42 (1773): 559
Town & Country Magazine 5 (1773): 603
Universal Catalogue [2] (1773) art. 1124

2174 PILKINGTON, John Carteret. *The Poet's Recantation, Humbly Inscribed to the Right Honourable Sir Edward Montague, Knight of the Bath; By his most Obedient Humble Servant, John Carteret Pilkington.* London, 1755 (Fol. 6d. Tovey) BODLEIAN

Reviewed: *Monthly Review* 12 (1755): 159

2175 PILKINGTON, Laetitia. *The Third and Last Volume of the Memoirs of Mrs. Laetitia Pilkington, Written by Herself. Wherein are occasionally interspersed, Variety of Poems: As also the Letters of several Persons of Distinction: With the Conclusive Part of the Life of the Inimitable Dean Swift.* London, 1754 (12mo. 3s. Griffiths) BRITISH LIBRARY

Reviewed: *Monthly Review* 11 (1754): 401–411

2176 *A Pindaric Ode on Beauty, occasioned by the late Royal Nuptials*
NOT SEEN (4to. 6d. Worcester printed by Butler)

Reviewed: *Monthly Review* 26 (1762): 320

2177 *A Pindarick Ode on Painting. Addressed to Joshua Reynolds, Esq.* London, 1767 (4to. 1s.6d. Griffin) HARVARD (HOUGHTON)

Reviewed: *Monthly Review* 39 (1768): 316
Critical Review 25 (1768): 393
Universal Museum 4 (1768): 317

2178 [PINEAU-DUCLOS, Charles]. *The Pleasures of Retirement, Preferable to the Joys of Dissipation; Exemplified in the Life and Adventures of the Count de B————. Written by Himself. In Letters to a Friend. Now first translated from the Original French. By a Lady.* London, 1774 (12mo. 3s. Wilkie. 1774) BRITISH LIBRARY

Reviewed: *Monthly Review* 51 (1774): 239
Critical Review 37 (1774): 475
Universal Catalogue 3 (1774) art. 885

2179 PIPER, John. *The Life of Miss Fanny Brown, (A Clergyman's Daughter:) With the History and remarkable Adventures of Mrs. Julep, an Apothecary's Wife. The Whole interspersed with A great Variety of Characters, Moral, Instructive and Entertaining. To which is added, A Description of the most Elegant Monuments in Westminster-Abbey; the Curiosities in and about London; and Remarks on several Cathedrals.* Birmingham, 1760 (12mo. 3s. Ross) BRITISH LIBRARY

Reviewed: *Monthly Review* 24 (1761): 469
Critical Review 11 (1761): 418
British Magazine 2 (1761): 326

2180 [PITT, Christopher]. *Poems by the celebrated translator of Virgil's Aeneid. Together with The*

Jordan, A Poem: In Imitation Of Spenser. By ————— ———— Esq; London, 1756 (4to. 1s. Cooper) BRITISH LIBRARY

Reviewed: *Monthly Review* 15 (1756): 533
Critical Review 2 (1756): 276–277

The Placid Man: or, Memoirs of Sir Charles Beville
See: JENNER, Charles

2181 *The Plagues of the Spleen: an Heroic Poem. With An Appendix, entitled, The Humourist: or, The Absent Man. By the inimitable Author of Telemachus.* London, 1752 (4to. 6d. Corbet) BRITISH LIBRARY

Reviewed: *Monthly Review* 7 (1752): 398

The Plain Dealer: a Comedy
See: BICKERSTAFFE, Isaac

2182 *The Plain Question, Was she ravished, or not?* London, n.d. [BEINECKE CAT.–177-?] (4to. 1s. Bingley) YALE (BEINECKE)

Reviewed: *Monthly Review* 38 (1768): 148
Critical Review 25 (1768): 66
Universal Museum 4 (1768): 36–37
Political Register 2 (1768): 120

2183 *Plain Truth, in Plain English. A Satire. By a Plain Man, in a Plain Dress*
NOT SEEN (4to. 1s. Bingley)

Reviewed: *Monthly Review* 39 (1768): 489
Critical Review 26 (1768): 473
Universal Museum 4 (1768): 652

The Platonic Wife
See: GRIFFITH, Elizabeth

PLAUTUS, [Titus Maccius Plautus] (translations)
See: THORNTON, Bonnell. *The Comedies of Plautus*
WARNER, Richard. *The Comedies of Plautus*

The Pleasures of Retirement
See: PINEAU-DUCLOS, Charles

POCOCK, Edward, *The Traveller*
See: CHAPPELOW, Leonard

2184 *A Poem for the better Success of his Majesty's Arms against the French this Spring, with Part of Admiral Byng's Tryal Versifyed, &c.*
NOT SEEN (8vo. 6d. Withers)

Reviewed: *Monthly Review* 16 (1757): 463

2185 *A Poem inscribed to the Memory of the Rt. Hon. William Beckford, Esq. late Lord Mayor of London. Dedicated to John Wilkes, Esq;*
NOT SEEN (12mo. 6d. Baldwin)

Reviewed: *Monthly Review* 43 (1770): 244
Critical Review 30 (1770): 74–75

2186 *A Poem occasioned by the Death of the most illustrious Prince William Augustus, Duke of Cumberland. Humbly inscribed to her Royal Highness Princess Amelia*
NOT SEEN (4to. 6d. Kearsly)

Reviewed: *Monthly Review* 34 (1766): 242–243

2187 *A Poem. Occasioned by the Militia Bill, Now Depending. Addressed to the Ladies of Great Britain. Written by a Gentlewoman, Author of the Elegy on the Bishop of Sodor and Man.* London, 1757 (Fol. 6d. Cooper) HARVARD (HOUGHTON)

Reviewed: *Monthly Review* 16 (1757): [571] 581

2188 *A Poem on Chess.* London, 1764 (4to. 1s. Hawkins) BRITISH LIBRARY

Reviewed: *Monthly Review* 30 (1764): 241
Critical Review 17 (1764): 237

2189 *A Poem on Satire.* London, 1764 [Harvard copy has half-title only.] (4to. 6d. Franklin) HARVARD (HOUGHTON)

Reviewed: *Critical Review* 19 (1765): 151

A Poem on the Battle of Minden
See: SWINNEY, Sidney

A Poem on the Countess of Pomfret's Benefaction
See: VIVIAN, John

2190 *A Poem on the Earthquake at Lisbon.* London, 1755 (4to. 6d. Owen) BRITISH LIBRARY

Reviewed: *Monthly Review* 14 (1756): 59

2191 *A Poem on the late Earthquake at Lisbon. To which is added, Thoughts in a Church-Yard.* London, n.d. [ESTC-1755] (4to. 6d. Dodsley) BRITISH LIBRARY

Reviewed: *Monthly Review* 14 (1756): 59
Critical Review 1 (1756): 162

2192 *A Poem, on the Merchants New-beautifying the Statue of King Charles the IId. In the Royal-Exchange. With many Historical Remarks to George I. By the Author of the True-Briton.* London, 1762 (4to. 1s. Hope) BODLEIAN

Reviewed: *Monthly Review* 27 (1762): 224–225
Critical Review 13 (1762): 166

A Poem on the Peace
See: ALLEN, Bennet

A Poem on the Pomfret Statues
See: MYTTON, Thomas

2193 *A Poem on the Royal Nuptials*
NOT SEEN (4to. 1s. Henderson)

Reviewed: *Monthly Review* 25 (1761): 397–398
Critical Review 12 (1761): 402–403
British Magazine 2 (1761): 662

A Poem Sacred to the Memory Of the late Reverend P. Doddridge, D.D.
See: MOORE, Henry

A Poem to the Memory of the Celebrated Mrs. Cibber
See: KEATE, George

A Poem written in An Empty Assembly-Room
See: CAMBRIDGE, Richard Owen. *An Elegy written in An Empty Assembly-Room*

Poems (Oxford, 1768)
See: MUNDY, Francis Noel Clarke

2194 *Poems.* London, 1774 (12mo. 2s. Snagg. 1774) YALE (STERLING)

Reviewed: *Monthly Review* 50 (1774): 484
Critical Review 37 (1774): 395–396
London Magazine 43 (1774): 144
Universal Catalogue 3 (1774) art. 327

2195 *Poems and Translations, by a young Gentleman of Cambridge*
NOT SEEN (4to. 1s.6d. Evans. 1773)

Reviewed: *Monthly Review* 49 (1773): 230
Critical Review 36 (1773): 155

Poems and Translations, by A Young Gentleman of Oxford
See: LECHMERE, Edward

Poems and Translations. By the Author of the Progress of Physic
See: COWPER, Ashley

Poems. By *****
See: JENYNS, Soame

Poems, by A Lady
See: PYE, J. Henrietta

2196 *Poems by a Youth*
NOT SEEN (4to. 2s. Higgins. 1774)

Reviewed: *Monthly Review* 51 (1774): 68
Critical Review 37 (1774): 394
Universal Catalogue 3 (1774) art. 737

Poems by eminent Ladies
See: COLMAN, George (the elder), and Bonnell THORNTON (eds.)

2197 *Poems, by J. C. late of Trinity-Hall Cambridge*
NOT SEEN (8vo. 1s. Kearsley. 1773)

Reviewed: *Monthly Review* 48 (1773): 410–411
Critical Review 35 (1773): 392–393
London Magazine 42 (1773): 196
Universal Catalogue [2] (1773) art. 473

2198 *Poems by Several Gentlemen of Oxford.* London, 1757 (8vo. 6d. Baldwin) HARVARD (HOUGHTON)

Reviewed: *Monthly Review* 17 (1757): 185
Critical Review 4 (1757): 184

Poems. By the Author of the Sentimental Sailor
See: MERCER, Thomas

Poems by the celebrated translator of Virgil's Aeneid
See: PITT, Christopher

Poems, chiefly Rural
See: RICHARDSON, William

Poems consisting chiefly of Translations from the Asiatick Languages
See: JONES, Sir William

Poems, consisting of Tales, Fables, Epigrams, &c. By Nobody
See: ROBERTSON, James

Poems for Young Ladies
See: GOLDSMITH, Oliver

Poems, From A Manuscript, written in the time of Oliver Cromwell
See: CAREY, Patrick

Poems. Laura, or, The Complaint. . . .
See: MARRIOTT, Sir James

Poems; Ludicrous, Satirical, and Moral
See: KENRICK, William

2199 *Poems Moral and Divine, on the Following Subjects: I. Man's Fall and Exaltation: or, The Christian Triumph. In Seven Cantos. II. Modern Infidelity: or, The Principles of Atheism exposed and refuted. Inscrib'd to a Friend. III. A Paraphrase of the following Psalms: CXIX, CXLIV, CXLII, CXX, XIII, CXLIV, and CXXX. IV. The Prince and the Patriot. In Three Dialogues. By an American Gentleman. To which is added, Some Account Of The Author.* London, 1756 (4to. 2s.6d. Rivington) BRITISH LIBRARY

Reviewed: *Monthly Review* 14 (1756): 59–60

2200 *Poems on Different Subjects. Containing a Versification of some Parts of The Psalms of David. The 'Squire and his Setting Dogs. A Receipt to make Modern Novels. A Riddle, &c.* London, 1774 (4to. 1s.6d. Kearsly) BRITISH LIBRARY

Reviewed: *Monthly Review* 52 (1775): 272
Critical Review 38 (1774): 151–152

Poems on Several Occasions (1762)
See: CARTER, Elizabeth

Poems on several Occasions (1769)
See: MOSS, Thomas

2201 *Poems, on several Occasions. By C. S. In his Majesty's Sea-Service.* London, 1768 (8vo. 2s.sewed. Hawes, &c. 1768) BODLEIAN

Reviewed: *Monthly Review* 40 (1769): 351

2202 *Poems on several occasions, never before printed. Part the first*
NOT SEEN (4to. 6d. Crowder and Woodgate)

Reviewed: *Monthly Review* 11 (1754): 318

2203 *Poems on Several Subjects*
NOT SEEN (8vo. 1s.6d. Johnson and Co.)

Reviewed: *Monthly Review* 39 (1768): 490–491
Critical Review 26 (1768): 380–381

2204 *Poems on several subjects. By a gentleman*
NOT SEEN (4to. 1s. Bristol printed and sold by Palmer there, and Owen in London)

Reviewed: *Monthly Review* 4 (1750–51): 473

Poems on several Subjects. By the Author of the Life of Socrates
See: COOPER, John Gilbert

Poems on various subjects. By a young lady eighteen years of age
See: PORTER, Anna Maria. *Original Poems on Various Subjects*

Poems on various Subjects. Viz. The Nunnery, The Magdalens . . .
See: JERNINGHAM, Edward

2205 *Poems: The Chimney-Sweeper and Laundress. The Practice of Physic. The Poet at Guildhall*
NOT SEEN (4to. 6d. Flexney)

Reviewed: *Monthly Review* 27 (1762): 225–226
Critical Review 14 (1762): 155

Poems, with a Dramatic Entertainment
See: PENNY, Anne

Poems written by a Gentleman of Oxford
See: MUNDY, Francis Noel Clarke. *Poems*

2206 *The Poet*. London, 1754 (4to. 6d. Cooper) BRITISH LIBRARY

Reviewed: *Monthly Review* 9 (1753): 478

The Poet; a Poem
See: STOCKDALE, Percival

2207 *A Poetic Chronology. By a Briton*
NOT SEEN (4to. 1s. Luckman of Coventry)

Reviewed: *Monthly Review* 29 (1763): 228
Critical Review 16 (1763): 71–72

Poetic Essays, on Nature, Men, and Morals
See: THOMPSON, Isaac

A Poetical Address, in Favour of the Corsicans
See: RICHARDSON, William

Poetical Blossoms
See: VALPY, Richard

2208 *A Poetical Description of Mr. Hogarth's Election Prints: In Four Cantos. Written under Mr. Hogarth's Sanction and Inspection.* London, 1759 (4to. 1s. Smith) BRITISH LIBRARY

Reviewed: *Monthly Review* 20 (1759): 476
Critical Review 7 (1759): 274–275

A Poetical Dictionary
See: DERRICK, Samuel

2209 *A Poetical Epistle from Admiral Byng, in the Infernal Shades, to his Friend L———d A————, an Inhabitant on Earth.* London, 1757 (Fol. 6d. Fuller) HARVARD (HOUGHTON)

Reviewed: *Monthly Review* 16 (1757): 287

2210 *A poetical Epistle from Shakespear in Elysium, to Mr. Garrick, At Drury-Lane Theatre. To which is added, a View from Heymon-Hill, near Shrewsbury. A Solitudinarian Ode.* London, 1752 (4to. 1s. Newbery) BRITISH LIBRARY

Reviewed: *Monthly Review* 6 (1752): 397

2211 *A Poetical Epistle, occasioned by the late Change in the Administration. Addressed to the Right Hon. William Pitt, Esq;*
NOT SEEN (4to. 6d. Hinton)

Reviewed: *Monthly Review* 15 (1756): 653

A Poetical Epistle, to Christopher Anstey
See: ROBERTS, William Hayward

2212 *A Poetical Epistle to Miss C——h——y: Occasioned by her appearing in the Character of Iphigenia At the late Jubilee Ball at Ranelagh: With A Digression on the D——ke, and the celebrated Mrs. C———b——r.* London, 1749 (4to. 6d. Printed for T. Andrew in the Strand) BRITISH LIBRARY

Reviewed: *Monthly Review* 1 (1749): 319

2213 *A Poetical Epistle to the Author of Verses addressed to John Wilkes, Esq; on his Arrival at Lynn*
NOT SEEN (4to. 6d. London, sold by the booksellers of Lynn and Cambridge. 1771)

Reviewed: *Monthly Review* 44 (1771): 341
Critical Review 32 (1771): 78

2214 *A Poetical Epistle to the Right Hon. Lord M********. By a Gentleman of the King's Bench Prison.* London, 1768 (4to. 1s.6d. Bingley) BRITISH LIBRARY

Reviewed: *Monthly Review* 39 (1768): 401
Critical Review 26 (1768): 383
Universal Museum 4 (1768): 597

2215 *Poetical Epistles, to the Author of the New Bath Guide, from a Genteel Family In ————shire.* London, 1767 (4to. 1s.6d. Dodsley) BRITISH LIBRARY

Reviewed: *Monthly Review* 36 (1767): 409
Critical Review 23 (1767): 220
Gentleman's Magazine 37 (1767): 262
London Magazine 36 (1767): 150

Poetical Essays (1772)
See: GREENE, Edward Burnaby

2216 *Poetical Essays, chiefly of a moral Nature. Written at different Periods of Time, by a young Man*
NOT SEEN (8vo. 1s.6d. Wheble. 1770)

Reviewed: *Monthly Review* 44 (1771): 260–261
Critical Review 31 (1771): 158–159
Gentleman's Magazine 41 (1771): 132

2217 *Poetical Essays, Spoken at the Annual Visitation of Tunbridge School.* London, 1773 (4to. 1s. Hawes. 1773) BRITISH LIBRARY

Reviewed: *Monthly Review* 48 (1773): 317
Universal Catalogue [2] (1773) art. 361

2218 *Poetical Impertinence: or, Advice Unask'd. In two Poems, the Good Wife: and the Good Husband. Containing Rules humbly proposed to those Ladies and Gentlemen, who are not intirely satisfied with the Examples of the Polite Husbands and Wives of this present Age.* London, 1752 (8vo. 1s. Russel) BRITISH LIBRARY

Reviewed: *Monthly Review* 6 (1752): 238

2219 *Poetical Justice: Or, the Trial of a Noble Lord, in the Court of Parnassus, for an Offence, lately found bailable in the Court of King's Bench*
NOT SEEN (4to. 1s. Murdoch)

Reviewed: *Monthly Review* 38 (1768): 248
Critical Review 25 (1768): 228

2220 *The Poetical Miscellany; consisting of Select Pieces from the Works of the following Poets, viz. Milton, Dryden, Pope, Addison, Gay, Parnel, Young, Thomson, Akenside, Philips, Gray, Watts, &c. For the Use of Schools.* London, 1762 (12mo. 3s. Becket and DeHondt) BRITISH LIBRARY

Reviewed: *Monthly Review* 27 (1762): 390
Critical Review 14 (1762): 319

2221 *The Poetical Retrospect; or, the Year 1769. A Poem*
NOT SEEN (4to. 2s. S. Noble)

Reviewed: *Monthly Review* 42 (1770): 327
Critical Review 29 (1770): 313–314

2222 *The Poetical Tell-Tale; or, Muses in Merry Story. By Prior, Pope, Gay, Swift, Parnell, Wesley, Fontaine, And other celebrated Poets, both French and English.* London, 1764 (12mo. 1s.6d. Fletcher) BRITISH LIBRARY

Reviewed: *Monthly Review* 29 (1763): 154

2223 *A Poetical Wreath of Laurel and Olive; humbly inscribed to the Right Honourable the Marquis of Granby. By the Author*
NOT SEEN (4to. 1s. Morley)

Reviewed: *Monthly Review* 28 (1763): 161
Critical Review 15 (1763): 230–231
British Magazine 4 (1763): 158

2224 *The Poet's Time well employed*
NOT SEEN (12mo. 3s. Dell)

Reviewed: *Monthly Review* 23 (1760): 412

2225 *The Poet's Wardrobe: or, Livery of the Muses: A Poem. Written in Hudibrastic Verse. And addressed (by Way of Letter) to a particular Friend*
NOT SEEN (8vo. 6d. Henley)

Reviewed: *Monthly Review* 36 (1767): 240–241
Critical Review 23 (1767): 220–221

2226 *The Point of Honour. A Novel.* 2 vols.
NOT SEEN (12mo. 6s. Noble)

Reviewed: *Monthly Review* 39 (1768): 84–85
Critical Review 26 (1768): 376
London Magazine 37 (1768): 276
Universal Museum 4 (1768): 429

2227 [POISSON] DE GOMEZ, [Madeleine Angelique]. *The London Merchant. A Tale. From the French of Madame de Gomez*
NOT SEEN (8vo. 1s.6d. Almon)

Reviewed: *Monthly Review* 37 (1767): 393
Critical Review 24 (1767): 157–158
Gentleman's Magazine 37 (1767): 415
Universal Museum 3 (1767): 429
Political Register 1 (1767): 314

POLIGNAC, Cardinal Melchior de. *Anti-Lucretius* (translations)
See: CANNING, George. *A Translation of Anti-Lucretius*
DOBSON, William. *Anti-Lucretius of God and nature*

2228 *Political Epistles on various Subjects of the present Times*
NOT SEEN (8vo. 1s. Nicoll)

Reviewed: *Monthly Review* 34 (1766): 164–165
[Epistles I and II]
Critical Review 21 (1766): 75
Gentleman's Magazine 36 (1766): 37 [Epistle I] and 91 [Epistle II]

2229 *Political Epistles on Various Subjects of the present Times*
NOT SEEN (4to. 1s. Nicoll)

Reviewed: *Monthly Review* 34 (1766): 242 [Epistle III]
Critical Review 21 (1766): 156
Gentleman's Magazine 36 (1766): 143 [Epistle III]

A Political Romance
See: STERNE, Laurence

2230 *Political Society: A Poetical Essay. Addressed to John Wilkes, Esq;* London, 1769 (4to. 2s. Flexney) BODLEIAN

Reviewed: *Monthly Review* 40 (1769): 336–337
Critical Review 27 (1769): 154–155
Town & Country Magazine [1] (1769): 101
Critical Memoirs 1 (1769): 257–258

The Politician. A Poem
See: GREENE, Edward Burnaby

Pollio: an Elegiac Ode
See: MICKLE, William Julius

Polly Honeycombe
See: COLMAN, George (the elder)

2231 *Polydore and Julia: or, the Libertine Reclaim'd. A Novel.* London, 1756 (12mo. 3s. Crowder) BRITISH LIBRARY

Reviewed: *Monthly Review* 15 (1756): 536
Critical Review 2 (1756): 283–284

Pomery-Hill. A Poem
See: FORTESCUE, James

Ponteach: or the Savages of America
See: ROGERS, Robert

2232 POOKE, George. *An Address to His Most Gracious Majesty, King George the Third, on the Most Happy Arrival, at London, of Her Serene Highness Princess Charlotte of Mecklenburgh-Strelitz, Who was that Day made our most Gracious Queen.* London, 1762 (8vo. 6d. Keith) BODLEIAN

Reviewed: *Monthly Review* 27 (1762): 158–160
Critical Review 14 (1762): 78
British Magazine 3 (1762): 438

2233 POOKE, George. *A collection of odes, including a descriptive pastoral ode, a pastoral dialogue, and an elegy on the supposed death of a gentleman*
NOT SEEN (4to. 1s. Cooper)

Reviewed: *Monthly Review* 17 (1757): 281–282
Critical Review 4 (1757): 278

2234 POPE, Alexander. *A Supplement to the Works of Alexander Pope Esq. Containing Such Poems, Letters, &c. as are omitted in the Edition published by the Reverend Dr. Warburton. To which is added, A Key to the Letters.* London, 1757 (12mo. 3s. Cooper) BRITISH LIBRARY

Reviewed: *Monthly Review* 17 (1757): 89
Critical Review 3 (1757): 300–306
Literary Magazine 2 (1757): 167–170

2235 POPE, Alexander. *The Works of Alexander Pope Esq. In Nine Volumes Complete. With his last Corrections, Additions, and Improvements; As they were delivered to the Editor a little before his Death. Together with the Commentaries and Notes of Mr. Warburton.* 9 vols. London, 1751 (8vo. 21.14s.bound. Knapton, Lintot, and Tonson and Co.) BRITISH LIBRARY

Reviewed: *Monthly Review* 5 (1751): 97–102

2236 POPPLE, William (trans.). *Horace's Art of Poetry Translated. Inscribed To the Right Honourable The Earl of Halifax.* London, 1753 (4to. 2s.6d. Millar) BRITISH LIBRARY

Reviewed: *Monthly Review* 9 (1753): 307–310

2237 [POQUELIN DE MOLIÈRE, Jean Baptiste]. *An Hour before Marriage; a Farce in two acts. As it was Attempted to be acted at the Theatre-Royal in Covent-Garden.* [Adaptation of *Le mariage forcé.*] London, 1772 (8vo. 1s. Johnston. 1772) BRITISH LIBRARY

Reviewed: *Monthly Review* 46 (1772): 457–458
Critical Review 33 (1772): 411
Universal Catalogue [1] (1772) art. 589

POQUELIN DE MOLIÈRE, Jean Baptiste (adaptations)
See: BICKERSTAFFE, Isaac. *The Hypocrite*
BICKERSTAFFE, Isaac. *Doctor Last in his Chariot*
MURPHY, Arthur. *The School for Guardians*

2238 PORTAL, Ab[raham]. *The Indiscreet Lover: a Comedy. As it was performed at the King's Theatre in the Haymarket, For the Benefit of the British Lying-in Hospital in Brownlow-Street.* London, 1768 (8vo. 1s.6d. Kearsly) BRITISH LIBRARY

Reviewed: *Monthly Review* 39 (1768): 81
Critical Review 25 (1768): 393
Universal Museum 4 (1768): 260

2239 PORTAL, Abraham. *Innocence. A Poetical Essay. In Two Books. Most humbly Inscribed to Her Royal Highness The Princess Augusta. By Abraham Portal, Author of Olinda and Sophronia, a Tragedy.* London, 1762 (8vo. 1s.6d. Dodsley) HARVARD (HOUGHTON)

Reviewed: *Monthly Review* 26 (1762): 149
Critical Review 13 (1762): 79
British Magazine 3 (1762): 102

2240 [PORTAL, Abraham]. *Nuptial Elegies.* London, 1774 (4to. 2s. Kearsley. 1774) BRITISH LIBRARY

Reviewed: *Monthly Review* 50 (1774): 231
Critical Review 37 (1774): 157
Gentleman's Magazine 44 (1774): 228–229
London Magazine 43 (1774): 144
Town & Country Magazine 6 (1774): 155
Universal Catalogue 3 (1774) art. 227

2241 PORTAL, Abraham. *Olindo and Sophronia. A Tragedy. The Story taken from Tasso.* 1st ed. reviewed; copy seen 2d ed.: London, 1758 (8vo. 1s.6d. Graham) BRITISH LIBRARY

Reviewed: *Monthly Review* 19 (1758): 94–96

2242 PORTAL, [Abraham]. *War. An Ode.* London, n.d. [ESTC-1763] (4to. 1s. Middleton) BRITISH LIBRARY

Reviewed: *Monthly Review* 31 (1764): 298–301
Critical Review 18 (1764): 320

2243 [PORTER, Anna Maria]. *Original Poems on various Subjects, By a Young Lady, Eighteen Years of Age.* London, n.d. [ESTC-1772?] (4to. 5s.sewed. Cadell, &c.) BRITISH LIBRARY

Reviewed: *Monthly Review* 46 (1772): 537–538
Critical Review 33 (1772): 328

2244 PORTEUS, Beilby. *Death, a Poetical Essay.* 1st ed. reviewed; copy seen 2d ed.: Cambridge, 1759 (4to. 1s. Whiston) BRITISH LIBRARY

Reviewed: *Monthly Review* 21 (1759): 429–432

The Portrait; a Burletta
See: COLMAN, George (the elder)

2245 *A Portrait; most humbly addressed to his Royal Highness George Prince of Wales*
NOT SEEN (4to. 1s. Wilkie)

Reviewed: *Monthly Review* 45 (1771): 151
Critical Review 32 (1771): 240
Gentleman's Magazine 41 (1771): 417

2246 *The Portrait of Life, or the various effects of Virtue and Vice delineated; As they daily appear on the great Theatre of the World. In a collection of Interesting Novels.* 2 vols. London, 1770 (12mo. 5s.sewed. Bell) BRITISH LIBRARY

Reviewed: *Monthly Review* 42 (1770): 71
Critical Review 29 (1770): 149
Town & Country Magazine 2 (1770): 120

2247 POST, Peregrine. *A Four Days Tour: or, Cursed Remarks and Pitiful Observations made on a Journey through part of the Land of Dumplings*
NOT SEEN (8vo. 1s.6d. Bladon, &c.)

Reviewed: *Monthly Review* 40 (1769): 430–431
London Magazine 38 (1769): 324–325
Town & Country Magazine [1] (1769): 435

The Posthumous Works of a late celebrated Genius deceased
See: GRIFFITH, Richard

2248 POTTER, John. *The Choice of Apollo: a Serenata. As performed at the Little Theatre in*

the Hay-Market. Written by John Potter. The Music composed by Mr. William Yates. London, 1765 (4to. 6d. Henderson) HARVARD (HOUGHTON)

Reviewed: *Monthly Review* 32 (1765): 234
Critical Review 19 (1765): 480

2249 POTTER, John. *The Curate of Coventry: A Tale. By John Potter, Author of the History and Adventures of Arthur O'Bradley.* 2 vols. London, 1771 (12mo. 5s.sewed. Newbery. 1771) BODLEIAN

Reviewed: *Monthly Review* 44 (1771): 418
Critical Review 31 (1771): 301–306
London Magazine 40 (1771): 322 and 510

2250 [POTTER, John]. *The History of the Adventures of Arthur O'Bradley.* 2 vols. London, 1769 (12mo. 5s.sewed. Becket) BRITISH LIBRARY

Reviewed: *Monthly Review* 40 (1769): 424–425
Critical Review 28 (1769): 69
Gentleman's Magazine 39 (1769): 261

2251 [POTTER, John]. *The Hobby-Horse: A Characteristical Satire on the Times. Printed from a Manuscript, found among the Papers of a late deceased Satirist*
NOT SEEN (4to. 1s. F. Newbery)

Reviewed: *Monthly Review* 36 (1767): 78
Critical Review 22 (1766): 471

2252 POTTER, [Robert]. *Holkham A Poem. To the Right Honourable The Earl of Leicester.* London, 1758 (Fol. 1s. Manby) BRITISH LIBRARY

Reviewed: *Monthly Review* 18 (1758): 278–279

2253 POTTER, [Robert]. *Kymber A Monody. To Sir Armine Wodehouse, Bart.* London, 1759 (4to. 1s. Pridden) BRITISH LIBRARY

Reviewed: *Monthly Review* 19 (1758): 636–637
Critical Review 6 (1758): 521
Gentleman's Magazine 28 (1758): 599

2254 POTTER, [Robert]. *Poems, by Mr. Potter.* London, 1774 (8vo. 3s.sewed. White. 1774) BRITISH LIBRARY

Reviewed: *Monthly Review* 51 (1774): 20–21
Critical Review 38 (1774): 150–151
Universal Catalogue 3 (1774) art. 482

2255 [POTTINGER, Israel]. *The Humorous Quarrel; or, The Battle of the Greybeards. A Farce. As it is Acted at Mr. Davis's Theatrical Booth on the Bowling-Green, During the Time of Southwark Fair.* London, n.d. (8vo. 1s. Pottinger) LIBRARY OF CONGRESS

Reviewed: *Monthly Review* 25 (1761): 240
Critical Review 12 (1761): 236

2256 [POTTINGER, Israel]. *The Methodist, a Comedy; Being a Continuation and Completion of the Plan of the Minor, Written by Mr. Foote, As it was intended to have been Acted at the Theatre Royal in Covent-Garden, but for obvious Reasons suppressed. With the original Prologue and Epilogue.* London, n.d. [ESTC-1761] (8vo. 1s.6d. Pottinger) BRITISH LIBRARY

Reviewed: *Monthly Review* 25 (1761): 392
Critical Review 12 (1761): 401

2257 POTTINGER, I[srael]. *Stanzas, sacred to Liberty. To which are added, The Farringdon Election, a Ballad*
NOT SEEN (4to. 1s. Bingley)

Reviewed: *Monthly Review* 40 (1769): 176
Critical Review 27 (1769): 155
London Magazine 38 (1769): 268
Critical Memoirs 1 (1769): 258–259 and 524
Town & Country Magazine [1] (1769): 101

POULLAIN DE SAINT FOIX, Germain François. *The Oracle*
See: CIBBER, Susanna Maria. *The Oracle*
BICKERSTAFFE, Isaac. *Daphne and Amintor*

POULLAIN DE SAINT FOIX, Germain François (adaptation)
See: *Three Comedies . . . Freely translated from Messrs. St. Foix and Fagan*

POUNCE, Peter (pseud.)
See: LEWIS, Richard

2258 POUNCIT, Giles. *A Tale. By Giles Pouncit, Gent. Canto I*
NOT SEEN (4to. 6d. Davis)

Reviewed: *Monthly Review* 25 (1761): 478 [2 cantos]
Critical Review 12 (1761): 402

2259 POUNCIT, Giles. *A Tale. Canto the Second*
NOT SEEN (4to. 6d. Davis)

Reviewed: *Monthly Review* 25 (1761): 478 [2 cantos]
Critical Review 12 (1761): 484

2260 *Le Pour et le Contre. Being a Poetical Display of the Merit and Demerit of the Capital Paintings exhibited at Spring Gardens.* London, 1767 (4to. 1s. Williams) BRITISH LIBRARY

Reviewed: *Monthly Review* 36 (1767): 407–408
Critical Review 23 (1767): 461–462

2261 *Poverty, a Poem*
NOT SEEN (4to. 1s. Baldwin)

Reviewed: *Monthly Review* 39 (1768): 401
Critical Review 26 (1768): 230
Universal Museum 4 (1768): 485

2262 *The Power of Fancy. A Poem. By the Author.* Oxford, 1773 (4to. 1s. Rivington) BRITISH LIBRARY

Reviewed: *Monthly Review* 49 (1773): 64
Critical Review 35 (1773): 473–474
London Magazine 42 (1773): 302

The Powers of the Pen
See: LLOYD, Evan

2263 [POWIS, T.]. *The Tablet of Cebes, or a Picture of Human Life. A Poem: copied from the Greek of Cebes the Theban. By a Gentleman of Oxford*
NOT SEEN (4to. 6d. Printed at Oxford and sold by Rivington and Co. London)

Reviewed: *Monthly Review* 21 (1759): 321–323

2264 [POYNTZ, Anne]. *Je Ne Sçai Quoi: or, a Collection of Letters, Odes, &c. Never Before Published. By a Lady.* London, 1769 (8vo. 5s. Sold by Wilkie. 1769) BODLEIAN

Reviewed: *Monthly Review* 40 (1769): 157–158
Critical Memoirs 1 (1769): 523–524

2265 *Prae-Existence: a Poem. Prae-Existentia: Poema Latine Redditum.* Bath, n.d. (8vo. 1s. Bath, printed for Leake and Frederick) BODLEIAN

Reviewed: *Monthly Review* 28 (1763): 183–185
Critical Review 15 (1763): 152–153

2266 *The Praises of Isis; a Poem. By a Gentleman of Cambridge.* London, 1755 (4to. 1s. Dodsley) BRITISH LIBRARY

Reviewed: *Monthly Review* 12 (1755): 107–109

2267 [PRATT, Ellis]. *The Art of dressing the Hair. A Poem. Humbly inscribed to the Members of the T. N. Club, By E. P. Philocosm. And Late Hair-Dresser to the said Society.* Bath, 1770 (4to. 1s.6d. Carnan, &c.) BRITISH LIBRARY

Reviewed: *Monthly Review* 43 (1770): 243
Critical Review 29 (1770): 464–467
Gentleman's Magazine 40 (1770): 625
London Magazine 39 (1770): 378
Town & Country Magazine 2 (1770): 378 and 436 [identical review repeated]

2268 [PRATT, Samuel Jackson]. *The Tears of Genius. Occasioned by the Death of Dr. Goldsmith. By Courtney Melmoth.* London, 1774 (4to. 1s.6d. Becket. 1774) BRITISH LIBRARY

Reviewed: *Monthly Review* 50 (1774): 406–407
Critical Review 38 (1774): 75–76
Gentleman's Magazine 44 (1774): 275–276
Town & Country Magazine 6 (1774): 437
Universal Catalogue 3 (1774) art. 635

2269 *The Precipitate Choice: or, the History of Lord Osssory and Miss Rivers. By a Lady.* 2 vols. London, 1772 (12mo. 5s.sewed. Jones. 1772) BRITISH LIBRARY

Reviewed: *Monthly Review* 46 (1772): 456–457
Critical Review 33 (1772): 255
London Magazine 41 (1772): 189
British Magazine & General Review 1 (1772): 467
Universal Catalogue [1] (1772) art. 413

2270 *The Prediction; or, the History of Miss Lucy Maxwell. By a Lady.* 3 vols.
NOT SEEN (12mo. 7s.6d. Chater, &c.)

Reviewed: *Monthly Review* 43 (1770): 326
  Critical Review 30 (1770): 306–309
  London Magazine 39 (1770): 580

2271 *The Present State of the Literati. A Satire.* London, 1752 (4to. 1s. Cooper) BRITISH LIBRARY

Reviewed: *Monthly Review* 6 (1752): 316

2272 *The present State of the Nation; or, Love's Labour Lost. A Poem. In eight Books*
NOT SEEN (12mo. 3s.6d. Bath printed, and sold by Newbery in London)

Reviewed: *Monthly Review* 47 (1772): 71
  Critical Review 33 (1772): 410
  Universal Catalogue [1] (1772) art. 600

2273 [PRÉVOST, Antoine François]. *The History of the Chevalier des Grieux, Written by Himself. Translated from the French*
NOT SEEN (8vo. 4s. B. White)

Reviewed: *Monthly Review* 37 (1767): 76–77
  Critical Review 24 (1767): 141–143
  London Magazine 36 (1767): 312–313
  Universal Museum 3 (1767): 428
  Political Register 1 (1767): 180–181

2274 *Pride: a Poem. Inscribed to John Wilkes, Esquire. By An Englishman.* London, 1766 (4to. 1s.6d. Almon) BRITISH LIBRARY

Reviewed: *Monthly Review* 34 (1766): 242
  Critical Review 21 (1766): 152–153
  Gentleman's Magazine 36 (1766): 143–144

The Priest Dissected
See: ANSTEY, Christopher

2275 *The Priest in Rhime; an Epistle to the Rev. and Learned Mr. Br-w-r. Concerning the Presentation of Mr. H----s to the Living of Al--nk--le, in Northamptonshire, &c. &c.* London, 1767 (4to. 1s. Cooke) BRITISH LIBRARY

Reviewed: *Monthly Review* 37 (1767): 394
  Critical Review 24 (1767): 387–388
  Gentleman's Magazine 37 (1767): 561
  Universal Museum 3 (1767): 597

2276 *The Priest in Rhyme: a Doggrell Versification of Kidgell's Narrative, relative to the Essay on Woman. By A Member of Parliament, A Friend to Mr. Wilkes, and to Liberty.* London, n.d. [ESTC-1763] (4to. 1s. Gretton) BRITISH LIBRARY

Reviewed: *Monthly Review* 29 (1763): 464–465
  Critical Review 16 (1763): 478–479

2277 [PRIME, Benjamin Young]. *The Patriot Muse, or Poems on some of the principal Events of the late War; together with a Poem on the Peace. By an American Gentleman*
NOT SEEN (8vo. 1s.6d. Bird)

Reviewed: *Monthly Review* 32 (1765): 153–154
  Critical Review 19 (1765): 71
  Candid Review 1 (1765): 45

The Prince of Abissinia
See: JOHNSON, Samuel

2278 *The Prince of Salermo*
NOT SEEN (3s. Roson)

Reviewed: *Critical Review* 29 (1770): 148–149

The Prince of Tunis
See: MACKENZIE, Henry

2279 *The Prisoner; an Epistle to J*** B****, Esq; Written by a Young Gentleman, now in the King's Bench Prison*
NOT SEEN (4to. 1s. Peat)

Reviewed: *Monthly Review* 39 (1768): 401
  Critical Review 26 (1768): 315

2280 *The Prisoner; or, Nature's Complaint to Justice. A Poem. By a Lady in Confinement.* London, 1758 (4to. 1s. Cabe) BRITISH LIBRARY

Reviewed: *Monthly Review* 20 (1759): 92
  Critical Review 6 (1758): 521
  Gentleman's Magazine 28 (1758): 600

Privilege. A Poem
See: GREENE, Edward Burnaby

2281 *Pro and Con; or, the Political Squabble: A Satirical Dialogue. Addressed to the Leaders of the Opposition. By a Lady*
NOT SEEN (4to. 1s. Nicoll)

Reviewed: *Monthly Review* 29 (1763): 226
Critical Review 16 (1763): 231

2282 PROBE-ALL, Timothy (pseud.). *The Quack: an Empirical Essay. By Timothy Probe-all, M.M.D. Professor of Physic for the Mind in the University of London, and Member of the Academy of Sciences in Grubstreet*
NOT SEEN (4to. 1s.6d. Wilkie)

Reviewed: *Critical Review* 18 (1764): 478

2283 *Proceedings at the Court of Apollo*. London, 1752 (Fol. 6d. Owen) BRITISH LIBRARY

Reviewed: *Monthly Review* 6 (1752): 317–318

The Progress of Envy
See: LLOYD, Robert

The Progress of Gallantry
See: GRAVES, Richard

2284 *The Progress of Lying. A Satire*. London, 1762 (4to. 1s. Nicoll) NEWBERRY

Reviewed: *Monthly Review* 26 (1762): 385
Critical Review 13 (1762): 363

2285 *The Progress of Physic; a Poem. With Notes and Observations from antient Authors. By a Physician*
NOT SEEN (Fol. 20pp. 1s.)

Reviewed: *Monthly Review* 2 (1749–50): 227–229

2286 *The Progress of Vanity and Virtue, or, the History of two Sisters*. 2 vols.
NOT SEEN (12mo. 5s. Fletcher)

Reviewed: *Monthly Review* 35 (1766): 146
Critical Review 21 (1766): 470

2287 *The Prologue, Interludes, and Epilogue to the Heauton-Timoroumenos of Terence, acted by the young gentlemen of Beverley School, at Christmas, 1756*
NOT SEEN (Fol. 1s. Hitch)

Reviewed: *Monthly Review* 16 (1757): 462
Critical Review 3 (1757): 74–78

A Prologue on Comic Poetry
See: COOKE, Thomas

Prolusions; or, select Pieces of antient Poetry
See: CAPELL, Edward (ed.)

2288 *The Prophecy of Famine: A Scots Pastoral. Part the Second. Inscribed to C. Churchill*
NOT SEEN (4to. 1s. Cabe)

Reviewed: *Monthly Review* 28 (1763): 488
Critical Review 15 (1763): 486

2289 *The Prophecy of Genius. Inscribed to the Revd. Author of the Prophecy of Famine*. London, 1763 (4to. 6d. Cabe) FOLGER

Reviewed: *Monthly Review* 28 (1763): 321–322
Critical Review 15 (1763): 323

2290 *The Prophecy of Liberty: A Poem. Humbly Inscrib'd to the Right Hon. Robert Lord Romney*. London, 1768 (4to. 1s. Pearch) BRITISH LIBRARY

Reviewed: *Monthly Review* 38 (1768): 334
Critical Review 25 (1768): 227
Universal Museum 4 (1768): 148

2291 *Propriety: a Poetical Essay. To which is added, A Poetical Epistle to a young Gentleman, On his Determination to appear upon the Stage. By the same Author*. London, 1773 (4to. 1s.6d. Becket. 1773) FOLGER

Reviewed: *Monthly Review* 48 (1773): 317
Critical Review 35 (1773): 315
London Magazine 42 (1773): 196
Town & Country Magazine 5 (1773): 266
Universal Catalogue [2] (1773) art. 457

2292 *The Prospect of Liberty. Addressed to The Gentlemen of the County of H-n-g-d-n*. London, 1767 (4to. 2s.6d. Bladon) BRITISH LIBRARY

Reviewed: *Monthly Review* 37 (1767): 315
Critical Review 24 (1767): 72–74
Gentleman's Magazine 37 (1767): 409–410
Universal Museum 3 (1767): 372

2293 *The Prostitutes of Quality; or Adultery a-la-mode. Being Authentic and genuine Memoirs of several Persons of the highest Quality.* London, 1757 (12mo. 3s. Cooke) BRITISH LIBRARY

Reviewed: *Monthly Review* 17 (1757): 478

Providence: or, Arandus and Emilec
See: MICKLE, William Julius

2294 *The Providential Adultery.* 2 vols. NOT SEEN (12mo. 5s.sewed. Hall)

Reviewed: *Critical Review* 31 (1771): 160
London Magazine 40 (1771): 322–323

2295 *The Prudential Lovers, or the History of Harry Harper.* 2 vols. London, 1773 (12mo. 6s. Bell. 1773) BRITISH LIBRARY

Reviewed: *Monthly Review* 49 (1773): 150
Critical Review 36 (1773): 397
London Magazine 42 (1773): 351
Town & Country Magazine 5 (1773): 669
Universal Catalogue [2] (1773) art. 841

Psalms and Spiritual Songs
See: HOOPER, William

The Psalms of David, Translated into Heroic Verse
See: WHEATLAND, Stephen, and Tipping SYLVESTER

Public Spirit; an Ode
See: VEROVICENSIS SENESCENS

2296 *Pug's Reply to Parson Bruin. Or A Polemical Conference occasioned by an Epistle to Wiliam Hogarth, Esq; by C. Churchill.* London, n.d. [ESTC-1763] (4to. 1s. Cooke) BRITISH LIBRARY

Reviewed: *Monthly Review* 29 (1763): 78
Critical Review 16 (1763): 70–71

2297 PULLEIN, Samuel (trans.). *The Silk-worm: a poem in two books. By M. Hieronymus Vida. Translated into English verse. By the reverend Samuel Pullein, of Trinity-college, Dublin*
NOT SEEN (8vo. large paper. 4s. Dodsley)

Reviewed: *Monthly Review* 8 (1753): 153–156

2298 *Punch, a Panegyric, Attempted in the Manner of Milton.* London, 1769 (4to. 1s. Wilkie) BRITISH LIBRARY

Reviewed: *Monthly Review* 40 (1769): 337
Critical Review 28 (1769): 72–74
Gentleman's Magazine 39 (1769): 158
London Magazine 38 (1769): 159
Critical Memoirs 1 (1769): 523

The Pursuits of Happiness
See: MACKENZIE, Henry

2299 *Put Money in your Purse: or the Golden Rule. A Conversation-Piece, Not in Painting, but Poesy. A Satire with Notes.* London, 1754 (Fol. 1s. A. Dodd) BRITISH LIBRARY

Reviewed: *Monthly Review* 10 (1754): 78–79
Gentleman's Magazine 24 (1754): 50

2300 *Put Money in your Purse: or the Golden Rule; a conversation piece, not in painting but poesy. A satire with notes*
NOT SEEN (Fol. 1s. Dodd)

Reviewed: *Monthly Review* 13 (1755): 157

2301 [PYE, Henry James]. *Beauty, A Poetical Essay. In Three Parts.* London, 1766 (4to. 1s. Becket) BRITISH LIBRARY

Reviewed: *Monthly Review* 34 (1766): 481
Critical Review 21 (1766): 391–392
Gentleman's Magazine 36 (1766): 241

2302 [PYE, Henry James]. *Elegies on Different Occasions.* London, 1768 (4to. 1s. Bathurst) CAMBRIDGE

Reviewed: *Monthly Review* 40 (1769): 90–91
Critical Review 27 (1769): 231–234
London Magazine 37 (1768): 666
Town & Country Magazine [1] (1769): 213

2303 [PYE, Henry James]. *Faringdon Hill. A Poem. In Two Books.* Oxford, 1774 (4to. 2s.6d. Oxford printed, and sold by Wilkie in London. 1774) BRITISH LIBRARY

Reviewed: *Monthly Review* 50 (1774): 484
Critical Review 37 (1774): 392
London Magazine 43 (1774): 244
Universal Catalogue 3 (1774) art. 638

2304 PYE, Henry James. *The Triumph of Fashion. A Vision.* London, 1771 (4to. 1s.6d. Griffin. 1771) NEWBERRY

Reviewed: *Monthly Review* 44 (1771): 416
Critical Review 31 (1771): 314
London Magazine 40 (1771): 367

2305 [PYE, J. Henrietta]. *Poems, by A Lady.* London, 1771 (12mo. 2s.sewed. Walter. 1771) BRITISH LIBRARY

Reviewed: *Monthly Review* 45 (1771): 149–150
Critical Review 31 (1771): 475
Gentleman's Magazine 41 (1771): 325
Town & Country Magazine 3 (1771): 480

2306 *Pynsent, a Poem.* London, 1766 (4to. 1s.6d. Williams) BRITISH LIBRARY

Reviewed: *Monthly Review* 34 (1766): 243
Critical Review 21 (1766): 156
Gentleman's Magazine 36 (1766): 90

2307 *Pynsent's Ghost: (A Parody on the Celebrated Ballad of William and Margaret:).* London, 1766 (4to. 1s. Almon) BRITISH LIBRARY

Reviewed: *Monthly Review* 35 (1766): 325
Critical Review 22 (1766): 233
Gentleman's Magazine 36 (1766): 430

Pythagoras an Ode
See: COOKE, Thomas

2308 *The Quack Doctors. A Satire. In Hudibrastic Stile*
NOT SEEN (4to. 1s. Moran)

Reviewed: *Monthly Review* 26 (1762): 386
Critical Review 13 (1762): 363

2309 *The Quarrel between Venus and Hymen: an Heroi-Satyrical Mythological Poem. In Imitation of the Antients: In VI. Cantos. Found among the Papers of a very learned Antiquarian, and published for the Benefit of Posterity, with Notes.* London, 1750–1 (8vo. 1s.6d. Printed for M. Cooper) BRITISH LIBRARY

Reviewed: *Monthly Review* 4 (1750–51): 28–33

Quebec: A poetical Essay, in Imitation of the Miltonic Stile
See: PATRICK, J.

Queen Tragedy Restor'd
See: HOPER, Mrs.

2310 [QUILLET, Claude]. *Advice to new-married persons; or, the art of having beautiful children. In four books. To which is added, the art of bringing up children, &c.*
NOT SEEN (12mo. 2s. Owen)

Reviewed: *Monthly Review* 11 (1754): 318
Gentleman's Magazine 24 (1754): 391.

2311 QUINTUS, Tertius Quartus (pseud.). *The Conciliad: or, The Triumph of Patriotism. A Poem. Translated from the Latin of Tertius Quartus Quintus.* 1st ed. reviewed; copy seen 3d ed.: London, 1762 (4to. 1s. Pridden) BRITISH LIBRARY

Reviewed: *Monthly Review* 25 (1761): 396–397
Critical Review 12 (1761): 397
British Magazine (1761): 662

RACINE, Louis. *Religion, a Poem*
See: ELPHINSTON, James (trans.)

2312 *The Ragged Uproar: or, the Oxford Roratory: a new Dramatic Satire; In many Scenes, and one very long Act. In which is introduced, The A-la-mode System of Fortune-Telling. Originally plann'd By Joan Plotwell; and continued by several truly Eminent Hands, well vers'd in the Art of Designing. The Whole Concluding with an important Scene of Witches, Gypsies, and Fortune-Tellers; a long jumbling Dance of Politicians; And An Epilogue spoken by Mary Squires, &c. flying on Broom-Sticks.* London, n.d. [ESTC-1754] (4to. 1s. G. Pote) BRITISH LIBRARY

Reviewed: *Monthly Review* 11 (1754): 235

2313 *The Rake of Taste, or the Elegant Debauchee: A True Story.* London, 1760 (8vo. 2s. Wicks) BRITISH LIBRARY

Reviewed: *Monthly Review* 23 (1760): 327
Critical Review 10 (1760): 327
London Magazine 29 (1760): 560
British Magazine 1 (1760): 665

2314 *The Rake; or, the Adventures of Tom Wildman. Exhibiting striking Pictures of Life, in all its variegated Scenes; interspersed with the Histories of several Personages of either Sex, well known in the Polite World. Written by Himself.* 2 vols.
NOT SEEN (12mo. 5s. Williams)

Reviewed: *Monthly Review* 49 (1773): 231–232

The Rambles of Mr. Frankly
See: BONHOTE, Elizabeth

2315 RAMSAY, Allan (ed.). *The Ever Green being a Collection of Scots Poems, Wrote by the Ingenious before 1600. Published by Allan Ramsay.* 2 vols. Edinburgh, 1761 (12mo. 5s. Edinburgh printed. Sold by Richardson in London) BRITISH LIBRARY

Reviewed: *Monthly Review* 26 (1762): 188–196

2316 RANGER, Honest (pseud.). *Ranger's Progress: Consisting of a Variety of Poetical Essays, Moral, Serious, Comic, and Satyrical. By Honest Ranger, Of Bedford-Row.* London, 1760 (8vo. 2s.6d. Kinnersley) BRITISH LIBRARY

Reviewed: *Monthly Review* 23 (1760): 243–245
Critical Review 10 (1760): 121–122
British Magazine 1 (1760): 546

2317 RANGER, Honest (pseud.). *A Visit to the Ideal World. By Honest Ranger.* London, 1763 (4to. 1s.6d. Flexney) FOLGER

Reviewed: *Monthly Review* 29 (1763): 74–75
Critical Review 15 (1763): 393

2318 *The Rape: A Poem, Humbly Inscribed to the Ladies.* 1st ed. reviewed; copy seen 2d ed.: London, 1768 (4to. 1s. Steare) BRITISH LIBRARY

Reviewed: *Monthly Review* 38 (1768): 70
Critical Review 25 (1768): 65–66
London Magazine 37 (1768): 42
Universal Museum 4 (1768): 36–37
Political Register 2 (1768): 120

The Rape of Pomona
See: COURTENAY, John

The Rape of the Smock
See: JACOB, Giles

2319 *The Rape of the Vineyard: or, Mock-Heroic Stanzas on the Mock-Heroic Expedition. Dedicated to the Right Honourable W---- P--t Esquire.* London, 1757 (Fol. 6d. J. Cooke, J. Coote) BRITISH LIBRARY

Reviewed: *Monthly Review* 17 (1757): 378–379
Critical Review 4 (1757): 465

2320 [RASBOTHAM, Dorning]. *Codrus: A Tragedy.* London, 1774 (8vo. 1s.6d. Johnson. 1774) BRITISH LIBRARY

Reviewed: *Monthly Review* 50 (1774): 409
Critical Review 37 (1774): 157–158
Gentleman's Magazine 44 (1774): 228
Universal Catalogue 3 (1774) art. 325

2321 *The Rational Lovers: or, the History of Sir Charles Leusum, and Mrs Frances Fermor.* 2 vols. London, 1769 (12mo. 6s. Noble) BRITISH LIBRARY

Reviewed: *Monthly Review* 40 (1769): 259
Critical Memoirs 1 (1769): 525

2322 *The Rational Rosciad. On a More extensive Plan than any thing of the kind hitherto published. In Two Parts. Viz. I. On the Stage in general and particular, and the Merits of the most celebrated Dramatic Writers. II. On the Merits of the principal Performers of both Theatres. By F.-- B-- L--.* London, 1767 (4to. 1s.6d. Wilkie) BRITISH LIBRARY

Reviewed: *Monthly Review* 36 (1767): 163
Critical Review 23 (1767): 60
Gentleman's Magazine 37 (1767): 77–78

2323 RAYNER, William. *Miscellanies In Prose and Verse, Original and Translated.* Ipswich, 1767 (4to. 3s.6d. Johnson) BRITISH LIBRARY

Reviewed: *Monthly Review* 38 (1768): 70
Critical Review 24 (1767): 469
Universal Museum 4 (1768): 36

The Reapers: or the Englishman out of Paris
See: FAVART, Charles Simon

2324 *Reason: A poem. To which is prefix'd, a Notion of Poetry: an essay*
NOT SEEN (4to. 1s. Cooper)

Reviewed: *Monthly Review* 18 (1758): 651
Critical Review 6 (1758): 171–174

2325 *The Recantation and Confession of Doctor Kenrick, L.L.D.* London, 1772 (4to. 1s. Allen) BRITISH LIBRARY

Reviewed: *Critical Review* 35 (1773): 70
London Magazine 41 (1772): 598
Universal Catalogue [1] (1772) art. 1456

2326 *The Reclaim'd Libertine; or, the History of the honourable Charles Belmont Esq; and Miss Melvill. In a Series of Letters. In Two Volumes.* London, 1769 (12mo. 6s. Noble) UNIVERSITY OF ILLINOIS

Reviewed: *Monthly Review* 40 (1769): 259
Critical Review 28 (1769): 373–375
London Magazine 38 (1769): 44–45

2327 *The Reclaimed Prostitute; or, the Adventures of Amelia Sidney.* 2 vols.
NOT SEEN (12mo. 5s. Roson)

Reviewed: *Monthly Review* 46 (1772): 165
Critical Review 33 (1772): 84
Gentleman's Magazine 42 (1772): 85
Town & Country Magazine 4 (1772): 100
Universal Catalogue [1] (1772) art. 92

2328 *The Recruiter for Germany*
NOT SEEN (4to. 6d. Williams)

Reviewed: *Monthly Review* 26 (1762): 320
Critical Review 13 (1762): 364

The Recruiting Serjeant. A Musical Entertainment
See: BICKERSTAFFE, Isaac

2329 *The Recruiting Serjeant. A Tale*
NOT SEEN (4to. 6d. Wilkie)

Reviewed: *Monthly Review* 34 (1766): 244
Critical Review 21 (1766): 231
Gentleman's Magazine 36 (1766): 145

2330 [REED, Isaac (ed.)]. *Musae Seatoniae. A complete Collection of the Cambridge Prize Poems, from the first institution of that Premium by the Rev. Mr. Tho. Seaton, in 1750, to the present time. To which are added, Two Poems, likewise written for the prize, by Mr. Bally and Mr. Scott.* London, 1772 (8vo. 3s.6d. Pearch, &c. 1772) BRITISH LIBRARY

Reviewed: *Monthly Review* 49 (1773): 148
London Magazine 42 (1772): 195
Universal Catalogue [2] (1773) art. 466

2331 [REED, Joseph]. *A British Philippic. Inscribed to the Right Honourable The Earl of Granville.* London, 1756 (4to. 1s. Kinnersley) BRITISH LIBRARY

Reviewed: *Monthly Review* 15 (1756): 85–86

2332 REED, J[oseph]. *Madrigal and Trulletta. A Mock-Tragedy. Acted (Under the Direction of Mr. Cibber) at the Theatre-Royal in Covent-Garden. With Notes by the Author, and Dr. Humbug, Critick and Censor-General.* London, 1758 (8vo. 1s.6d. Reeve) BRITISH LIBRARY

Reviewed: *Monthly Review* 19 (1758): 303
Critical Review 6 (1758): 168–170

2333 REED, J[oseph]. *The Register-Ofice: A Farce Of Two Acts. Acted at the Theatre-Royal in Drury-Lane.* London, 1761 (8vo. 1s. Davies) BRITISH LIBRARY

Reviewed: *Monthly Review* 24 (1761): 441
Critical Review 11 (1761): 412–413
British Magazine 2 (1761): 326

2334 [REED, Joseph]. *A Sop in the Pan for a Physical Critick: In a Letter to Dr. Sm*ll*tt, occasion'd by A Criticism on a late Mock-Tragedy, call'd Madrigal and Trulletta. By a Halter-Maker.* London, 1759 (8vo. 6d. Reeve) BRITISH LIBRARY

Reviewed: *Monthly Review* 20 (1759): 605

2335 REED, Joseph. *Tom Jones, a Comic Opera: As it is Performed at the Theatre-Royal in Covent-Garden.* London, 1769 (8vo. 1s.6d. Becket) BRITISH LIBRARY

Reviewed: *Monthly Review* 40 (1769): 65–68
Critical Review 27 (1769): 80
Gentleman's Magazine 39 (1769): 157
London Magazine 38 (1769): 42–43
Critical Memoirs 1 (1769): 60–63 and 521

2336 [REEVE, Clara]. *Original Poems on several Occasions. By C. R.* London, 1769 (4to. 5s. sewed. Harris) BRITISH LIBRARY

Reviewed: *Monthly Review* 41 (1769): 476
Critical Review 28 (1769): 378–379

2337 [REEVE, Clara (trans.)]. *The Phoenix; or, the History of Polyarchus and Argenis. Translated from the Latin. By a Lady.* [Translation of John BARCLAY's *Argenis*.] 4 vols. London, 1772 (12mo. 12s. Bell. 1772) BRITISH LIBRARY

Reviewed: *Monthly Review* 45 (1771): 503–504
Critical Review 32 (1771): 471
Gentleman's Magazine 41 (1771): 604
London Magazine 41 (1771): 32
Town & Country Magazine 4 (1771): 45

2338 *Reflections on the Ruins Of An Ancient Cathedral: to which is added, An Elegy on Winter.* Chelmsford, 1770 (4to. 1s. Newbery) UNIVERSITY OF ILLINOIS

Reviewed: *Monthly Review* 43 (1770): 244
Critical Review 30 (1770): 231–232
London Magazine 39 (1770): 268
Town & Country Magazine 2 (1770): 268

2339 *Regeneration, a Poem; shewing, from scripture and experience, the nature and necessity of being born again. With explanatory notes under each verse. By the author of the wonderful Signs of Christ's Coming, &c.*
NOT SEEN (8vo. 6d. Scott)

Reviewed: *Monthly Review* 16 (1757): 286

The Regicide
See: SMOLLETT, Tobias

2340 *The Register of Folly; or, Characters and Incidents at Bath and the Hot-Wells. In a Series of Poetical Epistles. By An Invalid.* London, 1773 (8vo. 2s.6d. sewed. Newbery. 1773) BRITISH LIBRARY

Reviewed: *Monthly Review* 49 (1773): 64
Critical Review 35 (1773): 473
Universal Catalogue [2] (1773) art. 475

REGNARD, Jean François (adaptation)
See: KING, Thomas. *Wit's Last Stake*

2341 *The Reign of George VI.* London, 1763 (12mo. 2s.6d. Nicoll) BODLEIAN

Reviewed: *Monthly Review* 30 (1764): 251–252
Critical Review 17 (1764): 305–306

The Relief, or, Day Thoughts
See: JONES, Henry

2342 *Religion: a Poem. By J. H. A. B. Formerly of Pembroke College, Oxon.* London, 1761 (4to. 1s. Lewis) BODLEIAN

Reviewed: *Monthly Review* 24 (1761): 354
Critical Review 12 (1761): 484
British Magazine 3 (1762): 44

2343 *Religious Conscience: or, the Morning and Evening Sacrifice. A Poem. In Imitation of Dr. Young's Night Thoughts.* London, 1755 (4to. 1s. Baker, Beechcroft, &c.) BRITISH LIBRARY

Reviewed: *Monthly Review* 12 (1755): 509–510

Reliques of Ancient English Poetry
See: PERCY, Thomas

2344 *The Remonstrance. A Poem.* London, 1764 (4to. 1s. Burnet) BODLEIAN

Reviewed: *Monthly Review* 30 (1764): 239–240
Critical Review 17 (1764): 316–317
General Magazine 1 (1764): 96–97

2345 *The Remonstrance. A Poem.* London, 1770 (4to. 2s.6d. Davenhill, &c.) BRITISH LIBRARY

Reviewed: *Monthly Review* 42 (1770): 326–327
Critical Review 29 (1770): 312–313
Town & Country Magazine 2 (1770): 214

2346 *The Rendezvous, or Covent-Garden Piazza: a Satire.* London, 1760 (4to. 1s. Thrush) YALE (BEINECKE)

Reviewed: *Monthly Review* 22 (1760): 167–168
Critical Review 9 (1760): 237

2347 RENWICK, William. *The Genuine Distress of Damon and Clelia. In a Series of Letters between The Late General Craufurd, Sir John Hussey Delaval, Bart. Sir Francis Blake Delaval, K.B. and Two Unfortunate Lovers.* 2 vols.

Bath, 1771 (12mo. 6s. Dodsley, &c.) BRITISH LIBRARY

Reviewed: *Monthly Review* 45 (1771): 331–332
Critical Review 32 (1771): 311–312
London Magazine 40 (1771): 570
Town & Country Magazine 3 (1771): 602

2348 *Report: or, the Political Lyar. A Satirical Epistle*
NOT SEEN (4to. 1s. Roberts)

Reviewed: *Monthly Review* 30 (1764): 241
Critical Review 17 (1764): 238

The Reprisal: or, the Tars of Old England
See: SMOLLETT, Tobias

2349 *The Request, a Poem*. London, 1762 (4to. 1s. Caston) YALE (BEINECKE) [N.B. May not be same poem; bookseller's name—Kent—differs from that given in *Monthly Review* and *Critical Review*.]

Reviewed: *Monthly Review* 27 (1762): 458–460
Critical Review 14 (1762): 397–398

Resignation In Two Parts
See: YOUNG, Edward

2350 *Resignation; or, Majesty in the Dumps; an Ode. Addressed To George Colman, Esq. Late Manager of the Theatre Royal in Covent-Garden*. London, 1774 (4to. 1s. Bew) BRITISH LIBRARY

Reviewed: *Critical Review* 37 (1774): 473
London Magazine 43 (1774): 399
Town & Country Magazine 6 (1774): 437

2351 [RESTIF DE LA BRETONNE, Nicolas Anne Edmé]. *Lucilla: or the Progress of Virtue. Translated from the French.* [Translation of *Lucile, ou les Progrès de la Vertu*.] London, 1770 (12mo. 3s. Lowndes, &c.) BRITISH LIBRARY

Reviewed: *Monthly Review* 42 (1770): 70–71
Critical Review 29 (1770): 366–367
London Magazine 39 (1770): 105

2352 *The Resurrection of Liberty; or, Advice to the Colonists: a Poem. By the Ghost of Churchill*
NOT SEEN (4to. 2s. Allen. 1774)

Reviewed: *Monthly Review* 51 (1774): 317
London Magazine 44 (1775): 39
Universal Catalogue 3 (1774) art. 1253

The Retort. By the Author
See: VAUGHAN, Thomas

The Reverie; or, a Flight to the Paradise of Fools
See: JOHNSTONE, Charles

2353 *Reveries Revived. A Poem*
NOT SEEN (8vo. 1s. No Bookseller's Name)

Reviewed: *Monthly Review* 42 (1770): 76
Critical Review 29 (1770): 234

A Review of the Poem entitled "The Patricians"
See: DELAMAYNE, Thomas Hallie

A Review of the Poem intitled "The Senators"
See: DELAMAYNE, Thomas Hallie

2354 *The Reward of Virtue; or the History of Miss Polly Graham. Intermixed with several curious and interesting incidents in the Lives of several Persons of both Sexes, remarkable for the singular Adventures which befel them. To which is added, a brief Description of Bounty-Hall, and its Inhabitants*
NOT SEEN (12mo. 2s.6d. Roson)

Reviewed: *Monthly Review* 41 (1769): 479

2355 *Reynard's Prosecution of The Unfortunate Bruin, assisted by the Wolfe, Ox, Ass, Ram, Beaver, &c. Together with the Sufferings of the Pard, Agent for the Unhappy Bruin; A Fable.* London, 1761 (4to. 1s. Ranger) UNIVERSITY OF ILLINOIS

Reviewed: *Monthly Review* 25 (1761): 231
Critical Review 12 (1761): 320

2356 *Rhapsodies. A Poem. Book I.* London, 1766 (4to. 2s.6d. Printed for the Author. Sold by Nicoll) YALE (BEINECKE)

Reviewed: *Monthly Review* 34 (1766): 481
Critical Review 21 (1766): 476

2357 *A Rhapsody in the House of Commons. Inscribed to the right honourable William Pitt, and Henry Bilson Legge, Esquires*
NOT SEEN (Fol. 6d. Wilkie)

Reviewed: *Monthly Review* 18 (1758): 651
Critical Review 5 (1758): 442–443

2358 *The Rhapsody: or, Every Man his own Companion*
NOT SEEN (8vo. 2s.6d. Griffin)

Reviewed: *Monthly Review* 38 (1768): 241
Critical Review 25 (1768): 74

2359 RICCOBONI, [Marie Jeanne]. *The Continuation of the Life of Marianne. To which is added The History of Ernestina, With Letters and other Miscellaneous Pieces. Translated from the French of Madame Riccoboni.* London, 1766 (12mo. 3s. Becket and De Hondt) BRITISH LIBRARY

Reviewed: *Monthly Review* 38 (1768): 72–73
Gentleman's Magazine 37 (1767): 80

2360 RICCOBONI, [Marie Jeanne]. *The History of Miss Jenny Salisbury; addressed to the Countess of Roscommond. Translated from the French of the celebrated Madame Riccoboni.* 2 vols. London, 1764 (12mo. 6s. Becket) BRITISH LIBRARY

Reviewed: *Monthly Review* 31 (1764): 475–478
Critical Review 18 (1764): 313–314

2361 [RICCOBONI, Marie Jeanne]. *The History of the Marquis de Cressy. Translated from the French.* London, 1765 (12mo. 2s.6d. Becket) BRITISH LIBRARY

Reviewed: *Monthly Review* 33 (1765): 87
Candid Review 1 (1765): 396–397

2362 [RICCOBONI, Marie Jeanne]. *The History of the Marquis of Cressy. Translated from the French*
NOT SEEN (12mo. 3s. Pottinger)

Reviewed: *Monthly Review* 20 (1759): 467

RICCOBONI, Marie Jeanne. *Letters from Elizabeth Sophia de Valiere*
See: MACEUEN, ––– (trans.)

RICCOBONI, Marie Jeanne. *Letters from Juliet Lady Catesby*
See: BROOKE, Frances (trans.)

2363 RICCOBONI, [Marie Jeanne]. *Letters from the Countess de Sancerre to the Count de Nancé, her Friend. By Madam Riccoboni. Translated from the French.* 2 vols. London, 1767 (12mo. 6s. Becket) BRITISH LIBRARY

Reviewed: *Monthly Review* 37 (1767): 67–68
Critical Review 23 (1767): 400
London Magazine 36 (1767): 205–206
Political Register 1 (1767): 486

2364 [RICH, John]. *The Spirit of Contradiction. A New Comedy of Two Acts, As it is Acted at the Theatre-Royal in Covent-Garden. By a Gentleman of Cambridge.* London, 1760 (8vo. 1s. Lowndes) BODLEIAN

Reviewed: *Monthly Review* 22 (1760): 333–336
Critical Review 9 (1760): 239–240

2365 RICHARDSON, John. *A Specimen of Persian Poetry; or Odes of Hafez, With an English Translation and Paraphrase. Chiefly from the Specimen Poeseos Persicae of Baron Revisky, Envoy from the Emperor of Germany to the Court of Poland. With Historical and Grammatical Illustrations, and a complete Analysis, for the assistance of those who wish to study the Persian Language.* London, 1774 (4to. 5s.3d.boards. Sold at No. 76 Fleet-street. 1774) BRITISH LIBRARY

Reviewed: *Monthly Review* 51 (1774): 165–166
Critical Review 37 (1774): 300–303
London Magazine 43 (1774): 447
Town & Country Magazine 6 (1774): 267
Universal Catalogue 3 (1774) art. 496

2366 [RICHARDSON, Samuel]. *A Collection Of the Moral and Instructive Sentiments, Maxims, Cautions, and Reflexions, Contained in the Histories of Pamela, Clarissa, and Sir Charles Grandison. Digested under Proper Heads, With References to the Volume, and Page, both in Octavo and Twelves, in the respective Histories. To which are subjoined, Two Letters from the Editor of those Works: The one, in Answer to a Lady who was solicitous for an additional Volume to the History of Sir Charles Grandison.*

The other, in Reply to a Gentleman, who had objected to Sir Charles's offer'd Compromise in the Article of Religion, had he married a Roman Catholic Lady. London, 1755 (12mo. 3s. Hitch, Rivington, &c.) BRITISH LIBRARY

Reviewed: *Monthly Review* 12 (1755): 235

2367 [RICHARDSON, Samuel]. *The History of Sir Charles Grandison. In a Series of Letters Published from the Originals, By the Editor of Pamela and Clarissa. In Seven Volumes.* [Title page to volume 7 also reads: *To which is added, An Historical and Characteristical Index. As Also, A Brief History, authenticated by Original Letters, of the Treatment which the Editor has met with from certain Booksellers and Printers in Dublin. Including Observations on Mr. Faulkner's Defence of himself, published in his Irish News-Paper of Nov. 3, 1753.*] London, 1754 (12mo. 19s. Rivington, &c.) UNIVERSITY OF PENNSYLVANIA

Reviewed: *Monthly Review* 10 (1754): 70–71
Gentleman's Magazine 23 (1753): 543

2368 [RICHARDSON, Samuel]. *The Paths of Virtue delineated; or, the History in Miniature Of the Celebrated Pamela, Clarissa Harlow, and Sir Charles Grandison, Familiarised and Adapted To the Capacities of Youth.* London, 1756 (12mo. 2s.6d. Baldwin) BRITISH LIBRARY

Reviewed: *Monthly Review* 14 (1756): 581–582
Critical Review 1 (1756): 315–316

2369 RICHARDSON, William. *Poems, chiefly Rural.* Glasgow, 1774 (8vo. 2s.6d.boards. Glasgow printed, and sold in London by Murray) BRITISH LIBRARY

Reviewed: *Monthly Review* 51 (1774): 94–96
Critical Review 38 (1774): 143–146
Town & Country Magazine 6 (1774): 464

2370 [RICHARDSON, William]. *A Poetical Address, in Favour of the Corsicans.* London, 1769 (4to. 1s. Almon) LILLY

Reviewed: *Monthly Review* 40 (1769): 250
Critical Review 27 (1769): 234
Town & Country Magazine [1] (1769): 213
Political Register 4 (1769): 321

2371 RICHWOULD, Mrs. *The South Sea Fortune, or the Chaplain advanced to the Saddle. Containing The genuine private Memoirs of a worthy Family in Gloucestershire, from the fatal Year 1720, to the Year 1748. Written by Mrs. Richwould, One of the most interested Parties.* 2 vols. London, 1758 (12mo. 6s. Wren) NEWBERRY

Reviewed: *Monthly Review* 19 (1758): 581

2372 RIDER, William (trans.). *Candidus: or, the Optimist. By Mr. De Voltaire. Translated into English. By W. Rider, M.A. Late Scholar of Jesus College, Oxford.* London, 1759 (1s.6d. Scott) BRITISH LIBRARY

Reviewed: *Gentleman's Magazine* 29 (1759): 233–235

2373 *The Rider; or, Humours of an Inn; A Farce of Two Acts: As it has been acted with general Approbation, and was Intended for the Theatres in London.* London, 1768 (8vo. 1s. Nicoll) BRITISH LIBRARY

Reviewed: *Monthly Review* 38 (1768): 412
Critical Review 25 (1768): 315 and 29 (1770): 72

2374 [RIDLEY, James]. *The History of James Lovegrove, Esq; In Four Books.* London, 1761 (12mo. 6s. Wilkie) BRITISH LIBRARY

Reviewed: *Monthly Review* 24 (1761): 352
Critical Review 11 (1761): 420
British Magazine 2 (1761): 326

2375 [RIDLEY, James]. *The Schemer Or, Universal Satirist. By That Great Philosopher Helter van Scelter. Illustrated with Notes Critical and Explanatory, by some of the first Personages of Europe.* London, 1763 (12mo. 3s. Wilkie) BRITISH LIBRARY

Reviewed: *Monthly Review* 28 (1763): 495
Critical Review 15 (1763): 396–397

2376 [RIDLEY, James]. *The Tales of the Genii: or, the Delightful Lessons of Horam, The Son of Asmar. Faithfully Translated from the Persian Manuscript; and Compared with the French and Spanish Editions Published in Paris and Madrid. By Sir Charles Morell, Formerly Am-*

bassador from the British Settlements in India to the Great Mogul. 2 vols. London, 1764 (8vo. 6s. Wilkie) BRITISH LIBRARY

Reviewed: *Monthly Review* 31 (1764): 478–479
Critical Review 18 (1764): 34–41 [vol. 1] and 19 (1765): 136–137 [vol. 2]
British Magazine 5 (1764): 433

The Ring. An Epistle, addressed to Mrs. L----m
See: HARRIS, Thomas

2377 *The Rise and Progress Of the Present Taste in Planting Parks, Pleasure Grounds, Gardens, &c. from Henry the Eighth to King George the Third. In a poetic Epistle to the Right Honourable Charles Lord Viscount Irwin.* London, 1767 (4to. 1s.6d. Moran) BRITISH LIBRARY

Reviewed: *Monthly Review* 37 (1767): 139–144
Critical Review 23 (1767): 460–461

2378 *The Rise and surprizing Adventures of Donald McGregor. A Novel.* 2 vols.
NOT SEEN (12mo. 4s. Williams)

Reviewed: *Monthly Review* 30 (1764): 488
Critical Review 17 (1764): 478
General Magazine 1 (1764): 301

2379 RITSO, George. *Kew Gardens. A Poem. Humbly inscribed to Her Royal Highness the Princess Dowager of Wales. By George Ritso.* London, 1763 (4to. 1s. Dodsley) UNIVERSITY OF CHICAGO

Reviewed: *Monthly Review* 29 (1763): 407–409
Critical Review 16 (1763): 394–395

The Rival Beauties; a Poetical Contest
See: SHERIDAN, Richard Brinsley

2380 *The Rival Mother: or, the History of the Countess de Salens, and Her two Daughters.* 2 vols. London, 1755 (12mo. 6s. Noble) BRITISH LIBRARY

Reviewed: *Monthly Review* 12 (1755): 237

2381 *The Rival Politicians; or, the Fox triumphant, a Fable, betwixt a Lion, a Wolf, and a Fox*
NOT SEEN (Fol. 6d. Sympson)

Reviewed: *Monthly Review* 16 (1757): 363

2382 *A Roast for a Scots Parson. A New Song, To Some Tune. With a Word to the Reader. By the Fool.* London, 1749 (8vo. 20pp. 6d. Printed for Dickinson, a Printseller on Ludgate Hill) BRITISH LIBRARY

Reviewed: *Monthly Review* 2 (1749–50): 104–105

2383 ROBERTS, George. *The Prospect, or Rural Sports; a Poem.* [British Library copy cropped] [ESTC: London? 1754?] (Fol. 1s. Cooper) BRITISH LIBRARY

Reviewed: *Monthly Review* 11 (1754): 233–234

2384 [ROBERTS, William Hayward]. *Arimant and Tamira: an Eastern Tale. In the manner of Dryden's fables. By a Gentleman of Cambridge.* London, 1707 [ESTC-1757] (4to. 1s. M. Cooper) BRITISH LIBRARY

Reviewed: *Monthly Review* 18 (1758): 183–184
Critical Review 5 (1758): 88

2385 ROBERTS, [William Hayward]. *Poems by Dr. Roberts of Eton College.* London, 1774 (8vo. 4s.bound. Wilkie. 1774) BRITISH LIBRARY

Reviewed: *Monthly Review* 51 (1774): 166
Critical Review 37 (1774): 213–214
Town & Country Magazine 6 (1774): 211–212
Universal Catalogue 3 (1774) art. 346

2386 [ROBERTS, William Hayward]. *A Poetical Epistle, to Christopher Anstey, Esq; on the English Poets, chiefly those, who have written in blank verse.* London, 1773 (4to. 1s. Wilkie. 1773) BRITISH LIBRARY

Reviewed: *Monthly Review* 48 (1773): 145–148
Critical Review 35 (1773): 52–54
Gentleman's Magazine 43 (1773): 34–35
London Magazine 42 (1773): 92
Universal Catalogue [2] (1773) art. 104

2387 ROBERTS, W[illiam] H[ayward]. *A poetical Essay on the Attributes of God. Part II.* London, 1771 (4to. 1s. Wilkie. 1771) BRITISH LIBRARY

Reviewed: *Monthly Review* 44 (1771): 492
Critical Review 32 (1771): 152
Gentleman's Magazine 41 (1771): 325

2388 ROBERTS, William Hayward. *A Poetical Essay, on the Existence of God. Part I.* London, 1771 (4to. 1s. Wilkie) BRITISH LIBRARY

Reviewed: *Monthly Review* 44 (1771): 261
Critical Review 31 (1771): 71–73
Gentleman's Magazine 41 (1771): 86 and 228
London Magazine 39 (1770): 677

2389 ROBERTS, W[illiam] H[ayward]. *A Poetical Essay, on the Providence of God. Part III.* London, 1771 (4to. 1s.6d. Wilkie) BODLEIAN

Reviewed: *Monthly Review* 45 (1771): 235
Critical Review 32 (1771): 152

2390 [ROBERTSON, James]. *Poems, consisting of Tales, Fables, Epigrams, &c. By Nobody* NOT SEEN (12mo. 2s.6d. Robinson and Roberts, &c. 1770)

Reviewed: *Monthly Review* 42 (1770): 144
Critical Review 29 (1770): 113–117

2391 ROBERTSON, James. *Poems on Several Occasions.* London, 1773 (12mo. 3s.6d. Davies, &c. 1773) BRITISH LIBRARY

Reviewed: *Monthly Review* 48 (1773): 413
Critical Review 35 (1773): 314
London Magazine 42 (1773): 195
Town & Country Magazine 5 (1773): 210
Universal Catalogue [2] (1773) art. 464

2392 ROBINSON, J. *The Methodists. An Eclogue* NOT SEEN (4to. 6d. Crouse at Norwich)

Reviewed: *Monthly Review* 29 (1763): 227–228
Critical Review 15 (1763): 486

ROBINSON, J. *Poems on Several Occasions*
See: ROBERTSON, James

2393 [ROBINSON, John]. *The History of Mr. Charles Chance, and Miss Clara Vellum.* London, 1767 (12mo. 3s. Noble) BRITISH LIBRARY

Reviewed: *Monthly Review* 36 (1767): 173
Critical Review 22 (1766): 468–469

2394 ROBINSON, John. *Poems of various Kinds Viz. Satires, Tales, Pastorals, Elegiac and Other Pieces.* Norwich, 1768 (8vo. 2s.6d. Knox) BRITISH LIBRARY

Reviewed: *Monthly Review* 38 (1768): 149
Critical Review 25 (1768): 67–69
Universal Museum 4 (1768): 36

2395 ROBINSON, John. *The Poet's Manual. A Satire.* London, 1767 (4to. 1s. Noble) BRITISH LIBRARY

Reviewed: *Monthly Review* 36 (1767): 240
Critical Review 23 (1767): 144

2396 ROBINSON, John. *Preferment: a Satire.* London, 1765 (4to. 1s. Nicoll) BRITISH LIBRARY

Reviewed: *Monthly Review* 32 (1765): 232
Critical Review 19 (1765): 234–235

2397 ROBINSON, John. *The Village Oppress'd a Poem. Dedicated to Dr. Goldsmith.* London, 1771 (4to. 1s. Robson. 1771) BRITISH LIBRARY

Reviewed: *Monthly Review* 44 (1771): 261
Critical Review 31 (1771): 73
Gentleman's Magazine 41 (1771): 86
London Magazine 40 (1771): 47
Town & Country Magazine 3 (1771): 102

2398 ROBSON, John. *The first book of the Psalms of David, translated into English verse, of Heroic measure. With arguments and notes* NOT SEEN (8vo. 2s. Sandby)

Reviewed: *Monthly Review* 24 (1761): 354

Rodogune: or The Rival Brothers
See: ASPINWALL, S.

Rodondo; or, the State Jugglers
See: DALRYMPLE, Hugh

2399 [ROGERS, Robert]. *Ponteach: or the Savages of America. A Tragedy.* London, 1766 (8vo. 2s.6d. Milan) BRITISH LIBRARY

Reviewed: *Monthly Review* 34 (1766): 242
Critical Review 21 (1766): 150
Gentleman's Magazine 36 (1766): 90

2400 ROGERS, Samuel. *The Choice; a Poem* NOT SEEN (4to. 1s. Richardson, &c.)

Reviewed: *Monthly Review* 50 (1774): 314
Critical Review 37 (1774): 474
Universal Catalogue 3 (1774) art. 364

2401 ROGERS, Samuel. *Poems on Several Occasions. Vol. 1.* London, 1764 (8vo. 5s. Dodsley) BODLEIAN

Reviewed: *Monthly Review* 31 (1764): 474
Critical Review 18 (1764): 379–381

2402 ROLT, Elizabeth. *Miscellaneous Poems.* London, 1768 (Small 8vo. 1s.sewed. Turpin) BRITISH LIBRARY

Reviewed: *Monthly Review* 39 (1768): 80
Critical Review 25 (1768): 465
Universal Museum 4 (1768): 317

2403 ROLT, [Richard]. *Almena: an English Opera. As it is performed At the Theatre-Royal in Drury-Lane.* London, 1764 (8vo. 1s. Becket) BRITISH LIBRARY

Reviewed: *Monthly Review* 31 (1764): 385–396
Critical Review 18 (1764): 400
General Magazine 1 (1764): 530–534

2404 ROLT, Richard. *An Elegiac Ode Sacred to the Memory of his late Royal Highness Edward Augustus, Duke of York. By Richard Rolt, Author of Cambria, Eliza, Almena, &c.* London, n.d. [FOLGER CAT.–1767; dedication dated 26 Oct. 1767] (4to. 1s. Garland) FOLGER

Reviewed: *Monthly Review* 37 (1767): 468
Critical Review 24 (1767): 384
Universal Museum 3 (1767): 596

2405 ROLT, Richard. *A Poem, sacred to the Memory of the late Sir Watkin Williams Wynne, Bart.* London, 1749 (4to. 26pp. 1s. Printed for Owen in Fleet-street) BRITISH LIBRARY

Reviewed: *Monthly Review* 1 (1749): 461–463

2406 [ROLT, Richard]. *The Royal Shepherd, an English Opera; As it is Performed At the Theatre-Royal in Drury-Lane. The Music composed by Mr. Rush.* [Adaptation from METASTASIO.] London, n.d. [ESTC-1764] (8vo. 1s. Owen) BRITISH LIBRARY

Reviewed: *Monthly Review* 30 (1764): 245–246
Critical Review 17 (1764): 311–312

2407 *The Romance of a Day; or, an Adventure in Greenwich-Park, last Easter.* London, 1760 (12mo. 1s. Pottinger) BRITISH LIBRARY

Reviewed: *Monthly Review* 23 (1760): 327
Critical Review 10 (1760): 241–242
London Magazine 29 (1760): 496
British Magazine 1 (1760): 602

2408 *The Romance of a Night: or, a Covent-Garden Adventure*
NOT SEEN (8vo. 1s. Nicoll)

Reviewed: *Monthly Review* 27 (1762): 386–387
Critical Review 14 (1762): 319

2409 ROSA, Salvator (pseud.). *The Group; composed of The Most Shocking Figures, though The Greatest In The Nation. Painted In an Elegy on the Saddest Subjects, The Living, Dead, and Damned; such as Hogarth, Dishonourable Right Honourables, &c.&c.&c. Inscribed to John Wilkes (who is above Title) and Charles Churchill. By Salvator Rosa. Or, rather, the real Friend of Mr. Wilkes.* London, 1763 (4to. 2s. Moran) BRITISH LIBRARY

Reviewed: *Monthly Review* 29 (1763): 468
Critical Review 16 (1763): 390

2410 *Rosamond, an Opera, altered from Mr. Addison, the Music entirely new, set by M. Arnold*
NOT SEEN (8vo. 1s. Davis, &c.)

Reviewed: *Monthly Review* 36 (1767): 409

Rosara; or, the Adventures of an Actress
See: CHIARI, Pietro

2411 *The Rosciad, a Poem.* London, 1750 (4to. 1s. Robinson) BRITISH LIBRARY

Reviewed: *Monthly Review* 4 (1750–51): 157–158
Gentleman's Magazine 20 (1750): 528

The Rosciad. By the Author
See: CHURCHILL, Charles

The Rosciad of C–v–nt G–rd–n
See: SHIRLEY, William

2412 *The Rose, a Comic Opera. In Two Acts, as it is performed at The Theatre-Royal in Drury-Lane. The Words by a Gentleman Commoner*

of Oxford. The Music by Doctor Arne. London, 1773 (8vo. 1s. Dilly. 1772) BODLEIAN

Reviewed: *Monthly Review* 47 (1772): 486
Critical Review 34 (1772): 471
Universal Catalogue [1] (1772) art. 1461

ROUSSEAU, Jean Baptiste (adaptation)
See: CAREY, George Savile. *The Magic Girdle*

ROUSSEAU, Jean Jacques (adaptations)
See: BURNEY, Charles. *The Cunning Man*
  KENRICK, William. *Eloisa*
  KENRICK, William. *Emilius and Sophia*
  NUGENT, Thomas. *Emilius*

The Rout. A Farce of two acts
See: HILL, John

2413 ROVER, William. *Scapin Triumphant; or a Journey to Petersfield and Portsmouth*
NOT SEEN (4to. 1s. Willock)

Reviewed: *Monthly Review* 16 (1757): 461

The Rover; or, Happiness at Last
See: BOYCE, Samuel

2414 ROWE, Thomas. *Pasquin, A New Allegorical Romance on the Times: with the Fortyfivead, a Burlesque Poem. Dedicated to the Right Honourable The Earl of Rochford, One of his Majesty's principal Secretaries of State. Published by the Editor, Thomas Rowe, Esq.* 2 vols. London, 1769 (12mo. 5s.sewed. Bladon) BRITISH LIBRARY

Reviewed: *Monthly Review* 41 (1769): 233
Critical Review 28 (1769): 147–149
Gentleman's Magazine 39 (1769): 404
Town & Country Magazine [1] (1769): 491

2415 *The Royal Conference or A Dialogue Between Their Majesties G****e the IId. of E***d. And L**s the XV. of F***e. With some Notes Critical and Explanatory.* N.p., 1756 [ESTC-London] (8vo. 6d. Cooper) BRITISH LIBRARY

Reviewed: *Monthly Review* 14 (1756): 575
Critical Review 1 (1756): 572

2416 *The Royal Favourite; a Poem: or, A Blot in the Great Fav'rite's 'Scutcheon, Which Ay--l--b'ry Witlings may make much on.* London, 1762 (4to. 6d. Pridden) UNIVERSITY OF ILLINOIS

Reviewed: *Monthly Review* 27 (1762): 460
Critical Review 14 (1762): 476–477
British Magazine 3 (1762): 662

The Royal Garland, a new Occasional Interlude
See: BICKERSTAFFE, Isaac

2417 *The Royal Manual. A Poem. Supposed to have been Written by Andrew Marvel. And now First Publish'd.* London, 1751 (4to. 23pp. 1s. B. Dod) BRITISH LIBRARY

Reviewed: *Monthly Review* 4 (1750–51): 371

The Royal Merchant
See: HULL, Thomas

The Royal Shepherd
See: ROLT, Richard

2418 RUGELEY, Rowland. *Miscellaneous Poems and Translations from La Fontaine and Others.* Cambridge, 1763 (8vo. 3s. Kearsly) BRITISH LIBRARY

Reviewed: *Monthly Review* 29 (1763): 468–470
Critical Review 16 (1763): 353–360

2419 *The Rural Christian; or, the Pleasures of Religion. An Allegorical Poem: In Four Books. To which are added, Sylvan Letters; or, the Benefit of Retirement. By a young Gentleman.* London, 1772 (8vo. 3s.6d. Buckland) BRITISH LIBRARY

Reviewed: *Monthly Review* 47 (1772): 490
Critical Review 34 (1772): 431–433
Town & Country Magazine 5 (1773): 32

2420 *The Rural Conference. A Pastoral. Inscribed to Mr. C. Churchill*
NOT SEEN (4to. 1s.6d. Williams)

Reviewed: *Monthly Review* 28 (1763): 322
Critical Review 15 (1763): 324

2421 *The Rural Maid, a Poem.* London, 1751 (4to. 6d. James) BRITISH LIBRARY

Reviewed: *Monthly Review* 5 (1751): 78

2422 RUSSEL, Thomas. *Elegies*. London, 1767 (4to. 1s.6d. Cadell) BRITISH LIBRARY

Reviewed: *Monthly Review* 36 (1767): 362–364
Critical Review 23 (1767): 225
Gentleman's Magazine 37 (1767): 173–174
Political Register 1 (1767): 486

2423 RUSSELL, W[illiam]. *Fables Moral and Sentimental. In Familiar Verse*. London, 1772 (Small 8vo. 3s. Flexney, &c. 1772) BRITISH LIBRARY

Reviewed: *Monthly Review* 47 (1772): 239–240
Critical Review 33 (1772): 409–410
British Magazine & General Review 1 (1772): 533

2424 [RUSSELL, William]. *Julia, a poetical Romance. By the Editor of the Essay on the Character, Manners, and Genius of Women*
NOT SEEN (8vo. 4s.sewed. Robinson. 1773)

Reviewed: *Monthly Review* 50 (1774): 232
Critical Review 37 (1774): 46–49
London Magazine 42 (1773): 611
Town & Country Magazine 6 (1774): 45
Universal Catalogue [2] (1773) art. 1316

2425 RUSSELL, William. *An Ode to Fortitude*. London, 1749 [1769] [ESTC-1769] (4to. 1s. Nicoll) BRITISH LIBRARY

Reviewed: *Monthly Review* 40 (1769): 333–335
Critical Review 27 (1769): 234–235
Critical Memoirs 1 (1769): 524
Political Register 4 (1769): 391
Universal Catalogue [1] (1772) art. 766

2426 [RUSSELL, William]. *Sentimental Tales*. 2 vols.
NOT SEEN (12mo. 5s.sewed. Wilkie. 1771)

Reviewed: *Monthly Review* 44 (1771): 333
Critical Review 31 (1771): 231–232
London Magazine 40 (1771): 163
Town & Country Magazine 3 (1771): 155

2427 [RYLAND, John Collett]. *The Life and Actions of Jesus Christ, from His Birth To His Resurrection, by way of Question And Answer, for the Education of Children and Youth. In Four Parts. By a Lover of Christ*. London, 1767 (12mo. 1s. Wilkie) BRITISH LIBRARY

Reviewed: *Monthly Review* 37 (1767): 152

2428 [SADLER, Thomas]. *The Merry Miller: or, The Country-Man's Ramble to London. A Farce of two Acts*. London, 1766 (8vo. 1s. Davenhill) BRITISH LIBRARY

Reviewed: *Critical Review* 21 (1766): 395

2429 [SAGREDO, Giovanni]. *L'Arcadia in Brenta. A new opera*
NOT SEEN (1s. Woodfall)

Reviewed: *Monthly Review* 11 (1754): 467

The Sailor's Song, to The South
See: YOUNG, Edward

2430 ST. PIERRE, William. *The History of two Persons of Quality, taken from memoirs written in the reign of Edward IV*
NOT SEEN (12mo. 3s. Noble)

Reviewed: *Monthly Review* 16 (1757): 452

Saint Thomas's Mount. A Poem
See: IRWIN, Eyles

2431 SALIGNAC DE LA MOTHE FÉNÉLON, François. *The Adventures of Telemachus; an Epic Poem. Translated into English Verse, from the French of Monsieur Fenelon, Archbishop of Cambray. In Two Volumes. Book I*
NOT SEEN (4to. 3s. Hawes. 1773)

Reviewed: *Monthly Review* 48 (1773): 408–409
Critical Review 36 (1773): 69–70

SALIGNAC DE LA MOTHE FÉNÉLON, François. *The Adventures of Telemachus* (translations)
See: BAGNALL, Gibbons (1756)
CLARKE, John (1773)
HAWKESWORTH, John (1768)

2432 *Salvation: A Poem*
NOT SEEN (4to. 10pp. 6d. Dixwell)

Reviewed: *Universal Catalogue* [2] (1773) art. 842

2433 *The Samians, a Tale*. London, 1771 (12mo. 1s.6d. Dodsley. 1771) BRITISH LIBRARY

Reviewed: *Monthly Review* 45 (1771): 156
Critical Review 31 (1771): 477–478
Town & Country Magazine 3 (1771): 379

2434 SAMSON, W. *The Conciliade: a Poem. Occasioned by the present Disputes between the Graduate and Licentiate Physicians* NOT SEEN (4to. 1s.6d. Newbery)

Reviewed: *Monthly Review* 38 (1768): 498
Critical Review 25 (1768): 392

Sanitas, Daughter of Aesculapius
See: COMBE, William

2435 *Satire, a Poem.* [MS note in Harvard copy ascribes this poem to a Mr. Roberts "of the Custom-house."] London, 1764 (4to. 1s. Nicoll) LILLY

Reviewed: *Monthly Review* 31 (1764): 232
Critical Review 18 (1764): 238

2436 *A Satire upon Physicians, or an English Paraphrase, With Notes and References, of Dr. King's most memorable Oration, Delivered at the Dedication of the Radclivian library in Oxford. To which is added, A curious Petition to an Hon. House, In Favour of Dr. King.* London, 1755 (8vo. 1s. Griffiths) BRITISH LIBRARY

Reviewed: *Monthly Review* 12 (1755): 378–379

The Satires of Juvenal Paraphrastically Imitated
See: GREENE, Edward Burnaby

2437 *Satires on the Times. In Two Parts.* London, 1763 (4to. 2s. Dodsley) BRITISH LIBRARY

Reviewed: *Monthly Review* 29 (1763): 466–468
Critical Review 16 (1763): 392–393

2438 *A Satirical Dialogue between A Sea Captain and his Friend in Town: humbly address'd To the Gentlemen who deform'd the Play of Othello, On Th--rs--y, M---- the 7th, 1750, at the Th–atre R–y–l in Dr--y L–ne: To which is added, a Prologue and Epilogue Much more suitable to the Occasion than their Own.* [ESTC: probably by William KENRICK.] London, n.d. [ESTC-1751] (6d. Sold by J. River, under St. Dunstan's Church, Fleet-street, and A. Pope, near the Change) BRITISH LIBRARY

Reviewed: *Monthly Review* 4 (1750–51): 374
Gentleman's Magazine 21 (1751): 142

Satirical Trifles
See: ALLEN, Bennet

2439 *The Satirist: a Poem.* London, 1771 (4to. 2s. Robson) BRITISH LIBRARY

Reviewed: *Monthly Review* 44 (1771): 174
Critical Review 31 (1771): 58–60
London Magazine 40 (1771): 104
Town & Country Magazine 3 (1771): 155

2440 [SAURIN, Bernard Joseph]. *Mirza and Fatima. An Indian Tale. Translated from the French.* London, 1754 (12mo. 3s. Osborne) HARVARD (WIDENER)

Reviewed: *Monthly Review* 11 (1754): 237–238

The Savages of Europe
See: LESUIRE, Robert Martin, and --- LOUVEL

2441 SAYER, John. *The Temple of Gnidus a Poem. From the French Prose of M. Secondat, Baron de Montesquieu. By John Sayer, M.A.* London, 1765 (4to. 1l.1s. Woodfall) BRITISH LIBRARY

Reviewed: *Monthly Review* 32 (1765): 478
Critical Review 20 (1765): 152–153

2442 *The Scale: or, Woman weighed with Man. A Poem. Inscribed to her Royal Highness The Princess Dowager of Wales. By J. M.* London, 1752 (4to. 1s.6d. Wilson and Durham) BRITISH LIBRARY

Reviewed: *Monthly Review* 7 (1752): 78

2443 *Scandal at Tunbridge-Wells. A Fable. To which is added The Country Dance Militant.* London, 1760 (Fol. 1s. Becket) BRITISH LIBRARY

Reviewed: *Monthly Review* 23 (1760): 331
Critical Review 10 (1760): 408

The Schemer Or, Universal Satirist
See: RIDLEY, James

2444 SCHOENAICH, Christoph Otto von, Baron. *Arminius: Or, Germania Freed. Translated*

from the Third Edition of the German Original, Written by Baron Cronzeck. With an Historical and Critical Preface, by the celebrated Professor Gottsched of Leipsic. 2 vols. London, 1764 (12mo. 5s. Becket and De Hondt) BRITISH LIBRARY

Reviewed: *Monthly Review* 32 (1765): 15–19
Critical Review 18 (1764): 353–360

2445 [SCHOMBERG, Ralph]. *The Death of Bucephalus: A Burlesque Tragedy. In Two Acts. As Acted, with Applause, at the Theatre in Edinburgh.* London, 1765 (8vo. 1s.6d. Johnston) BRITISH LIBRARY

Reviewed: *Monthly Review* 32 (1765): 483
Critical Review 19 (1765): 478–479
Gentleman's Magazine 35 (1765): 290
Candid Review 1 (1765): 427–429

2446 [SCHOMBERG, Ralph]. *IETRORHAPSODIA: or, A Physical Rhapsody.* [First word of title transliterated from Greek.] London, 1751 (4to. 1s. Robinson) BRITISH LIBRARY

Reviewed: *Monthly Review* 4 (1750–51): 305

2447 [SCHOMBERG, Ralph]. *The Judgment of Paris. An English Burletta. In Two Acts. As it is performed at the Theatre-Royal in the Hay-Market. The Music composed by Mr. Barthelemon.* London, 1768 (8vo. 1s. Becket) BRITISH LIBRARY

Reviewed: *Monthly Review* 39 (1768): 247
Critical Review 26 (1768): 150
Gentleman's Magazine 38 (1768): 479

2448 [SCHOMBERG, Ralph]. *Medico Mastix, or Physic Craft detected, a satirico didactic Poem*
NOT SEEN (4to. 1s. Evans)

Reviewed: *Monthly Review* 50 (1774): 314–315
Critical Review 37 (1774): 76
Town & Country Magazine 6 (1774): 100

2449 [SCHOMBERG, Ralph]. *The Theorists. A Satire. By the Author of Medico-Mastix.* Bath, 1774 (4to. 1s. Kearsly) BRITISH LIBRARY

Reviewed: *Monthly Review* 52 (1775): 93
Critical Review 38 (1774): 473

The School for Guardians
See: MURPHY, Arthur

2450 *The School for Husbands. Written by a Lady.* 2 vols.
NOT SEEN (12mo. 6s. Bew. 1774)

Reviewed: *Monthly Review* 50 (1774): 327
Critical Review 37 (1774): 317–318
London Magazine 43 (1774): 92
Universal Catalogue 3 (1774) art. 314

The School for Rakes
See: GRIFFITH, Elizabeth

The School for Wives. A Comedy
See: KELLY, Hugh

2451 *The School for Wives. In a Series of Letters.* London, 1763 (8vo. 3s. Dodsley) BRITISH LIBRARY

Reviewed: *Monthly Review* 28 (1763): 326–327
Critical Review 15 (1763): 130–133
British Magazine 4 (1763): 158

2452 *The School of Virtue, or polite Novelist. Consisting of Novels, Tales, Fables, Allegories, &c. &c. moral and entertaining in Prose and Verse*
NOT SEEN (12mo. 2s. Cooke)

Reviewed: *Monthly Review* 31 (1764): 399

The School of Woman
See: GENARD, François

2453 *The School-master, a characteristical poem. By a Gentleman of Cambridge*
NOT SEEN (4to. 6d. Payne)

Reviewed: *Monthly Review* 12 (1755): 381–382

Science; A Poem
See: FORTESCUE, James

2454 *The Scotch Marine: or, memoirs of the life of Celestina; a young lady, who secretly deserting her family, spent two years in strict amity, as a man, with her beloved Castor. Containing a relation of the various fortunes she ran with him in that time, without a discovery or suspicion of her sex. Her marriage after with Cario, a North-Briton, in New England; her voyage with* that gentleman to this kingdom; and their adventures here till their return to Scotland. Including a great diversity of surprising incidents. Printed from the original manuscript, for the justification of her character. 2 vols. NOT SEEN (12mo. 6s. Robinson)

Reviewed: *Monthly Review* 10 (1754): 148

The Scotch Parents
See: CARTER, John

2455 SCOTT, [James]. *Every Man the Architect of his own Fortune: or the Art Of Rising in the Church. A Satyre. By Mr. Scott, Fellow of Trinity-College in Cambridge.* London, 1763 (4to. 1s.6d. Bristow) BRITISH LIBRARY

Reviewed: *Monthly Review* 28 (1763): 317–318
Critical Review 15 (1763): 231–232
British Magazine 4 (1763): 158

2456 SCOTT, [James]. *Heaven: A Vision. By Mr. Scott, Fellow of Trinity-College, Cambridge.* Cambridge, 1760 (4to. 1s. Stanby) BRITISH LIBRARY

Reviewed: *Monthly Review* 24 (1761): 355–356
Critical Review 12 (1761): 233–235

2457 SCOTT, [James]. *An Hymn to Repentance. By Mr. Scott, Fellow of Trinity-College, Cambridge.* Cambridge, 1762 (4to. 6d. Beecroft) BRITISH LIBRARY

Reviewed: *Monthly Review* 27 (1762): 426–429
Critical Review 14 (1762): 399
British Magazine 3 (1762): 606

2458 SCOTT, James. *Odes on Several Subjects.* Cambridge, 1761 (4to. 1s. Sandby) BRITISH LIBRARY

Reviewed: *Monthly Review* 24 (1761): 400–402
Critical Review 11 (1761): 462–465
British Magazine 2 (1761): 382

2459 SCOTT, J[ames]. *The Perils of Poetry: an Epistle to a Friend. By J. Scott, Fellow of Trinity-College in Cambridge.* London, 1766 (4to. 1s.6d. Griffin) BRITISH LIBRARY

Reviewed: *Monthly Review* 34 (1766): 403
Critical Review 21 (1766): 231–232
Gentleman's Magazine 36 (1766): 145–146

2460 SCOTT, [James]. *Purity of Heart: a Moral Epistle. By Mr. Scott, Fellow of Trinity-College, Cambridge.* Cambridge, 1761 (4to. 6d. Bentham, Cambridge) BRITISH LIBRARY

Reviewed: *Monthly Review* 25 (1761): 465–466
Critical Review 12 (1761): 398

2461 SCOTT, [James]. *The Redemption, a Monody.* Cambridge, 1763 (4to. 1s. Wilson and Fell) BRITISH LIBRARY

Reviewed: *Monthly Review* 29 (1763): 556–558
Critical Review 16 (1763): 474–475

2462 SCOTT, James. *A Spousal Hymn, or, an Address to his Majesty on his Marriage.* London, 1761 (4to. 1s. Dodsley) BRITISH LIBRARY

Reviewed: *Monthly Review* 25 (1761): 229
Critical Review 12 (1761): 232–233
British Magazine 2 (1761): 550

2463 [SCOTT, John]. *Elegy, Written At Amwell, in Hertfordshire, MDCCLXVIII.* London, 1769 (4to. Printed by Dryden Leach, for the Author) BRITISH LIBRARY

Reviewed: *Monthly Review* 41 (1769): 475–476

2464 [SCOTT, John]. *Four Elegies: Descriptive and Moral.* London, 1760 (4to. 1s. Buckland, Dodsley, &c.) BRITISH LIBRARY

Reviewed: *Monthly Review* 23 (1760): 68–73
Critical Review 9 (1760): 320
British Magazine 1 (1760): 140 [324]

2465 [SCOTT, John, Major]. *An Epistle from Oberea, Queen of Otaheite, to Joseph Banks, Esq. Translated by T. Q. Z. Esq. Professor of the Otaheite Language in Dublin, and of all the Languages of the undiscovered Islands in the South Sea; And enriched with Historical and Explanatory Notes.* London, 1774 (4to. 1s. Almon. 1774) BRITISH LIBRARY

Reviewed: *Monthly Review* 49 (1773): 503–504
Critical Review 37 (1774): 62–65
London Magazine 42 (1773): 611
Town & Country Magazine 6 (1774): 100
Universal Catalogue [2] (1773) art. 1307

2466 [SCOTT, John, Major]. *A Second Letter from Oberea, Queen of Otaheite, to Joseph Banks,*

Esq; Translated from the Original, Brought over by his Excellency Otapairoo, Envoy Extraordinary and Plenipotentiary from the Queen of Otatheite, To the Court of Great Britain, Lately arrived in his Majesty's Ship the Adventure, Capt. Furneaux. With some curious and entertaining Anecdotes of this celebrated Foreigner before and since his Arrival in England; Together with explanatory Notes from the Queen's former Letter, and from Dr. Hawkesworth's Voyages. London, n.d. [BODLEIAN CAT.–1774] (4to. 1s. Johnson) BODLEIAN

Reviewed: *Monthly Review* 51 (1774): 394
Critical Review 38 (1774): 152
Town & Country Magazine 6 (1774): 464

2467 SCOTT, Joseph Nicol. *An Essay towards a Translation of Homer's Works, In Blank Verse, With Notes.* London, 1755 (4to. 2s. Osborn, &c.) BRITISH LIBRARY

Reviewed: *Monthly Review* 12 (1755): 355–370
Gentleman's Magazine 25 (1755): 143

2468 SCOTT, Mary. *The Female Advocate; a Poem: Occasioned by Mr. Duncombe's Feminead.* London, 1775 (4to. 2s. Johnson. 1774) BRITISH LIBRARY

Reviewed: *Monthly Review* 51 (1774): 387–390
Critical Review 38 (1774): 218–220
Gentleman's Magazine 44 (1774): 375–377
Town & Country Magazine 6 (1774): [548]
Universal Catalogue 3 (1774) art. 1174

2469 SCOTT, Robert. *Elegies. By Robert Scott.* London, 1764 (4to. 1s. Burnet) NEWBERRY

Reviewed: *Monthly Review* 30 (1764): 487
Critical Review 17 (1764): 395
General Magazine 1 (1764): 244

2470 SCOTT, Robert. *Poems on Various Occasions.* London, 1765 (8vo. 2s. Burnet) BRITISH LIBRARY

Reviewed: *Monthly Review* 34 (1766): 478–479
Critical Review 21 (1766): 315

2471 [SCOTT, Sarah]. *Agreeable Ugliness: or, the Triumph of the Graces. Exemplified in the real Life and Fortunes of a young Lady of some Distinction.* London, 1754 (12mo. 3s. Dodsley) BRITISH LIBRARY

Reviewed: *Monthly Review* 10 (1754): 144–145

2472 [SCOTT, Sarah]. *A Description of Millenium Hall, and the Country Adjacent: Together with the Characters of the Inhabitants, And such Historical Anecdotes and Reflections, as May excite in the Reader proper Sentiments of Humanity, and lead the Mind to the Love of Virtue. By a Gentleman on his Travels.* London, 1762 (12mo. 2s.6d. Newbery) BRITISH LIBRARY

Reviewed: *Monthly Review* 27 (1762): 389–390
Critical Review 14 (1762): 463–464
British Magazine 4 (1763): 46

2473 [SCOTT, Sarah]. *The History of Cornelia.* London ed. reviewed; copy seen: Dublin, 1750 (12mo. 271pp. 3s. Printed for A. Millar.) BRITISH LIBRARY

Reviewed: *Monthly Review* 3 (1750): 59–61

2474 [SCOTT, Sarah]. *The History of Sir George Ellison.* 2 vols. London, 1766 (12mo. 6s. Millar) BRITISH LIBRARY

Reviewed: *Monthly Review* 35 (1766): 43–46
Critical Review 21 (1766): 281–288

2475 [SCOTT, Sarah]. *A Journey through Every Stage of Life, Described in a Variety of Interesting Scenes, Drawn from Real Characters. By a Person of Quality.* 2 vols. London, 1754 (12mo. 6s. Millar) BRITISH LIBRARY

Reviewed: *Monthly Review* 10 (1754): 237

2476 [SCOTT, Sarah]. *The Test of Filial Duty. In a Series Of Letters between Miss Emilia Leonard, and Miss Charlotte Arlington. A Novel.* 2 vols. London, 1772 (12mo. 6s.bound. Carnan. 1772) BRITISH LIBRARY

Reviewed: *Monthly Review* 46 (1772): 165
Critical Review 33 (1772): 182
Town & Country Magazine 4 (1772): 99
Universal Catalogue [1] (1772) art. 131

2477 [SCOTT, Thomas]. *The Anglers. Eight Dialogues in Verse.* London, 1758 (12mo. 1s. Dilly) BRITISH LIBRARY

Reviewed: *Monthly Review* 18 (1758): 629–631
Critical Review 6 (1758): 87–88

2478 SCOTT, Thomas. *The Book of Job, in English Verse; translated from the original Hebrew; with Remarks, Historical, Critical, and Explanatory.* London, 1771 (4to. 11.1s. Cadell, &c. 1771) BRITISH LIBRARY

Reviewed: *Monthly Review* 46 (1772): 373–382
Critical Review 35 (1773): 450–455
Gentleman's Magazine 41 (1771): 366–369

2479 SCOTT, Thomas. *Lyric Poems, Devotional and Moral.* London, 1773 (8vo. 3s.6d. Buckland. 1773) BRITISH LIBRARY

Reviewed: *Monthly Review* 50 (1774): 213–214
Critical Review 37 (1774): 155–156
Universal Catalogue [2] (1773) art. 374

2480 SCOTT, Thomas. *The Table of Cebes, or, the Picture of Human Life. In English verse. With Notes.* London, 1754 (4to. 1s.6d. Dodsley) BRITISH LIBRARY

Reviewed: *Monthly Review* 11 (1754): 502–508
Gentleman's Magazine 24 (1754): 601

2481 SCOTT, [William]. *Epigrams of Martial, &c. with Mottos from Horace, &c. Translated, imitated, adapted, and addrest to the Nobility, Clergy, and Gentry. With Notes moral, historical, explanatory, and humorous.* London, 1773 (12mo. 3s.6d.sewed. Wilkie) BRITISH LIBRARY

Reviewed: *Monthly Review* 48 (1773): 65
Critical Review 35 (1773): 147–149
London Magazine 42 (1773): 40
Town & Country Magazine 5 (1773): 134
Universal Catalogue [2] (1773) art. 132

2482 SCOTT, William. *An Ode In Honour of his Royal Highness the Prince of Wales's Birth-Day. August 12, 1766, As Intended to have been performed before Their Majesties at Kew.* London, n.d. [BODLEIAN CAT.–1766?] (4to. 1s. Wilkie) BODLEIAN

Reviewed: *Monthly Review* 35 (1766): 235
Critical Review 22 (1766): 155
Gentleman's Magazine 36 (1766): 384

The Scourge, a Satire
See: GREENE, Edward Burnaby

2483 *A Scourge for False Patriots; or, Mother Hubberd's Tale of the Ape and the Fox. Part the Second. Dedicated without Permission to John Wilkes, Esq.* London, n.d [HOUGHTON CAT.–1770?] (4to. 2s.6d. Snagg) HARVARD (HOUGHTON)

Reviewed: *Monthly Review* 49 (1773): 505
Critical Review 38 (1774): 236–237
Town & Country Magazine 6 (1774): [548]
Universal Catalogue [2] (1773) art. 1304

The Scribleriad
See: CAMBRIDGE, Richard Owen

SCRIBLERIUS FLAGELLARIUS (pseud.). *A Whipping for the Welch Parson*
See: KENRICK, William

2484 SCRIBLERUS, Martin, Jun. (pseud.). *The Prospect: a Lyric Essay. By Martin Scriblerus, Jun.* London, 1769 (4to. 1s. Tomlinson) BODLEIAN

Reviewed: *Monthly Review* 40 (1769): 340–341
Critical Review 27 (1769): 397
Town & Country Magazine (1769): 269

2485 SCRIBLERUS MINIMUS (pseud.). *The Modern Justice, in Imitation of The Man of Taste. By Scriblerus Minimus. Written in the Year 1753.* London, 1755 (4to. 6d. Baldwin) BRITISH LIBRARY

Reviewed: *Monthly Review* 12 (1755): 231

A Sea-Piece
See: YOUNG, Edward

2486 SEALLY, John. *Moral Tales, after the Eastern Manner; by Mr. Seally.* 2 vols. London, n.d. [ESTC-1780?] (12mo. 6s.bound. Goldsmith) BRITISH LIBRARY

Reviewed: *Universal Catalogue* [2] (1773) art. 376

The Search after Happiness
See: MORE, Hannah

The Seasons. In Imitation of Spenser
See: MENDEZ, Moses

2487 *The second Chapter of the Prophet Joel versified. By T. A. Student of Trinity College, Cambridge*
NOT SEEN (4to. 6d. Beecroft)

Reviewed: *Monthly Review* 42 (1770): 486
Town & Country Magazine 2 (1770): 491

A Second Letter from Oberea
See: SCOTT, John, Major

2488 *The Secret Expedition. A Farce; (In Two Acts) As it has been represented upon the Political Theatre of Europe, with the Highest Applause.* London, 1757 (8vo. 6d. Scot) BRITISH LIBRARY

Reviewed: *Monthly Review* 17 (1757): 379
Critical Review 5 (1758): 75

The Secret History of Zeokinisul
See: JOLYOT DE CRÉBILLON, Claude Prosper (le fils)

2489 *Secret memoirs of the late count Saxe, marshal of France, &c.*
NOT SEEN (12mo. 2s. Wren)

Reviewed: *Monthly Review* 6 (1752): 75–76

SEDAINE, Michel Jean (translations)
See: DIBDIN, Charles. *The Deserter*
O'BRIEN, William. *The Duel*

2490 *The Sedan. A Novel. In which Many New and Entertaining Characters are introduced.* 2 vols. London, 1757 (12mo. 6d. Baldwin) BRITISH LIBRARY

Reviewed: *Monthly Review* 17 (1757): 477

2491 *Sedition. A Poem*
NOT SEEN (4to. 1s. Nicoll)

Reviewed: *Monthly Review* 42 (1770): 327
Critical Review 29 (1770): 233

2492 *A Select Collection of the Psalms of David, As Imitated or Paraphrased by the most Eminent English Poets, Viz. Mr. Addison, Mr. Blacklock, Mr. Barton, Mr. Daniel, Sir John Denham, Dr. Gibbs, King James I, Mrs. Leapor, Milton, Mrs. Masters. Mrs. Rowe, Sir Philip Sidney, Dr. Trapp, Mrs. Tollet, Dr. Woodford, And several Others. Together with Some Originals never before Printed. To which is added, An Appendix of several Divine Hymns and Poems, Not to be found in any other Collection.* London, 1756 (12mo. 3s. Hooper, &c.) BRITISH LIBRARY

Reviewed: *Monthly Review* 16 (1757): 364

2493 *The Self-Deceived: or, the History of Lord Byron.* 2 vols. London, 1773 (12mo. 5s. Noble. 1773) BRITISH LIBRARY

Reviewed: *Monthly Review* 48 (1773): 416
Critical Review 35 (1773): 395
London Magazine 42 (1773): 195
Universal Catalogue [2] (1773) art. 483

The Senators
See: DELAMAYNE, Thomas Hallie

Sensibility, a Poem
See: JOHNSON, Samuel (1739?–1798)

2494 *Sentimental Fables. Designed chiefly for the Use of the Ladies.* London, 1772 (8vo. 6s.bound. Robinson. 1772) BRITISH LIBRARY

Reviewed: *Monthly Review* 47 (1772): 57–61
Critical Review 37 (1774): 140–143
Universal Catalogue [1] (1772) art. 745

A Sentimental Journey through France and Italy
See: STERNE, Laurence

The Sentimental Sailor
See: MERCER, Thomas

2495 *The Sentimental Spy: a Novel.* 2 vols. London, 1773 (12mo. 5s. Lowndes. 1773) BRITISH LIBRARY

Reviewed: *Monthly Review* 48 (1773): 417
Critical Review 35 (1773): 394
London Magazine 42 (1773): 149
Universal Catalogue [2] (1773) art. 480

Sentimental Tales
See: RUSSELL, William

2496 *Sentiments On the Death of the Sentimental Yorick. By one of Uncle Toby's illegitimate Children. With Rules for Writing Modern Elegies.* London, 1768 (4to. 1s. Steare) HARVARD (HOUGHTON)

Reviewed: *Monthly Review* 38 (1768): 323
Critical Review 25 (1768): 220

A Series of Genuine Letters between Henry and Frances
See: GRIFFITH, Elizabeth and Richard

Sethona; a Tragedy
See: DOW, Alexander

The Seventeenth Epistle Of the First Book of Horace Imitated
See: NEVILE, Thomas

SEYMOUR, W. *Odes on the Four Seasons.*
See: SHAW, Cuthbert

SHADWELL, Charles (adaptation)
See: THOMPSON, Edward. *The Fair Quaker*

2497 SHAKESPEARE, William. *The Beauties of Shakespear: Regularly selected from each Play. With a General Index, Digesting them under Proper Heads. Illustrated with Explanatory Notes, and Similar Passages from Ancient and Modern Authors. By William Dodd, B.A. Late of Clare-Hall, Cambridge.* 2 vols. London, 1752 (12mo. Waller) BRITISH LIBRARY

Reviewed: *Monthly Review* 6 (1752): 316–317

2498 SHAKESPEARE, William. *Bell's Edition of Shakespeare's Plays, As they are now performed at the Theatres Royal in London; Regulated from the Prompt Books of each House. By Permission; with Notes Critical and Illustrative; By the Authors of the Dramatic Censor.* [Ed. Francis Gentleman.] 9 vols. London, 1774 (8vo. 15s.sewed. Bell. 1774) BRITISH LIBRARY

Reviewed: *Monthly Review* 50 (1774): 144–147
Universal Catalogue 3 (1774) art. 117

2499 SHAKESPEARE, William. *Hamlet, Prince of Denmark. A Tragedy. By William Shakespeare. Collated with The Old And Modern Editions.* London, 1773 (8vo. 3s. Bowyer & Nichols) BRITISH LIBRARY

Reviewed: *Monthly Review* 48 (1773): 413
Critical Review 35 (1773): 230

2500 SHAKESPEARE, William. *Julius Caesar, a Tragedy. By William Shakespeare. Collated with The Old And Modern Editions.* London, 1774 (8vo. 3s. Owen) BRITISH LIBRARY

Reviewed: *Monthly Review* 51 (1774): 69

2501 SHAKESPEARE, William. *King Lear. A Tragedy. By William Shakespeare. Collated with The Old And Modern Editions.* London, 1770 (8vo. 3s.sewed. White) BRITISH LIBRARY

Reviewed: *Monthly Review* 44 (1771): 243–244
Critical Review 30 (1770): 436–439
Town & Country Magazine 3 (1771): 155

2502 SHAKESPEARE, William. *Macbeth. A Tragedy. By William Shakespeare. Collated with The Old And Modern Editions.* London, 1773 (8vo. 3s. Owen) BRITISH LIBRARY

Reviewed: *Monthly Review* 51 (1774): 69

2503 SHAKESPEARE, William. *Mr. William Shakespeare his Comedies, Histories, and Tragedies, set out by himself in quarto, or by the Players his Fellows in folio, and now faithfully republish'd from those Editions in ten Volumes octavo; with an Introduction: Whereunto will be added, in some other Volumes, Notes, critical and explanatory, and a Body of Various Readings entire.* [Ed. Edward Capell.] London, n.d. [ESTC-1768] (8vo. 21.2s. Tonson) BRITISH LIBRARY

Reviewed: *Monthly Review* 39 (1768): 271–276
Critical Review 26 (1768): 321–323

2504 SHAKESPEARE, William. *Othello, The Moor of Venice. A Tragedy. By William Shakespeare. Collated with The Old And Modern Editions.* London, 1773 (8vo. 3s.sewed. Owen. 1773) BRITISH LIBRARY

Reviewed: *Monthly Review* 49 (1773): 65

2505 SHAKESPEARE, William. *The Plays of William Shakespeare, in eight volumes, with*

the Corrections and Illustrations of Various Commentators. To which are added Notes by Sam. Johnson. London, 1765 (8vo. 2l.8s. Tonson) BRITISH LIBRARY

Reviewed: *Monthly Review* 33 (1765): 285–301 and 374–389
Critical Review 20 (1765): 321–33 and 401–411 and 21 (1766): 13–26 and 81–88
Gentleman's Magazine 35 (1765): 479–482, 499–500, and 554–555
Annual Register 8 (1765): 311–318

2506 SHAKESPEARE, William. *The Plays of William Shakespeare, in Six Volumes. 2d Edit.* NOT SEEN (4to. 3l.13s.6d. Payne)

Reviewed: *Critical Review* 31 (1771): 306–307

2507 SHAKESPEARE, William. *The Plays of William Shakespeare. In Ten Volumes. With the Corrections and Illustrations of Various Commentators; To which are added Notes by Samuel Johnson and George Steevens. With an Appendix.* London, 1773 (8vo. 3l. Bathurst) BRITISH LIBRARY

Reviewed: *Monthly Review* 49 (1773): 419–424
Critical Review 36 (1773): 345–358 and 401–416
Town & Country Magazine 5 (1773): 669

2508 SHAKESPEARE, William. *Poems written by Mr William Shakespeare.* N.p., n.d. [ESTC: London, 1775] (8vo. 3s. Evans) BRITISH LIBRARY

Reviewed: *Monthly Review* 51 (1774): 483–484
Critical Review 38 (1774): 473

2509 [SHAKESPEARE, William]. *Tarquin and Lucrece, or, the Rape: A Poem* [*The Rape of Lucrece*] NOT SEEN (8vo. 1s. Nicoll)

Reviewed: *Critical Review* 25 (1768): 228

2510 SHAKESPEARE, William. *Twenty of the Plays of Shakespeare, Being the whole Number printed in Quarto during his Life-time, or before the Restoration, Collated where there were different Copies, and Publish'd from the Originals, by George Steevens, Esq; In Four Volumes.* London, 1766 (8vo. 1l. Tonson) BRITISH LIBRARY

Reviewed: *Monthly Review* 34 (1766): 237–238
Critical Review 21 (1766): 26–33

SHAKESPEARE, William (adaptations)

Coriolanus
See: SHERIDAN, Thomas. *Coriolanus*

Cymbeline
See: HAWKINS, William. *Cymbeline*
MARSH, Charles. *Cymbeline*

King Lear
See: COLMAN, George (the elder). *The History of King Lear*

Love's Labour's Lost
See: *The Students. A Comedy*

A Midsummer Night's Dream
See: COLMAN, George (the elder). *A Fairy Tale*
GARRICK, David. *The Fairies*

The Taming of the Shrew
See: GARRICK, David. *Catharine and Petruchio*

The Tempest
See: GARRICK, David. *The Tempest. An Opera*

Timon of Athens
See: CUMBERLAND, Richard. *Timon of Athens*
LOVE, James. *Timon of Athens*

Two Gentlemen of Verona
See: VICTOR, Benjamin. *The Two Gentlemen of Verona*

The Winter's Tale
See: GARRICK, David. *Florizel and Perdita*
MARSH, Charles. *The Winter's Tale*

Shakespeare: An Epistle to Mr. Garrick
See: LLOYD, Robert

2511 *Shakespeare's Garland. Being a Collection of New Songs, Ballads, Roundelays, Catches, Glees, Comic-Serenatas, &c. performed at the Jubilee at Stratford Upon Avon. The Musick by Dr. Arne, Mr. Barthelimon, Mr. Ailwood, and Mr. Dibdin.* London, 1769 (8vo. 1s. Becket) BRITISH LIBRARY

Reviewed: *Monthly Review* 41 (1769): 238
Critical Review 28 (1769): 234–236

Gentleman's Magazine 39 (1769): 447
London Magazine 38 (1769): 538

2512 *The Sham Beggar. A Comedy. In Two Acts. As it is now acting at the Theatre in Dublin with very great Applause.* Dublin printed, London reprinted; 1756 (8vo. 1s. Henderson) BRITISH LIBRARY

Reviewed: *Monthly Review* 14 (1756): 447
Critical Review 1 (1756): 483
Gentleman's Magazine 26 (1756): 200

2513 *The Sham Fight: or, Political Humbug. A State Farce, In Two Acts. As it was acted by some Persons of Distinction in the M--d--n, and elsewhere.* London, 1756 (8vo. 1s. Sold at Hogarth's Head, Fleetstreet) BRITISH LIBRARY

Reviewed: *Monthly Review* 15 (1756): 312–313
Critical Review 2 (1756): 280

2514 SHARP, William, jun. *An Englishman's Remonstrance: Inscribed to the Right Honourable Brass Crosby, Lord Mayor of London.* London, 1771 (8vo. 1s. Almon. 1771) HARVARD (HOUGHTON)

Reviewed: *Monthly Review* 45 (1771): 326
Critical Review 32 (1771): 326

2515 SHARP, William, jun. *Sincerity: a Poem.* London, 1763 (4to. 1s.6d. Flexney) NEWBERRY

Reviewed: *Monthly Review* 28 (1763): 397–398
Critical Review 15 (1763): 324–325

2516 SHARPE, Timothy. *The Cabinet for Wit: or, an Infallible Recipe to cure Stupidity.* London, 1751 (8vo. 1s. More, near St. Paul's) BODLEIAN

Reviewed: *Monthly Review* 4 (1750–51): 473

2517 [SHAW, Cuthbert]. *Corruption. A Satire. Inscribed to the Right Honourable Richard Grenville, Earl Temple. By the Author of The Monody to the Memory of a Young Lady.* London, 1768 (4to. 2s.6d. Bladon) HARVARD (Houghton)

Reviewed: *Monthly Review* 39 (1768): 487–489
Critical Review 26 (1768): 474–474

2518 [SHAW, Cuthbert]. *The Four Farthing-Candles. A Satire. Inscribed to A------ D--, Esq;* London, 1762 (4to. 1s. Morley) BODLEIAN

Reviewed: *Monthly Review* 26 (1762): 231
Critical Review 13 (1762): 272
British Magazine 3 (1762): 158

2519 SHAW, Cuthbert. *Liberty. A Poem. Humbly Inscrib'd to The Right Hon. the Earl of Darlington, by Cuthbert Shaw, Usher of the Free-School, in Darlington.* Durham, 1756 (4to. 1s. Manby) HARVARD (HOUGHTON)

Reviewed: *Monthly Review* 14 (1756): 575–576

2520 [SHAW, Cuthbert]. *Monody to the Memory of a Young Lady who died in Child-bed. By an afflicted husband.* London, 1768 (4to. 1s. Nicoll) BRITISH LIBRARY

Reviewed: *Monthly Review* 39 (1768): 400–401
Critical Review 26 (1768): 314
London Magazine 37 (1768): 611

2521 [SHAW, Cuthbert]. *Odes, on the Four Seasons. By W. Seymour.* Bury St. Edmonds, 1760 (4to. 1s. Printed at Bury St. Edmonds; and sold by Millar &c. in London) BRITISH LIBRARY

Reviewed: *Monthly Review* 22 (1760): 516
Critical Review 9 (1760): 322
British Magazine 1 (1760): 140 [324]

2522 [SHAW, Cuthbert]. *The Race. By Mercurius Spur, Esq. with Notes. By Faustinus Scriblerus.* London, 1765 (4to. 2s.6d. Flexney) BRITISH LIBRARY

Reviewed: *Monthly Review* 32 (1765): 153
Critical Review 19 (1765): 73
Gentleman's Magazine 35 (1765): 40
Candid Review 1 (1765): 125–127

2523 [SHAW, Cuthbert]. *The Race. By Mercurius Spur, Esq; with Notes. By Faustinus Scriblerus. The Second Edition. With large Additions and Alterations.* London, 1766 (4to. 2s.6d. Flexney) BODLEIAN

Reviewed: *Monthly Review* 34 (1766): 321–323
Critical Review 21 (1766): 315

The She Gallant
See: O'KEEFFE, John

2524 [SHEBBEARE, John]. *A Love Epistle, in Verse. Found at Paris, In the Cell of an Irish Carthusian, after his Death; And sent to the Honourable R...... T...... Esq; by Monsieur M--R--V--X*. London, 1753 (4to. 1s. Owen) BRITISH LIBRARY

Reviewed: *Monthly Review* 8 (1753): 238

2525 [SHEBBEARE, John]. *Lydia, or Filial Piety. A Novel. By the author of the Marriage-Act, a Novel. And Letters on the English Nation.* 4 vols. London, 1755 (12mo. 6s. Scott) BRITISH LIBRARY

Reviewed: *Monthly Review* 12 (1755): 478

2526 SHEBBEARE, John. *Lydia, or Filial Piety. A Novel. By John Shebbeare, M.D. Reg. Acad. Scient. Paris. Consoc. The Second Edition, with corrections and alterations.* 2 vols. London, 1769 (12mo. 5s.sewed. Davies) BRITISH LIBRARY

Reviewed: *Critical Review* 27 (1769): 471

2527 [SHEBBEARE, John]. *The Marriage-act. A Novel. Containing a Series of Interesting Adventures.* 2 vols. London, 1754 (12mo. 6s. Hodges) BRITISH LIBRARY

Reviewed: *Monthly Review* 11 (1754): 395

2528 SHEELES, James. *Threnodia Northumbria. A Funeral Pindaric Poem Sacred to the Memory of the Right Honourable The Lady Elizabeth Anne Frances Percy.* London, 1761 (4to. 1s. Dodsley) BODLEIAN

Reviewed: *Monthly Review* 25 (1761): 79
Critical Review 12 (1761): 77

2529 SHENSTONE, William. *The Works in Verse and Prose, of William Shenstone, Esq; Most of which were never before printed. In Two Volumes, With Decorations.* [Ed. R. Dodsley.] London, 1764 (8vo. 12s. Dodsley) BRITISH LIBRARY

Reviewed: *Monthly Review* 30 (1764): 378–379 and 450–463
Critical Review 17 (1764): 338–344
General Magazine 1 (1764): 198

2530 [SHEPHERD, Richard]. *Hector, a Dramatic Poem.* London, 1770 (4to. 2s.6d. Flexney) BRITISH LIBRARY

Reviewed: *Monthly Review* 42 (1770): 409
Critical Review 29 (1770): 392–393

2531 [SHEPHERD, Richard]. *The Nuptials. A Didactick Poem. In Three Books.* London, 1761 (4to. 2s.6d. Flexney) BRITISH LIBRARY

Reviewed: *Monthly Review* 26 (1762): 65–68
Critical Review 12 (1761): 452–456
British Magazine 3 (1762): 44

2532 [SHEPHERD, Richard]. *An Ode to Love.* London, n.d. [ESTC-1755?] (4to. 6d. Scott) BRITISH LIBRARY

Reviewed: *Monthly Review* 15 (1756): 447–450

2533 [SHEPHERD, Richard]. *Odes Descriptive and Allegorical.* London, 1761 (4to. 1s.6d. Cooper) BRITISH LIBRARY

Reviewed: *Monthly Review* 24 (1761): 139–141
Critical Review 11 (1761): 158–159
British Magazine 2 (1761): 161

The Shepherds Lottery
See: MENDEZ, Moses

2534 [SHERIDAN, Frances]. *The Discovery. A Comedy. As it is Performed At the Theatre-Royal, In Drury-Lane. Written by the Editor of Miss Sidney Bidulph.* London, 1763 (8vo. 1s.6d. Davies) BRITISH LIBRARY

Reviewed: *Monthly Review* 28 (1763): 167
Critical Review 15 (1763): 96–112
British Magazine 4 (1763): 98

2535 [SHERIDAN, Frances]. *The Dupe, a Comedy. As it is now Acting at the Theatre-Royal In Drury-Lane, By His Majesty's Servants. By the Author of the Discovery.* London, 1764 (8vo. 1s.6d. Millar) BODLEIAN

Reviewed: *Monthly Review* 29 (1763): 464
Critical Review 16 (1763): 429–435

2536 [SHERIDAN, Frances]. *The History of Nourjahad. By the Editor of Sidney Bidulph.* London, 1767 (12mo. 3s. Dodsley) BRITISH LIBRARY

Reviewed: *Monthly Review* 37 (1767): 314
Critical Review 24 (1767): 34–44
Gentleman's Magazine 37 (1767): 365–366
London Magazine 36 (1767): 362–364
Political Register 1 (1767): 178
Universal Museum 3 (1767): 372

2537 [SHERIDAN, Frances]. *Memoirs of Miss Sidney Bidulph, Extracted from Her Own Journal, And now First Published. In Three Volumes.* London, 1761 (12mo. 9s. Dodsley) HARVARD (HOUGHTON)

Reviewed: *Monthly Review* 24 (1761): 260–266
Critical Review 11 (1761): 186–198
London Magazine 30 (1761): 168
British Magazine 2 (1761): 212

2538 [SHERIDAN, Frances]. [*Memoirs of Miss Sidney Bidulph*] *Conclusion of the Memoirs of Miss Sidney Bidulph, As prepared for the Press By the Late Editor of the Former Part. Vols. IV and V.* London, 1770 (12mo. 6s.6d. Dodsley) BRITISH LIBRARY

Reviewed: *Monthly Review* 37 (1767): 238
Critical Review 23 (1767): 274–278
London Magazine 36 (1767): 150
Political Register 1 (1767): 483

2539 [SHERIDAN, Richard Brinsley]. *The Love Epistles of Aristaenetus: Translated from The Greek into English Metre.* London, 1771 (8vo. 3s.bound. Wilkie. 1771) BRITISH LIBRARY

Reviewed: *Monthly Review* 45 (1771): 511
Critical Review 32 (1771): 206–208
Gentleman's Magazine 41 (1771): 604
London Magazine 40 (1771): 415
Town & Country Magazine 3 (1771): 536

2540 [SHERIDAN, Richard Brinsley, and others]. *The Rival Beauties; a Poetical Contest.* London, n.d. [ESTC-1772] (4to. 1s.6d. Griffin. 1772) BRITISH LIBRARY

Reviewed: *Monthly Review* 46 (1772): 625
Critical Review 33 (1772): 491
London Magazine 41 (1772): 337
British Magazine & General Review 2 (1772): 64
Universal Catalogue [1] (1772) art. 870

2541 [SHERIDAN, Thomas]. *Coriolanus: or the Roman Matron. A Tragedy. Taken from Shakespear and Thomson. As it is Acted at the Theatre-Royal in Covent-Garden. To which is added, The Order of the Ovation.* London, 1755 (8vo. 6d. Millar) BRITISH LIBRARY

Reviewed: *Monthly Review* 12 (1755): 80

The Shipwreck
See: FALCONER, William

2542 [SHIRLEY, William]. *The Apology. Addressed to the Reviewers. By ---, Esq; Author of The Rosciad of Covent-Garden* NOT SEEN (4to. 1s. Gretton)

Reviewed: *Monthly Review* 26 (1762): 473

2543 [SHIRLEY, William]. *A Bone for the Chroniclers to pick; or A Take-Off Scene From behind the Curtain. A Poem. By a Candid Observer of Men and Things.* London, 1758 (8vo. 6d. Scott) FOLGER

Reviewed: *Monthly Review* 19 (1758): 502
Critical Review 6 (1758): 345–346
Gentleman's Magazine 28 (1758): 492–493

2544 SHIRLEY, William. *Edward The Black Prince; or, the Battle of Poictiers: an Historical Tragedy. Attempted after the Manner of Shakespear. As it is acted at the Theatre-Royal in Drury-Lane, by His Majesty's Servants.* London, 1750 (8vo. 1s.6d. Printed by Tonson and Draper) BRITISH LIBRARY

Reviewed: *Monthly Review* 2 (1749–50): 213–219

2545 SHIRLEY, William. *Electra, a Tragedy.* London, 1765 (4to. 5s. Newbery) BRITISH LIBRARY

Reviewed: *Monthly Review* 33 (1765): 83
Critical Review 19 (1765): 354–358
Candid Review 1 (1765): 388–393

2546 [SHIRLEY, William]. *An Epistle to the Author of The Four Farthing Candles. By the Author of the Rosciad of C–v–nt-G–rd–n.* London, 1762 (4to. 6d. Gretton) CAMBRIDGE

Reviewed: *Monthly Review* 26 (1762): 232
Critical Review 13 (1762): 272

2547 [SHIRLEY, William]. *The Rosciad of C–v–nt–G–rd–n. By the Author*. London, 1762 (4to. 1s.6d. Gretton) BODLEIAN

Reviewed: *Monthly Review* 26 (1762): 231
Critical Review 13 (1762): 272

2548 *The Sibyl. A Novel. By a Lady. In Two Volumes*. London, 1769 (12mo. 5s.sewed. Johnson and Payne) HARVARD (HOUGHTON)

Reviewed: *Monthly Review* 41 (1769): 74
Critical Review 27 (1769): 389
London Magazine 38 (1769): 325

The Sick Monkey
See: GARRICK, David

The Siege of Aquileia
See: HOME, John

The siege of Calais, an Historical Novel
See: TENCIN, Claudine Alexandrine Guerin de

2549 *The Siege of Quebec*. London, 1769 (4to. 1s. Fletcher) BODLEIAN

Reviewed: *Monthly Review* 42 (1770): 76
Critical Review 28 (1769): 464

2550 *The Siege of the Castle of Aesculapius; An Heroic Comedy. As it is acted at the Theatre in Warwick-Lane*. London, 1768 (8vo. 1s. Bladon) BRITISH LIBRARY

Reviewed: *Monthly Review* 38 (1768): 245–246
Critical Review 25 (1768): 60
Gentleman's Magazine 38 (1768): 133
Universal Museum 4 (1768): 93

2551 *A Simile*. London, 1759 (Fol. 6d. Cooper) BRITISH LIBRARY

Reviewed: *Monthly Review* 20 (1759): 279

2552 *Simplicity: or, Domestic Poems*. London, 1773 (4to. 2s. Dodsley. 1773) BRITISH LIBRARY

Reviewed: *Monthly Review* 49 (1773): 504
Critical Review 36 (1773): 314
Gentleman's Magazine 43 (1773): 570
Universal Catalogue [2] (1773) art. 1110

SINGLE, Simon (pseud.)
See: CAREY, Henry. *Cupid and Hymen*

2553 *Sir Amorous Whimsy; or, the Disappointed Macaroni. A poetical Tale*
NOT SEEN (4to. 1s. Evans. 1772)

Reviewed: *Monthly Review* 47 (1772): 324
Critical Review 34 (1772): 317
London Magazine 41 (1772): 491
Town & Country Magazine 4 (1772): 603

Sir Harry Gaylove
See: MARISHALL, Jean

The Sisters; or the History of Lucy and Caroline Sanson
See: DODD, William

Six Pastorals . . . By P––– N–––
See: NEWBY, Peter

2554 SIXTUS, Quartus Quintus (pseud.). *The Quack-Iliad: or, Sick Lady and Quack-Doctor, an Allegorical Poetical Tale*
NOT SEEN (4to. 6d. Pridden)

Reviewed: *Monthly Review* 25 (1761): 479
Critical Review 12 (1761): 483

2555 *A Sketch of Happiness in Rural Life, and of the Misery that attended an Indiscreet Passion*
NOT SEEN (Small 8vo. 1s.6d. Millan)

Reviewed: *Monthly Review* 41 (1769): 74–76

2556 *A Sketch of the Beau-Monde. Inscribed to Charles Hastings, Esq. Part I*. London, 1764 (4to. 1s. Burd) BODLEIAN

Reviewed: *Monthly Review* 30 (1764): 323
Critical Review 17 (1764): 393–394

2557 *A Sketch of the Present Times, and the Time to Come: In an Address to Kitty Fisher*. London, 1762 (4to. 1s. Waller) FOLGER

Reviewed: *Monthly Review* 26 (1762): 149–150
Critical Review 13 (1762): 166

2558 SKINN, A[nn]. *The Old Maid; or, History of Miss Ravensworth. In a Series of Letters. By Mrs. Skinn, Late Miss Masterman, of York*. 3

vols. London, 1771 (12mo. 7s.6d.sewed. Bell, &c.) BRITISH LIBRARY

Reviewed: *Monthly Review* 43 (1770): 500
Critical Review 30 (1770): 478–479
London Magazine 39 (1770): 632

2559 SLACK, John. *An Address to one of the Greatest, Gallantest, Most Loyal, and Humane Gentlemen in the World. By John Slack, A.M. Residentiary at Bristol, and sometime Fellow of Broughton College, Oxford Road.* London, 1762 (4to. 1s. Hinxman) BODLEIAN

Reviewed: *Monthly Review* 26 (1762): 154
Critical Review 13 (1762): 159–160

2560 SLADE, John. *The Adventures of Jerry Buck.* London, 1754 (12mo. 3s. Osborne) BRITISH LIBRARY

Reviewed: *Monthly Review* 10 (1754): 238

2561 SLADE, John. *Love and Duty. A Tragedy.* London, 1756 (8vo. 1s.6d. Griffiths) BRITISH LIBRARY

Reviewed: *Monthly Review* 14 (1756): 579
Critical Review 2 (1756): 84

2562 SLADE, J[ohn]. *The Loves of Hero and Leander; a Poetical Translation, from the Greek of Musaeus.* London, 1753 (4to. 1s. Owen) BODLEIAN

Reviewed: *Monthly Review* 8 (1753): 392

2563 SLADE, John. *The Transmigrating Soul; or, An Epitome of Human Nature. A Moral Satire.* London, 1760 (8vo. 3s. Dodsley) BRITISH LIBRARY

Reviewed: *Monthly Review* 23 (1760): 239–240
Critical Review 9 (1760): 494

2564 SMACKUM, Whackum (pseud.). *The Scrubs of Parnassus: or, All in the Wrong. A comi-tragical heroic Poem, in Hudibrastic Verse, addressed To the Authors of the Rosciad, the Fribbleriad, the Churchiliad, the Naiads of Fleet-Ditch, and the Gentlemen of both Theatres.* London, 1761 (4to. 1s.6d. Williams) BRITISH LIBRARY

Reviewed: *Monthly Review* 24 (1761): 444
Critical Review 11 (1761): 495–496
British Magazine 2 (1761): 382

2565 *The small Talker; A Series of Letters from a Lady in the West of England, to Lady Anne D———, abroad*
NOT SEEN (12mo. 2s.6d. Johnson and Payne)

Reviewed: *Monthly Review* 41 (1769): 74
Critical Review 27 (1769): 388–389
London Magazine 38 (1769): 269

2566 SMART, Christopher. *Hannah. An Oratorio. Written by Mr. Smart. The Musick composed by Mr. Worgan. As Performed at the King's Theatre in the Hay-market.* London, n.d. [ESTC-1764] (4to. 1s. Tonson) BRITISH LIBRARY

Reviewed: *Monthly Review* 30 (1764): 325

2567 SMART, C[hristopher]. *The Hilliad: an Epic Poem.* London, 1753 (4to. 2s. Newbery) BRITISH LIBRARY

Reviewed: *Monthly Review* 8 (1753): 151

2568 SMART, Christopher. *Hymn to the Supreme Being, on Recovery from a dangerous Fit of Illness.* London, 1756 (4to. 6d. Newbery) BRITISH LIBRARY

Reviewed: *Monthly Review* 15 (1756): 202
Critical Review 1 (1756): 482

2569 SMART, Christopher. *An Occasional Prologue and Epilogue to Othello, As it was acted at the Theatre-Royal in Drury-Lane, On Thursday the 7th of March 1751, By Persons of Distinction for their Diversion.* London, n.d. (6d. Carman) BODLEIAN

Reviewed: *Gentleman's Magazine* 21 (1751): 142–143

2570 SMART, Christopher. *Ode to the Right Honourable the Earl of Northumberland, on his being appointed Lord Lieutenant of Ireland. Presented on the Birth-day of Lord Warkworth.* London, 1764 (4to. 1s. Dodsley) BRITISH LIBRARY

Reviewed: *Monthly Review* 31 (1764): 231
Critical Review 18 (1764): 79
General Magazine 1 (1764): 350–351

2571 SMART, Christopher. *On the Goodness of the Supreme Being. A Poetical Essay.* Cambridge, 1756 (4to. 6d. Newbery) BRITISH LIBRARY

Reviewed: *Monthly Review* 14 (1756): 554–557

2572 SMART, Christopher. *On the Immensity of the Supreme Being. A Poetical Essay.* Cambridge, 1751 (4to. 6d. Newbery) BODLEIAN

Reviewed: *Monthly Review* 4 (1750–51): 508–510
Gentleman's Magazine 21 (1751): 239

2573 SMART, Christopher. *On the Omniscience of the Supreme Being. A Poetical Essay.* Cambridge, 1752 (4to. 6d. Bathurst, Newbery, &c.) BRITISH LIBRARY

Reviewed: *Monthly Review* 7 (1752): 474–475

2574 SMART, Christopher. *On the Power of the Supreme Being. A Poetical Essay.* Cambridge, 1754 (4to. 6d. Bathurst) BRITISH LIBRARY

Reviewed: *Monthly Review* 10 (1754): 78
Gentleman's Magazine 24 (1754): 49

2575 SMART, Christopher. *The Parables of our Lord and Saviour Jesus Christ. Done Into Familiar Verse, With Occasional Applications, for the Use And Improvement Of Younger Minds.* London, 1768 (8vo. 3s. Owen) BRITISH LIBRARY

Reviewed: *Monthly Review* 38 (1768): 409
Critical Review 25 (1768): 310
Universal Museum 4 (1768): 205

2576 SMART, [Christopher]. *Poems by Mr. Smart.* London, n.d. [Cropped] [ESTC-1763?] (4to. 1s. Fletcher) BRITISH LIBRARY

Reviewed: *Monthly Review* 29 (1763): 227
Critical Review 16 (1763): 72

2577 SMART, Christopher. *Poems on Several Occasions.* London, 1752 (4to. 10s.6d. Newbery) BRITISH LIBRARY

Reviewed: *Monthly Review* 7 (1752): 131–143

2578 SMART, [Christopher]. *Poems On several Occasions. viz. Munificence and Modesty. Female Dignity. To Lady Hussey Delaval. Verses from Catullus, after Dining with Mr. Murray. Epitaphs. On the Dutchess of Cleveland. On Henry Fielding, Esq. On the Rev. James Sheeles. Epitaph from Demosthenes.* London, n.d. [ESTC-1763] (4to. 1s. Fletcher and Co.) BRITISH LIBRARY

Reviewed: *Monthly Review* 29 (1763): 398
Critical Review 16 (1763): 395–396

2579 SMART, Christopher. *A Poetical Translation of the Fables of Phaedrus, with The Appendix of Gudius, And an accurate Edition of the Original on the opposite Page. To which is added, A Parsing Index For the Use of Learners.* London, 1765 (12mo. 3s. Dodsley) BRITISH LIBRARY

Reviewed: *Monthly Review* 32 (1765): 74–75
Critical Review 19 (1765): 46–47

2580 SMART, [Christopher]. *A Solemn Dirge, Sacred to the Memory of His Royal Highness Frederic Prince of Wales, As it was Sung by Mr. Lowe, Miss Burchell, and others, at Vauxhall. Written by Mr Smart. The Music compos'd By Mr. Worgan, M.B.* London, 1751 (6d. Carman) BRITISH LIBRARY

Reviewed: *Gentleman's Magazine* 21 (1751): 190

2581 SMART, Christopher. *A Song to David.* London, 1763 (4to. 1s. Fletcher) BRITISH LIBRARY

Reviewed: *Monthly Review* 28 (1763): 320–321
Critical Review 15 (1763): 324

2582 SMART, Christopher. *A Translation of the Psalms of David, attempted in the Spirit of Christianity, and adapted to the Divine Service.* London, 1765 (4to. 10s.6d. Bathurst) BRITISH LIBRARY

Reviewed: *Monthly Review* 33 (1765): 241
Critical Review 20 (1765): 208–216

2583 SMART, Christopher. *The Works of Horace, translated into Verse. With a Prose Interpretation, for the help of Students. And Occasional*

Notes. 4 vols. London, 1767 (8vo. 1l. Flexney) BRITISH LIBRARY

Reviewed: *Critical Review* 24 (1767): 94–105
Political Register 1 (1767): 486

2584 SMART, Christopher. *The Works of Horace, Translated Literally into English Prose; For the Use of those who are desirous of acquiring or recovering a competent Knowledge of the Latin Language.* 2 vols. London, 1756 (12mo. 5s. Newbery) BRITISH LIBRARY

Reviewed: *Monthly Review* 16 (1757): 32–36

The Smartiad
See: HILL, John

2585 SMILEWELL, Samuel (pseud.). *The Art of Joking; or, an Essay on Witticism; in the Manner of Mr. Pope's Essay on Criticism: With Proper Examples to the Risible Rules. To which is added, the Laws of Laughing, and the Contrast, or A Joke and a Jest, In small compass exprest.* London, n.d. [ESTC-1780?] (12mo. 1s. Dervelle) BRITISH LIBRARY

Reviewed: *Monthly Review* 50 (1774): 220
Universal Catalogue 3 (1774) art. 241

2586 SMITH, Edmund. *Thales. A Monody, Sacred to the Memory of Dr. Pococke. In Imitation of Spenser. From an authentic Manuscript of Mr. Edmund Smith, formerly of Christ-Church, Oxon.* London, 1751 (4to. 6d. Newbery) BRITISH LIBRARY

Reviewed: *Monthly Review* 4 (1750–51): 303

2587 SMITH, George. *Six Pastorals: Videlicet, I. The Country Lovers II. The Contest. III. Winter. IV. Two Boys. V. The Complaint of Daphnis. VI The Happy Meeting. To which are added, Two Pastoral Songs.* London, 1770 (4to. 2s. Dodsley) BRITISH LIBRARY

Reviewed: *Monthly Review* 43 (1770): 285–288
Gentleman's Magazine 40 (1770): 625
Critical Review 29 (1770): 475–476
London Magazine 39 (1770): 319

2588 [SMITH, James]. *The Art of Living in London: a Poem, in Two Cantos.* London, 1768 (4to. 2s. Griffin) BRITISH LIBRARY

Reviewed: *Monthly Review* 40 (1769): 89–90
Critical Review 27 (1769): 73–74
Gentleman's Magazine 39 (1769): 45
London Magazine 38 (1769): 104

2589 SMITH, Michael. *Christianity unmasqued; or Unavoidable Ignorance preferable to Corrupt Christianity. A Poem. In Twenty-one Cantos.* London, 1771 (8vo. 4s.sewed. Turpin. 1771) BRITISH LIBRARY

Reviewed: *Monthly Review* 45 (1771): 151
Critical Review 32 (1771): 225–227

2590 [SMITH, William]. *A Letter from a Gentleman in London, to his friend in Pennsylvania; with a Satire; containing Some Characteristical Strokes upon the Manners and Principles of the Quakers.* London, 1756 (Scott) LIBRARY OF CONGRESS

Reviewed: *Gentleman's Magazine* 26 (1756): 198

2591 *The Smithfield Rosciad. By the Author.* London, 1763 (4to. 2s.6d. Flexney) BRITISH LIBRARY

Reviewed: *Monthly Review* 30 (1764): 158
Critical Review 17 (1764): 75–76

2592 [SMOLLETT, Tobias]. *The Adventures of Ferdinand Count Fathom. By the Author of Roderick Random.* 2 vols. London, 1753 (12mo. 6s. Johnston) BRITISH LIBRARY

Reviewed: *Monthly Review* 8 (1753): 203–214

2593 [SMOLLETT, Tobias]. *The Adventures of Peregrine Pickle. In which are included, Memoirs of a Lady of Quality.* 4 vols. London, 1751 (12s.bound. Printed for the Author, and sold by Wilson in the Strand) BRITISH LIBRARY

Reviewed: *Monthly Review* 4 (1750–51): 355–364

2594 [SMOLLETT, Tobias]. *The Adventures of Sir Launcelot Greaves. By the Author of Roderick Random.* 2 vols. London, 1762 (12mo. 6s. Coote) BRITISH LIBRARY

Reviewed: *Monthly Review* 26 (1762): 391
Critical Review 13 (1762): 427–429

2595 [SMOLLETT, Tobias]. *The Expedition of Humphry Clinker. By the Author of Roderick*

Random. 3 vols. London, 1671 [1771] (12mo. 7s.6d.sewed. Johnston, &c. 1771) BRITISH LIBRARY

Reviewed: *Monthly Review* 45 (1771): 152
Critical Review 32 (1771): 81–88
Gentleman's Magazine 41 (1771): 317–321 and 417
London Magazine 40 (1771): 317–319 and 368–370
Town & Country Magazine 3 (1771): 323

2596 [SMOLLETT, Tobias]. *The History and Adventures of an Atom.* 2 vols. London, 1749 [1769] (12mo. 5s.sewed. Robertson and Roberts) BRITISH LIBRARY

Reviewed: *Monthly Review* 40 (1769): 441–455
Critical Review 27 (1769): 362–369
Gentleman's Magazine 39 (1769): 200–205
London Magazine 38 (1769): 262–263
Town & Country Magazine 1 (1769): 505–511
Critical Memoirs 1 (1769): 269
Political Register 4 (1769): 389–390

2597 SMOLLETT, T[obias]. *The History and Adventures of the renowned Don Quixote. Translated from the Spanish of Miguel de Cervantes Saavedra. To which is prefixed, Some Account of the Author's Life. By T. Smollett, M.D.* 2 vols. London, 1755 (4to. 2l.2s. Millar, &c.) BRITISH LIBRARY

Reviewed: *Monthly Review* 13 (1755): 196–202

2598 SMOLLETT, T[obias]. *Ode to Independence. By the late T. Smollett, M.D. With Notes and Observations.* Glasgow, 1773 (4to. 6d. Murray. 1773) BRITISH LIBRARY

Reviewed: *Monthly Review* 49 (1773): 500–502
Universal Catalogue [2] (1773) art. 1213

2599 [SMOLLETT, Tobias]. *The Regicide: or, James the First, of Scotland. A Tragedy. By the Author of Roderick Random.* London, 1749 (5s. London, printed by Subscription for the Benefit of the Author.) BRITISH LIBRARY

Reviewed: *Monthly Review* 1 (1749): 72–79

2600 [SMOLLETT, Tobias]. *The Reprisal: or, the Tars of Old England. A Comedy Of Two Acts, As it is Performed at the Theatre Royal in Drury-Lane.* London, 1757 (8vo. 1s. Baldwin) BRITISH LIBRARY

Reviewed: *Monthly Review* 16 (1757): 179
Critical Review 3 (1757): 157–160
Literary Magazine 2 (1757): 36–38

2601 SMYTH, W. H. *Love Triumphant. A Tale in Verse. By W. H. Smyth, Gent.* London, n.d. [UC CAT.–1757] (4to. 1s. Whiston) UNIVERSITY OF CHICAGO

Reviewed: *Monthly Review* 17 (1757): 185
Critical Review 3 (1757): 555–556

2602 [SMYTHIES, Miss ———]. *The Brothers. In Two Volumes. By the Author of the Stage-Coach, and Lucy Wellers.* London, 1758 (12mo. 6s. Dodsley) BRITISH LIBRARY

Reviewed: *Monthly Review* 20 (1759): 81
Critical Review 7 (1759): 79

2603 [SMYTHIES, Miss ———]. *The history of Lucy Wellers. Written by a Lady.* 2 vols. London, 1754 (12mo. 6s. Baldwin) BRITISH LIBRARY

Reviewed: *Monthly Review* 10 (1754): 75

2604 [SMYTHIES, Miss ———]. *The Stage-Coach. Containing the Character of Mr. Manly, and the History of his Fellow-Travellers.* 2 vols. London, 1753 (12mo. 6s. Osborne) BRITISH LIBRARY

Reviewed: *Monthly Review* 9 (1753): 394

2605 SMYTHIES, Humphry. *Precepts: A Poem. Addressed to the Toasts of Great Britain in general, but particularly to Miss *****.* London, 1753 (4to. 2s.6d. Newbery) BRITISH LIBRARY

Reviewed: *Monthly Review* 8 (1753): 392–393

The Snarlers
See: UNDERWOOD, Thomas

The Soldier. A Poem
See: THOMPSON, Edward

2606 *The Soldier's Amusement, a Novel. By the Author of the Memoirs of ****.* London, n.d.

(8vo. 1s. Warcus) UNIVERSITY OF ILLINOIS

Reviewed: *Monthly Review* 22 (1760): 549

The Soliloquy, a Poem
See: DOWNMAN, Hugh

2607 *A Soliloquy in a Grove.* London, 1756 (4to. 6d. Keith) BODLEIAN

Reviewed: *Monthly Review* 16 (1757): 95

2608 *A Soliloquy on the Eve of a late Coronation. The second Edition*
NOT SEEN (4to. 1s. Kearsley)

Reviewed: *Monthly Review* 25 (1761): 397
Critical Review 12 (1761): 403

Solitude: or, the Elysium of the Poets
See: OGILVIE, John

Solyman and Almena
See: LANGHORNE, John

2609 *Some Political and Literary Observations on reading some of the Works of the Reverend Mr. Churchill; and particularly the Conference. In a Letter to that Gentleman*
NOT SEEN (4to. 2s. Hinxman)

Reviewed: *Critical Review* 17 (1764): 306

Something New
See: GRIFFITH, Richard

2610 *A song: to be said or sung, by the good people of England, especially those who are Anti-Gallicans*
NOT SEEN (Fol. 1s. Sheepey)

Reviewed: *Monthly Review* 4 (1750–51): 479

The Songs and Recitative of Orpheus
See: GARRICK, David

Songs, Chorusses, &c. . . . in the new Entertainment of Harlequin's Jubilee
See: WOODWARD, Henry

The Songs, Chorusses, &c. in a new Dramatic Entertainment called A Christmas Tale
See: GARRICK, David

Songs, Chorusses, &c. in the Pastoral Entertainment of the Maid of the Oaks
See: BURGOYNE, John

Songs, Chorusses, &c. which are introduced in the new Entertainment of the Jubilee
See: GARRICK, David

The Songs, Chorusses, and Serious Dialogue of The Masque called the Institution of the Garter
See: GARRICK, David

Songs in the new Burletta of Midas
See: O'HARA, Kane

The Songs of Selma
See: MACPHERSON, James

A Sop in the Pan for a Physical Critick
See: REED, Joseph

SOPHOCLES (translation)
See: FRANCKLIN, Thomas. *The Tragedies of Sophocles*

2611 *Sophronia: a Poem, in Five Books.* London, 1756 (8vo. 1s.6d. Cooper) HARVARD (HOUGHTON)

Reviewed: *Monthly Review* 16 (1757): 183
Critical Review 2 (1756): 461–464

2612 *Sophronia: Or, Letters to the Ladies.* London, 1761 (12mo. 2s.6d. Johnston) BRITISH LIBRARY

Reviewed: *Monthly Review* 24 (1761): 352
Critical Review 11 (1761): 420
British Magazine 2 (1761): 326

2613 *The South Briton: A Comedy Of Five Acts: As it is performed at the Theatre in Smock-Alley, with great applause. Written by a Lady.* London, 1774 (8vo. 1s.6d. Williams. 1774) BRITISH LIBRARY

Reviewed: *Monthly Review* 50 (1774): 326
Critical Review 38 (1774): 237–238
Universal Catalogue 3 (1774) art. 324

2614 SOUTHERNE, Thomas. *Plays written by Thomas Southerne, Esq. now first collected. With An Account of the Life and Writings of the Author*. 3 vols. London, 1774 (12mo. 9s. Evans) BRITISH LIBRARY

Reviewed: *Critical Review* 38 (1774): 392–393
Universal Catalogue 3 (1774) art. 1066

SOUTHERNE, Thomas (adaptations)
See: GARRICK, David. *Isabella*
HAWKESWORTH, John. *Oroonoko*

The Spanish Lady, a Musical Entertainment
See: HULL, Thomas

2615 *Sparks: or, Small Poems morally turned*. London, 1752 (Fol. 1s. Cooper) BRITISH LIBRARY

Reviewed: *Monthly Review* 6 (1752): 155
Gentleman's Magazine 22 (1752): 95

2616 *A Specimen of a Book, intituled, Ane Compendious Booke, of Godly And Spiritual Sangs, collectit out of Sundrie Partes of the Scripture, with Sundrie of other Ballates changed out of Prophaine Sanges, for avoyding of Sinne and Harlotrie. With Augmentation of sundrie Gude and Godly Ballates, not contained in the first Edition*. Edinburgh, 1765 (8vo. 1s.6d. Edinburgh printed by Andro Hart, Nicoll) BRITISH LIBRARY

Reviewed: *Monthly Review* 34 (1766): 404
Critical Review 22 (1766): 77–78
Gentleman's Magazine 36 (1766): 146

A Specimen of Elegaic Poetry
See: BOYCE, Tho.

2617 SPENCER, John. *Hermas, or the Acarian Shepherds: a Poem. In Sixteen Books*. [Ed. by William HILTON.] Newcastle upon Tyne, 1772 (8vo. 8s.sewed. Newcastle printed. Sold by Murray in London) BRITISH LIBRARY

Reviewed: *Monthly Review* 47 (1772): 69
Critical Review 32 (1771): 390–391 and 33 (1772): 174
London Magazine 41 (1772): 188
Universal Catalogue [1] (1772) arts. 256 and 1022

2618 SPENSER, Edmund. *The Faerie Queene, by Edmund Spenser. A New Edition, with Notes critical and explanatory, by Ralph Church. M.A. Late Student of Christ Church, Oxon*. 4 vols. London, 1758 and 1759 (8vo. 11.1s.sheets. Faden) BRITISH LIBRARY

Reviewed: *Monthly Review* 20 (1759): 567–568
Critical Review 7 (1759): 103–106

2619 SPENSER, Edmund. *Spenser's Faerie Queene. A New Edition with a Glossary, And Notes explanatory and critical by John Upton Prebendary of Rochester and Rector of Great Rissington in Glocestershire*. 2 vols. London, 1758 (4to. 11.1s.sheets. Tonson) BRITISH LIBRARY

Reviewed: *Monthly Review* 20 (1759): 566–567

2620 *Spenser's Fairy Queen attempted in Blank Verse. Canto I*
NOT SEEN (4to. 1s. Davies)

Reviewed: *Monthly Review* 52 (1775): 111–113
Critical Review 38 (1774): 469–470
London Review 1 (1775): 231–232

The Spirit of Contradiction
See: RICH, John

2621 *The Spiritual Minor. A Comedy*. London, n.d. [ESTC-1763?] (8vo. 1s. Morgan) BRITISH LIBRARY

Reviewed: *Monthly Review* 29 (1763): 236
Critical Review 16 (1763): 74–75

The Spiritual Quixote
See: GRAVES, Richard

2622 SPOONER, Thomas. *Three Hundred Hymns*. London, 1762 (12mo. 3s. Dilly) BRITISH LIBRARY

Reviewed: *Monthly Review* 28 (1763): 70–71
Critical Review 15 (1763): 160
British Magazine 4 (1763): 158

The Spouter, or the Double Revenge
See: DELL, Henry

The Spouter: or, the Triple Revenge
See: MURPHY, Arthur

The Spouting-Club
See: LEWIS, Richard

2623 [SPRING, Thomas]. *A Familiar Epistle from A Student of the Middle Temple, London, to his Friend in Dublin. Written in the Year 1759.* Dublin, 1771 (4to. 2s.6d. Davies. 1771) BRITISH LIBRARY

Reviewed: *Monthly Review* 45 (1771): 412
Critical Review 32 (1771): 227–228
Gentleman's Magazine 41 (1771): 560

The Spring. A Pastoral
See: HARRIS, James

SPUR, Mercurius (pseud.)
See: SHAW, Cuthbert

The 'Squire and the Parson
See: JENYNS, Soame

The Stage-Coach
See: SMYTHIES, Miss

2624 *The Stage of Aristophanes.* London, 1774 (4to. 1s. Setchell. 1774) BRITISH LIBRARY

Reviewed: *Monthly Review* 51 (1774): 483
Critical Review 38 (1774): 237

2625 STAMMA, Louis. *The Kellyad: or a Critical Examination into the Merits of Thespis.* London, 1767 (4to. 2s. Williams) BRITISH LIBRARY

Reviewed: *Monthly Review* 36 (1767): 77
Critical Review 23 (1767): 61
Gentleman's Magazine 37 (1767): 34

2626 *The State-Farce: a Lyrick. Written at Clermont, and inscribed to His Grace the Duke of Newcastle.* London, 1756 (Fol. 6d. Cooper) BRITISH LIBRARY

Reviewed: *Monthly Review* 14 (1756): 260
Critical Review 1 (1756): 163

2627 *State Necessity Not considered as a Question of Law. A Poetical Sketch.* London, 1767 (4to. 1s. Kearsly) HARVARD (HOUGHTON)

Reviewed: *Monthly Review* 36 (1767): 241–242
Critical Review 23 (1767): 225–226

2628 *State Poems, (Relative to former and to future Times, And, Especially, To the present Critical Conjuncture) Entitled Britannia, The Ocean, Liberty, Eliza, George, the First, Dettingen.* London, 1755 (4to. 6d. Cooper) BRITISH LIBRARY

Reviewed: *Monthly Review* 12 (1755): 512

The Statesman Foil'd
See: DOSSIE, Robert

STATIUS (translation)
See: LEWIS, William Lillington. *The Thebaid of Statius*

2629 STAYLEY, George. *The Rival Theatres: or, A Play-House to be let. A Farce. To which is added, the Chocolate-Makers: or, Mimickry Exposed. An Interlude. With a Preface and Notes Commentary and Explanatory.* Dublin printed, London reprinted; 1759 (8vo. 1s. Reeve) BRITISH LIBRARY

Reviewed: *Monthly Review* 20 (1759): 463–464
Critical Review 7 (1759): 557

2630 [STEELE, Anne]. *Poems on Subjects chiefly Devotional. In Two Volumes. By Theodosia.* London, 1760 (8vo. 6s. Buckland, &c.) BODLEIAN

Reviewed: *Monthly Review* 22 (1760): 231–324
Critical Review 9 (1760): 154

2631 STEPHENS, Edward. *A Poem, In Blank Verse, on a Violent Storm, attended with Thunder and Lightning. To which is added, A Poem on Death; To Palmera.* London, 1751 (Fol. 6s. Cooper) BODLEIAN

Listed: *Monthly Review* 5 (1751): 77–78

2632 STEPHENS, Edward. *Poems on Various Subjects.* London, 1759 (8vo. 2s.6d.sewed. Dodsley) BRITISH LIBRARY

Reviewed: *Monthly Review* 22 (1760): 342–344

2633 [STERLING, James]. *An Epistle to the Hon. Arthur Dobbs, Esq; in Europe. From a Clergyman in America.* London, 1752 (4to. 2s.6d. Dodsley) BRITISH LIBRARY

Reviewed: *Monthly Review* 6 (1752):236–237

2634 [STERNE, Laurence]. *The Life and Opinions of Tristram Shandy, Gentleman.* 2 vols.

N.p., 1760 [ESTC: York, 1759] (12mo. 5s. Cooper) BRITISH LIBRARY

Reviewed: *Monthly Review* 21 (1759): 561–571
Critical Review 9 (1760): 73–74
London Magazine 29 (1760): 111–112
Annual Register 3 (1760): 247–249

2635 [STERNE, Laurence]. *The Life and Opinions of Tristram Shandy, Gentleman. Vols. III and IV.* London, 1761 (8vo. 5s. Dodsley) BRITISH LIBRARY

Reviewed: *Monthly Review* 24 (1761): 101–116
Critical Review 11 (1761): 314–317
London Magazine 30 (1761): 56, 100–102
British Magazine 2 (1761): 98

2636 [STERNE, Laurence]. *The Life and Opinions of Tristram Shandy, Gentleman. Vols. V and VI.* London, 1762 (8vo. 5s. Becket) BRITISH LIBRARY

Reviewed: *Monthly Review* 26 (1762): 31–41
Critical Review 13 (1762): 66–69
British Magazine 3 (1762): 44

2637 [STERNE, Laurence]. *The Life and Opinions of Tristram Shandy, Gentleman. Vols. VII and VIII.* London, 1765 (Small 8vo. 2s.each. Becket and De Hondt) BRITISH LIBRARY

Reviewed: *Monthly Review* 32 (1765): 120–139
Critical Review 19 (1765): 65–66
Candid Review 1 (1765): 91–92

2638 [STERNE, Laurence]. *The Life and Opinions of Tristram Shandy, Gentleman. Vol. IX.* London, 1767 (8vo. 2s. Becket) BRITISH LIBRARY

Reviewed: *Monthly Review* 36 (1767): 93–102
Critical Review 23 (1767): 135–138
Gentleman's Magazine 37 (1767): 75–76

2639 [STERNE, Laurence]. *A Political Romance, addressed to --- --- Esq. of York.* London, 1769 (12mo. Murdoch. 1769) BRITISH LIBRARY

Reviewed: *Monthly Review* 41 (1769): 485–486
Critical Review 29 (1770): 69–70
Gentleman's Magazine 40 (1770): 37

2640 [STERNE, Laurence]. *A Sentimental Journey through France and Italy. By Mr. Yorick.* 2 vols. London, 1768 (Small 8vo. 5s. Becket) BRITISH LIBRARY

Reviewed: *Monthly Review* 38 (1768): 174–185, 309–319
Critical Review 25 (1768): 181–185
London Magazine 37 (1768): 163
Universal Museum 4 (1768): 148
Political Register 2 (1768): 383

2641 [STEVENS, George Alexander]. *Albion Restored, or Time turned Oculist: A Masque.* London, 1758 (8vo. 1s. Seymour) BRITISH LIBRARY

Reviewed: *Monthly Review* 18 (1758): 491

2642 [STEVENS, George Alexander]. *The Birth-Day of Folly. An Heroi-Comical Poem, By Peter: With Notes Variorum, For the illustration of historical passages relating to the Hero of the Poem, and other remarkable Personages.* London, 1755 (4to. 1s. Cooper) BODLEIAN

Reviewed: *Monthly Review* 12 (1755): 383
Gentleman's Magazine 25 (1755): 190

2643 [STEVENS, George Alexander]. *The Court of Alexander. An Opera, In Two Acts. As it is performed at the Theatre Royal in Covent-Garden.* London, n.d. [FOLGER CAT.–1770] (8vo. 1s. Waller) FOLGER

Reviewed: *Monthly Review* 42 (1770): 73–74
Critical Review 29 (1770): 71
London Magazine 39 (1770): 45

2644 STEVENS, George Alexander. *Distress upon Distress: or, Tragedy In True Taste. A Heroi-Comi-Parodi-Tragedi-Farci-cal Burlesque. In Two Acts. By George Alexander Stevens. With All the Similies, Rants, Groans, Sighs, &c. entirely New. With Annotations, Dissertations, Explanations, Observations, Emendations, Quotations, Restorations, &c. By Sir Henry Humm. And Notes Critical, Classical and Historical, By Paulus Purgantius Pedasculus. Who has carefully Revised, Corrected and Amended it; Expunged the several Errors and Interpolations; Reconciled the various Readings, and Restored the Author to himself.*

London, 1752 (8vo. 1s.6d. Griffiths. From the Dublin edition) BRITISH LIBRARY

Reviewed: *Monthly Review* 7 (1752): 79
Gentleman's Magazine 22 (1752): 339

2645 STEVENS, George Alexander. *The Dramatic History of Master Edward, Miss Ann, Mrs. Llwhuddwhydd, and Others. The Extraordinaries of these Times. Collected from Zaphaniel's Original Papers.* London, 1743 [1763] (12mo. 3s.6d.sewed. Waller) BODLEIAN

Reviewed: *Monthly Review* 28 (1763): 328
Critical Review 15 (1763): 373–377

2646 [STEVENS, George Alexander]. *The French Flogged, or, The British Sailors in America, A Farce of Two Acts, As it was performed at the Theatre Royal Covent-Garden.* London, 1767 (8vo. 1s. Williams) BRITISH LIBRARY

Reviewed: *Monthly Review* 36 (1767): 238
Critical Review 23 (1767): 229

2647 [STEVENS, George Alexander]. *The History of Tom Fool.* 2 vols. London, 1760 (12mo. 6s. Waller) BRITISH LIBRARY

Reviewed: *Monthly Review* 23 (1760): 163–164
Critical Review 9 (1760): 494

2648 [STEVENS, George Alexander]. *The Humours of an Irish Court of Justice. A Dramatic Satyr. Written by an exil'd Freeman of that Country for his Amusement during his Retirement, and dedicated to the Lovers of Truth and Liberty.* London, n.d. [BLC-1750?] (8vo. 6d. No publisher's name to it) BRITISH LIBRARY

Reviewed: *Monthly Review* 5 (1751): 72

2649 STEVENS, George Alexander. *Religion: or, the Libertine Repentant. A Rhapsody.* London, 1751 (8vo. 6d. Reeve) BRITISH LIBRARY

Reviewed: *Monthly Review* 4 (1750–51): 377–378

2650 [STEVENS, George Alexander]. *Songs, Comic, and Satyrical.* Oxford, 1772 (8vo. 6d. Reeve) BRITISH LIBRARY

Reviewed: *Monthly Review* 46 (1772): 455–456
Critical Review 34 (1772): 70–71

Town & Country Magazine 4 (1772): 154
Universal Catalogue [1] (1772) art. 378

2651 [STEVENS, George Alexander]. *The Trip to Portsmouth; a Comic Sketch of One Act, With Songs.* London, n.d. [ESTC-1773] (12mo. 3s.sewed. Waller, &c. 1772) BRITISH LIBRARY

Reviewed: *Monthly Review* 49 (1773): 232
Universal Catalogue [2] (1773) art. 1033

2652 STEVENS, John. *Poetical Pieces. By Several Hands.* London, 1752 (8vo. 6d. Printed by subscription for the editor, J. Stephens) BRITISH LIBRARY

Reviewed: *Monthly Review* 6 (1752): 397–398

2653 [STEVENS, Thomas]. *The Castle-Builders; or, the History of William Stephens, of the Isle of Wight, Esq; lately deceased. A Political Novel, Never before published in any Language.* 1st ed. reviewed; copy seen 2d ed.: London, 1759 (8vo. 2s.6d. Cabe) BRITISH LIBRARY

Reviewed: *Monthly Review* 21 (1759): 81
Critical Review 7 (1759): 558

2654 [STEVENSON, John Hall]. *Crazy Tales.* London, 1762 (4to. 4s. Becket) BRITISH LIBRARY

Reviewed: *Monthly Review* 26 (1762): 450–454
Critical Review 13 (1762): 475–480
British Magazine 3 (1762): 382

2655 [STEVENSON, John Hall]. *Fables for grown Gentlemen: For the Year 1770.* London, 1770 (4to. 2s. Dodsley) BRITISH LIBRARY

Reviewed: *Monthly Review* 42 (1770): 132–135
Critical Review 29 (1770): 72–73
Town & Country Magazine 2 (1770): 72

2656 [STEVENSON, John Hall]. *Fables for Grown Gentlemen: or, A Fable for every Day in the Week.* London, 1761 (4to. 1s.6d. Dodsley) BRITISH LIBRARY

Reviewed: *Monthly Review* 26 (1762): 68–71
Critical Review 12 (1761): 459–462
British Magazine 2 (1761): 662

2657 [STEVENSON, John Hall]. *Hymn to Miss Laurence, in the Pump-Room at Bath*. London, 1755 (Fol. 6d. Dodsley) LILLY

Reviewed: *Monthly Review* 13 (1755): 297–298
Gentleman's Magazine 25 (1755): 335

2658 [STEVENSON, John Hall]. *Lyric Consolations. With the Speech of Alderman W——— delivered in A Dream, at the King's Bench Prison the Evening of his Inauguration*. London, 1769 (4to. 3s. Almon) BRITISH LIBRARY

Reviewed: *Monthly Review* 40 (1769): 351–352
Critical Review 27 (1769): 396–397
Critical Memoirs 1 (1769): 523
Political Register 4 (1769): 322

2659 [STEVENSON, John Hall]. *Makarony Fables; with the New Fable of the Bees. In Two Cantos. Addressed to the Society. By Cosmo, Mythogelastick Professor, and F.M.S.* London, 1768 (4to. 2s.6d. Almon) HARVARD (HOUGHTON)

Reviewed: *Monthly Review* 38 (1768): 247
Critical Review 25 (1768): 69–70
London Magazine 37 (1768): 43
Universal Museum 4 (1768): 36
Political Register 2 (1768): 113–115

2660 [STEVENSON, John Hall]. *A Nosegay and a Simile for the Reviewers. A Lyric Epistle*. London, 1760 (4to. 6d. Cooper) BODLEIAN

Reviewed: *Monthly Review* 23 (1760): 86
British Magazine 1 (1760): 433

2661 [STEVENSON, John Hall]. *A Pastoral Cordial, or, an Anodyne Sermon: preached before Their Graces N. and D. In the Country, By an Independent Teacher of the Truth*. London, 1763 (4to. 1s.6d. Hinxman) BRITISH LIBRARY

Reviewed: *Monthly Review* 28 (1763): 96–99
Critical Review 15 (1763): 74–76

2662 [STEVENSON, John Hall]. *A Pastoral Puke. A Second Sermon preached before The People called Whigs. By an Independent*. London, 1764 (4to. 1s.6d. Hinxman) BRITISH LIBRARY

Reviewed: *Monthly Review* 30 (1764): 415
Critical Review 17 (1764): 472

2663 [STEVENSON, John Hall]. *Two Lyric Epistles: One to my cousin Shandy, on his coming to Town; and the other to the Grown Gentlewomen, the Misses of*****. London, 1760 (4to. 1s. Dodsley) BRITISH LIBRARY

Reviewed: *Monthly Review* 22 (1760): 437–439
Critical Review 9 (1760): 322–323
British Magazine 1 (1760): 140 [324]

2664 [STEVENSON, John Hall]. *Two Lyrick Epistles: or; Margery the Cook-maid to the Critical Reviewers*. London, 1762 (4to. 1s. Thrush) BRITISH LIBRARY

Reviewed: *Monthly Review* 26 (1762): 151

2665 [STEVENSON, John Hall]. *Yorick's Sentimental Journey, continued. To which is prefixed, some Account of the Life and Writings of Mr. Sterne.* [Volumes are numbered III and IV and printed to match the 2 vols. of Sterne's *Sentimental Journey*.] 2 vols. London, 1769 (12mo. 5s. Bladon) BRITISH LIBRARY

Reviewed: *Monthly Review* 40 (1769): 428
Critical Review 27 (1769): 390
Gentleman's Magazine 39 (1769): 398
London Magazine 38 (1769): 323–324
Critical Memoirs [2] (1769): 195–198

2666 STEVENSON, William. *Original Poems on Several Subjects*. 2 vols. Edinburgh, 1765 (12mo. 5s. sewed. Hawes) BRITISH LIBRARY (vol. 1 only)

Reviewed: *Monthly Review* 33 (1765): 239–240
Critical Review 20 (1765): 124–134

2667 STEWART, James. *The Two English Gentlemen; or the Sham Funeral. A Comedy*. London, 1774 (8vo. 1s.6d. Bell. 1774) BRITISH LIBRARY

Reviewed: *Monthly Review* 50 (1774): 485
Critical Review 38 (1774): 76
Universal Catalogue 3 (1774) art. 483

2668 STILLINGFLEET, Benjamin. *Paradise Lost. An Oratorio. As it is performed at the Theatre-Royal in Covent-Garden. Altered and adapted to the Stage from Milton. Set to Music* by Mr. Smith. London, 1760 (4to. 1s. Dodsley) BRITISH LIBRARY

Reviewed: *Monthly Review* 22 (1760): 259

2669 STIRLING, John (trans.). *The Works of Horace. With The Original Text. And Reduc'd to the natural Order of Construction, with Accents to regulate the right Pronunciation, and a close and truly literal English Translation, rendering that Author exceedingly easy and familiar to every Reader. In a Method never attempted before, for the Use of all Lovers of that Prince of Lyrics.* London, 1751 and 1753 (12mo. 1s.6d. Baldwin) BRITISH LIBRARY

Reviewed: *Monthly Review* 7 (1752): 369–371 and 9 (1753): 472

2670 STOCK, J. P. *A Pastoral Elegy on the Death of his Royal Highness Will, Duke of Cumberland* NOT SEEN (4to. 6d. Peat)

Reviewed: *Monthly Review* 33 (1765): 405
Critical Review 20 (1765): 394–395

2671 STOCKDALE, Percival. *The Amyntas of Tasso. Translated from the original Italian by Percival Stockdale.* London, 1770 (8vo. 3s.6d.sewed. Davies. 1770) BRITISH LIBRARY

Reviewed: *Monthly Review* 42 (1770): 425–427
Critical Review 29 (1770): 214–220
Gentleman's Magazine 40 (1770): 621

2672 [STOCKDALE, Percival]. *Churchill Defended, a Poem: addressed to the Minority.* London, 1765 (4to. 2s. Flexney) BRITISH LIBRARY

Reviewed: *Monthly Review* 32 (1765): 76
Critical Review 19 (1765): 71–72
Candid Review 1 (1765): 35–37

2673 STOCKDALE, P[ercival]. *The Constituents, a Poem.* London, 1765 (4to. 1s. Flexney) BODLEIAN

Reviewed: *Monthly Review* 32 (1765): 154
Critical Review 19 (1765): 70–71
Candid Review 1 (1765): 51

2674 [STOCKDALE, Percival]. *The Poet; a Poem.* London, 1773 (4to. 2s.6d. Flexney. 1773) BRITISH LIBRARY

Reviewed: *Monthly Review* 49 (1773): 230
Critical Review 36 (1773): 305–307
London Magazine 42 (1773): 249
Town & Country Magazine 5 (1773): 602
Universal Catalogue [2] (1773) art. 593

2675 *The Storm; or, the History of Nancy and Lucy.* 2 vols. London, 1772 (12mo. 6s.bound. Noble. 1772) BODLEIAN (vol. 1 only)

Reviewed: *Monthly Review* 46 (1772): 164
Critical Review 33 (1772): 83
Universal Catalogue [1] (1772) art. 130

2676 STRAHAN, Alexander. *The Aeneid of Virgil. Translated into Blank Verse, by Alexander Strahan, Esq;* London, 1767 (12mo. 6s. Cadell) BRITISH LIBRARY

Reviewed: *Monthly Review* 37 (1767): 321–323
Critical Review 24 (1767): 124–127
Political Register 1 (1767): 266–269

2677 STRAHAN, Alexander. *The first six books of Virgil's Aeneid. Translated into blank verse* NOT SEEN (8vo. 4s. Strahan)

Reviewed: *Monthly Review* 9 (1753): 1–11

The Stratford Jubilee
See: GENTLEMAN, Francis

2678 STREIT, F[riedrich] W[ilhelm] (trans.). *Memoirs of the Count of P----; Shewing at once The Dreadful Consequences of Vice, and the Happiness of being Virtuous. A Novel, Translated from the German, by F. W. Streit, F. Ducal S. at Jenna.* 2 vols. London, 1767 (12mo. 6s. Dodsley) BRITISH LIBRARY

Reviewed: *Monthly Review* 37 (1767): 151–152
Critical Review 24 (1767): 194–198
London Magazine 36 (1767): 206

2679 [STUART, Charles, and John BONAR (eds.)]. *Miscellaneous Pieces of Poetry. Selected from Various Eminent Authors. Among which are interspersed A Few Originals.* Edinburgh, 1765 (Small 8vo. 3s. Edinburgh, printed for W. Gray) BRITISH LIBRARY

Reviewed: *Monthly Review* 33 (1765): 404–405
Critical Review 20 (1765): 176–180

2680 *The Students. A Comedy. Altered from Shakespeare's Love's Labours Lost, and Adapted to the Stage.* London, 1762 (8vo. 1s.6d. Hope) BRITISH LIBRARY

Reviewed: *Monthly Review* 26 (1762): 475
Critical Review 13 (1762): 441
British Magazine 3 (1762): 324

2681 *The Subscription Soldier, in Imitation of the Sixteenth Satire of Juvenal*
NOT SEEN (4to. 6d. Ross)

Reviewed: *Monthly Review* 22 (1760): 76–77

2682 SUCKLING, John. *The Works of Sir John Suckling. Containing his Poems, Letters, and Plays.* 2 vols. London, 1770 (12mo. 5s. Davies. 1770) BRITISH LIBRARY

Reviewed: *Monthly Review* 43 (1770): 264–268

2683 *Suicide, a Poem.* London, 1773 (4to. 1s. Hookham. 1773) BRITISH LIBRARY

Reviewed: *Monthly Review* 49 (1773): 504
London Magazine 42 (1773): 559
Universal Catalogue [2] (1773) art. 1206

The Sultan: or, Love and Fame
See: GENTLEMAN, Francis

2684 *The Summer-Day. A Poem: in four Cantos, Morning, Noon, Evening and Night.* London, 1769 (8vo. 4s. Robinson and Co. 1769) BRITISH LIBRARY

Reviewed: *Monthly Review* 42 (1770): 486
Critical Review 30 (1770): 224–227
Town & Country Magazine 2 (1770): 490

2685 *The Summer-House: or, the History of Mr. Morton and Miss Bamsted. In Two Volumes.* London, 1768 (12mo. 6s. Noble) HARVARD (HOUGHTON)

Reviewed: *Monthly Review* 38 (1768): 498–499
Critical Review 26 (1768): 60–62
London Magazine 37 (1768): 163
Universal Museum 4 (1768): 316
Political Register 3 (1768): 253

The Summer's Tale
See: CUMBERLAND, Richard

2686 *The Summons For the 18th of April, 1770. A Poem.* London, 1770 (4to. 1s.6d. Steidell) UNIVERSITY OF ILLINOIS

Reviewed: *Monthly Review* 42 (1770): 327
Critical Review 29 (1770): 392
Town & Country Magazine 2 (1770): 214

2687 *A Supplement to the Life and Opinions of Tristram Shandy, Gent. Serving to elucidate that Work. By the Author of Yorick's Meditations.* London, 1760 (8vo. 1s.6d. Pottinger) BRITISH LIBRARY

Reviewed: *Monthly Review* 23 (1760): 522
Critical Review 10 (1760): 485
London Magazine 29 (1760): 672

2688 *The Supposed Daughter; or, Innocent Impostor. In which is Comprised The Entertaining Memoirs of Two North-Country Families of Distinction, In a Series of Thirty Years. Many of the Adventures, altho' remarkably uncommon, are attested by Manuscripts, now in the Hands of the Compiler.* 3 vols. London, n.d. (12mo. 9s. Noble) BODLEIAN

Reviewed: *Monthly Review* 14 (1756): 453
Critical Review 1 (1756): 260–262

The Surprises of Love
See: CLELAND, John

Surry Triumphant
See: DUNCOMBE, John

2689 SWABY, Edward Lamport. *An Ode Most humbly Inscribed to the Right Hon. Lord Blakeney, on his Arrival to England from Minorca. To which is added, An Occasional Ode of Consolation Upon the Loss of Captain William Death, Late of the Terrible Privateer. By Mr. Swaby.* London, 1757 (Fol. 1s. Printed for the benefit of the Widow of Capt. Death, and to be had at her house in Old Gravel-lane, Wapping; at Lloyd's Coffee-house, Lombard-street; and at Mr. Woodfall's, Charing-cross.) HARVARD (HOUGHTON)

Reviewed: *Monthly Review* 16 (1757): 286

Swearing, a Satire
See: TAPERELL, J.

2690 SWIFT, Dean (pseud.). *BIBLIOMAXIA; or, the Battle of the Books. Translated from the Greek. Supposed to have been written by Dean Swift*
NOT SEEN (8vo. 1s. Hope)

Reviewed: *Monthly Review* 20 (1759): 81
Critical Review 7 (1759): 283
Gentleman's Magazine 29 (1759): 36

2691 SWIFT, Jonathan. *The Works of Dr. Jonathan Swift, Dean of St. Patrick's, Dublin. Vols. XIII and XIV*. London, 1762 (12mo. 6s. Dodsley) BODLEIAN

Reviewed: *Monthly Review* 27 (1762): 271–281
Critical Review 14 (1762): 177–184
British Magazine 3 (1762): 605

2692 SWIFT, Jonathan. *The Works of Dr. Jonathan Swift, Dean of St. Patrick's, Dublin. Collected and revised By Deane Swift, Esq; of Goodrich, in Herefordshire. Vols. 15, 16 and 17*. London, 1765 (Small 8vo. 2s.6d.sewed. Johnston) BODLEIAN

Reviewed: *Monthly Review* 33 (1765): 1–13, 147–156, 218–230 and 312–319
Critical Review 19 (1765): 344–350 and 420–432
Gentleman's Magazine 35 (1765): 238–240
Candid Review 1 (1765): 331–333

2693 SWINNEY, Sidney. *The Battle of Minden, a Poem. In Three Books. By Sidney Swinney, D.D. Fellow of the Royal and Antiquarian Societies. Enriched with Critical Notes by Two Friends, and with Explanatory Notes by the Author*. London, 1769 (4to. 10s.6d. Dodsley, &c. 1769) BRITISH LIBRARY

Reviewed: *Monthly Review* 41 (1769): 472–475

2694 SWINNEY, Sidney. *The Ninth Satire of Horace, Book the First, Imitated*. London, 1767 (4to. 1s.6d. Becket) BRITISH LIBRARY

Reviewed: *Monthly Review* 37 (1767): 315
Critical Review 24 (1767): 159
Universal Museum 3 (1767): 429

2695 [SWINNEY, Sidney]. *An Ode consecrated to the Memory of his Grace the Duke of Newcastle, late Chancellor of the University of Cambridge*
NOT SEEN (4to. 1s. Becket, &c.)

Reviewed: *Monthly Review* 40 (1769): 341
Critical Review 27 (1769): 235–236

2696 SWINNEY, Sidney. *A Poem on the Battle of Minden. Book the Second. Enriched with Critical Notes by Two Friends, and with Explanatory Notes by the Author*. [British Library copy is bound with the first book (see above, *Battle of Minden*) and has no separate title-page; dedication is dated January 1772.] (4to. 2s.6d. No publisher's name) BRITISH LIBRARY

Reviewed: *Critical Review* 33 (1772): 170–171

2697 *Sydenham, a Poem, addressed to The Right Honourable William Pitt, Esq;* London, 1761 (4to. 1s. Moran) YALE (BEINECKE)

Reviewed: *Monthly Review* 25 (1761): 396
Critical Review 12 (1761): 395

The Tablet of Cebes
See: POWIS, T.

2698 [TAIT, John]. *The Cave of Morar, the Man of Sorrows. A Legendary Tale. In Two Parts*. London, 1774 (4to. 2s. Davies. 1774) BRITISH LIBRARY

Reviewed: *Monthly Review* 50 (1774): 481–482
Critical Review 37 (1774): 472
Universal Catalogue 3 (1774) art. 639

2699 [TAIT, John]. *The Druid's Monument, a Tribute to the Memory of Dr. Oliver Goldsmith. By the Author of The Cave of Morar*. London, 1774 (4to. 6d. Davies) BRITISH LIBRARY

Reviewed: *Monthly Review* 51 (1774): 67
Critical Review 37 (1774): 473
London Magazine 43 (1774): 399
Universal Catalogue 3 (1774) art. 775

2700 *Tales from Fontaine; the first Satire and first Epistle of Horace; and a Letter to a Friend, on his repining at Old Age*
NOT SEEN (12mo. 2s.6d.sewed. Nourse)

Reviewed: *Monthly Review* 26 (1762): 384–385
Critical Review 13 (1762): 249–252
British Magazine 3 (1762): 213

2701 *Tales to kill Time: or, A New Method to cast off Care, and to cure Melancholy, Vapours, and all Hypochondriacal Complaints. By the Society of the Court of Momus.* London, 1757 (12mo. 2s. Baldwin) BRITISH LIBRARY

Reviewed: *Monthly Review* 17 (1757): 375

Tales, Translated from the Persian
See: DOW, Alexander

2702 TAPERELL, J. *Swearing, a Satire. With a Preface to the Swearer. Some Verses on the late Judgments of God, and on The Death of his Royal Highness Frederick Prince of Wales.* London, 1751 (8vo. 6d. Withers) BRITISH LIBRARY

Reviewed: *Monthly Review* 5 (1751): 76

2703 *Tarrataria: or, Don Quixote the Second. A Romantic, Poetical Medley. In Two Cantos. By a Traveller of Distinction. To which is added a Poem, intituled, Christianity against Deism and Immorality. By the same Author. A Work chiefly intended for His Majesty's Perusal.* London, 1761 (8vo. 1s.6d. Cooke) BRITISH LIBRARY

Reviewed: *Monthly Review* 24 (1761): 353
Critical Review 11 (1761): 412
British Magazine 2 (1761): 326

2704 TASSO, Torquato. *Godfrey of Bulloign; or the Gierusalemme Liberata of Torquato Tasso, abridged and altered. Inscribed to Lady M*****.* London, 1774 (8vo. 3s. Dodsley) BRITISH LIBRARY

Reviewed: *Monthly Review* 52 (1775): 113–115
Critical Review 38 (1774): 470–473

TASSO, Torquato (translations)
See: HOOLE, John. *Jerusalem Delivered*
STOCKDALE, Percival. *The Amyntas*

2705 *Taste. A Satire. In An Epistle to a Friend.* London, n.d. [Cropped; HARVARD CAT.–c. 1746] (Fol. 6d. Bizet) HARVARD (HOUGHTON)

Reviewed: *Monthly Review* 8 (1753): 472

Taste: An Epistle to a Young Critic
See: ARMSTRONG, John

2706 TASWELL, E. *Miscellanea Sacra: Containing the Song of Deborah and Barak; David's Lamentation over Saul and Jonathan, a Pindaric Poem; and the Prayer of Solomon at the Dedication of the Temple*
NOT SEEN (4to. 1s. Burd)

Reviewed: *Monthly Review* 22 (1760): 168

The Taxes, a Dramatic Entertainment
See: BACON, Phanuel

The Tears and Triumphs of Parnassus
See: LLOYD, Robert

2707 *The Tears of Britannia: an Elegiac Poem. Occasioned by The Death of his Most Sacred Majesty King George II.* London, 1760 (4to. 1s. Owen) BRITISH LIBRARY

Reviewed: *Monthly Review* 23 (1760): 527–528

2708 *The Tears of Cambria; a Poem: Inscribed to the Honourable Society of Ancient Britons*
NOT SEEN (4to. 1s.6d. Kearsly. 1773)

Reviewed: *Monthly Review* 48 (1773): 411–412
Critical Review 35 (1773): 394
London Magazine 42 (1773): 249
Universal Catalogue [2] (1773) art. 490

2709 *The Tears of Twickenham. A Poem.* London, 1766 (4to. 1s. White) HARVARD (HOUGHTON)

Reviewed: *Monthly Review* 34 (1766): 481
Critical Review 21 (1766): 393
Gentleman's Magazine 36 (1766): 240–241

2710 TEEDE, Richard. *Corin and Olinda: A Legendary Tale. In Three Parts.* London, 1774 (4to. 1s.6d. Hoggins, &c. 1774) BRITISH LIBRARY

Reviewed: *Monthly Review* 51 (1774): 166
Critical Review 37 (1774): 315
Universal Catalogue 3 (1774) art. 604
Town & Country Magazine 6 (1774): 268

2711 *The Tell-Tale: or, Anecdotes Expressive of the Characters of Persons Eminent for Rank, Learning, Wit, or Humour. Collected from the Best Authors and Best Companions: For the Improvement of Youth in Conversation.* 2 vols. London, 1756 (12mo. 4s. Baldwin) BRITISH LIBRARY

Reviewed: *Monthly Review* 13 (1755): 510

The Tempest. An Opera
See: GARRICK, David

TEMPLE, Launcelot (pseud.)
See: ARMSTRONG, John

2712 *The Temple Beau; or, the Town Coquets. A Novel.* London, 1754 (12mo. 2s.6d. Owen) BRITISH LIBRARY

Reviewed: *Monthly Review* 10 (1754): 148

2713 *The Temple of Compassion; a Poem: Addressed to a Lady, by an Officer in the Guards* NOT SEEN (4to. 1s. Ridley)

Reviewed: *Monthly Review* 44 (1771): 343–344
Critical Review 31 (1771): 157–158
Gentleman's Magazine 41 (1771): 82–84
Town & Country Magazine 3 (1771): 155

2714 *The Temple of Tragedy. A Poetical Essay* NOT SEEN (4to. 1s. Burnet)

Reviewed: *Monthly Review* 32 (1765): 75
Critical Review 18 (1764): 474–475

The Temple of Venus
See: THOMPSON, Edward

The Temple-Student
See: KEATE, George

2715 [TENCIN, Claudine Alexandrine Guerin de]. *The Female Adventurers.* 2 vols. NOT SEEN (12mo. 2s.6d.each. Folingsby)

Reviewed: *Monthly Review* 33 (1765): 490
Critical Review 20 (1765): 384–385

2716 [TENCIN, Claudine Alexandrine Guerin de]. *The Siege of Calais, an Historical Novel. Translated from the French.* 2 vols. London, 1751 (8vo. 3s.sewed. W. Wilson) YALE (STERLING)

Reviewed: *Monthly Review* 4 (1750–51): 476

2717 [TENDUCCI, Giusto Fernando]. *Amintas, an English Opera. As perform'd at the Theatre-Royal in Covent-Garden.* [Altered from Richard Rolt's *The Royal Shepherd.*] London, 1769 (8vo. 1s. Lowndes) BRITISH LIBRARY

Reviewed: *Monthly Review* 41 (1769): 478
Gentleman's Magazine 39 (1769): 600
London Magazine 38 (1769): 642

The tenth epistle of the first book of Horace Imitated
See: GREENE, Edward Burnaby

TERENCE (translations)
See: COLMAN, George (the elder). *The Comedies of Terence*
GORDON, ———. *The Comedies of Terence*

2718 TERES, T. *The Civil War of Geneva, or, the Amours of Robert Covelle, an Heroic Poem, in Five Cantos. Translated from the French of M. de Voltaire.* London, 1769 (12mo. 1s. Durham) BRITISH LIBRARY

Reviewed: *Monthly Review* 41 (1769): 94–98
Critical Review 27 (1769): 397
Gentleman's Magazine 39 (1769): 261

2719 TERES, T. *Richard in Cyprus. A Tragedy.* London, n.d. [ESTC-1769] (8vo. 1s. Blyth) BRITISH LIBRARY

Reviewed: *Monthly Review* 41 (1769): 478
Critical Review 28 (1769): 461–463

The Test of Filial Duty
See: SCOTT, Sarah

2720 *The Test of Friendship: or the History of Lord George B———. and Sir Harry Acton, Bart.* 2 vols.
NOT SEEN (12mo. 6s. Noble)

Reviewed: *Monthly Review* 40 (1769): 86
Critical Review 26 (1768): 312–313
London Magazine 37 (1768): 610
Universal Museum 4 (1768): 541

2721 *The Test of Friendship; or the Royal Adventurers*
NOT SEEN (12mo. 3s. Allen. 1773)

Reviewed: *Monthly Review* 48 (1773): 320
London Magazine 42 (1773): 196
Universal Catalogue [2] (1773) art. 260

2722 *The Theatre of Love. A Collection of Novels, (None of which were ever printed before) Containing, I. Frederick and Harriet: Or, The Discreet Parent. II. Miranda: or, The Favourite Daughter. III. Horatio: Or, The Sincere Friend. IV. Cordelia: Or, The Tender Mother. V. The Cruel Father. VI Clerimont: Or, The Generous Lover. VII. The Lovers Quarrel: Or, The Fatal Resolution. VIII. John and Joan: Or, The Mannerly Couple. IX. Celia: Or, The Generous Maid. X. Innocence in Distress: Or, Virtue Triumphant. XI. The Rival Sisters. XII. Hillario and Leonora: Or, The Unfortunate Lovers. XIII. Jenny: Or, The Female Fortune-Hunter.* London, 1759 (12mo. 3s. Reeve) BRITISH LIBRARY

Reviewed: *Monthly Review* 19 (1758): 498

2723 *The Theatrical Contention. A fable.* N.p., n.d. [ESTC: London, 1752] (Fol. 4d. Owen) BRITISH LIBRARY

Reviewed: *Monthly Review* 7 (1752): 398

2724 *The Theatrical Manager: a Dramatic Satire.* London, 1751 (8vo. 1s. Lowndes) BRITISH LIBRARY

Reviewed: *Monthly Review* 4 (1750–51): 305

2725 *Theatrical Portraits, epigrammatically delineated; wherein The Merit and Demerit of most of our Stage Heroes and Heroines are excellently Painted by some of the best Masters. Inscribed to the Performers of Both Theatres.* London, 1774 (4to. 1s. Bew. 1774) BRITISH LIBRARY

Reviewed: *Monthly Review* 51 (1774): 68
Critical Review 37 (1774): 396
Universal Catalogue 3 (1774) art. 657

Themistocles, a Satire on Modern Marriage
See: MONCRIEFF, John

THEOCRITUS (translation)
See: FAWKES, Francis. *The Idylliums*

THEODOSIA (pseud.)
See: STEELE, Anne

2726 THEOPHILA. *The History of Sir Charles Grandison spiritualized in Part. A Vision. With Reflections thereon. By Theophila*
NOT SEEN (12mo. 1s.6d. Keith)

Reviewed: *Monthly Review* 23 (1760): 255–256
Critical Review 10 (1760): 79

Thespis
See: KELLY, Hugh

2727 *Things as They Are.* London, 1768 (4to. 1s. Bingley) BODLEIAN

Reviewed: *Monthly Review* 39 (1768): 81
Critical Review 25 (1768): 465
Gentleman's Magazine 38 (1768): 386
London Magazine 37 (1768): 390
Political Register 3 (1768): 125

2728 *The Thistle.* London, 1773 (4to. 1s.6d. Bladon. 1773) BRITISH LIBRARY

Reviewed: *Monthly Review* 49 (1773): 65
Critical Review 35 (1773): 474
London Magazine 42 (1773): 302
Universal Catalogue [2] (1773) art. 734

Thomas and Sally: or, The Sailor's Return
See: BICKERSTAFFE, Isaac

2729 [THOMPSON, Edward]. *The Court of Cupid. By the Author of the Meretriciad. Containing the Eighth Edition of the Meretriciad, with great Additions.* 2 vols. London, 1770 (8vo. 5s. Moran) BRITISH LIBRARY

Reviewed: *Critical Review* 30 (1770): 233–234
London Magazine 39 (1770): 530

2730 [THOMPSON, Edward]. *The Courtesan. By the Author of the Meretriciad.* London, 1765 (4to. 2s.6d. Harrison) BRITISH LIBRARY

Reviewed: *Monthly Review* 32 (1765): 393
Critical Review 19 (1765): 313–315
Candid Review 1 (1765): 287

2731 [THOMPSON, Edward]. *The Demi-Rep. By N.O. Author of the Meretriciad.* 1st ed. reviewed; copy seen 2d ed.: London, 1756 [1766] (4to. 2s.6d. Moran) BRITISH LIBRARY

Reviewed: *Monthly Review* 34 (1766): 241–242
Critical Review 21 (1766): 150–151
Gentleman's Magazine 36 (1766): 91

2732 [THOMPSON, Edward]. *The Fair Quaker: or, The Humours of the Navy. Formerly written By Mr. Charles Shadwell, and now alter'd with great Additions and a New Character, by the Author. As it is now performed At the Theatre-Royal in Drury-Lane.* London, 1773 (8vo. 1s. Lowndes, &c. 1773) BRITISH LIBRARY

Reviewed: *Monthly Review* 49 (1773): 394–395
Critical Review 36 (1773): 465–467
Universal Catalogue [2] (1773) art. 1202

2733 [THOMPSON, Edward]. *The Meretriciad.* N.p., 1761 [NEWBERRY CAT.–London] (4to. 2s. Moran) NEWBERRY

Reviewed: *Monthly Review* 25 (1761): 231
Critical Review 12 (1761): 201–203
British Magazine 2 (1761): 550

2734 [THOMPSON, Edward]. *The Soldier. A Poem. Inscribed to The Honourable General Conway.* London, 1764 (4to. 1s.6d. Almon) BRITISH LIBRARY

Reviewed: *Monthly Review* 31 (1764): 232
Critical Review 18 (1764): 160

2735 [THOMPSON, Edward]. *The Temple of Venus. A gentle Satire on the Times. By the Author of the Meretriciad. Part the First.* London, 1763 (4to. 1s. Moran) BRITISH LIBRARY

Reviewed: *Monthly Review* 28 (1763): 318
Critical Review 15 (1763): 229–230
British Magazine 4 (1763): 158

2736 [THOMPSON, Edward]. *The Temple of Venus. Part the Second.* London, 1763 (4to. 1s.6d. Moran) BRITISH LIBRARY

Reviewed: *Monthly Review* 28 (1763): 487
Critical Review 16 (1763): 316

2737 [THOMPSON, Edward]. *Trinculo's Trip to the Jubilee.* London, 1769 (4to. 1s.6d. Moran) NEWBERRY

Reviewed: *Monthly Review* 41 (1769): 393–394
Critical Review 28 (1769): 378
London Magazine 38 (1769): 585

2738 [THOMPSON, Isaac]. *Poetic Essays, on Nature, Men, and Morals. Essay 1. Dr. Askew of Newcastle.* Newcastle upon Tyne & London, 1750 (4to. 29pp. 1s.6d. Printed for Hitch) BRITISH LIBRARY

Reviewed: *Monthly Review* 3 (1750): 34–37

2739 THOMPSON, William. *Poems on Several Occasions, To which is added Gondibert and Birtha, A tragedy.* Oxford, 1757 (8vo. 6s. Rivington and Fletcher) BRITISH LIBRARY

Reviewed: *Monthly Review* 18 (1758): 319–325
Critical Review 5 (1758): 415–419

2740 THOMSON, James. *The Works of James Thomson, With his last Corrections and Improvements. To which is prefixed, An Account of his Life and Writings.* [Ed. Patrick MURDOCH.] 2 vols. London, 1762 (4to. 2l.12s.6d. Millar) BRITISH LIBRARY

Reviewed: *Monthly Review* 26 (1762): 298–305
Critical Review 14 (1762): 122–130
British Magazine 3 (1762): 382

2741 THORN, Theophilus (pseud.). *The Demagogue.* London, 1766 (4to. 1s.6d. Robinson and Roberts) BRITISH LIBRARY

Reviewed: *Monthly Review* 34 (1766): 243
Critical Review 21 (1766): 137–139

2742 THORNTON, Bonnell. *The Battle of the Wigs. An Additional Canto to Dr. Garth's Poem of the Dispensary. Occasioned by The Disputes between the Fellows and Licentiates of the College of Physicians, in London.* London, 1768 (4to. 2s. Davies, &c.) BRITISH LIBRARY

Reviewed: *Monthly Review* 38 (1768): 142–143
Gentleman's Magazine 38 (1768): 132–133
London Magazine 37 (1768): 105
Universal Museum 4 (1768): 148
Political Register 2 (1768): 318

2743 THORNTON, Bonnell. *The Comedies of Plautus, translated into Familiar Blank Verse.* London, 1767 (8vo. 10s. Becket) BRITISH LIBRARY

Reviewed: *Monthly Review* 36 (1767): 177–189
Critical Review 23 (1767): 113–123
London Magazine 36 (1767): 47

2744 THORNTON, Bonnell. *An Ode on St. Caecilia's Day, adapted to The Antient British Musick: viz. The Salt-Box, the Jews Harp, the Marrow-Bones and Cleavers, the Hum-Strum, or Hurdy-Gurdy, &c. With an Introduction, Giving some Account of These Truly British Instruments.* London, 1763 (4to. 1s. Becket and De Hondt) BRITISH LIBRARY

Reviewed: *Monthly Review* 28 (1763): 479–481
Critical Review 15 (1763): 485

THORNTON, Bonnell (ed.). *Poems by eminent Ladies* (with George COLMAN)
See: COLMAN, George (the elder)

2745 *The Thought. A Poem. Address'd to the Ladies.* London, 1753 (Fol. 6d. Robinson) NEW YORK PUBLIC LIBRARY

Reviewed: *Monthly Review* 8 (1753): 238
Gentleman's Magazine 23 (1753): 150

2746 *Thoughts occasioned by the War*
NOT SEEN (4to. 6d. Keith)

Reviewed: *Monthly Review* 16 (1757): 363

2747 *Three Comedies; The Uneasy Man, The Financier, and The Sylph. Freely translated from Messrs. St. Foix and Fagan*
NOT SEEN (8vo. 2s.6d.sewed. Walter. 1771)

Reviewed: *Monthly Review* 45 (1771): 151
Critical Review 31 (1771): 397
Town & Country Magazine 3 (1771): 261

2748 *The Three Conjurers, a Political Interlude. Stolen from Shakespeare. As it was performed at sundry Places in Westminster, On Saturday the 30th of April, and Sunday the 1st of May. Most humbly dedicated to that distressed and unfortunate Gentleman, John Wilkes, Esq; Late Prisoner in the Tower, and late Colonel of the Militia for the County of Buckingham but still a Member of Parliament for Aylesbury.* London, n.d. [ESTC-1763] (4to. 1s. Cabe) BRITISH LIBRARY

Reviewed: *Monthly Review* 28 (1763): 491
Critical Review 15 (1763): 485

Threnodia Augustalis
See: GOLDSMITH, Oliver

TIBULLUS, Albius (translation)
See: GRAINGER, James. *A Poetical Translation of the Elegies of Tibullus*

2749 [TIMBURY, Jane]. *The Male-Coquette: or, the History of the Hon. Edward Astell.* 2 vols. London, 1770 (12mo. 5s.sewed. Robinson and Co.) BRITISH LIBRARY

Reviewed: *Monthly Review* 42 (1770): 72
Critical Review 28 (1769): 450–452
London Magazine 38 (1769): 640

2750 *The Times. A Modest Ode.* London, 1757 (Fol. 6d. Morgan) BRITISH LIBRARY

Reviewed: *Monthly Review* 16 (1757): 363
Critical Review 3 (1757): 380–381

2751 *The Times. A Poem*
NOT SEEN (4to. 1s.6d. Almon. 1769)

Reviewed: *Monthly Review* 40 (1769): 335–336
Critical Review 27 (1769): 471
Gentleman's Magazine 39 (1769): 260–261
Town & Country Magazine [1] (1769): 327
Political Register 4 (1769): 322–323

The Times. A Second Epistle to Flavian
See: CLELAND, John

The Times! An Epistle to Flavian
See: CLELAND, John

Timon of Athens, Altered from Shakespear
See: CUMBERLAND, Richard

Timon of Athens. As it is acted at the Theatre-Royal on Richmond-Green
See: LOVE, James

2752 [TIPHAIGNE DE LA ROCHE, Charles François]. *Amilec; or the Seeds of Mankind. Translated from the French.* [Translation of

Amilec, ou la graine d' hommes.] London, 1753 (12mo. 1s. Needham) BRITISH LIBRARY

Reviewed: *Monthly Review* 9 (1753): 228

'Tis Well it's no Worse
See: BICKERSTAFFE, Isaac

Tittle Tattle; or, Taste-A-la-Mode
See: FRIBBLE, Timothy

Titus Vespasian
See: CLELAND, John

2753 *To Francis Bindon, Esq; on a Picture of his Grace Dr. Hugh Boulter Lord Archbishop of Armagh, set up in the Work-house near Dublin, in Commemoration of his Charities in the Years 1739–40 and 1740–41. By T. D. H. Esq.* NOT SEEN (4to. 1s. Williams)

Reviewed: *Monthly Review* 36 (1767): 489–490
Critical Review 23 (1767): 400

2754 *To the Right Honourable Thomas Harley, late Lord Mayor of London. An Ethic Epistle* NOT SEEN (4to. 6d.)

Reviewed: *Monthly Review* 40 (1769): 340

The Tobacconist
See: GENTLEMAN, Francis

2755 TOLDERVY, William. *The History of Two Orphans.* 4 vols. London, 1756 (12mo. 12s. Owen) BRITISH LIBRARY

Reviewed: *Monthly Review* 15 (1756): 535
Critical Review 2 (1756): 340–343

2756 TOLLET, Elizabeth. *Poems on Several Occasions. With Anne Boleyn to Henry VIII. An Epistle.* London, 1755 (12mo. 2s.6d. Clarke) BRITISH LIBRARY

Reviewed: *Monthly Review* 13 (1755): 373–377

Tombo-Chiqui
See: CLELAND, John

2757 *A too hasty censure, February 15, 1757. And a too necessary retraction, March 20, 1757. Verses relative to the late unhappy A------l* NOT SEEN (Fol. 6d. Doughty)

Reviewed: *Monthly Review* 16 (1757): 363
Critical Review 3 (1757): 377

2758 [TOOKE, William]. *The Loves of Othniel and Achsah. Translated from the Chaldee.* 2 vols. London, 1769 (8vo. 6s.bound. Wilkie. 1769) BRITISH LIBRARY

Reviewed: *Monthly Review* 41 (1769): 272–278
Gentleman's Magazine 39 (1769): 261
London Magazine 38 (1769): 584
Critical Memoirs [2] (1769): 39–43

2759 TOURNAY, T[homas]. *Ambition, An Epistle to Paoli.* London, 1769 (4to. 2s.6d. Dilly. 1769) BODLEIAN

Reviewed: *Monthly Review* 40 (1769): 339–340
Critical Review 27 (1769): 311–313
Critical Memoirs [1] (1769): 522
Political Register 4 (1769): 387

2760 TOUSEY, G[eorge] P[hilip]. *Flights to Helicon: or, Petites Pieces, In Verse.* London, 1768 (12mo. 2s.6d. Newbery) BRITISH LIBRARY

Reviewed: *Monthly Review* 39 (1768): 486–487
Critical Review 26 (1768): 380
Universal Museum 4 (1768): 596

The Tower
See: GREENE, Edward Burnaby

2761 [TOWNLEY, James]. *High Life Below Stairs. A Farce of Two Acts. As it is performed at the Theatre-Royal in Drury-Lane.* London, 1759 (8vo. 1s. Newbery) BRITISH LIBRARY

Reviewed: *Monthly Review* 21 (1759): 449
Critical Review 8 (1759): 394–398
Gentleman's Magazine 29 (1759): 541–543
London Magazine 28 (1759): 631

2762 TOWNLY, Charles. *The Courtezans: a Comedy Of Two Acts: Founded On Truth; and Acted every Night at Drury-Lane and Covent-Garden.* London, 1760 (8vo. 1s. Lewis) BRITISH LIBRARY

Reviewed: *Monthly Review* 22 (1760): 435

2763 *A Tragi-Comic Dialogue, between the Ghost of an A------l, and the Substance of a G------l: Shewing the Difference between A*

Chop and a Pop. By an Antigallican. London, 1749 [1759] (4to. 6d. A. Moore, near St. Paul's) YALE (BEINECKE) [1749 must be misprint; poem concerns Admiral Byng whose court-martial took place at the end of 1756 and execution in March 1757.]

Reviewed: *Monthly Review* 21 (1759): 181
Critical Review 8 (1759): 257

2764 *Translations in Verse. Mr. Pope's Messiah, and Mr. Philips's Splendid Shilling in Latin; The Eighth Isthmian of Pindar in English*. Oxford, 1752 (4to. 1s. Oxford, printed for Fletcher, and sold by Rivington, London) BRITISH LIBRARY

Reviewed: *Monthly Review* 5 (1751): 452–454

2765 TRAPAUD, Elisha. *Aglaura. A Tale. Taken from the French in Marmontel's Moral Tales*. London, 1774 (4to. 1s. Brotherton. 1774) BRITISH LIBRARY

Reviewed: *Monthly Review* 51 (1774): 318
Critical Review 38 (1774): 152
Universal Catalogue [3] (1774) art. 1037

2766 [TRAPAUD, Elisha]. *The Oeconomy of Happiness. A Poem. By E. T.* London, 1772 (4to. 1s. Brotherton. 1772) BRITISH LIBRARY

Reviewed: *Monthly Review* 48 (1773): 160
Critical Review 34 (1772): 470
London Magazine 42 (1773): 92
Universal Catalogue [1] (1772) art. 1485

2767 *The Travels and Adventures of William Bingfield, Esq; containing, As surprizing a Fluctuation of Circumstances, both by Sea and Land, as ever befel one Man. With An accurate Account of the Shape, Nature, and Properties of that most furious, and amazing Animal, the Dog-Bird. Printed from his own Manuscript. With a Beautiful Frontispiece*. 2 vols. London, 1753 (12mo. 5s. Withers) BRITISH LIBRARY

Reviewed: *Monthly Review* 8 (1753): 77

2768 *The Travels of Mons. le Post-Chaise. Written by Himself*. London, 1753 (8vo. 1s. Swan) BRITISH LIBRARY

Reviewed: *Monthly Review* 8 (1753): 311

2769 *The Travels of Mr. Drake Morris, Merchant in London. Containing His Sufferings and Distresses in Several Voyages at Sea. Written by Himself*. London, 1755 (12mo. 3s. Baldwin) BRITISH LIBRARY

Reviewed: *Monthly Review* 11 (1754): 395

The Travels of the Imagination
See: MURRAY, James

2770 *The Travels of Zoroaster, King of the Bactrians. Composed chiefly for the Instruction of a Young Prince*. 3 vols. London, 1753 (12mo. 9s. Fuller) BRITISH LIBRARY

Reviewed: *Monthly Review* 9 (1753): 228–229

2771 TREYSSAC DE VERGY, [Pierre Henri]. *Henrietta, Countess Osenvor, a sentimental Novel, in a series of Letters To Lady Susannah Fitzroy*. 2 vols. London, 1770 (12mo. 6s. bound. Roson) BODLEIAN

Reviewed: *Monthly Review* 42 (1770): 488
Critical Review 30 (1770): 316

2772 TREYSSAC DE VERGY, [Pierre Henri]. *The Lovers: or the Memoirs of Lady Sarah B——— and The Countess P———. Published by Mr. Treyssac de Vergy, Counsellor in the Parliament of Paris*. London, 1769 (8vo. 5s. Roson) BRITISH LIBRARY

Reviewed: *Monthly Review* 41 (1769): 480–481
Critical Review 28 (1769): 353–357

2773 TREYSSAC DE VERGY, [Pierre Henri]. *The Lovers: or, the Memoirs of Lady Mary Sc—————, and the Hon. Miss Amelia B—————. Vol. II.* London, 1772 (8vo. 5s. Printed for the Editor, and sold by the Booksellers. 1772) BRITISH LIBRARY

Reviewed: *Monthly Review* 46 (1772): 263
Critical Review 33 (1772): 83
Gentleman's Magazine 42 (1772): 85
Universal Catalogue [1] (1772) art. 111

2774 TREYSSAC DE VERGY, [Pierre Henri]. *The Mistakes of the Heart: or, Memoirs of Lady Carolina Pelham and Lady Victoria Nevil. In a Series of Letters. Published by M. Treyssac de Vergy, Counsellor in the Parliaments of Paris*

and Bourdeaux. 3 vols. London, 1769 (12mo. 7s.6d.sewed. Murdoch) BRITISH LIBRARY

Reviewed: *Monthly Review* 40 (1769): 511
Critical Review 28 (1769): 282
Gentleman's Magazine 39 (1769): 261
London Magazine 38 (1769): 213
Critical Memoirs [2] (1769): 43–48
Town & Country Magazine [1] (1769): 213

2775 TREYSSAC DE VERGY, [Pierre Henri]. *The Mistakes of the Heart: or, Memoirs of Lady Carolina Pelham, and Lady Victoria Nevil. In a Series of Letters. Vol. IV. and last*
NOT SEEN (12mo. 2s.6d. Shatwell. 1771)

Reviewed: *Monthly Review* 46 (1772): 164
Critical Review 33 (1772): 182

2776 TREYSSAC DE VERGY, [Pierre Henri]. *Nature*
NOT SEEN (12mo. 3s. Murdoch)

Reviewed: *Critical Review* 30 (1770): 316
London Magazine 39 (1770): 580

2777 TREYSSAC DE VERGY, [Pierre Henri]. *The Palinode: or, The Triumphs of Virtue over Love. A sentimental Novel. In which are painted to the Life the Characters and Manners of some of the most celebrated Beauties in England*. 2 vols.
NOT SEEN (12mo. 5s.sewed. Woodfall and Evans)

Reviewed: *Monthly Review* 45 (1771): 73
Critical Review 32 (1771): 230
London Magazine 40 (1771): 226

2778 TREYSSAC DE VERGY, [Pierre Henri]. *The Scotchman; or, the World as it goes: a Novel. By Mr. Treyssac de Vergy*. 2 vols.
NOT SEEN (12mo. 5s.sewed. Brough)

Reviewed: *Monthly Review* 43 (1770): 66
Critical Review 30 (1770): 316–317
London Magazine 39 (1770): 268

2779 *The Trial for Murder, or, the Siege of Calais besieg'd; Inscribed to Lord ---- and Mons. de Belloy*. London, 1765 (4to. 2s.6d. Moran) HARVARD (HOUGHTON)

Reviewed: *Monthly Review* 33 (1765): 85
Critical Review 20 (1765): 72

2780 *The Trial of Abraham. In Four Cantos. Translated from the German*
NOT SEEN (8vo. 2s. Becket and DeHondt)

Reviewed: *Monthly Review* 30 (1764): 324
Critical Review 17 (1764): 180–184

The Trial of Dramatic Genius
See: HEARD, William. *The Tryal of Dramatic Genius*

The trial of Hercules
See: COOKE, Thomas. *The Tryal of Hercules*

The Trial of the Time-Killers.
See: BACON, Phanuel. *The Tryal of the Time-Killers*

2781 *The Trial: or, the History of Charles Horton, Esq. By a Gentleman.* 3 vols. London ed. reviewed; copy seen: Dublin, 1772 (12mo. 9s. Vernor) BRITISH LIBRARY

Reviewed: *Monthly Review* 46 (1772): 79
Critical Review 33 (1772): 83
Gentleman's Magazine 42 (1772): 85
Town & Country Magazine 4 (1772): 100
British Magazine & General Review 1 (1772): 337–340
Universal Catalogue [1] (1772) art. 101

Trinculo's Trip to the Jubilee
See: THOMPSON, Edward

2782 *The Trinket. A Novel. By a Lady*. London, 1774 (12mo. 3s. Lowndes. 1774) BRITISH LIBRARY

Reviewed: *Monthly Review* 50 (1774): 327
Critical Review 37 (1774): 475
London Magazine 43 (1774): 143
Universal Catalogue 3 (1774) art. 338

The Trip to Portsmouth
See: STEVENS, George Alexander

A Trip to Scotland
See: WHITEHEAD, William

2783 *Tristram Shandy at Ranelagh*
NOT SEEN (8vo. 1s. Dunstan)

Reviewed: *Monthly Review* 22 (1760): 548
London Magazine 29 (1760): 328

2784 *Tristram Shandy in a Reverie*
NOT SEEN (8vo. 1s. Williams)

Reviewed: *Monthly Review* 22 (1760): 549
Critical Review 9 (1760): 493

2785 *Triumph in Death, or Death Triumphant, exemplified in the Death of the late glorious, and ever blessed in Memory, Major General Wolfe*
NOT SEEN (4to. 6d. Thrush)

Reviewed: *Monthly Review* 21 (1759): 455
Critical Review 15 (1763): 237
London Magazine 28 (1759): 631

2786 *The Triumph of Benevolence; or, the History of Francis Wills*. 2 vols. London, 1772 (12mo. 5s.sewed. Verner, &c. 1772) BRITISH LIBRARY [ESTC: variously attributed to Arthur Murphy and to Oliver Goldsmith]

Reviewed: *Monthly Review* 46 (1772): 457
Critical Review 33 (1772): 255
London Magazine 41 (1772): 543
British Magazine & General Review 1 (1772): 340–342
Universal Catalogue [1] (1772) art. 432

2787 *The Triumph of Brutes. A Satire on this Caledonian Age*. London, 1763 (4to. 1s.6d. Pridden) FOLGER

Reviewed: *Monthly Review* 28 (1763): 238
Critical Review 15 (1763): 237
British Magazine 4 (1763): 158

2788 *The Triumph of Death. A Poem. In Memory of The Right Honourable Henry Pelham. Imitated from Petrarch*. London, 1754 (4to. 6d. Dodsley) BRITISH LIBRARY

Listed: *Monthly Review* 10 (1754): 305
Reviewed: *Gentleman's Magazine* 24 (1754): 146

The Triumph of Fashion; a Vision
See: PYE, Henry James

2789 *The Triumph of Love and Beauty; or, the History of Mr. Wallace and his family. In Four Books*. 2 vols. London, 1768 (no pub. details) UNIVERSITY OF PENNSYLVANIA

Reviewed: *London Magazine* 37 (1768): 276–277

2790 *The Triumphant Christian: or, a Sight of Heaven in Dying. A Poem, on the much lamented Death of Mr. Joseph Weatherill*
NOT SEEN (8vo. 4d. Buckland, Ward, &c.)

Reviewed: *Monthly Review* 5 (1751): 464

2791 *The Triumphs of Bigotry. A Poem, sacred to the peaceful Memory of Charistes. Inscribed to the Reverend Mr. Thomas Bradbury. By a Lady*. London, 1749 (4to. 14pp. 6d. Cooper) BRITISH LIBRARY

Reviewed: *Monthly Review* 2 (1740–50): 6–8

2792 *The Triumphs of Britannia. A Poem. Humbly inscribed to George Robert Fitzgerald, Esq.* London, 1773 (4to. 2s. Snagg. 1773) BRITISH LIBRARY

Reviewed: *Monthly Review* 49 (1773): 316
Critical Review 36 (1773): 315
Town & Country Magazine 5 (1773): 602
Universal Catalogue [2] (1773) art. 1115

2793 *The Triumphs of Bute. A Poem*. London, 1770 (4to. 1s. Swan) HARVARD (HOUGHTON)

Reviewed: *Monthly Review* 43 (1770): 484
Critical Review 30 (1770): 311–312
London Magazine 39 (1770): 580
Town & Country Magazine 2 (1770): 599

The Triumvirate: or, the Authentic Memoirs of A. B. and C.
See: GRIFFITH, Richard

2794 TRIVETT, Edward. *Hymns and Spiritual Songs. In Two Books. I. Collected from the Scriptures, and suited to the Gospel. II. Prepar'd for Baptism, and the Lord's Supper*. London, 1755 (12mo. 2s. Keith) BRITISH LIBRARY

Reviewed: *Monthly Review* 13 (1755): 459

TROTTER, Catharine
See: COCKBURN, Catharine

2795 *The Troublers of Israel. In Which The Principles Of Those Who turn The World Upside Down Are Displayed. With A Preface To The Rev. Dr. ----. To Which Is Prefixed, A Short*

Introductory Description Of Modern Enthusiasts. London, 1767 (4to. 1s.6d. Keith) YALE (STERLING)

Reviewed: *Monthly Review* 38 (1768): 70
Critical Review 25 (1768): 235

True Blue; or, the Press-Gang
See: CAREY, Henry

2796 *The True-Born Scot: inscribed to John Earl Of Bute.* London, 1764 (4to. 1s. Sumpter) YALE (BEINECKE)

Reviewed: *Monthly Review* 31 (1764): 232
Critical Review 18 (1764): 159
British Magazine 5 (1764): 433

2797 *The true Cause of a certain G-----l Officer's Conduct, on the first of August last, in which All former Explanations are Explained away.* London, 1759 (4to. 1s. Stephens) BRITISH LIBRARY

Reviewed: *Monthly Review* 21 (1759): 269
Critical Review 8 (1759): 257
London Magazine 28 (1759): 512

2798 *True Delicacy; or, the History of Lady Frances Tylney, and Henry Cecil, Esq;* 2 vols. London, 1769 (12mo. 6d. Noble) BRITISH LIBRARY

Reviewed: *Monthly Review* 39 (1768): [163]
Critical Review 27 (1769): 151
London Magazine 37 (1768): 445
Political Register 3 (1768): 128

True Merit, true Happiness
See: DIGARD DE KERGUETTE, Jean

2799 [TRUSLER, John]. *An Elegy on the Fears of Death. By the Author of The Difference between Words reputed Synonimous, after the Manner of Girard; Hogarth moralized, &c. &c.* London, n.d. [ESTC-1780?] (4to. 1s.6d. Bell. 1774) BRITISH LIBRARY

Reviewed: *Monthly Review* 50 (1774): 315-316
Critical Review 37 (1774): 315-316
Universal Catalogue 3 (1774) art. 215

Truth and Falshood: a Tale
See: FRANCKLIN, Thomas

Truth, in Rhyme: addressed to a certain Noble Lord
See: MALLET, David

The Tryal of Dramatic Genius
See: HEARD, William

The Tryal of the Time-Killers
See: BACON, Phanuel

2800 TUCKER, Nathaniel. *The Bermudian: a Poem.* London, 1774 (4to. 1s.6d. Cadell. 1774) BRITISH LIBRARY

Reviewed: *Monthly Review* 50 (1774): 371-375
Critical Review 38 (1774): 75
Gentleman's Magazine 44 (1774): 325
Town & Country Magazine 5 (1774): 437
Universal Catalogue 3 (1774) art. 510

2801 *Tunbridge Epistles, from Lady Margaret to The Countess of B**.* London, 1767 (4to. 1s.6d. Cadell) BRITISH LIBRARY

Reviewed: *Monthly Review* 36 (1767): 409
Critical Review 23 (1767): 218-220
Gentleman's Magazine 37 (1767): 262

A Turkish Tale. In Five Cantos
See: GRAY, George

2802 *Turncoat, a Parody Of the Tragedy of Athelstan. In One Act.* London, 1756 (8vo. 1s. Vaillant) BRITISH LIBRARY

Reviewed: *Monthly Review* 15 (1756): 202
Critical Review 1 (1756): 569-570

2803 TURNER, Daniel. *The Contrast; or the dying Profligate, and the dying Christian, in two Poetical Essays*
NOT SEEN (4to. 6d. Johnston)

Reviewed: *Monthly Review* 38 (1768): 149
Critical Review 25 (1768): 233-235
London Magazine 37 (1768): 43
Universal Museum 4 (1768): 148

2804 [TURNER, Daniel]. *The Fashionable Daughter. Being a Narrative of True and Recent Facts. By an Impartial Hand. In Four Parts.* London, 1774 (12mo. 3s. Domville. 1774) BRITISH LIBRARY

Reviewed: *Monthly Review* 50 (1774): 234–235
Critical Review 37 (1774): 77
London Magazine 43 (1774): 38

The Tutor; or, the History of George Wilson and Lady Fanny Melfont
See: KELLY, Hugh

2805 *'Twas Right to Marry him; or, the History of Miss Petworth.* 2 vols. London, 1774 (12mo. 6s. Noble. 1774) BRITISH LIBRARY

Reviewed: *Monthly Review* 50 (1774): 233
Critical Review 36 (1773): 476
Town & Country Magazine 6 (1774): 45
Universal Catalogue [2] (1773) art. 1333

2806 *'Twas Wrong to Marry Him; or, the History of Lady Dursley.* 2 vols. London, 1773 (12mo. 6s. Noble) UNIVERSITY OF PENNSYLVANIA

Reviewed: *Monthly Review* 48 (1773): 320
Critical Review 35 (1773): 78
London Magazine 42 (1773): 91
Town & Country Magazine 5 (1773): 210
Universal Catalogue [2] (1773) art. 128

The Twentieth Epistle of Horace To His Book
See: MARRIOTT, Thomas

2807 *The Twenty-Fourth of May. An Ode On his Royal Highness The Prince of Wales's Birth-Day. By J. M.* London, 1752 (4to. 6d. Wilson and Durham) BRITISH LIBRARY

Reviewed: *Monthly Review* 7 (1752): 78

2808 TWIGEM, Ferdinand (pseud.). *The Macaroni. A Satire.* London, 1773 (4to. 1s. Allen. 1773) BRITISH LIBRARY

Reviewed: *Monthly Review* 48 (1773): 319
Universal Catalogue [2] (1773) art. 379

2809 *Two Elegies*
NOT SEEN (Fol. 1s. Flexney)

Reviewed: *Monthly Review* 38 (1768): 408
Critical Review 25 (1768): 233
Universal Museum 4 (1768): 148

Two Elegies. I. The Bee. II. The Bulfinch.
See: CLEAVER, William

Two Epistles on Happiness: To a Young Lady
See: LLOYD, Robert

Two Gentlemen of Verona
See: VICTOR, Benjamin

Two Lyric Epistles
See: STEVENSON, John Hall

2810 *Two Lyric Essays. I. An Ode to Genius. II. An Ode to Independence.*
NOT SEEN (4to. 1s. Becket. 1772)

Reviewed: *Monthly Review* 46 (1772): 454–455
Critical Review 33 (1772): 170
Universal Catalogue [1] (1772) art. 272

Two Lyrick Epistles
See: STEVENSON, John Hall

2811 *Two New Comic Satiric Dialogues That lately passed in The Tower. The First, Between John Wilkes, Esq. Member of Parliament for Aylesbury, and Two of his Majesty's Lions. The Second, Between that Gentleman, and the Shade of the late Sir William W******m. In which are introduced several modern Political Characters and entertaining Anecdotes, with Explanatory Notes to the Whole. To which is added, A Genuine Account of the whole Proceedings against John Wilkes, Esq. from his Commitment to the Tower, to his Discharge in the Common-Pleas. With all the Speeches, Letters, &c. &c. &c.* London, 1763 (8vo. 6d. Pridden) CAMBRIDGE

Reviewed: *Monthly Review* 28 (1763): 489
Critical Review 15 (1763): 393

Two Novels. In Letters
See: GRIFFITH, Elizabeth and Richard

Two Odes (London, 1760)
See: COLMAN, George (the elder), and Robert LLOYD

2812 *Two Odes; to Fortitude, and an Easy Chair*
NOT SEEN (4to. 1s. Folingsby)

Reviewed: *Monthly Review* 46 (1772): 537
Critical Review 33 (1772): 328
Universal Catalogue [1] (1772) art. 590

2813 *Two Odes. To Indolence, and to Impudence.* London, 1762 (4to. 1s. Dodsley) BODLEIAN

Reviewed: *Monthly Review* 26 (1762): 473–474
Critical Review 13 (1762): 443–444
British Magazine 3 (1762): 324

2814 *Two pastorals in the manner of Mr. Pope's* NOT SEEN (1s.6d. Crowder)

Reviewed: *Gentleman's Magazine* 24 (1754): 534

Tyburn to the Marine Society. A Poem
See: MALLET, David

2815 TYPO, Dr. (pseud.). *The affecting History of two young Gentlewomen, who were ruined by their excessive Attachments to the Amusements of the Town. By Dr. Typo, P.T.M.* NOT SEEN (12mo. 1s. Baldwin)

Reviewed: *Monthly Review* 39 (1768): 410
Critical Review 26 (1768): 313–314
Universal Museum 4 (1768): 541

TYRTAEUS. *Elegies . . . translated into English Verse*
See: CLEAVER, William

2816 UNDERWOOD, T[homas]. *The Impartialist. A Poem.* London, 1767 (4to. 1s.6d. Webley) BRITISH LIBRARY

Reviewed: *Monthly Review* 36 (1767): 239
Critical Review 23 (1767): 143

2817 UNDERWOOD, T[homas]. *Liberty, a Poem. By T. Underwood, Late of St. Peter's College, Cambridge, Author of the Impartialist, &c.* London, 1768 (4to. 2s.6d. Bladon) HARVARD (Houghton)

Reviewed: *Monthly Review* 38 (1768): 248
Critical Review 25 (1768): 152
London Magazine 37 (1768): 111
Universal Museum 4 (1768): 93

2818 UNDERWOOD, T[homas]. *Poems, &c.* Bath, 1768 (8vo. 5s. Dodsley) BRITISH LIBRARY

Reviewed: *Monthly Review* 39 (1768): 80
Critical Review 25 (1768): 391–392
Universal Museum 4 (1768): 93

2819 UNDERWOOD, T[homas]. *The Snarlers. A Poem.* London, 1767 (4to. 1s.6d. Moran) BODLEIAN

Reviewed: *Monthly Review* 36 (1767): 79
Critical Review 23 (1767): 61

2820 UNDERWOOD, T[homas]. *A Word to the Wise. A Poetical Farce, Most respectfully addressed to the Critical Reviewers.* London, 1770 (8vo. 1s. Noteman) BODLEIAN

Reviewed: *Critical Review* 29 (1770): 316
London Magazine 39 (1770): 211

2821 *The Undutiful Daughter; or, the History of Miss Goodwin. In a Series of Letters. In Three Volumes.* London, 1771 (12mo. 7s.6d.sewed. Noble) UNIVERSITY OF ILLINOIS

Reviewed: *Monthly Review* 43 (1770): 400
Critical Review 30 (1770): 396–397
London Magazine 39 (1770): 631–632

2822 *The Unequal Alliance; or, the History of Lord Ashford.* 2 vols.
NOT SEEN (12mo. 5s.sewed. Noble)

Reviewed: *Monthly Review* 46 (1772): 539
Critical Review 33 (1772): 411–412
Universal Catalogue [1] (1772) art. 583

2823 *The Unexpected Wedding, in a Series of Letters.* London, 1768 (Small 8vo. 2s.6d. Becket) BRITISH LIBRARY

Reviewed: *Monthly Review* 38 (1768): 249
Critical Review 25 (1768): 212–213
Universal Museum 4 (1768): 204
Political Register 2 (1768): 384

2824 *The Unfashionable Wife. A Novel. In Two Volumes.* 2 vols. London, 1772 (12mo. 6s. Lowndes. 1772) LIBRARY OF CONGRESS

Reviewed: *Monthly Review* 46 (1772): 78
Critical Review 32 (1771): 392

2825 *The Unfortunate Beauty: Or Memoirs of Miss Anna Maria Soames, And several Others; A Narrative founded on Known Facts, interspersed with several uncommon Characters, and exemplified in the many Instances that befel them during the Course of many Years Court-*

ship and unsuccessful Love. London, 1757 (8vo. 3s. Scott) HARVARD (HOUGHTON)

Reviewed: *Monthly Review* 16 (1757): 452
Critical Review 4 (1757): 461

2826 *The unguarded Moment.* 2 vols. NOT SEEN (12mo. 5s.sewed. Almon. 1771)

Reviewed: *Monthly Review* 45 (1771): 74
Critical Review 31 (1771): 482

2827 *The Unhappy Memorable Old Song, (as it is called) Of the Hunting of Chevy Chase; imitated. In a Spick and Span New Ballad, accomodated to the Present Times.* London, 1761 (Fol. 6d. Taylor) BRITISH LIBRARY

Reviewed: *Monthly Review* 25 (1761): 399
Critical Review 12 (1761): 399

2828 *The Unhappy Wife, A Series of Letters. By a Lady.* 2 vols. London, 1770 (12mo. 5s.sewed. Newbery) BRITISH LIBRARY

Reviewed: *Monthly Review* 42 (1770): 250
Critical Review 29 (1770): 474–475
London Magazine 39 (1770): 378

The Union: or select Scots and English Poems
See: WARTON, Thomas (ed.)

The Upholsterer
See: MURPHY, Arthur

2829 *The Upper Gallery. A Poem.* London, 1753 (4to. 6d.) BRITISH LIBRARY

Reviewed: *Monthly Review* 8 (1753): 151

2830 UPTON, Robert. *Poems, on Several Occasions. Containing, I. On Retirement. A Miltonic Essay. II. Isaiah, chap.xi.versify'd. III. Rural Happiness. IV. Philander's Petition. V. The Fortunate Clown. VI. The Lucky Minute. VII. Advice to Daphne. VIII. Songs. IX. Epigrams.* London, 1750 (8vo. 1s. W. Reeve) BRITISH LIBRARY

Reviewed: *Monthly Review* 4 (1750–51): 303

2831 [VALPY, Richard]. *Poetical Blossoms; or, a Collection of Poems, Odes, and Translations. By a young Gentleman of the Royal Grammar School, Guildford.* Guildford, 1772 (4to. 2s.6d. Hawes, Clarke and Collins, 1774) BRITISH LIBRARY

Reviewed: *Monthly Review* 47 (1772): 408–410
London Magazine 41 (1772): 543
Universal Catalogue [1] (1772) art. 1294

VAN SCELTER, Helter (pseud.)
See: RIDLEY, James

2832 VANE, L. (trans.). *The History of the Life of Tamerlane the Great. From the Time of his being made Regent of Sachetay till his Death. Originally written in Arabic By Alhacen, a learned Arabian. Translated, abridged and methodized, from the French of Jean du Bec, Abbot of Mortemer. With Political Notes.* London, 1750 (8vo. 150pp. 3s.bound. Owen) BRITISH LIBRARY

Reviewed: *Monthly Review* 3 (1750): 45–47

2833 *The Vanity of Human Life, a Monody. Sacred to the Memory of The Most Hon. Francis Russel, Marquis of Tavistock.* London, 1767 (4to. 1s. Dodsley) BRITISH LIBRARY

Reviewed: *Monthly Review* 36 (1767): 409
Critical Review 23 (1767): 297

2834 *The Vanity of Human Wishes; or, the History of Sir James Scudamore, Bart.* London ed. reviewed; copy seen: Dublin, 1768 (12mo. 6s. Robinson and Roberts) BRITISH LIBRARY

Reviewed: *Monthly Review* 38 (1768): 248–249
Critical Review 25 (1768): 52–53
Universal Museum 4 (1768): 93
Political Register 2 (1768): 384

2835 *The Vanity of Philosophick Systems. A Poem. Addressed to the Royal Society.* London, 1761 (4to. 1s. Millar) BRITISH LIBRARY

Reviewed: *Monthly Review* 24 (1761): 470
Critical Review 11 (1761): 497

2836 [VAUGHAN, Thomas]. *The Retort. By the Author.* London, 1761 (4to. 1s. Flexney) BODLEIAN

Reviewed: *Monthly Review* 25 (1761): 477
Critical Review 12 (1761): 400
British Magazine 2 (1761): 606

2837 *The Veil Unrent; or, A Walk in the Tombs. A Poem. With the Death-bed Scene*
NOT SEEN (4to. 6d. T. Baldwin)

Reviewed: *Monthly Review* 41 (1769): 72

2838 *Venus Unmasked: or, an Inquiry into the Nature and Origin of the Passion of Love. Interspersed with Curious and Entertaining Accounts of several Modern Amours. In Two Volumes.* London, 1759 (12mo. 3s. Thrush) BRITISH LIBRARY

Reviewed: *Monthly Review* 21 (1759): 169–171

Ver-Vert: or, the Nunnery Parrot
See: COOPER, John Gilbert

2839 VERITAS (pseud.). *The Triumvirate, A Poetical Portrait. Taken from the Life, and finish'd after the manner of Swift. By Veritas, an unknown hand.* London, 1761 (4to. 1s. Kearsly) BODLEIAN

Reviewed: *Monthly Review* 25 (1761): 319–320
Critical Review 12 (1761): 318–319

2840 VERNON, William. *Poems on several Occasions. By William Vernon. A Private Soldier in the Buffs.* London, 1758 (12mo. 3s. Reeve) BRITISH LIBRARY

Reviewed: *Monthly Review* 19 (1758): 407–408

2841 VEROVICENSIS SENESCENS (pseud.). *Public Spirit; an Ode. By Verovicensis Senescens*
NOT SEEN (4to. 1s. Birmingham printed, and sold in London by Baldwin. 1773)

Reviewed: *Monthly Review* 48 (1773): 410
Critical Review 36 (1773): 155
London Magazine 42 (1773): 196
Universal Catalogue [2] (1773) art. 486

2842 *Verses Addressed to John Wilkes, Esq; on his Arrival at Lynn*
NOT SEEN (4to. 6d. Whittingham at Lynn, Baldwin in London. 1771)

Reviewed: *Monthly Review* 44 (1771): 259–260
Critical Review 31 (1771): 315
Gentleman's Magazine 41 (1771): 228

2843 *Verses Addressed to no Minister.* London, 1763 (4to. 6d. Nicoll) BRITISH LIBRARY

Reviewed: *Monthly Review* 29 (1763): 227
Critical Review 16 (1763): 232

2844 *Verses addressed to the King.* London, 1760 (4to. 6d. Dodsley) BODLEIAN

Reviewed: *Monthly Review* 23 (1760): 411
Critical Review 10 (1760): 406

Verses in Memory of a Lady
See: LANGHORNE, John

2845 *Verses Occasioned by Mr. Warburton's Late Edition of Mr. Pope's Works.* London, 1751 (8vo. 6d. Cooper) BRITISH LIBRARY

Reviewed: *Monthly Review* 5 (1751): 522–523

2846 *Verses occasioned by the Victory at Rosbach*
NOT SEEN (4to. 6d. Owen)

Reviewed: *Monthly Review* 18 (1758): 186

Verses on Miss C———s and Miss W———t
See: WARTON, Thomas

2847 *Verses on the Approach of Peace*
NOT SEEN (4to. 3d. Horsfield)

Reviewed: *Critical Review* 18 (1764): 473

2848 *Verses on the Coronation Of their Late Majesties King George II. and Queen Caroline, October 11, MDCCXXVII. Spoken by the Scholars of Westminster School, (some of them Now the Ornaments of the Nation).* London, 1761 (8vo. 2s. Dodsley) BRITISH LIBRARY

Reviewed: *Monthly Review* 25 (1761): 228
Critical Review 12 (1761): 235

Verses on the Demise of the late King
See: LOCKMAN, John

2849 *Verses to the memory of the late Sir Theodore Janssen, bart. father to the right hon. Stephen Theodore Janssen, esq; the present lord mayor. With notes, wherein is given a short historical account of him and his family*
NOT SEEN (Fol. 6d. Robinson)

Reviewed: *Monthly Review* 11 (1754): 399

2850 *Verses to the Right Honourable Robert Lord Clive, Baron Plassey*
NOT SEEN (4to. 6d. Johnston)

Reviewed: *Monthly Review* 25 (1761): 508
Critical Review 13 (1762): 79–80

2851 *Verses Written in London, on the Approach of Spring.* London, 1759 (4to. 1s. Dodsley) CAMBRIDGE

Reviewed: *Monthly Review* 20 (1759): 474–475

The Vestry, a Poem
See: ELLIOT, N.

2852 *The Vicar of Bray: a Tale.* 2 vols. London, 1771 (12mo. 5s.sewed. Baldwin) BRITISH LIBRARY

Reviewed: *Monthly Review* 44 (1771): 334
Critical Review 32 (1771): 78
London Magazine 40 (1771): 162

The Vicar of Wakefield
See: GOLDSMITH, Oliver

2853 *Vice, a Satire.* London, 1774 (4to. 1s. Bew. 1774) BRITISH LIBRARY

Reviewed: *Monthly Review* 51 (1774): 166
Critical Review 37 (1774): 157
London Magazine 43 (1774): 144
Town & Country Magazine 6 (1774): 155
Universal Catalogue 3 (1774) art. 247

The Viceroy: A Poem
See: LANGHORNE, John

2854 *The Vicissitudes of Fortune: or, the History of Miss Sedley. In Two Volumes.* London, 1773 (12mo. 5s.sewed. Jones. 1773) HARVARD (HOUGHTON)

Reviewed: *Monthly Review* 48 (1773): 320
Critical Review 34 (1772): 473
Universal Catalogue [1] (1772) art. 1490

2855 *The Victim. A Poem. Inscribed to John Wilkes, Esq.* London, 1768 (4to. 1s.6d. Steare) BRITISH LIBRARY

Reviewed: *Monthly Review* 39 (1768): 165
Critical Review 25 (1768): 309
London Magazine 37 (1768): 334
Universal Museum 4 (1768): 205

2856 [VICTOR, Benjamin]. *The Two Gentlemen of Verona. A Comedy, Written by Shakespeare. With Alterations and Additions. As it is performed at the Theatre-Royal in Drury-Lane.* London, 1763 (8vo. 1s. Tonson) BRITISH LIBRARY

Reviewed: *Monthly Review* 28 (1763): 75

VIDA, Marcus Hieronymus (translations)
See: CRANWELL, John. *The Christiad*
GRANAN, Edward. *The Christiad*
PULLEIN, Samuel. *The Silk-worm*

A View of Life in its several Passions
See: FORTESCUE, James

Village Memoirs
See: CRADOCK, Joseph

The Village Oppress'd a Poem
See: ROBINSON, John

The Village Wedding
See: LOVE, James

2857 *The Vindication: or, Day-Thoughts on Wisdom and Goodness: Occasioned by the Complaint; or, Night-Thoughts on Life, Death, and Immortality.* London, 1753 (4to. 1s. Noon) BRITISH LIBRARY

Reviewed: *Monthly Review* 9 (1753): 235–236

2858 VIRGIL (Publius VIRGILIUS MARO). *The works of Virgil, In Latin and English. The original Text correctly printed from the most authentic Edition, collated for this Purpose. The Aeneid Translated By the Rev. Mr. Christophr Pitt, The Eclogues and Georgics, with Notes on the Whole, By the Rev. Mr. Joseph Warton. With several New Observations By Mr. Holdsworth, Mr. Spence, and Others. Also, A Dissertation on the Sixth Book of the Aeneid, by Mr. Warburton. On the Shield of Aeneas, by Mr. W. Whitehead. On the Character of Japis, by the late Dr. Atterbury, Bishop of Rochester. And, Three Essays on Pastoral, Didactic and*

Epic Poetry, by the Editor. 4 vols. London, 1753 (8vo. 20s. Dodsley) BRITISH LIBRARY

Reviewed: *Monthly Review* 8 (1753): 161–176

VIRGIL (translations)
See: ANDREWS, Robert. *The Works of Virgil Englished*
HAWKINS, William. *The Aeneid of Virgil*
NEVILE, Thomas. *The Georgics*
PEACOCK, James. *The First Pastoral of Virgil*
STRAHAN, Alexander. *The Aeneid of Virgil*
STRAHAN, Alexander. *The first six books of Virgil's Aeneid*

Virginia. A Tragedy
See: CRISP, Samuel

2859 *Virtue. A Poem on the breaking out of the war between England and France, in 1756*
NOT SEEN (4to. 6d. Morgan)

Reviewed: *Monthly Review* 15 (1756): 319–320

2860 *Virtue, an Ethic Epistle.* London, 1759 (4to. 6d. Griffiths) HARVARD (HOUGHTON)

Reviewed: *Monthly Review* 19 (1758): 590–591
Critical Review 7 (1759): 81
Gentleman's Magazine 28 (1758): 600–601

2861 *Virtue in Distress; or, the History of Miss Sally Pruen, and Miss Laura Spencer. By a Farmer's Daughter in Glocestershire*
NOT SEEN (12mo. 3s. Fuller. 1772)

Reviewed: *Monthly Review* 46 (1772): 264
Critical Review 33 (1772): 327
British Magazine & General Review 1 (1772): 446
Universal Catalogue [1] (1772) art. 99

Virtue the source of Pleasure
See: BARNARD, Edward

2862 *Virtue triumphant, and Pride abased; In the Humorous History of Dickey Gotham, and Doll Clod; Digested from Antient Tractates, and the Records of those memorable Families, now extant at Addle Hall, in Nottinghamshire. By R. P. biographer.* 2 vols. London, 1753 (12mo. 6s. Cooper) BRITISH LIBRARY

Reviewed: *Monthly Review* 7 (1752): 470

2863 *The Virtuous Criminal; or, the History of Lord Stanley. Translated from the French. In Two Volumes.* London, 1759 (12mo. 6s. Noble) HARVARD (HOUGHTON)

Reviewed: *Monthly Review* 20 (1759): 81

2864 *The Vision. A divine poem*
NOT SEEN (Fol. 6d. Dodsley)

Reviewed: *Monthly Review* 8 (1753): 472

2865 *The Vision. A poem, addressed to Sir Crisp Gascoigne, knt.*
NOT SEEN (Fol. 6d. Cooper)

Reviewed: *Monthly Review* 10 (1754): 304
Gentleman's Magazine 24 (1754): 193

2866 *The Vision of Mirza; Versified from the Spectator, Number CLIX.* London, 1753 (Fol. 6d. Payne) BODLEIAN

Reviewed: *Monthly Review* 9 (1753): 478

Visions in Verse
See: COTTON, Nathaniel

2867 *The Visitation; or, an Interview between The Ghost of Shakespear and D–v–d G–rr–k, Esq;* London, 1755 (4to. 6d. Corbet) BRITISH LIBRARY

Reviewed: *Monthly Review* 13 (1755): 459

2868 *The Visitations of the Almighty. A Poem. Inscribed to Her Grace the Dutchess of Queensberry and Dover. Part the First.* London, 1759 (4to. 1s.6d. Woodfall) YALE (STERLING)

Reviewed: *Monthly Review* 20 (1759): 17–20
Critical Review 7 (1759): 79–80

2869 *The Visiting Day. A Novel.* 2 vols. London, 1768 (12mo. 6s. Lownds) BRITISH LIBRARY

Reviewed: *Monthly Review* 38 (1768): 499
Critical Review 26 (1768): 206–208
London Magazine 37 (1768): 276

2870 [VIVIAN, John]. *A Poem on the Countess of Pomfret's Benefaction to the University of Oxford.* Oxford, 1756 (4to. 6d. Rivington) BRITISH LIBRARY

Reviewed: *Monthly Review* 15 (1756): 202

2871 *The Voice of Britain*. London, 1764 (Fol. 6d. Wilson and Fell) BRITISH LIBRARY

Reviewed: *Monthly Review* 30 (1764): 69
Critical Review 17 (1764): 78

2872 *The Voice of Britain: A Poem on the late Glorious Dawn of Ancient Patriotism, and the later inglorious Frustration by the Dismission of the Right Honourable William Pitt, Esq;* NOT SEEN (4to. 6d. Major)

Reviewed: *Monthly Review* 16 (1757): 463
Critical Review 4 (1757): 92

2873 *The Voice of Truth, an Ode to His Royal Highness the Prince of Wales*. London, 1755 (4to. 1s. Cooper) BRITISH LIBRARY

Reviewed: *Monthly Review* 12 (1755): 380

2874 VOLTAIRE, [François Marie Arouet de]. *Candid: or, All for the Best. By M. de Voltaire*. London, 1759 (12mo. 1s.6d. Nourse) NEW YORK PUBLIC LIBRARY

Reviewed: *Monthly Review* 21 (1759): 83–85

VOLTAIRE, François Marie Arouet de (spurious continuation of translation of *Candide*)
See: *Candid: or, All for the Best . . . Part II*

2875 VOLTAIRE, [François Marie Arouet de]. *The Coffee-House, or Fair Fugitive. A Comedy Of Five Acts. Written by Mr. Voltaire. Translated from the French*. London, 1760 (4to. 1s. Dodsley) BRITISH LIBRARY

Reviewed: *Monthly Review* 23 (1760): 237
Critical Review 10 (1760): 241

2876 VOLTAIRE, [François Marie Arouet de]. *An Epistle of Mr. De Voltaire, Upon his Arrival at his Estate near the Lake of Geneva, in March, 1755. From the French*. London, 1755 (4to. 1s. Dodsley) BRITISH LIBRARY

Reviewed: *Monthly Review* 13 (1755): 285–287

2877 VOLTAIRE, [François Marie Arouet de]. *An Epistle of Mr. Voltaire, upon his arrival at his Estate near the Lake of Geneva, in March 1755. From the French*

NOT SEEN (4to. 1s. Hitch)

Reviewed: *Monthly Review* 14 (1756): 66–67

2878 VOLTAIRE, [François Marie Arouet de]. *The History of the Voyages of Scarmentado. A Satire. Translated from the French of M. De Voltaire*. London, 1757 (8vo. 6d. Vaillant) BRITISH LIBRARY

Reviewed: *Monthly Review* 16 (1757): 180
Critical Review 3 (1757): 175–176

2879 VOLTAIRE, [François Marie Arouet de]. *The Maid of Orleans. Written by Mons. de Voltaire. Translated from the French.* [Translation of *La pucelle d'Orleans*.] 2 vols. London, 1758 (12mo. 6s. No publisher's name) BRITISH LIBRARY

Reviewed: *Monthly Review* 19 (1758): 309
Critical Review 6 (1758): 346–347

2880 VOLTAIRE, [François Marie Arouet de]. *Micromegas: a Comic Romance. Being A Severe Satire upon the Philosophy, Ignorance, and Self-Conceit of Mankind. Together with A Detail of the Crusades: And a new Plan for the History of the Human Mind. Translated from the French of M. De Voltaire*. London, 1753 (12mo. 3s. Wilson & Durham) BRITISH LIBRARY

Reviewed: *Monthly Review* 7 (1752): 376–386

2881 VOLTAIRE, [François Marie Arouet de]. *The Orphan of China. A Tragedy. Translated from the French of M. De Voltaire. First Acted at Paris, on the 20th of August, 1755*. London, 1756 (8vo. 1s.6d. Baldwin) LIBRARY OF CONGRESS

Reviewed: *Monthly Review* 14 (1756): 64–66

2882 VOLTAIRE, [François Marie Arouet de]. *The Princess of Babylon. Translated from the French of M. de Voltaire*. London, 1768 (8vo. Bladon) BRITISH LIBRARY

Reviewed: *Monthly Review* 39 (1768): 124–126
Gentleman's Magazine 38 (1768): 336
Political Register 3 (1768): 60–64

2883 VOLTAIRE, [François Marie Arouet de]. *The Pupil of Nature; a True History, Found*

amongst the Papers of Father Quesnel. Translated from the original French of Mons. De Voltaire. London, 1771 (12mo. 2s. Carnan) BRITISH LIBRARY

Reviewed: *Monthly Review* 45 (1771): 329
Critical Review 32 (1771): 282–286
London Magazine 40 (1771): 414
Town & Country Magazine 3 (1771): 437

2884 VOLTAIRE, [François Marie Arouet de]. *Rome Preserv'd: a Tragedy. Translated from the French of M. de Voltaire.* London, 1760 (8vo. 1s.6d. Curtis) BRITISH LIBRARY

Reviewed: *Monthly Review* 24 (1761): 280–281
Critical Review 11 (1761): 78

2885 VOLTAIRE, [François Marie Arouet de]. *Semiramis: a Tragedy. Translated from the French of M. De Voltaire.* London ed. reviewed; copy seen: Dublin, 1760 (8vo. 1s.6d. Kearsly) BRITISH LIBRARY

Reviewed: *Monthly Review* 23 (1760): 247
Critical Review 10 (1760): 154–157
British Magazine 1 (1760): 546

2886 VOLTAIRE, [François Marie Arouet de]. *Socrates, a Tragedy Of Three Acts. Translated from the French of Monsieur de Voltaire.* London, 1760 (12mo. 1s. Dodsley) BRITISH LIBRARY

Reviewed: *Monthly Review* 22 (1760): 284–291
Critical Review 9 (1760): 221–225

2887 VOLTAIRE, [François Marie Arouet de]. *The Works of M. de Voltaire. Translated from the French. With Notes, Historical and Critical. By Dr. Smollett, and Others. Volume the First.* London, 1761 (12mo. In monthly volumes, 3s. each. Newbery, &c.) BRITISH LIBRARY

Reviewed: *Monthly Review* 29 (1763): 273–282
Critical Review 11 (1761): 377–381

VOLTAIRE, François Marie Arouet de (other translations and adaptations)
See: CELESIA, Dorothea. *Almida, a Tragedy*
COLMAN, George (the elder). *The English Merchant*
CRADOCK, Joseph. *Zobeide*
MURPHY, Arthur. *Alzuma*
MURPHY, Arthur. *No One's Enemy but His Own*
MURPHY, Arthur. *The Orphan of China*
TERES, T. *The Civil War of Geneva*

The Voluntary Exile
See: FREE, John

2888 *A Voyage to the World in the center of the earth. Giving an account of the manners, customs, laws, &c. of the inhabitants, &c. &c. &c.*
NOT SEEN (12mo. 3s. Crowder)

Reviewed: *Monthly Review* 12 (1755): 394–395

2889 *The Voyages and Adventures of the Chevalier Dupont. In Four Volumes. Translated from the French.* London, 1772 (12mo. 10s.sewed. Jones. 1772) BRITISH LIBRARY

Reviewed: *Monthly Review* 46 (1772): 625–626
Critical Review 33 (1772): 411
London Magazine 41 (1772): 28
British Magazine & General Review 1 (1772): 529–532
Universal Catalogue [1] (1772) art. 731

2890 *The Voyages, Travels, And Wonderful Discoveries of Capt. John Holmesby. Containing A Series of the most Surprising and Uncommon Events, which befel the Author, in his Voyage to the Southern Ocean, in the Year 1739.* London, n.d. [BODLEIAN CAT.–1757] (12mo. 3s. Noble) BODLEIAN

Reviewed: *Monthly Review* 17 (1757): 563

2891 WAGSTAFF, Walter. *The Pandaemonium Ballot; or, the Leadenheads at Loggerheads. In three Cantos*
NOT SEEN (8vo. 2s. Griffin. 1773)

Reviewed: *Monthly Review* 49 (1773): 65
Critical Review 35 (1773): 394
Universal Catalogue [2] (1773) art. 628

2892 [WAGSTAFFE, John]. *An Elegy, written in a Quakers Burial Ground. To which is added The Country Quaker.* London, 1764 (Fol. 1s. Keith) LIBRARY OF CONGRESS

Reviewed: *Monthly Review* 31 (1764): 230
Critical Review 18 (1764): 79–80
British Magazine 5 (1764): 433

2893 WALES, William. *An Ode to the Right Hon. William Pitt, Esq;*
NOT SEEN (Fol. 1s. Kearsley)

Reviewed: *Monthly Review* 27 (1762): 316
Critical Review 14 (1762): 318

2894 [WALL, Anne]. *The Life of Lamenther: a True History. Written by Herself. In Five Parts. Containing a just Account of the many Misfortunes she underwent, occasioned by the ill Treatment of an unnatural Father*. London, 1771 (8vo. 4s.6d.sewed. Evans) BRITISH LIBRARY

Reviewed: *Monthly Review* 46 (1772): 77–78
Critical Review 32 (1771): 471
Gentleman's Magazine 42 (1772): 84
London Magazine 40 (1771): 611

2895 WALLER, Edmund. *The Works of Edmund Waller, Esq. in Verse and Prose. To which is prefixed, The Life of the Author, By Percival Stockdale*. London, 1772 (8vo. 3s.6d. Waller) BRITISH LIBRARY

Reviewed: *Monthly Review* 48 (1773): 319
Critical Review 35 (1773): 50–52
London Magazine 41 (1772): 440
Town & Country Magazine 5 (1773): 94
Universal Catalogue [1] (1772) art. 1493

2896 [WALLIS, George]. *The Juvenaliad. A Satire*. York, n.d. [BODLEIAN CAT.–1774] (4to. 1s. Bell) BODLEIAN

Reviewed: *Monthly Review* 50 (1774): 232
Critical Review 37 (1774): 76
Universal Catalogue 3 (1774) art. 110

2897 WALLIS, George. *Perjury. A Satire*. York, n.d. [BODLEIAN CAT.–1774] (4to. 2s. York printed, and sold in London by Bell) BODLEIAN

Reviewed: *Monthly Review* 50 (1774): 484
Universal Catalogue 3 (1774) art. 762

2898 [WALPOLE, Horace]. *The Castle of Otranto, a Story. Translated by William Marshal, Gent. From the Original Italian of Onuphrio Muralto, Canon of the Church of St. Nicholas at Otranto*. London, 1765 (8vo. 3s. Lowndes) BRITISH LIBRARY

Reviewed: *Monthly Review* 32 (1765): 97–99
Critical Review 19 (1765): 50–51

2899 [WALPOLE, Horace]. *The Castle of Otranto, a Gothic Story. The Second Edition*. London, 1765 (8vo. 3s. Bathoe) BRITISH LIBRARY

Reviewed: *Monthly Review* 32 (1765): 394
Critical Review 19 (1765): 469
Candid Review 1 (1765): 241–245

2900 *The Wanderer: or, Memoirs of Charles Searle, Esq; containing His Adventures by Sea and Land. With Many remarkable Characters, and interesting Situations in Real Life; and a Variety of surprizing Incidents*. 2 vols. London, 1766 (12mo. 5s.sewed. Lowndes) BRITISH LIBRARY

Reviewed: *Monthly Review* 33 (1765): 490
Critical Review 20 (1765): 476

2901 [WARNER, Richard (trans.)]. *The Comedies of Plautus, translated into Familiar Blank Verse, By the Gentleman who translated The Captives. Vols. III and IV*. [Vols. 1 and 2 are translated by Bonnell THORNTON.] London, 1772 (8vo. 12s. Becket. 1772) BRITISH LIBRARY

Reviewed: *Monthly Review* 48 (1773): 249–262
Critical Review 35 (1773): 81–92
London Magazine 42 (1773): 91
Town & Country Magazine 5 (1773): 94

2902 [WARNER, Richard (trans.)]. *Comedies of Plautus, translated into Familiar Blank Verse, By the Gentleman who translated The Captives. Volume the Fifth and last*. London, 1774 (8vo. 6s.bound. Becket. 1774) BRITISH LIBRARY

Reviewed: *Monthly Review* 51 (1774): 1–10
Critical Review 38 (1774): 237
Universal Catalogue 3 (1774) art. 348

2903 WARTON, Joseph. *An Ode, Occasioned by reading Mr. West's Translation of Pindar*. London, 1749 (Fol. 8pp. 6d. Owen) BODLEIAN

Reviewed: *Monthly Review* 1 (1749): 238

2904 [WARTON, Thomas]. *New-Market. A Satire*. London, 1751 (no pub. details) BODLEIAN

Reviewed: *Monthly Review* 4 (1750–51): 160

2905 WARTON, Thomas. *Ode for Music, as perform'd at the Theatre in Oxford, On the Second of July, 1751. Being the Anniversary appointed by The late Lord Crew, Bishop of Durham, For the Commemoration of Benefactors to the University. By Tho. Warton, A.M. of Trinity Coll. Set to Music by Dr. Hayes, Professor of Music*. Oxford, n.d. [ESTC-1751] (no pub. details) BRITISH LIBRARY

Reviewed: *Gentleman's Magazine* 21 (1751): 335

2906 [WARTON, Thomas (ed.)]. *The Oxford Sausage: or, Select Poetical Pieces, Written by the most Celebrated Wits of the University of Oxford. Adorned with Cuts, Engraved in a New Taste, and Designed by the Best Masters*. London, 1764 (8vo. 2s.6d.sewed. Fletcher and Co.) BRITISH LIBRARY

Reviewed: *Monthly Review* 31 (1764): 232
Critical Review 18 (1764): 80
British Magazine 5 (1764): 377
General Magazine 1 (1764): 301

2907 [WARTON, Thomas (ed.)]. *The Union: or select Scots and English Poems*. Edinburgh, 1753 (12mo. 2s.sewed. Edinburgh printed) BRITISH LIBRARY

Reviewed: *Monthly Review* 9 (1753): 199–200

2908 [WARTON, Thomas]. *Verses on Miss C----s and Miss W----t*
NOT SEEN (4to. 12pp. 6d. Owen)

Reviewed: *Monthly Review* 1 (1749): 240

2909 *Water Poetry. A Collection of Verses written at Several Public Places, Most of them never before printed*. London, n.d. [ESTC-1771?] (8vo. 1s.6d. Pearch) BRITISH LIBRARY

Reviewed: *Monthly Review* 45 (1771): 236
Critical Review 32 (1771): 152–153
Gentleman's Magazine 41 (1771): 417
London Magazine 40 (1771): 462
Town & Country Magazine 3 (1771): 437

The Waterman
See: DIBDIN, Charles

The Way to Keep Him
See: MURPHY, Arthur

2910 *The Way To Lose Him; or, the History of Miss Wyndham. By the Author of the Way To Please Him*. 2 vols. London, 1773 (12mo. 5s. Noble. 1773) BRITISH LIBRARY

Reviewed: *Monthly Review* 48 (1773): 155
Critical Review 34 (1772): 398
London Magazine 41 (1772): 543
Town & Country Magazine 4 (1772): 660
Universal Catalogue [1] (1772) art. 1387

2911 *The Way To Please Him: or the History of Lady Sedley. By the Author of the Way to Lose Him*. 2 vols. London, 1773 (12mo. 5s. Noble. 1773) UNIVERSITY OF PENNSYLVANIA

Reviewed: *Monthly Review* 48 (1773): 155
Critical Review 34 (1772): 398
London Magazine 41 (1772): 543
Town & Country Magazine 4 (1772): 660
Universal Catalogue [1] (1772) art. 1386

2912 *The Wedding-Day; a Poem*. Oxford, 1771 (4to. 2s. Flexney) BRITISH LIBRARY

Reviewed: *Monthly Review* 45 (1771): 235
Critical Review 32 (1771): 310

2913 *The Wedding Day. In Three Parts. By a Citizen of London*. London, 1762 (8vo. 1s. Keith) BRITISH LIBRARY

Reviewed: *Monthly Review* 27 (1762): 391–393
Critical Review 14 (1762): 315

2914 *The Wedding-Night; or, the Perplex'd Lovers. A Tale*
NOT SEEN (8vo. 1s. Thrush)

Reviewed: *Monthly Review* 19 (1758): 503

The Wedding Ring
See: DIBDIN, Charles

2915 WEEKES, Nathaniel. *The Angel and Curate. A Poem*. London, 1765 (4to. 1s. Coote) BRITISH LIBRARY

Reviewed: *Monthly Review* 33 (1765): 86
Critical Review 19 (1765): 393

2916 WEEKES, [Nathaniel]. *Barbados a Poem. To Sir Thomas Robinson, Bart.* London, 1754 (4to. 2s. Dodsley) BRITISH LIBRARY

Reviewed: *Monthly Review* 11 (1754): 325–329
Gentleman's Magazine 24 (1754): 439

2917 WEEKES, Nath[aniel]. *The Choice of a Husband. An Epistle. To a Young Lady.* London, 1754 (4to. 1s. Dodsley) BRITISH LIBRARY

Reviewed: *Monthly Review* 10 (1754): 302–303
Gentleman's Magazine 24 (1754): 146

2918 [WEEKES, Nathaniel]. [*The Messiah, a Sacred Poem.*] *The Nativity, a Poem. Being the First Book of the Messiah, A Sacred Poem.* London, 1763 (4to. 2s.6d. Coote) BRITISH LIBRARY

Reviewed: *Monthly Review* 29 (1763): 399
Critical Review 17 (1764): 318–319

2919 [WEEKES, Nathaniel]. [*The Messiah, a Sacred Poem.*] *The Temptation a Poem. Being the Second Book of the Messiah, A Sacred Poem.* London, 1763 (4to. 2s.6d. Coote) BRITISH LIBRARY

Reviewed: *Monthly Review* 31 (1764): 73
Critical Review 17 (1764): 319–320

2920 [WEEKES, Nathaniel]. [*The Messiah, a Sacred Poem.*] *The Crucifixion a Poem. Being the Third Book of the Messiah, A Sacred Poem.* London, 1763 (4to. 2s.6d. Coote) BRITISH LIBRARY

Reviewed: *Monthly Review* 31 (1764): 73–74
Critical Review 17 (1764): 472

2921 [WEEKES, Nathaniel]. [*The Messiah, a Sacred Poem.*] *The Resurrection a Poem. Being the Fourth Book of the Messiah, A Sacred Poem.* London, 1764 (4to. 2s.6d. Coote) BRITISH LIBRARY

Reviewed: *Monthly Review* 31 (1764): 232
Critical Review 18 (1764): 320

2922 WEEKES, [Nathaniel]. *The Messiah; a sacred Poem. In Four Books* NOT SEEN (4to. 10s.6d. Coote)

Reviewed: *Monthly Review* 32 (1765): 155

2923 [WEEKES, Nathaniel]. *On the Abuse of Poetry. A Satire. To the Honourable Richard Savage Nassau, Esq;* London, 1752 (4to. 1s. Manby) BRITISH LIBRARY

Reviewed: *Monthly Review* 6 (1752): 79–80
Gentleman's Magazine 22 (1752): 47

2924 WEEKS, James Eyre. *A poetical prospect of the coast, town, and harbour of Workington. To which is annexed a correct edition of the poetical prospect of Whitehaven* NOT SEEN (8vo. 24pp. Whitehaven, printed by W. Masheder)

Listed: *Monthly Review* 7 (1752): 79

Wensleydale: or, Rural Contemplations, a Poem
See: MAUDE, Thomas

2925 WESLEY, Charles. *An Elegy on the late reverend George Whitefield, M.A. Who died September 30, 1770, In the 56th Year of his Age.* Bristol, 1771 (8vo. 6d. Keith) BRITISH LIBRARY

Reviewed: *Monthly Review* 44 (1771): 174
Critical Review 31 (1771): 75–76
Gentleman's Magazine 41 (1771): 86
Town & Country Magazine 3 (1771): 155

2926 WESLEY, Charles. *An Epistle To the Reverend Mr. John Wesley.* London, 1755 (8vo. 3d. Robinson) BRITISH LIBRARY

Reviewed: *Monthly Review* 12 (1755): 509

2927 WESLEY, Charles. *Short Hymns on Select Passages of the Holy Scriptures. By Charles Wesley, M.A. And Presbyter of the Church of England.* 2 vols. Bristol, 1762 (12mo. 6s. Bristol printed by E. Farley) BRITISH LIBRARY

Reviewed: *Monthly Review* 38 (1768): 51–55

2928 WEST, Gilbert. *Odes of Pindar, With several other Pieces in Prose and Verse, Translated from the Greek. To which is prefixed a Dissertation on the Olympick Games.* London, 1749 (4to. 550pp. Dodsley) BRITISH LIBRARY

Reviewed: *Monthly Review* 1 (1749): 38–51 and 92–123

2929 *West-country thoughts on east-country folly. Occasioned by the late very extraordinary rejoicings on the late very remarkable day. By a private gentleman of Cornwal*
NOT SEEN (Fol. 6d. Scott)

Reviewed: *Monthly Review* 18 (1758): 279–280
Critical Review 5 (1758): 267

The West Indian
See: CUMBERLAND, Richard

2930 WEYLAR, Maria. *Reveries Du Coeur: or, Feelings of the Heart. Attempted in Verse, by Maria Weylar.* London, 1770 (8vo. 2s.6d. Dodsley. 1770) BRITISH LIBRARY

Reviewed: *Monthly Review* 43 (1770): 326
London Magazine 39 (1770): 580
Town & Country Magazine 2 (1770): 598

What we must All come to
See: MURPHY, Arthur

2931 WHATELEY, [Mary]. *Original Poems on Several Occasions.* London, 1764 (8vo. 5s.sewed. Dodsley) BRITISH LIBRARY

Reviewed: *Monthly Review* 30 (1764): 445–450
Critical Review 18 (1764): 114–118
British Magazine 5 (1764): 377

2932 WHEATLAND, Stephen, and Tipping SYLVESTER. *The Psalms of David, Translated into Heroic Verse, In as Literal a Manner, As Rhyme and Metre will allow. With Arguments to each Psalm. And Explanatory Notes.* London, 1754 (12mo. 3s. Buckland) BRITISH LIBRARY

Reviewed: *Monthly Review* 11 (1754): 168–169

2933 WHEATLEY, Phillis. *Poems on Various Subjects, religious and moral. By Phillis Wheatley, Negro Servant to Mr. John Wheatley, of Boston, in New England.* London, 1773 (12mo. 2s. Bell. 1773) BRITISH LIBRARY

Reviewed: *Monthly Review* 49 (1773): 457–459
Critical Review 36 (1773): 232–233
London Magazine 42 (1773): 456
Town & Country Magazine 5 (1773): 546–547
Universal Catalogue [2] (1773) art. 1039

2934 WHIPCORD, Jasper Canonicus (pseud.). *The Pick-Lock, or, Voltaire's Hue and Cry after a certain celebrated Wit Stealer, and Dramatic Smuggler*
NOT SEEN (Fol. 1s. Williams)

Reviewed: *Monthly Review* 25 (1761): 396
Critical Review 12 (1761): 319

A Whipping for the Welch Parson
See: KENRICK, William

2935 WHITAKER, L. *Verses on the Approach of Peace. Written in December 1762*
NOT SEEN (Hull printed and sold by Horsfield in London)

Reviewed: *Monthly Review* 32 (1765): 75
Critical Review 18 (1764): 458–462

2936 WHITE, James (trans.). *The Clouds: a Comedy. Written by Aristophanes, The Wittiest Man of his Age, against Socrates, Who was the Wisest and Best. Now first intirely translated into English, With the Principal Scolia, And Notes Critical and Explanatory.* London, 1759 (12mo. 2s. Payne) BRITISH LIBRARY

Reviewed: *Monthly Review* 20 (1759): 462
Critical Review 8 (1759): 157–158

2937 WHITEHEAD, [Paul]. *An Epistle to Dr. Thompson.* London, n.d. [ESTC-1755] (4to. 1s. Owen) BRITISH LIBRARY

Reviewed: *Monthly Review* 13 (1755): 458–459

2938 WHITEHEAD, William. *A Charge to the Poets. By William Whitehead, Esq; Poet Laureat.* London, 1762 (4to. 1s. Dodsley) BRITISH LIBRARY

Reviewed: *Monthly Review* 26 (1762): 222–224
Critical Review 13 (1762): 268
British Magazine 3 (1762): 158

2939 WHITEHEAD, William. *Crèüsa, Queen of Athens. A Tragedy. As it is Acted at the Theatre Royal in Drury-lane By His Majesty's Servants.* London, 1754 (8vo. 1s.6d. Dodsley) BRITISH LIBRARY

Reviewed: *Monthly Review* 10 (1754): 374–384

2940 WHITEHEAD, William. *Elegies. With an Ode to the Tiber. Written Abroad. By William Whitehead, Esq; Register and Secretary to the Hon. Order of the Bath*. London, 1757 (4to. 1s. Dodsley) BRITISH LIBRARY

Reviewed: *Monthly Review* 16 (1757): 232–235
Critical Review 3 (1757): 136–139
Literary Magazine 2 (1757): 31

2941 WHITEHEAD, W[illiam]. *An Hymn to the Nymph of Bristol Spring. By Mr. W. Whitehead*. London, 1751 (4to. 1s.6d. Dodsley) BRITISH LIBRARY

Listed: *Monthly Review* 4 (1750–51): 305

2942 WHITEHEAD, William. *Plays and Poems*. 2 vols. London, 1774 (8vo. 9s.bound. Dodsley. 1774) BRITISH LIBRARY

Reviewed: *Monthly Review* 51 (1774): 318
Critical Review 37 (1774): 199–201
Town & Country Magazine 6 (1774): 156
Universal Catalogue 3 (1774) art. 366

2943 WHITEHEAD, W[illiam]. *Poems on Several Occasions, with the Roman Father, A Tragedy*. London, 1754 (8vo. 3s.6d. Dodsley) BRITISH LIBRARY

Reviewed: *Monthly Review* 9 (1753): 479–480

2944 WHITEHEAD, W[illiam]. *The Roman Father, a Tragedy. As it is Acted at the Theatre-Royal in Drury-Lane. By His Majesty's Servants*. London, 1750 (no pub. details) BRITISH LIBRARY

Reviewed: *Monthly Review* 2 (1749–50): 407–417

2945 WHITEHEAD, William. *The School for Lovers, a Comedy. As it is Acted at the Theatre Royal in Drury-Lane*. [Founded on *Le Testament* by Bernard le Bovier de FONTANELLE.] London, 1762 (8vo. 1s.6d. Dodsley) BODLEIAN

Reviewed: *Monthly Review* 26 (1762): 157–158
Critical Review 13 (1762): 135–138
British Magazine 3 (1762): 158

2946 [WHITEHEAD, William]. *A Trip to Scotland. As it is Acted at the Theatre Royal in Drury-Lane*. London, 1770 (8vo. 1s. Dodsley. 1770) BRITISH LIBRARY

Reviewed: *Monthly Review* 42 (1770): 145
Critical Review 29 (1770): 235–236

2947 WHITEHEAD, William. *Verses to the People of England. 1758*. London, 1758 (4to. 6d. Dodsley) BRITISH LIBRARY

Reviewed: *Monthly Review* 18 (1758): 334–335

2948 [WHYTE, Samuel (ed.)]. *A Collection of Poems, The Productions of the Kingdom Of Ireland: Selected from a Collection published in that Kingdom, intituled, The Shamrock; or, Hibernian Cresses*. London, 1773 (8vo. 3s. sewed. Bladon. 1773) BRITISH LIBRARY

Reviewed: *Monthly Review* 49 (1773): 148
Universal Catalogue [2] (1773) art. 730

2949 WHYTE, Samuel (ed.). *The Shamrock: or, Hibernian Cresses. A collection of Poems, Songs, Epigrams, &c. Latin as well as English, the Original Production of Ireland*. Dublin, 1772 (4to. Dublin printed. 1772) BRITISH LIBRARY

Reviewed: *Monthly Review* 47 (1772): 484–486
Critical Review 35 (1773): 71

2950 WIELAND, C[hristoph] M[artin]. *The History of Agathon, By Mr. C. M. Wieland. Translated from the German Original, with A Preface by the Translator*. London, 1773 (12mo. 12s. Cadell. 1773) BRITISH LIBRARY

Reviewed: *Monthly Review* 50 (1774): 176–182
Critical Review 37 (1774): 196–199
London Magazine 43 (1774): 143
Universal Catalogue 3 (1774) art. 313

2951 WIELAND, C[hristoph] M[artin]. *Reason Triumphant over Fancy; Exemplified in the singular Adventures of Don Sylvio de Rosalva. A History in which every marvellous Event occurs naturally. Translated from the German Original of Mr. C. M. Wieland. In Three Volumes*. London, 1761 (12mo. 9s. Wilkie, &c. 1773) JOHNS HOPKINS

Reviewed: *Monthly Review* 48 (1773): 126–129
Critical Review 35 (1773): 143–147
London Magazine 42 (1773): 39

Town & Country Magazine 5 (1773): 134
Universal Catalogue [2] (1773) art. 126

2952 *The Wig. A Burlesque-Satirical Poem. By the Author of More Fun.* London, 1765 (4to. 1s.6d. Flexney) BRITISH LIBRARY

Reviewed: *Monthly Review* 32 (1765): 76
Critical Review 19 (1765): 72–73
Candid Review 1 (1765): 31–32

2953 WIGNELL, J[ohn]. *A Collection of Original Pieces; consisting of Poems, Prologues, Epilogues, Songs, Epistles, Epigrams, Epitaphs, &c. &c. By J. Wignell. To which is added a Farce, of Two Acts, (Never perform'd) call'd, Love's Artifice: or, The Perplex'd Squire.* London, 1762 (8vo. 4s. Davies) LILLY

Reviewed: *Monthly Review* 28 (1763): 71–72
Critical Review 16 (1763): 191–194

2954 [WILKES, John]. *An Essay on Woman, in Three Epistles.* [This version, unlike the several fake versions of *An Essay on Woman*, has some clear resemblance to the original, although it is bowdlerized.] London, n.d. [ESTC-1763] (4to. 1s. Gretton) BRITISH LIBRARY

Reviewed: *Monthly Review* 29 (1763): 465
Critical Review 16 (1763): 479

2955 *Wilkes and Liberty: or, The Universal Prayer.* London, 1764 (4to. 1s.6d. Williams) BODLEIAN

Reviewed: *Monthly Review* 30 (1764): 415
Critical Review 17 (1764): 397
General Magazine 1 (1764): 242–243

2956 [WILKIE, William]. *The Epigoniad. A Poem. In Nine Books.* Edinburgh, 1757 (12mo. 6s. fine, 4s. common paper. Hamilton and Balfour) BODLEIAN

Reviewed: *Monthly Review* 17 (1757): 228–238
Critical Review 4 (1757): 27–35
Literary Magazine 2 (1757): 293–296

2957 WILKIE, William. *The Epigoniad. A Poem. In Nine Books. By William Wilkie, V.D.M. The Second Edition. Carefully Corrected and Improved. To which is Added, A Dream. In the Manner of Spenser.* London, 1769 (12mo. 3s. Millar) BRITISH LIBRARY

Reviewed: *Critical Review* 7 (1759): 323–324

2958 WILKIE, William. *Fables.* London, 1768 (8vo. 4s. Dilly) BRITISH LIBRARY

Reviewed: *Monthly Review* 39 (1768): 166–168
Critical Review 25 (1768): 360–366
Universal Museum 4 (1768): 259

2959 [WILKINSON, Edward]. *The Gamesters. A Poem. Addressed to The Mayor of C———.* N.p., 1774 [NEWBERRY CAT.–London] (12mo. 1s. Lewis. 1774) NEWBERRY

Reviewed: *Monthly Review* 50 (1774): 314
Universal Catalogue 3 (1774) art. 365

The Will of a certain Northern Vicar
See: COOPER, William

2960 WILLIAMS, Anna. *Miscellanies in Prose and Verse.* London, 1766 (4to. 5s. Davis) BRITISH LIBRARY

Reviewed: *Monthly Review* 34 (1766): 355–359
Critical Review 21 (1766): 291-[294]

WILLINGTON, James (pseud.)
See: GOLDSMITH, Oliver

2961 WILLS, [James]. *De Arte Graphica; or, the Art of Painting. Translated from the Original Latin of C. A. Du Fresnoy. By Mr. Wills. With Notes, miscellaneous and explanatory.* London, 1754 (4to. 2s.6d. Franklin) BRITISH LIBRARY

Reviewed: *Monthly Review* 10 (1754): 385–386

2962 [WILSON, John]. *The Earl of Douglas: a Dramatick Essay.* London, 1760 (8vo. 1s. Hitch) BRITISH LIBRARY

Reviewed: *Monthly Review* 23 (1760): 526–527
Critical Review 10 (1760): 483
British Magazine 2 (1761): 46

2963 *The Wiltshire Beau: or the Life and Adventures of Ben Barnard.* 2 vols.
NOT SEEN (12mo. 5s. Nicoll)

Reviewed: *Monthly Review* 32 (1765): 394
Critical Review 19 (1765): 471
Candid Review 1 (1765): 277

2964 *The Winter Evenings Companion. Being a New Collection of Diverting Essays, Merry Stories, Humorous Letters, Select Histories, Entertaining Novels, Adventures, &c. Among which are The Generous Husband; or, the History of Arabella. The History of Beau Bronze, the Fortune-Hunter. Conjugal Love: Or a good Example for married Ladies. The History of Tacitus and Corinna. The Secret History of the Slipper; or the Story of Lucius and Rosetta, a Fact. The Ungrateful Lover; or, the Amours of Lysander and Climene. The fatal Effect of too sudden Surprizes of Joy; or, the History of Florio and Fidelia. The Discreet Wife; or, the Lapsed Husband relaimed. The Dishonourable Lover. To which are added, A Choice Collection of Songs, sung this Season at Vauxhall, Ranelagh, Marybone, &c. Polite Tales, Fables, Poems and Epigrams. Also, The Jocular Companion: Or, a Curious Collection of brilliant Jests, Puns, Conundrums, &c.* London, n.d. [ESTC-1760?] (12mo. 1s.6d. Stamper) BRITISH LIBRARY

Reviewed: *Monthly Review* 5 (1751): 518

2965 *The Winter Medley: Or, Amusement for the Fire-Side. Containing a curious Collection of entertaining Stories, interesting Novels, remarkable Tales, curious Anecdotes, Essays, Allegories, Visions, and select Pieces of Poetry, &c.*
NOT SEEN (12mo. 2s. Snagg. 1774)

Reviewed: *Monthly Review* 50 (1774): 322
Universal Catalogue 3 (1774) art. 85

The Winter-Piece, a Poem
See: PHIPPS, Joseph

2966 *Wisdom. A poem*
NOT SEEN (4to. 6d. Owen)

Reviewed: *Monthly Review* 4 (1750–51): 478–479

2967 *The Wisdom of Plutus.* London, 1757 (4to. 1s. Cooper) YALE (BEINECKE)

Reviewed: *Monthly Review* 16 (1757): 463

2968 [WISE, Joseph]. *The Coronation of David. Written in M.DCC.LXIII. By a Sussex Clergyman.* Lewes, 1766 (8vo. 1s. Bladon) BRITISH LIBRARY

Reviewed: *Monthly Review* 34 (1766): 406
Critical Review 22 (1766): 73–74

2969 WISE, Joseph. *Providence. Book I*
NOT SEEN (8vo. 1s.6d. White)

Reviewed: *Monthly Review* 42 (1770): 250
Critical Review 29 (1770): 238–239
London Magazine 39 (1770): 320

2970 WISE, Joseph. *Providence. Written in 1764*
NOT SEEN (8vo. 1s. Bladon)

Reviewed: *Monthly Review* 35 (1766): 322
Critical Review 22 (1766): 156

2971 WISE, Joseph. *Providence. Written in 1764 and 1765.* Lewes, 1766 (8vo. 1s. Bladon) BODLEIAN

Reviewed: *Critical Review* 23 (1767): 143

2972 *The Wise Ones Bubbled, or, Lovers Triumphant: After a Series of above twenty Years of Separation and Residence in divers Foreign Parts, most the Time subject to the acutest Difficulties. With an account of their miraculous Meeting and Adventures, till they happily enjoyed the blessed Fruits of all their Toils for for each other. Printed from Mr. Parsons's own Manuscript.* 2 vols.
NOT SEEN (8vo. 6s. Wren)

Reviewed: *Monthly Review* 24 (1761): 349
Critical Review 11 (1761): 163
British Magazine 2 (1761): 161

2973 *The Wish: a Poem. By a Gentleman of Cambridge.* London, 1771 (4to. 1s. Dodsley) BRITISH LIBRARY

Reviewed: *Monthly Review* 45 (1771): 151
Critical Review 32 (1771): 78
Gentleman's Magazine 41 (1771): 417
Town & Country Magazine 3 (1771): 437

The Wishes of a Free People
See: HIFFERNAN, Paul

Wit's Last Stake
See: KING, Thomas

WODHULL, Michael. *An Epistle to *************
See: WODHULL, [Michael]. *A Poetical Epistle to **** *******

2974 WODHULL, [Michael]. *The Equality of Mankind. A Poem.* Oxford, 1765 (4to. 1s.6d. Becket) BRITISH LIBRARY

Reviewed: *Monthly Review* 34 (1766): 22–24
Critical Review 20 (1765): 468–469
Gentleman's Magazine 35 (1765): 584

2975 [WODHULL, Michael]. *Ode to Criticism. By a Gentleman of Oxford.* London, 1761 (Fol. 1s. Gonisten, Piccadilly) BRITISH LIBRARY

Reviewed: *Monthly Review* 24 (1761): 278–280

2976 WODHULL, [Michael]. *Ode to the Muses.* Oxford, 1760 (4to. 1s. Payne and Cropley) BRITISH LIBRARY

Reviewed: *Monthly Review* 23 (1760): 525–526
Critical Review 10 (1760): 246–248
British Magazine 1 (1760): 602

2977 WODHULL, [Michael]. *A Poetical Epistle to **** *******, M.A. Student of Christ-Church.* 1st ed. reviewed; copy seen 2d ed.: London, 1762 (4to. 1s. Payne) BRITISH LIBRARY

Reviewed: *Monthly Review* 25 (1761): 330–331
Critical Review 12 (1761): 236

2978 WODHULL, [Michael]. *Two Odes. By Mr. Wodhull. I. To Miss Sally Fowler. II. To the Dryads.* Oxford, 1763 (4to. Oxford, Printed by Jackson) BRITISH LIBRARY

Reviewed: *Monthly Review* 30 (1764): 30–34

2979 *Woffington's Ghost. A Poem. In Answer to the Meretriciad.* London, 1761 (4to. 1s. Woodgate) HARVARD (HOUGHTON)

Reviewed: *Monthly Review* 25 (1761): 478
Critical Review 12 (1761): 403

2980 [WOLLASTON, George]. *The Life and History of a Pilgrim, A Narrative founded on Fact. By George Wollaston, Esq;* Dublin printed, London reprinted; 1753 (12mo. 3s. Dublin printed, London re-printed, Whiston, Payne, &c.) NEWBERRY

Reviewed: *Monthly Review* 9 (1753): 226

2981 *Woman: a Fragment.* London, 1758 (4to. 1s. Withey) BODLEIAN

Reviewed: *Monthly Review* 19 (1758): 502–503
Critical Review 6 (1758): 259

2982 *Woman: an Epistle to C. Churchill, On his intended Publication, entitled, Woman: a Satyr. By A. B. C.* London, 1763 (4to. 1s. Williams) HARVARD (WIDENER)

Reviewed: *Monthly Review* 28 (1763): 72
Critical Review 14 (1762): 479
British Magazine 3 (1762): 662

The Woman of Fashion
See: GIBBES, Phebe

The Woman of Honor
See: CLELAND, John

2983 *Woodbury: or, the Memoirs of William Marchmont, Esq. and Miss Walbrook.* 2 vols. London, 1773 (12mo. 6s. Bell. 1773) UNIVERSITY OF PENNSYLVANIA

Reviewed: *Monthly Review* 48 (1773): 417
Critical Review 35 (1773): 395
London Magazine 42 (1773): 149
Universal Catalogue [2] (1773) art. 353

2984 *The Wooden Bowl. A Tale. To which is added, A Love-Match. Taken from Mr. Collet's Four celebrated Pieces, viz. Courtship, Elopement, Honey-moon, and Matrimony.* London, 1767 (4to. 1s. Moran) HARVARD (HOUGHTON)

Reviewed: *Monthly Review* 37 (1767): 394
Critical Review 24 (1767): 384
Universal Museum 3 (1767): 596
Political Register 1 (1767): 464

2985 [WOODFIN, A.]. *The Auction: A Modern Novel. In Two Volumes.* London, 1760 (12mo. 6s. Lownds) UNIVERSITY OF PENNSYLVANIA

Reviewed: *Monthly Review* 21 (1759): 573
Critical Review 8 (1759): 452–458
British Magazine 1 (1760): 40

2986 WOODFIN, A. *The Discovery: Or, Memoirs of Miss Marianne Middleton. By Mrs. Woodfin, Author of Harriot Watson, Sally Sable, and of the Auction, a Modern Novel.* 2 vols. London, 1764 (12mo. 5s.sewed. Lowndes) BRITISH LIBRARY

Reviewed: *Monthly Review* 30 (1764): 488–489
Critical Review 17 (1764): 398

2987 WOODFIN, Mrs. [A.]. *The History of Miss Harriot Watson. In Two Volumes. By Mrs. Woodfin, Author of The Auction.* London, 1762 (12mo. 5s. Lowndes) YALE (STERLING)

Reviewed: *Monthly Review* 28 (1763): 162
Critical Review 15 (1763): 62–66
British Magazine 4 (1763): 98

2988 [WOODFIN, A.]. *The History of Miss Sally Sable. By the author of the Memoirs of a Scotch Family.* 2 vols. London, n.d. [1757] [ESTC-1770?] [ESTC suggests 1770, but vol. 2 of novel has ads for two recent publications, both novels published in 1757.] (12mo. 6s. Noble) BRITISH LIBRARY

Reviewed: *Monthly Review* 17 (1757): 563
Critical Review 5 (1758): 28–32

2989 [WOODFIN, A.]. *Northern Memoirs: or, the History of a Scotch Family. Written by a Lady. In Two Volumes.* London, n.d. (12mo. 6s. Noble) NEWBERRY

Reviewed: *Monthly Review* 15 (1756): 656
Critical Review 2 (1756): 448–451

2990 WOODHOUSE, James. *Poems on several Occasions. By James Woodhouse, Journeyman Shoemaker. The second Edition, Corrected, With several additional pieces never before published.* [2d ed. of *Poems on Sundry Occasions.*] London, 1766 (8vo. 5s. Dodsley) BRITISH LIBRARY

Reviewed: *Monthly Review* 35 (1766): 415
Critical Review 21 (1766): 474

2991 WOODHOUSE, James. *Poems on Sundry Occasions. By James Woodhouse, a Journeyman Shoemaker.* London, 1764 (4to. 3s. Dodsley) BRITISH LIBRARY

Reviewed: *Monthly Review* 30 (1764): 415
Critical Review 17 (1764): 392–393
General Magazine 1 (1764): 198

Woodstock: an Elegy
See: DALRYMPLE, Hugh

2992 WOODWARD, [Henry]. *Songs, Chorusses, &c. As they are performed in the New Entertainment of Harlequin's Jubilee, at the Theatre Royal in Covent-Garden.* London, 1770 (8vo. 6d. Griffin) BRITISH LIBRARY

Reviewed: *Monthly Review* 42 (1770): 146
Critical Review 29 (1770): 147
London Magazine 39 (1770): 104

2993 *The World Lost and Regained by Love. An Allegorical Tale. To which is added, Iphis and Amaranta, or, Cupid Revenged.* London, 1760 (12mo. 2s.6d.sewed. Burd) YALE (STERLING)

Reviewed: *Monthly Review* 22 (1760): 460–464
Critical Review 10 (1760): 240–241
British Magazine 1 (1760): 602

2994 [WORSDALE, James]. *Gasconado the Great: a Tragi-Comi, Political, Whimsical Opera, As it was intended For the Entertainment of the Public, But rejected by the Managers of both Theatres.* London, 1759 (4to. 1s. Reeves) BRITISH LIBRARY

Reviewed: *Monthly Review* 20 (1759): 475–476
Critical Review 7 (1759): 462–463
Gentleman's Magazine 29 (1759): 233

2995 WOTY, W[illiam]. *The Blossoms of Helicon.* London, 1763 (12mo. 3s. Flexney) BRITISH LIBRARY

Reviewed: *Monthly Review* 28 (1763): 151–156
Critical Review 14 (1762): 456–462
British Magazine 3 (1762): 662

2996 [WOTY, William]. *Campanologia. A Poem, in praise of Ringing. By the Author of The*

Shrubs of Parnassus. London, 1761 (Fol. 1s. Coote) BRITISH LIBRARY

Reviewed: *Monthly Review* 25 (1761): 478

2997 WOTY, W[illiam]. *Church-Langton: a Poem*. Leicester, n.d. [ESTC-1767] (4to. 1s.6d. Flexney) BRITISH LIBRARY

Reviewed: *Monthly Review* 48 (1773): 319
Critical Review 35 (1773): 315
Town & Country Magazine 5 (1773): 304
Universal Catalogue [2] (1773) art. 363

2998 [WOTY, William]. *The Estate-Orators; a Town Eclogue*. London, 1774 (4to. 1s. Evans) NEWBERRY

Reviewed: *Monthly Review* 50 (1774): 316
Critical Review 37 (1774): 315
London Magazine 43 (1774): 198
Universal Catalogue 3 (1774) art. 360

2999 WOTY, W[illiam]. *The Female Advocate, a Poem*. London, 1770 (4to. 2s. Flexney. 1770) BRITISH LIBRARY

Reviewed: *Monthly Review* 42 (1770): 154
Critical Review 29 (1770): 443-446
London Magazine 39 (1770): 268

3000 [WOTY, William]. *The Graces: a Poetical Epistle. From a Gentleman To His Son*. London, 1774 (4to. 1s. Flexney. 1774) BRITISH LIBRARY

Reviewed: *Monthly Review* 52 (1775): 273
Critical Review 38 (1774): 473
London Review 1 (1775): 64

3001 WOTY, W[illiam]. *The Muse's Advice. Addressed to the Poets of the Age*. London, 1761 (4to. 1s. Flexney) YALE (STERLING)

Reviewed: *Monthly Review* 25 (1761): 479
Critical Review 12 (1761): 484

3002 WOTY, William. *The Poetical Works*. 2 vols. London, 1770 (12mo. 6s. Flexney) BRITISH LIBRARY

Reviewed: *Monthly Review* 42 (1770): 486
London Magazine 39 (1770): 212
Town & Country Magazine 2 (1770): 120

3003 [WOTY, William]. *The Shrubs of Parnassus. Consisting of a Variety of Poetical Essays, Moral and Comic. By J. Copywell, of Lincoln's-Inn, Esq*; London, 1760 (12mo. 3s. Newbery) BRITISH LIBRARY

Reviewed: *Monthly Review* 23 (1760): 64-68
Critical Review 9 (1760): 217-221
British Magazine 1 (1760): 139 [323]

3004 WRIGHT, Mr. *The Loss of the Handkerchief. An Heroic-Comic Poem, In Four Cantos. By Mr. Wright*. London, 1756 (8vo. 1s. Marshal) BRITISH LIBRARY

Reviewed: *Monthly Review* 16 (1757): 95
Critical Review 2 (1756): 475-476

3005 WRIGHT, G[eorge]. *The Gracious Warning; or, a Monody On the Death of the late Pious and Learned Joseph Nicoll Scott, M.D. With his Very Remarkable Dream concerning it: to which are added, Some Lines on the late Rev. Mr. Edward Hitchin, B.D*. London, 1774 (4to. 6d. Otridge, &c. 1774) BRITISH LIBRARY

Reviewed: *Monthly Review* 50 (1774): 232
Universal Catalogue 3 (1774) art. 108

WYCHERLEY, William (adaptations)
See: BICKERSTAFFE, Isaac. *The Plain Dealer*
GARRICK, David. *The Country Girl*
LEE, John. *The Country Wife*

3006 WYLD, William. *An Essay on the Character of Manilius, in an Epistle to Juvenis. In which is attempted A Description of the Distressed, the Miser and the Liberal. With Other Epistles on Several Subjects, in Blank Verse*. London, 1767 (8vo. 1s.6d. Richardson) BRITISH LIBRARY

Reviewed: *Monthly Review* 37 (1767): 468
Critical Review 24 (1767): 382-383

3007 WYLD, William. *Songs of Masonry*.
NOT SEEN (8vo. 6d. No bookseller's name)

Reviewed: *Monthly Review* 34 (1766): 481-482

3008 WYNNE, John Huddlestone. *Evelina: a Poem*. London, 1773 (4to. 2s.6d. Riley. 1773) BRITISH LIBRARY

Reviewed: *Monthly Review* 49 (1773): 147–148
Critical Review 36 (1773): 234
Universal Catalogue [2] (1773) art. 591

3009 [WYNNE, John Huddlestone]. *Fables of Flowers, for The Female Sex. With Zephyrus and Flora, A Vision. Written for the amusement of Her Highness The Princess Royal.* London, 1773 (12mo. 3s.bound. Riley. 1773) BODLEIAN

Reviewed: *Monthly Review* 48 (1773): 183–185
Critical Review 35 (1773): 232–233
London Magazine 42 (1773): 40
Universal Catalogue [2] (1773) art. 215

3010 WYNNE, John Huddlestone. *The Four Seasons, a Poem.* London, 1773 (4to. 2s.6d. Riley, &c. 1773) BRITISH LIBRARY

Reviewed: *Monthly Review* 50 (1774): 156
Critical Review 37 (1774): 224–227

3011 WYNNE, J[ohn] H[uddlestone]. *The Prostitute, a Poem.* London, 1771 (4to. 2s. Wheble. 1771) BRITISH LIBRARY

Reviewed: *Monthly Review* 44 (1771): 417
Critical Review 31 (1771): 229–230
Gentleman's Magazine 41 (1771): 228
London Magazine 40 (1771): 164

Yarico to Inkle
See: JERNINGHAM, Edward

3012 *Yorick's Meditations upon various Interesting and Important Subjects. Viz. Upon Nothing. Upon Something. Upon the Thing. Upon the Constitution. On Tobacco. On Noses. Upon Quacks. Upon Midwives. Upon the Homunculus. Upon Hobby-Horses. Upon Momus's Glass. Upon Digressions. On Obscurity in Writing. On Nonsense. Upon the Association of Ideas. Upon Cuckolds. Upon the Man in the Moon. Upon the Monades of Leibnitz. Upon Virtu. Upon Conscience. Upon Drunkeness. Upon a Close-stool. Meditations upon Meditations.* London, 1760 (12mo. 1s.6d. Stevens) BRITISH LIBRARY

Reviewed: *Monthly Review* 23 (1760): 84
Critical Review 10 (1760): 70–72
British Magazine 1 (1760): 489

Yorick's Sentimental Journey, continued
See: STEVENSON, John Hall

3013 [YOUNG, Arthur]. *The Adventures of Emmera, or the Fair American. Exemplifying the Peculiar Advantages of Society and Retirement.* 2 vols. London, 1767 (8vo. 6s. Nicoll) BRITISH LIBRARY

Reviewed: *Monthly Review* 36 (1767): 239
Critical Review 23 (1767): 272–274

3014 [YOUNG, Edward]. *The Brothers. A Tragedy. Acted at the Theatre Royal in Drury-Lane.* London, 1753 (8vo. 1s.6d. Dodsley) NEWBERRY

Reviewed: *Monthly Review* 8 (1753): 239–240

3015 YOUNG, Edward. *The Merchant, a naval Lyric, written in imitation of Pindar's Spirit, on the British Trade and Navigation* NOT SEEN (4to. 2s.6d. Swan)

Reviewed: *Monthly Review* 44 (1771): 490–491
Critical Review 31 (1771): 226–228
Gentleman's Magazine 41 (1771): 228
London Magazine 40 (1771): 163

3016 [YOUNG, Edward]. *Resignation In Two Parts. And a Postscript. To Mrs. B*******.* London, 1762 (4to. 2s. Owen) BRITISH LIBRARY

Reviewed: *Monthly Review* 26 (1762): 462–466
Critical Review 13 (1762): 461–464
British Magazine 3 (1762): 382

3017 [YOUNG, Edward]. *The Sailor's Song, to The South. A New Ballad: Occasion'd by the Rumour of War* [British Library copy cropped; BLC: London, 1750?] (Fol. 6d. Dodsley) BRITISH LIBRARY

Reviewed: *Monthly Review* 13 (1755): 296–297

3018 [YOUNG, Edward]. *A Sea-Piece: Containing I. The British Sailor's Exultation. II. His Prayer before Engagement. Occasion'd by the Rumour of War.* London, 1755 (4to. 6d. Dodsley) BRITISH LIBRARY

Reviewed: *Monthly Review* 13 (1755): 460

Young Scarron
See: MOZEEN, Thomas

3019 *The Younger Brother, a Tale.* 2 vols. London, 1770 & 1772 (12mo. 5s. sewed. Newbery) BRITISH LIBRARY

Reviewed: *Monthly Review* 46 (1772): 540
Critical Review 34 (1772): 77
Gentleman's Magazine 42 (1772): 329–331 and 375–377
Town & Country Magazine 4 (1772): 266
British Magazine & General Review 1 (1772): 457
Universal Catalogue [1] (1772) art. 587

The Younger Sister
See: DAWE, Anne

3020 *Youthful Amusements, in Verse: on Different Occasions.* London, 1757 (8vo. 1s. Owen) BRITISH LIBRARY

Reviewed: *Monthly Review* 17 (1757): 602–603

Zenobia: a Tragedy
See: MURPHY, Arthur

3021 *Zimri. An Oratorio. As it is perform'd at the Theatre-Royal in Covent-Garden. Set to Musick by Mr. Stanley.* London, 1760 (4to. 1s. Griffiths) BRITISH LIBRARY

Reviewed: *Monthly Review* 22 (1760): 260–261

3022 *La Zingara: or, the Gipsy. A Burletta. Set to Music By Mr. Barthelemon. As Performed at Mary-le-Bone Gardens, August the 21st, 1773.* London, n.d. [YALE CAT.–1773] (4to. 1s. Becket) YALE (STERLING)

Reviewed: *Monthly Review* 49 (1773): 233

Zobeide. A Tragedy
See: CRADOCK, Joseph

3023 ZOUCH, Thomas. *The Crucifixion: a Poetical Essay.* Cambridge, 1765 (4to. 1s. Dodsley) BRITISH LIBRARY

Reviewed: *Monthly Review* 34 (1766): 82–83
Critical Review 20 (1765): 392–394